SYMPOSIUM OF THE WHOLE

SYMPOSIUM OF THE WHOLE

A Range of Discourse Toward an Ethnopoetics

Edited with Commentaries
by

Jerome Rothenberg
&
Diane Rothenberg

UNIVERSITY OF CALIFORNIA PRESS
Berkeley   Los Angeles   London

UNIVERSITY OF CALIFORNIA PRESS
Berkeley and Los Angeles, California

UNIVERSITY OF CALIFORNIA PRESS, LTD.
London, England

Library of Congress Cataloging in Publication Data

Main entry under title:

Symposium of the whole.

  Bibliography: p. 485
  1. Poetry—History and criticism—Addresses, essays,
lectures.   2. Literature and society—Addresses, essays,
lectures.   3. Religion and poetry—Addresses, essays,
lectures.   I. Rothenberg, Jerome, 1931–
II. Rothenberg, Diane.
PN1081.S9   809.1   82-40092
ISBN 0-520-04530-0   AACR2

1 2 3 4 5 6 7 8 9

For Michel Benamou (1929–1978)

CONTENTS

THREE
Meanings

FOUR
Doings

FIVE
Contemporary Moves

PRE-FACE

1

When the industrial West began to discover—and plunder—"new" and "old" worlds beyond its boundaries, an extraordinary countermovement came into being in the West itself. Alongside the official ideologies that shoved European man to the apex of the human pyramid, there were some thinkers and artists who found ways of doing and knowing among other peoples as complex as any in Europe and often virtually erased from European consciousness. Cultures described as "primitive" and "savage"—a stage below "barbarian"—were simultaneously the models for political and social experiments, religious and visionary revivals, and forms of art and poetry so different from European norms as to seem revolutionary from a later Western perspective. It was almost, looking back at it, as if every radical innovation in the West were revealing a counterpart—or series of counterparts—somewhere in the traditional worlds the West was savaging.

The present gathering will center on the poetics of the matter and will map, from the perspective of the editors, a discourse on poetics (really a range of such discourses) that has been a vital aspect of twentieth-century poetry and art—with precedents going back two centuries and more. The poetics in question, which we will speak of as an "*ethno*poetics," reemerged after World War II (with its rampant and murderous racism) and the dislocations of the European colonial system during the postwar period.[1] Whenever it has appeared—and some version of it may be as old as human consciousness itself—it has taken the form of what Stanley Diamond, in a recently renewed "critique of civilization," calls "the search for the primitive" or, more precisely, the "attempt to define a primary human potential." (See below, p. 71.) The search as such is by no means confined to the "modern" world (though our concern with it will be just there) but is felt as well, say, in the words of ancient Heraclitus often cited by Charles Olson: "Man is estranged from that with which he is most familiar." And it is present too in the thought of those the West had cast as ultimate "primitives," as when the Delaware Indians tell us in their *Walum Olum*:

> in the beginning of the world
> all men had knowledge cheerfully
> all had leisure
> all thoughts were pleasant
>
> at that time all creatures were friends. . . .

[1] The word "ethnopoetics" suggested itself, almost too easily, on the basis of such earlier terms as ethnohistory, ethnomusicology, ethnolinguistics, ethnopharmacology, and so on. As such it refers to a redefinition of poetry in terms of cultural specifics, with an emphasis on those alternative traditions to which the West gave names like "pagan," "gentile," "tribal," "oral," and "ethnic." In its developed form, it moves toward an exploration of creativity over the fullest human range, pursued with a regard for particularized practice as much as unified theory and further "defined," as in this book, in the actual discourse.

The past is what it is—or was—but it is also something we discover and create through a desire to know what it is to be human, anywhere.

Some of the results of that search and its attendant yearnings are obvious by now—so much so that a principal defense against their power to transform us involves an attack on a primitivism debased by the attackers and abstracted thereby from its revolutionary potential. Such a primitivism is not in any case the stance of this collection. Nor is our interest directed backward toward a past viewed with feelings of decontextualized nostalgia. It is our contention, in fact, that the most experimental and future-directed side of Romantic and modern poetry, both in the Western world and increasingly outside it, has been the most significantly connected with the attempt to define an ethnopoetics.

There is a politics in all of this, and an importance, clearly, beyond the work of poets and artists. The old "primitive" models in particular—of small and integrated, stateless and classless societies—reflect a concern over the last two centuries with new communalistic and anti-authoritarian forms of social life and with alternatives to the environmental disasters accompanying an increasingly abstract relation to what was once a living universe. Our belief in this regard is that a re-viewing of "primitive" ideas of the "sacred" represents an attempt—by poets and others—to preserve and enhance primary human values against a mindless mechanization that has run past any uses it may once have had. (This, rather than the advocacy of some particular system, seems to us the contribution of the "primitive" to whatever world we may yet hope to bring about.) As a matter of history, we would place the model in question both in the surviving, still rapidly vanishing stateless cultures and in a long subterranean tradition of resistance to the twin authorities of state and organized religion.

What we're involved with here is a complex redefinition of cultural and intellectual values: a new reading of the poetic past and present which Robert Duncan speaks of as "a symposium of the whole." In such a new "totality," he writes (see below, p. 328), "all the old excluded orders must be included. The female, the proletariat, the foreign; the animal and vegetative; the unconscious and the unknown; the criminal and failure—all that has been outcast and vagabond must return to be admitted in the creation of what we consider we are." If that or some variant thereof is taken as the larger picture, it can provide the context in which to see most clearly the searches and discoveries in what we call "the arts." In painting and sculpture, say, the results of those searches are by now so well known that there's little surprise left in marking the change from Ruskin's late nineteenth-century comment, "There is no art in the whole of Africa, Asia, and America," to Picasso's exclamation on his first sighting of an African sculpture, "It is more beautiful than the Venus de Milo." Yet the obviousness of the change is itself deceptive. The "human" concerns demanded by the Dada poet Tristan Tzara—for an art that "lives first of all for the functions of dance, religion, music, and work"—remain largely submerged in the "aesthetic"; and it's a long way too from Picasso's classicizing admiration of the static art object to the reality of a tribal/oral "art in motion" (see below, p. 285) that brings all our scattered arts together.

This dream of a total art—and of a life made whole—has meant different things and been given different names throughout this century. "Intermedia" was a word for it in its 1960s manifestation—also "total theater" and "happenings"—behind which was the sense of what the nineteenth-century Wagnerian consciousness had called *Gesamt-*

kunstwerk and had placed—prefigured—at the imagined beginnings of the human enterprise. The difference in our own time was to smash that imperial and swollen mold—to shift the primary scene from Greece, say, to the barbaric or paleolithic past, or to the larger, often still existing tribal world, and to see in that world (however "outcast and vagabond" it had been made to look) a complexity of act and vision practiced by proto-poets/proto-artists who were true "technicians of the sacred." (See below, p. 99.) And along with this shift came the invention and revival of *specific* means: new materials and instruments (plastic and neon, film and tape) alongside old or foreign ones (stones, bones, and skin; drums, didjeridoos, and gamelans); ancient roles and modes of thought that had survived at the Western margins (sacred clowns and dancers, shamanistic ecstasies, old and new works of dream and chance); and a tilt toward ritual, not as "an obsessional concern with repetitive acts" but, as Victor Turner describes it, "an immense orchestration of genres in all available sensory codes: speech, music, singing; the presentation of elaborately worked objects, such as masks; wall-paintings, body-paintings; sculptured forms; complex, many-tiered shrines; costumes; dance forms with complex grammars and vocabularies of bodily movements, gestures, and facial expressions" (1977: 12).

The description, which fits both "them" and "us," holds equally true in the language arts—as this book will attempt to show—though by the nature of language itself (and the need to translate ourselves in—always—partial forms) the complexity and the interplay of new and old haven't been as clear there. Taken as a whole, then, the human species presents an extraordinary richness of verbal means—both of languages and poetries—closed to us until now by an unwillingness to think beyond the conventions and boundaries of Western literature. This "literature" as such goes back in its root meaning to an idea of writing—more narrowly and literally, the idea of alphabetic writing (*littera*, Lat. = letters) as developed in the West. In poetry, the result has been to exclude or set apart those oral traditions that together account for the greatest human diversity, an exclusion often covered over by a glorification of the oral past. Thus Marshall McLuhan—defining the words "tribal" and "civilized" on the basis of alphabetic literacy alone—can write: "Tribal cultures like those of the Indian and Chinese [!] may be greatly superior to the Western cultures in the range and delicacy of their expressions and perception," and in the same paragraph: "Tribal cultures cannot entertain the possibility of the individual or of the separate citizen" (1963: 86–87—but see Radin and Diamond, below, pp. 31, 71, for another view of the matter).

If the recovery of the oral is crucial to the present work, it goes hand in hand with a simultaneous expansion of the idea of writing and the text, wherever and whenever found. To summarize rapidly what we elsewhere present in extended form, the oral recovery involves a poetics deeply rooted in the powers of song and speech, breath and body, as brought forward across time by the living presence of poet-performers, with or without the existence of a visible/literal text. The range of such poetries is the range of human culture itself, and the forms they take (different for each culture) run from wordless songs and mantras to the intricacies (imagistic and symbolic) of multileveled oral narratives; from the stand-up performances of individual shamans and bards to the choreographies of massed dancers and singers, extended sometimes over protracted periods of time. From the side of visual and written language—which may, like the oral, be as old as the species itself—a fully human poetics would include all forms of what

Jacques Derrida calls *archécriture* (= primal writing): pictographs and hieroglyphs, aboriginal forms of visual and concrete poetry, sand paintings and earth mappings, gestural and sign languages, counting systems and numerologies, divinational signs made by man or read (as a poetics of natural forms) in the tracks of animals or of stars through the night sky.

That practices like these correspond to experimental moves in our own time isn't needed to justify them, but it indicates why we're now able to see them and to begin to understand as well the ways they differ from our own work. Other areas in which such correspondences hold true may be more involved with "idea" than "structure," though the distinction isn't always easy to maintain. Traditional divination work, for example— the Ifa oracles of Africa, say, or the Chinese *I Ching*—rests on the recognition of a world revealed moment by moment through processes of chance and synchronicity (i.e., the interrelatedness of simultaneous events), and these processes in turn inform one major segment of our avant-garde. Similarly, the widespread practice of exploring the "unknown" through the creation of new languages shows a strong sense of the *virtual* nature of reality (what Senghor speaks of as the traditional *surreal*) and the linguistic means to get it said. The idea of the surreal—at its most meaningful—also suggests the dreamworks so central to other cultures and so long submerged in ours. And from these, or through them, it's only a short step into a life lived in a state-of-myth ("reality at white heat," Radin called it) and to the recovery of archetypes (as image and/or symbol) that infuse our own work at its most heated: the animal and trickster side of us; the goddess and the feminine; the sense of "earth as a religious form" and of a living, even human, universe; and the commitment to imaginal geographies and journeys that lead into our own lives and minds. These are as old as the human, maybe older, and they come back to us, transformed, not so much when we shut out the immediate world around us as when we choose to work within it.

The twentieth century—and with it the attendant modernisms that have characterized our poetry and art—is by now winding down. It has been a long haul and a sometimes real adventure, but the work is in no way complete and some of the major points have still to be hammered home. My own choice has been to write from the side of a modernism that sees itself as challenging limits and changing ways of speaking/ thinking/doing that have too long robbed us of the freedom to be human to the full extent of our powers and yearnings. The struggle is immediate and the objects and attitudes to be destroyed or transformed appear on every side of us. But it isn't a question of our having no sense of history or of the human past—no sense of possibilities besides the most apparent. The clincher, in fact, is the transformation, beyond that, of our consciousness of the human in all times and places.

2

By the end of the 1960s, I first introduced the term "ethnopoetics" as a necessary part of a poetics (an idea of poetry) changed by a century of such experimentation and mapping. A number of often previously involved poets, anthropologists, and critics (Antin, Awoonor, Beier, Diamond, Hymes, McClure, Ortiz, Quasha, Snyder, Spanos, Tedlock, Tarn, et al.) responded immediately to the discourse around the term, while others, who remained aloof, were in their own terms implicit contributors to the issues clustered therein. What this marked wasn't so much a first invention as a recognition that the ethnopoetics, once it had entered our work, altered the nature of that work in all its aspects. And behind it was the century itself and a crisis in language and thought not of our making: an international avant-garde on the one hand, an American opening to history and myth on the other, and a de facto but rarely acknowledged collaboration between poets and scholars by whom the attack on the narrow view of literature (i.e., the "great" tradition) was simultaneously carried on. Few poets and artists—post-World War II—weren't somehow involved in these new mappings, for what had changed was our paradigm of what poetry was or now could come to be.

The explicit discourse—that around an ethnopoetics per se—involved the magazine *Alcheringa* (founded by Rothenberg and Tedlock in 1970) and included the 1975 gathering, at the Center for Twentieth Century Studies in Milwaukee, of the "first international symposium on ethnopoetics," which drew from many of the principal contributors as well as from others working in related areas.[2] (See Turner, "A Review of 'Ethnopoetics,' " below, p. 337.) On the one hand, this discourse explored an ongoing "intersection between poetry and anthropology," in Nathaniel Tarn's words, and on the other hand, between contemporary poets as the "marginal" defenders of an endangered human diversity and poets of other times and places who represented that diversity itself and many of the values being uncovered and recovered in the new poetic enterprises. The discourse opened as well to include what Richard Schechner called the "poetics of performance" across the spectrum of the arts, and it also tied in with movements of self-definition and cultural liberation among third world ethnic groups in the United States and elsewhere.

The present anthology is an attempt to present some highlights of that discourse—both over the last two decades and in relation to its own history—and to show as well how ethnographic revelations can change our ideas of poetic form and function. There is otherwise no claim to an ethnopoetics movement per se, and many of the present contributors in fact remain largely unaware of each other's work. Nor is there anything final or tidy about such an ethnopoetics, which works instead to churn up a whole range of issues about "art and life" (as those terms are used by practitioners like John Cage and Allan Kaprow)—not as a closed field but as an always shifting series of tendencies in the thought and practice of those who in any sense might be considered as participants. And the participants themselves are not only poets but—in an age of intermedia works and genre cross-overs—other artists as well; not only anthropologists and folklorists but the indigenous poets and shamans for whom the others often act as conduits to the world of print and text.

We have structured the book to present these issues historically, ethnographically, and from a number of contemporary points of view. Working from our two bases as poet

---

[2]Much of the ethnopoetic work at that time, my own included, was involved with the discovery and translation of the poetry itself and, for many, with the incorporation of related processes into their own works and lives. In that context—in books of my own making, say, such as *Technicians of the Sacred, Shaking the Pumpkin*, and *America a Prophecy*—the discourse *appeared* as a distinctly secondary event or one handled by example largely, though elsewhere it was clearly the event of primary importance. Our effort now, in contrast to those earlier workings, is to bring the talk *about* poetry—the discourse—forward, while still upholding the primacy of the poetic act.

and anthropologist, we have divided it into five sections—the first and the final ones dealing largely with theory and ideology, the middle ones with the particular insights derived from ethnographic and other descriptive approaches. Such a distinction—given the need for both good poetics and good anthropology to merge the particular and the general—is of course impossible to maintain in any absolute sense. Nor have we wished to do so, but to follow, in a number of instances, certain issues through all five sections of the book. The result intended, as should be clear by now, is no less than a new poetics.

The first section, ''Preliminary Moves,'' sets out the leading issues and proposes a representative (by no means complete) chronology of ethnopoetic predecessors, from the writings of Giambattista Vico in the eighteenth century to my own first ethnopoetics ''manifesto'' in 1968. In doing so, we've tried not to be merely historical but to select works that still hold up—Herder's clear vision of the tribal and non-Western, say, rather than Rousseau's ultimate disdain for them. And we've tried also to open the ethnopoetic into what David Antin (see below, p. 452) calls a ''human poetics'' instead of forcing it into the more restricted mold of the ''primitive.'' The themes set out in these works, and open to continuing modification, include the reinterpretation of the poetic past, the recurrent question of a primitive-civilized dichotomy (particularly in its post-Platonic, Western manifestations), the idea of a visionary poetics and of the shaman as a paradigmatic proto-poet, the idea of a great subculture and of the persistence of an oral poetics in all of the ''higher'' civilizations, the concept of wilderness and of the role of the poet as a defender of biological and psychic diversity, the issue of the monoculture and the issue of cultural imperialism, the question of communal and individual expression in traditional societies, the relation of culture and language to mental processes, the divergence of oral and written cultures (and their projected reconciliation), and the reemergence of suppressed and rejected forms and images (the goddess, the trickster, the human universe, etc.).

In the middle sections, drawn largely from the work of anthropologists and other scholars, many of these issues recur (along with others not previously discussed)—this time in relation to specific forms and events in both other-than-Western and alternative Western traditions. The second section, ''Workings,'' deals principally with operational descriptions of poetic and related linguistic forms. How do poems really ''work'' in such situations? What elements do they include, how are those elements put together, and what are the intended results? Is the poetry of oral cultures essentially different from that of written ones, and are written elements at work as well? With an eye to the expansion and transformation of our present ideas of poetic practice—and with our expanded practice as a key to the kinds of verbal acts that may now be viewed as ''poetry''—we've focused on a number of culturally specific ''workings'': the language of magic employing often untranslatable sounds, the processes of naming and imaging by means of language, the use of surrogate language forms (drum-language poems, in the present instance), the relation of visual forms to vocal ones, the employment of chance-related procedures in divination poetry—as well as the persistent question of the individual poet's voice in traditional and communal societies.

The question of transferability—whether or to what degree it's possible for us to adapt such culturally specific forms—is of course implicit throughout this presentation. The forms, the processes themselves, are always part of a larger nexus of meanings, and to get a grip on such a nexus is, it seems to us, essential to any new poetics, particularly one that stresses an intimate relation between "form" and "content." In our third section, "Meanings," we shift attention to conceptual questions of world view and symbolic process, with particular concern for the ways language shapes reality, for the kind of symbolmaking that approaches what William Blake called the "four-fold vision," for the use of paralinguistic modes (dreamings, psychedelics) to enhance language and meaning, and for culturally (and historically) particular views of certain of the imaginal beings most pertinent to a twentieth-century process of "mythopoetic" recovery.

In the fourth section, "Doings," we move directly to the matter of performance or enactment—ritual and theater—that has, in fact, been a dominant theme throughout the gathering. This approach through performance has so frequently been identified with ethnopoetics and the recovery of an oral impulse as to be almost indistinguishable. In tackling it head on (that is, in situ), the subjects range from Antonin Artaud's early intuition (1931) of a Balinese theater that goes "beyond language" and J. Stephen Lansing's recent exposition of a Balinese "poetics of the sounding of the text" to a broad survey of the performative sides of shamanism, particularized descriptions of sacred clowns and traditional cathartic rituals and songs, writings-in-space as an aspect of African dance, contemporary signing poetry in the "culture of the deaf," celebrations of the female aspect of God in the subculture of Jewish kabbalistic mysticism, and a final overview by Richard Schechner of the ongoing but ever-shifting relation between ritual and theater.

Schechner's essay acts in turn as a bridge to the last section of the book, "Contemporary Moves," which articulates some of the major issues of the earlier discourse while adding still others developed in the 1960s and 1970s. Though it's in the nature of such discourse to run over many issues and to produce as much opposition as agreement, the section is unified by the participants' common desire and need to chart and adjust the relation between traditional and contemporary modes of poetry. It begins with the overviews of a poet and an anthropologist and continues with several approaches to experimental translation from oral sources and with two pieces that deal with the process of oral transmission from the perspectives of a Native American poet and of a European-born poet-anthropologist. These are followed by a number of writings that explore the idea of poetic continuities—in Native American and Afro-American culture, in the survival of Coyote and related trickster figures in the work of several different American poets, and in the reinterpretation of the human past going back to our earliest paleolithic sources. The last several pieces—before Edmund Carpenter's coda-like "The Death of Sedna"—deal in various ways with the still-to-be-resolved question of the relation between written and oral forms of poetry and language—both "there" and "here."

Those familiar with the intentions and workings of contemporary poetry and art will likely see the relevance to our present practice of most of the inclusions. But because we hope to inform as wide an audience as possible, we offer a running commentary to place the pieces in context—concentrating in the first and last sections on authors, issues, and movements, and in the middle sections on the original cultural contexts or on the relation of traditional modes to contemporary concerns or to what we often take as losses or discontinuities in our own culture. For those who want to pursue the work still further, we've provided a cumulative bibliography of works mentioned throughout the anthology, adding a few others that have been of special importance to the ethnopoetic discourse. The bibliography in no sense pretends to completeness but attempts only to suggest the web of readings that underlies even as partial a selection as this one.

We are calling our book *Symposium of the Whole* after Robert Duncan's phrase already noted in this Pre-face. To this we have added the subtitle, *A Range of Discourse Toward an Ethnopoetics*. That means, quite literally, that we are, in spite of the privileges of editorship, trying to remain open to the variety of voices and stances around this subject and, above all, to see the work as a movement *toward* something that can in no sense be taken as presently achieved.

San Diego　　　　　　　　　　　　　　　　　　　　Jerome Rothenberg
1982

POST-SCRIPT and ACKNOWLEDGMENTS. In coming—as the custom is—to the matter of particular indebtedness, we're mindful that the book has been made possible by the efforts of many gifted people who have contributed to the possibility of an ethnopoetics from often divergent directions. Those represented in these pages are acknowledged by their presence, while those not represented are so numerous that we hesitate to name some, thereby seeming to slight others.

The book is dedicated to the memory of our friend, Michel Benamou, a literary scholar of distinction, who spent the last years of his life as director of the Center for Twentieth Century Studies in Milwaukee and as a devoted ally in the work of defining a new poetics. Through his presence we were able to believe that a genuine collaboration between artists and scholars was both possible and necessary for that "liberation of the creative forces from the tutelage of the advocates of power" described by the Dada poet Richard Huelsenbeck in the legendary days of the Cabaret Voltaire.

We are grateful also for the encouragement and good talk of our editor, Robert Zachary, who commissioned the book and gave us the privilege of gathering these works as a gift to those who wish to use them.

J. R.
D. R.

ONE
Preliminary Moves

Magic Words

Material reworked from The Netsilik Eskimos *(1931), representing field work by Knud Rasmussen (1879–1933), Danish explorer and ethnologist, of Eskimo ancestry on his mother's side. Nalungiaq, "just an ordinary woman" (she says), learned it from an old uncle, Unaraluk the shaman, whose helping spirits—his dead father and mother, the sun, a dog, and a sea scorpion—enabled him to "know everything about what was on the earth and under the earth, in the sea and in the sky."*

The idea of "magic words" will be running through these pages (see especially Malinowski, p. 107, below), and the convergence with poetry, as method and process, goes back in the West at least as far as the seventeenth- and eighteenth-century speculation on a golden "age of the gods." (Thus Vico, for example, immediately following.) Writes the contemporary poet Robert Creeley: "Mighty magic is a mother"; and the Dada poet Hugo Ball: "Perhaps the art which we are seeking is the key to every former art: a solomonic key that will open all the mysteries."

In the very earliest time,
when both people and animals lived on earth,
a person could become an animal if he wanted to
and an animal could become a human being.
Sometimes they were people
and sometimes animals
and there was no difference.
All spoke the same language.
That was the time when words were like magic.
The human mind had mysterious powers.
A word spoken by chance
might have strange consequences.
It would suddenly come alive
and what people wanted to happen could happen—
all you had to do was say it.
Nobody could explain this:
That's the way it was.

SOURCE: Translation in Edward Field, Eskimo Songs and Stories, *pages 7–8.*

GIAMBATTISTA VICO
The Age of the Gods
and the Origins of Language

The "Principles of New Science of Giambattista Vico concerning the Common Nature of the Nations" (first edition:1725) is a model work (comparative, evolutionary) for later history and anthropology: a view of the history of all societies as the account of their birth and development. But it's also a virtual speculative ethnopoetics in which the poetry of the "Nations" (= gentiles/gentes = Gk. ethnoi) already looms large. The core of the work, an extended section called "Poetic Wisdom," sets out a kind of aboriginal creativity-writ-large that comes back full circle into the projected "new science." Of that interplay between the new and old, the present translators tell us: "[The] creation [of Vico's new science] has been made possible by a return to the poetic wisdom by which the world of nations was first created. In devoting half the book to poetic wisdom, Vico exhibits scientific and religious wisdom seeking to know itself by recovering its own origins in vulgar or poetic or creative wisdom. In doing this, it becomes itself creative, or recreative . . . re-creates itself by re-creating the first science, that of augury or divination, out of which all the others grew" (pp. xli—xlii). Thus, as with any ethnopoetics worth its salt, "something more than literature is going on here."

This New Science or metaphysic, studying the common nature of nations in the light of divine providence, discovers the origins of divine and human institutions among the gentile nations, and thereby establishes a system of the natural law of the gentes, which proceeds with the greatest equality and constancy through the three ages which the Egyptians handed down to us as the three periods through which the world had passed up to their time. These are: (1) The age of the gods, in which the gentiles believed they lived under divine governments, and everything was commanded them by auspices and oracles, which are the oldest institutions in profane history. (2) The age of the heroes, in which they reigned everywhere in aristocratic commonwealths, on account of a certain superiority of nature which they held themselves to have over the plebs. (3) The age of men, in which all men recognized themselves as equal in human nature, and therefore there were established first the popular commonwealths and then the monarchies, both of which are forms of human government.

In harmony with these three kinds of nature and government, three kinds of language were spoken which compose the vocabulary of this Science: (1) That of the time of the families when gentile men were newly received into humanity. This, we shall find, was a mute language of signs and physical objects having natural relations to the ideas they wished to express. (2) That spoken by means of heroic emblems, or similitudes, comparisons, images, metaphors, and natural descriptions, which make up the

SOURCE: Translation in Thomas Goddard Bergin and Max Harold Fisch, The New Science of Giambattista Vico, *pages 20—22.*

great body of the heroic language which was spoken at the time the heroes reigned. (3) Human language using words agreed upon by the people, a language of which they are absolute lords, and which is proper to the popular commonwealths and monarchical states; a language whereby the people may fix the meaning of the laws by which the nobles as well as the plebs are bound. Hence, among all nations, once the laws had been put into the vulgar tongue, the science of laws passed from the control of the nobles. Hitherto, among all nations, the nobles, being also priests, had kept the laws in a secret language as a sacred thing. That is the natural reason for the secrecy of the laws among the Roman patricians until popular liberty arose.

Now these are the same three languages that the Egyptians claimed had been spoken before in their world, corresponding exactly both in number and in sequence to the three ages that had run their course before them. (1) The hieroglyphic or sacred or secret language, by means of mute acts. This is suited to the uses of religion, for which observance is more important than discussion. (2) The symbolic, by means of similitudes, such as we have just seen the heroic language to have been. (3) The epistolary or vulgar, which served the common uses of life. These three types of language are found among the Chaldeans, Scythians, Egyptians, Germans, and all the other ancient gentile nations; although hieroglyphic writing survived longest among the Egyptians, because for a longer time than the others they were closed to all foreign nations (as for the same reason it still survives among the Chinese), and hence we have a proof of the vanity of their imagined remote antiquity.

We here bring to light the beginnings not only of languages but also of letters, which philology has hitherto despaired of finding. We shall give a specimen of the extravagant and monstrous opinions that have been held up to now. We shall observe that the unhappy cause of this effect is that philologists have believed that among the nations languages first came into being and then letters; whereas (to give here a brief indication of what will be fully proved in this volume) letters and languages were born twins and proceeded apace through all their three stages. . . .

We find that the principle of these origins both of languages and of letters lies in the fact that the first gentile peoples, by a demonstrated necessity of nature, were poets who spoke in poetic characters. This discovery, which is the master key of this Science, has cost us the persistent research of almost all our literary life, because with our civilized natures we [moderns] cannot at all imagine and can understand only by great toil the poetic nature of these first men. The [poetic] characters of which we speak were certain imaginative genera (images for the most part of animate substances, of gods or heroes, formed by their imagination) to which they reduced all the species or all the particulars appertaining to each genus; exactly as the fables of human times, such as those of late comedy, are intelligible genera reasoned out by moral philosophy, from which the comic poets form imaginative genera (for the best ideas of the various human types are nothing but that) which are the persons of the comedies. These divine or heroic characters were true fables or myths, and their allegories are found to contain meanings not analogical but univocal, not philosophical but historical, of the peoples of Greece of those times.

Since these genera (for that is what the fables in essence are) were formed by most vigorous imaginations, as in men of the feeblest reasoning powers, we discover in them true poetic sentences, which must be sentiments clothed in the greatest passions and therefore full of sublimity and arousing wonder. Now the sources of all poetic locution are two: poverty of language and need to explain and be understood. Heroic speech followed immediately on the mute language of acts and objects that had natural relations to the ideas they were meant to signify, which was used in the divine times. Lastly, in the necessary natural course of human institutions, language among the Assyrians, Syrians, Phoenicians, Egyptians, Greeks, and Latins began with heroic verses, passed thence to iambics, and finally settled into prose. This gives certainty to the history of the ancient poets and explains why in the German language, particularly in Silesia, a province of peasants, there are many natural versifiers, and in the Spanish, French and Italian languages the first authors wrote in verse.

JOHANN GOTTFRIED HERDER
From a Correspondence on Ossian and the Songs of Ancient Peoples[1]

With Herder we get the outlines for an actual and still viable ethnopoetics—a concept of poetry "emancipated from rationalist or Christian context and strictures, opening to world horizons, the dimension of time and cultural relativism, and deepening its meaning as a profound mode of truth" (Feldman, Modern Mythology, p. 225). But the universal poetics Herder creates has a new and strict regard for cultural autonomies and particularities—allowing the reentry of the outcast European ("folk") past and the more distant poetries of peoples then falling to European domination. Herder's Volkslieder (1778) is a first anthology with ethnopoetic scope: "not only German but also Italian, French, Spanish, Estonian, Lithuanian, Lettish, Eskimo, Old Norse, Greek, Danish, medieval Latin, and Inca folk poems." His equation of "wildness" (= "savagery") with creative energy and freedom ("for that is the simple meaning of the word") leads to a new poetics of liberation that makes its way to the present through that Romanticism (not softheaded but sharp and clear) for which Herder was a shaping force.

Wrote his older contemporary, Rousseau, of the "civilized"/"savage" dichotomy: "Man is born free & is everywhere in chains," and his younger contemporary, Blake, turning toward amelioration: "Poetry fetter'd, fetters the Human Race."

---

[1]Ossian was the purported author of an "ancient Gaelic epic," *Fingal*, gathered and largely fabricated by James Macpherson (circa 1760)—about which much comment followed by the great European pre-Romantics. (Eds.)

SOURCE: Translation in Burton Feldman and Robert D. Richardson (eds.), The Rise of Modern Mythology, pages 228–230.

Your objections are strange. You yield to me on the matter of ancient Gothic songs, as you like to call them, rhymed poems, romances, sonnets, and such artful or even artificial stanzas, but not when it comes to the ancient unaffected songs of savage, uncivilized peoples. Savage, uncivilized peoples? I can hardly subscribe to your point of view. So you think that Ossian and his noble and great Fingal belong merely to a savage, uncivilized people? Even if he had idealized everything he wrote about, would someone who could idealize like that, or someone who found his nightly dreams, his daily example, his relaxation and greatest pleasure in such images, such stories—would he be savage and uncivilized? We find ourselves in the strangest places when trying to rescue our favorite opinions!

Know then, that the more savage, that is, the more alive and freedom-loving a people is (for that is the simple meaning of the word), the more savage, that is, alive, free, sensuous, lyrically active, its songs must be, if it has songs. The more distant a people is from artful cultivated thinking, language, and letters, the less will its songs be written for paper—dead literary verse. The lyrical, the living and therefore rhythmical elements of song, the living presentness of the imagery, the continuity and force of the contents and invention, the symmetry of words, syllables, even letters, the melody and the hundreds of other things that belong to and disappear with the living word, the songs of a language and a nation—on this and this alone depends the natures, the purpose, the whole miraculous power of these songs, their charm, the driving force that makes them the timeless song of the heritage and joy of our people. These arrows of a savage Apollo, pierce hearts and carry souls and thoughts with them. The longer a song is to last, the stronger and more sensuous the rousers of the soul must be, in order to defy the powers of time and changing circumstances of centuries—what do you say to that? . . .

You laugh at my enthusiasm for savages as Voltaire laughed at Rousseau for wanting to walk on all fours. Don't think because of that that I despise our customary civilized preferences in any way. The human race is fated to a progression of scenes, cultures, and customs; woe to the man who is dissatisfied with the scene he is supposed to appear in, act his part, and spend his life! But woe also to the philosopher of mankind and customs who considers his own scene the only one, and insists on dismissing the earliest scenes as the worst! Since they all belong in the whole of the continuous drama, each one demonstrates a new and remarkable side of mankind—and take care that I don't haunt you with some psychology from Ossian's poetry next time! The idea of it at least lies deep and vivid in my heart, and you might see many peculiar things. . . .

All unpolished peoples sing and act; they sing about what they do and thus sing histories. Their songs are the archives of their people, the treasury of their science and religion, their theogony and cosmogony, the deeds of their fathers and the events of their history, an echo of their hearts, a picture of their domestic life in joy and in sorrow, by bridal bed and graveside. Nature has given them a comfort against many of the miseries that oppress them and a substitute for many of the so-called blessings we enjoy: that is, love of freedom, leisure, ecstasy and song. Here everyone portrays himself and appears as he is. The warrior nation sings of brave deeds; the tender sings of love. A clever people makes up riddles; a people with imagination makes allegories, similes, living tableaux. The people with warm passions knows only passion, as the people under terrible conditions creates terrifying gods for itself. A small collection of such songs from the mouth of each nation, about the noblest conditions and deeds of their lives, in their own language but at the same time properly understood and explained, accompanied with music: how much it would enliven the chapter that the student of man reads most eagerly in every travelogue, "the nature and customs of the people! their science and letters, their games and dances, their music and mythology!" All of these would give us better concepts of the nation than we get through the gossip of a traveler or an "Our Father" copied down in their language! As a natural history describes plants and animals, so the peoples depict themselves here. We would gain an intuitive understanding of everything; and from the similarities or differences in language, contents, and tone among these songs, particularly of ideas of cosmology and the history of their forefathers, a great deal could be concluded with certainty about the ancestry, propagation, and intermingling of peoples.

WILLIAM BLAKE
From *The Marriage of Heaven & Hell*

As does his very different contemporary Goethe, Blake appears today as one of the first of the new poets to revive in his own work a more-than-literary role as ("visionary") shaper-of-the-real. (See Vico, above, p. 4.) Of the prevalence of such a mythopoetic mode in a larger human history, he wrote: "The antiquities of every Nation under Heaven, is no less sacred than that of the Jews. They are the same thing as Jacob Bryant, and all antiquaries have proved. How other antiquities came to be neglected and disbelieved, while those of the Jews are collected and arranged, is an enquiry, worthy of both the Antiquarian and the Divine" (from "A Descriptive Catalogue"). He thus unites a new vision of the past with an overthrowing of inherited conceptions of the past and present, through the acts of his own mind working on its own experience: "The Nature of my Work is Visionary or Imaginative it is an Endeavour to Restore (what the Ancients calld) the Golden Age" (from "A Vision of the Last Judgment").

The ancient Poets animated all sensible objects with Gods or Geniuses, calling them by the names and adorning them with the properties of woods, rivers, mountains, lakes, cities, nations, and whatever their enlarged & numerous senses could perceive.

SOURCE: The Poetry & Prose of William Blake, pages 37−38.

And particularly they studied the genius of each city & country. placing it under its mental deity.

Till a system was formed, which some took advantage of & enslav'd the vulgar by attempting to realize or abstract the mental deities from their objects; thus began Priesthood.

Choosing forms of worship from poetic tales.

And at length they pronouncd that the Gods had orderd such things.

Thus men forgot that All deities reside in the human breast.

A MEMORABLE FANCY

The Prophets Isaiah and Ezekiel dined with me, and I asked them how they dared so roundly to assert. that God spake to them; and whether they did not think at the time, that they would be misunderstood, & so be the cause of imposition.

Isaiah answer'd. I saw no God, nor heard any, in a finite organical perception; but my senses discover'd the infinite in every thing, and as I was then perswaded, & remain confirm'd; that the voice of honest indignation is the voice of God, I cared not for consequences but wrote.

Then I asked: does a firm perswasion that a thing is so, make it so?

He replied. All poets believe that it does, & in ages of imagination this firm perswasion removed mountains; but many are not capable of a firm perswasion of any thing.

Then Ezekiel said. The philosophy of the east taught the first principles of human perception   some nations held one principle for the origin & some another, we of Israel taught that the Poetic Genius (as you now call it) was the first principle and all the others merely derivative, which was the cause of our despising the Priests & Philosophers of other countries, and prophecying that all Gods would at last be proved to originate in ours & to be the tributaries of the Poetic Genius, it was this. that our great poet King David desired so fervently & invokes so patheticly, saying by this he conquers enemies & governs kingdoms; and we so loved our God. that we cursed in his name all the deities of surrounding nations, and asserted that they had rebelled; from these opinions the vulgar came to think that all nations would at last be subject to the jews.

This said he, like all firm perswasions, is come to pass, for all nations believe the jews code and worship the jews god, and what greater subjection can be.

I heard this with some wonder, & must confess my own conviction. After dinner I ask'd Isaiah to favour the world with his lost works, he said none of equal value was lost. Ezekiel said the same of his.

I also asked Isaiah what made him go naked and barefoot three years? he answerd, the same that made our friend Diogenes the Grecian.

I then asked Ezekiel. why he eat dung, & lay so long on his right & left side? he answerd. the desire of raising other men into a perception of the infinite this the North American tribes practise. & is he honest who resists his genius or conscience only for the sake of present ease or gratification?

HENRY DAVID THOREAU
In Wildness is
the preservation of the World

Thoreau brings the "wilderness" side of the proposition into focus: what the nineteenth century would have subsumed under the word "nature" and the later twentieth century under "ecology." The emphasis is in fact characteristically American, and the view of wilderness and wildness brings together ideas (social and personal) of place, of language, of body, and of mind. In the American instance, also, the persistent presence is that of the Indian ("the vengeful ghost lurking in the back of the troubled American mind"—G. Snyder), as one remembers the word "Indian" spoken by Thoreau on his death bed—or his vision and "yearning" while walking "the arrowheadiferous sands of Concord," whose arrowheads "are not fossil bones but, as it were, fossil thoughts, forever reminding me of the mind that shaped them. . . . The footprint, the mind-print of the oldest men" (Journal 1859).

The West of which I speak is but another name for the Wild; and what I have been preparing to say is, that in Wildness is the preservation of the World. Every tree sends its fibers forth in search of the Wild. The cities import it at any price. Men plow and sail for it. From the forest and wilderness come the tonics and barks which brace mankind. Our ancestors were savages. The story of Romulus and Remus being suckled by a wolf is not a meaningless fable. The founders of every state which has risen to eminence have drawn their nourishment and vigor from a similar wild source. It was because the children of the Empire were not suckled by the wolf that they were conquered and displaced by the children of the northern forests who were. . . .

In literature it is only the wild that attracts us. Dullness is but another name for tameness. It is the uncivilized free and wild thinking in Hamlet and the Iliad, in all the scriptures and mythologies, not learned in the schools, that delights us. As the wild duck is more swift and beautiful than the tame, so is the wild—the mallard—thought, which 'mid falling dews wings its way above the fens. A truly good book is something as natural, and as unexpectedly and unaccountably fair and perfect, as a wildflower discovered on the prairies of the West or in the jungles of the East. Genius is a light which makes the darkness visible, like the lightning's flash, which perchance shatters the temple of knowledge itself—and not a taper lighted at the hearthstone of the race, which pales before the light of common day.

English literature, from the days of the minstrels to the Lake Poets—Chaucer and Spenser and Milton, and even Shakespeare, included—breathes no quite fresh and, in this sense, wild strain. It is an essentially tame and civilized literature, reflecting Greece and Rome. Her wilderness is a greenwood, her wild man a Robin Hood. There is plenty of genial love of Nature, but no so much of Nature herself. Her chronicles inform us

SOURCE: *Henry David Thoreau, "Walking," from* Excursions (*Volume IX of the Riverside Edition of* The Writings of Henry David Thoreau), *pages 534, 539–541.*

when her wild animals, but not when the wild man in her, became extinct.

The science of Humboldt is one thing, poetry is another thing. The poet today, notwithstanding all the discoveries of science, and the accumulated learning of mankind, enjoys no advantage over Homer.

Where is the literature which gives expression to Nature? He would be a poet who could impress the winds and streams into his service, to speak for him; who nailed words to their primitive senses, as farmers drive down stakes in the spring, which the frost has heaved; who derived his words as often as he used them—transplanted them to his page with earth adhering to their roots; whose words were so true and fresh and natural that they would appear to expand like the buds at the approach of spring, though they lay half smothered between two musty leaves in a library—aye, to bloom and bear fruit there, after their kind, annually, for the faithful reader, in sympathy with surrounding Nature.

I do not know of any poetry to quote which adequately expresses this yearning for the Wild. Approached from this side, the best poetry is tame. I do not know where to find in any literature, ancient or modern, any account which contents me of that Nature with which even I am acquainted. You will perceive that I demand something which no Augustan nor Elizabethan age, which no *culture*, in short, can give. Mythology comes nearer to it than anything. How much more fertile a Nature, at least, has Grecian mythology its root in than English literature! Mythology is the crop which the Old World bore before its soil was exhausted, before the fancy and imagination were affected with blight; and which it still bears, wherever its pristine vigor is unabated. All other literatures endure only as the elms which overshadow our houses; but this is like the great dragon-tree of the Western Isles, as old as mankind, and, whether that does or not, will endure as long; for the decay of other literatures makes the soil in which it thrives.

The West is preparing to add its fables to those of the East. The valleys of the Ganges, the Nile, and the Rhine having yielded their crop, it remains to be seen what the valleys of the Amazon, the Plate, the Orinoco, the St. Lawrence, and the Mississippi will produce. Perchance, when, in the course of ages, American liberty has become a fiction of the past—as it is to some extent a fiction of the present—the poets of the world will be inspired by American mythology.

KARL MARX and FRIEDRICH ENGELS
The Rise of Bourgeois Rule and the Origin of World Literature

In Stanley Diamond's summation of a primitivist/Marxist "claim that our sense of primitive communal societies is the archetype for socialism," he writes: "Primitive cultures were for [Marx and Engels] the ground of all future movement. Moreover, Marx indicated that they served as the paradigm for the idea of socialism; socialism would achieve 'that which men had always dreamed about,' Marx believed" (Diamond 1974: 106, 108). The opening image of The Communist Manifesto—*"a specter is haunting Europe: the specter of communism"—is, therefore, not only the classic statement of a revolutionary European politics but an implicit argument toward a radical anthropology and ethnopoetics. The Marx-Engels ethnology (its most systematic work is Engels's* The Origin of the Family, Private Property, and the State) *draws from evolutionary anthropologists like Lewis Henry Morgan in positing a stateless/classless communalism as the primitive foundation of all human society and the model for a future escape from the "conflicts" and "alienations" of capitalism. In the present excerpt from* The Communist Manifesto, *the authors' sardonic view of the bourgeoisie is a virtual prophecy of twentieth-century moves (both capitalist and socialist) toward a universal monoculture. And it raises as well the thorny, often ambiguous issue of cultural imperialism—a central question for an ethnopoetics that would be other than a mere sentimentalization of the idea of human diversity. (For more recent views, see Carpenter, Baraka, and Césaire, below.)*

The bourgeoisie has played a most revolutionary role in history.

The bourgeoisie, whenever it has got the upper hand, has put an end to all feudal, patriarchal, idyllic relations. It has pitilessly torn asunder the motley feudal ties that bound man to his "natural superiors," and has left no other bond between man and man than naked self-interest, than callous "cash payment." It has drowned the most heavenly ecstasies of religious fervor, of chivalrous enthusiasm, of philistine sentimentalism, in the icy water of egotistical calculation. It has resolved personal worth into exchange value, and, in place of the numberless indefeasible chartered freedoms, has set up that single, unconscionable freedom—Free Trade. In one word, for exploitation, veiled by religious and political illusions, it has substituted naked, shameless, direct, brutal exploitation.

The bourgeoisie has stripped of its halo every occupation hitherto honored and looked up to with reverent awe. It has converted the physician, the lawyer, the priest, the poet, the man of science, into its paid wage-laborers.

The bourgeoisie has torn away from the family its sentimental veil, and has reduced the family relation to a mere money relation.

SOURCE: Karl Marx and Friedrich Engels, Basic Writings on Politics and Philosophy, *pages 9–11.*

The bourgeoisie has disclosed how it came to pass that the brutal display of vigor in the Middle Ages, which reactionaries so much admire, found its fitting complement in the most slothful indolence. It has been the first to show what man's activity can bring about. It has accomplished wonders far surpassing Egyptian pyramids, Roman aqueducts, and Gothic cathedrals; it has conducted expeditions that put in the shade all former migrations of nations and crusades.

The bourgeoisie cannot exist without constantly revolutionizing the instruments of production, and thereby the relations of production, and with them the whole relations of society. Conservation of the old modes of production in unaltered form, was, on the contrary, the first condition of existence for all earlier industrial classes. Constant revolutionizing of production, uninterrupted disturbance of all social conditions, everlasting uncertainty and agitation distinguish the bourgeois epoch from all earlier ones. All fixed, fast-frozen relations, with their train of ancient and venerable prejudices and opinions, are swept away, all new-formed ones become antiquated before they can ossify. All that is solid melts into air, all that is holy is profaned, and man is at last compelled to face with sober senses his real conditions of life and his relations with his kind.

The need of a constantly expanding market for its products chases the bourgeoisie over the whole surface of the globe. It must nestle everywhere, settle everywhere, establish connections everywhere.

The bourgeoisie has through its exploitation of the world market given a cosmopolitan character to production and consumption in every country. To the great chagrin of reactionaries, it has drawn from under the feet of industry the national ground on which it stood. All old-established national industries have been destroyed or are daily being destroyed. They are dislodged by new industries, whose introduction becomes a life and death question for all civilized nations, by industries that no longer work up indigenous raw material, but raw material drawn from the remotest zones; industries whose products are consumed, not only at home, but in every quarter of the globe. In place of the old wants, satisfied by the production of the country, we find new wants, requiring for their satisfaction the products of distant lands and climes. In place of the old local and national seclusion and self-sufficiency, we have intercourse in every direction, universal inter-dependence of nations. And as in material, so also in intellectual production. The intellectual creations of individual nations become common property. National one-sidedness and narrow-mindedness become more and more impossible, and from the numerous national and local literatures there arises a world literature. . . .

From "Mauvais Sang" [Bad Blood]

The center of an ethnopoetics in Rimbaud's work is his recovery (circa 1870 at age 16) of the shaman-like poet who "must become a seer, make oneself a seer . . . by a long, prodigious & systematic derangement of the senses." (Compare, e.g., the Copper Eskimo word for the shaman/songman [= poet]: "one who has eyes.") But along with that comes an early internalization of the once distant "savage"—a ferocious play, in Rimbaud's case, that fuses his imagined Gallic/pagan ancestors ("the race that sang under torture") with those contemporary outcasts and criminals (local and colonial) who become for him a kind of internalized "nigger" (nègre) set against the "sham niggers" of the reigning French politesse: la vie française, le sentier de l'honneur. In another form, this nègre will be exorcised and/or reconstituted by those such as the African and Caribbean Negritude poets (see below, p. 52).

I have the blue-white eye of my Gallic ancestors, their narrow skull and their clumsiness in fighting. I find my clothes as barbarous as theirs. Only I don't butter my hair.

The Gauls were the most inept flayers of beasts and scorchers of grass of their time.

From them too: idolatry and love of sacrilege; oh! all the vices, anger, lust—lust, magnificent—above all, lying and sloth.

I have a horror of all trades. Masters and workers—base peasants all. The hand that guides the pen is worth the hand that guides the plough.—What an age of hands! I shall never have my hand. Afterward domesticity leads too far. The decency of beggars sickens me. Criminals disgust like castrates: as for me, I am intact, and I don't care.

But who gave me so perfidious a tongue that it has guided and guarded my indolence till now? Without ever making use of my body for anything, and lazier than the toad, I have lived everywhere. Not a family of Europe that I do not know.—I mean families like my own that owe everything to the Declaration of the Rights of Man.—I have known all the sons of respectable families.

* * *

Had I but antecedents at some point in the history of France!

But no, nothing.

It is quite clear to me that I have always been of an inferior race. I cannot understand revolt. My race never rose except to pillage: like wolves with the beast they have not killed.

I remember the history of France, eldest daughter of the Church. A villein, I must have made the journey to the Holy Land; my head is full of roads through the Swabian plains, views of Byzantium, ramparts of Jerusalem: The cult of Mary, compassion for

SOURCE: *Arthur Rimbaud, A Season in Hell (tr. Louise Varèse), pages 7–19.*

14

the crucified Christ awake in me among a thousand profane phantasmagoria.—A leper, I am seated among pot-sherds and nettles, at the foot of a sun-eaten wall.—Later, a reiter, I must have bivouacked under German stars.

Ah! again: I dance the witches' sabbath in a red clearing with old women and children.

I can remember no farther back than this very land and Christianity. I shall never have done seeing myself in that past. But always alone; without family; and even the language that I spoke—what was it? I cannot see myself at the councils of Christ; nor at the councils of Lords—representatives of Christ.

What was I in the last century? I find no trace again until today. No more vagabonds, no more vague wars. The inferior race has over-run everything: the people—as we say the nation, reason, science.

Oh! Science! Everything has been revised. For the body and for the soul,—the viaticum,—there is medicine and philosophy,—old wives' remedies and popular songs rearranged. And the pastimes of princes and games they proscribed! Geography, cosmography, mechanics, chemistry! . . .

Science, the new nobility! Progress. The world marches on! Why shouldn't it turn?

It is the vision of numbers. We are going toward the *Spirit*. There's no doubt about it, an oracle, I tell you. I understand, and not knowing how to express myself without pagan words, I'd rather remain silent.

* * *

Pagan blood returns! The Spirit is near; why doesn't Christ help me by granting my soul nobility and liberty? Alas! The gospel has gone by! The gospel! The gospel.

Greedily I await God. I am of an inferior race for all eternity.

Here I am on the Breton shore. Let the towns light up in the evening. My day is done; I'm quitting Europe. Sea air will burn my lungs; strange climates will tan my skin. To swim, to trample the grass, to hunt, and above all to smoke; to drink liquors strong as boiling metal,—like my dear ancestors around their fires.

I'll return with limbs of iron, dark skin and furious eye; people will think to look at me that I am of a strong race. I will have gold: I will be idle and brutal. Women nurse those fierce invalids, home from hot countries. I'll be mixed up in politics. Saved.

Now I am an outcast. I loathe the fatherland. A very drunken sleep on the beach, that's best.

* * *

Still but a child, I admired the intractable convict on whom the prison doors are always closing; I sought out the inns and rooming houses he might have consecrated by his passing; *with his idea* I saw the blue sky, and labour flowering the country; in cities I sensed his doom. He had more strength than a saint, more common sense than a traveler—and he, he alone! the witness of his glory and his reason.

On highroads on winter nights, without roof, without clothes, without bread, a voice gripped my frozen heart: "Weakness or strength: why, for you it is strength. You do not know where you are going, nor why you are going; enter anywhere, reply to anything. They will no more kill you than if you were a corpse." In the morning I had a look so lost, a face so dead, that perhaps those whom I met *did not see me*.

In cities, suddenly, the mud seemed red or black like a mirror when the lamp moves about in the adjoining room, like a treasure in the forest! Good luck, I cried, and I saw a sea of flames and smoke in the sky; to the right, to the left all the riches of the world flaming like a billion thunder-bolts.

But to me debauch and the comradeship of women were denied. Not even a companion. I saw myself before an infuriated mob, facing the firing-squad, weeping out of pity for their being unable to understand, and forgiving!—Like Jeanne d'Arc!— "Priests, professors, masters, you are making a mistake in turning me over to the law. I have never belonged to this people; I have never been a Christian; I am of the race that sang under torture; laws I have never understood; I have no moral sense, I am a brute: you are making a mistake."

Yes, my eyes are closed to your light. I am a beast, a nigger. But I can be saved. You are sham niggers, you, maniacs, wildmen, misers. Merchant, you are a nigger; Judge, you are a nigger; General, you are a nigger; Emperor, old itch, you are a nigger: you have drunk of the untaxed liquor of Satan's still.—Fever and cancer inspire this people. Cripples and old men are so respectable they are fit to be boiled.—The smartest thing would be to leave this continent where madness stalks to provide hostages for these wretches. I enter the true kingdom of Ham.

Do I know nature yet? Do I know myself?—*No more words*. I bury the dead in my belly. Shouts, drums, dance, dance, dance, dance! I cannot even see the time when, white men landing, I shall fall into nothingness.

Hunger, thirst, shouts, dance, dance, dance, dance!

EMILE DURKHEIM
On Ritual and Theater

Durkheim (1858–1917) has exerted a major and continuing influence on contemporary social theory (structural-functionalism, structuralism, etc.) through his investigations of the relation of social to mental structures. In "non-alienated" simple societies, he viewed this relationship as an instance of "collective mind"—as when he and Marcel Mauss wrote: "Logical relations are in a sense domestic relations . . . and the unity of knowledge is nothing else than the unity of the collectivity extended to the universe" (1963: 84). Durkheim brings to the present context an emphasis on the collective nature of tribal ritual and art, leading, from our perspective, toward later experiments with the creation and/or revival of participatory performance— those of Schechner (see below, p. 311), say, or the proposition of Jackson Mac Low, by which the new performance poet would "create a situation wherein she or he

SOURCE: Emile Durkheim, The Elementary Forms of the Religious Life *(tr. Joseph Ward Swain), pages 424–427.*

*invites other persons & the world in general to be co-creators . . . within the free
society of equals which it is hoped the work will help to bring about" (1979: 75).
Schechner's "efficacy-entertainment dyad" reflects the perception—by Durkheim
and others such as Jane Harrison or, later, Victor Turner—of the dramatic nature of
religious ritual and its continuing presence in even those performances that seem to
signal its demise. For Durkheim, this was a question of "collective mind," while
with an anthropologist like Radin (see below, p. 31), we get the balancing concept
of the extreme individuality of "primitive man."*

Not only do [ritual representations] employ the same processes as the real drama, but
they also pursue an end of the same sort: being foreign to all utilitarian ends, they make
men forget the real world and transport them into another where their imagination is
more at ease; they distract. They sometimes even go so far as to have the outward
appearance of a recreation: the assistants may be seen laughing and amusing themselves
openly.

Representative rites and collective recreations are even so close to one another that
men pass from one sort to the other without any break of continuity. The characteristic
feature of the properly religious ceremonies is that they must be celebrated on a
consecrated ground, from which women and noninitiated persons are excluded. But
there are others in which this religious character is somewhat effaced, though it has not
disappeared completely. They take place outside the ceremonial ground, which proves
that they are already laicized to a certain degree; but profane persons, women and
children, are not yet admitted to them. So they are on the boundary between the two
domains. They generally deal with legendary personages, but ones having no regular
place in the framework of the totemic religion. They are spirits, more generally
malevolent ones, having relations with the magicians rather than the ordinary believers,
and sorts of bugbears, in whom men do not believe with the same degree of seriousness
and firmness of conviction as in the proper totemic beings and things. As the bonds by
which the events and personages represented are attached to the history of the tribe relax,
these take on a proportionately more unreal appearance, while the corresponding
ceremonies change in nature. Thus men enter into the domain of pure fancy, and pass
from the commemorative rite to the ordinary corrobbori, a simple public merrymaking,
which has nothing religious about it and in which all may take part indifferently. Perhaps
some of these representations, whose sole object now is to distract, are ancient rites,
whose character has been changed. In fact, the distinction between these two sorts of
ceremonies is so variable that it is impossible to state with precision to which of the two
kinds they belong.

It is a well-known fact that games and the principal forms of art seem to have been
born of religion and that for a long time they retained a religious character. We now see
what the reasons for this are: it is because the cult, though aimed primarily at other ends,
has also been a sort of recreation for men. Religion has not played this role by hazard or
owing to a happy chance, but through a necessity of its nature. Though, as we have
established, religious thought is something very different from a system of fictions, still

the realities to which it corresponds express themselves religiously only when religion transfigures them. Between society as it is objectively and the sacred things which express it symbolically, the distance is considerable. It has been necessary that the impressions really felt by men, which served as the original matter of this construction, should be interpreted, elaborated and transformed until they became unrecognizable. So the world of religious things is a partially imaginary world, though only in its outward form, and one which therefore lends itself more readily to the free creations of the mind. Also, since the intellectual forces which serve to make it are intense and tumultous, the unique task of expressing the real with the aid of appropriate symbols is not enough to occupy them. A surplus generally remains available which seeks to employ itself in supplementary and superfluous works of luxury, that is to say, in works of art. There are practices as well as beliefs of this sort. The state of effervescence in which the assembled worshippers find themselves must be translated outwardly by exuberant movements which are not easily subjected to too carefully defined ends. In part, they escape aimlessly, they spread themselves for the mere pleasure of so doing, and they take delight in all sorts of games. Besides, in so far as the beings to whom the cult is addressed are imaginary, they are not able to contain and regulate this exuberance; the pressure of tangible and resisting realities is required to confine activities to exact and economical forms. Therefore one exposes oneself to grave misunderstandings if, in explaining rites, he believes that each gesture has a precise object and a definite reason for its existence. There are some which serve nothing; they merely answer the need felt by worshippers for action, motion, gesticulation. They are to be seen jumping, whirling, dancing, crying and singing, though it may not always be possible to give a meaning to all this agitation.

Therefore religion would not be itself if it did not give some place to the free combinations of thought and activity, to play, to art, to all that recreates the spirit that has been fatigued by the too great slavishness of daily work: the very same causes which called it into existence make it a necessity. Art is not merely an external ornament with which the cult has adorned itself in order to dissimulate certain of its features which may be too austere and too rude; but rather, in itself, the cult is something æsthetic. Owing to the well-known connection which mythology has with poetry, some have wished to exclude the former from religion; the truth is that there is a poetry inherent in all religion. The representative rites which have just been studied make this aspect of the religious life manifest; but there are scarcely any rites which do not present it to some degree. . . .

ERNEST FENOLLOSA

From *The Chinese Written Character as a Medium for Poetry*

Fenollosa's long essay, written circa 1908, is the outstanding instance of the impact on contemporary practice not simply of another poetry but of the inherent poetics of another language—its written as well as spoken form. Ezra Pound, who had translated Japanese Noh plays with Fenollosa, arranged for the essay's posthumous publication, writing in introduction: "In his search through unknown art, Fenollosa, coming upon unknown motives and principles unrecognized in the West, was already led into many modes of thought since fruitful in 'new' Western painting and poetry. . . . The later movements in art have corroborated his theories." In spite of subsequent questioning of its accuracy, Fenollosa's freeing of poetry from the limits of a partial grasp of the potentialities of language influenced not only Pound and William Carlos Williams and their generation and followers but also later groups, such as the "concrete poets," seeking the (semiotic) immediacy of the graphic/ visual ideogram ("a splendid flash of concrete poetry," Fenollosa wrote prophetically, below, p. 24). Or again, Charles Olson's summation from the side of speech: "Why Fenollosa wrote the damned best piece on language since when, is because, in setting Chinese directly over against American, he reasserted these resistant primes in our speech, put us back to the origins of their force not as history but as living oral law to be discovered in speech as directly as it is in our mouths" (1967: 18). (For more on the poetics of language systems per se and their influence on thought and world view, see Whorf, "An American Indian Model of the Universe," below, p. 191.)

My subject is poetry, not language, yet the roots of poetry are in language. In the study of a language so alien in form to ours as is Chinese in its written character, it is necessary to inquire how these universal elements of form which constitute poetics can derive appropriate nutriment.

In what sense can verse, written in terms of visible hieroglyphics, be reckoned true poetry? It might seem that poetry, which like music is a *time art*, weaving its unities out of successive impressions of sound, could with difficulty assimilate a verbal medium consisting largely of semipictorial appeals to the eye.

Contrast, for example, Gray's line:

The curfew tolls the knell of parting day

SOURCE: *Ernest Fenollosa,* The Chinese Written Character as a Medium for Poetry, *pages 6–15, 23–28.*

with the Chinese line:

月   耀   如   晴   雪

Moon   *Rays*   *Like*   *Pure*   *Snow*

Unless the sound of the latter be given, what have they in common? It is not enough to adduce that each contains a certain body of prosaic meaning; for the question is, how can the Chinese line imply, *as form*, the very element that distinguishes poetry from prose?

On second glance, it is seen that the Chinese words, though visible, occur in just as necessary an order as the phonetic symbols of Gray. All that poetic form requires is a regular and flexible sequence, as plastic as thought itself. The characters may be seen and read, silently by the eye, one after the other:

Moon rays like pure snow.

Perhaps we do not always sufficiently consider that thought is successive, not through some accident or weakness of our subjective operations but because the operations of nature are successive. The transferences of force from agent to object, which constitute natural phenomena, occupy time. Therefore, a reproduction of them in imagination requires the same temporal order.[1]

Suppose that we look out of a window and watch a man. Suddenly he turns his head and actively fixes his attention upon something. We look ourselves and see that his vision has been focused upon a horse. We saw, first, the man before he acted; second, while he acted; third, the object toward which his action was directed. In speech we split up the rapid continuity of this action and of its picture into its three essential parts or joints in the right order, and say:

Man sees horse.

It is clear that these three joints, or words, are only three phonetic symbols, which stand for the three terms of a natural process. But we could quite as easily denote these three stages of our thought by symbols equally arbitrary, *which had no basis in sound*; for example, by three Chinese characters:

人   見   馬

Man   *Sees*   *Horse*

If we all knew *what division* of this mental horse-picture each of these signs stood

for, we could communicate continuous thought to one another as easily by drawing them
as by speaking words. We habitually employ the visible language of gesture in much this
same manner.

But Chinese notation is something much more than arbitrary symbols. It is based
upon a vivid shorthand picture of the operations of nature. In the algebraic figure and in
the spoken word there is no natural connection between thing and sign: all depends upon
sheer convention. But the Chinese method follows natural suggestion. First stands the
man on his two legs. Second, his eye moves through space: a bold figure represented by
running legs under an eye, a modified picture of an eye, a modified picture of running
legs, but unforgettable once you have seen it. Third stands the horse on his four legs.

The thought-picture is not only called up by these signs as well as by words, but far
more vividly and concretely. Legs belong to all three characters: they are *alive*. The
group holds something of the quality of a continuous moving picture.

The untruth of a painting or a photograph is that, in spite of its concreteness, it
drops the element of natural succession.

Contrast the Laocoön statue with Browning's lines:

> *I sprang to the stirrup, and Joris, and he*
> .   .   .   .   .
> *And into the midnight we galloped abreast.*

One superiority of verbal poetry as an art rests in its getting back to the fundamental
reality of *time*. Chinese poetry has the unique advantage of combining both elements. It
speaks at once with the vividness of painting, and with the mobility of sounds. It is, in
some sense, more objective than either, more dramatic. In reading Chinese we do not
seem to be juggling mental counters, but to be watching *things* work out their own fate.

Leaving for a moment the form of the sentence, let us look more closely at this
quality of vividness in the structure of detached Chinese words. The earlier forms of
these characters were pictorial, and their hold upon the imagination is little shaken, even
in later conventional modifications. It is not so well known, perhaps, that the great
number of these ideographic roots carry in them a *verbal idea of action*. It might be
thought that a picture is naturally the picture of a *thing*, and that therefore the root ideas of
Chinese are what grammar calls nouns.

But examination shows that a large number of the primitive Chinese characters,
even the so-called radicals, are shorthand pictures of actions or processes.

For example, the ideograph meaning 'to speak' is a mouth with two words and a
flame coming out of it. The sign meaning 'to grow up with difficulty' is grass with a
twisted root. But this concrete *verb* quality, both in nature and in the Chinese signs,
becomes far more striking and poetic when we pass from such simple, original pictures
to compounds. In this process of compounding, two things added together do not
produce a third thing but suggest some fundamental relation between them. For
example, the ideograph for a 'messmate' is a man and a fire.

A true noun, an isolated thing, does not exist in nature. Things are only the
terminal points, or rather the meeting points, of actions, cross-sections cut through
actions, snapshots. Neither can a pure verb, an abstract motion, be possible in nature.

The eye sees noun and verb as one: things in motion, motion in things, and so the Chinese conception tends to represent them.[2]

The sun underlying the bursting forth of plants=spring.

The sun sign tangled in the branches of the tree sign=east.

'Rice-field' plus 'struggle'=male.

'Boat' plus 'water'=boat-water, a ripple.

Let us return to the form of the sentence and see what power it adds to the verbal units from which it builds. I wonder how many people have asked themselves why the sentence form exists at all, why it seems so universally necessary *in all languages*? Why *must* all possess it, and what is the normal type of it? If it be so universal, it ought to correspond to some primary law of nature.

I fancy the professional grammarians have given but a lame response to this inquiry. Their definitions fall into two types: one, that a sentence expresses a 'complete thought'; the other, that in it we bring about a union of subject and predicate.

The former has the advantage of trying for some natural objective standard, since it is evident that a thought can not be the test of its own completeness. But in nature there is *no* completeness. On the one hand, practical completeness may be expressed by a mere interjection, as 'Hi! there!', or 'Scat!', or even by shaking one's fist. No sentence is needed to make one's meaning more clear. On the other hand, no full sentence really completes a thought. The man who sees and the horse which is seen will not stand still. The man was planning a ride before he looked. The horse kicked when the man tried to catch him. The truth is that acts are successive, even continuous; one causes or passes into another. And though we may string ever so many clauses into a single compound sentence, motion leaks everywhere, like electricity from an exposed wire. All processes in nature are interrelated; and thus there could be no complete sentence (according to this definition) save one which it would take all time to pronounce.

In the second definition of the sentence, as 'uniting a subject and a predicate,' the grammarian falls back on pure subjectivity. *We* do it all; it is a little private juggling between our right and left hands. The subject is that about which *I* am going to talk; the predicate is that which *I* am going to say about it. The sentence according to this definition is not an attribute of nature but an accident of man as a conversational animal.

If it were really so, then there could be no possible test of the truth of a sentence. Falsehood would be as specious as verity. Speech would carry no conviction.

Of course this view of the grammarians springs from the discredited, or rather the useless, logic of the Middle Ages. According to this logic, thought deals with abstractions, concepts drawn out of things by a sifting process. These logicians never inquired how the 'qualities' which they pulled out of things came to be there. The truth of all their little checker-board juggling depended upon the natural order by which these powers or properties or qualities were folded in concrete things, yet they despised the 'thing' as a mere 'particular,' or pawn. It was as if Botany should reason from the leaf-patterns woven into our table-cloths. Valid scientific thought consists in following as closely as may be the actual and entangled lines of forces as they pulse through things. Thought deals with no bloodless concepts but watches *things move* under its microscope.

The sentence form was forced upon primitive men by nature itself. It was not we

---

[2]Axe *striking* something; dog *attending* man=dogs him.

who made it; it was a reflection of the temporal order in causation. All truth has to be expressed in sentences because all truth is the *transference of power*. The type of sentence in nature is a flash of lightning. It passes between two terms, a cloud and the earth. No unit of natural process can be less than this. All natural processes are, in their units, as much as this. Light, heat, gravity, chemical affinity, human will, have this in common, that they redistribute force. Their unit of process can be represented as:

term	*transference*	*term*
from	*of*	*to*
which	*force*	*which*

If we regard this transference as the conscious or unconscious act of an agent we can translate the diagram into:

agent	*act*	*object*

In this the act is the very substance of the fact denoted. The agent and the object are only limiting terms.

It seems to me that the normal and typical sentence in English as well as in Chinese expresses just this unit of natural process. It consists of three necessary words: the first denoting the agent or subject from which the act starts, the second embodying the very stroke of the act, the third pointing to the object, the receiver of the impact. Thus:

Farmer	*pounds*	*rice*

The form of the Chinese transitive sentence, and of the English (omitting particles), exactly corresponds to this universal form of action in nature. This brings language close to *things*, and in its strong reliance upon verbs it erects all speech into a kind of dramatic poetry.

A different sentence order is frequent in inflected languages like Latin, German or Japanese. This is because they are inflected, i.e., they have litle tags and word-endings, or labels, to show which is the agent, the object, etc. In uninflected languages, like English and Chinese, there is nothing but the order of the words to distinguish their functions. And this order would be no sufficient indication, were it not the *natural order*—that is, the order of cause and effect.

It is true that there are, in language, intransitive and passive forms, sentences built out of the verb 'to be,' and, finally, negative forms. To grammarians and logicians these have seemed more primitive than the transitive, or at least exceptions to the transitive. I had long suspected that these apparently exceptional forms had grown from the transitive or worn away from it by alteration, or modification. This view is confirmed by Chinese examples, wherein it is still possible to watch the transformation going on.

The intransitive form derives from the transitive by dropping a generalized, customary, reflexive or cognate object: 'He runs (a race).' 'The sky reddens (itself).' 'We breathe (air).' Thus we get weak and incomplete sentences which suspend the picture and lead us to think of some verbs as denoting states rather than acts. Outside grammar the word 'state' would hardly be recognised as scientific. Who can doubt that when we say 'The wall shines,' we mean that it actively reflects light to our eye?

The beauty of Chinese verbs is that they are all transitive or intransitive at pleasure. There is no such thing as a naturally intransitive verb. The passive form is evidently a correlative sentence, which turns about and makes the object into a subject. That the object is not in itself passive, but contributes some positive force of its own to the action, is in harmony both with scientific law and with ordinary experience. The English passive voice with 'is' seemed at first an obstacle to this hypothesis, but one suspected that the true form was a generalised transitive verb meaning something like 'receive,' which had degenerated into an auxiliary. It was a delight to find this the case in Chinese.

In nature there are no negations, no possible transfers of negative force. The presence of negative sentences in language would seem to corroborate the logicians' view that assertion is an arbitrary subjective act. *We* can assert a negation, though nature can not. But here again science comes to our aid against the logician: all apparently negative or disruptive movements bring into play other positive forces. It requires great effort to annihilate. Therefore we should suspect that, if we could follow back the history of all negative particles, we should find that they also are sprung from transitive verbs. It is too late to demonstrate such derivations in the Aryan languages, the clue has been lost; but in Chinese we can still watch positive verbal conceptions passing over into so-called negatives. Thus in Chinese the sign meaning 'to be lost in the forest' relates to a state of non-existence. English 'not'=the Sanskrit *na*, which may come from the root *na*, to be lost, to perish.

Lastly comes the infinitive which substitutes for a specific colored verb the universal copula 'is,' followed by a noun or an adjective. We do not say a tree 'greens itself,' but 'the tree is green'; not that 'monkeys bring forth live young,' but that 'the monkey is a mammal.' This is an ultimate weakness of language. It has come from generalising all intransitive words into one. As 'live,' 'see,' 'walk,' 'breathe,' are generalised into states by dropping their objects, so these weak verbs are in turn reduced to the abstractest state of all, namely bare existence.

There is in reality no such verb as a pure copula, no such original conception; our very word *exist* means 'to stand forth,' to show oneself by a definite act. 'Is' comes from the Aryan root *as*, to breathe. 'Be' is from *bhu*, to grow.

In Chinese the chief verb for 'is' not only means actively 'to have,' but shows by its derivation that it expresses something even more concrete, namely 'to snatch from the

moon with the hand.''   Here the baldest symbol of prosaic analysis is

transformed by magic into a splendid flash of concrete poetry. . . .

One of the most interesting facts about the Chinese language is that in it we can see, not only the forms of sentences, but literally the parts of speech growing up, budding forth one from another. Like nature, the Chinese words are alive and plastic, because *thing* and *action* are not formally separated. The Chinese language naturally knows no grammar. It is only lately that foreigners, European and Japanese, have begun to torture this vital speech by forcing it to fit the bed of their definitions. We import into our reading of Chinese all the weakness of our own formalisms. This is especially sad in poetry, because the one necessity, even in our own poetry, is to keep words as flexible as possible, as full of the sap of nature.

Let us go further with our example. In English we call 'to shine' a *verb in the infinitive*, because it gives the abstract meaning of the verb without conditions. If we want a corresponding adjective we take a different word, 'bright.' If we need a noun we say 'luminosity,' which is abstract, being derived from an adjective. To get a tolerably concrete noun, we have to leave behind the verb and adjective roots, and light upon a thing arbitrarily cut off from its power of action, say 'the sun' or 'the moon.' Of course there is nothing in nature so cut off, and therefore this nounising is itself an abstraction. Even if we did have a common word underlying at once the verb 'shine,' the adjective 'bright' and the noun 'sun,' we should probably call it an 'infinitive of the infinitive.' According to our ideas, it should be something extremely abstract, too intangible for use.

The Chinese have one word, *ming* or *mei*. Its ideograph is the sign of the sun together with the sign of the moon. It serves as verb, noun, adjective. Thus you write literally, 'the sun and moon of the cup' for 'the cup's brightness.' Placed as a verb, you write 'the cup sun-and-moons,' actually 'cup sun-and-moon,' or in a weakened thought, 'is like sun,' i.e., shines. 'Sun-and-moon cup' is naturally a bright cup. There is no possible confusion of the real meaning, though a stupid scholar may spend a week trying to decide what 'part of speech' he should use in translating a very simple and direct thought from Chinese to English. . . .

I trust that this digression concerning parts of speech may have justified itself. It proves, first, the enormous interest of the Chinese language in throwing light upon our forgotten mental processes, and thus furnishes a new chapter in the philosophy of language. Secondly, it is indispensable for understanding the poetical raw material which the Chinese language affords. Poetry differs from prose in the concrete colors of its diction. It is not enough for it to furnish a meaning to philosophers. It must appeal to emotions with the charm of direct impression, flashing through regions where the intellect can only grope.[3] Poetry must render what is said, not what is merely meant. Abstract meaning gives little vividness, and fullness of imagination gives all. Chinese poetry demands that we abandon our narrow grammatical categories, that we follow the original text with a wealth of concrete verbs.

But this is only the beginning of the matter. So far we have exhibited the Chinese characters and the Chinese sentence chiefly as vivid shorthand pictures of actions and processes in nature. These embody true poetry as far as they go. Such actions are *seen*, but Chinese would be a poor language, and Chinese poetry but a narrow art, could they not go on to represent also what is unseen. The best poetry deals not only with natural images but with lofty thoughts, spiritual suggestions and obscure relations. The greater part of natural truth is hidden in processes too minute for vision and in harmonies too large, in vibrations, cohesions and in affinities. The Chinese compass these also, and with great power and beauty.

You will ask, how could the Chinese have built up a great intellectual fabric from mere picture writing? To the ordinary Western mind, which believes that thought is

---

[3]Cf. principle of Primary apparition, 'Spirit of Romance.' E. P.

concerned with logical categories and which rather condemns the faculty of direct imagination, this feat seems quite impossible. Yet the Chinese language with its peculiar materials has passed over from the seen to the unseen by exactly the same process which all ancient races employed. This process is metaphor, the use of material images to suggest immaterial relations.[4]

The whole delicate substance of speech is built upon substrata of metaphor. Abstract terms, pressed by etymology, reveal their ancient roots still embedded in direct action. But the primitive metaphors do not spring from arbitrary *subjective* processes. They are possible only because they follow objective lines of relations in nature herself. Relations are more real and more important than the things which they relate. The forces which produce the branch-angles of an oak lay potent in the acorn. Similar lines of resistance, half-curbing the out-pressing vitalities, govern the branching of rivers and of nations. Thus a nerve, a wire, a roadway, and a clearing-house are only varying channels which communication forces for itself. This is more than analogy, it is identity of structure. Nature furnishes her own clues. Had the world not been full of homologies, sympathies, and identities, thought would have been starved and language chained to the obvious. There would have been no bridge whereby to cross from the minor truth of the seen to the major truth of the unseen. Not more than a few hundred roots out of our large vocabularies could have dealt directly with physical processes. These we can fairly well identify in primitive Sanskrit. They are, almost without exception, vivid verbs. The wealth of European speech grew, following slowly the intricate maze of nature's suggestions and affinities. Metaphor was piled upon metaphor in quasi-geological strata.

Metaphor, the revealer of nature, is the very substance of poetry. The known interprets the obscure, the universe is alive with myth. The beauty and freedom of the observed world furnish a model, and life is pregnant with art. It is a mistake to suppose, with some philosophers of aesthetics, that art and poetry aim to deal with the general and the abstract. This misconception has been foisted upon us by mediaeval logic. Art and poetry deal with the concrete of nature, not with rows of separate 'particulars,' for such rows do not exist. Poetry is finer than prose because it gives us more concrete truth in the same compass of words. Metaphor, its chief device, is at once the substance of nature and of language. Poetry only does consciously[5] what the primitive races did unconsciously. The chief work of literary men in dealing with language, and of poets especially, lies in feeling back along the ancient lines of advance.[6] He must do this so that he may keep his words enriched by all their subtle undertones of meaning. The original metaphors stand as a kind of luminous background, giving color and vitality, forcing them closer to the concreteness of natural processes. Shakespeare everywhere teems with examples. For these reasons poetry was the earliest of the world arts; poetry, language and the care of myth grew up together.

I have alleged all this because it enables me to show clearly why I believe that the

---

[4]Compare Aristotle's *Poetics*: 'Swift perception of relations, hallmark of genius.' E. P.

[5]*Vide* also an article on 'Vorticism' in the *Fortnightly Review* for September 1914. 'The language of exploration' now in my 'Gaudier-Brzeska.' E. P.

[6]I would submit in all humility that this applies in the rendering of ancient texts. The poet, in dealing with his own time, must also see to it that language does not petrify on his hands. He must prepare for new advances along the lines of true metaphor, that is interpretative metaphor, or image, as diametrically opposed to untrue, or ornamental, metaphor. E. P.

Chinese written language has not only absorbed the poetic substance of nature and built with it a second work of metaphor, but has, through its very pictorial visibility, been able to retain its original creative poetry with far more vigor and vividness than any phonetic tongue. Let us first see how near it is to the heart of nature in its metaphors. We can watch it passing from the seen to the unseen, as we saw it passing from verb to pronoun. It retains the primitive sap, it is not cut and dried like a walking-stick. We have been told that these people are cold, practical, mechanical, literal, and without a trace of imaginative genius. That is nonsense.

Our ancestors built the accumulations of metaphor into structures of language and into systems of thought. Languages today are thin and cold because we think less and less into them. We are forced, for the sake of quickness and sharpness, to file down each word to its narrowest edge of meaning. Nature would seem to have become less like a paradise and more and more like a factory. We are content to accept the vulgar misuse of the moment.

A late stage of decay is arrested and embalmed in the dictionary.

Only scholars and poets feel painfully back along the thread of our etymologies and piece together our diction, as best they may, from forgotten fragments. This anaemia of modern speech is only too well encouraged by the feeble cohesive force of our phonetic symbols. There is little or nothing in a phonetic word to exhibit the embryonic stages of its growth. It does not bear its metaphor on its face. We forget that personality once meant, not the soul, but the soul's mask. This is the sort of thing one can not possibly forget in using the Chinese symbols.

In this Chinese shows its advantage. Its etymology is constantly visible. It retains the creative impulse and process, visible and at work. After thousands of years the lines of metaphoric advance are still shown, and in many cases actually retained in the meaning. Thus a word, instead of growing gradually poorer and poorer as with us, becomes richer and still more rich from age to age, almost consciously luminous. Its uses in national philosophy and history, in biography and in poetry, throw about it a nimbus of meanings. These centre about the graphic symbol. The memory can hold them and use them. The very soil of Chinese life seems entangled in the roots of its speech. The manifold illustrations which crowd its annals of personal experience, the lines of tendency which converge upon a tragic climax, moral character as the very core of the principle—all these are flashed at once on the mind as reinforcing values with accumulation of meaning which a phonetic language can hardly hope to attain. Their ideographs are like bloodstained battle-flags to an old campaigner. With us, the poet is the only one for whom the accumulated treasures of the race-words are real and active. Poetic language is always vibrant with fold on fold of overtones and with natural affinities, but in Chinese the visibility of the metaphor tends to raise this quality to its intensest power.

I have mentioned the tyranny of mediaeval logic. According to this European logic, thought is a kind of brickyard. It is baked into little hard units or concepts. These are piled in rows according to size and then labeled with words for future use. This use consists in picking out a few bricks, each by its convenient label, and sticking them together into a sort of wall called a sentence by the use either of white mortar for the positive copula 'is,' or of black mortar for the negative copula 'is not.' In this way we produce such admirable propositions as 'A ring-tailed baboon is not a constitutional assembly.'

Let us consider a row of cherry trees. From each of these in turn we proceed to take an 'abstract,' as the phrase is, a certain common lump of qualities which we may express together by the name cherry or cherry-ness. Next we place in a second table several such characteristic concepts: cherry, rose, sunset, iron-rust, flamingo. From these we abstract some further common quality, dilutation or mediocrity, and label it 'red' or 'redness.' It is evident that this process of abstraction may be carried on indefinitely and with all sorts of material. We may go on forever building pyramids of attenuated concept until we reach the apex 'being.'

But we have done enough to illustrate the characteristic process. At the base of the pyramid lie *things*, but stunned, as it were. They can never know themselves for things until they pass up and down among the layers of the pyramids. The way of passing up and down the pyramid may be exemplified as follows: We take a concept of lower attenuation, such as 'cherry'; we see that it is contained under one higher, such as 'redness.' Then we are permitted to say in sentence form, 'Cherryness is contained under redness,' or for short, '(The) cherry is red.' If, on the other hand, we do not find our chosen subject under a given predicate we use the black copula and say, for example, '(The) cherry is not liquid.'

From this point we might go on to the theory of the syllogism, but we refrain. It is enough to note that the practised logician finds it convenient to store his mind with long lists of nouns and adjectives, for these are naturally the names of classes. Most textbooks on language begin with such lists. The study of verbs is meagre, for in such a system there is only one real working verb, to wit, the quasi-verb 'is.' All other verbs can be transformed into participles and gerunds. For example, 'to run' practically becomes a case of 'running.' Instead of thinking directly, 'The man runs,' our logician makes two subjective equations, namely: The individual in question is contained under the class 'man'; and the class 'man' is contained under the class of 'running things.'

The sheer loss and weakness of this method are apparent and flagrant. Even in its own sphere it can not think half of what it wants to think. It has no way of bringing together any two concepts which do not happen to stand one under the other and in the same pyramid.

It is impossible to represent change in this system or any kind of growth.

This is probably why the conception of evolution came so late in Europe. *It could not make way until it was prepared to destroy the inveterate logic of classification.*

Far worse than this, such logic can not deal with any kind of interaction or with any multiplicity of function. According to it, the function of my muscles is as isolated from the function of my nerves, as from an earthquake in the moon. For it the poor neglected things at the bases of the pyramids are only so many particulars or pawns.

Science fought till she got at the things.

All her work has been done from the base of the pyramids, not from the apex. She has discovered how functions cohere in things. She expresses her results in grouped sentences which embody no nouns or adjectives but verbs of special character. The true formula for thought is: The cherry tree is all that it does. Its correlated verbs compose it. At bottom these verbs are transitive. Such verbs may be almost infinite in number.

In diction and in grammatical form science is utterly opposed to logic. Primitive men who created language agreed with science and not with logic. Logic has abused the language which they left to her mercy.

Poetry agrees with science and not with logic. . . .

TRISTAN TZARA
A Note on Negro Poetry/Oceanian Art

As an avant-garde extremist and co-founder of the Dada movement—Zurich 1916 in the midst of World War I—Tzara called for "a great negative work of destruction" against the European nation-state as a "state of madness, the aggressive complete madness of a world left in the hands of bandits who vandalize and destroy the centuries." But the constructive side of the work included a project to recoup the model of a primal art and poetry, toward which he assembled, using numerous scholarly sources, a first anthology of tribal/oral poems from a fiercely modernist perspective—poèmes nègres, never published in his lifetime—and read from it at Dada soirées and cabaret performances. In much the same way, his Dada colleague (later Dada rival) Richard Huelsenbeck banged out "African" rhythms on a tomtom while chanting Dada poems—"to drum literature into the ground," the poet Hugo Ball said about him. Of his own "modernism" 's rejection of "modernism" itself, Tzara later said: "You are making a mistake if you take Dada for a modern school, or even for a reaction against present-day schools. . . . Dada isn't at all modern, it's rather a return to a quasi-buddhist religion of indifference" (Lecture on Dada 1922).

A NOTE ON NEGRO POETRY (1918)

"I don't even want to know that there were men before me" (Descartes), but some essential and simple laws, pathetic and muffled fermentation of a solid earth.

To fix on the point where the forces have accumulated, from whence the formulated sense springs, the invisible radiance of substance, the natural relation, but hidden and just, naively, without explanation.

To round off and regulate into shapes, into constructs, the images according to their weight, color and matter; or to map the arrangements of the values, the material and lasting densities, subordinating nothing to them. Classification of the comic operas sanctioned by the aesthetic of accessories. (O, my drawer number ABSOLUTE.)

I abhor to enter a house where the balconies, the "ornaments," are carefully stuck to the wall. Yet the sun, the stars continue to vibrate and hum freely in space, but I loathe to identify the explanatory hypotheses (asphyxiant probable) with the principle of life, activity, certainty.

The crocodile hatches the future life, rain falls for the vegetal silence, one isn't a creator by analogy. The beauty of the satellites—the teaching of light—will satisfy us, for we are God only for the country of our knowledge, in the laws

SOURCE: *Tristan Tzara,* Oeuvres Complètes, *volume 1, pages 400–401; volume 4, pages 301–302.*

according to which we live experience on this earth, on both sides of our equator, inside our borders. Perfect example of the infinite we can control: the sphere.

To round off and regulate into shapes, into constructs, the images according to their weight, color and matter; or to map the arrangements of the values, the material and lasting densities through personal decision and the unswerving firmness of sensibility, comprehension adequate to the matter transformed, close to the veins and rubbing against them in the pain for the present, definite joy. One creates an organism when the elements are ready for life. Poetry lives first of all for the functions of dance, religion, music and work.

[Tr. Pierre Joris]

OCEANIAN ART (1951)

Against the aesthetic concerns of an Apollinaire—who thought of art as a more or less intentional *product* of man, somehow separable from his inner nature— DADA opposed a grander concept wherein the art of primitive peoples, with its overlap of social and religious functions, appeared as the direct expression of their life. DADA, which foresaw an age of "Dadaist spontaneity," intended to make poetry a way of life rather than a subsidiary manifestation of intelligence and will. For DADA, art was one of the forms—common to all mankind—of a poetic activity whose deep roots commingled with the primitive structures of sentient life. DADA attempted to put this theory into practice—to join Black African and Oceanian art to the life of the mind and its expressions on an immediate and contemporary level—by organizing improvised soirées of Black dance and music. The issue for DADA was to recover from the depths of consciousness the exalted source of the poetic function.

The dominance of the human over the aesthetic, which DADA brought to light in the arts of primitive peoples, was a concern picked up by the Surrealists. If African art was the chief support for the plastic experiments of the cubist painters, it was through the new poetry that Oceanian art was discovered. By placing that art—and artistic activity in general—on the plane of mind (*esprit*) and by interpreting it as a directive for the freeing-up of the imagination, the Surrealist painters, coming after DADA, enlarged the domain where art had camped and where it ran the risk of choking on its own principle of perfection.

[Tr. Jerome Rothenberg]

PAUL RADIN
Reality at White Heat

Born in Lodz, Poland, Radin (1883–1959) became a leading figure in the Boasian school of American anthropology. His special genius lay in revealing and asserting the dominance of the individual in the stateless communal cultures of the aboriginal world. Not only that but "an individualism run riot," a "ruthless realism," and a high imagination, in a human nexus he summarized as follows:

> If one were asked to state briefly and succinctly . . . the outstanding positive features of aboriginal civilizations, I, for one, would have no hesitation in answering that there are three: the respect for the individual, irrespective of age or sex; the amazing degree of social and political integration achieved by them; and the existence there of a concept of personal security which transcends all governmental forms and all tribal and group interests and conflicts. (1953, 1971: 11)

In Primitive Man as Philosopher, *Radin focused on a kind of speculative, reality-shaping poetry (= "philosophy") for which his book acted as an early and germinal gathering. As a maker of texts, he contributed masterworks such as* The Trickster *(see below, p. 206) and the Winnebago ritual drama he called* The Road of Life and Death, *and he transmitted such native autobiographies as* Crashing Thunder *and* The Autobiography of a Winnebago Indian, *always oriented toward the presentation of the communal, individual self.*

It is one of the salient traits of so-called primitive man, . . . that he allows a full and appreciative expression to his sensations. He is preeminently a man of practical common sense just as is the average peasant. Now this does not merely mean manual dexterity or an exclusive interest in the purely material side of life. It has much deeper implications. This tough-mindedness leads to a recognition of all types of realities, realities which primitive man sees in all their directness and ruggedness, stripped of all that false and sentimental haze so universal among civilized peoples. We cannot dwell upon this point now but will return to it later. Here we desire merely to point out that primitive man is endowed with an overpowering sense of reality and possesses a manner of facing this reality, which to a western European implies an almost complete lack of sensitiveness. And this is true of even the more avowedly intellectual among them, such as the medicine-men and the leaders of the ceremonies. It is true that the facts of everyday life, in every primitive community, are clothed in a magical and ritualistic dress, yet it is not unfair to say that it is not the average native who is beguiled into an erroneous interpretation of this dress but the ethnologist.

To illustrate what I mean I shall give an example that came under my own

SOURCE: Paul Radin, Primitive Man as Philosopher, *pages 19–29.*

observation. An American Indian, pursued by the enemy, took refuge in a cave where he could easily defend himself against direct attack but where escape was apparently completely cut off. This particular individual was not religious. He had during his lifetime had so little interest in getting into the proper *rapport* with the deities of his tribe that he knew the conventional methods of addressing them but little else. In his dilemma, with death staring him in the face, he mechanically offers tobacco to the spirits. That much he knew. But he did not know what to say nor whom to address. So he prayed—if we are inclined to call this a prayer—"To you, O spirits, whoever you are, wherever you are, here is tobacco. May I be saved!" Through an almost miraculous piece of good luck the enemy fled and he was saved. "By the will of God," a devout Christian would have ejaculated; in Indian phraseology, "The spirits have heard me." Here, if anywhere, we might have expected an almost mystical feeling of heavenly intervention and a well-nigh complete obliteration of the mere workaday world. Yet nothing of the kind occurred to this very hard-minded individual. He sought to explain nothing. I can picture him saying to himself in his humorous way—for he was the professional humorist in the tribe— "Let the medicine-men explain; they like such things. All I know is that I was pursued by the enemy; I took refuge in a cave; my attackers withdrew and here I am." The ritualistic paraphernalia were all there but they did not obscure his vision of the nature of a true fact.

This man was of course an unusual specimen of the tough-minded species. So much will have to be granted unhesitatingly. Yet this intense realism, this refusal to be deluded by the traditional phraseology employed, is a salient feature of most primitive communities. That there are many individuals who take the phraseology more seriously we know. The medicine-man, the thinker, the poet, these insist upon a less matter-of-fact explanation and clearly enjoy the wrappings. Did they not in fact devise these explanations and are they not continually elaborating them? But in spite of the inner necessity that prompts them to prefer a supermundane formula they, too, are deeply rooted in the workaday-world conception of reality.

Nothing, for instance, is more thoroughly ingrained in the minds of many American Indians than the fact that a supernatural warrant must be obtained for any undertaking of importance no matter how practical its nature. The Indian will tell you simply enough that if a deity has bestowed his power upon an individual in a vision and permitted him to go on a warpath, he may do so. Yet if one visualizes concretely the hazardous nature of such an enterprise in a small tribe, it is but natural to assume that any community allowing a young man to risk his own life and possibly that of others on the strength of communication in a dream, must be profoundly imbued with a religious spirit. Unfortunately this whole picture is wrong. It changes as soon as we obtain fuller details about the matter. Then we discover that no individual is ever allowed to proceed on even a private war party unless his dream experience has been communicated to the chief of the tribe or else to some highly respected elder. Such men are always exceedingly devout. They certainly may be expected to take religious sanctions at their face value. Yet it was just these custodians of the tribal tradition who were most careful to see that the practical aspects of the situation did not militate too markedly against success. If, in their opinion, the undertaking was unwarranted—whether because they thought the leader too inexperienced, the possibility for adequate preparation unfavorable, the strength of the enemy possibly too great, or what not—they refused to give their sanction and forbade it. Quite naturally they couched this prohibition in a religious phraseology. "The spirits have not blessed you with sufficient power'' is the Winnebago formula, for instance.

The intense belief in the existence of the spirits and of their direct participation in the affairs of man is not to be questioned, any more than is the acceptance of the magical. But this in no way interferes with their full realization of all the facts involved in any given situation. In other words, though primitive man may describe life in a religious terminology it is not to be inferred that in the vast majority of cases he regards a purely mundane happening as due to supernatural agency. This is indicated clearly by the great care taken among many tribes not to demand impossible tasks from their deities. One does not ask rain from a cloudless sky during the dry season, nor security against capsizing in a canoe when foolishly setting out during a terrific storm.

Primitive man, in short, does not consider the deities or a magical rite as conditioning reality but as an accessory to it, as constraining it. Both the deity and the rite are aids for the proper functioning of a series of habitually connected individual or social events. The religious and magical content seems the all-important factor to us who are mere spectators; to primitive man they are, as we have said, simply aids, stimuli for the attainment of a goal.

Thus viewed the facts of primitive life take on a new psychological orientation. The attainment of a goal, the clear realization of a specific objective, becomes the main factor. Everything else is either completely slurred or regarded as secondary. Even rites, beliefs, motor activities, may all become functionless and accidental. Primitive man may not in our sense of the term provide for the morrow but he attempts something perhaps far more important—he bends all his energies, inward and outward, toward ensuring the success of his objective on the morrow. With this determination steadily before him he completely identifies himself with the goal to be obtained. He prepares for it, previsions it, preënacts it, and preattains it. Select any example at random—a war party among the Winnebago. In a dream communication from the spirits he ascertains the necessary number of moccasins and the necessary amount of food to be consumed on the expedition; he is told how many men he is to take along and how many of the enemy he is to kill. His divine certificate is then closely scrutinized by experienced elders and if it is accepted, then in the ceremony preparatory to his actually starting out he previsions his enemy. He destroys his courage, deprives him of his power of running, paralyzes his actions, and blunts his weapons. Thus protected and his enemy correspondingly weakened and constrained, he proceeds to the attack.

All these facts are admirably and convincingly illustrated by a very unusual document obtained by [Frank] Russell from the Pima Indians of Arizona (1908: 357). It represents a speech given by the war chief urging the people to go on the warpath against the Apache. I shall give it in full:

> Yes, my poor brother-in-law, this land was covered with herbage. The mountains were covered with clouds. The sunlight was not bright and the darkness was not dense. All was rolling before our eyes. It was thought that the time had come for considering these things in council, my brothers. Then wood was gathered and a fire kindled, the flames of which burst forth, reaching to the sky and causing a portion of the earth to fold over, disclosing the underside where a reddish mountain stood. After these things had happened the enterprise was decided upon.
>
> Then my breast was tightened and my loins girded; my hunger was appeased;

sandals with strings were made for my feet; my canteen was made ready. I went about the country, from mountain to village, beneath the sheds and trees, offering all an opportunity to join me. Returning home I thought I saw my brother when I was in a trance. I tried to grasp him and my arms embraced nothing but myself. I somehow caught in my palm what I thought to be this power; turning this over I found it to be but a creation of my imagination, and again I was disappointed. I was unkempt and rough and my tears moistened the land.

The plan occurred to me to ask Nasia, the old woman magician, for aid. Thinking that I saw her I ran toward the eastward and finally reached her. I said, "Yes, you who make the bows of the Apache like a *kiaha* and crush his arrow-heads, you who paint triangles and curves on the *kiaha* bottoms with the arrow foreshafts of the Apache dipped in his blood, you who twist the hair of the Apache and tie your *kiaha* with it." Thus I addressed her and she gave me a bundle of power which I grasped under my arm and ran with it to my home.

I thought of Vikaukam and prayed for his aid. When I finally reached him I said, "Yes, your house is built of Apache bows and bound with their arrows, you use his bowstrings and sinew to tie these withes. You use Apache headdresses and moccasins to cover your house. Within it you have square piles of Apache hair. At the corners of the piles cigarettes give off wreaths of smoke resembling white, black, glittering, purple, and yellow blossoms." Thus I spake and he gave me power which I carried away beneath my arm.

I thought of South Doctor and finally prayed to him. I said to him, "Yes, you who can make the Apache bow as harmless as a rainbow, his arrows like the white tassels of grass, his arrow shafts like soft down, his arrowheads like thin, dry mud, his arrow poison like the water fern upon the pools, his hair like rain clouds."

Thus I spake and he gave me power which I grasped under my arm and journeyed westward with four slackenings of speed. The home magician gave me a seat of honor. The cigarette smoked and I took it and, drawing in a cloud of smoke, I prayed to Old Woman Magician, saying, "Yes, you make the Apache bow like a game ring, you crush his arrow shafts and make headbands of them, you split his arrow foreshafts, color them with Apache blood, and make game sticks of them; his arrowheads you make like pottery paddles, you make a girdle of Apache hair."

Thus I spake and he gave me his power, which I caught under my arm and ran home, with four slackenings of speed. The home magician gave me a seat of honor. The cigarette smoked and I took it and, drawing in a cloud of smoke, breathed it forth in the direction of the enemy. The power grew and shone on and on until it slowly disclosed the enemy. The Pima magician desired that the earth move, the trees take on their leaves, the land be softened and improved, that all be straightened and made correct. The place was one where food was increased and they were gathered about it. Their springs were made larger and they were gathered about them. Their game was gathered together. Some of the enemy were in the west and they said, "We know that harm may come to us if we go to that place, but we will not heed our own misgivings." They started on their journey and camped on the way. In the morning they arose and continued, reaching their friends' camp during the day, where they saluted them. In the distant east were other enemies who heard that their friends were gathering. When they heard of it they said, "We know that harm may come of it if we go to that place, but we must go." They started on their journey and camped once before arriving and saluting their friends. They took the sun's rays and painted triangles on their blankets.

While this was happening among them my young men were preparing to fight. They rushed upon them like flying birds and swept them from the earth. Starting out upon my trail I reached the first water, whence I sent my swiftest young men to carry the message of victory to the old people at home. Before the Magician's door the earth was swept, and there my young men and women danced with headdresses and flowers on their heads. The wind rose and, cutting off these ornaments, carried them to the sky and hung them there. The rain fell upon the high places, the clouds enveloped the mountains, the torrents descended upon the springs and fell upon the trees.

You may think this over, my relatives. The taking of life brings serious thoughts of the waste; the celebration of victory may become unpleasantly riotous.

This is a reality at white heat and it is in such a heightened atmosphere that primitive man frequently lives. Since it is so frequent and accustomed an atmosphere, he is generally calm outwardly, although this varies from time to time and moments occur where pandemonium seems to reign. When, therefore, we see his life obviously permeated with religious beliefs and with rites and rituals at every step, we assume that all this emotional intensity is due to the religious and magical background in which he is enveloped. And here it is that many observers and investigators commit what is a fundamental error of interpretation; first, by assuming that there exists, in the minds of most natives, a cause and effect relation, and second, by stressing the wrong end of what constitutes, in each tribe, the habitually determined sequence of acts and beliefs. We can easily agree with Professor Lévy-Bruhl when he contends that any analysis of this sequence is, strictly speaking, nonexistent or, at least, rare, without nevertheless following him farther along his argument. In his famous work *Les Fonctions Mentales dans les Sociétés Inférieures* he implies that no primitive people are capable of logical differentiation or of a logical selection of data. He is certainly in error on this point. . . . But he errs in an equally fundamental way when he unconsciously assumes that every analysis must be the work of the rational faculties.

Lévy-Bruhl is by training and nurture too much of an intellectual to appreciate how adequately sensations, emotions, and intuitions may determine a selection, and how such a selection can be on a par with a so-called rational analysis. For him any such selection implies a prelogical mentality and is not a true or correct analysis. Be this as it may, it is this nonintellectual analysis that is typical of much of primitive thought. But another element must not be forgotten, namely, that the selection is in its turn predetermined by being oriented toward a socially and individually determined goal. This goal, it may be said, is to fix what is to be interpreted as real. It thus follows that reality becomes largely pragmatic. What happens is true. So markedly developed is this pragmatic test for reality that even when the event that occurs is more or less definitely contradictory to the specific cultural background, it carries conviction. . . .

LEO FROBENIUS
Paideuma

One of the first Westerners to recognize the actual achievement of traditional African art, Frobenius (1873–1938) spent many years in Africa, gathered and translated African oral traditions, and founded the Institute for Cultural Morphology in Frankfurt as a repository for (largely facsimiles of) prehistoric and African paintings and engravings. He was, in anthropological terms, a leading German diffusionist who advocated a complex, multifactorial approach to the analysis of cultural transmission, but in British and American anthropology, for example, his reputation is by now minimal. At the same time, he has profoundly influenced at least two major and largely unrelated directions in twentieth-century poetry—the American line of Pound and Williams/Olson and Duncan, etc. (see Pound's estimate of him, immediately following), and the African and French Caribbean line of Negritude poets. In Léopold Sédar Senghor's summation: "It was Leo Frobenius who gave us both the vision and the explanation [of "black values," etc.] at the very moment when, having completed our studies, we were entering upon active militant life, with the concept and the idea of Negritude under our belts. It was Frobenius who helped us to give the word its most solid, and at the same time its most human significance" ("Foreword," Leo Frobenius: An Anthology, p. viii).

Frobenius's principal contributions in this regard are his concept of Paideuma and his attempt to bridge the historical separation between African and European cultures. But the effect of his translation of African masterworks (e.g., his twelve-volume gathering, Atlantis) should not be underestimated.

MECHANISTIC AND INTUITIVE TYPES OF ENQUIRY

There are two main ways of apprehending reality, which may be called the mechanistic and the intuitive. The former seeks to establish laws as a means of understanding the processes and phenomena of the external world and of human consciousness. The strength of this method lies in its power to elicit such laws; its weakness is that it cannot avoid setting up an unnatural opposition between the norm and the abnormal, the regular and the irregular, the rule and the exception. Whatever diverges from the law is treated as second-class reality, so that the observer loses his power of comprehensive and impartial judgment. The mechanistic principle is, like a railroad track, the shortest means of reaching a given end, but it prevents us from taking a broad survey of the country as we pass through it.

The intuitive approach, on the other hand, is based on the conception of structure. It is content to perceive the main phenomena and assign to them, as sympathetically as possible, a place in the general structure. In this way the intuitive observer can, with full

SOURCE: Translation in Eike Haberland (ed.), Leo Frobenius: An Anthology, pages 19–21, 24–27.

understanding, enter into all the vicissitudes of reality.

In the mechanistic view the world consists of a system of facts which can be analysed into cause and effect, elements and combinations, and from which it is possible to deduce relationships of universal validity. It is a type of biological or psychological approach based on albumen tests, laws of association, motives and impulses, ganglion cells and nerve tissues, all duly classified and reduced to dry formulae. The intuitive observer, by contrast, seeks to enter with his whole being into the lawless profusion of spiritual activity, at the same time distinguishing the significant from the trivial, the expressive from the merely accidental. He surrenders to the inner logic of growth, evolution and maturity, a realm which system and experiment are powerless to unlock. Instead of petrified laws and formulae, he discovers symbolic events and types of living, breathing reality.

The mechanistic approach is nowadays very much in vogue, and the intuitive correspondingly rare. I am not here using these terms to denote philosophical doctrines. Both, in their way, are comprehensive, penetrating, almost compulsive modes of thought, with their own claim to interpret reality. Nor am I suggesting that there is anything especially new or superior about the intuitive method. As for novelty, Goethe himself took a thoroughly intuitive view of the world, though this was overlaid by the development of nineteenth-century specialization, so that he was not wrong in predicting that his work would never be popular—even though tags from *Faust* are on everybody's lips. As for superiority, every culture that we know of has oscillated between the two poles of mechanism and intuition. However, in advancing the theory that we are moving into a new cultural era, the advent of which can be felt rather than proved, I am bound to support the revival of an intuitive attitude.

It must also be stressed that there is no such thing as an absolutely mechanistic or an absolutely intuitive outlook. It is a question rather of the predominance of one or other of two tendencies which, in a sense to be explained in more detail, we may call the factual and the daemonic.

Since 1904, when I was introduced to the sphere of African cultures, my life has been crowded with experiences and impressions for which I can never be sufficiently grateful. I look back on periods of independence during which I was responsible for the lives and activities of comrades who helped me to gather a rich harvest of information and experience, and again on years of hard work between expeditions, studying and classifying the material we had brought home. Its wealth is such that I shall never be able to publish it all to the world, and this made it all the more important to put my collections and manuscripts in order, with the help of an increasing army of assistants in the field and in Germany. The scholar's den of 1894 turned into a research institute which it was my task to direct and animate, either on the spot or during my absence on expeditions. The fruits of my practical experience had to be compared with others' descriptions, with the relevant literature and with museum exhibits from elsewhere. The handful of ideas and theories with which I had started grew into hundreds; my staff of assistants increased steadily. Work which had been within the compass of a single individual demanded to be made accessible to a host of workers and enquirers, within the framework of a vast organization.

All this could not fail to affect the manner in which I had envisaged my task in 1895. At that time I was concerned with Africa and European prehistory in the light of a few broad concepts such as the geographical exploration of cultures and the "age of the sun god." But, on the one hand, the more I travelled about Africa and observed its different cultures, the more conscious I became of what was typical and organic rather than unique and individual; and, on the other, familiarity with the dark continent gave me a keener insight into the forms of modern European culture, which in many cases I beheld from a considerable distance of space and time.

Another change was that I came to distinguish more sharply between cultures and human beings. In Africa I made the acquaintance of obscure races with powerful cultural forms, while in Europe one might encounter advanced human beings with a vestigial culture, or vice versa. In the remotest corners of Africa one might find men and women of lofty views, deep religion and an exalted poetic sense, whereas Europe with all its achievements was not free from pettiness, envy and all the vices and distempers in Pandora's box. It is not a question of whether human beings are better in one continent or the other: they are in fact the same throughout, except for a few qualities which they imbibe as part of their cultural inheritance.

The following lines are not intended to depict one culture or another, but rather to help the reader to apprehend what I have called the "Paideuma," that is to say the spiritual essence of culture in general. What I have to say does not answer the question "This is how things are," but rather "This is how they are to be understood." My investigation is not concerned with modern psychology or physiology: it is obliged to pursue its own way, so as to remove from the path what would otherwise be gross and insurmountable obstacles. At the same time it is a modest enquiry, and in a sense an unscientific one. This may be perceived in the use of a special terminology and forms of language which are not readily intelligible, because their subject-matter is not. In particular, I have found it necessary for certain purposes to replace the word "culture" by the special term "Paideuma" as above defined.

POETIC COMPOSITION

The work on mythology which I completed in 1894 led me to put the basic question regarding the origin of fables, myths, and poetry.

To us Northerners in our "scientific" superiority, the answer is usually clear enough: we use a facile term like "imagination" and consider ourselves dispensed from further thought. Let me recall here an episode that I described in *Schwarze Seelen* [Black Souls]. On my visit to a certain part of Africa, an old missionary who had lived there for years told me that there were no folktales worth mentioning. A few weeks later I read him some stories of merit that I had collected: he was astonished and exclaimed: "They must have made them up for your benefit." We discussed the matter, and he admitted that Europeans, whether townsfolk or peasants, could certainly not have "invented" a body of well-constructed oral literature in so short a time. When I pressed the point he also agreed that the natives' myths, properly so called, were as limited in form and content as the world of their own experience, so that "imagination" could not be invoked to account for the stories. He was thus finally obliged to admit that they must have been handed down from distant times and places.

True fables, myths and fairy-tales present themselves to us in perfected form as an inheritance from remote ages. Hans Andersen and Hauff are men of letters, and their works have nothing in common with true folktales except an external similarity of language and subject matter. No one will ever again be able to invent a story of the kind that peasant grandmothers, a hundred years ago, used to relate to a spellbound group of children; and, what is more, our own children will never feel that particular spell again, for nowadays they read stories from books instead of listening to them. They no longer cluster at the feet of an old dame who herself half-believes the story she is telling. If a kindly aunt or uncle ''tells the children a story'' they do so with detachment, not as a part of their ordinary life: the story is something they can vaguely remember or have come across in a book or magazine devoted to this sort of entertainment. I can speak of this from my own knowledge, for I remember as a child sitting in twilight at the feet of my old grandmother and sharing the magic experience of a story that enthralled us both. It is sad to reflect that one will not be able to impart this feeling to others. The Grimm brothers learnt stories in this fashion by word of mouth, and strictly speaking we no longer possess the stories—we can only read them or, still worse, hear them recited at literary evenings. We have lost the world of living magic, in which we absorbed and shared the experience of our ancestors. The old forms are no more than shadows on the horizon, whose fascination we can guess at but not feel.

So much for the disappearance of this type of experience—but what must have been the exhilaration of its beginning! This is what I went to seek for in Africa. I embarked on my first journey with high hopes, choosing an area in which different races lived in close proximity. At first, however, I was disappointed. The villages along the Kwilu river, west of the Kasai, were inhabited by cannibal tribes who were constantly fighting one another, and whose only common interests in the intellectual sphere were magic spells and lawsuits (*milonga*). Old people were almost an unknown species. As soon as anyone's hair began to grey, he or she was arraigned for cannibalism in violation of law, was sentenced to ordeal by poison and, having succumbed to this, was eaten by the rest of the tribe. Clearly the Kwilu area was not one in which to explore the development of mental culture. All I was able to collect in the way of stories were a few remnants of fables, withered leaves from a long-dead tree, of which one could guess what they were but scarcely how they had come into being.

I had better luck two hundred miles further east, in the middle reaches of the Kasai, a region inhabited by the gloomy, laconic Bakuba and the cheerful Baluba; the latter were given to trade and travelling and had some excellent stories to tell. I encouraged this propensity by making it known that I was prepared to reward storytellers generously, and it was not long before I had assembled a whole company of them. In this way I learnt important things about the narrative art: for instance, while animal fables might be related in the daytime, other tales belonged to the twilight, the hearth or the campfire. Stories of all kinds were related word for word as they had been handed down, and if the narrator got a word wrong he was often corrected by his audience. Gesture and intonation were even more important than the text itself, and the best storytellers laid great weight on ''atmosphere.'' I realized this one day when I repeated a story I had just heard and the narrator denied that he had said any such thing. After much discussion it was explained to me that the gestures, intonation and so forth carried a separate and quite different meaning from the words themselves. A translation could not give the sense of the original, since it failed to reproduce its living soul.

It follows that while verbal transcriptions of native stories may be of great value to the linguist, and while literal translations are an aid to the study of form and subject matter, including their historical development, neither of these forms of reproduction is sufficient to convey the paideumatic quality of the original. Translations reflect it in the same sort of degree as a sheet of music represents a song. As the spirit of a work of imagination is destroyed by literal translation, such a work can only be preserved by a different mode of communication which may be compared to a spiritual rebirth. This process begins in the narrator's consciousness, appeals to the intuition of the hearer and spectator, and reduces language to a kind of mechanical instrument.

A missionary in the Luluaburg district set about teaching the native children French. For this purpose he translated some of Aesop's fables and made the children learn them by heart, first the Baluba and then the French version. Some of the fables are very similar to Baluba ones, and one might have supposed that they would be readily assimilated to the native stock, but not at all. Many of the tribe became acquainted with the "white man's writings" (*mukanda na m'putu*), and I had many opportunities of noticing that they aroused lively interest. But when I asked some intelligent people one day whether they thought our European stories (*tushimuni*) as good as their own, they asked in surprise "Have the Europeans got *tushimuni* too?" When I reminded them of the fables they laughed and said those were *mukanda*, not *tushimuni*. I tried to discover what the difference was, and received the following illuminating answer.

"In the *tushimuni* everything is alive—*gabuluku* (small antelopes), *ngulu* (wild boar), *kashiama* (leopard). When the tale is told, you can hear them all speak. But the *mukanda* only tells you what happened to them once upon a time. *Tushimuni* can happen today, tomorrow or yesterday; *mukanda* are things that happened once and for all, dead things." To make himself clearer, one of the men talking to me pointed to an elephant's skull in front of the hut and said: "That *nsevu* (elephant) is dead—he can't live again, and neither can the *mukanda*. But the *tushimuni* is just as much alive as the *nsevu* that comes every night and browses on our manioc fields. The *mukanda* are dead bones, the *tushimuni* are living flesh."

The sharp distinction made by these simple yet receptive tribesmen is of great importance, and it would be hard to express better the difference between written and oral tradition. In terms of the theory expounded [here], writing and science belong to what may be called a "factual" world, divorced from living tradition and experience. Its opposite is the "daemonic" world of poetic or artistic rapture, as we may find it in a musician performing a Beethoven sonata or an old peasant woman telling children a fairy story. Clearly the despised African is closer to a daemonic or intuitive apprehension of the core of his civilization than are we intellectualized Westerners, from whom the Paideuma is hidden by an accumulation of soulless, objective facts. . . .

EZRA POUND
The Value of Leo Frobenius

Pound's gift to a possible ethnopoetics comes largely from his idea of culture and mind as "vortex"—opening the poem to a range of historical and cultural particulars: Chinese and Japanese, Egyptian, Provençal, gnostic and subterranean, contemporary U.S. and European, as well as a gesture toward the Euro-African bridge via Frobenius. Of the vortex in general, Pound wrote, manifesto fashion, in 1914: "All experience rushes into this vortex. All the energized past, all the past that is living and worthy to live. All MOMENTUM, which is the past bearing upon us." With this end in view, Frobenius's idea of Paideuma, *here discussed, "validated the Cantos"—Pound's epic life-work then in progress—"and underwrote Pound's notion that the Cantos were 'the tale of the tribe' " (Hugh Kenner,* The Pound Era, *p. 507). Or Pound again: "It is dawn at Jerusalem while midnight hovers above the Pillars of Hercules. All ages are contemporaneous in the mind."*

The value of Leo Frobenius to civilization is not for the rightness or wrongness of this opinion or that opinion but for the kind of thinking he does (whereof more later).

He has in especial seen and marked out a kind of knowing, the difference between knowledge that has to be acquired by particular effort and knowing that is in people, "in the air." He has accented the value of such record. His archaeology is not retrospective, it is immediate.

Example: the peasants opposed a railway cutting. A king had driven into the ground at that place. The engineers dug and unearthed the bronze car of Dis, two thousand years buried.

It wd. be unjust to Frazer to say that his work was *merely* retrospective. But there is a quite different phase in the work of Frobenius.

"Where we found these rock drawings, there was always water within six feet of the surface." That kind of research goes not only into past and forgotten life, but points to tomorrow's water supply.

This is not *mere* utilitarianism, it is a double charge, a sense of two sets of values and their relation.

To escape a word or a set of words loaded up with dead association Frobenius uses the term Paideuma for the tangle or complex of the inrooted ideas of any period.

Even were I to call this book the New Learning I shd. at least make a bow to Frobenius. I have eschewed his term almost for the sole reason that the normal anglo-saxon loathes a highsounding word, especially a greek word unfamiliar.

The Paideuma is not the Zeitgeist, though I have no doubt many people will try to sink it in the latter romantic term. Napoleon said he failed for opposing the spirit of his time.

As I understand it, Frobenius has seized a word not current for the express purpose

SOURCE: *Ezra Pound,* Guide to Kulchur, *pages 57–59.*

of scraping off the barnacles and ''atmosphere'' of a long-used term.

When I said I wanted a new civilization, I think I cd. have used Frobenius' term.

At any rate for my own use and for the duration of this treatise I shall use Paideuma for the gristly roots of ideas that are in action.

I shall leave ''Zeitgeist'' as including also the atmospheres, the tints of mental air and the idées reçues, the notions that a great mass of people still hold or half hold from habit, from waning custom.

The ''New Learning'' under the ideogram of the mortar can imply whatever men of my generation can offer our successors as means to the new comprehension.

A vast mass of school learning is DEAD. It is as deadly as corpse infection.

CH'ING MING, a new Paideuma will start with that injunction as has every conscious renovation of learning.

正名

Having attained a clear terminology whereof no part can be mistaken for any other, the student might consider another point raised by Frobenius when interviewed by Dr Monotti.

''It is not what a man says, but the part of it which his auditor considers important, that measures the quantity of his communication.''

FEDERICO GARCÍA LORCA
The Duende

Lorca's poetry of the late 1920s/early 1930s fuses Surrealist concerns with that sense of native culture (Andalusian and Gypsy), a true Paideuma (see above, p. 36), which permeates this essay. "Characteristically," writes Arturo Barea, "Lorca took his Spanish term for daemonic inspiration from the Andalucían idiom. While to the rest of Spain the duende *is nothing but a hobgoblin, to Andalucía it is an obscure power which can speak through every form of human art, including the art of personality"* (Lorca: The Poet and His People). *The duende essay, originally a lecture, followed a year in New York City (1929–1930), during which Lorca wrote his most deliberately surrealistic book,* Poet in New York—*a response to the urban surreal and to the presence of a lingering African surreality (see Senghor, below, p. 120) he sensed there:*

> Negroes, Negroes, Negroes, Negroes.
> The blood has no doors in your night face upwards.
> There is no blushing. Furious blood under the skins,
> alive in the thorn of the dagger and in the breast of
> landscapes,
> under the pincers and the broom of the celestial Moon
> of Cancer.

But such "negritude," which might be sensed in Spain as well, is ancillary to the native duende; *nor are the authorities of that* duende *the masters of "high European culture" but those like Manuel Torres, "a man of exemplary blood culture" and of a music that opens to "black sounds."*

Whoever inhabits that bull's hide stretched between the Jucar, the Guadalete, the Sil, or the Pisuerga—no need to mention the streams joining those lion-colored waves churned up by the Plata—has heard it said with a certain frequency: "Now that has real *duende!*" It was in this spirit that Manuel Torres, that great artist of the Andalusian people, once remarked to a singer: "You have a voice, you know all the styles, but you will never bring it off because you have no *duende.*"

In all Andalusia, from the rock of Jaen to the shell of Cádiz, people constantly speak of the *duende* and find it in everything that springs out of energetic instinct. That marvelous singer, "El Librijano," originator of the *Debla*, observed, "Whenever I am singing with *duende*, no one can come up to me"; and one day the old gypsy dancer, "La Malena," exclaimed while listening to Brailowsky play a fragment of Bach: "Olé! That has *duende!*"—and remained bored by Gluck and Brahms and Darius Milhaud. And Manuel Torres, to my mind a man of exemplary blood culture, once uttered this splendid phrase while listening to Falla himself play his "Nocturno del Generalife": "Whatever

SOURCE: *Federico García Lorca,* Poet in New York *(tr. Ben Belitt), pages 154–166.*

has black sounds, has *duende.*'' There is no greater truth.

These "black sounds" are the mystery, the roots that probe through the mire that we all know of, and do not understand, but which furnishes us with whatever is sustaining in art. Black sounds: so said the celebrated Spaniard, thereby concurring with Goethe, who, in effect, defined the *duende* when he said, speaking of Paganini: "A mysterious power that all may feel and no philosophy can explain."

The *duende*, then, is a power and not a construct, is a struggle and not a concept. I have heard an old guitarist, a true virtuoso, remark, "The *duende* is not in the throat, the *duende* comes up from inside, up from the very soles of the feet." That is to say, it is not a question of aptitude, but of a true and viable style—of blood, in other words; of what is oldest in culture: of creation made act.

This "mysterious power that all may feel and no philosophy can explain," is, in sum, the earth-force, the same *duende* that fired the heart of Nietzsche, who sought it in its external forms on the Rialto Bridge, or in the music of Bizet, without ever finding it, or understanding that the *duende* he pursued had rebounded from the mystery-minded Greeks to the dancers of Cádiz or the gored, Dionysian cry of Silverio's *siguiriya.*

So much for the *duende*; but I would not have you confuse the *duende* with the theological demon of doubt at whom Luther, on a Bacchic impulse, hurled an inkwell in Nuremberg, or with the Catholic devil, destructive, but short on intelligence, who disguised himself as a bitch in order to enter the convents, or with the talking monkey that Cervantes' mountebank carried in the comedy about jealousy and the forests of Andalusia.

No. The *duende* I speak of, shadowy, palpitating, is a descendant of that benignest daemon of Socrates, he of marble and salt, who scratched the master angrily the day he drank the hemlock; and of that melancholy imp of Descartes, little as an unripe almond, who, glutted with circles and lines, went out on the canals to hear the drunken sailors singing.

Any man—any artist, as Nietzsche would say—climbs the stairway in the tower of his perfection at the cost of a struggle with a *duende*—not with an angel, as some have maintained, or with his muse. This fundamental distinction must be kept in mind if the root of a work of art is to be grasped.

The Angel guides and endows, like Saint Raphael, or prohibits and avoids like Saint Michael, or foretells, like Saint Gabriel.

The Angel dazzles; but he flies over men's heads and remains in mid-air, shedding his grace; and the man, without any effort whatever, realizes his work, or his fellow-feeling, or his dance. The angel on the road to Damascus, and he who entered the crevice of the little balcony of Assisi, or that other angel who followed in the footsteps of Heinrich Suso, *commanded*—and there was no resisting his radiance, for he waved wings of steel in an atmosphere of predestination.

The Muse dictates and, in certain cases, prompts. There is relatively little she can do, for she keeps aloof and is so full of lassitude (I have seen her twice) that I myself have had to put half a heart of marble in her. The Poets of the Muse hear voices and do not know where they come from; but surely they are from the Muse, who encourages and at times devours them entirely. Such, for example, was the case of Apollinaire, that great poet ravaged by the horrible Muse with whom the divinely angelic Rousseau painted him. The Muse arouses the intellect, bearing landscapes of columns and the false taste of laurel; but intellect is oftentimes the foe of poetry because it imitates too much: it elevates the poet to a throne of acute angles and makes him forget that in time the ants can devour him, too, or that a great, arsenical locust can fall on his head, against which the Muses who live inside monocles or the lukewarm lacquer roses of insignificant salons, are helpless.

Angel and Muse approach from without; the Angel sheds light and the Muse gives form (Hesiod learned of them). Gold leaf or chiton-folds; the poet finds his models in his laurel coppice. But the *Duende*, on the other hand, must come to life in the nethermost recesses of the blood.

And repel the Angel, too—kick out the Muse and conquer his awe of the fragrance of the violets that breathe from the poetry of the eighteenth century, or of the great telescope in whose lenses the Muse dozes off, sick of limits.

The true struggle is with the *Duende*.

The paths leading to God are well known, from the barbaric way of the hermit, to the subtler modes of the mystic. With a tower, then, like Saint Theresa, or with three roads, like St. John of the Cross. And even if we must cry out in Isaiah's voice: "Truly, thou art the hidden God!" at the end and at last, God sends to each seeker his first fiery thorns.

To seek out the *Duende*, however, neither map nor discipline is required. Enough to know that he kindles the blood like an irritant, that he exhausts, that he repulses, all the bland, geometrical assurances, that he smashes the styles; that he makes of a Goya, master of the grays, the silvers, the roses of the great English painters, a man painting with his knees and his fists in bituminous blacks; that he bares a Mosen Cinto Verdaguer to the cold of the Pyrenees or induces a Jorge Manrique to sweat out his death on the crags of Ocaña, or invests the delicate body of Rimbaud in the green domino of the saltimbanque, or fixes dead fish-eyes on the Comte de Lautréamont in the early hours of the boulevard.

The great artists of southern Spain, both gypsies and flamenco, whether singing or dancing or playing on instruments, know that no emotion is possible without the mediation of the *Duende*. They may hoodwink the people, they may give the illusion of *duende* without really having it, just as writers and painters and literary fashionmongers without *duende* cheat you daily; but it needs only a little care and the will to resist one's own indifference, to discover the imposture and put it and its crude artifice to flight.

Once the Andalusian singer, Pastora Pavon, "The Girl with the Combs," a sombre Hispanic genius whose capacity for fantasy equals Goya's or Raphael el Gallo's, was singing in a little tavern in Cádiz. She sparred with her voice—now shadowy, now like molten tin, now covered over with moss; she tangled her voice in her long hair or drenched it in sherry or lost it in the darkest and furthermost bramble bushes. But nothing happened—useless, all of it! The hearers remained silent.

There stood Ignacio Espeleta, handsome as a Roman turtle, who was asked once why he never worked, and replied with a smile worthy of Argantonio: "How am I to work if I come from Cádiz?"

There, too, stood Héloise, the fiery aristocrat, whore of Seville, direct descendant of Soledad Vargas, who in the thirties refused to marry a Rothschild because he was not of equal blood. There were the Floridas, whom some people call butchers, but who are really millennial priests sacrificing bulls constantly to Geryon; and in a corner stood that imposing breeder of bulls, Don Pablo Murabe, with the air of a Cretan mask. Pastora Pavon finished singing in the midst of total silence. There was only a little man, one of those dancing mannikins who leap suddenly out of brandy bottles, who observed sarcastically in a very low voice: "*Viva* Paris!" As if to say: We are not interested in aptitude or techniques or virtuosity here. We are interested in something else.

Then the "Girl with the Combs" got up like a woman possessed, her face blasted like a medieval weeper, tossed off a great glass of Cazalla at a single draught, like a potion of fire, and settled down to singing—without a voice, without breath, without nuance, throat aflame—but with *duende*! She had contrived to annihilate all that was nonessential in song and make way for an angry and incandescent *Duende*, friend of the sand-laden winds, so that everyone listening tore at his clothing almost in the same rhythm with which the West Indian negroes in their rites rend away their clothes, huddled in heaps before the image of Saint Barbara.

The "Girl with the Combs" had to *mangle* her voice because she knew there were discriminating folk about who asked not for form, but for the marrow of form—pure music spare enough to keep itself in air. She had to deny her faculties and her security; that is to say, to turn out her Muse and keep vulnerable, so that her *Duende* might come and vouchsafe the hand-to-hand struggle. And then how she sang! Her voice feinted no longer; it jetted up like blood, ennobled by sorrow and sincerity, it opened up like ten fingers of a hand around the nailed feet of a Christ by Juan de Juni—tempestuous!

The arrival of the *Duende* always presupposes a radical change in all the forms as they existed on the old plane. It gives a sense of refreshment unknown until then, together with that quality of the just-opening rose, of the miraculous, which comes and instils an almost religious transport.

In all Arabian music, in the dances, songs, elegies of Arabia, the coming of the *Duende* is greeted by fervent outcries of *Allah! Allah! God! God!*, so close to the *Olé! Olé!* of our bull rings that who is to say they are not actually the same; and in all the songs of southern Spain the appearance of the *Duende* is followed by heartfelt exclamations of God *alive!*—profound, human, tender, the cry of communion with God through the medium of the five senses and the grace of the *Duende* that stirs the voice and the body of the dancer—a flight from this world, both real and poetic, pure as Pedro Soto de Roja's over the seven gardens (that most curious poet of the seventeenth century), or Juan Calimacho's on the tremulous ladder of tears.

Naturally, when flight is achieved, all feel its effects: the initiate coming to see at last how style triumphs over inferior matter, and the unenlightened, through the I-don't-know-what of an authentic emotion. Some years ago, in a dancing contest at Jerez de la Frontera, an old lady of eighty, competing against beautiful women and young girls with waists supple as water, carried off the prize merely by the act of raising her arms, throwing back her head, and stamping the little platform with a blow of her feet; but in the conclave of muses and angels foregathered there—beauties of form and beauties of smile—the dying *Duende* triumphed as it had to, trailing the rusted knife blades of its wings along the ground.

All the arts are capable of *duende*, but it naturally achieves its widest play in the fields of music, dance, and the spoken poem, since these require a living presence to interpret them, because they are forms which grow and decline perpetually and raise their contours on the precise present.

Often the *Duende* of the musician passes over into the *Duende* of the interpreter, and at other times, when musician and poet are not matched, the *Duende* of the interpreter—this is interesting—creates a new marvel that retains the appearance—and the appearance only—of the originating form. Such was the case with the *duende*-ridden Duse who deliberately sought out failures in order to turn them into triumphs, thanks to her capacity for invention; or with Paganini who, as Goethe explained, could make one hear profoundest melody in out-and-out vulgarity; or with a delectable young lady from the port of Santa María whom I saw singing and dancing the horrendous Italian ditty, "O Marie!" with such rhythms, such pauses, and such conviction that she transformed an Italian gewgaw into a hard serpent of raised gold. What happened, in effect, was that each in his own way found something new, something never before encountered, which put lifeblood and art into bodies void of expression.

In every country, death comes as a finality. It comes, and the curtain comes down. But not in Spain! In Spain the curtain goes up. Many people live out their lives between walls till the day they die and are brought out into the sun. In Spain, the dead are more alive than the dead of any other country of the world: their profile wounds like the edge of a barber's razor. The quip about death and the silent contemplation of it are familiar to the Spanish. From the "Dream of the Skulls" of Quevedo, to the "Putrescent Bishop" of Valdés Leal; from La Marbella of the seventeenth century who, dying in childbirth on the highway, says:

> The blood of my entrails
> Covers the horse.
> And the horses' hooves
> Strike fire from the pitch.

to a recent young man from Salamanca, killed by a bull, who exclaimed:

> My friends, I am dying.
> My friends, it goes badly.
> I've three handkerchiefs inside me,
> And this I apply now makes four.

there is a balustrade of flowering nitre where hordes peer out, contemplating death, with verses from Jeremiah for the grimmer side or sweet-smelling cypress for the more lyrical—but in any case, a country where all that is most important has its final metallic valuation in death.

The knife and the cart wheel and the razor and the stinging beard-points of the shepherds, the shorn moon and the fly, the damp lockers, the ruins and the lace-covered saints, the quicklime and the cutting line of eaves and balconies: in Spain, all bear little grassblades of death, allusions and voices perceptible to the spiritually alert, that call to our memory with the corpse-cold air of our own passing. It is no accident that all Spanish art is bound to our soil, so full of thistles and definitive stone; the lamentations of Pleberio or the dances of the master Josef Maria de Valdivielso are not isolated instances, nor is it by chance that from all the balladry of Europe the Spanish inamorata disengages herself in this fashion:

> "If you are my fine friend
> Tell me—why won't you look at me?"
>   "The eyes with which I look at you
>   I gave up to the shadow."
> "If you are my fine friend
> Tell me—why don't you kiss me?"
>   "The lips with which I kissed you
>   I gave up to the clay."
> "If you are my fine friend
> Tell me—why won't you embrace me?"
>   "The arms that embrace you
>   I have covered up with worms."

Nor is it strange to find that in the dawn of our lyricism, the following note is sounded:

> Inside the garden
> I shall surely die.
> Inside the rosebush
> They will kill me.
> Mother, Mother, I went out
> Gathering roses,
> But surely death will find me
> In the garden.
> Mother, Mother, I went out
> Cutting roses,
> But surely death will find me
> In the rosebush.
> Inside the garden
> I shall surely die.
> In the rosebush
> They will kill me.

Those heads frozen by the moon that Zurbarán painted, the butter-yellows and the lightning-yellows of El Greco, the narrative of Father Sigüenza, all the work of Goya, the presbytery of the Church of the Escorial, all polychrome sculpture, the crypt of the ducal house of Osuna, the death with the guitar in the chapel of the Benavente in Medina de Río Seco—all equal, on the plane of cultivated art, the pilgrimages of San Andrés de Teixido where the dead have their place in the procession; they are one with the songs for the dead that the women of Asturias intone with flame-filled lamps in the November night, one with the song and dance of the Sibyl in the cathedrals of Mallorca and Toledo, with the obscure "In Recort" of Tortosa, and the innumerable rites of Good Friday that, with the arcane Fiesta of the Bulls, epitomize the popular triumph of Spanish death. In all the world, Mexico alone can go hand-in-hand with my country.

When the Muse sees death on the way, she closes the door, or raises a plinth, or promenades an urn and inscribes an epitaph with a waxen hand, but in time she tears down her laurels again in a silence that wavers between two breezes. Under the truncated arch of the Ode, she joins with funereal meaning the exact flowers that the Italians of the fifteenth century depicted, with the identical cock of Lucretius, to frighten off an unforeseen darkness.

When the Angel sees death on the way, he flies in slow circles and weaves with tears of narcissus and ice the elegy we see trembling in the hands of Keats and Villasandino and Herrera and Becquer and Juan Ramón Jiménez. But imagine the terror of the Angel, should it feel a spider—even the very tiniest—on its tender and roseate flesh!

The *Duende*, on the other hand, will not approach at all if he does not see the possibility of death, if he is not convinced he will circle death's house, if there is not every assurance he can rustle the branches borne aloft by us all, that neither have, nor may ever have, the power to console.

With idea, with sound, or with gesture, the *Duende* chooses the brim of the well for his open struggle with the creator. Angel and Muse escape in the violin or in musical measure, but the *Duende* draws blood, and in the healing of the wound that never quite closes, all that is unprecedented and invented in a man's work has its origin.

The magical virtue of poetry lies in the fact that it is always empowered with *duende* to baptize in dark water all those who behold it, because with *duende*, loving and understanding are simpler, there is always the *certainty* of being loved and being understood; and this struggle for expression and for the communication of expression acquires at times, in poetry, finite characters.

Recall the case of that paragon of the flamenco and daemonic way, Saint Theresa—flamenca not for her prowess in stopping an angry bull with three magnificent passes—though she did so—nor for her presumption in esteeming herself beautiful in the presence of Fray Juan de la Miseria, nor for slapping the face of a papal nuncio; but rather for the simple circumstance that she was one of the rare ones whose *Duende* (not her Angel—the angels never attack) pierced her with an arrow, hoping thereby to destroy her for having deprived him of his ultimate secret: the subtle bridge that links the five senses with the very center, the living flesh, living cloud, living sea, of Love emancipated from Time.

Most redoubtable conqueress of the *Duende*—and how utterly unlike the case of Philip of Austria who, longing to discover the Muse and the Angel in theology, found himself imprisoned by the *Duende* of cold ardors in that masterwork of the Escorial, where geometry abuts with a dream and the *Duende* wears the mask of the Muse for the eternal chastisement of the great king.

We have said that the *Duende* loves ledges and wounds, that he enters only those areas where form dissolves in a passion transcending any of its visible expressions.

In Spain (as in all Oriental countries where dance is a form of religious expression) the *Duende* has unlimited play in the bodies of the dancers of Cádiz, eulogized by

Martial, in the breasts of the singers, eulogized by Juvenal, and in all the liturgy of the bulls—that authentic religious drama where, in the manner of the Mass, adoration and sacrifice are rendered a God.

It would seem that all the *duende* of the classical world is crowded into this matchless festival, epitomizing the culture and the noble sensibility of a people who discover in man his greatest rages, his greatest melancholies, his greatest lamentations. No one, I think, is amused by the dances or the bulls of Spain; the *Duende* has taken it on himself to make them suffer through the medium of the drama, in living forms, and prepares the ladders for a flight from encompassing reality.

The *Duende* works on the body of the dancer like wind works on sand. With magical force, it converts a young girl into a lunar paralytic; or fills with adolescent blushes a ragged old man begging handouts in the wineshops; or suddenly discovers the smell of nocturnal ports in a head of hair, and moment for moment, works on the arms with an expressiveness which is the mother of the dance of all ages.

But it is impossible for him ever to repeat himself—this is interesting and must be underscored. The *Duende* never repeats himself, any more than the forms of the sea repeat themselves in a storm.

In the bullfight, the *Duende* achieves his most impressive advantage, for he must fight then with death who can destroy him, on one hand, and with geometry, with measure, the fundamental basis of the bullfight, on the other.

The bull has his orbit, and the bullfighter has his, and between orbit and orbit is the point of risk where falls the vertex of the terrible byplay.

It is possible to hold a Muse with a *muleta* and an Angel with *banderillas*, and pass for a good bullfighter; but for the *faena de capa*, with the bull still unscarred by a wound, the help of the *Duende* is necessary at the moment of the kill, to drive home the blow of artistic truth.

The bullfighter who moves the public to terror in the plaza by his audacity does not *fight* the bull—that would be ludicrous in such a case—but, within the reach of each man, puts his life at stake; on the contrary, the fighter bitten by the *Duende* gives a lesson in Pythagorean music and induces all to forget how he constantly hurls his heart against the horns.

Lagartijo with his Roman *duende*, Joselito with his Jewish *duende*, Belmonte with his baroque *duende*, and Cagancho with his gypsy *duende*, from the twilight of the ring, teach poets, painters, and musicians four great ways of the Spanish tradition.

Spain is the only country where death is the national spectacle, where death blows long fanfares at the coming of each Spring, and its art is always governed by a shrewd *duende* that has given it its distinctive character and its quality of invention.

The *Duende* that, for the first time in sculpture, fills the cheeks of the saints of the master Mateo de Compostela with blood, is the same spirit that evokes the lamentations of St. John of the Cross or burns naked nymphs on the religious sonnets of Lope.

The *Duende* who raises the tower of Sahagun or tesselates hot brick in Calatayud or Teruel, is the same spirit that breaks open the clouds of El Greco and sends the constables of Quevedo and the chimaeras of Goya sprawling with a kick.

When it rains, he secretly brings out a *duende*-minded Velasquez, behind his monarchical grays; when it snows, he sends Herrera out naked to prove that cold need not kill; when it burns, he casts Berruguete into the flames and lets him invent a new space for sculpture.

The Muse of Góngora and the Angel of Garcilaso must yield up the laurel wreath when the *Duende* of St. John of the Cross passes by, when

> The wounded stag
> peers over the hill.

The Muse of Gonzalo de Berceo and the Angel of the Archpriest of Hita must give way to the approaching Jorge Manrique when he comes, wounded to death, to the gates of the Castle of Belmonte. The Muse of Gregorio Hernandez and the Angel of José de Mora must retire, so that the *Duende* weeping blood-tears of Mena, and the *Duende* of Martínez Montañes with a head like an Assyrian bull's, may pass over, just as the melancholy Muse of Cataluña and the humid Angel of Galicia must watch, with loving terror, the *Duende* of Castile, far from the hot bread and the cow grazing mildly among forms of swept sky and parched earth.

The *Duende* of Quevedo and the *Duende* of Cervantes, one bearing phosphorescent green anemones and the other the plaster flowers of Ruidera, crown the altarpiece of the *Duende* of Spain.

Each art has, by nature, its distinctive *Duende* of style and form, but all roots join at the point where the black sounds of Manuel Torres issue forth—the ultimate stuff and the common basis, uncontrollable and tremulous, of wood and sound and canvas and word.

Black sounds: behind which there abide, in tenderest intimacy, the volcanoes, the ants, the zephyrs, and the enormous night straining its waist against the Milky Way.

Ladies and gentlemen: I have raised three arches, and with clumsy hand I have placed in them the Muse, the Angel, and the *Duende*.

The Muse keeps silent; she may wear the tunic of little folds, or great cow-eyes gazing toward Pompeii, or the monstrous, four-featured nose with which her great painter, Picasso, has painted her. The Angel may be stirring the hair of Antonello da Messina, the tunic of Lippi, and the violin of Masolino or Rousseau.

But the *Duende*—where is the *Duende*? Through the empty arch enters a mental air blowing insistently over the heads of the dead, seeking new landscapes and unfamiliar accents; an air bearing the odor of child's spittle, crushed grass, and the veil of a Medusa announcing the unending baptism of all newly created things.

AIMÉ CÉSAIRE and RENÉ DEPESTRE
On Negritude

"Negritude" was—from one of its directions—a culmination of Surrealist concepts of an alternative consciousness "opposed to the values of Europe" and "violently departing once and for all from the ways of thinking and feeling which have made life no longer bearable." (Thus: André Breton, the master of French Surrealism, in his preface—1943—to the Martinican poet Aimé Césaire's Notebook of a Return to the Native Land.*) The young French-speaking black poets (Césaire, Senghor, et al.) who launched the movement in the 1930s tied all that to this particular culture or network of cultures—"Africa," then colonized—from which they themselves had been estranged. With an arrogance that set a model for such ethnopoetic insurgency, they took their name from the corrosive word* nègre *(= nigger), simultaneously exorcising and accepting their "negritude":*

> . . . the Negro pimp, the Negro Lascar, and all the zebras shaking themselves in various ways to get rid of their stripes in a dew of fresh milk. And in the midst of all that I say right on! my grandfather dies, I say right on! the old negritude progressively cadavers itself.
>
> [Césaire, *Notebook* . . . , tr. C. Eshleman]

And Senghor, from a point in Africa closer to the source: "Negritude is the sum total of the values of the civilization of the African world: . . . communal warmth, the image-symbol and the cosmic rhythm which instead of dividing and sterilizing, unified and made fertile." (See also, below, p. 119.)

In the accompanying dialogue, Césaire discourses with the Haitian poet René Depestre.

René Depestre: How did you come to develop the concept of Negritude?

Aimé Césaire: I have a feeling that it was somewhat of a collective creation. I used the term first, that's true. But it's possible we talked about it in our group. It was really a resistance to the politics of assimilation. Until that time, until my generation, the French and the English—but especially the French—had followed the politics of assimilation unrestrainedly. We didn't know what Africa was. Europeans despised everything about Africa, and in France people spoke of a civilized world and a barbarian world. The barbarian world was Africa, and the civilized world was Europe. Therefore the best thing one could do with an African was to assimilate him: the ideal was to turn him into a Frenchman with black skin.

R.D.: Haiti experienced a similar phenomenon at the beginning of the nineteenth century. There is an entire Haitian pseudo-literature, created by authors who allowed themselves to be assimilated. The independence of Haiti, our first independence, was a violent attack against the French presence in our country, but our first authors did

SOURCE: *Aimé Césaire,* Discourse on Colonialism *(tr. Joan Pinkham), pages 72–79.*

not attack French cultural values with equal force. They did not proceed toward a decolonization of their consciousness.

A.C.: This is what is known as *bovarisme*. In Martinique also we were in the midst of *bovarisme*. I still remember a poor little Martinican pharmacist who passed the time writing poems and sonnets which he sent to literary contests, such as the Floral Games of Toulouse. He felt very proud when one of his poems won a prize. One day he told me that the judges hadn't even realized that his poems were written by a man of color. To put it in other words, his poetry was so impersonal that it made him proud. He was filled with pride by something I would have considered a crushing condemnation.

R.D.: It was a case of total alienation.

A.C.: I think you've put your finger on it. Our struggle was a struggle against alienation. That struggle gave birth to Negritude. Because Antilleans were ashamed of being Negroes, they searched for all sorts of euphemisms for Negro: they would say a man of color, a dark-complexioned man, and other idiocies like that.

R.D.: Yes, real idiocies.

A.C.: That's when we adopted the word *nègre*, as a term of defiance. It was a defiant name. To some extent it was a reaction of enraged youth. Since there was shame about the word *nègre*, we chose the word *nègre*. I must say that when we founded *L'Etudiant noir*, I really wanted to call it *L'Etudiant nègre*, but there was a great resistance to that among the Antilleans.

R.D.: Some thought that the word *nègre* was offensive.

A.C.: Yes, too offensive, too aggressive, and then I took the liberty of speaking of *négritude*. There was in us a defiant will, and we found a violent affirmation in the words *nègre* and *négritude*.

R.D.: In *Return to My Native Land* you have stated that Haiti was the cradle of Negritude. In your words, "Haiti, where Negritude stood on its feet for the first time." Then, in your opinion, the history of our country is in a certain sense the prehistory of Negritude. How have you applied the concept of Negritude to the history of Haiti?

A.C.: Well, after my discovery of the North American Negro and my discovery of Africa, I went on to explore the totality of the black world, and that is how I came upon the history of Haiti. I love Martinique, but it is an alienated land, while Haiti represented for me the heroic Antilles, the African Antilles. I began to make connections between the Antilles and Africa, and Haiti is the most African of the Antilles. It is at the same time a country with a marvelous history: the first Negro epic of the New World was written by Haitians, people like Toussaint l'Ouverture, Henri Christophe, Jean-Jacques Dessalines, etc. Haiti is not very well known in Martinique. I am one of the few Martinicans who know and love Haiti.

R.D.: Then for you the first independence struggle in Haiti was a confirmation, a demonstration of the concept of Negritude. Our national history is Negritude in action.

A.C.: Yes, Negritude in action. Haiti is the country where Negro people stood up for the first time, affirming their determination to shape a new world, a free world.

R.D.: During all of the nineteenth century there were men in Haiti who, without using the term Negritude, understood the significance of Haiti for world history. Haitian authors, such as Hannibal Price and Louis-Joseph Janvier, were already speaking of the need to reclaim black cultural and aesthetic values. A genius like Anténor Firmin wrote in Paris a book entitled *De l'égalité des races humaines*, in which he tried to re-evaluate African culture in Haiti in order to combat the total and colorless assimilation that was characteristic of our early authors. You could say that beginning with the second half of the nineteenth century some Haitian authors—Justin Lhérisson, Frédéric Marcelin, Fernand Hibbert, and Antoine Innocent—began to discover the peculiarities of our country, the fact that we had an African past, that the slave was not born yesterday, that voodoo was an important element in the development of our national culture. Now it is necessary to examine the concept of Negritude more closely. Negritude has lived through all kind of adventures. I don't believe that this concept is always understood in its original sense, with its explosive nature. In fact, there are people today in Paris and other places whose objectives are very different from those of *Return to My Native Land*.

A.C.: I would like to say that everyone has his own Negritude. There has been too much theorizing about Negritude. I have tried not to overdo it, out of a sense of modesty. But if someone asks me what my conception of Negritude is, I answer that above all it is a concrete rather than an abstract coming to consciousness. What I have been telling you about—the atmosphere in which we lived, an atmosphere of assimilation in which Negro people were ashamed of themselves—has great importance. We lived in an atmosphere of rejection, and we developed an inferiority complex. I have always thought that the black man was searching for his identity. And it has seemed to me that if what we want is to establish this identity, then we must have a concrete consciousness of what we are—that is, of the first fact of our lives: that we are black; that we were black and have a history, a history that contains certain cultural elements of great value; and that Negroes were not, as you put it, born yesterday, because there have been beautiful and important black civilizations. At the time we began to write people could write a history of world civilization without devoting a single chapter to Africa, as if Africa had made no contributions to the world. Therefore we affirmed that we were Negroes and that we were proud of it, and that we thought that Africa was not some sort of blank page in the history of humanity; in sum, we asserted that our Negro heritage was worthy of respect, and that this heritage was not relegated to the past, that its values were values that could still make an important contribution to the world.

R.D.: That is to say, universalizing values. . . .

A.C.: Universalizing, living values that had not been exhausted. The field was not dried up: it could still bear fruit, if we made the effort to irrigate it with our sweat and plant new seeds in it. So this was the situation: there were things to tell the world. We were not dazzled by European civilization. We bore the imprint of European civilization but we thought that Africa could make a contribution to Europe. It was also an affirmation of our solidarity. That's the way it was: I have always recognized that what was happening to my brothers in Algeria and the United States had its repercussions in me. I understood that I could not be indifferent to what was happening in Haiti or Africa. Then, in a way, we slowly came to the idea of a sort of black civilization spread throughout the world. And I have come to the realization that there was a ''Negro situation'' that existed in different geographical areas, that Africa was also my country. There was the African continent, the Antilles, Haiti; there were Martinicans and Brazilian Negroes, etc. That's what Negritude meant to me.

R.D.: There has also been a movement that predated Negritude itself—I'm speaking of the Negritude movement between the two world wars—a movement you could call pre-Negritude, manifested by the interest in African art that could be seen among European painters. Do you see a relationship between the interest of European artists and the coming to consciousness of Negroes?

A.C.: Certainly. This movement is another factor in the development of our consciousness. Negroes were made fashionable in France by Picasso, Vlaminck, Braque, etc.

R.D.: During the same period, art lovers and art historians—for example Paul Guillaume in France and Carl Einstein in Germany—were quite impressed by the quality of African sculpture. African art ceased to be an exotic curiosity, and Guillaume himself came to appreciate it as the ''life-giving sperm of the twentieth century of the spirit.''

A.C.: I also remember the *Negro Anthology* of Blaise Cendrars.

R.D.: It was a book devoted to the oral literature of African Negroes. I can also remember the third issue of the art journal *Action*, which had a number of articles by the artistic vanguard of that time on African masks, sculptures, and other art objects. And we shouldn't forget Guillaume Apollinaire, whose poetry is full of evocations of Africa. To sum up, do you think that the concept of Negritude was formed on the basis of shared ideological and political beliefs on the part of its proponents? Your comrades in Negritude, the first militants of Negritude, have followed a different path from you. There is, for example, Senghor, a brilliant intellect and a fiery poet, but full of contradictions on the subject of Negritude.

A.C.: Our affinities were above all a matter of feeling. You either felt black or did not feel black. But there was also the political aspect. Negritude was, after all, part of the left. I never thought for a moment that our emancipation could come from the right—that's impossible. We both felt, Senghor and I, that our liberation placed us on the left, but both of us refused to see the black question as simply a social question. There are people, even today, who thought and still think that it is all simply a matter of the left taking power in France, that with a change in the economic conditions the black question will disappear. I have never agreed with that at all. I think that the economic question is important, but it is not the only thing.

R.D.: Certainly, because the relationships between consciousness and reality are extremely complex. That's why it is equally necessary to decolonize our minds, our inner life, at the same time that we decolonize society.

A.C.: Exactly, and I remember very well having said to the Martinican Communists, in those days, that black people, as you have pointed out, were doubly proletarianized and alienated: in the first place as workers, but also as blacks, because after all we are dealing with the only race which is denied even the notion of humanity. . . .

ROBERT GRAVES
The White Goddess

The "return of the goddess" is one of the central events of a poetics of recovery, a symposium of the whole, etc. From Blake on ("The Eternal Female groand! it was heard all over the Earth"), her image accompanies many of our most radical language experiments, summoning up past images (e.g., Shekinah, Sophia, Kali), leading to a male-centered vision of the muse, as with Graves in what follows, and to a revitalized feminism exploring its own numinosity. But the goddess is linked as well with a geocentric/Gaiacentric vision ("the earth as a religious form" [Eliade]) and thus with contemporary stabs at reclaiming an ecological wholeness—a realization, in Lucy Lippard's words, that "the history of the domination of nature has inexorably been tied to attitudes to gender." The image appears throughout this volume: as the suppressed gnostic feminism restored through an assiduous scholarship (p. 217), in kabbalistic ceremonies around the "bride of God" (p. 303), in personal visions of an animal goddess that parallel old tribal forms (pp. 156, 441), in the despairing image that concludes this book (p. 480).

To much of this, Graves's white-goddess-as-the-source-of-poetry was, beyond his taste for it, a clear incitement. (See Snyder, below, p. 94, for a contemporary statement of the poetry-goddess connection in an ecological framework.)

The Goddess is a lovely, slender woman with a hooked nose, deathly pale face, lips red as rowan-berries, startlingly blue eyes and long fair hair; she will suddenly transform herself into sow, mare, bitch, vixen, she-ass, weasel, serpent, owl, she-wolf, tigress, mermaid or loathsome hag. Her names and titles are innumerable. In ghost stories she often figures as "The White Lady," and in ancient religions, from the British Isles to the Caucasus, as the "White Goddess." I cannot think of any true poet from Homer onwards who has not independently recorded his experience of her. The test of a poet's vision, one might say, is the accuracy of his portrayal of the White Goddess and of the island over which she rules. The reason why the hairs stand on end, the eyes water, the throat is constricted, the skin crawls and a shiver runs down the spine when one writes or reads a true poem is that a true poem is necessarily an invocation of the White Goddess, or Muse, the Mother of All Living, the ancient power of fright and lust—the female spider or the queen-bee whose embrace is death. Housman offered a secondary test of true poetry: whether it matches a phrase of Keats's, "everything that reminds me of her goes through me like a spear." This is equally pertinent to the Theme. Keats was writing under the shadow of death about his Muse, Fanny Brawne; and the "spear that roars for blood" is the traditional weapon of the dark executioner and supplanter.

Sometimes, in reading a poem, the hairs will bristle at an apparently unpeopled and eventless scene described in it, if the elements bespeak her unseen presence clearly enough: for example, when owls hoot, the moon rides like a ship through scudding

SOURCE: Robert Graves, The White Goddess, *pages 12–13.*

cloud, trees sway slowly together above a rushing waterfall, and a distant barking of dogs is heard; or when a peal of bells in frosty weather suddenly announces the birth of the New Year.

Despite the deep sensory satisfaction to be derived from Classical poetry, it never makes the hair rise and the heart leap, except where it fails to maintain decorous composure; and this is because of the difference between the attitudes of the Classical poet, and of the true poet, to the White Goddess. This is not to identify the true poet with the Romantic poet. "Romantic," a useful word while it covered the reintroduction into Western Europe by the writers of verse-romances of a mystical reverence for woman, has become tainted by indiscriminate use. The typical Romantic poet of the nineteenth century was physically degenerate, or ailing, addicted to drugs and melancholia, critically unbalanced and a true poet only in his fatalistic regard for the Goddess as the mistress who commanded his destiny. The Classical poet, however gifted and industrious, fails to pass the test because he claims to be the Goddess's master—she is his mistress only in the derogatory sense of one who lives in coquettish ease under his protection. Sometimes, indeed, he is her bawdmaster: he attempts to heighten the appeal of his lines by studding them with "beauties" borrowed from true poems. In Classical Arabic poetry there is a device known as "kindling" in which the poet induces the poetic atmosphere with a luscious prologue about groves, streams and nightingales, and then quickly, before it disperses, turns to the real business in hand—a flattering account, say, of the courage, piety and magnanimity of his patron or sage reflexions on the shortness and uncertainty of human life. In Classical English poetry the artificial kindling process is often protracted to the full length of the piece. . . .

CLAUDE LÉVI-STRAUSS

From *Tristes Tropiques*

The founder of "structural anthropology," Lévi-Strauss globalizes Durkheim's "collective mind" and here carries it into the heart of the city—the contemporary world of the new wilderness. Beneath the primitive-civilized dichotomy, he asserts a deep structure, a principle of psychic unity that offers a way out of the anomie caused not only by a breakdown of the social bond but by rejection of the underlying unity of mind and nature. The resultant proposition is a new science— based like that of Vico (see above, p. 4) on the reshaping of a primary "poetic wisdom"—and a recognition of the actual "work of the artist, the poet, the composer," celebrated by him elsewhere as a species of "savage thought . . . to which our civilization accords the status of a national park" (see below, p. 91). From our vantage, his own large, synthesizing works reflect the processes he

SOURCE: Claude Lévi-Strauss, Tristes Tropiques (tr. John Russell), pages 126–127.

describes (bricolage, etc.) and project a universalizing poetics that not only avoids an antiquarian response to "savage mind" but leads toward one side of a possible ethnopoetics—just as that of Whorf (see below, p. 191) might be seen as leading to the other.

It's a long time since we ceased to worship the sun; and with our Euclidean turn of mind we jib at the notion of space as qualitative. But it is independently of ourselves that the great phenomena of astronomy or meteorology have their effect—an effect as discreet as it is ineluctable—in every part of the globe. We all associate the direction east-to-west with achievement, just as every inhabitant of the temperate zone of the southern hemisphere associates the north with darkness and cold and the south with warmth and light. None of all this comes out, of course, in our considered behavior. But urban life offers a stange contrast. It represents civilization at its most complex and in its highest state of refinement; but by the sheer human concentration which it represents within a limited space, it precipitates and sets in motion a number of unconscious attitudes. Infinitesimal as these are in themselves, they can produce a considerable effect when a large number of people are reacting to them at the same time and in the same manner. Thus it is that every town is affected by the westward drive, with wealth gravitating to one side and poverty to the other. What is at first sight unintelligible becomes clear if we realize that every town has the privilege (though some would see in it rather a form of servitude) of bringing to our notice, as if under a microscope, the incessant and insect-like activity of our ancestral and still-far-from-extinct superstitions.

And can they really be called superstitions? I see these predilections as a form of wisdom which primitive peoples put spontaneously into practice; the madness lies rather in our modern wish to go against them. These primitive peoples attained quickly and easily to a peace of mind which we strive for at the cost of innumerable rebuffs and irritations. We should do better to accept the true conditions of our human experience and realize that it is not within our power to emancipate ourselves completely from either its structure or its natural rhythms. Space has values peculiar to itself, just as sounds and scents have their colours and feelings their weight. The search for correspondences of this sort is not a poets' game or a department of mystification, as people have dared to say of Rimbaud's *sonnet des voyelles*: that sonnet is now indispensable to the student of language who knows the basis, not of the colour of phenomena, for this varies with each individual, but of the relation which unites one phenomenon to another and comprises a limited gamut of possibilities. These correspondences offer the scholar an entirely new terrain, and one which may still have rich yields to offer. If fish can make an aesthetic distinction between smells in terms of light and dark, and bees classify the strength of light in terms of weight—darkness is heavy, to them, and bright light light—just so should the work of the painter, the poet, and the composer and the myths and symbols of primitive Man seem to us: if not as a superior form of knowledge, at any rate as the most fundamental form of knowledge, and the only one that we all have in common; knowledge in the scientific sense is merely the sharpened edge of this other knowledge. More penetrating it may be, because its edge has been sharpened on the hard stone of fact, but this penetration has been acquired at the price of a great loss of substance; and it is only efficacious in so far as it can penetrate far enough for the whole bulk of the instrument to follow the sharpened point.

The sociologist has his part to play in the elaboration of this worldwide, concrete humanism. For the great manifestations of Society have this in common with the work of art: that they originate at the level of unconscious existence—*because* they are collective, in the first case, and *although* they are individual, in the second; but the difference is not of real importance—is, indeed, no more than apparent—because the first is produced *by*, and the second *for*, the public; and the public supplies them both with their common denominator and determines the conditions in which they shall be created. . . .

MIRCEA ELIADE
The Epilogue to *Shamanism*

An experimental novelist earlier along (his objective, in the Rumanian phrase, to "sabotage history"), Eliade became a historian of religion and the greatest living reinterpreter of the sacred dimensions of religion and thought, setting these against a contemporary "desacralization of nature" through an impressive sweep of disciplines and cultures (shamanism, yoga, alchemy, etc.). His large work on shamanism is still the best guide to the subject, reinforcing an intuition long held of the shaman as artist and thinker as well as "medicine man, priest and psychopompus." In the present co-editor's book, Technicians of the Sacred *(the title itself is a take-off from Eliade's "specialist of the sacred" who masters the "techniques of ecstasy," etc.), the shaman is viewed as a "proto-poet" and paradigm for the later visionary artist. (The accompanying excerpt shows Eliade's own ruminations on the matter.)*

Defining the scope of shamanism, Eliade wrote: "Shamanism is a religious phenomenon characteristic of Siberian and Ural-Altaic peoples. The word 'shaman' is of Tungus origin and it has passed, by way of Russian, into European scientific terminology. But shamanism . . . must not be considered as limited to those countries. It is encountered, for example, in Southeast Asia, Oceania, and among many North American aboriginal tribes" (1967: 423).

There is no solution of continuity in the history of mysticism. More than once we have discerned in the shamanic experience a "nostalgia for paradise" that suggests one of the

SOURCE: *Mircea Eliade,* Shamanism: Archaic Techniques of Ecstasy *(tr. Willard R. Trask), pages 508–511.*

oldest types of Christian mystical experience. As for the "inner light," which plays a part of the first importance in Indian mysticism and metaphysics as well as in Christian mystical theology, it is . . . already documented in Eskimo shamanism. We may add that the magical stones with which the Australian medicine man's body is stuffed are in some degree symbolic of "solidified light."

But shamanism is important not only for the place that it holds in the history of mysticism. The shamans have played an essential role in the defense of the psychic integrity of the community. They are pre-eminently the antidemonic champions; they combat not only demons and disease, but also the black magicians. The exemplary figure of the shaman-champion is Dto-mba Shi-lo, the mythical founder of Na-khi shamanism, the tireless slayer of demons. The military elements that are of great importance in certain types of Asian shamanism (lance, cuirass, bow, sword, etc.) are accounted for by the requirements of war against the demons, the true enemies of humanity. In a general way, it can be said that shamanism defends life, health, fertility, the world of "light," against death, diseases, sterility, disaster, and the world of "darkness."

The shaman's combativeness sometimes becomes an aggressive mania; in certain Siberian traditions shamans are believed to challenge one another constantly in animal form. But such a degree of aggressiveness is rather exceptional; it is peculiar to some Siberian shamanisms and the Hungarian *táltos*. What is fundamental and universal is the shaman's struggle against what we could call "the powers of evil." It is hard for us to imagine what such a shamanism can represent for an archaic society. In the first place, it is the assurance that human beings are not alone in a foreign world, surrounded by demons and the "forces of evil." In addition to the gods and supernatural beings to whom prayers and sacrifices are addressed, there are "specialists in the sacred," men able to "see" the spirits, to go up into the sky and meet the gods, to descend to the underworld and fight the demons, sickness, and death. The shaman's essential role in the defense of the psychic integrity of the community depends above all on this: men are sure that *one of them* is able to help them in the critical circumstances produced by the inhabitants of the invisible world. It is consoling and comforting to know that a member of the community is able to *see* what is hidden and invisible to the rest and to bring back direct and reliable information from the supernatural worlds.

It is as a further result of his ability to travel in the supernatural worlds and to *see* the superhuman beings (gods, demons, spirits of the dead, etc.) that the shaman has been able to contribute decisively to the *knowledge of death*. In all probability many features of "funerary geography," as well as some themes of the mythology of death, are the result of the ecstatic experiences of shamans. The lands that the shaman sees and the personages that he meets during his ecstatic journeys in the beyond are minutely described by the shaman himself, during or after his trance. The unknown and terrifying world of death assumes form, is organized in accordance with particular patterns; finally it displays a structure and, in course of time, becomes familiar and acceptable. In turn, the supernatural inhabitants of the world of death become *visible*; they show a form, display a personality, even a biography. Little by little the world of the dead becomes knowable, and death itself is evaluated primarily as a rite of passage to a spiritual mode of being. In the last analysis, the accounts of the shamans' ecstatic journeys contribute to "spiritualizing" the world of the dead, at the same time that they enrich it with wondrous forms and figures. . . .

The shaman's adventures in the other world, the ordeals that he undergoes in his ecstatic descents below and ascents to the sky, suggest the adventures of the figures in popular tales and the heroes of epic literature. Probably a large number of epic "subjects" or motifs, as well as many characters, images, and clichés of epic literature, are, finally, of ecstatic origin, in the sense that they were borrowed from the narratives of shamans describing their journeys and adventures in the superhuman worlds.

It is likewise probable that the pre-ecstatic euphoria constituted one of the universal sources of lyric poetry. In preparing his trance, the shaman drums, summons his spirit helpers, speaks a "secret language" or the "animal language," imitating the cries of beasts and especially the songs of birds. He ends by obtaining a "second state" that provides the impetus for linguistic creation and the rhythms of lyric poetry. Poetic creation still remains an act of perfect spiritual freedom. Poetry remakes and prolongs language; every poetic language begins by being a secret language, that is, the creation of a personal universe, of a completely closed world. The purest poetic act seems to re-create language from an inner experience that, like the ecstasy or the religious inspiration of "primitives," reveals the essence of things. It is from such linguistic creations, made possible by pre-ecstatic "inspiration," that the "secret languages" of the mystics and the traditional allegorical languages later crystallize.

Something must also be said concerning the dramatic structure of the shamanic séance. We refer not only to the sometimes highly elaborate "staging" that obviously exercises a beneficial influence on the patient. But every genuinely shamanic séance ends as a *spectacle* unequaled in the world of daily experience. The fire tricks, the "miracles" of the rope-trick or mango-trick type, the exhibition of magical feats, reveal another world—the fabulous world of the gods and magicians, the world in which *everything seems possible*, where the dead return to life and the living die only to live again, where one can disappear and reappear instantaneously, where the "laws of nature" are abolished, and a certain superhuman "freedom" is exemplified and made dazzlingly *present*.

It is difficult for us, modern men as we are, to imagine the repercussions of such a *spectacle* in a "primitive" community. The shamanic "miracles" not only confirm and reinforce the patterns of the traditional religion, they also stimulate and feed the imagination, demolish the barriers between dream and present reality, open windows upon worlds inhabited by the gods, the dead, and the spirits.

These few remarks on the cultural creations made possible or stimulated by the experiences of shamans must suffice. A thorough study of them would exceed the limits of this work. What a magnificient book remains to be written on the ecstatic "sources" of epic and lyric poetry, on the prehistory of dramatic spectacles, and, in general, on the fabulous worlds discovered, explored, and described by the ancient shamans.

CHARLES OLSON
Human Universe

*"We are estranged from that with which we are most familiar," wrote Olson,
quoting ancient Heraclitus, and he set out on a search through the American and
human past—Pleistocene, pre-Biblical Mediterranean (Sumerian, Hittite, etc.),
Norse, Mayan, and American Indian—with a conviction "that the reality the
Trobriand Islanders hearken to" (at least the process of getting at it, reenacting it as
myth) "is not at all a local or primitive one, is as much our own as theirs, whatever
the differences" (Olson 1978: 67). And on a local level—and here was his major
contribution—he put a renewed value on geographical and historical particulars of
place ("localism is the new history"), but especially his own home-place of
Gloucester, Mass., which as "Maximus" he addressed in one of the true epic poems
of the modern period (see Olson 1960). It was his genius to recast old ideas with
new force, to rediscover "myth" as living speech, as the thing said ("not a question
of truth or falsehood, but only: has he got the story straight, that is, does he tell it
right?"), and to rediscover "history" as, in its origins, to find-out-for-oneself. In the
early 1950s, he set off on such a self-finding to the Yucatan, where the present essay
was written—underlying which, a recognition of the force of culture as creative
localism and, withal, an irritation with its limits, a desire later confessed to "put an
end to nation, put an end to culture, put an end to divisions of all sorts. . . . We have
our picture of the world & that's the creation" (1969: 36).*

There are laws, that is to say, the human universe is as discoverable as that other. And as
definable.

The trouble has been, that a man stays so astonished he can triumph over his own
incoherence, he settles for that, crows over it, and goes at a day again happy he at least
makes a little sense. Or, if he says anything to another, he thinks it is enough—the
struggle does involve such labor and some terror—to wrap it in a little mystery: ah, the
way is hard but this is what you find if you go it.

The need now is a cooler one, a discrimination, and then, a shout. Der Weg stirbt,
sd one. And was right, was he not? Then the question is: was ist der Weg?

I

The difficulty of discovery (in the close world which the human is because it is ourselves
and nothing outside us, like the other) is, that definition is as much a part of the act as is
sensation itself, in this sense, that life *is* preoccupation with itself, that conjecture about
it is as much of it as its coming at us, its going on. In other words, we are ourselves both
the instrument of discovery and the instrument of definition.

SOURCE: Charles Olson, Human Universe, *pages 3–15.*

Which is of course, why language is a prime of the matter and why, if we are to see some of the laws afresh, it is necessary to examine, first, the present condition of the language—and I mean language exactly in its double sense of discrimination (logos) and of shout (tongue).

We have lived long in a generalizing time, at least since 450 B.C. And it has had its effects on the best of men, on the best of things. Logos, or discourse, for example, has, in that time, so worked its abstractions into our concept and use of language that language's other function, speech, seems so in need of restoration that several of us got back to hieroglyphs or to ideograms to right the balance. (The distinction here is between language as the act of the instant and language as the act of thought about the instant.)

But one can't any longer stop there, if one ever could. For the habits of thought are the habits of action, and here, too, particularism has to be fought for anew. In fact, by the very law of the identity of definition and discovery, who can extricate language from action? (Though it is one of the first false faces of the law which I shall want to try to strike away, it is quite understandable—in the light of its identity—that the Greeks went on to declare all speculation as enclosed in the "UNIVERSE of discourse." It is their word, and the refuge of all metaphysicians since—as though language, too, was an absolute, instead of (as even man is) instrument, and not to be extended, however much the urge, to cover what each, man and language, is in the hands of: what we share, and which is enough, of power and of beauty, not to need an exaggeration of words, especially that spreading one, "universe." For discourse is hardly such, or at least only arbitrarily a universe. In any case, so extended (logos given so much more of its part than live speech), discourse has arrogated to itself a good deal of experience which needed to stay put—needs now to be returned to the only two universes which count, the two phenomenal ones, the two a man has need to bear on because they bear so on him: that of himself, as organism, and that of his environment, the earth and planets.

We stay unaware how two means of discourse the Greeks appear to have invented hugely intermit our participation in our experience, and so prevent discovery. They are what followed from Socrates' readiness to generalize, his willingness (from his own bias) to make a "universe" out of discourse instead of letting it rest in its most serviceable place. (It is not sufficiently observed that logos, and the reason necessary to it, are only a stage which a man must master and not what they are taken to be, final discipline. Beyond them is direct perception and the contraries which dispose of argument. The harmony of the universe, and I include man, is not logical, or better, is post-logical, as is the order of any created thing.) With Aristotle, the two great means appear: logic and classification. And it is they that have so fastened themselves on habits of thought that action is interfered with, absolutely interfered with, I should say.

Nor can I let the third of the great Greeks, Plato, go free—he who had more of a sort of latitude and style my tribe of men are apt to indulge him for. His world of Ideas, of forms as extricable from content, is as much and as dangerous an issue as are logic and classification, and they need to be seen as such if we are to get on to some alternative to the whole Greek system. Plato may be a honey-head, as Melville called him, but he is precisely that—treacherous to all ants, and where, increasingly, my contemporaries die, or drown the best of themselves. Idealisms of any sort, like logic and like classification, intervene at just the moment they become more than the means they are, are allowed to become ways as end instead of ways *to* end, END, which is never more than this instant, than you on this instant, than you, figuring it out, and acting, so. If there is any absolute, it is never more than this one, you, this instant, in action.

Which ought to get us on. What makes most acts—of living and of writing—unsatisfactory, is that the person and/or the writer satisfy themselves that they can only make a form (what they say or do, or a story, a poem, whatever) by selecting from the full content some face of it, or plane, some part. And at just this point, by just this act, they fall back on the dodges of discourse, and immediately, they lose me, I am no longer engaged, this is not what I know is the going-on (and of which going-on I, as well as they, want some illumination, and so, some pleasure). It comes out a demonstration, a separating out, an act of classification, and so, a stopping, and all that I know is, it is not there, it has turned false. For any of us, at any instant, are juxtaposed to any experience, even an overwhelming single one, on several more planes than the arbitrary and discursive which we inherit can declare.

It is not the Greeks I blame. What it comes to is ourselves, that we do not find ways to hew to experience as it is, in our definition and expression of it, in other words, find ways to stay in the human universe, and not be led to partition reality at any point, in any way. For this is just what we do do, this is the real issue of what has been, and the process, as it now asserts itself, can be exposed. It is the function, *comparison*, or its bigger name, *symbology*. These are the false faces, too much seen, which hide and keep from us the active intellectual states, metaphor and performance. All that comparison ever does is set up a series of reference points: to compare is to take one thing and try to understand it by marking its similarities to or differences from another thing. Right here is the trouble, that each thing is not so much like or different from another thing (these likenesses and differences are apparent) but that such an analysis only accomplishes a *description*, does not come to grips with what really matters: that a thing, any thing, impinges on us by a more important fact, its self-existence, without reference to any other thing, in short, the very character of it which calls our attention to it, which wants us to know more about it, its particularity. This is what we are confronted by, not the thing's "class," any hierarchy, of quality or quantity, but the thing itself, and its *relevance* to ourselves who are the experience of it (whatever it may mean to someone else, or whatever other relations it may have).

There must be a means of expression for this, a way which is not divisive as all the tag ends and upendings of the Greek way are. There must be a way which bears *in* instead of away, which meets head on what goes on each split second, a way which does not—in order to define—prevent, deter, distract, and so cease the act of, discovering.

I have been living for some time amongst a people who are more or less directly the descendants of a culture and civilization which was a contrary of that which we have known and of which we are the natural children. The marked thing about them is, that it is only love and flesh which seems to carry any sign of their antecedence, that all the rest which was once a greatness different from our own has gone down before the poundings of our way. And, now, except as their bodies jostle in a bus, or as they disclose the depth and tenacity of love among each other inside a family, they are poor failures of the modern world, incompetent even to arrange that, in the month of June, when the rains have not come far enough forward to fill the wells, they have water to wash in or to drink. They have lost the capacity of their predecessors to do anything in common. But they do one thing no modern knows the secret of, however he is still by nature possessed of it:

they wear their flesh with that difference which the understanding that it is common leads to. When I am rocked by the roads against any of them—kids, women, men—their flesh is most gentle, is granted, touch is in no sense anything but the natural law of flesh, there is none of that pull-away which, in the States, causes a man for all the years of his life the deepest sort of questioning of the rights of himself to the wild reachings of his own organism. The admission these people give me and one another is direct, and the individual who peers out from that flesh is precisely himself, is a curious wandering animal like me—it is so very beautiful how animal human eyes are when the flesh is not worn so close it chokes, how human and individuated the look comes out of a human eye when the house of it is not exaggerated.

This is not easy to save from subjectivism, to state so that you understand that this is not an observation but a first law to a restoration of the human house. For what is marked about these Lermeros with whom I live (by contrast, for example, to the people of the city nearby) is that, here, the big-eared, small-eyed creatures stay as the minority they must always have been before garages made them valuable and allowed them out of their holes to proliferate and overrun the earth. Nothing is accident, and man, no less than nature, does nothing without plan or the discipline to make plan fact. And if it is true that we now live in fear of our own house, and can easily trace the reason for it, it is also true that we can trace reasons why those who do not or did not so live found out how to do other than we.

My assumption is, that these contemporary Maya are what they are because once there was a concept at work which kept attention so poised that (1) men were able to stay so interested in the expression and gesture of all creatures, including at least three planets in addition to the human face, eyes and hands, that they invented a system of written record, now called hieroglyphs, which, on its very face, is verse, the signs were so clearly and densely chosen that, cut in stone, they retain the power of the objects of which they are the images; (2) to mass stone with sufficient proportion to decorate a near hill and turn it into a fire-tower or an observatory or one post of an enclosure in which people, favored by its shadows, might swap camotes for sandals; and (3) to fire clay into pots porous enough to sieve and thus cool water, strong enough to stew iguana and fish, and handsome enough to put ceremony where it also belongs, in the most elementary human acts. And when a people are so disposed, it should come as no surprise that, long before any of these accomplishments, the same people did an improvement on nature—the domestication of maize—which remains one of the world's wonders, even to a nation of Burbanks, and that long after all their accomplishments, they still carry their bodies with some of the savor and the flavor that the bodies of the Americans are as missing in as is their irrigated lettuce and their green-picked refrigerator-ripened fruit. For the truth is, that the management of external nature so that none of its virtu is lost, in vegetables or in art, is as much a delicate juggling of her content as is the same juggling by any one of us of our own. And when men are not such jugglers, are not able to manage a means of expression the equal of their own or nature's intricacy, the flesh does choke. The notion of fun comes to displace work as what we are here for. Spectatorism crowds out participation as the condition of culture. And bonuses and prizes are the rewards of labor contrived by the monopolies of business and government to protect themselves from the advancement in position of able men or that old assertion of an inventive man, his own shop. All individual energy and ingenuity is bought off—at a suggestion box or the cinema. Passivity conquers all. Even war and peace die (to be displaced by world government?) and man reverts to only two of his components, inertia and gas.

It is easy to phrase, too easy, and we have had enough of bright description. To say that in America the goods are as the fruits, and the people as the goods, all glistening but tasteless, accomplishes nothing in itself, for the overwhelming fact is, that the rest of the world wants nothing but to be the same. Value is perishing from the earth because no one cares to fight down to it beneath the glowing surfaces so attractive to all. Der Weg stirbt.

II

Can one restate man in any way to repossess him of his dynamic? I don't know. But for myself a first answer lies in his systemic particulars. The trouble with the inherited formulations which have helped to destroy him (the notion of himself as the center of phenomenon by fiat or of god as the center and man as god's chief reflection) is that both set aside nature as an unadmitted or suppressed third party, a sort of Holy Ghost which was allowed in once to touch men's tongues and then, because the fire was too great, was immediately banished to some sort of half place in between god and the devil—who actually, of course, thereby became the most powerful agent of all. The result, we have been the witnesses of: discovering this discarded thing nature, science has run away with everything. Tapping her power, fingering her like a child, giving her again her place, but without somehow, remembering what truth there was in man's centering the use of anything, god, devil, or holy ghost, in himself, science has upset all balance and blown value, man's peculiar responsibility, to the winds.

If unselectedness is man's original condition (such is more accurate a word than that lovely riding thing, chaos, which sounds like what it is, the most huge generalization of all, obviously making it necessary for man to invent a bearded giant to shape it for him) but if likewise, selectiveness is just as originally the impulse by which he proceeds to do something about the unselectedness, then one is forced, is one not, to look for some instrumentation in man's given which makes selection possible. And it has gone so far, that is, science has, as to wonder if the fingertips, are not very knowing knots in their own rights, little brains (little photo-electric cells, I think they now call the skin) which, immediately, in responding to external stimuli, make decisions! It is a remarkable and usable idea. For it is man's first cause of wonder how rapid he is in his taking in of what he does experience.

But when you have said that, have you not done one of two things, either forever damned yourself by making "soul" mechanical (it has long been the soul which has softly stood as a word to cover man as a selecting internal reality posed dangerously in the midst of those externals which the word chaos generously covers like Williams' paint) or you have possibly committed a greater crime. You have allowed that external reality is more than merely the substance which man takes in. By making the threshold of reception so important and by putting the instrumentation of selection so far out from its traditional place (the greatest humanist of them all opened a sonnet, "Poor soul, the centre of my sinful earth''), you have gone so far as to imply that the skin itself, the meeting edge of man and external reality, is where all that matters does happen, that man and external reality are so involved with one another that, for man's purposes, they had better be taken as one.

It is some such crime by which I am willing to hazard a guess at a way to restore to man some of his lost relevance. For this metaphor of the senses—of the literal speed of light by which a man absorbs, instant on instant, all that phenomenon presents to him—is a fair image as well, my experience tells me, of the ways of his inner energy, of the ways of those other things which are usually, for some reason, separated from the external pick-ups—his dreams, for example, his thoughts (to speak as the predecessors spoke), his desires, sins, hopes, fears, faiths, loves. I am not able to satisfy myself that these so-called inner things are so separable from the objects, persons, events which are the content of them and by which man represents or re-enacts them despite the suck of symbol which has increased and increased since the great Greeks first promoted the idea of a transcendent world of forms. What I do see is that each man, does make his own special selection from the phenomenal field and it is true that we begin to speak of personality, however I remain unaware that this particular act of individuation is peculiar to man, observable as it is in individuals of other species of nature's making (it behooves man now not to separate himself too jauntily from any of nature's creatures).

Even if one does follow personality up, does take the problem further in to those areas of function which may seem more peculiarly human (at least are more peculiarly the concern of a humanist), I equally cannot satisfy myself of the gain in thinking that the process by which man transposes phenomena to his use is any more extricable from reception than reception itself is from the world. What happens at the skin is more like than different from what happens within. The process of image (to be more exact about transposition than the "soul" allows or than the analysts do with their tricky "symbol-maker") cannot be understood by separation from the stuff it works on. Here again, as throughout experience, the law remains, form is not isolated from content. The error of all other metaphysic is descriptive, is the profound error that Heisenberg had the intelligence to admit in his principle that a thing can be measured in its mass only by arbitrarily assuming a stopping of its motion, or in its motion only by neglecting, for the moment of the measuring, its mass. And either way, you are failing to get what you are after—so far as a human being goes, his life. There is only one thing you can do about kinetic, re-enact it. Which is why the man said, he who possesses rhythm possesses the universe. And why art is the only twin life has—its only valid metaphysic. Art does not seek to describe but to enact. And if man is once more to possess intent in his life, and to take up the responsibility implicit in his life, he has to comprehend his own process as intact, from outside, by way of his skin, in, and by his own powers of conversion, out again.

For there is this other part of the motion which we call life to be examined anew, that thing we overlove, man's action, that tremendous discharge of force which we overlove when we love it for its own sake but which (when it is good) is the equal of all intake plus all transposing. It deserves this word, that it is the equal of its cause only when it proceeds unbroken from the threshold of a man through him and back out again, without loss of quality, to the external world from which it came, whether that external world take the shape of another human being or of the several human beings hidden by the generalization "society" or of things themselves. In other words, the proposition here is that man at his peril breaks the full circuit of object, image, action at any point. The meeting edge of man and the world is also his cutting edge. If man is active, it is exactly here where experience comes in that it is delivered back, and if he stays fresh at the coming in he will be fresh at his going out. If he does not, all that he does inside his house is stale, more and more stale as he is less and less acute at the door. And his door is where he is responsible to more than himself. Man does influence external reality, and it can be stated without recourse to the stupidities of mysticism (which appears to love a mystery as much outside as it does in). If man chooses to treat external reality any differently than as part of his own process, in other words as anything other than relevant to his own inner life, then he will (being such a froward thing, and bound to use his energy willy-nilly, nature is so subtle) use it otherwise. He will use it just exactly as he has used it now for too long, for arbitrary and willful purposes which, in their effects, not only change the face of nature but actually arrest and divert her force until man turns it even against herself, he is so powerful, this little thing. But what little willful modern man will not recognize is, that when he turns it against her he turns it against himself, held in the hand of nature as man forever is, to his use of himself if he choose, to his disuse, as he has.

What gets me is, how man refuses to acknowledge the consequences of his disposing of himself at his own entrance—as though a kiss were a cheap thing, as though he were. He will give a Rimbaud a lot of lip and no service at all, as though Rimbaud were a sport of nature and not a proof. Or a people different from himself—they will be the subject of historians' studies or of tourists' curiosity, and be let go at that, no matter how much they may disclose values he and his kind, you would think, could make use of. I have found, for example, that the hieroglyphs of the Maya disclose a placement of themselves toward nature of enormous contradiction to ourselves, and yet I am not aware that any of the possible usages of this difference have been allowed to seep out into present society. All that is done is what a Toynbee does, diminish the energy once here expended into the sieve phonetic words have become to be offered like one of nature's pastes that we call jewels to be hung as a decoration of knowledge upon some Christian and therefore eternal and holy neck. It is unbearable what knowledge of the past has been allowed to become, what function of human memory has been dribbled out to in the hands of these learned monsters whom people are led to think "know." They know nothing in not knowing how to reify what they do know. What is worse, they do not know how to pass over to us the energy implicit in any high work of the past because they purposely destroy that energy as dangerous to the states for which they work—which it is, for any concrete thing is a danger to rhetoricians and politicians, as dangerous as a hard coin is to a banker. And the more I live the more I am tempted to think that the ultimate reason why man departs from nature and thus departs from his own chance is that he is part of a herd which wants to do the very thing which nature disallows—that energy can be lost. When I look at the filth and lumber which man is led by, I see man's greatest achievement in this childish accomplishment—that he damn well can, and does, destroy destroy destroy energy every day. It is too much. It is too much to waste time on, this idiot who spills his fluids like some truculent and fingerless chamaco hereabouts who wastes water at the pump when birds are dying all over the country in this hottest of the months and women come in droves in the morning begging for even a tasa of the precious stuff to be poured in the amphoras they swing on their hips as they swing their babies. Man has made himself an ugliness and a bore.

It was better to be a bird, as these Maya seem to have been, they kept moving their heads so nervously to stay alive, to keep alerted to what they were surrounded by, to watch it even for the snake they took it to be or that larger bird they had to be in awe of, the zopilote who fed on them when they were dead or whom they looked at of a morning in a great black heap like locusts tearing up a deer that had broken his wind or leg in the night. Or even Venus they watched, as though they were a grackle themselves and could attack her vertically in her house full of holes like a flute through which, they thought, when she had the upper hand she spread down on them, on an east wind, disease and those blows on their skin they call granitos. When she was new, when she buzzed the morning sky, they hid in their houses for fear of her, Shoosh Ek, for fear of her bite, the Wasp she was, the way she could throw them down like that electrical stick which, last year, pinched one of these fishermen on his cheek, in all the gulf hit him as he sat in the prow of his cayuco with a line out for dogfish of a day and laid him out dead, with no more mark burned on him than that little tooth of a kiss his wife was given as cause when they brought him out over the beach as he might have hauled in a well-paying shark.

Or to be a man and a woman as Sun was, the way he had to put up with Moon, from start to finish the way she was, the way she behaved, and he up against it because he did have the advantage of her, he moved more rapidly. In the beginning he was only young and full of himself, and she, well, she was a girl living with her grandfather doing what a girl was supposed to be doing, making cloth. Even then he had the advantage of her, he hunted, instead, and because he could hunt he could become a humming-bird, which he did, just to get closer to her, this loveliness he thought she was and wanted to taste. Only the trouble was, he had to act out his mask, and while he was coming closer, one tobacco flower to another toward the house, her grandfather brought him down with a clay shot from a blow gun. And sun fell, right into moon's arms, who took him to her room to mother him, for she was all ready to be a wife, a man's second mother as a wife is in these parts where birds are so often stoned and need to be brought back to consciousness and, if they have their wings intact, may fly away again. As sun was. Only he could also talk, and persuaded moon to elope with him in a canoe. But there you are: there is always danger. Grandfather gets rain to throw his fire at them and though sun converts to turtle and is tough enough to escape alive, moon, putting on a crab shell, is not sufficiently protected and is killed.

Which is only part of it, that part of it which is outside and seems to have all of the drama. But only seems. For dragonflies collect moon's flesh and moon's blood in thirteen hollow logs, the sort of log sun had scooped his helpless runaway boat out of, thinking he had made it, had moon finally for his own. Foolish sun. For now here he is back again, after thirteen days, digging out the the thirteen logs, and finding that twelve of them contain nothing but all the insects and all the snakes which fly and crawl about the earth of man and pester people in a hot climate so that a lot die off before they are well begun and most are ready, at any instant, for a sickness or a swelling, and the best thing to do is to lie quiet, wait for the poison to pass. For there is log 13, and it reveals moon restored to life, only moon is missing that part which makes woman woman, and deer alone, only deer can give her what he does give her so that she and sun can do what man and woman have the pleasure to do as one respite from the constant hammering.

But you see, nothing lasts. Sun has an older brother, who comes to live with sun and moon, and sun has reason to suspect that something is going on between moon and the big star, for this brother is the third one of the sky, the devilish or waspish one who is so often with moon. By a trick, sun discovers them, and moon, dispirited, sitting off by herself on the river bank, is persuaded by the bird zopilote to go off with him to the house of the king of the vultures himself. And though a vulture is not, obviously, as handsome a thing as the sun, do not be fooled into thinking that this bird which can darken the sky as well as feed on dead things until they are only bones for the sun to whiten, has not his attractions, had not his attractions to moon, especially the king of them all. She took him, made him the third of her men, and was his wife.

But sun was not done with her, with his want of her, and he turned to that creature which empowered her, the deer, for aid. He borrowed a skin, and hiding under it—knowing as hot sun does the habits of vultures—he pretends to be a carcass. The first vulture comes in, landing awkwardly a distance off, hobbles his nervous way nearer until, as he is about to pick apart what he thinks is a small deer, sun leaps on his back and rides off to where moon is. He triumphantly seizes her, only to find that she is somewhat reluctant to return.

At which stage, for reasons of cause or not, sun and moon go up into the sky to assume forever their planetary duties. But sun finds there is one last thing he must do to the moon before human beings are satisfied with her. He must knock out one of her eyes, they complain she is so bright and that they cannot sleep, the night is so much the same as his day, and his day is too much anyhow, and a little of the sweetness of the night they must have. So he does, he puts out her eye, and lets human beings have what they want. But when he does more, when, occasionally, he eclipses her entirely, some say it is only a sign that the two of them continue to fight, presumably because sun cannot forget moon's promiscuity, though others say that moon is forever erratic, is very much of a liar, is always telling sun about the way people of the earth are as much misbehavers as she, get drunk, do the things she does, in fact, the old ones say, moon is as difficult to understand as any bitch is.

O, they were hot for the world they lived in, these Maya, hot to get it down the way it was—the way it is, my fellow citizens.

STANLEY DIAMOND
Plato and the Definition of the Primitive[1]

At the heart of Diamond's engaged and committed anthropology is the image of a "search for the primitive"—as "an attempt to define a primary human potential," to transcend thereby the "primitive-civilized dichotomy" that he traces back to the origins of the political state, with its antagonism to ambivalence and to the concrete instance in favor of a "Platonic abstraction, the essence of civilized modalities of thought." (Compare Olson's "we have lived long in a generalizing time," p. 63, above.) More than any contemporary anthropologist of note, with the possible exception of Victor Turner, Diamond insists on an internalized poetics as crucial to anthropology (beyond that, to human survival), specifically a poetics that deals with the function of the "poet-thinker" (Radin) in traditional ("primitive") societies and of the poet-artist in the contemporary world "perpetually recovering his primitivism." If the extent of Diamond's commitment to this image (which he connects herein with the archetypal Trickster figure as "the personification of human ambiguity") sets him apart from most of his contemporaries, it is, as he makes clear, a commitment that unites him with a major lineage in revolutionary Western thought. "Authentically primitive and maximally civilized traits," he writes and proceeds to demonstrate empirically, "are as antithetical as it is possible for cultural attributes to become within the limits of the human condition. This is, however, the present fact of history and it constitutes the problem of this society, for the sickness of civilization consists, I believe, in its failure to incorporate (and only then to move beyond the limits of) the primitive" (1974: 129).

The origin and nature of the state is a subject peculiarly appropriate to cultural anthropology, for states first arise through the transformation and obliteration of typically primitive institutions. Thinkers of the most diverse backgrounds and intentions have throughout history grasped this cardinal fact of state formation. Lao-tzu, Rousseau, Marx and Engels, Maine, Morgan, Maitland, Tonnies and many contemporary students of society have understood that there is a qualitative distinction between the structure of primitive life and civilization. Moreover, they have, more or less explicitly, sensed the

[1]Throughout this [essay], I have used the term *God* metaphorically, since Plato's notion of the deity is, historically and technically, somewhat different from ours. But Plato's meaning is nonetheless conveyed, and the implications of my argument are in no way affected. Similarly, the definition of the essence as an idea in the *mind of God* is neo-Platonic, most notably developed by Malebranche.

SOURCE: Stanley Diamond, In Search of the Primitive, pages 176–202.

contradictions inherent in the transition from kinship or primitive society, to civilized or political society. This momentous transition, this great transformation in the life of man, this social and cultural trauma, has led to a passionate and ancient debate about the merits of primitive existence as opposed to civilization. The debate has frequently been waged in utopian terms. Some utopias face backward to a sometimes fantastic image of the primitive, others face forward to the complete triumph of the rational state. Although I have no intention of engaging in this debate, it seems to me that it is the opposition to the primitive which lies at the root of Plato's utopia, and that is the theme I intend to pursue here. In opposing the primitive, Plato helps us define both it and the state.

THE OPPOSITION TO THE PRIMITIVE

The *Republic* can be considered a projection of the idealized, total city-state, conjured out of the ruins of fourth-century Athens and influenced by the Spartan oligarchy. But in its perfection, it transcends these local boundaries and becomes a classic model of the state to which Western scholars have turned for centuries in debating the good life and its relation to political society. This tension between the local and the universal is evident in all utopian constructs, whether merely literary, or socially realized; it is preeminently true of the *Republic*. Plato maintains certain landmarks of the city-state, but he takes us on a "journey of a thousand years." This span of time is reckoned, perhaps, too modestly, for all subsequent political societies commanded by a permanent, self-proclaimed, benevolent élite, and all élitist social theory, are adumbrated in the *Republic*.

The *Republic*, of course, is more than a political tract. It is also a psychology, an esthetics and a philosophy, but it is all these things within a political context. There is hardly any facet of Plato's vision, however abstruse, nor any action he believed imperative which is not colored or dictated by political considerations. The *Republic* is, in short, a work of enormous scope, but it is saturated with politics, with ideology. This point deserves emphasis because Plato has traditionally been considered the very image of the pure philosopher, and the *Republic* has been extolled as the masterwork, in which most of his major ideas appear, impressively interwoven. As Emerson put it, "Plato is philosophy and philosophy Plato. . . ." The New England Platonist goes further, ceding to Plato Omar's "fanatical compliment" to the Koran: "Burn the libraries, for their value is in this book." The phrase sticks—it is an appropriately Platonic sentiment, and it is a political remark.

What then are the political assumptions underlying the *Republic*? To begin with, Plato's personal political bias is clear. He was an aristocrat who experienced the decay of the Athenian "democracy." He was a philosopher in a society that put Socrates to death. He avoided the rough-and-tumble of politics and shrank from any actual political role in his own society for which his birth and training may have qualified him. Yet he seems to have been obsessed with the idea of politics; the political problem for Plato seems to have consisted in how to abolish politics.

It is possible, therefore, to view the *Republic* as the idealization and rationalization of Plato's personal motives. His ideal state is, after all, a utopian aristocracy, ruled by philosophers who have become kings, and the political problem has ceased to exist. But this is too close an exercise in the sociology of knowledge. Plato's personal motives are unquestionably important; they help fix the precise form of the republic, but they do not determine its broader cultural-historical meaning. In Cornford's words:

> The city-state was a frame within which any type of constitution could subsist; a despotism, an oligarchy, or a democracy. Any Greek citizen of Plato's day, rich or poor, would have been completely puzzled, if he had been told that he had no interest in maintaining the structure of the city-state. The democrat, in particular, would have replied: "Do you really think that an oriental despotism, where all men but one are slaves, is a higher and happier type of society? Or would you reduce us to the level of those savages with all their queer customs described by Herodotus?" [1950:129]

Plato's oligarchic inclinations, then, cannot be considered contradictory to the basic structure of the city-state; the exact form of his republic is less significant than its overall statism. The political assumptions underlying the *Republic* are simply the assumptions of political society, of the state, writ large and idealized. We must remember that classical Greece could look back to its own archaic and primitive past; moreover, it lived on the fringe of a "barbarian" Europe. Thus, the forms and usages of primitive society, even when these were being transformed into organs of the state or abolished in favor of state institutions, were by no means strange to the Greeks, as Fustel de Coulanges, Engels, Morgan, Bury and others have emphasized. Bury, for example, in tracing the early history of Greece, speaks of the authority of the state growing and asserting itself against the comparative independence of the family, and he remarks further that "in the heroic age . . . the state had not emerged fully from the society. No laws were enacted and maintained by the state" (1956: 56).

It seems likely then that Plato had ample opportunity to react against concrete primitive elements in Greek society and cultural tradition while envisioning his utopian state. Only the classical scholars, with the aid of a more fully developed classical anthropology, can establish the degree to which this was possible, but it is not essential to my argument. Plato could have been acting out of sheer political instinct, logically constructing the perfect political society and rejecting those institutions and modes of behavior which could not be coordinated with it, that is, the primitive modes. In any case, the fact of opposition to the primitive is clear in the *Republic*, as is Plato's sure sense of the strategy of political society. And this, I believe, is the larger cultural-historical meaning of his work, conceived, as it was in the morning of European civilization. Indeed the Heavenly City may be viewed as that essence of which all realized polities are inadequate reflections.

DENYING THE FAMILY

Although the themes that will concern us in the *Republic* are very subtly interwoven and sometimes lack precise definition, I shall consider them separately without trying to reconstruct Plato's full argument.

There is, first of all, the suggestion that Socrates makes about the initiation of the republic:

> They will begin by sending out into the country all the inhabitants of the city who are more than ten years old, and will take possession of their children, who will be unaffected by the habits of their parents; these they will train in their own habits and laws, I mean in the laws which we have given them: and in this way the State and constitution of which we were speaking will soonest and most easily attain happiness, and the nation which has such a constitution will gain most. [303][2]

The republic is to begin, then, by severing the bonds between the generations and by obliterating the primary kinship ties. This is, of course, an extreme statement of the general process through which states arise, which is by releasing the individual from kinship controls and obligations and thus making him subject to the emerging civil laws. There is, however, a remarkably exact parallel to Socrates' suggestion in native Dahomean usage as reported by Norris, one of the early chroniclers of the Slave Coast. In the Dahomean proto-state, "children are taken from their mothers at an early age, and distributed to places remote from their village of nativity, where they remain with little chance of being ever seen, or at least recognized, by their parents afterwards. The motive for this is that there may be no family connections or combinations, no associations that might prove injurious to the King's unlimited power" (Diamond 1951: 26).

But we must never forget that Plato has no intention of outlining the process of state formation per se; he is, in our view, idealizing that process, hence the purpose of setting up the republic in the manner described is seen as beneficent.

I might add, parenthetically, that the attempt to weaken or sever the ties between the generations is also a typical utopian and quasi-revolutionary aim. The most recent instance is the Israeli kibbutz, where the collective rearing of children is motivated by the desire to produce a generation quite different in character from the parental image of the Shtetl Jew (Diamond 1957: 71–99). As a matter of fact, wherever a massive shift in political power and structure is contemplated or wherever a radical rearrangement of public loyalties is demanded, the family, the psychic transmission belt between the generations, tends to be attacked not merely in terms of any particular form but as a primary social unit. This is evident in rather different ways in the work of many reformists, among a number of so-called Marxists, and in Nazi theory and practice.

Plato's modest proposal for initiating the republic, then, can be seen in both a revolutionary and a cultural-historical perspective. The *Republic* begins, appropriately enough, in opposition to the antecedent kin and generational ties. And we shall see that this imperative is extended to the rearing of the guardians within the republic. That is, state and family, echoing the old antagonism between political and primitive organization, are seen to be antithetical, even after the establishment of the ideal polity.

[2]All quotations from *The Republic*, unless otherwise indicated, are from Jowett 1914, volume 2.

THE DIVISION OF LABOR AND CLASS

Primitive societies that are not in transition to one or another archaic form of the state (that is, that are not proto-states) may function through rank and status systems and always function through kin or transfigured kin units, the latter being associations whose members are not necessarily reckoned as kin but which pattern themselves on kin forms. They are, however, devoid of class or caste. Further, primitive societies do not manifest the highly specialized division of labor which is one of the major aspects of the rise of class and caste systems. In these related respects, Plato's republic represents the reverse of primitive usage and is the state brought to its highest power. To clarify, let us begin with his vision of an absolute division of labor.

In the republic, no man is to engage in more than a single task. Indeed, the ultimate definition of justice, which Socrates pursues as perhaps the major aim of the entire dialogue, consists in each person doing the work "for which he was by nature fitted" within the class to which he constitutionally belongs. And "at that [occupation] he is to continue working all his life long and at no other" (68). Later on, Socrates elaborates this point as follows: "In our State, and in our State only, we shall find a shoemaker to be a shoemaker, and not a pilot also, and a soldier a soldier, and not a trader also, and the same throughout." He emphasizes: in "our State . . . human nature is not twofold or manifold, for one man plays one part only" (102).

In other words, it is imagined that the identity of the individual is exhausted by the single occupation in which he engages. The occupational status, so to speak, becomes the man, just as his class position is, in a wider sense, said to be determined by his nature. In this way, the existence of the state is guaranteed, but the life of the person is constricted and diminished. The division of labor is, of course, an expression of the socially available technology. The point is that Plato not only sensed the congruence of the elaborate division of labor with state organization, but carried it to its furthest reach and then gave it the name of justice.

The contrast with primitive usage could hardly be more striking. Primitives learn a variety of skills; a single family unit, as among the Nama, Anaguta or Eskimo, may make its own clothing, tools and weapons, build its own houses, and so on. Even in a transitional society such as the Dahomean proto-state it is expected that every man, whatever his occupation, know three things well: how to cut a field, how to build a wall and how to roof a house. Moreover, the average primitive participates directly in a wide range of cultural activities relative to the total available in his society, and he may move, in his lifetime, through a whole series of culturally prescribed statuses. He plays, in short, many parts, and his nature is viewed as manifold. The relevance of this to Plato's conception of the drama will be considered below, but it is first necessary to examine the class structure of his republic and its implications.

The republic is to be divided into three classes: the guardians, or ruling élite; the auxiliaries, including the soldiers; and the lowest class, consisting of all those engaged in economic production, particularly the artisans and farmers. We see at once that the manual laborers are at the base of the social hierarchy, being considered constitutionally unfit to rule themselves. This is of course a quite typical attitude, however rationalized, and we find it associated with the rise of civilization almost everywhere. In early states, the intellectual gradually emerges from the class of scribes or priests; his connections with the ruling groups are primary. The artisans and farmers grow out of the submerged primitive community, which is transformed into a reservoir of workers for the state through direct conscription of labor, taxation, slavery, or related means.

But whatever the details of the process, and they vary in different areas, the subordination of primitive artisan and cultivator is a function of state formation. An Egyptian document dating from the New Kingdom is pertinent, in that it reflects this state of affairs, long consolidated:

> Put writing in your heart that you may protect yourself from hard labor of any kind and be a magistrate of high repute. The scribe is released from manual tasks; it is he who commands. . . . Do you not hold the scribe's palette? That is what makes the difference between you and the man who handles an oar.
>
> I have seen the metal worker at his task at the mouth of his furnace with fingers like a crocodile's. He stank worse than fish spawn. Every workman who holds a chisel suffers more than the men who hack the ground; wood is his field and the chisel his mattock. At night when he is free, he toils more than his arms can do; even at night he lights [his lamp to work by]. . . . The stonecutter seeks work in every hard stone; when he has done the great part of his labor his arms are exhausted, he is tired out. . . . The weaver in a workshop is worse off than a woman; [he squats] with his knees to his belly and does not taste [fresh] air. He must give loaves to the porters to see the light. [Childe 1955: 149]

This process and the attendant attitudes are, I believe, ideally reflected in the *Republic*. They develop in Plato's cave, in the turmoil of history, but they are presented to us in a purified, philosophic and ultimate form.

Now the classes in the ideal state are relatively fixed; they tend to be castes, rationalized on a eugenic basis. But Plato provides for both a modicum of social mobility and the predominant freezing of the entire structure through the medium of a "royal lie," that is, through propaganda, a term that Cornford considers more appropriate, and a condition which we shall take up in connection with the exile of the dramatist. Socrates states:

> Citizens . . . God has framed you differently. Some of you have the power of command, and in the composition of these he has mingled gold, wherefore also they have the greatest honor; others he has made of silver, to be auxiliaries; others again to be husbandmen and craftsmen he has composed of brass and iron; and the species will generally be preserved in the children. But . . . a golden parent will sometimes have a silver son, or a silver parent a golden son. And God proclaims as a first principle to the rulers, and above all else, that there is nothing which they should so anxiously guard . . . as the purity of the race. . . . If the son of a golden or silver parent has an admixture of brass and iron, then nature orders a transportation of ranks and the eye of the ruler must not be pitiful towards the child because he has to descend in the scale and become a husbandman or artisan, just as there

may be sons of artisans who having an admixture of gold or silver in them are raised to honor, and become guardians or auxiliaries. For an oracle says that when a man of brass or iron guards the state, it will be destroyed. Such is the tale; is there any possibility of making our citizens believe in it? [129]

The class structure of the republic, then, is based on a theory of human nature, assimilated to Plato's doctrine of essences. Here we confront a perfect example of the convergence of characteristic Platonic concepts to an immediate political issue, a technique that weaves throughout the dialogue and accounts in part for its great dialectic density. The final nature of the individual is viewed as unambiguous, since human nature is a matter of distinct and single higher and lower essences, subdivided further into occupational essences. That is to say, the division of labor and class in the *Republic* is reflected in the division into essences or vice versa, if you will. The important point is that the whole structure is guaranteed by human nature, watched over by the guardians, justified by philosophy and sanctified by God, as the allegory states.

At the peak of the pyramid stand the guardians. They are said to have a pure intuition of the good; they live in the place of light above the cave and are, in a sense, divine; or at least they have intimations of divinity. Shall we call them divine kings? It matters little, for all kings have been considered holy since the primary differentiation of the king from the local primitive chief. The holiness of the king is the sanctification of civil power, as opposed to the common traditions which are symbolized in the person of the local chief and may thus render *him* sacred. The ultimate other-worldliness of the guardians or philosopher kings is, I believe, a reflection of the process through which civil power was first sanctified as the primitive community was transformed into political society. We should recall that Plato was impressed by the Egyptian theocracy and may have visited Egypt, where the concept of divine rule was as old as the state itself. In any event, the elite tradition of the guardians is the opposite of the communal tradition of primitive peoples.

Yet neither the divinity of the kings, who shape the end of the republic, nor the sterling quality of their auxiliaries is sufficient to ensure their devotion to the state. This can be achieved most readily through a completely collective life and training. Socrates says: "The wives of our guardians are to be common, and their children are to be common, and no parent is to know his own child, nor any child his parent." The children are to be reared collectively by special nurses who "dwell in a separate quarter." The mothers will nurse them but "the greatest possible care" will be taken that no mother recognizes her own child nor will suckling be "protracted too long." The mother will "have no getting up at night or other trouble, but will hand over all this sort of thing to the nurses and attendants" (187, 191–192).

Further, the guardians and their helpers, under a regime of spartan simplicity, are to live in common houses, dine in common and hold no property; and they are not to engage in economically productive work. The obvious aim is to disengage them from all connections and motives which might diminish their dedication to the state. Plato clearly sensed the antagonism between state and family, and in order to guarantee total loyalty to the former, he simply abolished the latter. Moreover, his distrust of kin ties in the ideal state leads him to invoke the aid of a "royal lie," possibly the first half of the propaganda-myth quoted above. Socrates, simulating embarrassment, says:

> I really know not how to look you in the face, or in what words to utter the
> audacious fiction, which I propose to communicate gradually, first to the rulers,
> then to the soldiers, and lastly to the people. They are to be told that their youth was
> a dream, and the education and training they received from us, an appearance only;
> in reality during all that time they were being formed and fed in the womb of the
> earth, where they themselves and their arms and appurtenances were manufac-
> tured; when they were completed, the earth, their mother, sent them up; and so
> their country being their mother and also their nurse, they are bound to advise for
> her good, and to defend her against attacks, and her citizens they are to regard as
> children of the earth and their brothers. [129]

This is, of course, a direct statement of the conflict between kin and political
principles. The territorial state is to receive the loyalty previously accorded the kin
group, and this can only be done by personifying the state, an essentially impersonal
structure. Plato remarks that the fiction is an old Phoenician tale of ''what has often
occurred before now in other places'' (128). Certainly, the myth is precisely of the type
we would expect in societies in transition from kin to civil structure, that is, in societies
engaged in a primary kin-civil conflict.

There is a peculiar parallel with Dahomean usage here, not in the form of myth but
in actual social convention. In Dahomey, every important official in the emerging state
structure had a female counterpart within the king's compound. This woman, termed his
''mother,'' had precedence at ''court,'' acting as a sort of buffer between the official and
the king and personalizing the purely material relationship involved. The bureaucrats
were mustered from the local villages, the conquered and subordinate areas; they had no
kin ties with the royal clan or dynastic lineage. The system of ''civil mothers'' thus
symbolized the new connections that had begun to develop in distinction to the old kin
loyalties. The idea of the motherland, or fatherland, although expressed in kin terms,
seems coincident with the rise of the state, at the point where the problem of political
loyalty begins. This, I believe, is the meaning of Plato's fiction, concretely revealed in
Dahomean usage.

It should be noted that Plato confines the fiction of the ''earth-born heroes'' to the
guardians and auxiliaries. The ordinary people, composed of brass and iron, are to live
under ordinary family circumstances. No extraordinary behavior of any kind is expected
of them, certainly no unusual loyalty to the state. Their worldly concerns, their emotional ties and their inferior natures are conceived as making such behavior impossible.
The soldiers guard the city, the guardians rule it; acquiescence and temperance, a living
up to their own limited possibilities, are the demands made on the mass of people. That,
and the labor which supports the upper classes. The economic producers are, of course,
deprived of political means; in the ideal state this was visualized as the solution to the
political problem. Yet Plato seems uncertain. He speaks of the soldiers selecting a spot
''whence they can best suppress insurrection, if any prove refractory within'' (130), and
also of their maintaining ''peace among our citizens at home . . . [that they may not]
have the power to harm us'' (128).

One further point is worth consideration. The selectively bred but family-less upper classes are to refer to all peers as brothers and sisters and to the members of the older generation as father and mother, seemingly congruent with extended family or clan usage. However, the upper classes represent what can be technically termed a collective, not a community; the relational forms are retained, but the substance is lacking. What we confront here is a rather interesting politicization of kin terminology, as in the case of the Dahomean "civil mothers," in direct opposition to primitive behavior. The latter is always based on concrete and complex family relationships which may then be extended outward to include remote relatives, strangers or even natural phenomena. But as we have seen, the mothers of the upper classes are not to know their own children. They are to be relieved of all domestic and maternal responsibility and thus converted into ideal instruments of the state, fully equal, in this respect, to the men.

The above is a rough outline of class structure and function in the *Republic*. In general, it is the antithesis of what Kroeber, for one, has called "primitive democracy" (1948: 281).

CENSORSHIP OF THE DRAMATIST

There is, I believe, a keystone in the soaring arch of Plato's argument, an imperative on which it must inevitably rest. In this imperative, the statism of the republic culminates, as does its opposition to the primitive.

The dramatists, the makers of tragedy and comedy, the "imitative poets," as Plato calls them, are to be exiled and their works abolished or heavily censored. Socrates says:

> When any one of these pantomimic gentlemen, who are so clever that they can imitate anything, comes to us, and makes a proposal to exhibit himself and his poetry, we will fall down and worship him as a sweet and holy and wonderful being; but we must also inform him that in our State such as he are not permitted to exist; the law will not allow them. [102]

Plato has already given us a reason for this, quoted above in connection with the division of labor: "[in] our State human nature is not twofold or manifold, for one man plays one part only." The "pantomimic gentlemen," Homer or Aeschylus, for example, have no place in the class and occupational structure of the republic, assimilated, as it is, to the doctrine of essences or ultimate forms. Socrates makes this clear to Adeimantos: "Human nature appears to have been coined into yet smaller pieces, and to be as incapable of imitating many things well, as of performing well the actions of which the imitations are copies" (98).

But before pursuing Plato's theory of art, which emerges so logically out of the dialogue, let us examine some of the simpler reasons for establishing a "censorship of the writers of fiction" (73) and the implications thereof.

The poets are perceived as impious and corrupters of youth. They misrepresent the nature of God, which is absolutely good, by spinning tales of rage and ribaldry in heaven. If at all possible, children in the ideal state should be told that conflict is unholy and has never existed among the gods or between citizens. The wicked must always be represented as miserable, "because they require to be punished, and are benefitted by receiving punishment from God,'' but God must never, in verse or prose, be considered the author of evil, for such a fiction would be suicidal in ''any well-ordered commonwealth.'' The poets, such as Euripides, must not be permitted to say that suffering is the work of God, or if it is of God, they ''must devise some explanation . . . such as we are seeking.'' The task of the poet, then, is to justify the ways of God to man, to buttress morality in the republic. And the ultimate impiety is to speak, with Homer, of ''Zeus, who is the dispenser of good *and* evil to us'' (75–78).

Moreover, the poets are inappropriately emotional. They portray death and the underworld in lurid terms; they lament the fallen warrior and rail against fortune, whereas, in the republic, ''the good man . . . will not sorrow for his departed friend [or son, or brother], as though he had suffered anything terrible, [since he] is sufficient for himself . . . and therefore is least in need of other men'' (86). What is worse, the poets portray famous men, heroes, even the gods themselves, in undignified postures of grief or frenzy. Nor can Homeric laughter, whether indulged in by men or gods, be tolerated; in men it leads to ''violent reaction[s],'' and it is a falsification of the nature of God. Hence, such verses from the *Iliad* as ''inextinguishable laughter arose among the blessed gods, when they saw Hephaestus bustling about the mansion,'' must be excised (88).

Finally, the heresy of the poets is expressed in the conception of God as a magician, ''and of a nature to appear insidiously now in one shape, and now in another—sometimes himself changing and passing into many forms, sometimes deceiving us with the semblance of such 'transformations' '' (78). For, ''the gods are not magicians who transform themselves, neither do they deceive mankind in any way'' (82).

Thus far, then, there are three related reasons for Plato's antagonism to the poets. First, they ascribe a dual nature to the gods—the gods are the authors of good *and* evil. Second, they portray the gods as extravagantly emotional, sometimes obscenely so, as in the case of Zeus, who, at the sight of Hera, ''forgot . . . all [his plans] in a moment through his lust'' (91). Third, they present the gods in a variety of shapes and deceptive appearances.

I submit that Plato's objections betray a direct antagonism against the transformer, or trickster, image of the gods; that this image is ''one of the oldest expressions of mankind,'' has been conclusively shown by Paul Radin ([1956], 1972). The Trickster is an authentically primitive figure, appearing in his sharpest form among primitive peoples—a bestial, human and divine being, knowing ''neither good nor evil, yet . . . responsible for both.'' Trickster ''is at the mercy of his passions and appetites,'' is devoid of values, ''yet through his actions all values come into being.'' At the same time, all figures associated with Trickster, for example the ''various supernatural beings'' and man, possess his traits. Thus, Plato says the poets must not be permitted to ''persuade our youth that the Gods are the authors of evil, and that heroes are no better than men''; for ''everybody will begin to excuse his own vice when he is convinced that similar wickednesses are always being perpetrated by 'the kindred of the Gods, the relatives of Zeus.' '' He gives as an example ''the tale of Theseus, son of Poseidon, or of Peirithous, son of Zeus, [who went forth] to perpetrate a horrid rape'' (93).

In his never ending search for himself, Trickster changes shape and experiments with a thousand identities. He has enormous power, is enormously stupid, is ''creator and destroyer, giver and negator.'' Trickster is the personification of human ambiguity.

He is the archetype of the comic spirit, the burlesque of the problem of identity, the ancestor of the clown, the fool of the ages, the incarnation of existential absurdity.

This existential absurdity is the converse of what can be termed "political" absurdity. The latter is the result of the effort to train men to respond on command, in terms of signals rather than symbols. So, for example, hazing at a military academy or in any other bureaucracy systematically conditions a recruit *not* to inquire into the meaning of the absurd act which he is compelled to perform. He obeys without question, and it is assumed he will do so in the future when appropriately stimulated. The absurdities which define conventional bureaucratic behavior do not, of course, originate in existential reflection on the absurdity of life—which is a source of creative energy—but in the reduction of men to reflexes in a system, which is the death of the creative instinct. The image of the wooden soldier fits precisely here. Political structures which manipulate persons hardly generate loyalty, skill, or initiative. That first and most basic bureaucracy, the "regular" army, dominated by career officers, predictably fails when confronted with the spontaneity and inventiveness of the guerrilla band, functioning on a higher symbolic level, stimulated by the immediacy of their associations and the consistencies of their goals. Plato was correct in assuming that the guardians would need rigorously trained auxiliaries to "suppress insurrection" in the ideal state; he was wrong in assuming they could succeed.

Inevitably, Trickster must be banished from the republic, wherein identity is a matter of pure, ideal, unambiguous forms and where men are to be totally and strategically socialized. The poets who have created or inherited Trickster's image of the world are, it follows, to be silenced. Once again, Plato's opposition to the primitive is clear, if not necessarily conscious.

It would be possible to claim that Plato's negative image of the poets themselves is that of the Trickster, for has he not called them "pantomimic gentlemen" and "imitators"? And may we not add that Plato sensed and distrusted the old connection between art and magic? This is a sensible, if superficial, interpretation; to deepen it we must explore Plato's theory of art and its implications.

Plato regarded the art of the tragic and comic dramatists, along with that of the painters, as essentially imitative, as dealing with appearances only. The painter, for example, paints a bed, but this image is "thrice removed" from the truth. The ideal form or essence of the bed is created by God; this is the eternal bed which the philosopher kings can intuit; it is the bed in truth and goodness, of one nature, essentially inimitable and complete. At a second remove from the truth is the tangible bed created by the artisan, the particular bed, which is a "semblance of existence," but not existence entire as manifested in God's bed (380). But the bed of the painter is sheer imitation, being neither useful nor ideal. In no sense can it be considered a *creation*. Further, all artists, save those who echo the needs of the state by composing "hymns to the Gods and praises of famous men" (396), are deceivers who, in effect, presume to create but cannot. The painter, for example, does not know how to make a bed nor does he know anything of the work of the cobbler or carpenter whom he may represent. Socrates states: "The imitator has no knowledge worth mentioning of what he imitates. Imitation is only a kind of play or sport, and the tragic poets, whether they write in Iambic or Heroic verse, are imitators in the highest degree." Nor can the artist-imitator have any knowledge of good or evil "and may be expected, therefore, to imitate only what appears good to the ignorant multitude'' (389). Plato seems to mean here that the intuition into pure existence aided by the study of mathematics, a basic subject for the guardians, is also the apprehension of the good, or at least a prerequisite to it. The artist reproduces appearances only, and these vary; pure essence cannot be reproduced, only intuited. Since the artist has no knowledge of the good, he can have no knowledge of evil, nor does he possess any understanding of the useful, for he is once removed from the particulars that he copies and hence thrice removed from the truth. A perfectly antithetical view of the artist is Goya's statement in the catalogue to *Los Caprichos*: ''Painting, like poetry, selects from the universe the material she can best use for her own ends. She unites and concentrates in one fantastic figure circumstances and characters which nature has distributed among a number of individuals. Thanks to the wise and ingenious combination, the artist deserves the *name of inventor and ceases to be a mere subordinate copyist*'' (italics added).

The absolute, reciprocal antagonism of the true artist and Platonism could not be more pertinently expressed. But this antagonism, it must be said, is not necessarily directed against a belief in God or religious passion as such, only against the removal of God from the concretely human, that is, against the turning of God into an abstraction. All religious art of any stature and all religious artists worthy of the name, from the Byzantines and Giotto through Michelangelo to Blake and Rouault (confining the example to a fragment of the Western tradition), inscribe their vision in the flesh and see God either as an aspect of man's nature or as a perception to which every man is capable of attaining, usually out of his agony. Hence, God may be apprehended by the artist as objectively real, yet always in the most ordinary, unexpected, various but human guises. The institutionalized and abstract God of the church and the philosophers is never the God of the artist, though called by the same name. The human distance between Plato's God and Blake's is infinite.

But whether or not we accept the terms in which it is couched, Plato's argument has extraordinary power and beauty. The philosopher expressed completely what many who have subsequently shared his attitudes have only dimly perceived; the artist is dangerous, as life is dangerous; he sees too much, because that is all he desires to do, and he presumes to create, to erect man into the role of the creator. But his vision is incomplete, he cannot penetrate to the objective order of the universe, the handiwork of God. And to men of Plato's temperament that objective order, the pure anatomy of reason, is as essential as breathing. Yet if the artist would accept the eternal order and thus learn humility, if he could convert his art into a public strategy in behalf of an abstract idea of the good, the state would find a place for him. Let the protagonists of Homer and of poetry in general prove their worth, and they will be returned from exile. Moreover, there is a passionate tie between the artist and the ''ignorant multitude.'' The artist does not believe in abstract systems; he deals with felt and ordered emotional ideas and believes that order is attained through the contradictions, the tense unities of everyday experience. Thus, the artist himself may be unstable, a changeling, and this is a threat to any establishment. Plato is entirely consistent. He was, it seems, a man of a certain type, incapable of tolerating ambiguity, positive in his conviction of an objective, superhuman good. He believed in God with the cool passion of a mathematician, and he believed at least abstractly that the perfectly just city could be established through perfectly rational and perfectly autocratic means. He began as a poet, and so he must have understood in his own being the old argument between poetry and philosophy to which he occasionally refers. In evicting the dramatist, Plato reveals himself, the nature of the republic and the functions of art; his motives, of course, are above suspicion.

The poets, then, are to be exiled from the ideal state. There is simply no room for them; they are the first superfluous men. The philosopher kings intuit the universal, ultimate forms, God creates them, and the multitude lives among and constructs their particular manifestations. Hence, the class structure of the republic reflects the doctrine of forms or essences. It descends from the superior, from the abstract, created by God and grasped by the guardians, to the inferior, to the particular, grasped by the craftsmen and ordinary citizens, who live in a world of ordinary, useful, sensuous things. Here we encounter Platonism enthroned, a political hierarchy perfectly mated to a conceptual one. The ''fleshy'' Homer, who also presumes to create, is a threat to this structure, and cannot be tolerated.

The class division between the universal and particular, between the institutionalized intellectuals and the economic men reflects a condition that develops with ancient civilization as opposed to primitive [culture]. This is not to say that temperamental distinctions do not exist among primitives, for they do, as Radin has brilliantly shown in his analysis of the thinker and man of action. The point is that among primitives such distinctions complement each other, the concrete and the abstract interpenetrate, ''thinker'' and ''man of action'' are tied together; sometimes, as Radin points out, they meet in the same individual, and in any case, such differences are not politicized. Just as soon as the latter occurs, in early states or as idealized in the *Republic*, there is both an impoverishment and a denial of the sources of human creativity. Further, in early states in the real world, the differential worth often ascribed to people in the various occupations within the broader classes is a political rationalization, generated from the top down. For not only did accidents of birth and training determine social fate, but the point of view from which evaluations were made was that of the scribes, the priests, the nobility. In the *Republic*, in the ideal world, Plato's division of labor and conceptual capacity is said to be genetically determined. The social accident is nullified, yet the division remains artificial because it isolates the abstract from the concrete, the intellectual from the emotional, and considers the craftsman and the farmer useful but inferior beings, not from the perspective of the priest or noble, but from that of Plato's philosophy.

I submit, further, that the Platonic definition of the abstract has become so entrenched in Western thought that the frequently encountered attitude toward primitives, that they are incapable of or deficient in this capacity, is a manifestation of it. Conversely, the attempt to prove that primitives are capable of abstracting too often centers on the types of abstraction emerging out of the history of Western culture, which would seem quite irrelevant. While it is true that no primitive group is made up of Platonists in the technical sense of that term (for primitives tend to live, as Radin has put it, ''in a blaze of reality'') and the various politico-conceptual divisions generic to the state have not yet been established, this does not mean that they do not think abstractly. In the basic sense, every linguistic system is a system of abstractions; each sorting out of experience and conclusion from it is an abstract endeavor; every tool is a symbol of abstract thinking. Indeed, all cultural convention, all custom, is testimony to the generic human capacity for abstracting. But such abstractions are indissolubly wedded to the concrete. They are nourished by the concrete, and they are, I believe, ultimately induced, not deduced. They are not, in short, specifically Platonic abstractions, and they do not have the politicized psychological connotations of the latter.

For Plato there is an order in the universe that escapes the human eye. That order is, as we have seen, composed of forms or essences which must ultimately be conceptualized; they cannot be perceived by the senses. There is a radical split between perceptions and conceptions in Platonic discourse, a split that has been elaborated endlessly in Western science to the point of morbidity and at the expense of the senses. Reality has become increasingly reified and, at the same time, thrown into question; the conceived object has been detached not only from the perceiving subject, but from itself. When a Platonist looks at an object, the reflection in his eye represents an inferior order of reality; he has no faith in either the perception or the object realized in the world. The object exists only as the shadow of a conceptual meta-reality, *as an instance of a class*, an analytic construction. The majority of civilized men, it is assumed, see only superficially (they are not "seers"), and they look at the object in a utilitarian, unthinking way. Being incapable of probing more deeply into, analyzing, the nature of their experience, they see but do not *see*. Therefore, they are compelled by their limited conceptual capacity to follow those who can *see*.

The expectation of a superior interpretation of what we apprehend is built into the use of our everyday language. That anticipation is an imperative of neither vocabulary or syntax, but of the cultural arrangement of meaning generic to the civilizational process, as Plato understood so well.

Tylor is equally acute although his evolutionary enthnocentrism is insupportable:

> It may be said in concluding the subject of Images and Names, that the effect of an inability to separate, so clearly as we do, *the external object from the mere thought or idea of it in the mind, shows itself very fully and clearly in the superstitious beliefs and practices of the untaught man.* . . . Between our clearness of separation of what is in the mind from what is out of it, and the mental confusion of the lowest savages of our own day, there is a vast interval. [1964: 126]

Most broadly defined, then, the language of theoretical science is also the language of political society. The ordinary man, it is imagined, bears witness only to the ordinary object. The priest or scientist—or being more rigorously Platonic, the priest trained as a scientist—conceives a metaphysical or theoretical construct, and that construct constitutes the specifically Platonic definition of the abstract. When we talk about the object in our usual Platonic mode, then, we are talking either metaphysics or theoretical science (not technics); and we are also talking politics, the latter because of the presumed inaccessibility of ultimate reality to the mass of civilized men, except through the conceptual mediation of their perceptions by statesmen, priests and scientists.

For the Platonic abstraction is, above all, the basis of the deductive, theoretical proposition which serves as the ground of what we call science. The notion of systematic forms (or, alternatively put, of underlying formal systems *governing* perceived reality, that is, the notion of logically deducible, conceptual meta-realities) dominates our definition of science, of *knowing*. In the Platonic view, these conceptions are eternal. They do not enter directly into the perceived world; they are the unmoved sources of all process, dialectic or otherwise; and they have no history. They are the ultimate structures, regularities, laws governing the universe; and they find their analogue in the laws governing the Republic.

But there is another way of relating to the object. Looking, for example, can be an intensely perceptual experience. The object may be seen in its absolute singularity through, let us say, the eye of a Vermeer. It erupts as a unique thing in the world, irreducible to an exclusive, a priori class, yet subject to a variety of relationships, a thing which may have been made, used, exchanged and which nonetheless may reveal different aspects according to the quality of light, position among other objects, meaning to those who relate to it. Or it may exist as a thing in nature, its being contained in its existence.

The uniqueness of the object inheres in the immediate, concentrated response of the unaided, humanly experienced eye. The object is *connotative*. Through the structure of analogy and metaphor that defines discourse among primitive people, it reveals a manifold and spontaneous reality. No decisive denotative statement can be made about the object, no mathematical or metaphysical statement can define it. This heightened perception is, of course, an aspect of the definition of art and commands a focus on the singularity of the object to such a degree that everything seems at once marvelous, strange, familiar and unexpected. No category can exhaust such an object; it saturates the perceiving subject. That is what William Blake, who despised Plato, meant when he said that he could look at a knothole in a tree until he became terrified. This existential perception, which is also that of the artist and the mystic, cannot be trimmed to fit a metaphysical class, and it is the converse of a theoretical construct.

Yet all three ways of looking—the utilitarian, the Platonic, and the poetic—are abstract and relational. What is at stake is the type of abstraction involved. The non-Platonic or ''concrete'' abstractions comprise the customary mode of primitive thinking,[3] not generically but culturally, and also define the mode of the artist who has been politically alienated from the ordinary man. Yet, despite everything, the artist is more closely aligned with the ordinary man, now differentiated from his primitive estate, than he is with the priest, scientist or statesman. Like the ordinary man, he ambivalently perceives his dependence on the structures the priest, scientist and statesman command. Like the ordinary man, he focuses on the object; but for him the object has become incandescent. He is perpetually recovering his primitivism.

Plato's theory of cognition is, therefore, not only an aspect of his esthetics, but logically defines his sense of justice or, rather, demonstrates once again how astonishingly integrated, how final his thinking is. Justice, the aim of the *Republic*, confined one man to one vocation; that principle of esthetic and political order is extended to assume single ''realities'' behind a multitude of ''appearances.'' Indeed, Plato's ontological ethic inheres precisely in this: for a man to engage in many jobs is to deny his essential nature, for men to concentrate on the uniquenes of things in this world is to deny their essential natures, and for men to presume above their natural stations is to deny the essential nature of the State. Justice in the *Republic* inheres in the given structure and indivisibility of essences.

---

[3]Robert Redfield understood this as follows: The patterns of thinking of a city man where a multitude of unfamiliar experiences are dealt with by relating them to convenient classes are different from those of a remote rural dweller, whose social objects are all unique and known by their individual characters (1930: 222–223).

This is not only a reflection of the political imperatives of civilization—it is, at the same time, the basis for a definition of evil (violation of the order) and an affirmation of the meaning of virtue (appreciation of the order). In the Platonic order, we discover the link between political, metaphysical and scientific classification and, therefore, the significance of the Platonic abstraction, the essence of civilized modalities of thought.

PRIMITIVE RITUAL DRAMA

Plato's opposition to the drama and the dramatist is directly associated with the class and ideational structure of the *Republic*. At its root, this is also an opposition to the primitive, not merely with reference to the old tie between artist and magician but, more comprehensively, in connection with the form and meaning of the primitive ritual drama.

In the ritual drama, art and life converge; life itself is seen as a drama, roles are symbolically acted out, dangers confronted and overcome and anxieties faced and resolved. Relations among the individual, society, and nature are defined, renewed, and reinterpreted. I am, of course, defining the primitive ritual drama in the broadest possible way, that is, as comprising those ceremonies which cluster around life crises or discontinuities, either of the individual or of the group at large. Generally speaking, the latter are concerned with crises arising from the group's relation to the natural environment, while the former are concerned with personal crises, that is, with the individual's relation to himself and the group. In all ritual dramas, however, despite the relative emphasis on the group or the individual, there is an apparent continuity from the individual's setting in the group to the group's setting in nature. Moreover, the problems of identity and survival are always the dominant themes, and it is for this reason that we can, I believe, term these primitive ceremonials dramas.

To clarify, let us consider those ceremonials which devolve upon personal crises, such as death, marriage, puberty or illness. These can be considered "existential" situations; that is, people die, marry, sicken, become sexually mature and economically responsible in all societies. In primitive societies, such ordinary human events are made meaningful and valuable through the medium of the dramatic ceremonies. Here we confront man raising himself above the level of the merely biological, affirming his identity and defining his obligations to himself and to the group. The ritual drama, then, focuses on ordinary human events and makes them extraordinary and, in a sense, sacramental.

At the same time, the ceremonials we are speaking of enable the individual to maintain integrity of self while changing life roles. The person is freed to act in new ways without crippling anxiety or becoming a social automaton. The person discharges the new status but the status does not become the person. This, I believe, is the central psychological meaning of the theme of death and rebirth, of constant psychic renewal, which is encountered so frequently in primitive ceremonials. It is an organic theme; what one is emerges out of what one was. There is no mechanical separation, only an organic transition extending over a considerable time, often crowded with events and never traumatic, but modulated and realistic in its effects.[4]

[4] I use the term "traumatic" here in the sense of deep, psychic trauma. This is not to deny the pain and suffering often involved in primitive rituals, but the personal and traditional meanings infusing them, the conventional structuring of the situation, strip these experiences of the unwitting and pathological ramifications of trauma.

Hence, the ceremonies of personal crisis are prototypically dramatic in two related ways. They affirm the human struggle for values within a social setting, while confirming individual identity in the face of ordinary "existential" situations such as death or puberty. These ceremonial dramas constitute a shaping and an acting out of the raw materials of life. All primitives have their brilliant moments on this stage, each becomes the focus of attention by the mere fact of his humanity; and in the light of the ordinary-extraordinary events, his kinship to others is clarified. Moreover, these ritual dramas, based on the typical crisis situations, seem to represent the culmination of all primitive art forms; they are, perhaps, the primary form of art around which cluster most of the esthetic artifacts of primitive society—the masks, poems, songs, myths, above all the dance, that quintessential rhythm of life and culture.

Ritual dramas are not automatic expressions of the folk spirit. They were created, just as were the poems, dances and songs that heighten their impact, by individuals moving in a certain cultural sequence, formed by that tradition and forming it. Whether we call these individuals "poet-thinkers," "medicine men" or "shamans," (terms used by Paul Radin) seems unimportant. Plainly, they were individuals who reacted with unusual sensitivity to the stresses of the life cycle and were faced, in extreme cases, with the alternative of breaking down or creating meaning out of apparent chaos. Let us call them primitive dramatists. The meanings they created, the conflicts they symbolized and sometimes resolved in their own "pantomimic" peformances, were felt by the majority of so-called ordinary individuals. There was, of course, magic here too; but, more deeply, there was a perception of human nature that tied the group together. The primitive dramatist served as the lightning rod for the commonly experienced anxieties, which, in concert with his peers and buttressed by tradition, the primitive individual was able to resolve. This is not to say that the primitive dramatist simply invented meanings promiscuously. It was always done within a given socio-economic and natural setting. But he shaped dramatic forms through which the participants were able to clarify their own conflicts and more readily establish their own identities.

There was an organic tie, then, between the primitive dramatist and the people at large, the tie of creation and response, which is in itself a type of creation. The difference was that the dramatist lived under relatively continuous stress, most people only periodically so. Thus the dramatist was in constant danger of breakdown, of ceasing to function or of functioning fantastically in ways that were too private to elicit a popular response. In this prototypical primitive situation, we can, I think, sense the connection that binds the psychotic to the shaman whom we have called a dramatist and the dramatist to the people at large. The distinctions are a matter of degree. The very presence of the shaman-dramatist is a continuous reminder that life often balances on the knife edge between chaos and meaning and that meaning is created or apprehended by man coming, as it were, naked into the world.

THE INEVITABILITY OF GREEK DRAMA

The Greek drama is the direct heir of the primitive ritual drama, as Cornford, Murray, and Harrison have helped establish. Indeed, it retains various technical ritual elements: the chorus, the conscience of the play, was a vestige of group participation. The plays of Sophocles were watched with an air of "ritual expectancy," Aristophanes was performed at the Dionysiac festivals, and the themes of Greek drama had the style of ritual (Fergusson n.d.: 40).

Thus we can begin to apprehend why Plato found it necessary to exile the dramatist, as the very prototype of the artist, from the republic. The dramatist is tied to the "ignorant multitude," he presumes to create meanings and reveal conflicts, he senses in his own being the ambiguity of man, and he is concerned with the ordinary-extraordinary things, with values as a problem and the common human struggle for personal identity. Such men are dangerous precisely because they view life as problematical in the best of states; they clarify what others feel. Hence, they must either be confined to composing "hymns to the Gods and praises of famous men" or exiled.

We must remember that in the *Republic* the problem of identity is presumably solved in terms of a political interpretation of higher and lower human natures. Such an institutionalized human identity is entirely contrary to the dramatist's perceptions; it is equally foreign to the mind of primitive man. The dramatist, as a dramatist, cannot believe in such stark and ultimate separations between men or within the individual man. When Shakespeare writes his tragedies of kings, he plays out their conflicts against a specific socio-economic background, but in the end he tells all of us about ourselves, and the "multitude" in the pit responds. And was not Shakespeare, in a sense, all the characters he constructed, what Plato would call a gross "imitator"?

Nor can the dramatist deny the sensuous, earthy things, since his plots are based on the "existential" situations: marriage, death, the coming to maturity, sickness of mind and body, the recurring issues in the inner relations among men, the very themes that served as the occasions for the primitive drama of personal crisis. Let me put it as plainly as I can. In the end, the dramatist must either become an antagonist to Plato's perfectionist God, or he must cease being a dramatist. Within his own lights, the philosopher was right.

If the dramatist is a tragedian, then he is grimly concerned with the problem of identity, self-definition, integrity; for tragedy is no more than the dissolution of personal identity and social value through behavior to which the hero is compelled and of which he is, sooner or later, aware. And by that awareness, he transcends himself in one final blinding moment, as did Oedipus at Colonus. The civilized tragic drama is, then, a free elaboration on the theme of identity, celebrated in the primitive ritual.

If the dramatist is a comedian, then he burlesques the problem of identity, he laughs it out of court, he stands aside and lets men make fools of themselves; men, he tells us, with Aristophanes, are everything but what they presume to be. The civilized comic drama, then, is based on the trickster's primitive image of the world, on identity, as it were, turned inside out. It is a celebration of the failure of identity.

Among primitives, the most serious rituals (those ancestral to the modern tragedy) and the ancient comic spirit of the trickster are often mingled. In Wintun, Pueblo, and Kond ceremonials, for example, "in nearly every instance it is the very thing which is regarded with greatest reverence or respect which is ridiculed," as Steward states (1931: 187—207). The Dionysiac tradition of the satyr (or trickster) play following the tragic trilogy echoes this primitive usage.

It should be clear, then, that on every major count Plato's exile of comedy and tragedy was inevitable; for the dramatist, in his elemental—or, better, primitive—nature, would have worked havoc with the structure of the ideal state and its ideology of identities.

But if one exiles or diminishes the artist, then who helps discover and dramatize the people to themselves? And if the people are considered incapable of attaining to real understanding, a view obviously not held here but essential to the *Republic*, then how are value and meaning to be transmitted to them? Plato answers this question, although he does not ask it. The royal or noble lie, the manufactured or applied myth filtering down from above, that is, official propaganda, is to provide the popular *raison d'être* of the republic. The youth are to be told, in morality tales, that they live in the best of all possible worlds. We have already quoted the fictions which justify the class structure. These lies, these political myths as opposed to primitive myths, are the means for fixing personal and social identity for the majority of people in the ideal state in the absence of the artist, both as a specialized figure and as an inherent aspect of the personality of every man.

But if the philosopher kings can lie in the name of the public good and in the interests of a higher truth accessible only to them, the common people cannot. Socrates says: "It seems that our rulers will have to administer a great quantity of falsehood and deceit for the benefit of the ruled" (Lindsay 1940: 148). And further, "for a private man to lie to them in return is to be deemed a more heinous fault than for the patient or the pupil of a gymnasium not to speak the truth about his own bodily illnesses to the physician or to the trainer, or for a sailor not to tell the captain what is happening about the ship and the rest of the crew" (89).

Plato was a sober, shrewd, sometimes witty, but hardly comic, idealist; he constructed his heavenly city, brick by brick, with great care and impeccable intentions. When he has finished—and what a craftsman he was—we confront a shining, impervious structure, a luminous monolith, a society with no problems, no conflicts, no tensions, individual or collective. As the *Republic* approaches its end of perfect justice and harmony, it becomes perfectly inhuman. It is so abstractly and ruthlessly wise, so canny and complete an exercise in statecraft, that were we to disregard Plato's temperament, we should have to consider him one of the most skilled totalitarian thinkers in history, the first state utopian, as opposed to the primitive utopians. His historic fault, which speaks to us across millennia, is not merely in his anthropology, it is not in his intoxication with God, abstract though that was, but rather that he, who so fastidiously shunned politics, should have insisted upon the politicization of his faith. Even Cornford, an eloquent defender of Plato, sees him finally as president of the Nocturnal Council, an inquisitor. His prisoner, of course, is Socrates.

GARY SNYDER

Poetry and the Primitive: Notes on Poetry as an Ecological Survival Technique

"As a poet I hold the most archaic values on earth. They go back to the Paleolithic: the fertility of the soil, the magic of animals. The power-vision in solitude, the terrifying initiation and rebirth, the love and ecstasy of the damned, the common work of the tribe."

More than most poets, Snyder has been a model of these values put into practice, engaged with experimental and traditional religion and with an experimental—still tentative—communal life. "Forming the New Society / Within the shell of the Old," he writes (quoting the old Wobbly motto) in his first book, Myths and Texts ([1960], 1978: 44). And somewhere in that process, as a young student in the 1950s, he made the shift (he tells us) from being the "anthropologist" to being the "informant." But, like other poets as informants, he has kept his eye on history as well—to trace the patterns and the movement of a "great subculture of illuminati . . . a powerful undercurrent in all higher civilizations . . . which runs . . . without break from Paleo-Siberian Shamanism and Magdalenian cave-painting; through megaliths and Mysteries, astronomers, ritualists, alchemists and Albigensians; gnostics and vagantes, right down to Golden Gate Park" (1969: 105, 115). On its Eastern side, too, it encompasses (often from the perspective of his own participation) "Taoism; . . . and the Zen Buddhists up till the early Sung; within Islam the Sufis; in India the various threads [that] converged to produce Tantrism," etc. In short, a link between primitive and civilized, archaic and modern, toward an expanded poetics and politics—as a function of life.

BILATERAL SYMMETRY

"Poetry" as the skilled and inspired use of the voice and language to embody rare and powerful states of mind that are in immediate origin personal to the singer, but at deep levels common to all who listen. "Primitive" as those societies which have remained non-literate and non-political while necessarily exploring and developing in directions that civilized societies have tended to ignore. Having fewer tools, no concern with history, a living oral tradition rather than an accumulated library, no overriding social goals, and considerable freedom of sexual and inner life, such people live vastly in the present. Their daily reality is a fabric of friends and family, the field of feeling and energy that one's own body is, the earth they stand on and the wind that wraps around it; and various areas of consciousness.

SOURCE: Gary Snyder, Earth House Hold, *pages 117–130.*

At this point some might be tempted to say that the primitive's real life is no different from anybody else's. I think this is not so. To live in the "mythological present" in close relation to nature and in basic but disciplined body/mind states suggests a wider-ranging imagination and a closer subjective knowledge of one's own physical properties than is usually available to men living (as they themselves describe it) impotently and inadequately in "history"—their mind-content programmed, and their caressing of nature complicated by the extensions and abstractions which elaborate tools are. A hand pushing a button may wield great power, but that hand will never learn what a hand can do. Unused capacities go sour.

Poetry must sing or speak from authentic experience. Of all the streams of civilized tradition with roots in the paleolithic, poetry is one of the few that can realistically claim an unchanged function and a relevance which will outlast most of the activities that surround us today. Poets, as few others, must live close to the world that primitive men are in: the world, in its nakedness, which is fundamental for all of us—birth, love, death; the sheer fact of being alive.

Music, dance, religion, and philosophy of course have archaic roots—a shared origin with poetry. Religion has tended to become the social justifier, a lackey to power, instead of the vehicle of hair-raising liberating and healing realizations. Dance has mostly lost its connection with ritual drama, the miming of animals, or tracing the maze of the spiritual journey. Most music takes too many tools. The poet can make it on his own voice and mother tongue, while steering a course between crystal clouds of utterly incommunicable non-verbal states—and the gleaming daggers and glittering nets of language.

In one school of Mahayana Buddhism, they talk about the "Three Mysteries." These are Body, Voice and Mind. The things that are what living *is* for us, in life. Poetry is the vehicle of the mystery of voice. The universe, as they sometimes say, is a vast breathing body.

With artists, certain kinds of scientists, yogins, and poets, a kind of mind-sense is not only surviving but modestly flourishing in the twentieth century. Claude Lévi-Strauss (*The Savage Mind*) sees no problem in the continuity: ". . . it is neither the mind of savages nor that of primitive or archaic humanity, but rather mind in its untamed state as distinct from mind cultivated or domesticated for yielding a return. . . We are better able to understand today that it is possible for the two to coexist and interpenetrate in the same way that (in theory at least) it is possible for natural species, of which some are in their savage state and others transformed by agriculture and domestication, to coexist and cross . . . whether one deplores or rejoices in the fact, there are still zones in which savage thought, like savage species, is relatively protected. This is the case of art, to which our civilization accords the status of a national park."

MAKING LOVE WITH ANIMALS

By civilized times, hunting was a sport of kings. The early Chinese emperors had vast fenced hunting reserves; peasants were not allowed to shoot deer. Millennia of experience, the proud knowledge of hunting magic—animal habits—and the skills of wild plant and herb gathering were all but scrubbed away. Much has been said about the frontier in American history, but overlooking perhaps some key points: the American confrontation with a vast wild ecology, an earthly paradise of grass, water, and game—was mind-shaking. Americans lived next to vigorous primitives whom they could not help but respect and even envy, for three hundred years. Finally, as ordinary men supporting their families, they often hunted for food. Although marginal peasants in Europe and Asia did remain part-time hunters at the bottom of the social scale, these Americans were the vanguard of an expanding culture. For Americans, "nature" means wilderness, the untamed realm of total freedom—not brutish and nasty, but beautiful and terrible. Something is always eating at the American heart like acid: it is the knowledge of what we have done to our continent, and to the American Indian.

Other civilizations have done the same, but at a pace too slow to be remembered. One finds evidence in T'ang and Sung poetry that the barren hills of central and northern China were once richly forested. The Far Eastern love of nature has become fear of nature: gardens and pine trees are tormented and controlled. Chinese nature poets were too often retired bureaucrats living on two or three acres of trees trimmed by hired gardeners. The professional nature-aesthetes of modern Japan, tea-teachers and flower-arrangers, are amazed to hear that only a century ago dozens of species of birds passed through Kyoto where today only swallows and sparrows can be seen; and the aesthetes can scarcely distinguish those. "Wild" in the Far East means uncontrollable, objectionable, crude, sexually unrestrained, violent; actually ritually polluting. China cast off mythology, which means its own dreams, with hairy cocks and gaping pudenda, millennia ago; and modern Japanese families participating in an "economic miracle" can have daughters in college who are not sure which hole babies come out of. One of the most remarkable intuitions in Western thought was Rousseau's Noble Savage: the idea that perhaps civilization has something to learn from the primitive.

Man is a beautiful animal. We know this because other animals admire us and love us. Almost all animals are beautiful and paleolithic hunters were deeply moved by it. To hunt means to use your body and senses to the fullest: to strain your consciousness to feel what the deer are thinking today, this moment; to sit still and let your self go into the birds and wind while waiting by a game trail. Hunting magic is designed to bring the game to you—the creature who has heard your song, witnessed your sincerity, and out of compassion comes within your range. Hunting magic is not only aimed at bringing beasts to their death, but to assist in their birth—to promote their fertility. Thus the great Iberian cave paintings are not of hunting alone—but of animals mating and giving birth. A Spanish farmer who saw some reproductions from Altamira is reported to have said, "How beautifully this cow gives birth to a calf!" Breuil has said, "The religion of those days did *not* elevate the animal to the position of a god . . . but it was *humbly entreated* to be fertile." A Haida incantation goes:

> "The Great One coming up against the current
>   begins thinking of it.
> The Great One coming putting gravel in his mouth
>   thinks of it
> You look at it with white stone eyes—
>   Great Eater begins thinking of it."

People of primitive cultures appreciate animals as other people off on various trips. Snakes move without limbs, and are like free penises. Birds fly, sing, and dance; they gather food for their babies; they disappear for months and then come back. Fish can breathe water and are brilliant colors. Mammals are like us, they fuck and give birth to babies while panting and purring; their young suck their mothers' breasts; they know terror and delight, they play.

Lévi-Strauss quotes Swanton's report on the Chickasaw, the tribe's own amusing game of seeing the different clans as acting out the lives of their totemic emblems: "The Raccoon people were said to live on fish and wild fruit, those of the Puma lived in the mountains, avoided water of which they were very frightened and lived principally on game. The Wild Cat clan slept in the daytime and hunted at night, for they had keen eyes; they were indifferent to women. Members of the Bird clan were up before daybreak: 'They were like real birds in that they would not bother anybody . . . the people of this clan have different sorts of minds, just as there are different species of birds.' They were said to live well, to be polygamous, disinclined to work, and prolific . . . the inhabitants of the 'bending-post-oak' house group lived in the woods . . . the High Corncrib house people were respected in spite of their arrogance: they were good gardeners, very industrious but poor hunters; they bartered their maize for game. They were said to be truthful and stubborn, and skilled at forecasting the weather. As for the Redskunk house group: they lived in dugouts underground."

We all know what primitive cultures don't have. What they *do* have is this knowledge of connection and responsibility which amounts to a spiritual ascesis for the whole community. Monks of Christianity or Buddhism, "leaving the world" (which means the games of society) are trying, in a decadent way, to achieve what whole primitive communities—men, women, and children—live by daily; and with more wholeness. The Shaman-poet is simply the man whose mind reaches easily out into all manners of shapes and other lives, and gives song to dreams. Poets have carried this function forward all through civilized times: poets don't sing about society, they sing about nature—even if the closest they ever get to nature is their lady's queynt. Class-structured civilized society is a kind of mass ego. To transcend the ego is to go beyond society as well. "Beyond" there lies, inwardly, the unconscious. Outwardly, the equivalent of the unconscious is the wilderness: both of these terms meet, one step even farther on, as *one*.

One religious tradition of this communion with nature which has survived into historic Western times is what has been called Witchcraft. The antlered and pelted figure painted on the cave wall of Trois Frères, a shaman-dancer-poet, is a prototype of both Shiva and the Devil.

Animal marriages (and supernatural marriages) are a common motif of folklore the world around. A recent article by Lynn White puts the blame for the present ecological crisis on the Judaeo-Christian tradition—animals don't have souls and can't be saved; nature is merely a ground for us to exploit while working out our drama of free will and salvation under the watch of Jehovah. The Devil? "The Deivill apeired vnto her in the liknes of ane prettie boy in grein clothes . . . and at that tyme the Deivil gaive hir his markis; and went away from her in the liknes of ane blak dowg." "He wold haw carnall dealling with ws in the shap of a deir, or in any vther shap, now and then, somtyme he vold be lyk a stirk, a bull, a deir, a rae, or a dowg, etc, and haw dealling with us.''

The archaic and primitive ritual dramas, which acknowledged all the sides of human nature, including the destructive, demonic, and ambivalent, were liberating and harmonizing. Freud said *he* didn't discover the unconscious, poets had centuries before. The purpose of California Shamanism was ''to heal disease and resist death, with a power acquired from dreams.'' An Arapaho dancer of the Ghost Dance came back from his trance to sing:

> ''I circle around, I circle around
>
> The boundaries of the earth,
> The boundaries of the earth
>
> Wearing the long wing feathers as I fly
> Wearing the long wing feathers as I fly.''

THE VOICE AS A GIRL

''Everything was alive—the trees, grasses, and winds were dancing with me, talking with me; I could understand the songs of the birds.'' This ancient experience is not so much—in spite of later commentators—''religious'' as it is a pure perception of beauty. The phenomenal world experienced at certain pitches is totally living, exciting, mysterious, filling one with a trembling awe, leaving one grateful and humble. The wonder of the mystery returns direct to one's own senses and consciousness: inside and outside; the voice breathes, ''Ah!''

Breath is the outer world coming into one's body. With pulse—the two always harmonizing—the source of our inward sense of rhythm. Breath is spirit, ''inspiration.'' Expiration, ''voiced,'' makes the signals by which the species connects. Certain emotions and states occasionally seize the body, one becomes a whole tube of air vibrating; all voice. In mantra chanting, the magic utterances, built of seed-syllables such as OM and AYNG and AH, repeated over and over, fold and curl on the breath until—when most weary and bored—a new voice enters, a voice speaks through you clearer and stronger than what you know of yourself; with a sureness and melody of its own, singing out the inner song of the self, and of the planet.

Poetry, it should not have to be said, is not writing or books. Non-literate cultures with their traditional training methods of hearing and reciting, carry thousands of poems—death, war, love, dream, work, and spirit-power songs—through time. The voice of inspiration as an ''other'' has long been known in the West as The Muse. Widely speaking, the muse is anything other that touches you and moves you. Be it a mountain range, a band of people, the morning star, or a diesel generator. Breaks through the ego-barrier. But this touching-deep is as a mirror, and man in his sexual nature has found the clearest mirror to be his human lover. As the West moved into increasing complexities and hierarchies with civilization, Woman as nature, beauty, and The Other came to be an all-dominating symbol; secretly striving through the last three millennia with the

Jehovah or Imperator God-figure, a projection of the gathered power of anti-nature social forces. Thus in the Western tradition the Muse and Romantic Love became part of the same energy, and woman as nature the field for experiencing the universe as sacramental. The lovers bed was the sole place to enact the dances and ritual dramas that link primitive people to their geology and the Milky Way. The contemporary decline of the cult of romance is linked to the rise of the sense of the primitive, and the knowledge of the variety of spiritual practices and paths to beauty that cultural anthropology has brought us. We begin to move away now, in this interesting historical spiral, from monogamy and monotheism.

Yet the muse remains a woman. Poetry is voice, and according to Indian tradition, voice, vāk (vox)—is a Goddess. Vāk is also called Sarasvati, she is the lover of Brahma and his actual creative energy; she rides a peacock, wears white, carries a book-scroll and a vīna. The name Sarasvati means "the flowing one." "She is again the Divine in the aspect of wisdom and learning, for she is the Mother of Veda; that is of all knowledge touching Brahman and the universe. She is the Word of which it was born and She is that which is the issue of her great womb, Mahāyoni. Not therefore idly have men worshipped Vāk, or Sarasvati, as the Supreme Power."

As Vāk is wife to Brahma ("wife" means "wave" means "vibrator" in Indo-European etymology) so the voice, in everyone, is a mirror of his own deepest self. The voice rises to answer an inner need; or as BusTon says, "The voice of the Buddha arises, being called forth by the thought of the living beings." In esoteric Buddhism this becomes the basis of a mandala meditation practice: "In their midst is Nayika, the essence of *Ali*, the vowel series—she possesses the true nature of Vajrasattva, and is Queen of the Vajra-realm. She is known as the Lady, as Suchness, as Void, as Perfection of Wisdom, as limit of Reality, as Absence of Self."

The conch shell is an ancient symbol of the sense of hearing, and of the female; the vulva and the fruitful womb. At Koptos there is a bas-relief of a four-point buck, on the statue of the god Min, licking his tongue out toward two conches. There are many Magdalenian bone and horn engravings of bear, bison, and deer licking abstract penises and vulvas. At this point (and from our most archaic past transmitted) the mystery of voice becomes one with the mystery of body.

How does this work among primitive peoples in practice? James Mooney, discussing the Ghost Dance religion, says "There is no limit to the number of these [Ghost Dance] songs, as every trance at every dance produces a new one, the trance subject after regaining consciousness embodying his experience in the spirit world in the form of a song, which is sung at the next dance and succeeding performances until superseded by other songs originating in the same way. Thus a single dance may easily result in twenty or thirty new songs. While songs are thus born and die, certain ones which appeal especially to the Indian heart, on account of their mythology, pathos, or peculiar sweetness, live and are perpetuated."

Modern poets in America, Europe, and Japan, are discovering the breath, the voice, and trance. It is also for some a discovery to realize that the universe is not a dead thing but a continual creation, the song of Sarasvati springing from the trance of Brahma. "Reverence to Her who is eternal, Raudrī, Gaurī, Dhātri, reverence and again reverence, to Her who is the Consciousness in all beings, reverence and again reverence. . . . Candī says.''

HOPSCOTCH AND CATS CRADLES

The clouds are "Shining Heaven" with his different bird-blankets on.

—Haida

The human race, as it immediately concerns us, has a vertical axis of about 40,000 years and as of A.D. 1900 a horizonal spread of roughly 3,000 different languages and 1,000 different cultures. Every living culture and language is the result of countless cross-fertilizations—not a ''rise and fall'' of civilizations, but more like a flowerlike periodic absorbing—blooming—bursting and scattering of seed. Today we are aware as never before of the plurality of human life-styles and possibilities, while at the same time being tied, like in an old silent movie, to a runaway locomotive rushing headlong toward a very singular catastrophe. Science, as far as it is capable of looking ''on beauty bare'' is on our side. Part of our being modern is the very fact of our awareness that we are one with our beginnings—contemporary with all periods—members of all cultures. The seeds of every social structure or custom are in the mind.

The anthropologist Stanley Diamond has said ''The sickness of civilization consists in its failure to incorporate (and only then) to move beyond the limits of the primitive.'' Civilization is, so to speak, a lack of faith, a human laziness, a willingness to accept the perceptions and decisions of others in place of your own—to be less than a full man. Plus, perhaps, a primate inheritance of excessive socializing; and surviving submission/dominance traits (as can be observed in monkey or baboon bands) closely related to exploitative sexuality. If evolution has any meaning at all we must hope to slowly move away from such biological limitations, just as it is within our power to move away from the self-imposed limitations of small-minded social systems. We all live within skin, ego, society, and species boundaries. Consciousness has boundaries of a different order, ''the mind is free.'' College students trying something different because ''they do it in New Guinea'' is part of the real work of modern man: to uncover the inner structure and actual boundaries of the mind. The third Mystery. The charts and maps of this realm are called mandalas in Sanskrit. (A poem by the Sixth Dalai Lama runs ''Drawing diagrams I measured / Movement of the stars / Though her tender flesh is near / Her mind I cannot measure.'') Buddhist and Hindu philosophers have gone deeper into this than almost anyone else but the work is just beginning. We are now gathering all the threads of history together and linking modern science to the primitive and archaic sources.

The stability of certain folklore motifs and themes—evidences of linguistic borrowing—the deeper meaning of linguistic drift—the laws by which styles and structures, art-forms and grammars, songs and ways of courting, relate and reflect each other are all mirrors of the self. Even the uses of the word ''nature,'' as in the seventeenth-century witch Isobel Gowdie's testimony about what it was like to make love to the Devil—''I found his nature cold within me as spring-well-water''—throw light on human nature.

Thus nature leads into nature—the wilderness—and the reciprocities and balances by which man lives on earth. Ecology: "eco" (*oikos*) meaning "house" (cf. "ecumenical"): Housekeeping on Earth. Economics, which is merely the housekeeping of various social orders—taking out more than it puts back—must learn the rules of the greater realm. Ancient and primitive cultures had this knowledge more surely and with almost as much empirical precision (see H. C. Conklin's work on Hanunoo plant-knowledge, for example) as the most concerned biologist today. Inner and outer: the Brihadāranyaka Upanishad says, "Now this Self is the state of being of all contingent beings. In so far as a man pours libations and offers sacrifice, he is in the sphere of the gods; in so far as he recites the Veda he is in the sphere of the seers; in so far as he offers cakes and water to the ancestors, in so far as he gives food and lodging to men, he is of the sphere of men. In so far as he finds grass and water for domestic animals, he is in the sphere of domestic animals; in so far as wild beasts and birds, even down to ants, find something to live on in his house, he is of their sphere."

The primitive world view, far-out scientific knowledge and the poetic imagination are related forces which may help if not to save the world or humanity, at least to save the Redwoods. The goal of Revolution is Transformation. Mystical traditions within the great religions of civilized times have taught a doctrine of Great Effort for the achievement of Transcendence. This must have been their necessary compromise with civilization, which needed for its period to turn man's vision away from nature, to nourish the growth of the social energy. The archaic, the esoteric, and the primitive traditions alike all teach that beyond transcendence is Great Play, and Transformation. After the mind-breaking Void, the emptiness of a million universes appearing and disappearing, all created things rushing into Krishna's devouring mouth; beyond the enlightenment that can say "these beings are dead already; go ahead and kill them, Arjuna" is a loving, simple awareness of the absolute beauty and preciousness of mice and weeds.

Tsong-kha-pa tells us of a transformed universe:

"1. This is a Buddha-realm of infinite beauty
 2. All men are divine, are subjects
 3. Whatever we use or own are vehicles of worship
 4. All acts are authentic, not escapes."

Such authenticity is at the heart of many a primitive world view. For the Anaguta of the Jos plateau, Northern Nigeria, North is called "up"; South is called "down." East is called "morning" and West is called "evening." Hence (according to Dr. Stanley Diamond in his *Anaguta Cosmography*), "Time flows past the permanent central position . . . they live at a place called noon, at the center of the world, the only place where space and time intersect." The Australian aborigines live in a world of ongoing recurrence—comradeship with the landscape and continual exchanges of being and form and position; every person, animals, forces, all are related via a web of reincarnation—or rather, they are "interborn." It may well be that rebirth (or interbirth, for we are actually mutually creating each other and all things while living) is the objective fact of existence which we have not yet brought into conscious knowledge and practice.

It is clear that the empirically observable interconnectedness of nature is but a corner of the vast "jewelled net" which moves from without to within. The spiral (think of nebulae) and spiral conch (vulva/womb) is a symbol of the Great Goddess. It is charming to note that physical properties of spiral conches approximate the Indian notion of the world-creating dance, "expanding form"—"We see that the successive chambers of a spiral Nautilus or of a straight Orthoceras, each whorl or part of a whorl of a periwinkle or other gastropod, each additional increment of an elephant's tusk, or each new chamber of a spiral foraminifer, has its leading characteristic at once described and its form so far described by the simple statement that it constitutes a *gnomon* to the whole previously existing structure" (D'Arcy Thompson).

The maze dances, spiral processions, cats cradles, Micronesian string star-charts, mandalas and symbolic journeys of the old wild world are with us still in the universally distributed childrens' game. Let poetry and Bushmen lead the way in a great hop forward:

In the following game of long hopscotch, the part marked H is for Heaven: it is played in the usual way except that when you are finishing the first part, on the way up, you throw your tor into Heaven. Then you hop to 11, pick up your tor, jump to the very spot where your tor landed in Heaven,
and say, as fast as you can,
the alphabet forwards and backwards,
your name, address and telephone number (if you have one),
your age,
and the name of your boyfriend or girl-friend (if you have
one of those).

[Patricia Evans, *Hopscotch*]

JEROME ROTHENBERG
Pre-Face to
Technicians of the Sacred

"Therefore, in outline: (1) the traditions in question add to any reconsideration of poetry as 'vision' & 'communion' a series of authentic instances (historical & cultural) in which such functions were realized; (2) they provide the idea of the oral & mythic as self-corrective tellings, & the evidence of how it works; (3) they give a functional dimension to 'meaning' or 'significance' in the poetic act: the evidence that even apparently minimal forms may have a great complexity of function ('the smallest things can turn you on'—P. Blackburn) . . . but at the same time, an expanded notion of alternative poetic & linguistic structures; (4) they point to the existence of what Gary Snyder calls 'models of basic nature-related cultures': . . . towards a fusion of ecology & poetics; (5) they lead to a recognition that cultures like species are irreplaceable once extinct: the product of millennia; (6) in the American Indian instance, etc., they afford a means of enlarging our experience of the continent—in time & space; (7) they comprise a necessary body of knowledge at a time when 'the wave of the future would seem to be the growing awareness of Europeans that they are themselves on the other side of the frontier of developing and expanding people . . . (when) we are being told (and a few are listening) that Europe is brutal and brilliant, successful—and dead.' (Thus the anthropologist, Paul Bohannan, 1966.)" [J. R., Pre-Faces: 17–18]

PRIMITIVE MEANS COMPLEX

That there are no primitive languages is an axiom of contemporary linguistics where it turns its attention to the remote languages of the world. There are no half-formed languages, no underdeveloped or inferior languages. Everywhere a development has taken place into structures of great complexity. People who have failed to achieve the wheel will not have failed to invent & develop a highly wrought grammar. Hunters & gatherers innocent of all agriculture will have vocabularies that distinguish the things of their world down to the finest details. The language of snow among the Eskimos is awesome. The aspect system of Hopi verbs can, by a flick of the tongue, make the most subtle kinds of distinction between different types of motion.

What is true of language in general is equally true of poetry & of the ritual-systems of which so much poetry is a part. It is a question of energy & intelligence as universal constants &, in any specific case, the direction that energy & intelligence (= imagination) have been given. No people today is newly born. No people has sat in sloth for the thousands of years of its history. Measure everything by the Titan rocket & the transistor radio, & the world is full of primitive peoples. But once change the unit of value to the poem or the dance-event or the dream (all clearly artifactual situations) & it becomes

SOURCE: *Jerome Rothenberg, Technicians of the Sacred, pages xix–xxiv.*

apparent what all those people have been doing all those years with all that time on their hands.

Poetry, wherever you find it among the "primitives"[1] (literally *everywhere*), involves an extremely complicated sense of materials & structures. Everywhere it involves the manipulation (fine or gross) of multiple elements. If this isn't always apparent, it's because the carry-over (by translation or interpretation) necessarily distorts where it chooses some part of the whole that it can meaningfully deal with. The work is foreign & its complexity is often elusive, a question of gestalt or configuration, of the angle from which the work is seen. If you expect a primitive work to be simple or naïve, you will probably end up seeing a simple or naïve work; & this will be abetted by the fact that translation can, in general, only present as a single work, a part of what is actually there. The problem is fundamental for as long as we approach these works from the outside—& we're likely fated to be doing that forever.

It's very hard in fact to decide what precisely are the boundaries of "primitive" poetry or of a "primitive" poem, since there's often no activity differentiated as such, but the words or vocables are part of a larger total "work" that may go on for hours, even days, at a stretch. What we would separate as music & dance & myth & painting is also part of that work, & the need for separation is a question of "our" interest & preconceptions, not of "theirs." Thus the picture is immediately complicated by the nature of the work & the media that comprise it. And it becomes clear that the "collective" nature of primitive poetry (upon which so much stress has been placed despite the existence of individualized poems & clearly identified poets) is to a great degree inseparable from the amount of materials a single work may handle.

Now all of this is, if so stated, a question of technology as well as inspiration; & we may as well take it as axiomatic for what follows that where poetry is concerned, "primitive" means complex.

WHAT IS A "PRIMITIVE" POEM?

Poems are carried by the voice & are sung or chanted in specific situations. Under such circumstances, runs the easy answer, the "poem" would simply be the words-of-the-song. But a little later on the question arises: what *are* the words & where do they begin & end? The translation, as printed, may show the "meaningful" element only, often no more than a single, isolated "line"; thus

> A splinter of stone which is white (Bushman)
> Semen white like the mist (Australian)

[1] The word "primitive" is used with misgivings & put in quotes, but no way around it seems workable. "Non-technological" & "non-literate," which have often been suggested as alternatives, are too emphatic in pointing to supposed "lacks" &, though they feel precise to start with, are themselves open to question. Are the Eskimo snow-workers, e.g., really "non-" or "pre-technological"? And how does the widespread use of pictographs & pictosymbols, which can be "read" by later generations, affect their users' non-literate status? A major point throughout this book is that these peoples (& they're likely too diverse to be covered by a single name) are precisely "technicians" where it most concerns them—specifically in their relation to the "sacred" as something they can actively create or capture. That's the only way in fact that I'd hope to define "primitive": as a situation in which such conditions flourish & in which the "poets" are (in Eliade's phrase) the principal "technicians of the sacred."

My-shining-horns (Chippewa: single word)
etc.

but in practice the one "line" will likely be repeated until its burden has been exhausted. (Is it "single" then?) It may be altered phonetically & the words distorted from their "normal" forms. Vocables with no fixed meaning may be intercalated. All of these devices will be creating a greater & greater gap between the "meaningful" residue in the translation & what-was-actually-there. We will have a different "poem" depending where we catch the movement, & we may start to ask: Is something within this work the "poem," or is everything?

Again, the work will probably not end with the "single" line & its various configurations—will more likely be preceded & followed by other lines. Are all of these "lines" (each of considerable duration) separate poems, or are they the component parts of a single, larger poem moving toward some specific (ceremonial) end? Is it enough, then, if the lines happen in succession & aren't otherwise tied? Will some further connection be needed? Is the group of lines a poem if "we" can make the connection? Is it a poem where no connection is apparent to "us"? If the lines come in sequence on a single occasion does the unity of the occasion connect them into a single poem? Can many poems be a single poem as well? (They often are.)

What's a sequence anyway?

What's unity?

THE UNITY OF "PRIMITIVE" THOUGHT & ITS SHATTERING

The anthology shows some ways in which the unity is achieved—in general by the imposition of some constant or "key" against which all disparate materials can be measured. A sound, a rhythm, a name, an image, a dream, a gesture, a picture, an action, a silence: any or all of these can function as "keys." Beyond that there's no need for consistency, for fixed or discrete meanings. An object is whatever it becomes under the impulse of the situation at hand. Forms are often open. Causality is often set aside. The poet (who may also be dancer, singer, magician, whatever the event demands of him) masters a series of techniques that can fuse the most seemingly contradictory propositions.

But above all there's a sense-of-unity that surrounds the poem, a reality concept that acts as a cement, a unification of perspective linking

poet & man
man & world
world & image
image & word
word & music
music & dance
dance & dancer
dancer & man
man & world
etc.

all of which has been put in many different ways—by Cassirer notably as a feeling for "the solidarity of all life" leading toward a "law of metamorphosis" in thought & word.

Within this undifferentiated & unified frame with its open images & mixed media, there are rarely "poems" as we know them—but we come in with our analytical minds & shatter the unity. It has in fact been shattered already by workers before us.

PRIMITIVE & MODERN: INTERSECTIONS & ANALOGIES

Like any collector, my approach to delimiting & recognizing what's a poem has been by analogy: in this case (beyond the obvious definition of poems as words-of-songs) to the work of modern poets. Since much of this work has been revolutionary & limit-smashing, the analogy in turn expands the range of what "we" can see as primitive poetry. It also shows some of the ways in which primitive poetry & thought are close to an impulse toward unity in our own time, of which the poets are forerunners. The important intersections (analogies) are:

(1) the poem carried by the voice: a "pre"-literate situation of poetry composed to be spoken, chanted or, more accurately, sung; compare this to the "post-literate" situation, in McLuhan's good phrase, or where-we-are-today;

> written poem as score
> public readings
>
> poets' theaters
> jazz poetry
> rock poetry etc.

(2) a highly developed process of image-thinking: concrete or non-causal thought in contrast to the simplifications of Aristotelian logic, etc., with its "objective categories" & rules of non-contradiction; a "logic" of polarities; creation thru dream, etc.; modern poetry (having had & outlived the experience of rationalism) enters a post-logical phase;

> Blake's multi-images
> symbolisme
> surrealism
>
> deep-image
>
> random poetry
> composition by field etc.

(3) a "minimal" art of maximal involvement; compound elements, each clearly articulated, & with plenty of room for fill-in (gaps in sequence, etc.): the "spectator" as (ritual) participant who pulls it all together;

> concrete poetry

(4) an "intermedia" situation, as further denial of the categories: the poet's techniques aren't limited to verbal maneuvers but operate also through song, non-verbal sound, visual signs, & the varied activities of the ritual event:

> picture poems
> prose poems
>
> happenings
> total theater

here the "poem" = the work of the "poet" in whatever medium, or (where we're able to grasp it) the totality of the work:

(5) the animal-body-rootedness of "primitive" poetry: recognition of a "physical" basis for the poem within a man's body—or as an act of body & mind together, breath &/or spirit; in many cases too the direct & open handling of sexual imagery & (in the "events") of sexual activities as key factors in creation of the sacred;

(6) the poet as shaman, or primitive shaman as poet & seer thru control of the means just stated: an open "visionary" situation prior to all system-making ("priesthood") in which the man creates thru dream (image) & word (song), "that Reason may have ideas to build on" (W. Blake).

poets as film-makers etc.

dada
lautgedichte (sound poems)

beast language

line & breath
projective verse etc.

sexual revolution etc.

Rimbaud's voyant
Rilke's angel
Lorca's duende

beat poetry
psychedelic see-in's, be-in's, etc.

individual neo-shamanisms, etc.
works directly influenced by the "other" poetry or by analogies to "primitive art": ideas of negritude, tribalism, wilderness, etc.

What's more, the translations themselves may create new forms & shapes-of-poems with their own energies & interest—another intersection that can't be overlooked.

In all this the ties feel very close—not that "we" & "they" are identical, but that the systems of thought & the poetry they've achieved are, like what we're after, distinct from something in the "west," & we can now see & value them because of it. What's missing are the in-context factors that define them more closely group-by-group: the sense of the poems as part of an integrated social & religious complex; the presence in each instance of specific myths & locales; the fullness of the living culture. Here the going is rougher with no easy shortcuts through translation: no simple carry-overs. If our world is open to multiple influences & data, theirs is largely self-contained. If we're committed to a search for the "new," most of them are tradition-bound. (The degree to which "they" are can be greatly exaggerated.) If the poet's purpose among us is "to spread doubt [& create illusion]" (N. Calas), among them it's to overcome it.

That they've done so *without denying the reality* is also worth remembering. . . .

TWO
Workings

BRONISLAW MALINOWSKI
The Meaning of Meaningless Words and the Coefficient of Weirdness

Malinowski lays down one major line of British functionalism, as A. R. Radcliffe-Brown lays down the other (structural-functionalism). But if Radcliffe-Brown's version has the greater theoretical carry-over at present, Malinowski has set a model for anthropological fieldwork and its attendant theory and has had an extraordinary impact as a teacher of later anthropologists and on a range of Western and Third World thought outside of anthropology itself. His principal writings in this regard come out of his extended work in the Trobriands and other islands off the southeast tip of New Guinea (1912–1916), and include such books as Argonauts of the Western Pacific, Sex and Repression in Savage Society, *and* Coral Gardens and Their Magic. *The last, in its account of Trobriand ecology and "the language of magic and gardening," is truly a major work of twentieth-century poetics. The key to the force of song and narrative set out therein recurs, for example, in Malinowski's description of myth and the attendant process of myth-making in the later but very influential* Magic, Myth, and Religion. *From a functionalist perspective, myth establishes the "charter" of a society and creates the group's coherence— "not merely [as] a story told," he writes, "but [as] a reality lived" (1948: 100). The implications of this favoring of* enactment *over* explanation *are enormous, culminating in one instance in Charles Olson's summary, circa 1953, of the link, through Malinowski, between Trobriand poetics, for example, and our own:*

> [Malinowski's] emphasis . . . strikes away the idea that a story is symbolical (that it stands for something, instead of being that something); and at the same time that it is meant to explain anything. . . .
>
> Malinowski is asserting the primary truth that the human fact is that there is *no* desire to explain—there is solely the desire to experience: that this is what is meant by *knowing*: to know is to experience, & vice versa: to experience is to know (*histōr*). That is, *to tell about it*, and *to tell about it as others have told it*, is one act, simply, that the reality itself is one, now, & then. [*Olson*, number 10: 64]

The reader who wishes to explore further the connections between "meaningless words" in traditional and contemporary practice (e.g., "sound poetry") might begin with the present co-editor's Technicians of the Sacred *(1968: 386–391).*

Magical formulae differ from other texts considerably, both as regards their intrinsic nature and the place which we have given them in our scheme of presentation. As to its intrinsic nature, the language of magic is sacred, set and used for an entirely different

SOURCE: Bronislaw Malinowski, Coral Gardens and Their Magic, *volume 2,* The Language of Magic and Gardening, *pages 213–222.*

purpose to that of ordinary life. As regards presentation, it was necessary in the course of our narrative account to make the garden magician recite his spells in a rhythmic, elaborated English version of the native text. This was justified because, in native, the language of magic, with its richness of phonetic, rhythmic, metaphorical and alliterative effects, with its weird cadences and repetitions, has a prosodic character which it is desirable to bring home to the English reader. At the same time, just because the language of magic is regarded as sacred, too great liberties must not be taken with it: or at least, such liberties as are taken must be checked against an exact statement of how much is contained in the native original and how much is added by the legitimate process of bringing out implications. . . .

It follows that those difficulties which we have encountered in the free translation of ordinary texts become much greater here. If . . . all ordinary terms which have to be translated are yet untranslatable, this puzzling quality becomes much more pronounced when we deal with words which are avowedly meaningless. For the magician in the Trobriands as elsewhere deals out verbal elements of the *abracadabra, sesame, hocus pocus* type, that is, words the function of which is not 'meaning' in the ordinary sense, but a specific magical influence which these words are believed to exercise. In what way the 'meaning of meaningless words' can be conveyed is a paradoxical problem of linguistic theory which will have to be confronted here. . . .

The most difficult problem, perhaps, in connexion with magical formulae and, according to our conception of language, the central problem, is that concerning the function of a magical utterance. To us the meaning of any significant word, sentence or phrase is *the effective change* brought about by the utterance within the context of the situation to which it is wedded. We have seen how this meaning has to be understood in the active pragmatic speech which passes between a group of people engaged in some concerted task; an order given and carried out, an advice or co-ordinating instruction followed. We have also seen how words of praise or encouragement act, and how they have a dynamic significance. We have enquired into the nature of meaning when speech is used for planning, for education, for narrative or conversation.

Now a magical formula is neither a piece of conversation, nor yet a prayer, nor a statement or communication. What is it? What is the sociological setting of a spell, what is its purpose, what is the function of magical words? In order to elicit the meaning of an ordinary utterance we found that we had to ascertain the social context; the purpose, aim and direction of the accompanying activities—practical, sociable, or generally cultural; and finally the function of the words, i.e., the effective change which they produce within concerted action. But in a magical formula the purpose seems to be imaginary, sociological co-operation non-existent and the rôle of words just to be uttered into the void.

Let us look more closely at the facts, however. When the magician mumbles over some herbs in his hut—is it just an empty monologue? No audience of listeners is supposed to be necessary to the effectiveness of the spell; therefore, according to our definition of meaning, the words would appear to be plainly meaningless. What is the point of his ritually uttered magical comments when, in striking the soil of the garden, he says: "I am striking thee, O soil"? Does he address the land, or his stick, or any people who chance to be present? Or again, on other occasions, does he talk to the herbs, or to a stone, or to one or other of the two saplings, or to spirits which, even if present, are not believed to do anything? When he addresses a spider or a bush-hen, a lawyer-cane or a dolphin, what sort of co-operative act, if any, is involved?

Some of these questions we are in a position to answer. Let us start from the purpose of magic. Imaginary it is from our point of view, but is this a reason for dismissing it as socially and culturally irrelevant? Certainly not. Magic happens in a world of its own, but this world is real to the natives. It therefore exerts a deep influence on their behaviour and consequently is also real to the anthropologist. The situation of magic—and by this I mean the scene of action pervaded by influences and sympathetic affinities, and permeated by *mana*—this situation forms the context of spells. It is created by native belief, and this belief is a powerful social and cultural force. Consequently we must try to place the utterances of magic within their appropriate context of native belief and see what information we can elicit which may help us towards the understanding of spells and the elucidation of words.

All the acts of magic, from the first oblation to the spirits to the last fragment of a banana spell, consist, from the dogmatic point of view, in one type of performance. Each rite is the ''production'' or ''generation'' of a force and the conveyance of it, directly or indirectly, to a certain given object which, as the natives believe, is affected by this force. In the Trobriands we have, then, the production and application of Melanesian *mana*, the magical force for which there is no name in our ethnographic province, but which is very much present there in the reality of belief and behaviour.

Take the principal spell of Omarakana garden magic, which begins with the word *vatuvi* [show the way]. The magician, after certain preparations and under the observance of certain rules and taboos, collects herbs and makes of them a magical mixture. Parallel with his actions and in concert with him, the members of the community make other preparations, notably the provision of fish for a gift to the magician and the spirits, and for a festive eating. The magician, after ritually and with an incantation offering some of this fish to the ancestral spirits, recites the main spell, *vatuvi*, over the magical mixture. Let me remind you of how he does this. He prepares a sort of large receptacle for his voice—a voice-trap we might almost call it. He lays the mixture on a mat and covers this with another mat so that his voice may be caught and imprisoned between them. During the recitation he holds his head close to the aperture and carefully sees to it that no portion of the herbs shall remain unaffected by the breath of his voice. He moves his mouth from one end of the aperture to the other, turns his head, repeating the words over and over again, rubbing them, so to speak, into the substance. When you watch the magician at work and note the meticulous care with which he applies this most effective and most important verbal action to the substance; when afterwards you see how carefully he encloses the charmed herbs in the ritual wrappings prepared, and in a ritual manner—then you realise how serious is the belief that the magic is in the breath and that the breath is the magic. . . .

To the Trobriander the spell is a sequence of words, more or less mysterious, handed down from immemorial times and always taught by an accredited magician to his successors; it is received by the first human wielder of the magic from some supernatural agency, or else brought by the first ancestors who came from underground, where they had led an existence in which magic apparently was already in use. The myths about the beginnings of magic are not altogether consistent and sometimes not even clear. Theology, from Australian totemism or Trobriand magical lore to scholastic disputes, modern faculties of divinity and the councils of Christian Science or Theosophy—is always controversial and inconsistent. But on the whole we find in the Trobriands one fundamental belief—that the magic of gardening was first effectively exercised by such cultural heroes as Tudava, Malita, Gere'u and others, and a much more precise belief that each garden magic has come from underground on the very spot where it is now being practised, or else that it has been introduced to this spot and naturalised there. Furthermore, the belief is very strong that supremacy in differential fertility is due to the fact of one magical system being better than the others. Also the element of luck, whether good or bad, is always accounted for by magic.

The important point for us is, however, that in whatever manner magic has come into the possession of man, the spell as such has existed from the very beginning of things, *quod semper*, *quod ab initio*. . . . It is regarded as a specific quality of a relevant aspect of the world. Fertility and the growth of yams matter to man, and cannot be mastered by human forces alone. Hence there is magic, there always was magic, and the magic resides in the spell. When speaking of things sacred and ritual, the Trobriander would fully endorse the truth of *in principio erat verbum*. Though the natives would not be able to formulate it themselves, this is in brief their dogma; and though they also would not be able to tell it simply and in an abstract manner, wherever there is an important human activity, which is at the same time dangerous, subject to chance and not completely mastered by technical means—there is always for the Trobriander a magical system, a body of rites and spells, to compensate for the uncertainty of chance and to forearm against bad luck. . . .

How far does this dogmatic background help us in understanding the wording of magic? If the main principle of magical belief is that words exercise power in virtue of their primeval mysterious connexion with some aspect of reality, then obviously we must not expect the words of Trobriand magic to act in virtue of their ordinary colloquial meaning. A spell is believed to be a primeval text which somehow came into being side by side with animals and plants, with winds and waves, with human disease, human courage and human frailty. Why should such words be as the words of common speech? They are not uttered to carry ordinary information from man to man, or to give advice or an order. The natives might naturally expect all such words to be very mysterious and far removed from ordinary speech. And so they are to a large extent, but by no means completely. We shall see that spells are astoundingly significant and translatable and we shall also see why this is so.

But the fact remains that unless the reader is forewarned that a great deal of the vocabulary of magic, its grammar and its prosody, falls into line with the deeply ingrained belief that magical speech must be cast in another mould, because it is derived from other sources and produces different effects from ordinary speech, he will constantly be at cross-purposes with the principles according to which the translation of magical utterance has to proceed. If the ordinary criteria of grammar, logic and consistency were applied, the translator would find himself hopelessly bogged by Trobriand magic.

Take the very first formula, for example. This is a direct address to ancestral spirits—a man-to-man communication we might say; hence in parts it is lucid and grammatical. And then comes the sentence: "Vikita, Iyavata, their myth head his." After much consultation with informants and etymological research in their company, I had to conclude that in no sense can these words be set equivalent to any ordinary prose sentence. The meaning of the magical expression is simply the intrinsic effect which, in native belief, it exerts on the spirits and indirectly on the fertility of the soil. The commentaries of the natives, however, reveal the mythological references connected with the names Vikita and Iyavata. Those who are versed in the magical tradition of this spell can interpret the significance of these words and tell us why they are ritually effective.

In what way, then, can we translate such a jumble of words, "meaningless" in the ordinary sense? The words are supposed to exercise a mystical effect *sui generis* on an aspect of reality. This belief is due to certain properties and associations of these words. They can therefore be translated in one sense and in one sense only: we must show what effect they are believed to produce, and marshal all the linguistic data available to show how and why they produce this effect.

To take another example, the exordium of the most important spell:

> Vatuvi, vatuvi, vatuvi, vatuvi. Vitumaga, i-maga.
> Vatuvi, vatuvi, vatuvi, vatuvi. Vitulola, i-lola.

The better one knows the Trobriand language the clearer it becomes that these words are not words of ordinary speech. As actually recited in the spell they are pronounced according to a special phonology, in a sing-song, with their own rhythm and with numerically grouped repetitions. The word *vatuvi* is not a grammatical form ever found in ordinary speech. The compounds *vitulola*, *vitumaga*, are again weird and unusual; in a way, nonsense words. Words like *vatuvi* or the root *lola* are clipped; but there are other words which are compounded, built up, developed. . . .

In some formulae we are able to translate the words clearly and satisfactorily after our magically illumined commentator has given us their esoteric meaning. Thus we are told that *gelu* is a magical word for "bush-hen," in ordinary speech *mulubida*; that *kaybwagina* is a clipped form of *mitakaybwagina*, which is the mystical name for the millipede, known in ordinary speech as *mwanita*. Some of the animals, it is true, are called by their ordinary names. . . . But even these ordinary words, by association with others . . . not used in common speech, and with proper names of spots which are not comprehensible without a mythological and topographical commentary, are incorporated into a complex prosodic structure, specifically magical in character. We could discover such characteristic structures, usually rhythmical and symmetrical, in almost every formula. . . .

Again we have in many spells what might be called negative comparison on the pattern "this is not (here the object to be charmed or a part of it is named) . . . but it is (here a pattern or ideal object is named)." Thus, for instance, we have "this is not thy eye, thy eye is as the black ant's" or "this is not thy flight, thy flight is as a parrot's." . . .

The same features can be found in any formula: most words can be translated if we know for what reason they are used in the spell. If, for example, we know that the dolphin is big and long as the tubers should become, that its weaving in and out of the rising and falling waves is associated with the winding and interweavng of the luxuriant vines whose rich foliage means a plentiful taytu harvest, we can not only translate the word "dolphin," but several sentences based on this allusion; above all, we can understand the structure of the whole spell. The same applies to the bush-hen in [another formula], whose large nest is associated with the swelling round the taytu plant when tubers are plentiful. . . .

Thus all magical verbiage shows a very considerable coefficient of weirdness, strangeness and unusualness. The better we know the Trobriand language the more clearly and immediately can we distinguish magic from ordinary speech. The most grammatical and least emphatically chanted spell differs from the forms of ordinary address. Most magic, moreover, is chanted in a sing-song which makes it from the outset profoundly different from ordinary utterances. The wording of magic is correlated with a very complicated dogmatic system, with theories about the primeval mystical power of words, about mythological influences, about the faint co-operation of ancestral spirits, and, much more important, about the sympathetic influence of animals, plants, natural forces and objects. Unless a competent commentator is secured who, in each specific case, will interpret the elements of weirdness, the allusions, the personal names or the magical pseudonyms, it is impossible to translate magic. Moreover, as a comparison of the various formulae has shown us, there has developed a body of linguistic practice— use of metaphor, opposition, repetition, negative comparison, imperative and question with answer—which, though not developed into any explicit doctrine, makes the language of magic specific, unusual, quaint.

HOWARD NORMAN
Born Tying Knots

The concern with names and naming enters our poetics with Whitman's exultant assertions (in An American Primer) that "names are magic" and that "no country can have its own poems without it have its own names" (1949: 577, 583) and even more emphatically in Gertrude Stein's later description of names as the key to the origins of poetry:

> Nouns are the names of anything. Think of all that early poetry, think of Homer, think of Chaucer, think of the Bible and you will see what I mean you will really realize that they were drunk with nouns, to name to know how to name earth sea and sky and all that was in them was enough to make them live and love in names, and that is what poetry is it is a state of knowing and feeling a name. [1935, 1957: 233]

The ethnopoetic exploration of naming has drawn from a wide range of poetries and cultures (here the Swampy Cree of northern Canada) and from speculations on the

SOURCE: *Howard Norman,* The Wishing Bone Cycle: Narrative Poems from the Swampy Cree Indians, *pages 47–49.*

presumed "concreteness" (= nominalism) of "primitive" thought that may relate to such twentieth-century dicta as William Carlos Williams's "no ideas but in things." (See below, p. 171).

Norman's entry into ethnopoetics comes through the experience of Cree language and culture going back to early childhood. A zoologist by profession, he has explored a total ecology that includes the realities of the imaginal and mythic world.

Affiliations with animals are the most common sources of Swampy Cree personal names (i.e., those not designated under the auspices of the church). The names are acquired several ways. A boy called "Loud Lynx," for example, may have inherited the name from a grandfather who said it still had useful powers. Or his parents may have requested a shaman to interpret his next dream or vision into a name.[1] In this case, the shaman consents, and in the dream or vision a loud lynx indeed appears. The shaman would then have carried out his responsibility in naming the child accordingly. In either case, however, the boy lives under the protection and guidance of the lynx.[2]

The name "Born Tying Knots" was given (*without* the aid of a shaman) because of an incident at birth in which the umbilical cord was *knotted* around the baby's toes. Subsequently,

> . . . he heard his birth
> story.
> It caused him to begin tying knots again.
> He tied things up near his home,
> TIGHT, as if everything might float away
> in a river.

In this way one is led to speculate upon the ways names affect subsequent behavior (or to consider how much any name-origin is simply the *teller's* embellishment).

The following account of an entirely different but coincidental kind of meaning event was told in August, 1973, by Yakwama yetum ("He Is Cautious"):

> I'd found a good name to fill up with someone. I'll tell you about it. I was standing on a high place, much to the north. I was travelling there, in that northern land. I saw a herd of caribou. They were feeding. There were many but I picked one out and watched him. Soon, the reason I picked *him* out became clear to me. He began a jerking his head up and down fast. He did this many times. Also, he tried to trip

---

[1] The dream, or vision, might not include an animal at all. The name "Turned Over Twice," for instance, came out of a shaman's vision of a boy sleeping near a cliff. The boy (in the vision) turned over once, nearing the cliff-edge, then turned back over safely. I never found out if the vision (and, consequently, the name) was in fact oracular.

[2] I use the lynx in the general sense of an animal namesake. Affiliations with specific animals are complex or simple, depending on the position and power of that animal as a totem figure.

one front leg with the other [as if] trying to trip himself! The whole herd was moving slowly. They were walking. But this was not enough moving for him. No, he had to be restless in other ways. I watched him more. Then I went back home. I told some new parents: I have a good, strong name. It is "Restless Caribou." They took the name for their son. This was after I told them the story. That's what happened.

On the other hand, if any unnamed boy (say, among a *group* of playing children)[3] was observed to be especially restless, it would be feasible to name him "Restless Caribou." In this way he "earns" (*kuskëtumowab*) the name for himself.

All of the name-origins translated in this chapter are earned names derived from various childhood episodes, affinities, special talents, even obsessions. Samuel Makidemewabe, in his capacity as one of the tribal historians, was invited to many naming ceremonies, at which the circumstances initiating each name were told to him. Or, as he said: "Names were brought to me from all over." You will notice that Makidemewabe spoke of all these naming incidents as if they occurred in his presence, which to him was less a matter of fact than a way of becoming intimate with the story. "I brought these stories home," he said, "and tell them *here*."[4]

Makidemewabe said: "To say the name is to begin the story." Over the years, I heard many personal names, then brought them to Makidemewabe. For me, then, to bring the name was to hear the story. This worked several ways. Often he would have his facts about a particular name right at hand. Other times, he would ask for time to "recall" the name's story. Though it was never requested, I told each story back to him many times in Cree before translating.

Finally, words Makidemewabe spoke loudly in his *tellings* are represented in my translations by capital letters; those he spoke softly, by italics. [One such story follows:]

TREE OLD WOMAN

She stood close to a tree and wrinkled
her face, TIGHT,
and this was her tree-bark face.
It felt like bark, too, when you ran fingers over it.

Tree old woman,
even when she was young.

Then her face would smooth out
into a young girl again. Once, after doing
her tree-bark face, she said,
"I *was* a tree and I saw a woodpecker

---

[3]I purposely use *group* as a correlate to *herd* because personal namings (and tales, songs, etc.) are often acutely attentive to animal behavior.

[4]Makidemewabe lived mainly in two communities: one near Walker Lake, the other north of the Hayes River in Manitoba.

who wanted my head! That's why
I smoothed out my face so quickly!''

We looked up in the trees for that woodpecker,
but it wasn't there. So, our eyes
turned back to her. She was gone too!
We found her in a lake. She was holding on
to some shore reeds
with her legs floating out behind.
She looked up at us WITH THE WRINKLED FACE
OF A FROG! We were certain of it!
Then she smoothed her face out,
saying, ''The largest turtle in the world
was swimming for me, thinking I was a frog!
That's why I smoothed my face out
so quickly!''

We didn't even look
for that turtle.

This time we kept our eyes on her
as she went to sit
by an old man, the oldest
in the village.
She sat down next to him.

Their two faces were close together,
and hers began
to wrinkle up again.

RAMÓN MEDINA SILVA

How the Names are Changed
on the Peyote Journey

The poetry of reversals described by the mara'akáme *(shaman), Ramón Medina
Silva, of San Sebastián, Mexico, is part of the Huichol peyote hunt and ritual (see
below, p. 225). The tactic is common to the languages, acts, and dream-work of
shamans and sacred clowns throughout the world. Its Crow Indian manifestation,
for example, took the form of warrior societies of "contraries" (Crazy Dogs) whose
behavior included "saying the opposite of what you mean & making others say the
opposite of what they mean in return" (Rothenberg 1972: 195). As a more deeply
rooted philosophy of contradictions, it reentered Western thought through eighteenth-century dialecticians and poets like Hegel and Blake ("without contraries
is no progression") or from another angle, as an aspect of Freud's description of the
"dream-work," which he related to verbal procedures in "the most ancient languages": "The way in which dreams treat the category of contraries and contradictions is highly remarkable. It is simply disregarded. 'No' seems not to exist as far as
dreams are concerned. . . . Dreams feel themselves at liberty, moreover, to represent any element by its wishful contrary; so there is no way of deciding at a first
glance whether any element that admits of a contrary is present in the dream-
thoughts as a positive or as a negative" (1900, 1965: 353). (For more on reversals,
contraries, and dream-work, see below, pp. 201, 225, 270, and 332.*

Well, let's see now. I shall speak about how we do things when we go and seek the
peyote, how we change the names of everything. How we call the things we see and do
by another name for all those days. Until we return. Because all must be done as it must
be done. As it was laid down in the beginning. How it was when the mara'akáme who is
Tatewarí[1] led all those great ones to Wirikuta. When they crossed over there, to the
peyote country. Because that is a very sacred thing, it is the most sacred. It is our life, as
one says. That is why nowadays one gives things other names. One changes everything.
Only when they return home, then they call everything again that it is.

    When everything is ready, when all the symbols which we take with us, the gourd
bowls, the yarn discs, the arrows, everything has been made, when all have prayed
together we set out. Then we must change everything, all the meanings. For instance: a
pot which is black and round, it is called a head. It is the mara'akáme who directs
everything. He is the one who listens in his dream, with his power and his knowledge. He
speaks to Tatewarí, he speaks to Kauyumari.[2] Kauyumari tells him everything, how it

---

[1]Huichol name for the deity with whom the shaman has a special affinity, roughly translatable as Our
Grandfather Fire.

[2]Kauyumari is a trickster hero, quasi-deified and roughly translatable as Sacred Deer Person.

SOURCE: Translation in Barbara Myerhoff, The Peyote Hunt, *pages 236–239.*

must be. Then he says to his companions, if he is the leader of the journey to the peyote, look, this thing is this way, and this is how it must be done. He tells them, look, now we will change everything, all the meanings, because that is the way it must be with the *hikuritámete* (peyote pilgrims). As it was in ancient times, so that all can be united. As it was long ago, before the time of my grandfather, even before the time of his grandfather. So the mara'akáme has to see to everything, so that as much as possible all the words are changed. Only when one comes home, then everything can be changed back again to the way it was.

"Look," the mara'akáme says to them, "it is when you say 'good morning,' you mean 'good evening,' everything is backwards. You say 'goodbye, I am leaving you,' but you are really coming. You do not shake hands, you shake feet. You hold out your right foot to be shaken by the foot of your companion. You say 'good afternoon,' yet it is only morning."

So the mara'akáme tells them, as he has dreamed it. He dreams it differently each time. Every year they change the names of things differently because every year the mara'akáme dreams new names. Even if it is the same mara'akáme who leads the journey, he still changes the names each time differently.

And he watches who makes mistakes because there must be no error. One must use the names the mara'akáme has dreamed. Because if one makes an error it is not right. That is how it is. It is a beautiful thing because it is right. Daily, daily, the mara'akáme goes explaining everything to them so that they do not make mistakes. The mara'akáme says to a companion, "Look, why does that man over there watch us, why does he stare at us?" And then he says, "Look, what is it he has to stare at us?" "His eyes," says his companion. "No," the mara'akáme answers, "they are not his eyes, they are tomatoes." That is how he goes explaining how everything should be called.

When one makes cigarettes for the journey, one uses the dried husks of maize for the wrappings. And the tobacco, it is called the droppings of ants. Tortillas one calls bread. Beans one calls fruit from a tree. Maize is wheat. Water is tequila. Instead of saying, "Let us go and get water to drink," you say, "Ah, let us take tequila to eat." *Atole* [maize broth], that is brains. Sandals are cactus. Fingers are sticks. Hair, that is cactus fiber. The moon, that is a cold sun.

On all the trails on which we travel to the peyote country, as we see different things we make this change. That is because the peyote is very sacred, very sacred. That is why it is reversed. Therefore, when we see a dog, it is a cat, or it is a coyote. Ordinarily, when we see a dog, it is just a dog, but when we walk for the peyote it is a cat or a coyote or even something else, as the mara'akáme dreams it. When we see a burro, it is not a burro, it is a cow, or a horse. And when we see a horse, it is something else. When we see a dove or a small bird of some kind, is it a small bird? No, the mara'akáme says, it is an eagle, it is a hawk. Or a piglet, it is not a piglet, it is an armadillo. When we hunt the deer, which is very sacred, it is not a deer, on this journey. It is a lamb, or a cat. And the nets for catching deer? They are called sewing thread.

When we say come, it means go away. When we say "shh, quiet," it means to shout, and when we whistle or call to the front we are really calling to a person behind us. We speak in this direction here. That one over there turns because he already knows how it is, how everything is reversed. To say, "Let us stay here," means to go, "let us go," and when we say "sit down," we mean, "stand up." It is also so when we have crossed

over, when we are in the country of the peyote. Even the peyote is called by another
name, as the mara'akáme dreamed. Then the peyote is flower or something else.

It is so with Tatewarí, with Tayaupa.[3] The mara'akáme, we call him Tatewarí. He
is Tatewarí, he who leads us. But there in Wirikuta, one says something else. One calls
him "the red one." And Tayaupa, he is "the shining one." So all is changed. Our
companion who is old, he is called the child. Our companion who is young, he is the old
one. When we want to speak of the machete, we say "hook." When one speaks of wood,
one really means fish. Begging your pardon, instead of saying "to eat," we say "to
defecate." And, begging your pardon, "I am going to urinate" means "I am going to
drink water." When speaking of blowing one's nose, one says "give me the honey."
"He is deaf" means "how well he hears." So everything is changed, everything is
different or backwards.

The mara'akáme goes explaining how everything should be said, everything,
many times, or his companions would forget and make errors. In the late afternoon,
when all are gathered around Tatewarí, we all pray there, and the mara'akáme tells how
it should be. So for instance he says, "Do not speak of this one or that one as serious. Say
he is a jaguar. You see an old woman and her face is all wrinkled, coming from afar, do
not say, 'Ah, there is a man,' say 'Ah, here comes a wooden image.' You say, 'Here
comes the image of Santo Cristo.' Or if it is a woman coming, say 'Ah, here comes the
image of Guadalupe.' "

Women, you call flowers. For the woman's skirts, you say, "bush," and for her
blouse you say "palm roots." And a man's clothing, that too is changed. His clothing,
you call his fur. His hat, that is a mushroom. Or it is his sandal. Begging your pardon, but
what we carry down here, the testicles, they are called avocados. And the penis, that is
his nose. That is how it is.

When we come back with the peyote, the peyote which has been hunted, they
make a ceremony and everything is changed back again. And those who are at home,
when one returns they grab one and ask, "What is it you called things? How is it that now
you call the hands hands but when you left you called them feet?" Well, it is because
they have changed the names back again. And they all want to know what they called
things. One tells them, and there is laughter. That is how it is. Because it must be as it
was said in the beginning, in ancient times.

[3]Our Father Sun.

LÉOPOLD SÉDAR SENGHOR
Speech and Image:
An African Tradition
of the Surreal

Emerging from the Negritude movement of the 1930s (see above, p. 52), Senghor became the first and long-reigning president of Senegal from the time of its independence in 1960. His poetics drew from a base in African oral tradition, illuminated by and in turn illuminating the explorations of European Surrealism, etc. For the "surreal image" per se, the reader might turn to Pierre Reverdy's classic "definition," circa 1918, often cited by the French Surrealists:

> The Image is a pure creation of the mind.
> It cannot spring from a comparison but from the bringing together of two more or less distant realities.
> The more distant and accurate the relation between the two realities brought together, the stronger the image will be—the more emotive power and poetic reality it will possess.

(Cf. Isidore Ducasse, le Comte de Lautreamont: ". . . as beautiful as the chance encounter of a sewing machine and an umbrella on a dissecting table.")

Speech seems to us the main instrument of thought, emotion and action. There is no thought or emotion without a verbal image, no free action without first a project in thought. This is even more true among peoples who disdained the written word. This explains the power of speech in Africa. The word, the spoken word is the expression *par excellence* of the life-force, of being in its fullness. God created the world through the Word. We shall see how later. For the human being, speech is the living and life-giving breath of man at prayer. It possesses a magical virtue, realizing the law of participation and, by its intrinsic power, creating the thing named. So that all the other arts are only specialized aspects of the great art of speech. In front of a picture made up of a tracery of geometrical forms in white and red representing a chorus of birds or a tree at sunrise, the artist explained: "These are wings, these are songs. These are birds."

The African languages are characterized first of all by the richness of their vocabulary. There are sometimes twenty different words for an object according to its form, weight, volume and colour, and as many for an action according to whether it is single or repeated, weakly or intensely performed, just beginning or coming to an end. In Fulani, nouns are divided into twenty-one genders which are not related to sex. The classification is based sometimes on the meaning of the words or the phonetic qualities and sometimes on the grammatical category to which they belong. Most significant in this respect is the verb. On the same root in Wolof can be constructed more than twenty

SOURCE: Léopold Sédar Senghor, Prose & Poetry *(tr. John Reed and Clive Wake), pages 84–85.*

verbs expressing different shades of meaning, and at least as many derivative nouns. While modern Indo-European languages emphasize the abstract notion of time, African languages emphasize the *aspect*, the concrete way in which the action of the verb takes place. These are essentially *concrete* languages. In them words are always pregnant with images. Under their value as signs, their sense value shows through.

The African image is not then an image by equation but an image by *analogy*, a surrealist image. Africans do not like straight lines and false *mots justes*. Two and two do not make four, but five, as Aimé Césaire has told us. The object does not mean what it represents but what it suggests, what it creates. The Elephant is Strength, the Spider is Prudence; Horns are the Moon and the Moon is Fecundity. Every representation is an image, and the image, I repeat, is not an equation but a *symbol*, an ideogramme. Not only the figuration of the image but also its material . . . stone, earth, copper, gold, fibre— and also its line and colour. All language which does not tell a story bores them, or rather, Africans do not understand such language. The astonishment of the first Europeans when they found that the "natives" did not understand their pictures or even the logic of their arguments!

I have spoken of the surrealist image. But as you would suppose, African surrealism is different from European surrealism. European surrealism is empirical. African surrealism is mystical and metaphysical. André Breton writes in *Signe Ascendant*: "The poetic analogy (meaning the European surrealist analogy) differs functionally from the mystical analogy in that it does not presuppose, beyond the visible world, an invisible world which is striving to manifest itself. It proceeds in a completely empirical way." In contrast, the African surrealist analogy presupposes and manifests the hierarchized universe of life-forces.

RICHARD DAUENHAUER
Koyukon Riddle-Poems

The riddle in verbal culture is part of the stock-in-trade of academic folklore, but its relation to the poetic image (see above, p. 119) has rarely been explored. The workings presented here were originally published in the Riddle and Poetry Handbook, *developed by Richard Dauenhauer as a project of the Alaska Native Education Board in Anchorage. With Nora Dauenhauer, a native Tlingit speaker, Dauenhauer has for some years engaged in translation projects (Tlingit into English, English into Tlingit) aimed at Tlingit-speaking audiences.*

In 1913, Father Julius Jetté, S.J. published a two-part article on the riddles of the Koyukon Indians, an Athapaskan group living on the Yukon and Koyukuk Rivers in the interior of western Alaska. [Jetté 1913:181−201; 630−651.] The Jetté article contains 110 riddles, each presented in the original Koyukon accompanied by a literal interlinear translation, a free translation, explication, and commentary. The workings here are based on the Jetté collection, to which the serious student of riddles is directed.

According to Jetté's introduction, the genre was associated with the return of light, and riddling was done only after the winter solstice. But even at the turn of the century, when Jetté was in the field, the riddle genre was on its way out as a viable medium of entertainment and verbal art. Today riddling is almost extinct in Koyukon, although it is still practiced by some tradition bearers, and has been experienced in context by some fieldworkers. [David Henry, Summer Institute of Linguistics, personal communication.]

The riddles in Jetté are a fine example of the highly developed verbal art of a tradition of poetic imagination which has declined and has in general been lost in the last 70 years—a period characterized by two generations of suppression of Native language and culture and by disruption of the language and intellectual community by the educational establishment and other government agencies, some of which continue to advocate and enforce total English replacement of Native languages rather than competence, comfort, and pride in both Native language and English. I hope these workings suggest that their Koyukon originals are hardly the creations of a conceptually and verbally impoverished people in need of intellectual transfusions from a paternalistic benefactor.

The riddles in Jetté exemplify the poetic use of everyday language and the imaginative juxtaposition of everyday images, of seeing something in terms of something else, and verbalizing that picture through manipulation of the wonderful and indefinite potential of language. With suppression and eradication of Native Alaskan intellectual traditions, and with the diminished possibilities for transmitting oral tradition because of language loss among the younger generations, a situation has developed in which even the average fluent speaker of Koyukon—though no fault of his or her own—is no longer familiar with riddles and riddle style.

SOURCE: Alcheringa, new series, volume 3, number 1, 1977, pages 85−90.

For example, each riddle in the Jetté collection begins with the formula "tła-dzor-kara'ana" ("riddle me"). None of the younger speakers of whom I have inquired were familiar with the formula, even though they are fluent in Koyukon. Also, younger speakers (30−60 age group) find much of the grammar bewildering. For example, a verbal prefix indicating a tree-like object would logically never occur with a first person subject pronoun—unless, as in the riddle style, the speaker is a tree, and the grammatical manipulation is a clue. Such grammatical combinations seem to have delighted the old-time riddle composers, but strike the younger speakers as totally non-sensical and incorrect. Because of such problems, any attempt to transliterate and update Jetté's transcription into the modern writing system used for teaching the language in Koyukon area schools and at the University level has been postponed. . . .

[In working from Jetté,] I have made one major change: I have treated the riddles as imagist poems, and have changed the riddle format to that of a poem, giving the clues in the first part of the poem, and the answer in the second. . . . My reason for treating the riddles as poems is to focus on the act of imagination contained in the riddle, rather than to obscure it. Because so many of the comparisons are culture-specific, they would not be "fair" put in riddle form in translation; but the images are striking and can easily be appreciated in poem format. Moreover, I consider these riddles poems, and the change in format simply discloses the poem that is underlyingly there. If more than one of the workings sounds like Pound's "In a Station of the Metro," I contend that the similarity derives not as much from my ear and style as translator as from the common underlying structure—the use of analogy in juxtaposition of images. It wouldn't be hard at all to make the Pound poem into a Koyukon riddle. . . . However, I should restate that the originals are riddles, and these workings are poems based on, designed to reflect, but not translate, riddles. These workings are in a different genre from the original. I should also clarify that for present purposes I have chosen to treat the riddle genre as literature, although some folklorists have demonstrated that for other purposes riddles may or should be considered games. Also it has been shown how for many traditions the answer is not to be guessed, but transmitted catechism-like with the riddle. Jetté considered this the case in Koyukon, though riddles are guessed in other contemporary Alaskan Athapaskan traditions.

The differences between these workings and the Jetté versions are mainly organization (poem format rather than riddle), rhythm, and choice of synonym. I have tried to retain the images and comparisons of the original, as well as the comparative devices: i.e., metaphor and simile are retained as in the original. In all cases I have dropped the opening formula "riddle me."

I chose to omit some riddles for two reasons: either they were not very imaginative, or at least did not appear so in the poem format (Jetté #55: I make chips; an axe), or they were so technical as to end up too cumbersome in translation. This latter category is truly magnificent, and I urge all interested readers to consult Jetté for such riddles as I could not attempt to do justice to! Several of these deal with internal organs of game animals as disclosed in the butchering process. In Jetté #90, for example, the fat particles on the stomach and intestinal membrane encountered at a specific stage of skinning an otter are compared to a particular formation of mare's tail cirrus clouds! Adding to the complexity of the translation problem is the poetic and descriptive term for the cloud formation in

Koyukon, compared to the English metaphor that would introduce horse hair into the otter skinning. With all this as background, I submit my working in progress of Jetté #90:

> The sun
> drives them through the sky;
> light clouds:
> fat globs on the gut.

At least one riddle is a verbal doodle. Jetté #83 is a beautiful comparison of a particular type of snare to a person bending over—the snare loop being the head, the tie-downs the arms, the balancing pivot-post the legs to the knees, and the heavy counterweight pole being the back, upper legs, and buttocks sticking out.

Another riddle contains metapoetry: singing an old song when a new composition is called for is compared to a lazy hunter who comes across last year's arrow and uses it again, rather than taking pride in his work. Such is the world of the Koyukon riddle imagination. I find it impressive, and I hope these workings in an alien genre do justice to the riddles themselves and to the creative genius that composed and transmitted them.

1/J1

Like a spruce tree
lying on the ground:
the back-hand
of (the) bear.

2/J2

We whistle
by the cliffs and gulches:
(the) bear, breathing
or the wind
on a brittle piece of
birch bark,
or wind
blowing on a small, dry spruce.

3/J4

Water dripping
from an ice-spear tip:
water dripping
from the beaver's nose.

4/J5

Like bones
piled up in the stream bed:
sticks
the beaver gnaws.

5/J7

Flying upward,
ringing bells in silence:
the butterfly.

6/J10

Muddy-light
dark-fresh
like two streams merging:
eagle feet.

7/J14

Small dots
on the skyline:
when the birds return.

8/J27

At the water hole
the ice-spear
trembles in the current:
a swimming otter's tail.

9/J36

Smoke-like
it spreads out in the water:
butchered salmon blood.

10/J39

The hilltop trail
running close beside me:
a thing on which
the wolf has peed.

11/J42

Like fine hair
on the penis of a squirrel:
veins in birchwood.

12/J59

Like water bursting
through a beaver dam:
flames
from the fire drill.

13/J62

Behind the woodpile
we lie in sheepskin blankets:
last year's
excrement.

14/J64

Like a herd
trailing up the hill:
the graveyard,
tombstones carved
with animal designs.

15/J70

I reach
beyond the mountains:
the sun
or moon.

16/J80

Grease-like, like
sun on water, streaking
in opposite directions:
sled runner tracks
on snow.

17/J106

I found my
last year's arrow:
using the same
song of mourning
twice.

18/J108

I broke my bow
shooting at a caribou:
the northern lights.

19/J109

Like a herd
bedded down on snow:
bare ground at break-up
where the snow is gone.

20/J110

On the beach,
mirage-like:
a fish trap,
being rolled by wind.

TREVOR COPE

Izibongo: Zulu Praise-Poems

The praise-poem as a stringing-together of new or inherited praise-names (e.g., Yoruba oriki, Zulu izibongo, Basuto lithoko, Hausa kirari) is found throughout much of Africa. "Such words or phrases," writes Ruth Finnegan, "occur frequently within the more complex form of a complete poem" (1970: 111), and the praise-poem itself can become extremely complex and diversified. But the basic method holds—a kind of "collaging" in which the individual poet takes off from the work of the collectivity, adding to it as last in a line of makers. His art therefore is one of creation and assemblage—the weighing of line against line (Rothenberg 1968: 418).

More on related forms of African praise poetry—drumming, divination and abuse forms—is included on pages 129, 147, and 165 of this volume. The impulse toward cumulative "praises" and/or descriptions of self and others is almost universal (see, for example, the chants of María Sabina, p. 475, below).

PRAISES AND PRAISE-POEMS

The word *izibongo* means "praises." It is a plural noun of which the singular means "surname": one's *isibongo* is the name of one's clan. Several early linguists give the meaning of *isibongo* as a "praise" or "surname," but nowadays the word means "surname" only. However, a clan name is the personal name of its founder, and personal names are essentially praise-names. Zulu (the sky), Qwabe (a musical bow), Mkhize (drizzle), Ndwandwe (a tall person), Vilakazi (a large lazy person), Nyembezi (a teardrop), Luthuli (dust), were the names of the founders of these clans, and these are as obviously praise-names as "Shakespear." Praise-names are not always flattering, and this is also true of Zulu praises. They are naturally inclined to be in praise of a person, but they may just as well be in criticism of him. Bryant writes that "for every man a number of praises is coined by his companions. These are simply short sentences commemorative of notable actions and events in his life" (1929, 1965: 39), and he adds that these actions need not be laudable nor the events pleasant. A man may receive praises from his parents and from members of his family in general, as well as from his companions, particularly his fellows in his age-set regiment. He may even give himself praises, as Godongwane, the son of the Mthethwa chief, is reputed to have given himself the name of Dingiswayo ("He who is caused to be in need") because of his experiences, by which name he was then and is now generally known. When a young man dances his solo (to *giya*) at a festivity, such as a wedding, his friends shout out these praises that have been bestowed upon him by virtue of his personality, his actions, and even events associated with him for which he is not directly responsible. When a man of distinction is rewarded for his services by the chief with grants of cattle and land and with political position, he then establishes a great kraal and appoints a personal praiser, who will collect, polish,

SOURCE: *Trevor Cope,* Izibongo: Zulu Praise-Poems, *pages 25–30.*

and perfect his praises, so that they constitute what we call a "praise-poem." The development from praises to praise-poems is not paralleled by the development of any new word to designate the product, so that the praises of the meanest man, which could comprise something in the nature of "long-legged one who ran to Zungu's without stopping," and the praises of the kings, which occur as stanzas of several verses in strings extending up to twenty minutes' time in recital, are likewise known as *izibongo*. Certainly there is no difference in kind, but there is a considerable difference in development. The praises of chiefs and important men benefit from the services of professional praisers, whereas the praises of the common man are simply the spontaneous tributes of his fellows.

The most primitive type of praise-poem is simply a collection of praises. This is the type of praise-poem of the common man, who, although he may have achieved a degree of fame, has not yet attained a position of political prominence. The praise-poem of a chief or politically prominent person (even a woman who combines royal blood with an outstanding personality) shows the operation of poetic art upon the basic simple praises, particularly in the use of alliteration and parallelism to give structural formality. In the royal praise-poems of the eighteenth century these praises are expanded into couplets and triplets, and in the royal praise-poems of the nineteenth century they are expanded into stanzas.

THE PRAISER OR *IMBONGI*

Anyone can tell tales, anyone can sing songs, anyone can shout out praises to encourage a man engaged in a fight or performing an exhibition (to *giya*), which is in its actions a fight with an imaginary enemy. Anyone can also compose tales, songs, and praises, but the praise-poem of a chief requires a specialist for its composition and proper performance. The specialization is more in the performance than in the composition, for the composition of a praise-poem is a matter of collection and perfection rather than of creation. The collection is sometimes made by borrowing from the praise-poems of other chiefs. Especially in the earlier poems there are praises in common currency, such as the praise incorporating the image of the ford with slippery stones, which so aptly describes treacherous slyness. . . . Nevertheless, the art of the professional praiser requires natural ability and special application. An excellent memory is an essential qualification, for he has to memorize not only the praises of the chief but the praises of all his ancestors as well, and he has to memorize them so perfectly that on occasions of tribal importance they pour forth in a continuous stream or torrent. Although he may vary the order of the sections or stanzas of the praise-poem, he may not vary the praises themselves. He commits them to memory as he hears them, even if they are meaningless to him, as they sometimes are when they have been handed down for generations.

The fact that the praiser is a specialist is reflected in his dress, which in the old days used to be a fantastic costume of furs and feathers and animal-tails, no less fantastic than that of the witchdoctor, who is also a specialist. The praiser (*imbongi*) and the witchdoctor (*isangoma*) don the dress of their respective professions only when they are performing these functions. At other times they wear the ordinary dress and carry out the ordinary duties of daily life. There is another parallel between the *imbongi* and the *isangoma*: just as the latter is the intermediary between man and the supernatural world of magic and the ancestral spirits, so the former is in a sense the intermediary between the chief and his subjects, for, when he presents the chief to the people in his recitation, he is also representing the opinion of the people to the chief. Thus the praise-poem contains criticism as well as praise. The special position of the praiser enables him to criticize with impunity certain aspects of the chief's personality or actions, either by overt criticism or covertly by the omission of praise. Senzangakhona is praised for his beauty and criticized for his obstinacy; there is significantly no mention of the aggressiveness for which his grandfather was praised or of the shrewdness for which his father was praised. Cetshwayo's praiser expresses the anxiety and disapproval of the people when he warns him strongly not to provoke the white man in Natal.

Just as everyone can compose praises, so everyone can recite praises. In times of trouble or insecurity it is the duty of the head of the family to sacrifice a beast to the ancestral spirits and to recite their praises as he does so. Although he cannot recite with the dramatic delivery of the professional praiser, he does his best to imitate the conventional style. Even if he is a chief, he himself has to call upon the ancestral spirits on these occasions by reciting their praises, as many as he remembers, for he is the most direct descendant.

METHOD OF DELIVERY

The praiser recites the praises at the top of his voice and as fast as possible. These conventions of praise-poem recitation, which is high in pitch, loud in volume, fast in speed, create an emotional excitement in the audience as well as in the praiser himself, whose voice often rises in pitch, volume, and speed as he progresses, and whose movements become more and more exaggerated, for it is also a convention of praise-poem recitation that the praiser never stands still. Even when the head of the family, who is not a professional praiser, recites the praises of his ancestors on an occasion of importance to the family, such as a wedding, he walks up and down as he does so. The professional praiser at court accompanies his recitation of the chief's praises not only by walking but by leaping about with gesticulations as the excitement increases. He suits the actions to the words, the words to the actions; the performance is indeed dramatic. Movement, both visible and audible, is the essence of praise-poem recitation.

The most important convention of praise-poem recitation from the linguistic point of view is the elimination of the normal downdrift intonation. Zulu is a tonal language in which every syllable bears a significant tone. These tones cannot be eliminated without distortion or complete loss of meaning. It is the overall downdrift intonation of the sentence that is absent in praise-poem recitation, which has the same effect as that created by the elimination of intonation in the priestly recitation of prayers in orthodox churches. This effect is a sense of seriousness and occasion, but it is not accompanied by a sense of serenity in the case of the Zulu praise-poems, for they are not recited smoothly and quietly but shouted with great gusto, so that the accompaniment to the sense of seriousness and occasion is emotional uplift and excitement.

The downdrift intonation is not altogether eliminated; it is absent only until the end of the stanza, when it occurs all at once, together with its concomitant penultimate vowel lengthening and tone falling. This exaggerated cadence clearly concludes the stanza. Rycroft has made a special study of the tonal and intonational aspects of praise-poem recitation, and his findings are most interesting (Rycroft 1960). He also shows that the significant tones, normally difficult to discern because of the overlay of downdrift intonation, are clearly discernible in praise-poem recitation when this downdrift intonation is eliminated.

The position with regard to cadences is in fact not so simple as we have described. A stanza is certainly always concluded with a final cadence, but there may be non-final cadences also within the stanza. The difference between final and non-final cadences is that the former are more exaggerated than the latter, and a longer pause ensues. The pause at the end of a final cadence may be prolonged in order to give the praiser time to collect his thoughts and recover his breath. At this point the audience sometimes participates with shouts of approval and cries of *musho, musho* (literally "say him, say him") to encourage the praiser to greater efforts. The degree of audience participation depends upon the nature of the occasion, whether serious, joyful, or sorrowful.

Thus the praise-poem is recited in stanzas (the nineteenth-century poems) or in sections (the eighteenth-century poems) marked by final cadence. The stanza is usually a single well-developed praise. It may consist of several sentences, but it has a unity of content which makes it a stable unit. The section on the other hand is a string of praises. It is therefore not a stable unit, and it may be broken by final cadences into several sections, at the discretion of the praiser. Both stanzas and sections may contain non-final cadences in addition to the concluding final cadences; these indicate the praises within the section, and sometimes the constituent parts (statements, extensions, developments) of the stanza. The ultimate unit is the verse, which is normally grammatically complete in itself as a sentence or clause, and is normally a breath-unit. Many more breaths are taken in praise-poem recitation than in normal speech, for the method of delivery demands that the lungs be always fully inflated. The frequent intakes of breath and the consequent short units of recitation contribute to the spirit of excitement.

RUTH FINNEGAN
Drum Language and Literature

"Of very great interest and importance is the possibility of transferring the whole system of speech symbolism into other terms than those that are involved in the typical process . . . a transfer, direct or indirect, from the typical symbolism of language as spoken and heard. . . . The ease with which speech symbolism can be transferred from one sense to another, from technique to technique, itself indicates that the mere sounds of speech are not the essential fact of language, which lies rather in the classification, in the formal patterning, and in the relating of concepts" (Sapir 1921: 19–21).

The process Sapir points to is also one of translation and of moves-across-media that have been given new importance in contemporary works (e.g., text-sound poetry and music, poésie sonore, and art-language works). The following article by Ruth Finnegan deals with only one of a wide range of surrogate language systems and transmedial poetries that have been part of the human repertory "then" and "now." Finnegan's own descriptions are based mainly on Rattray 1923; Carrington 1944, 1949a, 1949b; and Nketia 1963.

I

A remarkable phenomenon in parts of West and Central Africa is the literature played on drums and certain other musical instruments. That this is indeed a form of literature rather than music is clear when the principles of drum language are understood. Although its literary significance has been overlooked in general discussions of African oral literature (e.g., Bascom 1964, 1965a; Berry 1961; Herskovits 1946, 1960), expression through drums often forms a not inconsiderable branch of the literature of a number of African societies.

Communication through drums can be divided into two types. The first is through a conventional code where pre-arranged signals represent a given message; in this type there is no directly linguistic basis for the communication. In the second type, that used for African drum literature and the form to be considered here, the instruments communicate through direct representation of the spoken language itself, simulating the tone and rhythm of actual speech. The instruments themselves are regarded as speaking and their messages consist of words. Such communication, unlike that through conventional signals, is intended as a *linguistic* one; it can only be fully appreciated by translating it into words, and any musical effects are purely incidental.

This expression of words through instruments rests on the fact that the African languages involved are highly tonal; that is, the meanings of words are distinguished not only by phonetic elements but by their tones, in some cases by tone alone. It is the tone patterns of the words that are directly transmitted, and the drums and other instruments

SOURCE: Abridged from Ruth Finnegan, Oral Literature in Africa, pages 481–499.

involved are constructed so as to provide at least two tones for use in this way. The intelligibility of the message to the hearer is also sometimes increased by the rhythmic pattern, again directly representing that of the spoken utterance.

It might seem at first sight as if tonal patterns, even when supplemented by rhythm, might provide but a slight clue to the actual words of the message. After all, many words in a given language possess the same combination of tones. However, there are various devices in "drum language" to overcome this. There is, of course, the obvious point that there are conventional occasions and types of communication for transmission on the drum, so that the listener already has some idea of the range of meanings that are likely at any given time. More significant are the stereotyped phrases used in drum communications. These are often longer than the straightforward prose of everyday utterance, but the very extra length of the drum stereotypes or holophrases leads to greater identifiability in rhythmic and tonal patterning.

The principle can be illustrated from the Kele people of the Stanleyville area of the Congo, whose drum language has been extensively studied by Carrington (Carrington 1944, 1949*a*, and 1949*b*). In the Kele language the words meaning, for example, "manioc," "plantain," "above," and "forest" all have identical tonal and rhythmic patterns. By the addition of other words, however, a stereotyped drum phrase is made up through which complete tonal and rhythmic differentiation is achieved and the meaning transmitted without ambiguity. Thus "manioc" is always represented on the drums with the tonal pattern of "the manioc which remains in the fallow ground," "plantain" with "plantain to be propped up," and so on. Among the Kele there are a great number of these "proverb-like phrases" (Carrington 1949*a*: 38) to refer to nouns. "Money," for instance, is conventionally drummed as "the pieces of metal which arrange palavers," "rain" as "the bad spirit son of spitting cobra and sunshine," "moon" or "month" as "the moon looks down at the earth," "a white man" as "red as copper, spirit from the forest" or "he enslaves the people, he enslaves the people who remain in the land," while "war" always appears as "war watches for opportunities." Verbs are similarly represented in long stereotyped phrases. Among the Kele these drum phrases have their own characteristic forms—marked by such attributes as the use of duplication and repetition, derogatory and diminutive terms, specific tonal contrasts, and typical structures (Carrington 1949*b*: 47−54), and it is evident that they not only make for clear differentiation of intended meanings but also, in Carrington's words, are often "poetical in nature and constitute an important part of the oral literature of the tribe" (op. cit.: 47).

The sort of communication that can be sent using these drum phrases can be illustrated from the Kele drum representation of a simple message. It will be noticed how much longer the drum form is, both because of the repetition necessary to make the meaning clear and the use of the lengthy stereotyped phrases. The message to be conveyed is: "The missionary is coming up river to our village tomorrow. Bring water and firewood to his house." The drum version runs:

> White man spirit from the forest
> of the leaf used for roofs[1]

---

[1]Generic drum name for European. The reference is to the very large leaves used for roof tiles, compared to the Bible.

comes up-river, comes up-river
when to-morrow has risen
on high in the sky
to the town and the village
of us
come, come, come, come
bring water of *lɔkɔila* vine
bring sticks of firewood
to the house with shingles high up above[2]
of the white man spirit from the forest
of the leaf used for roofs.

[Carrington 1949*a*: 54]

Expression through drums, once thought so mysterious by visitors who failed to grasp its principles, thus turns out to be based directly on actual words and their tones. In a sense drum language fulfils many of the functions of writing, in a form, furthermore, better suited to tonal languages than an alphabetical script. Its usefulness too is undeniable in regions of dense forest where the only possible way of communicating, apart from actually sending messengers, was by sound. (Drum messages can be heard at a distance of between three to seven miles, according to Carrington 1949*b*: 25.)

This type of drum communication is known to occur widely in the Congo, Cameroons, and West Africa (particularly the coastal areas). The same principle—that of representing the tones of actual speech through stereotyped phrases—is also used for ''spoken'' communication through other instruments such as horns, flutes, or gongs.[3] Among some peoples such as the Ashanti or the Yoruba, drum language and literature are very highly developed indeed. In such cases, drumming tends to be a specialized and often hereditary activity, and expert drummers with a mastery of the accepted vocabulary of drum language and literature were often attached to a king's court. This type of expression is a highly skilled and artistic one and adds to the verbal resources of the language.

II

The relevance of drum language for oral literature is not confined to utilitarian messages with a marginally literary flavour. As will emerge clearly from some further examples, this type of medium can also be used for specifically literary forms, for proverbs, panegyric, historical poems, dirges, and in some cultures practically any kind of poetry. Something of the range and variety of this literature can be seen in the following examples, beginning with relatively simple messages, more typical of the Congo area

---

[2] Common drum phrase for house.

[3] Strictly the term ''gong'' should be used to refer to the hollow wooden ideophones or ''slit-gongs'' typical of the Congo area; whereas ''drum,'' which I have used in a wide sense here, should be confined to membranophones such as the Ashanti ''talking drums,'' a pair of hide-covered drums, one sounding a high, the other a low tone. Other media mentioned for this type of communication include horns, bells, yodelling of various types, sticks, a blacksmith's hammer and anvil, stringed instruments, and whistling.

and going on to some of the complex poetry found most characteristically in the southern areas of West Africa.

Among the Kele in the Congo, drum communication is used for formalized announcements. There are drum messages about, for instance, births, marriages, deaths, and forthcoming hunts or wrestling matches. A death is publicized on the drum by a special alert signal and the words, beaten out in drum language,

> You will cry, you will cry, you will cry
> Tears in the eyes
> Wailing in the mouth

> [Carrington 1949a: 58]

followed by the name and village of the dead man. The announcement of an enemy's approach is also transmitted by a special alert and the drummed tones which represent the words:

> War which watches for opportunities
> has come to the town
> belonging to us
> today as it has dawned
> come, come, come, come.

> [Ibid.: 61−62]

Another stock communication is the announcement of a dance, again with the drum speaking in standardized and repetitive phrases:

> All of you, all of you
> come, come, come, come,
> let us dance
> in the evening
> when the sky has gone down river
> down to the ground.

> [Ibid.: 65]

A final Kele message warns that rain is imminent and advises those in the forest or near the village to take shelter:

> Look out, look out, look out, rain,
> bad spirit, son of the spitting snake
> do not come down, do not come down, do not come down
> to the clods, to the earth
> for we men of the village
> will enter the house
> do not come down, do not come down, do not come down.

> [Carrington 1949b: 88]

Not all the peoples choose the same topics for these standardized drum announcements. Among the Akan, for instance, births, ordinary deaths, and marriages are not
normally publicized on drums (Nketia 1963: 43). However, the use of drums to
announce some emergency and, in particular, to call to arms seems very common
indeed. In some cases this takes a very elaborate and poetic form. Compare, for instance,
the simple and relatively straightforward call to fight among the Tumba of the Congo—

> Make the drum strong;
> strengthen your legs,
> spear, shaft and head,
> and the noise of moving feet;
> think not to run away

> [R. T. Clarke 1934: 39]

—with the literary and emotional quality typical of the specialized military drumming of
the Akan of Ghana, exemplified in one of their drum calls:

> Bodyguard as strong as iron,
> Fire that devours the nations,
> Curved stick of iron,
> We have leapt across the sea,
> How much more the lagoon?
> If any river is big, is it bigger than the sea?
> Come Bodyguard, come Bodyguard,
> Come in thick numbers,
> Locusts in myriads,
> When we climb a rock it gives way under our feet.
> Locusts in myriads,
> When we climb a rock it breaks into two.
> Come Bodyguard, come Bodyguard,
> In thick numbers.

> [Nketia 1963: 111−112]

Besides messages and announcements, drum language is also used for names. This
is one of the most common forms of drum expression and occurs even among people who
do not seem to have other more complicated drum poetry. Among the Hausa, for
instance, praise names and titles of rulers are poured forth on drums or horns on certain
public occasions (Smith 1957: 29), and the Lyele proverb names (*surnoms-devises*) are
commonly performed in the analogous whistle language (Nicolas 1950: 87); in both
cases this amounts to special praise and flattery of the individuals named.

Personal drum names are usually long and elaborate. In the Benue-Cross River
area of Nigeria, for instance, they are compounded of references to a man's father's
lineage, events in his personal life, and his own personal name (Armstrong 1954: 361).
Similarly among the Tumba of the Congo, all-important men in the village (and
sometimes others as well) have drum names: these are usually made up of a motto

emphasizing some individual characteristic, then the ordinary spoken name; thus a Belgian government official can be alluded to on the drums as "A stinging caterpillar is not good disturbed" (Clarke 1934: 38). Carrington describes the Kele drum names in some detail. Each man has a drum name given him by his father, made up of three parts: first the individual's own name; then a portion of his father's name; and finally the name of his mother's village. Thus the full name of one man runs "The spitting cobra whose virulence never abates, son of the bad spirit with the spear, Yangɔndɛ." Other drum names (i.e., the individual's portion) include such comments as "The proud man will never listen to advice," "Owner of the town with the sheathed knife," "The moon looks down at the earth / son of the younger member of the family," and, from the nearby Mba people, "You remain in the village, you are ignorant of affairs" (Carrington 1949a: 41 ff.; 1949b: 87, 107).

These drum names often play a significant part in the societies in which they occur. Their use in the conveying of messages is quite clear—the elaborateness of the names in this context has the directly utilitarian function of differentiating the tonal patterns without the possibility of ambiguity. They are also frequently used in the context of dances, entertainments, and festivals: they call on those present to encourage or to praise them by singling them out. As an Idoma informant told Armstrong, "when an African hears his name drummed, he must jump up for joy even from his sick bed" (Armstrong 1954: 360−361). . . .

In some areas, particularly much of southern West Africa, drum literature takes a more highly specialized form. There are drum proverbs, panegyric, and other poetry for drums, horns, or flutes, and sometimes state history is transmitted. . . .

Panegyric poetry is a genre to which public and ceremonial performance in drum language is particularly suited, whether the actual medium happens to be in fact drums, gongs, or wind instruments. Especially in parts of West Africa, praise poetry on drums and other instruments may take a complex and specialized form and is particularly common on public or state occasions. For Southern Nigeria, for instance, Armstrong quotes the following praise; it is taken from a performance in the royal court of the chief of Igumale, and is spoken by a flute. Throughout the poem the chief is praised in the imagery of a leopard:

> Akpa killed those who have horses *coza loga*.[4]
> The leopard in power is no toy!
> The mouth of him who goes wrongly and pays a fine is what is
>   guilty![5]
> *Ogo tikpa logwu gokpaawaga!*[6]
> When the land is dry ("strong") they will wait for the rains![7]
> When the leopard is on the way, the animals fear.
> When the kite calls, it is noon.[8]

[4]Title of a person present.

[5]i.e., "keep quiet everybody!"

[6]Meaning unknown; a title?

[7]i.e., "A patient person"; title of someone present.

[8]i.e., "A precise man"; title of someone present.

The locusts swarm![9]
Big, powerful man *cuna zegba*.
When there is a lion, there is a leopard![10]
The Chief, a full-bodied leopard in the hole!
The horses, here they are![11]
When the Chief did this, did that, they said it is not fitting. The
    Chieftaincy is not a plaything!
When the girls have no husbands, they say they belong to the Chief!
The girl from the corner with shame in her head, let her take shame
    from her head, for dancing is no plaything![12]
The leopard and the Chief have claws, have claws; the leopard and
    the Chief are coming today!
When the good thing is coming into public, what will the singer do
    today?
He who sits on the (royal) stool, Lion of lions, Chief, it is of him that
    I worry; the leopard and the Chief are no plaything!
He who is fitted for the kingship, let him be king! It is God who makes
    the King!

[Armstrong 1954: 362−363]

Again, one could quote from the elaborate drum praises so freely used among the
Yoruba. The rulers of the old kingdom of Ede, for example, are still praised on the
talking drum every month and in the course of all important festivals. These eulogies are
built up on a series of praise verses. Thus in the drum praise of Adetoyese Laoye, the
eleventh ruler, we have the building up of praises (mingled, as so often, with admoni-
tion) with the whole poem bound together by both the subject (the king) and the recurrent
image of the tree:

Adetoyese Akanji, mighty elephant.
One can worship you, as one worships his head.[13]
Son of Moware.
You enter the town like a whirlwind.
You, son of Odefunke.
Egungun[14] blesses quickly when you worship him.
Orisha[14] blesses more quickly when you worship him.
My father Akanji is an orisha.
The more devoutly you worship him
The greater blessings you receive from Adetoyese Akanji.

[9]i.e., "the people have all come together."
[10]i.e., "Here is a chief"; chiefly praise.
[11]i.e., "The royal people have assembled."
[12]i.e., "Come on, girls, get out and dance!"
[13]"Head" here stands for the Yoruba "ori" which means: head, good fortune or luck. People sacrifice to their
head as thanksgiving for success, etc.
[14]Yoruba spirits.

Bless, and bless me continuously,
Akanji, and do not leave me unblessed.
Do not attempt to shake a tree trunk.
One who shakes a tree trunk, shakes himself.
One who tries to undo you, you who are as short as death,
He will only undo himself.
A wine tapper cannot tap wine from a coconut palm.[15]
An elephant eats up the entire roots of an oro tree.
Do not behead me, I am not among them
I am not among the conspirators.
Conspirators, the hair on whose heads
Is ugly and ruffled.
A serious case may worry one but it will come to an end.
A serious case worries one, as if it will never be settled.
The case will be settled, and the slanderers and gossipers
Will be put to shame.
You met them in front, and you greet and greet them.
You met them behind you, and you greet and greet them
Your being courteous does not please them, like being insolent.
Keep on being insolent to them and their fathers!
It is unusual for one to greet his father's slave and prostrate.
You Adetoyese Akanji, bend one foot to greet them,
You leave the other unbent![16]
You, a notorious confuser! You confused everybody by your ap-
    pearance![17] Akanji you confused all those
Who tie cloth round their waists, without carrying a child[18]
I beg you in the name of God the great king, confuse me not!
Do not allow me to starve.
The leaves on a tree, do not allow the tree to feel the scorching sun.
You are a lucky person to wear the crown
A person who is on the throne
When the town prospers,
Is a lucky person to wear the crown.

[Oba Adetoyese Laoye I 1965]

. . . Among the Akan and the Yoruba, drum poetry also appears in invocations to spirits of various kinds. Longer Akan poems sometimes open with stanzas calling on the spirits associated with the drum itself—the wood and its various components—or invoke certain deities or ancient and famous drummers. Important rituals are also commonly opened or accompanied by the suitable drum poems. ''The Awakening'' is one which must be performed before dawn on the day of the Akan Adae festival:

---

[15]They are trying to do the impossible.
[16]Trying to conciliate your opponents, show respect—but not too much because you are the oba (king).
[17]During the chieftaincy dispute all the contestants were confused by the sudden appearance of Adetoyese Laoye.
[18]Policemen. The reference is to the cummerbund on the Native Authority Police uniform. During the contest police had to be transferred from Ede because they were alleged to favour one of the contestants.

The Heavens are wide, exceedingly wide.
The Earth is wide, very very wide.
We have lifted it and taken it away.
We have lifted it and brought it back,
From time immemorial.
The God of old bids us all
Abide by his injunctions.
Then shall we get whatever we want,
Be it white or red.
It is God, the Creator, the Gracious one.
"Good morning to you, God, Good morning."
I am learning, let me succeed.

[Nketia 1963: 44]

III

Drum language, it is clear, is a medium that can be put to a wide range of uses. Its appearance in messages, in names, in poetry, and in the performance of proverbs has been illustrated. It can also be employed to comment on or add to some current activity. Armstrong, for example, describes the actions of a chief drummer at a dance in the Benue-Cross River area, in words that could be applied elsewhere too: he

> maintains a running commentary on the dance, controls the line dancers with great precision, calls particular persons by name to dance solo, tells them what dance to do, corrects them as they do it, and sends them back into line with comment on the performance. He does this by making his drum talk, even above the sound of four or five other drums in the "orchestra."

[Armstrong 1954: 360]

In this example, the "speaking" and comment of the drum form a linguistic complement, as it were, to the musical and balletic aspects of the artistic event as a whole. Among the Kele, the talking drum accompanies wrestling matches, saluting contestants as they enter the ring, uttering comment and encouragement throughout the fight, and ending up with praise for the victor (Carrington 1949a: 63−64). Similar literary contributions are made by the drums among the Akan even to the otherwise mundane duty of carrying the chief. It is raised to a state ceremonial by the conventions surrounding it and by the drum poetry that accompanies and comments on it: the drums say "I carry father: I carry father, he is too heavy for me," to which the bass drum replies, in conventional form, "Can't cut bits off him to make him lighter" (Nketia 1963: 135). In funerals too, Akan drums play their part, echoing the themes of dirges and heralding the occasion with messages of condolence and farewell (ibid.: 64). Such comment by drums can take so elaborate a form as to be classed as full drum poetry in its own right. In this case it covers the sorts of drum proverbs, panegyrics, and histories already quoted, forming a specialized type of poetry apparently most characteristic of certain traditional states of West Africa.

Expression by drums or other instruments can also be an alternative medium to the human voice through which ordinary poetry can be represented. Thus among the Yoruba each of their many types of poetry can be recited on the drum as well as spoken, and the *oriki* (praise) poems are as frequently drummed as sung. With the Akan some poems can be drummed or sung, others are designed specifically for voice, drums, or horns respectively.

Many different kinds of communications, then, can be conveyed through the medium of drum language—messages, public announcements, comment, and many types of poetry—and the same sorts of functions can be fulfilled as by the corresponding speech forms, with the additional attributes of the greater publicity and impressiveness of the drum performance. In spite of its wide range of uses, however, drum communication is in certain respects a somewhat limited medium. There are limitations, that is, on the types of communications that can be transmitted; the stereotyped phrases for use in drum languages do not cover every sphere of life, but only the content conventionally expected to be communicated through drums.[19] Furthermore, in certain societies at least (for example, the Yoruba and the Akan), drumming is a highly specialized activity, with a period of apprenticeship and exclusive membership, so that to a greater extent than in most forms of spoken art, drum literature is a relatively esoteric and specialized form of expression, understood by many (at least in its simpler forms) but probably only fully mastered and appreciated by the few.[20] In the case of some peoples the response to such limitations has been the creation of a highly elaborate and conventional mode of artistic expression through drums—with the apparent corollary that in this very specialized and difficult medium the scope for individual variation and improvization seems to be correspondingly limited and the stress laid on technical mastery rather than on verbal originality.[21]

In conclusion it must be stressed again that what is transmitted in drum language is a direct representation of the *words* themselves. This is worth repeating, because for someone unacquainted with this medium it is not easy to grasp that the drums actually speak words, that from the point of view both of the analyst and of the people involved, the basis is a directly linguistic one. From this it follows that the content and style of drum communication can often be assessed as *literature*, and not primarily as music, signal codes, or incidental accompaniment to dancing or ceremonies. Some of the items of drum language—the "proverb-like" phrases of Kele drum language, for instance, or the whistled names in the Upper Volta—are only marginally literary. Other forms, however, in particular the drum poems of southern Ghana, Nigeria, and Dahomey,

[19]Or so it seems. With the exception of some remarks in Rattray, op. cit., 1923, pp. 256–7, the sources do not discuss this point directly.

[20]Not much has been written about the distribution of this skill among the population generally and further study of this question is desirable. Its prevalence in the contemporary scene also demands research; clearly it is at times highly relevant as, for instance, in the use of drum language over the radio during the Nigerian civil war to convey a message to certain listeners, and conceal it from others.

[21]Again, further evidence on this point would be welcome. Of the Akan Nketia makes the point that all drum texts are "traditional" (apart from the nonsense syllables sometimes included in them which may be invented) and that many are known in the same form to drummers in widely separated areas (1963: 48).

unmistakably fall into the category of highly developed oral literature. But whatever the assessment of individual examples it is clear that it is both correct and illuminating to analyse drum language in terms of its literary significance. Among the people who practise it, drum literature is clearly a part, albeit through a highly specialized and unusual medium, of their whole oral literature.

NANCY MUNN

Guruwari Designs

Munn's instance of a traditional tie between oral and visual language is from the Walbiri of northwestern Australia. The visual side (hand and eye) of ethnopoetics has generally been ignored in favor of the oral side (mouth and ear). Fundamental relations between writing/drawing and speaking/singing, although clear enough within such cultures as the Walbiri, have received little real attention from without. A series of propositions in this regard has come from the French philosopher, Jacques Derrida, whose elevation of other-than-alphabetic forms of writing should simultaneously help establish the equality of oral modes of poetry. Of the universality of his grammatology (discourse on writing), which must necessarily be an ethnogrammatology, he writes: "No reality or concept would correspond to the expression 'society without writing'" (1967, 1974). Furthermore, the relation of visual designs and verbal songs to "mapping"—as presented by Munn—ties up with the insistence of a poet like Charles Olson that topos (place) again be recognized as a fundamental poetic (we might add ethnopoetic) power. (See also Schieffelin's discussion of Gisaro "mapping" with songs, below, p. 281.) Other writers dealing with the relation between written and oral modes include Barthes on the Japanese theatrical face (below, p. 145), Thompson on Ngebe "action writing" (below, p. 285), Munn on "the idea of writing in an oral poet" (below p. 475), and Klima and Bellugi on the gestural poetry of the deaf (below, p. 291).

In Walbiri thought there is a close relation between graphic forms and the country, or ground (*walya*), since the term *guruwari* can be used in a general sense to refer to any visible mark left by an ancestor in the country, and in addition, *guruwari* in the abstract aspect of "ancestral powers" are lodged in the country. Among the most prominent of the graphs that Walbiri draw in the sand are track prints of animals and birds and circle or circle-line notations referring to places and journeys. An examination of these apparently simple forms can lead us into a closer examination of Walbiri thought concerning

SOURCE: Nancy Munn, Walbiri Iconography, pages 119−126, 131−133, 145−149.

the association between *guruwari* designs and the country.

Footprints are impressed in the sand by holding the hand in various special positions; their production is a casual play activity in which men, women, and children may indulge. The circle or circle-line notation commonly appears during general conversation about journeys and places. The circle signifies a locale and the line a path or movement from place to place; a group of circles may be used to specify the relative orientation of locales. Although both types of graphs are generally available among men and women, men apply them more widely, giving them a featured place in their storytelling repertory and ancestral designs.

Looked at in the context of the wider graphic system, track-print imitations (called *wulya*, "foot," "footprints") constitute a special class of elements and figures, for they are essentially translations of natural sand markings into artifactual ones of human making.

Each element or figure signifies the print made by one or more species, for example, there is one type of print for marsupial mouse and opossum (that is, they belong to a single visual category), another for the varieties of kangaroo, and a third for human beings. A figure may consist of a number of the same elements (footprints) or of the footprints ranged on either side of a "tail" (a meandering or straight line).

One man impressing track prints on the sand accompanied this activity with a commentary, for example, "the man ran away"; "he ran south." In another instance a man elaborated the depiction of a kangaroo print that he was demonstrating to me into a hunting scene. After the prints were impressed, he drew a circle to indicate the location of the kangaroo sleeping under a tree, and another slightly farther off to indicate the location of the hunter. "He throws a spear!" said the narrator and swiftly drew a line from the hunter to the kangaroo.

Prints used to tell stories in this way carry a standard signification. They convey the species, number (when over three or four, "many"), and direction of individuals moving through the country. As one young Walbiri man put it, the graphs can be "read." What is "read" obviously replicates the signaling value of the prints in ordinary hunting contexts.

Figures 1 and 2 illustrate how some men made use of track prints to tell stories in drawings that they made for me on paper.[1] In these typical narrative improvisations the prints are combined with a few additional elements (a water hole, a nest of eggs, a snake) to convey a narrative situation such as "an emu, seeing a snake, became afraid and went away east."

Clearly, a graph that signifies the footprint of a species such as opossum or kangaroo may, when transferred to a narrative about ancestors, signify the footprints of kangaroo or possum ancestors, and this is actually a characteristic feature of men's use of the footprints in storytelling. In the paper drawings of figure 2, track prints used to recount ancestral incidents tell us of the number and direction of movement of certain ancestors passing through a particular locale. It happens that in the drawing of figure 2.2, the fact that the actors are ancestors is graphically signaled by the presence of a ceremonial string cross in the drawing, but no such graphic cue is available in figure 2.1,

---

[1]Illustrations taken from paper drawings that men did for me are used here . . . as "visual texts" in much the way verbal texts may be used in the study of cultural expression and conceptualization.

Track prints used to tell stories. After charcoal (1, 2, 4) and pencil crayon (3) drawings. The drawings were done by different men, but at the same time. The snake is a traditional form, but water hole and grass (3) are nontraditional in style.

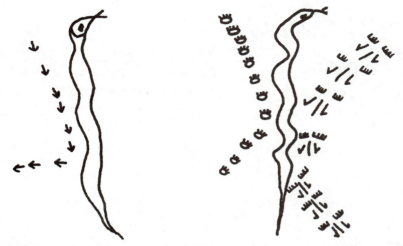

1. Emu and snake   2. Dog, kangaroo, and snake

1. An emu saw a snake and, becoming afraid, ran away eastward. The upper set of prints depicts the emu running away. East is left in this picture.

2. Seeing a snake, a dog turned away westward; a kangaroo also saw the snake and went east. East is right in this picture.

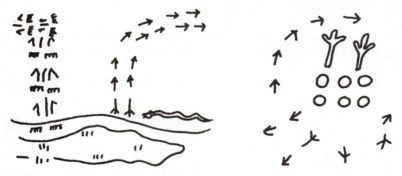

3. Kangaroo and emu   4. Emu and eggs

3. A kangaroo and emu come down to the water to drink.

4. An emu, leaving its nest, goes to a water hole. Prints at bottom left apparently indicate the return.

FIGURE 1.   Track-print stories and designs.

although here also the informant regarded the drawing as an ancestral scene. The same drawing could equally well have been used to portray a scene of daily life.

In still other cases a man may regard a particular set of prints as a *guruwari* design belonging to an ancestor of that species; as designs, track prints can occur independently or fixed into larger graphic composites. When the prints occur independently only

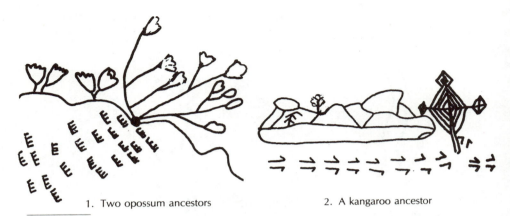

1. Two opossum ancestors

2. A kangaroo ancestor

1. Two opossum ancestors went into the ground at a site called Waraginbiri. The base of the little bush is the point at which they entered the ground.

2. A kangaroo ancestor came to Wanabi, took the large string cross, which is a ceremonial object, out of his body and left it there. A number of other kangaroos who were traveling behind him (not shown in the drawing) came up and saw it. A rocky hill with trees is shown behind the string cross.

FIGURE 2.   Track prints representing ancestral journeys. After pencil crayon drawings.

extragraphic factors, such as the medium and social context in which they appear or the informant's assertion that the graph is an ancestral design, cue the difference between instances of this kind and those in which the prints are simply used to recount ancestral movements (without also being regarded as designs). Thus paintings on the cave walls at Rugari, an important emu site west of Yuendumu, are the *guruwari* of ancestral emus who came to the site and walked around there (fig. 3.1). At the same time, the prints provide narrative information on their direction of travel and indicate their presence at the site.

Indeed, only a fine line divides the use of the graphs simply to recount ancestral

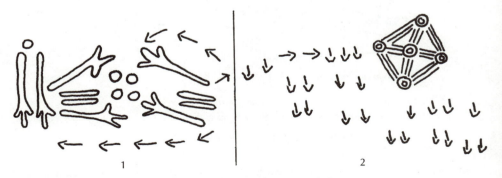

Emu *guruwari* on the cave walls at the site Rugari. After cave paintings

1. Prints of an emu standing over its eggs.

2. Prints of a large number of emus who came to the site. The circle-line figure signifies that they walked around the site. Each circle is a camp.

FIGURE 3.   Track prints as *guruwari* designs.

movements and their use as designs, since the term *guruwari* may refer not only to ancestral designs as such but also to the track prints of the ancestor, the actual prints made by him as he travels along. When a man identifies conventional prints as *guruwari*, he may mean that they depict the footprints of the ancestor, and therefore are his *guruwari*, or he may be indicating that the prints are a particular ancestral design. Actually, for Walbiri, the one tends to imply the other: the ancestor's footprints are his designs in the sense that they are among those "marks" or vestiges of his passage in the country through which he is identified and fixed forever in the consciousness of living Walbiri. Here we meet again with the circle of reality and reference so characteristic of Walbiri thinking about designs and ancestral events: designs are among the marks made by ancestors in the country and they also *represent* such marks. . . .

The most general premise behind the Walbiri conception of ancestral times is that all ancestors traveled routes which can be located in the country. The major topographical features are viewed as having been created through ancestral events, and may be thought of as metamorphoses of parts of an ancestor's body, or as due to his bodily imprints in the country. As a result, an ancestor can be "followed" (*bura*, to follow, as in hunting, to come behind), literally kept track of, through his site associations. Each ancestral journey begins with an emergence from the ground and is finalized in a return to the ground, whether at the site of emergence or at some place far distant from it. Ancestors are thought to remain today inside the ground.

This concept of locale and journey provides the framework for men's songs and narratives about ancestral events. Some songs consist simply of site names, and the term for song, *yiri*, also means "name," as well as "visible mark." Used in a broad sense *yiri* includes *guruwari* (visible marks of the ancestor), although in a narrower sense it refers to the verbal forms only. A sequence of songs or what the Walbiri call a "line" provides names of the sites associated with an ancestor as well as references to events along the track. Walbiri men think of the songs as having an exact sequence, correlated with the sequence of sites.[2]

Similarly, the typical ancestral narrative is built upon a framework of site sequences, a mode of narrative order which, as we have seen, is not used by Walbiri women, who typically build their stories on a micro-temporal scaffolding of the daily life cycle rather than on the macro-time of the journey. The journey model is the more inclusive, since it can include the daily cycle of activities (for example, some of men's narrative accounts describe daily hunting and gathering activities at the sites along a route).

Some accounts of an ancestral track consist almost entirely of lists of site names connected by phrases indicating the movement of the ancestors between sites. This provides a kind of minimal account of an ancestral journey. The same track may, of course, be rich in events that take place along the route, but the site-path framework is brought into relief by this sort of narration. An abstract from one such minimal account will suggest the pattern:

> They slept at Wabadi ["small yam"]. The two kangaroos rested. They go on to Bigili [Vaughan Springs]. Afterward they go on to Walguru ["stone axe"]. On they went. The two kangaroos went on. . . . They slept at Ngalyirba. Afterward

---

[2]The sequence is not, however, carried out precisely in ceremonial, and of course the sequence itself is always subject to the vagaries of individual memory.

they went on to Bangunubunda [where] they scooped out wooden dishes. . . . They went on to Winidjara [where] howling dogs pursued them. They fled. . . . Afterward they went to Ganibaguru. They sat down, sat down, sat down [i.e., for a long time]. They went into the distance to another country.

Not only are men's myth narratives constructed through the site-path framework but so also is the stereotype for dreams in which men may see designs and songs for *bulaba* (public camp ceremonies). The Walbiri view is that a dreamer first hears a *guruwalba* singing on a tree, perhaps while he is still half-awake. Then he follows the ancestor's track from place to place, and the various *guruwari* and songs are revealed to him. In the latter situation he appears to be merged with the ancestor. For example, a snake *bulaba* being performed during my stay at Yuendumu was said to have been dreamed by two Yanmadjiri men at a settlement to the northeast. According to my informants the dreamers followed the track or line of the snake as he moved from site to site. A line of men dancing in the ceremony was also said to "follow up" the track of the ancestor.[3]

DESIGNS AND SONGS

Walbiri postulate close associations between the *guruwari* designs associated with a single ancestor and the songs detailing the events of his track. The fact that the term *yiri* can cover both verbal forms and visual marks also points to the Walbiri view that designs and songs constititute a single complex. Not only is their association expressed in the norms of ritual behavior, but it can also be observed in the way men handle the meanings of designs and songs, since they tend to treat them as complementary channels of communication about an ancestor. For instance, one man sang the following song while drawing meander lines representing smoke in a design for a fire ancestor:

walunggana	*miraranggana*
fire	"big smoke"[4]

This song was part of a narrative to which the design referred and was in the song line associated with a *bulaba* ceremony currently being performed in the camp.

In another instance, a design being painted on the body of a dancer during ceremonial preparations was explained to me as a depiction of the tail and boomerang (both items specified by a single graphic element) of an opossum ancestor. Men then continued their explanation by singing a song belonging to the ceremony that had been sung during the preparations: "Opossum travels on, opossum tail." Pointing to the design, they added that the opossum walked a long way. Designs and songs are thus treated as complementary channels of communication; each is a repository of narrative meaning, and the production of one may evoke the other. The treatment of *guruwari*

[3]Informants used the term *ganari-li*, which they translated as "line up," "we follow'm up."

[4]Song words often take a special form, or are foreign terms; translation is therefore chancy. My informant gave the meaning "big smoke" for *miraranggana*. According to Kenneth Hale (n.d.), the term *mirawari* means "mirage"; in my data it also appears as the name of an ancestral site associated with rain, fire, and smoke and thus may, perhaps, be related to the song word.

designs and songs in this manner is clearly a specialized form of the general tendency to perceive figures in the graphic system as stores of narrative, potentially verbalizable meaning, or to use them in conjunction with verbalization to communicate such meanings. For the Walbiri, graphs do indeed ''speak.''

The interlocking of verbal and visual-graphic forms is a pervasive feature of Walbiri *eidos*, one which characterizes both the masculine and feminine subcultures; it is operative both in the casual social contexts of storytelling and conversation and in ceremonial contexts where the two forms function as coordinate parts of a construction process through which the qualities and potency of the ancestors are reembodied.

In ceremonials, songs combine with designs to infuse the event with *djugurba* qualities, as well as to represent *djugurba* meanings. Unlike the designs and other visual constructions, songs lack spatial localization and can pervade the activity as a whole. Thus a synthesis of spatially localized and nonlocalized media is required to form the sensual qualities of the event.

Indeed, it seems that in positing the close association of songs and designs in their cosmological assumptions about the nature of the world Walbiri are expressing symbolically the relation for them of verbal language and graphic or, more generally, nonverbal communication as a whole. Songs are in a sense symbols of oral language, and ancestral designs are symbols of visual or graphic ''language.'' The ancestors are in effect ''talking about'' the things that happen to them in both visual-graphic and verbal ways, and such ''talking'' objectivates the world around them, giving it social, communicable reality.

ROLAND BARTHES
The Written Face

Barthes's essay is presented here as an extension, by ethnopoetic means, of the "question of writing" discussed in the previous headnote.

The Japanese theatrical face is not painted (powdered), it is written. This unforeseen movement occurs: though painting and writing have the same original instrument, the brush, it is not painting, however, which seduces writing with its decorative style, its sprawling, caressing touch, its representative space (as no doubt would have happened with us in the West, for whom the civilized future of a function is always its esthetic ennoblement); on the contrary, it is the act of writing which subjugates the pictorial

SOURCE: The Drama Review, *volume 15, number 3, 1971, pages 80−83.*

gesture, so that painting is always only writing. This theatrical face (masked in Noh, drawn in Kabuki, artificial in Bunraku) is made from two substances: the white of the paper, the black of the inscription (reserved for the eyes).

The function of the white of the face is apparently not to make the complexion unnatural, or to caricature it (as is the case with Western clowns, for whom flour and plaster are just an incitement to daub their faces), but only to efface the prior trace of features, to make of the face an empty expanse of dull material which no natural substance (flour, dough, plaster, or silk) can succeed in animating with any texture, sweetness, or reflection. The face is only *the thing to be written on*; but this future tense itself has already been written by the hand which whitened its eyebrows, the protuber- ance of its nose, the planes of its cheeks and gave the page of flesh the black boundary of a head of hair compact as stone. The whiteness of the face—not at all candid, but heavy, disgustingly thick, like sugar—simultaneously signifies two contradictory movements: immobility (what we would "morally" call "impassivity") and fragility (which we would likewise, and as unsuccessfully, call "emotivity"). By no means *on* this surface, but engraved, incised in it, are the precisely elongated slashes of eyes and mouth. The eyes—crossed, uncircled by the rectilinear eyelids, with no circles under them (circles under the eyes: the truly expressive value of the Western face—fatigue, morbidness, eroticism)—open out directly on the face, as if they were the black empty depth of writing, "the night of the inkwell"; or, rather, the face is drawn like a sheet of water toward the black (but not at all somber) well of the eyes. Reduced to the elementary signifiers of writing—the blank of the page and the hollows of its incisions—the face banishes all the signified, that is, all expressivity: this writing writes nothing (or writes: "*nothing*"). Not only does it not "lend" (naively accountable accounting word) itself to any emotion, to any meaning (not even that of impassivity, of inexpressivity), it copies no characters: the transvestite (for women's roles are played by men) is not a boy powdered to look like a woman, with a copious supply of nuances, veristic touches, costly simulations, but a pure signifier whose *underneath* (verity) is neither clandestine (jealously masked) nor surreptitiously pointed out (by a smirking wink at the virility of the actor in the supporting role as done by Western transvestites, opulent blondes whose coarse hands or big feet infallibly belie their hormonal chests), but is simply *absented*. The actor, in his face, neither plays at being a woman nor copies her, but only signifies her; if, as Mallarmé says, writing is made of "the gestures of the idea," the transvestite is here the gesture of feminity, not its plagiarism. It follows that it is not at all remarkable—that is, not at all *marked* (which would be inconceivable in the West, where transvestism is already, in itself, badly thought of and poorly tolerated, purely transgressive)—to see a fifty-year-old actor (very famous and respected) playing the role of a shy young woman in love, because youth, like femininity, is not a natural essence here, the verity of which one madly pursues. The refinement of the code, its precision— which is indifferent to any related copy of an organic type (to create the real, physical body of a young woman)—results in, or is justified by, absorbing and fading all feminine reality, through a subtle diffraction of the signifier. Signified, but not represented, Woman is an idea (not a nature); as such, she is brought back into the classificatory action and into the verity of her pure difference. The Western transvestite wants to be *a* woman; the Oriental actor seeks only to combine Woman's signs.

Nevertheless, in that these signs are extreme—not because they are emphatic (I rather think they are not), but because they are intellectual, being, like writing, "gestures of the idea"—they purify the body of any expressivity: one might say that by dint of being signs, they exhaust meaning. Thus is explained the conjunction of sign and impassivity (an improper word, I repeat, since it is moral, expressive) which marks Asian theatre. . . .

[Tr. Sandy MacDonald]

RUTH FINNEGAN

The Divination Poetry of Ifa[1]

Though divination as such has had minimal impact on contemporary poetry, the underpinnings of divination in systematic chance procedures relate closely to processes used by experimental poets and artists, from the Dada work of Duchamp, Arp, and Tzara to its fuller development by Jackson Mac Low and John Cage. For this, the traditional system most drawn from is that of the Chinese I Ching, as modified by Carl Jung's speculation on "synchronicity," the "acausal connections" between things happening at the same time (Wilhelm/Baynes 1950). But it's in the widespread African practices that we find a still actively creative, large, and complex body of oral poetry accompanying a system of self-recognitions and self-placements based on an elaborate cosmology and an underlying principle of random meetings.

Of the place of Ifa divination in Africa and beyond, Finnegan writes: "Similar or identical systems are found among the Fon of Dahomey and Ewe of Togo as well as some other Nigerian peoples. Its elaborateness has led some to speculate about possible external origins, but it is now generally agreed that Ifa has a long history in West Africa and that, for recent centuries at any rate, the center of distribution has been Yoruba country in Southern Nigeria" (1970: 191). A very readable translation of selections from the Ifa repertory (16 major odus and 25 additional castings from a possible 256) is Judith Gleason's A Recitation of Ifa *(1973), based on workings by the Ifa priest, Awotunde Aworinde.*

---

[1]The main sources used are G. Parrinder 1961, ch. 13; R. C. Abraham 1958 (under *Ifa*); Bascom 1941, 1943; Abimbola 1964, 1965; Gbadamosi and Beier 1959: 25 ff.; R. Prince 1964; and Morton-Williams *et al.* 1966. Full bibliographies can be found in Maupoil 1961, who discusses in detail the very similar Fa divination system in Dahomey.

SOURCE: Ruth Finnegan, Oral Literature in Africa, *pages 191–203.*

Before discussing Ifa literature, it is necessary to describe something of the mechanism and beliefs of the Yoruba divination system. Ifa, the Yoruba oracle, is one among the pantheon of Yoruba gods, and as such appears in many (and sometimes contradictory) stories and myths, often under his alternative title of Orunmila. In one myth, for instance, the gods are depicted as hungry because they received few sacrifices. The trickster god, Eshu, then showed Ifa the system of divination so that as a result men could be helped through the diviners' skill, while, at the same time, the gods would benefit through the sacrifices and thank-offerings that human beings would be commanded to make by their diviners. Ifa has a special position among the gods. He is both the deity who acts as the intermediary between men and gods, and also in a sense is the impersonal principle of divination by which mankind has access to what is otherwise hidden from them. Ifa thus, as god and as oracle, plays a central part in Yoruba religious and everyday life:

> Ifa is the master of today;
> Ifa is the master of tomorrow;
> Ifa is the master of the day after tomorrow;
> To Ifa belongs all the four days
> Created by Orisa into this world.
>
> [Abimbola 1965: 4]

The Ifa divination system is a highly elaborate one. It rests on a series of mathematical permutations, the principle of which must be grasped in order to understand the way in which certain pieces of literature are associated with each of these. The permutations of figures (*odu*) are based on two columns of four units each, and the different combinations which these eight units may form between them. The total number of figures is 256, each with its own name and associated literature. It is only after obtaining one of the figures to form the basis of his utterance that the diviner can proceed to the divination itself.

There are two main ways of obtaining the figures. The first, less elaborate mechanism consists of a chain or cord of eight half-seeds (often split mango stones), divided into two portions of four half-seeds each. When this is thrown down by the diviner, the resultant figure makes two columns of four units each, the exact combination depending on whether the seeds have fallen convex- or concave-side-up. The other way of obtaining a figure, a longer method used in important consultations, is with a set of sixteen palm-nuts and a small board. The diviner throws or passes the nuts rapidly from one hand to the other. If either one or two nuts are left in the right hand, the throw is valid and he makes a corresponding mark on his board: a double mark for one nut, a single for two. The process is repeated eight times and eight marks are thus made in the dust on the tray; these start from the bottom right-hand side and are laid out in the form of two parallel columns of four sets of marks each. This gives the same result as the eight-seed chain, the double mark corresponding to a seed convex-side-up, a single mark to the concave.

TABLE 1
Table showing the Names and Structure of the Columns which form the Basis of Ifa Figures (odu)
(from Parrinder, 1961: 141; Abraham 1958: 276)

1. *ogbe*	2. *ọyẹku*	3. *iwori*	4. *odi*
I	II	II	I
I	II	I	II
I	II	I	II
I	II	II	I
5. *irosun*	6. *ọwara*	7. *ọbara*	8. *ọkọnrọn*
I	II	I	II
I	II	II	II
II	I	II	II
II	I	II	I
9. *ogunda*	10. *ọsa*	11. *ika*	12. *oturopọn*
I	II	II	II
I	I	I	II
I	I	II	I
II	I	II	II
13. *otuwa*	14. *irẹtẹ*	15. *ọsẹ*	16. *ofun*
I	I	I	II
II	I	II	I
I	II	I	II
I	I	II	I

Note. The order of the *odu* figures also has some significance in the full divination process. That given here is the order most commonly found, but there are regional variations (see Bascom 1961).

It is the figure thus produced that determines the diviner's utterances to his client. As can be seen from the table, each column of four can fall in any of sixteen permutations. When the two columns are considered together, as they are by Ifa diviners, the total number of different figures that can be produced is 16 × 16 = 256. Of this number, 16 are the leading figures or *odu* proper: these are the combinations of two identical columns. Thus the double figure based on the column called *ọyẹku* and known as *ọyẹku meji* appears as

$$
\begin{array}{cc}
\text{II} & \text{II} \\
\text{II} & \text{II} \\
\text{II} & \text{II} \\
\text{II} & \text{II}
\end{array}
$$

while the double figure *iwori meji*, based on the *iwori* column, is

$$
\begin{array}{cc}
\text{II} & \text{II} \\
\text{I} & \text{I} \\
\text{I} & \text{I} \\
\text{II} & \text{II}
\end{array}
$$

The remaining 240 figures, those in which the two columns differ, are considered secondary, and, though often referred to by the same term as for the principal figures (*odu*), are strictly *omo odu*, "children of *odu*." An example of one of these secondary *odu* would be that name *iwori obara*, a combination of the *obara* and *iwori* columns (the right-hand one being named first in the Yoruba title):

$$
\begin{array}{cc}
\text{I} & \text{II} \\
\text{II} & \text{I} \\
\text{II} & \text{I} \\
\text{II} & \text{II}
\end{array}
$$

Once the diviner has thrown his figure, the divination proper can begin. Each figure has several pieces of literature (*ese*) specifically connected with it, and it is in the words associated with the figure thrown that the answer to the client's query must be found. There is no definite number of pieces for each *odu*, but a diviner would not normally begin to practise unless he knew at least four for each (thus involving mastery of at least one thousand in all); good diviners are said to know about eight of the pieces for each of the 256 figures and many more for the important figures (Bascom 1941: 43, 50). It is commonly believed that the number of pieces for each figure is ideally sixteen, in keeping with the mathematical symmetry of the system as a whole. But there seems to be no such fixed correspondence in actual practice, and the number and to some extent the content of the verses vary with individual capacity and with the locality.

The practical point of these pieces is to guide the inquirer by suggesting a sacrifice or type of worship, by indicating his likely fortune, and by referring to a precedent from which he can judge his own case. Since more than one piece can be quoted for whatever figure is thrown, these are recited at random one after the other, and it is for the client, not the diviner, to select which applies to his particular case. The consultation thus proceeds through poetic allusion and analogy rather than through straight answers to specific questions—and it is this quality which leads to its development as a corpus of literature and gives depth and meaning to the bare injunctions with which the divination may open.

The pieces associated with each figure fall into a general pattern. Each usually opens with a mention of the sacrifices and other actions the client must carry out to have success. This first part is relatively prosaic; it may run, for instance:

> This person is intending to marry a new wife. He is warned to make sacrifice to Osun so that the wife may be prosperous. He is warned never to flog the wife if he wants peace in his home. He should make sacrifice with fifteen cowries and a big hen. Ifa says that if he observes all these warnings, success will be his. [Abimbola 1965: 15]

This is followed by the main part of the piece, expressed in poetic language and sometimes chanted all through. This part is concerned with setting out a precedent in terms of a previous divination. First often comes the name of the priest of Ifa who is said to have made the prophecy in the precedent cited, and the name of the client(s) for whom he was divining—these may be people, deities, animals, plants, inanimate objects. Thus the client may be told that on the previous occasion

> The-big-and-terrible-Rainbow[2]
> Cast Ifa for the Iroko tree
> Of the town of Igbo.
>   [Abimbola 1965: 16]

Another diviner is referred to as "Oropa Niga; to fight and stir up dust like Buffalo; parched dust on the top of a rock" (Bascom 1943:128) or as "I-have-no-time-to-waste." It will be seen that this section often involves elaborate and poetic names which may have symbolic meaning. Second in this main part of the piece there usually comes a poem (sometimes elaborated in a prose story) which describes the occasion of the previous divination. As will emerge from the examples given below, the subject-matter of this part is most varied. There are variations in length: sometimes there is only a fragmentary allusion (perhaps not much more than a poetic proverb), while at others there is a long and dramatic narration. Finally, the client told the result of the previous divination described and thus, indirectly, what he can expect himself. Very often the conclusion pointedly shows that on the previous occasion the one who performed the due sacrifices prospered, while the negligent met disaster. Sometimes the whole recitation is then closed by a chorus which is chanted in unison by the diviner, his pupils, and the client.

Within this general pattern there is plenty of scope for variation in the actual pieces recited. They differ greatly in length. Abimbola reports several that can be recited for more than half an hour, while others take only one or two minutes (Abimbola 1965: 13). The plots and the people involved in them are also of many different kinds. They include just about all the topics that can be met in narrative stories throughout the continent. This great variety is hardly surprising when one considers that even a mediocre diviner must know at least a thousand of these precedents with their accompanying verses and stories. They can be about animals, gods, legendary humans, natural phenomena like rivers or hills, plants, and even inanimate things like metals or shells, and they may take the form of a simple story about a man going on a journey, an account of the founding of a town, a philosophical discussion of the merits and demerits of monogamy—"there is . . . no limit to the subject-matter which *ese* Ifa may deal with " (ibid.: 14). The outcome often takes an aetiological form with the present nature of some plant or animal traced to its imaginary actions in the story—in particular its obedience or disobedience to the injunctions laid on it by the oracle; its characteristics in the world today thus provide a kind of imaginative validation of the truth of the story.

The sort of plots involved can be seen from a few brief synopses (quoted from the convenient summaries in Bascom 1941: 46, 48, 45).

1. It is because Maizebeer, Bamboo-wine, and Palm-wine refused to sacrifice that a

---

[2]Praise name of the diviner.

person who has been intoxicated recovers from his stupefied condition after
sleeping.

2. Lizard was told to make a sacrifice, part of which was to enable him to marry, and
part of which was to ensure that his wife would continue to love him. Lizard
sacrificed only the first part, and after he had married, his wife left him. It is
because he is looking for his wife in the tree-tops that he raises himself on his
forelegs and peers from side to side.

3. When Brass, Lead, and Iron were told to sacrifice, Iron said that the diviners were
just lying, that events had been predestined by Olorun [God], and that their course
could not be altered by sacrificing. Only Brass and Lead sacrificed, and because of
this they can be buried for many years without rotting, while Iron rusts away in a
short time.

4. When the 165 kinds of trees in the forest were told to sacrifice, only three did as
they were told. The others replied that they did not have enough money. When
Eshu [a god] reported this to the gods, a storm was sent to the forest. It pulled up
the larger trees by the roots, or broke them down; but the *atori* bush and the *ariran*
and *esun* grasses, who had sacrificed, simply bent down while the storm passed
over them.

5. Orunmila [another name for the god Ifa] was told to include a knife as a part of a
sacrifice, lest he be taken as a thief on a journey he was considering. He postponed
the sacrifice, and when he stole some kola-nuts on the way, he escaped capture
only after having been cut on the palm of his hand. The owner of the nuts asked the
king to gather everyone together so that he might identify the thief by this cut.
Frightened, Orunmila went to the diviners, who doubled the sacrifice. While
everyone slept Eshu took one of the knives and cut the palms of everyone,
including the unborn children. (It is because of this that people have lines on their
palms.) When the owner of the nuts demanded that Orunmila open his hand,
Orunmila showed that everyone, including the king himself, had the same scars;
and because he had been falsely accused, he was given a great deal of wealth.

6. Stout Foreigner was told to sacrifice so as to find good fortune; he sacrificed, and
everything to which he turned his hand became good.

The actual poems and prose narratives which give full expression to these plots are
of course much more lengthy and elaborate than the bald summaries just quoted. The last
one, for instance, seems to be the piece quoted in full in another source, and is associated
with the fourth of the sixteen principal *odus*. The allusive verse is, as often, explained
and expanded in the straightforward prose narrative which follows it:

Ifa sees the prospect of greatness for this person in a strange land. He should make
sacrifice with four pigeons, a good garment of his, and a shoe.

> I arrived in good time,
> I travelled in good time,
> I am the only man who travels in time of fortune
> When valuable objects of wealth are being deposited I entered
>   unannounced like the heir to the wealth

I am not the heir to the wealth, I am only good at travelling in time
   of fortune.

(These people) divined for the fat stranger[3]
Who would enter unannounced
On the day the property of the dead king of Benin was being shared.[4]

   The fat stranger was going to Benin in search of a suitable place to practise his
Ifa. He was told that he would prosper in Benin but he was warned to make
sacrifice. After making the sacrifice he made for Benin. He entered Benin just as
the King of that city died. He thought that would not speak well of him—a
renowned diviner (*babaláwo*)—if he did not say his condolences to the people of
Benin. But he did not know that whenever the properties of a dead king were being
shared out in Benin a good portion usually goes to the fortunate stranger who
entered just in time. On arriving at the place where the properties were being
shared, the fat stranger was given a good portion of the property.

   After gathering the materials given him, he made for his native land. He
started to sing in praise of his diviners (who divined for him before he went to
Benin) while in turn his diviners praised Ifa. He made a party for his neighbours.
There the *àràn*[5] was beaten, and it gave its pleasant melodies. Unconciously, as he
stretched his legs, he started to dance. On opening his mouth the song of the
diviners was already on his lips.

He said it happened, just as his Ifa priests said it would.

I arrive in good time,
I travelled in good time,
I am the only man who travels in time of fortune
When valuable objects of wealth are being deposited I entered
   unannounced like the heir to the wealth
I am not the heir to the wealth, I am only good at travelling in time
   of fortune.
(These people) divined for the fat stranger
Who would enter unannounced
On the day the property of the dead king of Benin was being shared.
Who will help us reconstruct this city?
Only the fat stranger will help us reconstruct this city.
                                             [Abimbola 1964: 7−8]

                         *   *   *

   Those who memorize and recite such poems are members of a highly trained and
respected profession. The Ifa diviners (*babaláwo*, lit. "father of mysteries") spend
several years learning the literature for their profession. The minimum seems to be three
years: the first is often spent learning the names and structure of the *odu*, the second and
third learning some of the literature of each as well as the actual practice of divination and
its rituals. But sometimes seven or ten years are spent in apprenticeship to a qualified

[3]*Gòdògbò*—fat or bold, and at the same time tall and stately.
[4]Benin has the reputation of great wealth among the Yoruba—"Benin the place of money."
[5]Drum connected with Ifa.

diviner, and the general opinion is, not surprisingly, that an Ifa diviner continues to learn as long as he lives. In some areas at least it is also a strictly organized profession with a head diviner (*olori-awo*) in each quarter of a town or village and several grades of diviners under him. It is clear also that both they and others regard their skill seriously. Though it is presumably possible in principle for dishonest individuals to exploit the system, there seems to be no question of the system as a whole being a piece of calculated trickery. As will be clear even from the few examples cited (see p. 152, no. 3), however, the Yoruba themselves admit the existence of individual scepticism on the subject. Nevertheless, the general belief is not only that the diviners themselves are genuine but that what they say represents the accumulated wisdom of generations, a belief strengthened by the fact that diviners themselves approach their own problems through Ifa consultation.

That Ifa divination and its literature should be regarded as seriously as this is not surprising when one considers the nature of the consultation. Only one point need be repeated in this connection. For each figure that is thrown the diviner does not repeat just one poem (and associated story), but at least four or so, either in outline or in full. Not only are these mostly expressed in allusive and poetic language, but the diviner himself does not know in advance the specific problem the questioner has in mind, and it is left to the client to make his choice among the several verses recited; there is always likely to be at least one which will appear relevant to him, particularly in view of the fact that what is described is not an exact prediction for the future but a poetically described precedent. ''The diviner's role is to recite and explain, the supplicant's role is to discern the precise canto in which *Ifa* is speaking to him, and *Ifa* may speak in veiled ways'' (Prince 1964: 9). In view of this literary and thus in a sense unfalsifiable nature of Ifa, the respect given to diviners and the continued popularity of Ifa divining among Christians and Muslims as well as pagans is not any cause for surprise.

Ifa, then, covers a whole corpus of literature consisting not only of straightforward injunctions to sacrifice, of meaningful and elaborate names and (sometimes) prose stories, but also of a body of allusive and complex poetry. This literature cannot be said to form a definitive and fixed canon. Not only does the number of pieces associated with each figure differ from diviner to diviner, but there are also regional differences in the pieces themselves as well as in the formal order of the figures. Each piece is separate and complete in itself, and may contradict other comparable pieces. The literature itself is fluid in the sense that there may be changes in the pieces, with new material merged and added by individual diviners which is then accepted as authoritative by their followers. But in spite of this lack of fixity and comprehensiveness, it remains true that the Ifa utterances form part of a conventional and vast scheme, hugely conceived, one that is known and recited by serious and highly qualified specialists but which has not yet been systematically collected in written form in anything approaching the scale of its conception.

DONALD L. PHILIPPI

First Person Voice in Ainu Epic

The device presented here—of a projective first person narration on a possibly shamanistic base—points to a linkage of the male and female singers with other "non-human entities" in what Philippi calls "a form of inter-species communication in which gods or humans speak of experiences to members of their own or other species." In saying this, he reveals a traditional way not only of knowing but of experiencing and projecting a total natural environment—as Gary Snyder describes it in his "foreword" to these songs: "The life of mountains and rivers flowed from their group experience, through speech and hands, into a fabric of artifacts and tales that was a total expression of their world, and themselves . . . [suggesting] to us with great clarity that this life support system is not just a mutual food factory, it is mysteriously beautiful" (Philippi 1979: ix). The recovery of some part of this process underlies many of the contemporary works referred to elsewhere in the present volume, among which the reader might compare the Ainu "Song of the Wolf Goddess" with Diane di Prima's experience of a related being prior to her own poem, Loba *(below, p. 441).*

The Ainu are the non-Japanese ethnic group forming the native population of the northern Japanese island of Hokkaido.

One of the most striking features of the epic songs is that they consistently use first-person narration. That is, the entire story is told in the first person singular from the point of view of the "speaker," who narrates his experiences subjectively using the pronoun "I." There is no attempt at an objective approach using third-person narration, and we encounter no impersonal Muse or Spirit of Song which intervenes and takes over the narrative. Everything from start to finish is a monologue told by a single speaker. The only exception is in a few cases where there are shifts from one speaker to another. Even here, however, the diction remains in the first person singular; only the identity of the speaker is shifted.

At the beginning of every epic song, we have no way of knowing who the speaker is. We cannot even tell whether the speaker is male or female, human or divine. During the course of the narrative, the speaker will describe the circumstances of his or her upbringing and life and will sometimes quote the words spoken by others to him or around him (or her, as the case may be). The name of the hero or heroine will thus be introduced in overheard dialogues or in two-way conversations between the speaker and another character. Since the landscape and events in each epic are viewed through the consciousness of the speaker, sometimes there are hiatuses in the narrative when the speaker loses consciousness or dies. In such cases, the epics use this formula:

rai hene ya	Was I dead?
mokor hene ya	was I asleep?

SOURCE: *Donald L. Philippi,* Songs of Gods, Songs of Humans: The Epic Tradition of the Ainu, *pages 26–28, 75–77.*

a-e-kon ramuhu	my mind
shitne kane	was clouded
tanak kane	and dazed.

The story resumes later on when the hero or heroine recovers consciousness or is restored to life.

The reason for this consistent adoption of first-person narration in all of the Ainu epic poetry is not hard to find. . . . The age-old north Asiatic practice of shamanism is an all-pervasive influence in Ainu life. The words spoken during shamanic seances assume the form of utterances of the deities themselves, borrowing the mouth of the shaman.

Ainu literature is, thus, basically a literature of self-revelation by a speaker. The process of self-revelation is gradual. No matter who the speaker may be, male or female, human or divine, the action always unfolds just as it occurs to the speaker. Not only does the speaker reveal himself by degrees to the audience; he also finds out about himself as the tale progresses. In many cases, the speaker at the beginning of a song does not even know his own name or background. His identity and his origins are revealed to him by other characters as the story moves on.

During the performance of the song, the epic reciter in a way assumes a different personality, temporarily becoming the speaker through the use of the first-person pronouns. The psychological mechanism is, one would suspect, rather similar to that of the experiences of a shaman in a trance. The person who is speaking is no longer the reciter, but the personality of the hero or heroine. We must take each revelation on its own terms, that is, as a subjective view into the inner world of a particular god or human. Since the content of an epic song is the autobiography of a particular epic personality, it is quite possible that the epic reciter might refuse, or be unable to provide elucidation about the content, just as a shaman would probably deny any knowledge of the contents of the utterances which had come through his mouth in a trance.

SONG OF WOLF GODDESS

This *kamui yukar* [mythic epic] was recorded in writing by Kubodera from the reciter Hiraga Etenoa on . . . September 6, 1932. It was sung with two burdens: *Heurur heurur* and *Uɔkar kanto*. Except for the word *kanto* (sky, heaven), both the burdens are semantically unclear.

Wolves (*horkeu*) figure prominently in Ainu mythic songs and tales. They were not regarded as being harmful predators by the Ainu. In fact, the wolves inhabiting Hokkaido in the past caught the plentiful deer for food and did not trouble the Ainu, who admired them greatly for their intelligence and skill at hunting. The Wolf God of the Upper Heavens (*rikun kanto ta horkeu kamui*) is a favorite character in epics, and sometimes the younger sister of this Wolf God is the mother of the *yukar* epic hero Poiyaunpe. She is a goddess of very beautiful appearance who wears white robes.

The wolf goddess in this song is living with her cubs in the land of the humans. She is attacked by an evil monster bear (*wen arsarush*). The cubs cry out to summon their father from the Upper Heavens. He arrives and defeats the monster bear, and the wolves go home to the Upper Heavens. . . .

I was among my cubs
on a meadow beside a brook.
This was the way
I continued to live
on and on until

One day
downstream
noises were heard.
I looked and saw
an evil monster bear,
a vile demon bear,
with his lower fangs
jutting out beyond
his upper jaw,
with his upper fangs
jutting out beyond
his lower jaw,
and with his inner gums
exposed.
The evil monster bear,
the vile demon bear
came this way.
As soon as he caught sight of me,
he glared at me
with his eyes wide open.
Then he attacked me.

After that
we fought each other,
rolling over each other
and rolling under each other
as we wrestled
on the meadow beside the brook.
We took turns
seizing each other by the teeth
and shaking each other about,
as we wrestled together
going in this direction and that.
As we continued to fight,
I bit out
small chunks of flesh
and large chunks of flesh
of the evil monster bear.

In his turn
he bit out
small chunks of my flesh
and large chunks of my flesh.
We continued
to take turns doing this.

The evil monster bear
had
ordinary heart strings[1]
six in number
and metal heart strings
six in number.
I also
had
ordinary heart strings
six in number
and metal heart strings
six in number.

We each continued
to take turns
in cutting
the other's ordinary heart strings
one by one
and the other's metal heart strings
one by one.
As we continued fighting each other,
by this time
I still had left
one heart string,
an ordinary heart string,
and one heart string,
a metal heart string
which he had been unable to get at.
The evil monster bear,
he also
still had left
one heart string,
a metal heart string,
and one heart string,
an ordinary heart string,
which I had been unable to get at.
            "Hear us,

---

[1]*Sampe-at*, cords on which the heart is suspended. The bear has six ordinary strings and six metal strings. Each one of these must be cut before he can be killed.

our father,
who must be
in the Upper Heavens,
in the high skies!
Come quickly
to rescue
our mother!
An evil monster bear,
a vile demon bear
looks as if he is
about to kill
our mother.
Our father,
come quickly
to rescue
our mother!''

The gods my children
cried out these words.

Then,
right away,
the Wolf God,
the most weighty deity,
came down
from the Upper Heavens.
In an instant
he gave a mighty kick
to the evil monster bear
the vile demon bear
and kicked him down
to the Underworld,
the dank land.

Afterward,
we went home
to the Upper Heavens
together with
our cubs.

ALBERT B. LORD

Songs and the Song

The distinction made by Lord and his predecessor, Milman Parry, is between poems "memorized," in a transcriptional writing system, and poems "remembered," in an oral or word-of-mouth tradition. The latter are never absolutely fixed as text or reference ("the oral poem even in the mouth of the same singer is ever in a state of change" [Parry 1932: 14]) and are finally inseparable from their performance (i.e., the idea here presented, that performance = composition). In focusing on surviving European oral epics, Lord and Parry put great stress on the use of traditional "tags" and "epithets" (formulas) that the epic singers reorganize and expand in relation to a set line or measure. This formulaic model has by now become a standard academic approach, "applicable to all oral poetries" (Parry and Lord 1954: 4), and often in the service of those without a particular commitment to orally based &/or alternative modes of poetry. But it's clear by now, over a wider range of oral and other-than-Western traditions, that the possibilities of improvisation and new invention in oral poetry may be much greater than supposed, and that conventional

SOURCE: Albert B. Lord, The Singer of Tales, pages 99–102.

written poetries may show an equally high degree of formularization. (For more on the question of the individual poet/singer, see Awoonor, below, p. 162.)

As long as one thought of the oral poet as a singer who carried in his head a song in more or less the exact form in which he had learned it from another singer, as long as one used for investigation ballads and comparatively short epics, the question of what an oral song is could not arise. It was, we assumed, essentially like any other poem; its text was more or less fixed. But when we look more closely at the process of oral composition and come to appreciate more fully the creative role of the individual singer in carrying forward the tradition, we must begin to query our concept of a song.

When the singer of tales, equipped with a store of formulas and themes and a technique of composition, takes his place before an audience and tells his story, he follows the plan which he has learned along with the other elements of his profession. Whereas the singer thinks of his song in terms of a flexible plan of themes, some of which are essential and some of which are not, we think of it as a given text which undergoes change from one singing to another. We are more aware of change than the singer is, because we have a concept of the fixity of a performance or of its recording on wire or tape or plastic or in writing. We think of change in content and in wording; for, to us, at some moment both wording and content have been established. To the singer the song, which cannot be changed (since to change it would, in his mind, be to tell an untrue story or to falsify history), is the essence of the story itself. His idea of stability, to which he is deeply devoted, does not include the wording, which to him has never been fixed, nor the unessential parts of the story. He builds his performance, or song in our sense, on the stable skeleton of narrative, which is the song in his sense.

When one asks a singer what songs he knows, he will begin by saying that he knows the song, for example, about Marko Kraljević when he fought with Musa, or he will identify it by its first lines. In other words, the song is the story of what someone did or what happened to some hero, but it is also the song itself expressed in verse. It is not just a story; it is not merely a tale divorced from its telling. Sulejman Makić said that he could repeat a song that he had heard only once, *provided that he heard it to the gusle.*[1] This is a most significant clue. The story in the poet-singer's mind is a story in song. Were it not for remarks like that of Makić, we might be led to think that the singer needs only "a story," which he then retells in the language of verse. But now we know that the story itself must have the particular form which it has only when it is told in verse.

Any particular song is different in the mouth of each of its singers. If we consider it in the thought of a single singer during the years in which he sings it, we find that it is different at different stages in his career. Its clearness of outline will depend upon how many times he sings it; whether it is an established part of his repertory or merely a song which he sings occasionally. The length of the song is also important, because a short

[1] A South Slavic (e.g., Serbocroatian) one-stringed instrument. [Eds.]

song will naturally tend to become more stable the more it is sung.

In some respects the larger themes and the song are alike. Their outward form and their specific content are ever changing. Yet there is a basic idea or combination of ideas that is fairly stable. We can say, then, that a song is the story about a given hero, but its expressed forms are multiple, and each of these expressed forms or tellings of the story is itself a separate song, in its own right, authentic and valid as a song unto itself. We must distinguish then two concepts of song in oral poetry. One is the general idea of the story, which we use when we speak in larger terms, for example, of the song of the wedding of Smailagić Meho, which actually includes all singings of it. The other concept of song is that of a particular performance or text, such as Avdo Mededović's song, "The Wedding of Smailagić Meho," dictated during the month of July, 1935.

Our real difficulty arises from the fact that, unlike the oral poet, we are not accustomed to thinking in terms of fluidity. We find it difficult to grasp something that is multiform. It seems to us necessary to construct an ideal text or to seek an original, and we remain dissatisfied with an ever-changing phenomenon. I believe that once we know the facts of oral composition we must cease trying to find an original of any traditional song. From one point of view each performance is an original. From another point of view it is impossible to retrace the work of generations of singers to that moment when some singer first sang a particular song.

We are occasionally fortunate enough to be present at a first singing, and we are then disappointed, because the singer has not perfected the song with much practice and by the test of repeated performance. Even after he has—and it may change much as he works it over—it must be accepted and sung by other singers in order to become a part of the tradition, and in their hands it will go through other changes, and so the process continues from generation to generation. We cannot retrace these steps in any particular song. There was an original, of course, but we must be content with the texts that we have and not endeavor to "correct" or "perfect" them in accordance with a purely arbitrary guess at what the original might have been.

Indeed, we should be fully aware that even had we this "original," let us say, of the wedding of Smailagić Meho, we would not have the original of the basic story, that is, the song of the young man who goes forth into the world to win his spurs. We would have only the application of this story to the hero Meho. Each performance is the specific song, and at the same time it is the generic song. The song we are listening to is "the song"; for each performance is more than a performance; it is a re-creation. Following this line of thinking, we might term a singer's first singing of a song as a creation of the song in his experience. Both synchronically and historically there would be numerous creations and re-creations of the song. This concept of the relationship between "songs" (performances of the same specific or generic song) is closer to the truth than the concept of an "original" and "variants." In a sense each performance is "an" original, if not "the" original.

The truth of the matter is that our concept of "the original," of "the song," simply makes no sense in oral tradition. To us it seems so basic, so logical, since we are brought up in a society in which writing has fixed the norm of a stable first creation in art, that we feel there must be an "original" for everything. The first singing in oral tradition does not coincide with this concept of the "original." We might as well be prepared to face the fact that we are in a different world of thought, the patterns of which do not always fit our cherished terms. In oral tradition the idea of an original is illogical.

It follows, then, that we cannot correctly speak of a ''variant,'' since there is no ''original'' to be varied! Yet songs are related to one another in varying degrees; not, however, in the relationship of variant to original, in spite of the recourse so often made to an erroneous concept of ''oral transmission''; for ''oral transmission,'' ''oral composition,'' ''oral creation,'' and ''oral performance'' are all one and the same thing. Our greatest error is to attempt to make ''scientifically'' rigid a phenomenon that is fluid.

But if we are pursuing a will-o'-the-wisp when we seek an original, we are deluded by a mirage when we try to construct an ideal form of any given song. If we take all the extant texts of the song of Smailagić Meho and from them extract all the common elements, we have constructed something that never existed in reality or even in the mind of any of the singers of that song. We have simply then the common elements in this restricted number of texts, nothing more, nothing less.

It seems to me highly significant that the words ''author'' and ''original'' have either no meaning at all in oral tradition or a meaning quite different from the one usually assigned to them. The anonymity of folk epic is a fiction, because the singer has a name. We have created for ourselves in regard to both these terms problems that are not of any major importance.

It should be clear from the foregoing that the author of an oral epic, that is, the text of a performance, is the performer, the singer before us. Given normal eyesight on the part of the spectator, he is not multiple, but single. The author of any of our texts, unless an editor has tampered with it, is the man who dictated, sang, chanted, or otherwise gave expression to it. A performance is unique; it is a creation, not a reproduction, and it can therefore have only one author.

Actually, only the man with writing seems to worry about this, just as only he looks for the nonexistent, illogical, and irrelevant ''original.'' Singers deny that they are the creators of the song. They learned it from other singers. We know now that *both* are right, each according to his meaning of ''song.'' To attempt to find the first singer of a song is as futile as to try to discover the first singing. And yet, just as the first singing could not be called the ''original,'' so the first man to sing a song cannot be considered its ''author,'' because of the peculiar relationship, already discussed, between his singing and all subsequent singings. From that point of view a song has no ''author'' but a multiplicity of authors, each singing being a creation, each singing having its own single ''author.'' . . .

Some Ewe Poets

A major African poet and himself a native Ewe-speaker, Awoonor's first-hand assessment of the individuality of the Ewe song-poets puts to rest the common view of the anonymous/collective nature of all tribal poetry. His own work in English, he tells us, has "attempted to incorporate the features of the Ewe dirge" and other forms of oral poetry, "borrowing liberally from [such poets as] Akpalu" in what Awoonor calls "a deliberate act of falling back upon a tradition which has been ignored in our missionary education and whose practice has been labeled paganistic by our Christian mentors" (1975: 202, 208).

The calling of the [Ewe] poet is intuitive. At times it is hereditary but only in the sense that a son may possess the talent of his father. A poet emerges, he is born, out of the traditions of songs, and he is the bearer of exceptional skill in words and has the talent to weave those words into coherent poetic statements. Among the young men's and women's drumming groups, the *heno* (poet-cantor) will be obvious. He makes up the songs, perfects them, rearranges them, organizes them, and, in turn, teaches his followers in rehearsals, or *hakpa*. His talent is self-evident, immediately recognizable in the association on which the particular drum is based and for which he creates poetry. He may have as an assistant another singer, preferably a woman, whose function is to teach this material to the women and thus provide the female choral counterpart in voice or accompaniment during the *hamekoko*. Female poets also are about, but their role is limited to exclusive women drums, which are not as common as the joint drums. Our young poet, of clear voice and an acclaimed ability to weave words, create allusions, and "speak," may grow from association to association. Some of these may center around old drums, some may be new drums created by the *heno*.

To have the ability to create song, the Ewe believes, is a gift from the gods. So in the Ewe pantheon there is a god of songs, or *hadzivodu*. He is the inspirer and the creator of songs. The poet, or *heno*, is only an instrument in the god's hands. That is why every poet who has a god of songs must pour libation and offer prayers to his god before he appears in public to perform. Singing, like all other aspects of Ewe life, is not a purely secular act. Its sacred nature lies in the power of the god to intervene and take away a poet's voice. In the phenomenon of *halo*, or the poetry of abuse, the *heno* is aware of rival forces marshaled against him. Among these forces are workers in evil medicine. But evil medicine, it is believed, cannot affect you if the gods do not approve. So the poet must be at harmony with both household and public gods.

Many traditional poets do not accept any necessity for a *hadzivodu* in their work. They achieve the spiritual rapport they need only with their household or public gods who are their protectors. Some, however, specifically acquire a *hadzivodu* and make him personal to themselves. The poet, if he means to acquire one, goes to the diviners who

SOURCE: *Kofi Awoonor,* The Breast of the Earth: A Survey of the Culture and Literature of Africa South of the Sahara, *pages 115–125.*

establish contact with the god and serve as intermediaries between him and the poet. Through divination and revelation, information is transmitted to the poet as to what kind of objects he must acquire. He acquires a brass pan, white clay modeled into human form, a selection of herbs, a fly whisk, fowls, and drinks for offering. A day is set for the "placing" of the god, a day on which he is to be "established." When the ceremony, marked by offerings of drink and food, and libation is over, the poet goes home with his god image. To this he makes offerings and pours libation at the appropriate season. There may be a few taboos to observe.

Other poets are born poets. But they are aware of the power of the muse. Their song, they may say, comes to them in their sleep and they wake up at the moment of its arrival and record it in their heads. Sometimes if it comes, by the time they wake up it has fled. Then they know they must make offerings to household gods and deities who will see to it that when the muse comes, the song stays. These are born poets, gifted with the power of words, who yet acknowledge the power of a divinity as the essence of song with which they must be in accord.

What is very striking about the Ewe oral tradition is the individuality of the poets. Even though their work has full meaning only within the all-embracing scope of the folk tradition, the individual genius and talent of the poets come into full play, contradicting the popular notion that performers are generally following rigidly laid down patterns in their art.

The dirge tradition owes its development to the work of Vinoko Akpalu, now about ninety years old. This is yet another example of a whole tradition owing its development and expansion to the work of one man. Akpalu's dirge pattern is not very rigid; yet it utilizes certain recurrent forms which reveal a structural regularity. For example, the poem opens with a statement about the mourner's condition or predicament, then moves into a general lamentation, and ends with a message, supplication, or prayer to those gone ahead into the spirit world. As with other oral poetic forms such syntactic devices as repetition of lines or whole segments, parallelism, alliteration, assonance, and pun are frequently used. The dirge also contains imagery drawn from nature, symbolism, and allusions and other regular poetic devices. But the main preoccupation of the dirge poet is himself, for the dirge is more a personal lament, full of self-pity. Here is a typical sample of Akpalu's dirges:

> Soon I would be dead and gone from amongst you.   *1*
> This branch will break off.
> The sons of men have gathered in counsel,
> debating how they will deal with Akpalu.
> Death is within my homestead.   *5*
> My mother's children, soon I shall be gone from amongst you.
> This branch will fall.
> Someone find me tears to shed.
> Vinoko says he wished he had some tears to shed;
> a mother-in-law may get back a thing, but not one's tears.   *10*
> I say I wish I had some tears to shed.
> Some people write
> to deny the blood that binds us,

> that Akpalu should be severely dealt with,
> that Agoha's ring should cease.   *15*
> The sons of men are in counsel,
> debating just how to deal with Akpalu.
> The singer's death is not from any distant place.
> Death is within my homestead.
> Children of my mother, soon I would be dead and gone   *20*
> from amongst you.
> This branch will break off.

The first line, the opening statement, does not refer to the dead person at all, but to the imminent death that stares the mourner in the face. Line 2 refers to the mourner as the branch. This image comes from the Ewe conception of the family as a tree, with the ancestors as the genealogical center, and the principal homestead the trunk, and all the members the branches. This line also indicates that the "you" of the first line refers to the members of the poet's family. This is again stressed in line 5, "Death is within my homestead." The belief is commonplace that the death that kills a man is within his very homestead. This is further explained in the proverb: "The insect that will bite you has its home in your cover cloth."

"My mother's children" in line 6 again refers to the kinsmen. All kinsmen are regarded as sharing the same blood, thus they are symbolically one's mother's children since they can all trace a common ancestry. Line 6 is a variation on line 1, just as line 7 is an approximate repetition of line 2. Line 8 connotes the overwhelming nature of his sorrow and, very obliquely, the burden of the threats being made against him by his own kinsmen. "Someone find me tears to shed" expresses the breathless inability to weep while in the grip of this sorrow. When events are overly painful, the impact is beyond tears. The emphasis here is on the treachery of the kinsmen, which is so painful as to hurt the mourner even beyond the capacity of seeking relief in tears. Line 9 is a repetition of line 8, with a variation achieved through the stress on the poet's own name, Vinoko. Line 10 reveals the power of the mother-in-law in kinship and familial relationship. The mother-in-law can make an unlimited number of demands on the man because she still retains a great amount of power over her daughter. She can ask and receive many things, but in this instance if she asks the poet to shed tears, there will be none forthcoming. This line is a repetitive variation on the lines 8 and 9, which yet forestalls line 11. The whole section from line 9 to line 11, therefore, constitutes a segmented whole. Lines 12 to 17 represent another segment; this describes the activities of his enemies. First they deny the kinship relationship between him and them and ask for stringent measures against him. (It was said that this poem was inspired by a lawsuit that developed between the poet and some of his own relatives; in the process of this suit, Akpalu was brought before the council of the elders charged with defamation and slander in an earlier song.) Lines 16 and 17 are again repetitions of lines 3 and 4. The last five lines revert to the opening lines, emphasizing the closeness of death to the poet and lamenting his imminent departure to the world beyond. The tight structure of this poem is evidenced in the use of repetition of individual lines and of segments and also in the integrity and completeness of the segments themselves in terms of ideas, sentiment, and imagery. . . .

What is significant about Akpalu's poetry is his sense of loneliness and betrayal and his deep sense of despair. When this writer spoke to him in the summer of 1970, he was alone in his little hut by the lagoon at Anyako in eastern Ghana, his eyesight failing. He was keenly aware of his place in the tradition of the dirge among the Ewe. His worry was what would happen to the style which he had spent his lifetime establishing and perfecting. But it is evident from my own studies that his dirge poetic style is well established, and hundreds of younger poets have followed Akpalu's footsteps in adding more poems and songs to this exciting type of oral poetry.

Two other poets whose work I came into contact with represent another variety of the Ewe poetic medium and, as in the case of Akpalu, significant evidence of the important role of the individual poet. These were the *halo* poets Komi Ekpe and Amega Dunyo. These two poets in their earliest works had been part of the *halo*, or poetry of abuse, tradition, long a feature of Ewe poetic tradition. *Halo* expresses itself in invective, satire, and insults. Two sections of a village or two separate villages may engage in *halo* for years.

The first poet, Komi Ekpe, now an old man, started singing when he was about twenty, just before the First World War. He has a *hadzivodu*, a personal god of songs, from whom he claims he receives poetic inspiration in his sleep. The god was his protector during fierce contests of *halo*. Before he sings or makes a public appearance, he offers his god a drink offering. Ekpe's poetic skill rests in his verbal versatility. He moves from light-hearted poetry full of exaggerated abuse and invective to heavy sorrowful and sententious poetry that borrows heavily from the dirge. This second type of poetry stresses his intense loneliness (he has buried all his children, he says). His abuse poetry is recognized for its vitriolic sharpness. He is a man of wit with a devastatingly wicked tongue. This writer was shown a respectable elder who had moved out of the village of Tsiame because of Ekpe's persistent verbal assaults on him at wakes and funerals. Ekpe has sung widely outside his own home town. His forte is sarcasm, allusion to events which are part of local history to which he makes references in order to clinch a point, and a generally effective sense of humor. Here is a sample of Ekpe's *halo* poetry as translated by this writer:

> She with the jawbone of a cow *1*
> falling upon her chest like sea egret's beak,
> Her waist flat,
> earlobes hanging, oversize intestines,
> it was you who took my affairs to Sokpe *5*
> and asked him to sing against me.
> I do not refuse;
> I am not afraid of song.
> I shall stay at home; if anyone likes,
> let him come; whatever he has, *10*
> let him say it;
> I shall listen.
> I was far up north
> when Kunye of the mad ram's face
> came and insulted me. *15*
> There is no one. I shall tell

a little tale to the slave;
let him open wide his ears and listen.
They heaped slave-insults upon Aheto's head
and he swore a lengthy oath   20
full of boasts and boasts
that he was not a slave.
Atomi came and said it.
We caught him, sold him to Zogbede.
Zogbede bought him with his own wealth   25
Your grandmother was taken from Yosu
from there she came to Tsiame.
The people of Dagbame, do you wear underclothes?
A small underpant was put upon your grandmother
and she burst into tears.   30

The poem opens with an insult directed against a particular woman member of the opposing side. Lines 1 to 4 are an accumulation of abuse. The images used—the jawbone of a cow, the sea egret's beak—underlie a specific nature of the Ewe insult as it tends to concentrate on such items as lack of good looks, ungainly gait, and ugliness in general. Lines 5 and 6 state the provocation the poet has had. He had obviously been attacked in song by another *halo* poet, Sokpe, at the instigation of the woman. Lines 7 to 12 contain expressions of boast and of patient anticipation of a verbal fight. Another opponent, Kunye, in line 14 is described as a man with the face of a mad ram. Lines 16 to 30 form an important segment of the poem in that it plows into the opponent's antecedents. *Halo* does not concentrate only on the immediate opponents—it extends its insults to the opponent's ancestors. One of the most fearsome insults centers around slavery. As pointed out above, domestic slavery was a feature of traditional Africa. It functioned as a substitute for prisons. Offenders—criminals—debtors especially, were sold into slavery or went into servitude under those to whom they owed money. A chronic indigent might be sold very far from home by his own relatives in order to pay the embarrassing debts which he incurred as a result of profligacy and reckless living. Reference to this becomes an insult to his offspring—a skeleton in the family, or clan, cupboard, as it were—engendering shame and embarrassment. This kind of insult is calculated to shut up an opponent for good. The fact remains, however, that *halo* also depends on inventiveness, and an insult may be based on sheer fiction.

The second poet, Dunyo, primarily a *halo* poet, was also impressive as a poet of the long lament. He had been an opponent of Ekpe in the *halo* during their youth. What is striking about Dunyo is the overwhelming ennui and deep sense of despair which was engendered by the death of a kinsman and a friend called Zanu in most of his work. Dunyo is now about eighty but still an active poet of the *adzima* drumming association which he founded himself. His style is that of the long lament which is highly personal, allusively clear about such wide questions as man and his destiny in the world. Here is an example of Dunyo's work:

Our adzima drums have stepped out;
who will listen to the songs of sorrow?
Who put death's rope on the ram's neck

and yet the ram refused to move?
Call the poet's supporters, call his chorus.   5
I do not know what I've done.
We went afar looking for wealth;
Ekuadzi went to the land of spirits
leaving his kinsmen behind.
Mothers of children cried into sobs.   10
The winds of the grave blow here.
My mother's child died;
Death is adamant, death is very adamant.
Shall I sing the Christian's song
about angels circling a throne   15
and the heavens opened
so my mother's child shall see the promised kingdom?
The boat has arrived on the other shore.
Who heard the songs of sorrow?
Dunyo says not nay; he agrees.   20
Go and tell the elders that
when they go to death's homeland
and see how affairs are,
let them come and inform their offspring.
I will stay till Zanu returns;   25
if it were so, I will await his return.
And so Death locked the door waiting for me,
waiting to come and uproot
what lies in life's field.
I leave the rest to the chorus.   30
I leave the rest to my songsters.

"Adzima drums" refers to Dunyo's own association. Line 2 establishes that this is a lament, a "song of sorrow." This type of announcement is also commonly heard in the dirge in which the poet-cantor calls upon his audience to listen to his song. In line 3 the poet sees himself as the sacred ram on the way to the sacrifice. Lines 3 and 4 ask a rhetorical question. When the death rope is put on the ram's neck, it cannot refuse to move. The poet is now the ram on whose neck this rope is placed. His enemies have planned his death and his ancestors concur, so he cannot refuse to go. Line 5 is a call to the community who may perhaps insulate him against the frightening loneliness of his pending fate. Lines 7, 8, and 9 are statements about the meaning of his destiny. Ekuadzi, his own kinsman, went by foot to *avlime*, the land of spirits, to seek the meaning of this life. At his death, there was great mourning, as suggested by line 10. After this brief diversion, the poem returns to the world of the living, stating the imminence of death in the line, "The winds of the grave blow here." The inexorable and destructive adamancy of death is stated in lines 12 and 13, with the usual technique of repetition being used in line 13. There is a hopelessness that expresses itself in the poet's search for an answer and in the desire to go as far as into the Christian Church for the knowledge. This segment—lines 14 to 17—shows how ready the traditional poem is to absorb imagery, ideas, and motifs from other cultures, in this case Christianity. Line 18 makes a reference to the Ewe mythology of crossing Kuto, the river that separates the world of the living from that of the dead. Line 20 is a reaffirmation of his readiness already stated in line 4. Lines 21 to 26 constitute a message to the dead, to the elders who have gone ahead to *avlime*. The message is for the elders to return to the living world to inform their offspring how affairs stand in the land of the dead. Zanu is the poet's close relation who had died and around whom most of Dunyo's songs center. Line 27, "And so Death locked the door waiting for me," expresses the idea of death as the predator, in this case, the slaver who waits inside the locked gates in life's field, ready to strike. The last two lines constitute absolute resignation, a giving up of the struggle.

From the foregoing discussions, it would be seen that oral literature covers a wide field and is diverse in subject matter, technique, and style. What seems to be an important truth is that practitioners of this traditional art possess an individuality and genius of their own, even though their art exists and has meaning within the *Gestalt* of the group. Individual poets suffer from the same, sad sense of loneliness which marks them as sensitive human beings. Their work is realizable fully only within the context of the whole group since their art has its impact within the specific genius of the language, culture, and the system of beliefs and philosophy of that group. This does not mean that types and styles of this literature do not travel farther afield than its own place of origin. Poets, praise singers, and storytellers and the materials they deal with exist in continuous development and flux. A great deal of this literature still exists, for about eighty percent of Africa is still rural. The social, political, and economic conditions may differ, but the literary or aesthetic outlook remains the same, firmly based in man's infinite ability to manipulate language at a highly complex and sophisticated level in order to communicate the primary sensations pertaining to life, history, men, gods, destiny, and death.

THREE
Meanings

JOHN FIRE/LAME DEER
The Meaning of Everyday Objects

What Lame Deer says here of the resonance and meaning of "ordinary, common things" among the Lakota (Sioux) had burst into Western consciousness as well—if not as the common practice he implies, then as a central issue of poetics from the first Romantics to the later modernists and "post"-modernists. Thus Blake, for example, in 1802 ("A Letter to Thomas Butts"), writes:

> What to others a trifle appears
> Fills me full of smiles or tears
> For double the vision my Eyes do see
> And a double vision is always with me
> With my inward Eye 'tis an old Man grey
> With my outward a Thistle across my way

and again, in "A Vision of the Last Judgment" (1810):

> When the Sun rises do you not see a round Disk of fire somewhat like a Guinea O no no I see an Innumerable company of the Heavenly host crying Holy Holy Holy is the Lord God Almighty I question not my Corporeal or Vegetative Eye any more than I would question a Window concerning a Sight I look thro it & not with it.

Something like that—but with the objects/things held onto even more strongly—turns up in William Carlos Williams's outcry in the 1920s:

> —Say it, no ideas but in things—
> nothing but the blank faces of the houses
> and cylindrical trees
> bent, forked by preconception and accident
> split, furrowed, creased, mottled, stained
> secret—into the body of the light . . .

And again, Charles Olson (see above, p. 62): "Man is estranged from that with which he is most familiar."

For more on Lame Deer specifically, see Paula Gunn Allen's essay on page 173 of this volume, and on American Indian philosophy and poetry ("reality at white heat"), see the excerpt from Paul Radin, above, page 31.

What do you see here, my friend? Just an ordinary old cooking pot, black with soot and full of dents.

It is standing on the fire on top of that old wood stove, and the water bubbles and

SOURCE: *John Fire/Lame Deer and Richard Erdoes,* Lame Deer Seeker of Visions: The Life of a Sioux Medicine Man, *pages 77—78.*

moves the lid as the white steam rises to the ceiling. Inside the pot is boiling water, chunks of meat with bone and fat, plenty of potatoes.

It doesn't seem to have a message, that old pot, and I guess you don't give it a thought. Except the soup smells good and reminds you that you are hungry. Maybe you are worried that this is dog stew. Well, don't worry. It's just beef—no fat puppy for a special ceremony. It's just an ordinary, everyday meal.

But I'm an Indian. I think about ordinary, common things like this pot. The bubbling water comes from the rain cloud. It represents the sky. The fire comes from the sun which warms us all—men, animals, trees. The meat stands for the four-legged creatures, our animal brothers, who gave of themselves so that we should live. The steam is living breath. It was water; now it goes up to the sky, becomes a cloud again. These things are sacred. Looking at that pot full of good soup, I am thinking how, in this simple manner, Wakan Tanka takes care of me. We Sioux spend a lot of time thinking about everyday things which in our mind are mixed up with the spiritual. We see in the world around us many symbols that teach us the meaning of life. We have a saying that the white man sees so little, he must see with only one eye. We see a lot that you no longer notice. You could notice if you wanted to, but you are usually too busy. We Indians live in a world of symbols and images where the spiritual and the commonplace are one. To you symbols are just words, spoken or written in a book. To us they are part of nature, part of ourselves—the earth, the sun, the wind and the rain, stones, trees, animals, even little insects like ants and grasshoppers. We try to understand them not with the head but with the heart, and we need no more than a hint to give us the meaning.

What to you seems commonplace to us appears wondrous through symbolism. This is funny, because we don't even have a word for symbolism, yet we are all wrapped up in it. You have the word, but that is all.

PAULA GUNN ALLEN

The Sacred Hoop: A Contemporary Indian Perspective on American Indian Literature

Born in Cubero, New Mexico, and affiliated with Laguna Pueblo, Paula Gunn Allen is one of the Native American poets concerned with the question of sources and survivals into the industrial/postindustrial world. The issue of traditional continuities (and discontinuities)—and the meanings derived therefrom—has been central to Third and Fourth World cultures and to others threatened by internal imperialisms and the movement toward a global monoculture.

For more on Lame Deer, frequently mentioned herein, see the excerpt and commentary immediately preceding.

Literature is a facet of a culture. Its significance can be best understood in terms of its culture, and its purpose is meaningful only when the assumptions it is based on are understood and accepted. It is not much of a problem for the person raised in the culture to see the relevance, the level of complexity, or the symbolic significance of his culture's literature. He is from birth familiar with the assumptions that underlie both his culture and its literature and art. Intelligent analysis in this circumstance becomes a matter of defining smaller assumptions peculiar to the locale, idiom, and psyche of the writer.

The study of nonwestern literature poses a problem for the western reader. He naturally tends to see alien literature in terms that are familiar to him, however irrelevant they may be to the literature he is considering. Because of this, students of American Indian literature have applied the terms "primitive," "savage," "childlike," or "heathen" to Indian literature. They have labeled its literature folklore, even though the term specifically applies only to that part of it that is the province of the general populace.

The great mythic[1] and ceremonial cycles of the American Indian peoples are neither primitive in any meaningful sense of the term, nor are they necessarily the province of the folk; much of the material on the literature is known only to educated, specialized persons who are privy to the philosophical, mystical, and literary wealth of their own tribe.

Much of the literature that was in their keeping, engraved perfectly and completely in their memories, was not known to the general run of men and women. Because of this, much of that literature has been lost as the last initiates of particular tribes and societies within the tribes died, leaving no successor.

[1]Mythic: 1. Narratives that deal with metaphysical, spiritual, and cosmic occurrences which recount the spiritual past and the "mysteries" of the tribe. 2. Sacred story. The *Word* in its cosmic, creative sense. This usage follows the literary usage rather than the common or vernacular sense of fictive or not-real narrative dealing with primitive, irrational explanations of the world. 3. Trans-rational.

SOURCE: Abraham Chapman, Literature of the American Indians, *pages 111–130.*

Most important, American Indian literature is not similar to western literature because the basic assumptions about the universe and, therefore, the basic reality experienced by tribal peoples and westerners are not the same, even at the level of "folk-lore." This difference has confused non-Indian students for centuries, because they have been unable or unwilling to grant this difference and to proceed in terms of it.

For example, the two cultures differ greatly in terms of the assumed purpose for the existence of literature. The purpose of Native American literature is never one of pure self-expression. The "private soul at any public wall" is a concept that is so alien to native thought as to constitute an absurdity. The tribes do not celebrate the individual's ability to feel emotion, for it is assumed that all people are able to do so, making expression of this basic ability arrogant, presumptuous, and gratuitous. Besides, one's emotions are one's own: to suggest that another should imitate them is an imposition on the personal integrity of others. The tribes seek, through song, ceremony, legend, sacred stories (myths), and tales to embody, articulate, and share reality, to bring the isolated private self into harmony and balance with this reality, to verbalize the sense of the majesty and reverent mystery of all things, and to actualize, in language, those truths of being and experience that give to humanity its greatest significance and dignity. The artistry of the tribes is married to the essence of language itself, for in language we seek to share our being with that of the community, and thus to share in the communal awareness of the tribe. In this art the greater self and all-that-is are blended into a harmonious whole, and in this way the concept of being that is the fundamental and sacred spring of life is given voice and being for all. The Indian does not content himself with simple preachments of this truth, but through the sacred power of utterance he seeks to shape and mold, to direct and determine the forces that surround and govern our lives and that of all things.

There is an old Keres song that says:

> I add my breath to your breath
> That our days may be long on the Earth
> That the days of our people may be long
> That we may be one person
> That we may finish our roads together
> May my father bless you with life
> May our Life Paths be fulfilled.

In this way we learn how we can view ourselves and our songs so that we may approach both rightly. Breath is life, and the intermingling of breaths is the purpose of good living. It is in essence the great principle on which all productive living must rest, for relationships between all the beings of the Universe must be fulfilled so that our life paths may also be fulfilled.

This idea is apparent in the Plains tribes' idea of a medicine wheel (Storm 1972: 4) or sacred hoop (Neihardt/Black Elk 1961: 35). The concept is one of singular unity that is dynamic and encompassing, including, as it does, all that is in its most essential aspect, that of life. In his introduction to Geronimo's autobiography, Frederick Turner III characterizes the American Indian cultures as static (Geronimo 1968: 7), a concept that is not characteristic of our own view of things; for as any American Indian knows, all of life is living—that is, dynamic and aware, partaking, as it does, in the life of the All-Spirit, and contributing, as it does, to the ongoing life of that same Great Mystery. The tribal systems are static in the sense that all movement is related to all other movement, that is, harmonious and balanced or unified; they are not static in the sense that they do not allow or accept change. Even a cursory examination of tribal systems will show that we have undergone massive changes and still retained those characteristics of outlook and experience that are the bedrock of tribal life (McNickle 1973: 12–13). So the primary assumptions we make can be seen as static only in that they acknowledge the essential harmony of all things, and in that we see all things as of equal value in the scheme of things, denying the qualities of opposition, dualism, and isolationism (separatism) that characterize non-Indian thought in the world. Civilized Christians believe that God is separate from man and does as He wishes without the creative participation of any of His creatures, while the non-Christian tribesman assumes a place in creation that is dynamic, creative, and responsive, and he allows his brothers, the rocks, the trees, the corn, and the nonhuman animals (the entire biota, in short) the same and even greater privilege. The Indian participates in destiny on all levels, including that of creation. Thus this passage from a Cheyenne tale: Maheo, the All-Spirit, created four things out of the void—the water, the light, the sky-air, and the peoples of the water.

"How beautiful their wings are in the light," Maheo said to his Power, as the birds wheeled and turned, and became living patterns against the sky.

The loon was the first to drop back to the surface of the lake. "Maheo," he said, looking around, for he knew that Maheo was all about him, "You have made us sky and light to fly in, and you have made us water to swim in. It sounds ungrateful to want something else, yet still we do. When we are tired of swimming and tired of flying, we should like a dry solid place where we could walk and rest. Give us a place to build our nests, please, Maheo."

"So be it," answered Maheo, "but to make such a place I must have your help, all of you. By myself, I have made four things. . . . Now I must have help if I am to create more, for my Power will only let me make four things by myself." [Marriott/Rachlin 1968: 39]

In this passage we see that even the All-Spirit, whose "being was a Universe," possesses limitations on his Power as well as a sense of proportion and respect for the Powers of his creatures. Contrast this with the Judeo-Christian God who makes everything and tells everything how it may and may not function if it is to gain his respect and blessing, and [whose] commandments don't allow for change or circumstance. The Indian universe is one based on dynamic self-esteem, while the Christian universe is based on a sense of sinfulness and futility. To the Indian, the ability of all creatures to share in the process of life (creation) makes us all sacred.

The Judeo-Christian God created a perfect environment for his creatures, leaving them only one means of exercising their creative capacity and their ability to make choices and thus exercise their intelligence, and that was in disobeying him and destroying the perfection he had bestowed on them. The Cheyennes' creator is somewhat wiser, for he allows them to have unmet needs which they can, working in harmony with him, meet. They can exercise their intelligence and their will in a creative, positive manner and so fulfill themselves without destroying others. Together Maheo and the water-beings create the earth, and with the aid of these beings, Maheo creates first man and first woman and the creatures and environment they will need to live good and satisfying lives on earth.

Of interest, too, is the way the loon prays: he looks around him as he addresses Maheo, for "he knew that Maheo was all about him," just as earlier, when the snow-goose asked if the water fowl could sometimes get out of the water, she addressed him in these words: ". . . I do not know where you are, but I know you must be everywhere. . . ." (ibid.: 6−7). In these words we see two things: that the creatures are respectful but not servile, and that the idea that Maheo is all around them is an active reality. As he is not thought of as superior in a hierarchical sense, he is not seen as living "up there." Here again, the Indian sense of space relationships is different from that of the West. The one sees space as essentially circular or spherical in nature, while the other views space (and thus all relationships within that space) as laddered. The circular concept requires that all "points" which make up the sphere of being be significant in their identity and function, while the linear model assumes that some "points" are more significant than others. In the one, significance is significant, and is a necessary factor of being in itself, while in the other, significance is a function of placement on an absolute scale which is fixed in time and space. In essence, what we have is a direct contradiction of Turner's notion about the Native American universe versus that of the western: it is the Indian universe that moves and breathes continuously, and the western universe that is fixed and static. The Christian attitude toward salvation is a reflection of this basic stance, for one can only be "saved" by belief in a savior who came and will never come again, and the idea that "once a saint always a saint" is an indication of the same thing.

In the Native American system, there is no idea that nature is somewhere over there while man is over here, nor that there is a great hierarchical ladder of being on which ground and trees occupy a very low rung, animals a slightly higher one, and man a very high one indeed—especially "civilized" man. All are seen to be brothers or relatives (and in tribal systems relationship is central), all are offspring of the Great Mystery, children of our mother, and necessary parts of an ordered, balanced, and living whole. This concept applies to what non-Natives think of as the supernatural as well as to the more tangible (phenomenal) aspects of the universe. Native American thought makes no such dualistic division, nor does it draw a hard-and-fast line between what is material and what is spiritual, for the two are seen to be two expressions of the same reality—as though life has twin manifestations that are mutually interchangeable and, in many instances, virtually identical aspects of a reality that is, essentially, more spirit than matter, or that more correctly, manifests its very spiritness in a tangible way. The closest analogy in western thought is the Einsteinian understanding of matter as a special state or condition of energy. Yet even this concept falls short of the Native American understanding, for Einsteinian energy is essentially stupid, while energy in the Indian view is intelligence manifesting yet another way.

To the non-Indian, man is the only intelligence in phenomenal existence (often in any form of existence). To the more abstractionist and less intellectually vain Indian, man's intelligence arises out of the very nature of being, which is, of necessity, intelligent in and of itself, as an attribute of being. Again, this idea probably stems from the Indian conception of a circular, dynamic universe: where all things are related, are of one family, then what attributes man possesses are naturally going to be attributes of all beings. Awareness of being is not seen as an abnormality peculiar to one species, but, because of the sense of relatedness (instead of isolation) the Indian feels to what exists, it is assumed to be a natural by-product of existence itself.

In English, one can divide the universe into two parts—one which is natural and one which is "supernatural." Man has no real part in either, being neither animal nor spirit. That is, the supernatural is discussed as though it were apart from people, and the natural as though people were apart from it. This necessarily forces English-speaking people into a position of alienation from the world that they live in. This isolation is entirely foreign to Native American thought. At base, every story, every song, every ceremony, tells the Indian that he is part of a living whole, and that all parts of that whole are related to one another by virtue of their participation in the whole of being. Incidentally, the American practice of forbidding Indian children to speak their own language forces them into isolation from their sense of belonging, or at best, creates a split in their perception of wholeness. This practice was specifically undertaken in the last century as a means of destroying the person's adherence to "heathenish" attitudes, values and beliefs. It was felt that a person who spoke only English would necessarily forget his own way, and that one who spoke a Native language could not be assimilated into white culture. Those who decided on this policy spoke of "civilizing" Indian people, through the agency of alienation, isolation, and "individuation." Other aspects of this centuries-long process have included de-tribalization of land holdings and living arrangements, and prohibition of religious ceremonies and observances, forcing on American Indians the very sense of isolation that plagues and destroys other Americans.

In Native American thought, God is known as the All-Spirit, and others are also spirit—more spirit than body, more spirit than intellect, more spirit than mind. The natural state of existence is whole. Thus healing chants and ceremonies emphasize restoration of wholeness, for disease is a condition of division and separation from the harmony of the whole. Beauty is wholeness. Health is wholeness. Goodness is wholeness. A witch—a person who uses the powers of the universe in a perverse or inharmonious way—is called a two-hearts: one who is not whole but split in two at the center of being. The circle of being is not physical; it is dynamic and alive. It is what lives and moves and knows, and all the life-forms we recognize—animals, plants, rocks, winds—partake of this greater life. It is acknowledgement of this that allows healing chants such as this from the [Navajo] Night Chant to heal (make the person whole again).

> Happily I recover.
> Happily my interior becomes cool.
> Happily I go forth.
> My interior feeling cool, may I walk.
> No longer sore, may I walk.
> As it used to be long ago, may I walk.
> Happily, with abundant dark clouds, may I walk.
> Happily, with abundant showers, may I walk.
> Happily, with abundant plants, may I walk.
> Happily, on a trail of pollen, may I walk.
> Happily, may I walk.

Because of the basic assumption of the wholeness or unity of the universe, our natural and necessary relationship to all life is evident; all phenomena we witness, within or "outside" ourselves are, like us, intelligent manifestations of the intelligent Universe from which they arise as do all things of earth and the cosmos beyond. Thunder and rain are specialized aspects of this universe, as is the human race. And consequently the unity of the whole is preserved and reflected in language, literature, and thought, and arbitrary divisions of the universe of being into "divine" and "worldly," "natural" and "unnatural" do not occur.

Literature takes on more meaning when considered in terms of some relevant whole (like life itself), so let us consider some of the relationships between definite Native American literary forms and the symbols usually found within them. The two forms basic to Native American literature are the Ceremony and the Myth. The Ceremony is the ritual enactment of a specialized perception of cosmic relationships, while the Myth is a prose record of that relationship. Thus, the *wiwanyag wachipi* (Sun Dance) is the ritual enactment of the relationship the Plains people see between consecration of the human spirit to *Wakan Tanka* in his manifestation as Sun or Light and Life-Bestower. Through purification, participation, sacrifice, and supplication, the participants act as instruments or transmitters of increased power and wholeness (which works itself out in terms of health and prosperity) from *Wakan Tanka*.

The formal structure of a ceremony is as holistic as the universe it purports to reflect and respond to, for the ceremony contains other forms such as incantation, song (dance), and prayer, and it is itself the central mode of literary expression, from which all allied songs and stories derive. For the Oglala, all the ceremonies are related to one another in various explicit and implicit ways, as though each was one face of a multifaceted prism. This interlocking of the basic forms has led to much confusion among non-Indian collectors and commentators, and this complexity makes all simplistic treatments of Native American literature more confusing than helpful. Indeed, it is the non-Indian tendency to separate things from one another—be they literary forms, species or persons—that causes a great deal of unnecessary difficulty and misinterpretation of Native American life and culture. It is reasonable, from an Indian point of view, that all literary forms should be interrelated, given the basic idea of the unity and relatedness of all the phenomena of life. Separation of parts into this or that is not agreeable to Native American systems, and the attempt to separate what are essentially unitary phenomena distorts them.

For example, to say that a ceremony contains songs and prayers is misleading, for prayers are one form of address and songs are another. It is more appropriate to say that songs, prayers, dances, drums, ritual movements, and dramatic address are compositional elements of a ceremony. It is equally misleading to single out the *wiwanyag wachipi* and treat it as an isolated ceremony, for it must of necessity include the *inipi* (rite of purification) and did, at its point of origin, contain the *hanblecyeyapi* (vision quest)—which was how it was learned of in the first place.[2] Actually, it might best be seen as a communal vision quest.

The purpose of a ceremony is integration: the individual is integrated, fused, with his fellows, the community of people is fused with that of the other kingdoms, and this larger communal group with the worlds beyond this one. A "raising" or expansion of individual consciousness naturally accompanies this process. The isolate, individualistic

---

[2]This is an inference I am making from the account of the appearance of White Buffalo Cow Woman to Kablaya as recounted by Black Elk in *The Sacred Pipe*, recorded and edited by Joseph Epes Brown (New York: Penguin Books, 1971), pp. 67–100.

personality is shed, and the person is restored to conscious harmony with the universe. Alongside this general purpose of realization of ceremonies, each specific ceremony has its own specific purpose. This specific purpose usually varies from tribe to tribe, and may be culture-specific—for example, the rain dances of the Southwest are peculiar to certain groups such as the Pueblos, and are not found among some other tribes, or war ceremonies which make up a large part of certain plains tribes' ceremonial life are unknown among many tribes of California (Kroeber/Heizer 1968: 28–30). But all ceremonies—whether for war or healing—create and support the sense of community which is the bedrock of tribal life. This community is not merely that of members of the tribe, but necessarily includes all orders of beings that people the tribe's universe.

It is within this context that the formal considerations of Native American literature can best be understood. The structures which embody expressed and implied relationships between men and other beings as well as the symbols which signify and articulate them are designed to accomplish this integration of the various orders of beings. It is assumed that beings other than the human participants are present at ceremonial enactments, and the ceremony is composed for their understanding participation as well as that of the human beings who are there. It is also understood that the human participants include those members of the tribe who are not physically present, for it is the community as community which enacts the ceremony, and not simply the separate persons attending it.

Thus devices such as repetition and lengthy passages of "meaningless syllables" take on meaning within the context of the dance. Repetition has an entrancing effect. Its regular recurrence creates a state of consciousness best described as "oceanic." It is hypnotic, and this exact state of consciousness is what is aimed for. The individual's attention must become diffused. The distractions of ordinary life must be put to rest, so that the larger awareness can come into full consciousness and functioning. In this way, the person becomes literally "one with the Universe," for the individual loses consciousness of mere individuality and shares the quality of consciousness that characterizes most orders of being.

The most significant and noticeable structural device is repetition, which serves to entrance and to unify—both the participants and the ceremony. In some sense, it operates analogously to a chorus in western forms, serving to reinforce the theme and refocus the attention on central concerns, while intensifying the participants' involvement with the enactment. One suits one's words and movements (if one of the dancers) to the repetitive pattern. Soon breath, heartbeat, thought, and word are one. The structure of repetition lends itself best to the purpose of integration or fusion, allowing thought and word to coalesce into one rhythmic whole that is not as jarring to the ear as rhyme but which unifies in larger units which are more consistent with the normal attention span of an adult.

Margot Astrov suggests that this characteristic device stems from two causes: one which is psychic and one which is magical:

> . . . this drive that forces man to express himself in rhythmic patterns has its ultimate source in psychic needs, for example the need of spiritual ingestion and proper organization of all the multiform perceptions and impressions rushing forever upon the individual from without and within. . . . Furthermore, repetition, verbal and otherwise, means accumulation of power. [Astrov 1962: 12]

She finds evidence that the first, or the need to organize perception, predominates in the ceremonies of tribes such as the Apaches, while the second, a "magically creative quality" is more characteristic of others, such as the Navajo. In other words, some tribes appear to stress form while others stress content, but in either case, the tribe will make its selection in terms of which emphasis is best likely to serve the purpose of fusion with the cosmic whole, which is dependent on the emphasis which is most congenial to the literary and psychic sense of the tribe.

It is important to remember when considering rhythmic aspects of native poetic forms that all ceremony is chanted, drummed, and danced. Indians will frequently refer to a piece of music as a "dance" instead of a song, because song without dance is very rare, as is song without drum or other percussive instrument. It is also important to note that the drum does not "accompany" the song, for that implies separation between instrument and voice where no separation in the performing sense is recognized. These aspects combine to form an integral whole, and accompaniment is as foreign to the ceremony, as is performance before an audience. Where the ceremony is enacted before people who are neither singing nor dancing, their participation is nevertheless assumed. For participation is a matter of attention and attunement and not of activity versus passivity.

Repetition is of two kinds, incremental and simple. In the first various modes will occur. Perhaps a stanza will be repeated in its entirety four times—once for each of the directions, or six, once for each lateral direction with above and below added, or seven, which will be related to those mentioned with the addition of the center of these. Alternatively, the repetition may be of a phrase only, as in the *Yei be chi* [Night Chant] quoted above, or of a phrase, repeated four times with one word, the ceremonial name for each of four mountains, say, or significant colors, animals, or powers, inserted in the appropriate place at each repetition, as in this Navajo mountain chant:

Seated at home behold me,
Seated amid the rainbow;
Seated at home behold me,
Here at the Holy Place!

                    Yea, seated at home behold me.

At Sisnajinni, and beyond it,

                    Yea, seated at home behold me;

The Chief of Mountains, and beyond it,

                    Yea, seated at home behold me;

In Life Unending, and beyond it,

                    Yea, seated at home behold me;

In Joy Unchanging, and beyond it,

                    Yea, seated at home behold me.

Seated at home behold me,
Seated amid the rainbow;
Seated at home behold me,
Here at the Holy Place!

                    Yea, seated at home behold me.

At Tsods*ch*l, and beyond it,

                    Yea, seated at home behold me;

The Chief of Mountains, and beyond it,

          Yea, seated at home behold me;

In Life Unending, and beyond it,

          Yea, seated at home behold me;

In Joy Unchanging, and beyond it,

          Yea, seated at home behold me.

Seated at home behold me,
Seated amid the rainbow;
Seated at home behold me,
Here at the Holy Place!

          Yea, seated at home behold me.

At Doko-oslid, and beyond it,

          Yea, seated at home behold me;

The Chief of Mountains, and beyond it,

          Yea, seated at home behold me;

In Life Unending, and beyond it,

          Yea, seated at home behold me;

In Joy Unchanging, and beyond it,

          Yea, seated at home behold me.

Seated at home behold me,
Seated amid the rainbow;
Seated at home behold me,
Here at the Holy Place!

          Yea, seated at home behold me.

At Depenitsa, and beyond it,

          Yea, seated at home behold me;

The Chief of Mountains, and beyond it,

          Yea, seated at home behold me;

In Life Unending, and beyond it,

          Yea, seated at home behold me;

In Joy Unchanging, and beyond it,

          Yea, seated at home behold me.

[Curtis 1968: 356][3]

It has been said that this device is caused by the nature of oral literature; that repetition ensures attention and remembrance, but if this is a factor at all, it is a peripheral one, for nonliterate people have memories that are more finely developed than those of literate people. The child learns early to remember complicated instructions, long stories verbatim, multitudes of details about plants, animals, kinship, and other social relationships, privileges and responsibilities, all "by heart." Since a person can't run to a bookshelf or a notebook to look up either vital or trivial information, reliance on memory becomes very important in everyday life. The highly developed memory of everyday is not likely to turn into a poorly developed one on ceremonial occasions, so the use of repetition for adequate memorization is not important.

[3]I have reproduced this part of the chant in its entirety though the Curtis version has only one verse with a note regarding the proper form.

Another reason that is given by folklorists for the widespread use of repetition in oral ceremonial literature is touched on by Ms. Astrov in her discussion of the "psychic" basis of the device:

> A child repeats a statement over and over for two reasons. First, in order to make himself familiar with something that appears to him to be threateningly unknown and thus to organize it into his system of familiar phenomena; and, second, to get something he wants badly. [Astrov 1962: 12]

It is assumed that repetition is childish on two counts: that it (rather than rational thought) familiarizes and defuses threat, and that the person, irrationally, believes that repetition of a desire verbally will ensure its gratification. Let us ignore the obvious fact that shamans, dancers, and other adult participants of the ceremony are not children, and instead concentrate on actual ceremonies to see if they contain factors which are or might appear "threatening" to the tribe or if they simply repeat wishes over and over. There is nothing in the passages quoted so far that could be construed as threatening, unless beauty, harmony, health, strength, rain, breath, life unending, or sacred mountains can be so seen. Nor is there any threatening unknown mentioned in the songs and chants she includes in her collection; there are threatening situations, such as death or great powers, but while these constitute true unknowns to many civilized people, they are familiar to the tribes. And, by her own admission, death or severe illness are approached in positive ways, as in this death song:

> From the middle
> Of the great water
> I am called by the spirits.
>   [Ibid.: 50]

"Light as the last breath of the dying," she comments, "these words flutter out and seem to mingle with the soft fumes and mists that rise from the river in the morning," which hardly seems a threatening description. She continues:

> It is as though the song, with the lightness of a bird's feather, will carry the departing soul up to where the stars are glittering and yonder where the rainbow touches the dome of the sky. [Ibid.]

Throughout her discussion of Indian songs, she does not indicate a sense that the singers feel threatened by the chants, but rather that they express a serenity and even joy in the face of what might seem frightening to a child. Nor do there appear any passages in an extensive collection that are the equivalent of "God Won't You Buy Me a Color TV," which weaken the childhood-magic theory of repetition.

The failure of folklorists to comprehend the true psychic nature of structural devices such as ceremonial repetition stems from the projection of one set of cultural assumptions onto another culture. People of western cultures, particularly those in professions noted for their "objectivity," are not going to interpret "psychic" in its extramundane sense, but rather in its more familiar psychological sense. The twin assumptions that repetition serves to quiet childish "psychic" needs and to give the participants in a ceremony the assurance that they are exerting control over external phenomena—"getting something they want badly"—are projections. The ceremonial participants do indeed believe that they can exert control over natural phenomena, but not because they have childishly repeated some syllables. Rather, they assume that all of reality is "internal" in some sense, that the dichotomy of the isolated individual versus the "out there" does not exist more than apparently, and that ceremonial observance can serve to transcend this delusion, unite people with the All-Spirit, and from a position of unity within this larger self, effect certain results such as healing one who is ill, ensuring that natural events move in their accustomed way, or bringing prosperity to the tribe.

The westerner's bias against nonordinary states of consciousness is as unthinking as the Indian's belief *in* them is said to be. The bias is created by an intellectual climate which has been carefully fostered in the west for centuries, and which is only beginning to yield to masses of data which contradict it. It is a cultural bias which has had many unfortunate side-effects, only one of which is the deep misunderstanding of tribal literatures which has for so long found an untouchable nest in the learned and popular periodicals which deal with tribal culture.

In his four-volume treatise on nonordinary reality, Carlos Castaneda has described what living in the universe as a shaman is like. Unfortunately, he does not indicate that this experience is rather commoner to ordinary people than extraordinary, that the state of consciousness created through ceremony and ritual and that detailed in mythic cycles is exactly that of the "man of knowledge." He makes the whole thing sound exotic, strange, beyond the reach of most persons; yet the great body of American Indian literature suggests a quite different conclusion. It is in the context of psychic journey that this literature can best be approached. It is only in the context of the consciousness of the universe that it can be understood.

Native American thought is essentially mystical and psychic in nature. Its distinguishing characteristic is a kind of magicalness—not the childish sort espoused by Ms. Astrov, but on the order of an enduring sense of the fluidity and malleability (or creative flux) of things. This is a reasonable attitude in its own context, derived quite logically from the central assumptions that characterize tribal thought. Things are not perceived as inert but as viable, as alive; and living things are subject to processes of growth and change as a necessary component of their aliveness. Since all that is in existence is alive, and all that is alive must grow and change, all existence can be manipulated under certain conditions and according to certain laws. These conditions and laws, called ritual or magic in the west, are known to Native Americans as "walking in a sacred manner" (Sioux), "standing in the center of the world" (Navajo), or "having a tradition" (Pomo).

Given this attitude, the symbolism incorporated in Native American ceremonial literature is not symbolic in the sense usually understood: that is, the four mountains in the "Mountain Chant" do not stand for four other mountains. They are those exact mountains perceived psychically, as it were, or mystically. Red, used by the Oglala, doesn't stand for sacred or earth, but is the quality of a being, the color of it, when perceived "in a sacred manner" or from the point of view of earth herself. That is, red is a psychic quality, not a material one, though it has a material dimension, of course. But its material aspect is not its essential one; or as Madame Blavatsky put it, the physical is not a principle, or as Lame Deer suggests, the physical aspect of existence is representative of what is real.

> The meat stands for the four-legged creatures, our animal brothers, who gave of themselves so that we should live. The steam (from the stew-pot) is living breath. It was water; now it goes up to the sky, becomes a cloud again. . . .
>
> We Sioux spend a lot of time thinking about everyday things, which in our mind are mixed up with the spiritual. We see in the world around us many symbols that teach us the meaning of life. We have a saying that the white man sees so little, he must see with only one eye. We see a lot that you no longer notice. You could notice if you wanted to, but you are usually too busy. We Indians live in a world of symbols and images where the spiritual and the commonplace are one. To you symbols are just words, spoken or written in a book. To us they are part of nature, part of ourselves, even little insects like ants and grasshoppers. We try to understand them not with the head but with the heart, and we need no more than a hint to give us the meaning.
>
> [Lame Deer/Erdoes 1972: 108–109]

Not only are the "symbols" statements of perceived reality rather than metaphorical or "poetic" statements, but the formulations which are characterized by brevity and repetition are also expressions of that perception. Life is seen as part of oneself; a hint to convey which particular part is all that is needed to convey meaning. This accounts for the "purity" and "simplicity" which apparently characterized Native American literature, but it is simple in the sense of what is known and familiar, not in the sense of childish or primitive.

In a sense, all that exists is perceived as symbolic to the Indian; it is this that has given currency to the concept of the Indian as one who is close to the earth; he is close to the earth, but not as a savage (primitive form of civilized man), or as a child (another version of the same idea), but as a person who assumes that the earth is alive in the same sense that he is alive. He sees this aliveness in nonphysical terms, in terms that are familiar to the mystic or the psychic, and this gives rise to a mystical sense of reality that is an ineradicable part of his being. . . .

This attitude is not anthropomorphism. No Indian would take his perception as the basic unit of universal consciousness (or as the only one). We believe instead that the basic unit of consciousness is the All-Spirit, the living fact of intelligence from which all other perceptions arise and derive their power.

> I live, but I will not live forever.
> Mysterious moon, you only remain,
> Powerful sun, you alone remain,
> Wonderful earth, you remain forever.
> All of us soldiers must die.[4]
>
> [Marriott 1968: 118]

[4]Crazy Dog Society song of the Kiowa People.

Nor is this attitude superstitious. It is based very solidly on experience, and it is experience which is shared to whatever degree by most of the members of the tribal group. It is experience which is verified by hundreds and thousands of years of experience, and it is a result of actual perception—sight, taste, hearing, smell—as well as more indirect social and natural phenomena. In the west, if a person points to a building and says "there is a building" and other people, looking in the direction indicated agree, then we say that the building is there. If that building can be entered, walked through, touched, and this is done by many people, we say the building is really there.

In the same way, metaphysical reality is encountered and verified by Indians. No one's experience is idiosyncratic. When the singer tells of journeying to the west and climbing under the sky, the journey is one that many have gone on in the past and will go on in the future. And every traveler will describe the same sights and sounds, and will enter and return in like fashion.

This peculiarity of psychic travel has been noticed by many westerners, who attempt to explain it in psychological terms, such as the "collective unconscious" predicated by Jung. But they are saying that our imaginations are very similar; that the unconscious life of man is the same. The experiences, sights, sounds, and so forth encountered on psychic journeys are presumed to be imaginary and hallucinatory, just as thoughts are believed to be idiosyncratic events of no real consequence. Nowhere in the literature on ceremonialism have I encountered a western writer willing to suggest that the "spiritual and the commonplace are one" (Lame Deer/Erdoes 1972: 115). Many argue that these hallucinations are good, others that they are the product of a diseased mind, but none suggests that one may *actually* be "seated amid the rainbow."

So symbols in Native American systems are not symbolic in the usual sense of the term. The words articulate reality—not "psychological" or imagined reality, not emotive reality captured metaphorically in an attempt to fuse thought and feeling, but that reality where thought and feeling are one, where objective and subjective are one, where speaker and listener are one, where sound and sense are one.

There are many kinds of Native American literature, and they can be categorized in various ways, but given the assumptions behind the creation and performance of the literature, a useful division might be along functional lines rather than along more mechanistic ones.

It might be said that the basic purpose of any culture is to maintain the ideal status quo. What creates differences among cultures, and literatures, is how that system goes about this task, and this in turn depends on (as much as maintains) basic assumptions about the nature of life and man's place in it. The ideal status quo is generally expressible in terms of "peace, prosperity, good health, and stability." Western cultures lean more and more heavily on technological and scientific methods of maintenance, while traditional cultures such as those of American Indian tribes tend toward mystical and philosophic methods. Because of this tendency, literature plays a central role in the traditional cultures which it is unable to play in technological ones. Thus, the purpose of a given "work" is of central importance to understanding its deeper significance.

The most basic division is ceremonial literature and popular literature, rather than the western "prose and poetry" distinction. Ceremonial literature includes all literature that is accompanied by ritual actions and music and which produces mythic (metaphysi-

cal) states of consciousness and/or conditions. This literature may appear to the westerner as either prose or poetry, but its distinguishing characteristic is that it is sacred,
whether to greater or lesser degree. "Sacred," like "power" and "medicine," has a
very different significance to tribespeople than to members of the "civilized" world. It
does not mean something that is of religious significance and therefore believed in with
deep emotional fervor, "venerable, consecrated or sacrosanct," as *Random House
Unabridged* has it, but rather that it is filled with an intangible but very real power or
force, for good or bad, as Lame Deer says in his discussion of symbolism:

> *Four* is the number that is most *wakan*, most sacred. Four stands for Tatuye
> Tope—the four quarters of the earth. One of its chief symbols is Umane, which
> looks like this:

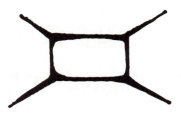

> It represents the unused earth force. By this I mean that the Great Spirit pours a
> great, unimaginable amount of force into all things—pebbles, ants, leaves,
> whirlwinds—whatever you will. . . .
>   This force is symbolized by the Umane. In the old days men used to have an
> Umane altar made of raised earth in their tipis on certain special occasions. It was
> so *wakan* you couldn't touch it or even hold your hand over it. [Ibid.: 115]

In this statement, Lame Deer isn't saying that one was forbidden to touch the altar.
He is saying that one *couldn't* touch it. The Umane doesn't represent the power, it is the
power. "Sacred," "power," and "medicine" are related terms. Having power means
being able to use this extra force without being harmed by it—it is a particular talent
possessed to greater or lesser degree, and "medicine" is a term used for the personally
owned force which one has power through; medicine is powerful in itself, but its power
can usually only be used by certain persons.
     So ceremonial literature is sacred; it has power. It frequently uses language of its
own, archaisms, "meaningless" words, or special words that are not used in everyday
conversation. It can be divided into several subcategories, some of which will appear in
some tribes but not in others, and other types which will be found throughout Native
America. Ceremonial literature includes healing songs; initiation songs; planting, har-
vesting, other agricultural songs; hunting songs; blessing songs of various kinds, such as
for new houses, journeys—new undertakings; dream-related songs; war songs; personal
power songs; food-preparation songs; purification songs; vision-seeking songs; and the
major ceremonial cycles which include origin and creation cycles, migration and

celebration of new laws, and legendary or "mythic" occurrences. Each of these serves the purpose of holding the society together; of creating harmony, restoring balance, ensuring prosperity and unity; and establishing right relationships within the social and natural world. At base they all restore the psychic unity of the people, the terms of their existence, and their sense of reality, order, and propriety. The most central of these perform this function at levels which are far more intense than others, and these are the great Ceremonies which, more than any single phenomenon, distinguish one tribe from another.

Every people has a responsibility with regard to the workings of the universe; today as yesterday, human beings play an intrinsic role in the ongoing creation. This role is largely determined by the place where the tribe lives, and will change when that people changes its location. In the Southwest, the Zuni dance Shalako every winter at the solstice so that the sun will turn in his course and move once again toward summer. Cosmic cycles such as Shalako or Wúwuchim are related to life-processes on earth and, by virtue of natural relationship, within the universe. They are aimed toward forces far bigger than the community or the individual, though each is inescapably dependent on the other, "circles within circles" as Lame Deer says, "with no beginning and no end" (ibid.: 112).

MARÍA SABINA

The Mushrooms of Language

Of the use of the psychedelic Psilocybe *mushroom in pre-Conquest Mexico, an early Spanish chronicler wrote: "They pay a sorcerer who eats them [the mushrooms] and tells what they have taught him. He does so by means of a rhythmic chant in full voice." The practice is continued today by shamans ("Wise Ones") among the Mazatec Indians of northeastern Oaxaca. But it isn't the shamans who speak directly; it's the mushrooms, called "saint children," and "little ones," and "flesh of god," that give them language. "If you ask a shaman where his imagery comes from"—Henry Munn tells us in his essay, "The Mushrooms of Language"— "he is likely to reply: I didn't say it, the mushrooms did. No mushroom speaks, only man speaks, but he who eats these mushrooms, if he is a man of language, becomes endowed with an inspired capacity to speak. The shamans who eat them . . . are the oral poets of the people, the doctors of the word, the seers and oracles, the ones possessed by the voice, 'It is not I who speak,' said Heraclitus, 'it is the logos' "* (Harner 1973: 88).

An outstanding shaman among the Mazatecs, María Sabina—born circa 1894—came to be known outside the village of Huautla de Jiménez largely through

---

SOURCE: Alvaro Estrada, María Sabina: Her Life & Chants (tr. Henry Munn), pages 46–50.

the writings and recordings of ethnomycologist R. Gordon Wasson. Unlettered and speaking only Mazatec, María Sabina conceived of the key to Language and to her own Language-centered chanting in the form of a book or as "little luminous objects that fall from heaven" to be caught, "word after word with my hands." (For more of which, see H. Munn, "Writing in the Imagination of an Oral Poet," below, page 475.)

> *. . . with words we live and grow.*

Some years, I don't know how many, after I became a widow for the first time, my sister María Ana got sick. She felt pains in her stomach; they were sharp stabs that made her double up and groan from pain. Each time I saw her she was worse. If she felt more or less well, she began her housework; but, without her being able to control herself, there came a moment when she fainted in the path.

Her fainting spells occurred more frequently later.

With great fear for her health, I contracted Curers to heal her, but I could see with anxiety that her illness got worse. One morning she didn't get up from her bed; she trembled and groaned. I felt preoccupied as never before. I called various Curers but it was useless; they couldn't cure my sister.

That afternoon, seeing my sister stretched out, I imagined her dead. My only sister. No, that couldn't be. She couldn't die. I knew that the *saint children* had the power. I had eaten them as a little girl and remembered that they didn't do harm. I knew that our people ate them to heal their sicknesses. So I made a decision; that same night I would take the holy mushrooms. I did it. To her I gave three pairs. I ate many in order for them to give me immense power. I can't lie: I must have eaten thirty pairs of the "landslide" variety.

When the *children* were working inside my body, I prayed and asked God to help me cure María Ana. Little by little I felt that I could speak with more and more facility. I went close to the sick woman. The *saint children* guided my hands to press her hips. Softly I massaged her where she said it hurt. I spoke and sang. I felt that I sang beautifully. I said what those *children* obliged me to say.

I went on pressing my sister, her stomach and her hips. Finally a lot of blood came out. Water and blood as if she were giving birth. I didn't get frightened because I knew that the *Little One Who Springs Forth* was curing her through me. Those *saint children* gave me advice and I carried it out. I attended my sister until the bleeding stopped. Afterward she left off groaning and slept. My mother sat down next to her to attend to her.

I couldn't sleep. The *little saints* continued working in my body. I remember that I had a vision: some people appeared who inspired me with respect. I knew they were the Principal Ones of whom my ancestors spoke. They were seated behind a table on which there were many written papers. I knew that they were important papers. There were a number of Principal Ones, six or eight of them. Some looked at me, others read the papers on the table, others appeared to be searching for something among the same papers. I knew that they weren't of flesh and bone. I knew that they weren't beings of water or tortilla. I knew that it was a revelation that the *saint children* were giving me. Right away I heard a voice. A voice that was sweet but authoritarian at the same time. Like the voice of a father who loves his children but raises them strictly. A wise voice that said: "These are the Principal Ones." I understood that the mushrooms were speaking to me. I felt an infinite happiness. On the Principal Ones' table a book appeared, an open book that went on growing until it was the size of a person. In its pages there were letters. It was a white book, so white it was resplendent.

One of the Principal Ones spoke to me and said: "María Sabina, this is the Book of Wisdom. It is the Book of Language. Everything that is written in it is for you. The Book is yours, take it so that you can work." I exclaimed with emotion: "That is for me. I receive it."

The Principal Ones disappeared and left me alone in front of the immense Book. I knew that it was the Book of Wisdom.

The Book was before me, I could see it but not touch it. I tried to caress it but my hands didn't touch anything. I limited myself to contemplating it and, at that moment, I began to speak. Then I realized that I was reading the Sacred Book of Language. My Book. The Book of the Principal Ones.

I had attained perfection. I was no longer a simple apprentice. For that, as a prize, as a nomination, the Book had been granted me. When one takes the *saint children*, one can see the Principal Ones. Otherwise not. And it's because the mushrooms are saints; they give wisdom. Wisdom is Language. Language is in the Book. The Book is granted by the Principal Ones. The Principal Ones appear through the great power of the *children*.

I learned the wisdom of the Book. Afterward, in my later visions, the Book no longer appeared because I already had its contents in my memory.

The vigil in which I cured my sister María Ana I conducted as the ancient Mazatecs did. I used candles of pure wax; flowers, white lilies and gladiolas (all kinds of flowers can be used as long as they have scent and color); copal and San Pedro as well.

In a brazier I burned the copal and with the smoke incensed the *saint children* that I held in my hands. Before eating them, I spoke to them. I asked them for favor. That they bless us, that they teach us the way, the truth, the cure. That they give us the power to follow the tracks of evil in order to be done with it. I said to the mushrooms: "I will take your blood. I will take your heart. Because my conscience is pure, it is clean like yours. Give me truth. May Saint Peter and Saint Paul be with me." When I felt dizzy, I blew out the candles. The darkness serves as a background for what is seen.

In that same vigil, after the Book disappeared, I had another vision: I saw the Supreme Lord of the Mountains, Chicon Nindó. I saw a man on horseback come toward my hut. I knew—the voice told me—that that being was an important person. His mount was beautiful: a white horse, white as foam. A beautiful horse.

The personage reined up his mount at the door of my hut. I could see him through the walls. I was inside the house but my eyes had the power to see through any obstacle. The personage waited for me to go out.

With decision I went out to meet him. I stood next to him.

Yes, it was Chicon Nindó, he who lives on Nindó Tocosho, he who is the Lord of the Mountains. He who has the power to enchant spirits. He who himself cures the sick.

To whom turkeys are sacrificed, to whom the Curers give cacao in order for him to cure.

I stood next to him and went closer. I saw that he didn't have a face though he wore a white sombrero. His face, yes, his face was like a shadow.

The night was black; the clouds covered the sky but Chicon Nindó was like a being covered by a halo. I became mute.

Chicon Nindó didn't say a word. All of a sudden he set his mount into motion to continue on his way. He disappeared along the path, in the direction of his dwelling place: the enormous Mountain of the Adoration, Nindó Tocosho. He lives there, while I live on Fortress Mountain, the closest one to Nindó Tocosho. That makes us neighbors. Chicon Nindó had come because in my wise Language I had called him.

I entered the house and had another vision: I saw that something fell from the sky with a great roar, like a lightning bolt. It was a luminous object that blinded. I saw that it fell through a hole in one of the walls. The fallen object turned into a kind of vegetal being, covered by a halo like Chicon Nindó. It was like a bush with flowers of many colors; in its head it had a great radiance. Its body was covered with leaves and stalks. There it stood, in the center of the hut. I looked straight at it. Its arms and legs were like branches and it was soaked with freshness and behind it appeared a red background. The vegetal being lost itself in this red background until it disappeared completely. When the vision vanished, I was sweating, sweating. My sweat wasn't warm but cool. I realized that I was crying and that my tears were crystals that tinkled when they fell on the ground. I went on crying but I whistled and clapped, sounded and danced. I danced because I knew that I was the great Clown woman and the Lord clown woman. At dawn I slept placidly. I slept, but it wasn't a deep sleep; rather I felt that I was rocking in a revery . . . as if my body were swaying in a gigantic hammock, suspended from the sky, which swung between the mountains.

I woke up when the world was already in sunlight. It was morning. I touched my body and the ground to make sure that I had returned to the world of humans. I was no longer near the Principal Ones. Seeing what surrounded me, I looked for my sister María Ana. She was asleep. I didn't want to wake her. I also saw that a part of the walls of the hut had fallen down, that another was about to fall. Now I believe that while the *saint children* worked in my body, I myself knocked over the wall with the weight of my body. I suppose that when I danced I hit against the wall and toppled it over. In the following days the people who passed asked what had happened to the house. I limited myself to telling them that the rains and winds of the last few days had weakened the mud-wattled walls and finally overthrown them.

And María Ana got better. She was healed once and for all. To this day she lives in good health with her husband and her children near Santa Cruz de Juarez.

From that cure on I had faith in the *saint children*. People realized how difficult it was to cure my sister. Many people learned of it and in a few days they came in search of me. They brought their sick. They came from places far away. I cured them with the Language of the *children*. The people came from Tenango, Rio Santiago, or San Juan Coatzospan. The sick arrived looking pale, but the mushrooms told me what the remedy was. They advised me what to do to cure them. People have continued to seek me. And since I received the Book I have become one of the Principal Ones. If they appear, I sit down with them and we drink beer or *aguardiente*. I have been among them since the time when, gathered together behind a table with important papers, they gave me wisdom, the perfect word: the Language of God.

Language makes the dying return to life. The sick recover their health when they hear the words taught by the *saint children*. There is no mortal who can teach this Language.

After I had cured my sister María Ana, I understood that I had found my path. The people knew it and came to me to cure their sick. In search of a cure came those who had been enchanted by elves, those who had lost their spirit from fright in the woods, at the river, or along the path. For some there was no remedy and they died. I cure with Language, the Language of the *saint children*. When they advise me to sacrifice chickens, they are placed on the parts where it hurts. The rest is Language.

BENJAMIN LEE WHORF
An American Indian
Model of the Universe

The ways in which the structure of a language may shape the reality of its speakers are nowhere more elegantly set down than in Whorf's studies of Hopi and other American Indian languages. "We dissect nature along lines laid down by our native language," he writes of the differences in linguistic pattern from language to language—and the consequences (= "thought worlds") arising therefrom. Or, summarizing the enterprise shared with linguists such as Edward Sapir (the so-called Sapir-Whorf hypothesis):

> Actually, thinking is most mysterious, and by far the greatest light upon it that we have is thrown by the study of language. This study shows that the forms of a person's thoughts are controlled by inexorable laws of pattern of which he is unconscious. These patterns are the unperceived intricate systematizations of his own language—shown readily enough by a candid comparison with other languages, especially those of a different linguistic family. His thinking itself is in a language—in English, in Sanskrit, in Chinese. And every language is a vast pattern-system, different from others, in which are culturally ordained the forms and categories by which the personality not only communicates, but also analyses nature, notices or neglects types of relationship and phenomena, channels his reasoning, and builds the house of his consciousness.

[Whorf 1956: 252]

Though open to real questions—how absolute is the grip of language? what other factors shape reality and action? how is any communication or translation possible across languages?—Whorf's linguistic determinism has sharpened an awareness (relating too to a possible poetics) not only of those minute particulars of language that define or condition the means of any poetry but also of the limits within which

SOURCE: *Benjamin Lee Whorf, Language, Thought, and Reality, pages 57–64.*

its poets work or which they sometimes strive to overcome. Wrote Wittgenstein, as a
philosopher of science and language often not far from a poetics: "Philosophy, as
we use the word, is a fight against the fascination which forms of expression exert
upon us" (1958: 27).

I find it gratuitous to assume that a Hopi who knows only the Hopi language and the cultural ideas of his own society has the same notions, often supposed to be intuitions, of time and space that we have, and that are generally assumed to be universal. In particular, he has no general notion or intuition of TIME as a smooth flowing continuum in which everything in the universe proceeds at an equal rate, out of a future, through a present, into a past; or, in which, to reverse the picture, the observer is being carried in the stream of duration continuously away from a past and into a future.

After long and careful study and analysis, the Hopi language is seen to contain no words, grammatical forms, constructions or expressions that refer directly to what we call "time," or to past, present, or future, or to enduring or lasting, or to motion as kinematic rather than dynamic (i.e., as a continuous translation in space and time rather than as an exhibition of dynamic effort in a certain process), or that even refer to space in such a way as to exclude that element of extension or existence that we call "time," and so by implication leave a residue that could be referred to as "time." Hence, the Hopi language contains no reference to "time," either explicit or implicit.

At the same time, the Hopi language is capable of accounting for and describing correctly, in a pragmatic or operational sense, all observable phenomena of the universe. Hence, I find it gratuitous to assume that Hopi thinking contains any such notion as the supposed intuitively felt flowing of "time," or that the intuition of a Hopi gives him this as one of its data. Just as it is possible to have any number of geometries other than the Euclidean which give an equally perfect account of space configurations, so it is possible to have descriptions of the universe, all equally valid, that do not contain our familiar contrasts of time and space. The relativity viewpoint of modern physics is one such view, conceived in mathematical terms, and the Hopi Weltanschauung is another and quite different one, nonmathematical and linguistic.

Thus, the Hopi language and culture conceals a METAPHYSICS, such as our so-called naïve view of space and time does, or as the relativity theory does; yet it is a different metaphysics from either. In order to describe the structure of the universe according to the Hopi, it is necessary to attempt—insofar as it is possible—to make explicit this metaphysics, properly describable only in the Hopi language, by means of an approximation expressed in our own language, somewhat inadequately it is true, yet by availing ourselves of such concepts as we have worked up into relative consonance with the system underlying the Hopi view of the universe.

In this Hopi view, time disappears and space is altered, so that it is no longer the homogeneous and instantaneous timeless space of our supposed intuition or of classical Newtonian mechanics. At the same time, new concepts and abstractions flow into the picture, taking up the task of describing the universe without reference to such time or space—abstractions for which our language lacks adequate terms. These abstractions, by approximations of which we attempt to reconstruct for ourselves the metaphysics of the Hopi, will undoubtedly appear to us as psychological or even mystical in character. They are ideas which we are accustomed to consider as part and parcel either of so-called animistic or vitalistic beliefs, or of those transcendental unifications of experience and intuitions of things unseen that are felt by the consciousness of the mystic, or which are given out in mystical and (or) so-called occult systems of thought. These abstractions are definitely given either explicitly in words—psychological or metaphysical terms—in the Hopi language, or, even more, are implicit in the very structure and grammar of that language, as well as being observable in Hopi culture and behavior. They are not, so far as I can consciously avoid it, projections of other systems upon the Hopi language and culture made by me in my attempt at an objective analysis. Yet, if MYSTICAL be perchance a term of abuse in the eyes of a modern Western scientist, it must be emphasized that these underlying abstractions and postulates of the Hopian metaphysics are, from a detached viewpoint, equally (or to the Hopi, more) justified pragmatically and experientially, as compared to the flowing time and static space of our own metaphysics, which are *au fond* equally mystical. The Hopi postulates equally account for all phenomena and their interrelations, and lend themselves even better to the integration of Hopi culture in all its phases.

The metaphysics underlying our own language, thinking, and modern culture (I speak not of the recent and quite different relativity metaphysics of modern science) imposes upon the universe two grand COSMIC FORMS, space and time; static three-dimensional infinite space, and kinetic one-dimensional uniformly and perpetually flowing time—two utterly separate and unconnected aspects of reality (according to this familiar way of thinking). The flowing realm of time is, in turn, the subject of a threefold division: past, present, and future.

The Hopi metaphysics also has its cosmic forms comparable to these in scale and scope. What are they? It imposes upon the universe two grand cosmic forms, which as a first approximation in terminology we may call MANIFESTED and MANIFESTING (or, UNMANIFEST) or, again, OBJECTIVE and SUBJECTIVE. The objective or manifested comprises all that is or has been accessible to the senses, the historical physical universe, in fact, with no attempt to distinguish between present and past, but excluding everything that we call future. The subjective or manifesting comprises all that we call future, BUT NOT MERELY THIS; it includes equally and indistinguishably all that we call mental—everything that appears or exists in the mind, or, as the Hopi would prefer to say, in the HEART, not only the heart of man, but the heart of animals, plants, and things, and behind and within all the forms and appearances of nature in the heart of nature, and by an implication and extension which has been felt by more than one anthropologist, yet would hardly ever be spoken of by a Hopi himself, so charged is the idea with religious and magical awesomeness, in the very heart of the Cosmos, itself.[1] The subjective realm (subjective from our viewpoint, but intensely real and quivering with life, power, and potency to the Hopi) embraces not only our FUTURE, much of which the Hopi regards as more or less predestined in essence if not in exact form, but also all mentality, intellection, and emotion, the essence and typical form of which is the striving of

---

[1] This idea is sometimes alluded to as the "spirit of the Breath" (*hikwsu*) and as the "Mighty Something" (*ʔaʔne himu*), although these terms may have lower and less cosmic though always awesome connotations.

purposeful desire, intelligent in character, toward manifestation—a manifestation which is much resisted and delayed, but in some form or other is inevitable. It is the realm of expectancy, of desire and purpose, of vitalizing life, of efficient causes, of thought thinking itself out from an inner realm (the Hopian HEART) into manifestation. It is in a dynamic state, yet not a state of motion—it is not advancing toward us out of a future, but ALREADY WITH US in vital and mental form, and its dynamism is at work in the field of eventuating or manifesting, i.e., evolving without motion from the subjective by degrees to a result which is the objective. In translating into English, the Hopi will say that these entities in process of causation "will come" or that they—the Hopi—"will come to" them, but, in their own language, there are no verbs corresponding to our "come" and "go" that mean simple and abstract motion, our purely kinematic concept. The words in this case translated "come" refer to the process of eventuating without calling it motion—they are "eventuates to here" (*pew'i*) or "eventuates from it" (*angqö*) or "arrived" (*pitu*, pl. *öki*) which refers only to the terminal manifestation, the actual arrival at a given point, not to any motion preceding it.

This realm of the subjective or of the process of manifestation, as distinguished from the objective, the result of this universal process, includes also—on its border but still pertaining to its own realm—an aspect of existence that we include in our present time. It is that which is beginning to emerge into manifestation; that is, something which is beginning to be done, like going to sleep or starting to write, but is not yet in full operation. This can be and usually is referred to by the same verb form (the EXPECTIVE form in my terminology of Hopi grammar) that refers to our future, or to wishing, wanting, intending, etc. Thus, this nearer edge of the subjective cuts across and includes a part of our present time, viz., the moment of inception, but most of our present belongs in the Hopi scheme to the objective realm and so is indistinguishable from our past. There is also a verb form, the INCEPTIVE which refers to this EDGE of emergent manifestation in the reverse way—as belonging to the objective, as the edge at which objectivity is attained; this is used to indicate beginning or starting, and in most cases there is no difference apparent in the translation from the similar use of the expective. But, at certain crucial points, significant and fundamental differences appear. The inceptive, referring to the objective and result side, and not like the expective to the subjective and causal side, implies the ending of the work of causation in the same breath that it states the beginning of manifestation. If the verb has a suffix which answers somewhat to our passive, but really means that causation impinges upon a subject to effect a certain result—i.e., "the food is being eaten," then addition of the INCEPTIVE suffix in such a way as to refer to the basic action produces a meaning of causal cessation. The basic action is in the inceptive state; hence whatever causation is behind it is ceasing; the causation explicitly referred to by the causal suffix is hence such as WE would call past time, and the verb includes this and the incepting and the decausating of the final state (a state of partial or total eatenness) in one statement. The translation is "it stops getting eaten." Without knowing the underlying Hopian metaphysics, it would be impossible to understand how the same suffix may denote starting or stopping.

If we were to approximate our metaphysical terminology more closely to Hopian terms, we should probably speak of the subjective realm as the realm of HOPE or HOPING. Every language contains terms that have come to attain cosmic scope of reference, that crystallize in themselves the basic postulates of an unformulated philosophy, in which is couched the thought of a people, a culture, a civilization, even of an era. Such are our words "reality, substance, matter, cause," and as we have seen "space, time, past, present, future." Such a term in Hopi is the word most often translated "hope"—*tunátya*—"it is in the action of hoping, it hopes, it is hoped for, it thinks or is thought of with hope," etc. Most metaphysical words in Hopi are verbs, not nouns as in European languages. The verb *tunátya* contains in its idea of hope something of our words "thought," "desire," and "cause," which sometimes must be used to translate it. The word is really a term which crystallizes the Hopi philosophy of the universe in respect to its grand dualism of objective and subjective; it is the Hopi term for SUBJECTIVE. It refers to the state of the subjective, unmanifest, vital and causal aspect of the Cosmos, and the fermenting activity toward fruition and manifestation with which it seethes—an action of HOPING; i.e., mental-causal activity, which is forever pressing upon and into the manifested realm. As anyone acquainted with Hopi society knows, the Hopi see this burgeoning activity in the growing of plants, the forming of clouds and their condensation in rain, the careful planning out of the communal activities of agriculture and architecture, and in all human hoping, wishing, striving, and taking thought; and as most especially concentrated in prayer, the constant hopeful praying of the Hopi community, assisted by their exoteric communal ceremonies and their secret, esoteric rituals in the underground kivas—prayer which conducts the pressure of the collective Hopi thought and will out of the subjective into the objective. The inceptive form of *tunátya*, which is *tunátyava*, does not mean "begins to hope," but rather "comes true, being hoped for." Why it must logically have this meaning will be clear from what has already been said. The inceptive denotes the first appearance of the objective, but the basic meaning of *tunátya* is subjective activity or force; the inceptive is then the terminus of such activity. It might then be said that *tunátya* "coming true" is the Hopi term for objective, as contrasted with subjective, the two terms being simply two different inflectional nuances of the same verbal root, as the two cosmic forms are the two aspects of one reality.

As far as space is concerned, the subjective is a mental realm, a realm of no space in the objective sense, but it seems to be symbolically related to the vertical dimension and its poles the zenith and the underground, as well as to the "heart" of things, which corresponds to our word "inner" in the metaphorical sense. Corresponding to each point in the objective world is such a vertical and vitally INNER axis which is what we call the wellspring of the future. But to the Hopi there is no temporal future; there is nothing in the subjective state corresponding to the sequences and successions conjoined with distances and changing physical configurations that we find in the objective state. From each subjective axis, which may be thought of as more or less vertical and like the growth-axis of a plant, extends the objective realm in every physical direction, though these directions are typified more especially by the horizontal plane and its four cardinal points. The objective is the great cosmic form of extension; it takes in all the strictly extensional aspects of existence, and it includes all intervals and distances, all seriations and number. Its DISTANCE includes what we call time in the sense of the temporal relation between events which have already happened. The Hopi conceive time and motion in the objective realm in a purely operational sense—a matter of the complexity and magnitude of operations connecting events—so that the element of time is not separated from whatever element of space enters into the operations. Two events in the past occurred a long "time" apart (the Hopi language has no word quite equivalent to our "time") when many periodic physical motions have occurred between them in such a way as to traverse much distance or accumulate magnitude of physical display in other ways. The Hopi metaphysics does not raise the question whether the things in a distant village exist at the same present moment as those in one's own village, for it is frankly pragmatic on this score and says that any "events" in the distant village can be compared to any events in one's own village only by an interval of magnitude that has both time and space forms in it. Events at a distance from the observer can only be known objectively when they are "past" (i.e., posited in the objective) and the more distant, the more "past" (the more worked upon from the subjective side). Hopi, with its preference for verbs, as contrasted to our own liking for nouns, perpetually turns our propositions about things into propositions about events. What happens at a distant village, if actual (objective) and not a conjecture (subjective) can be known "here" only later. If it does not happen "at this place," it does not happen "at this time"; it happens at "that" place and at "that" time. Both the "here" happening and the "there" happening are in the objective, corresponding in general to our past, but the "there" happening is the more objectively distant, meaning, from our standpoint, that it is further away in the past just as it is further away from us in space than the "here" happening.

As the objective realm displaying its characteristic attribute of extension stretches away from the observer toward that unfathomable remoteness which is both far away in space and long past in time, there comes a point where extension in detail ceases to be knowable and is lost in the vast distance, and where the subjective, creeping behind the scenes as it were, merges into the objective, so that at this inconceivable distance from the observer—from all observers—there is an all-encircling end and beginning of things where it might be said that existence, itself, swallows up the objective and the subjective. The borderland of this realm is as much subjective as objective. It is the abysm of antiquity, the time and place told about in the myths, which is known only subjectively or mentally—the Hopi realize and even express in their grammar that the things told in myths or stories do not have the same kind of reality or validity as things of the present day, the things of practical concern. As for the far distances of the sky and stars, what is known and said about them is supposititious, inferential—hence, in a way subjective—reached more through the inner vertical axis and the pole of the zenith than through the objective distances and the objective processes of vision and locomotion. So the dim past of myths is that corresponding distance on earth (rather than in the heavens) which is reached subjectively as myth through the vertical axis of reality via the pole of the nadir—hence it is placed BELOW the present surface of the earth, though this does not mean that the nadir-land of the origin myths is a hole or cavern as we should understand it. It is *Palátkwapi* "At the Red Mountains," a land like our present earth, but to which our earth bears the relation of a distant sky—and similarly the sky of our earth is penetrated by the heroes of tales, who find another earthlike realm above it.

It may now be seen how the Hopi do not need to use terms that refer to space or time as such. Such terms in our language are recast into expressions of extension, operation, and cyclic process provided they refer to the solid objective realm. They are recast into expressions of subjectivity if they refer to the subjective realm—the future, the psychic-mental, the mythical period, and the invisibly distant and conjectural generally. Thus, the Hopi language gets along perfectly without tenses for its verbs.

OGOTEMMÊLI, per MARCEL GRIAULE
The Fertilizing Word

The conversations between Ogotemmêli, an elder of the Dogon in the Western Sudan, and the ethnographer, Marcel Griaule, took place over thirty-three successive days in October 1946. During that time, according to Griaule, Ogotemmêli "laid bare the framework of a world system: ... a cosmogony as rich as that of Hesiod, poet of a dead world, and a metaphysics that has the advantage of being expressed in a thousand rites and actions in the life of a multitude of living beings" (1965: 3). That "system"—or the part of it presented to Griaule—sets up a vast web of correspondences between physical and mental objects, and a process of language in which a metaphysical/creative/fertilizing "word" is, so to speak, the germ of meaning in this world. As Griaule's daughter, Geneviève Calame-Griaule, writes of it: "Man seeks his reflection in all the mirrors of an anthropomorphic universe where each blade of grass, each little fly is the carrier of a word. The Dogon call it, word of the world, aduno sͻ:, the symbol" (Turner 1974: 159).

The god Nummo—lord of water and of speech—is one of the androgynous twins of Amma (God) and of their mother, Earth. From his mouth comes "a warm vapor which conveys, and itself constitutes, speech," and through the fibers of his fringed skirt ("full of water and words [and] placed over his mother's genitalia") language comes to earth. "Thus clothed," Griaule goes on, "the earth had a language, the first language of this world" (1965: 20). The developing relation between speech and Earth (as human body) makes a poetics and linguistics of extraordinary, even kabbalistic, power.

The conversation of the previous day had made plain the power of the human word. The voice of man can arouse God and extend divine action.

This, no doubt, was only to be expected, since God himself, acting through his son the Nummo, had three times reorganized the world by means of three successive Words, each more explicit and more widespread in its range than the one before it. There had been also the regeneration of the eight men and their rebirth as Water Spirits through the voice of the Nummo who, by speaking to himself, fertilized himself.

Where did it come from, this Word, which diffused itself along the spiral curves of the breath as it issued from the face, and what paths did it take within the human being?

It was not in the nature of Ogotemmêli to give direct answers to such questions.

"The Nummo," he said, "who is water and heat, enters the body in the water one drinks, and communicates his heat to the bile and the liver. The life-force, which is the bearer of the Word, which *is* the Word, leaves the mouth in the form of breath, or water vapour, which is water and is Word."

He repeated what he had said the day before, that the Word came from the deepest

SOURCE: *Marcel Griaule,* Conversations with Ogotemmêli, *pages 138–143.*

and most secret part of the being, namely, the liver. But he preferred to follow the original line of his thought, and not to answer questions.

He reminded them that the first Word had been pronounced in front of the genitalia of a woman; the first skirt had been plaited, that is, "spoken," by the Nummo in front of his mother.

The Word finally came from the anthill, that is, from the mouth of the seventh Nummo, which is to say from a woman's genitalia.

The second Word, contained in the craft of weaving, emerged from a mouth, which was also the primordial sex organ, in which the first childbirths took place.

"Issuing from a woman's sexual part," said Ogotemmêli, "the Word enters another sexual part, namely the ear."

In the symbolism of the body already discussed by the old man, the ear was bi-sexual: the external ear was male, and the auditory aperture female. But in fact the Word, according to its nature, can enter by two apertures in a woman—the ear or the sexual organ.

Bad words enter by the ear and pass into the throat, the liver, and finally the womb. The unpleasant smell of the female sexual parts comes from the bad words heard by the ear. The smell, apparently, completing a cycle of words.

On the other hand good words, though taken in by the ear, go directly to the sexual parts where they encircle the womb as the copper spiral encircles the sun. This Word of water provides and maintains the moisture necessary for procreation, and the Nummo, by this means, introduces a germ of water into the womb. He changes the water of the Word into a germ, and gives it the appearance of a human being but the essence of a Nummo. Or rather, the Nummo, present in the moist sexual organ, as in all water, by means of efficacious words which mingle with the woman's seed, moulds a tiny watery creature in his own image.

Thus at the very beginning of human life is to be found a divine germ which lies waiting in the womb of every fertile woman. It is shaped by the Nummo: but the living matter of which it is composed is produced by human action. All good words, whether spoken by the mouths of men or women, enter the bodies of all women, and prepare them for future mating and childbirth.

This is because the germ thus formed of water cannot grow or develop; it is in a state of expectation. It can however be destroyed by evil influences. It is motionless, and the flow of good words, even if it were unceasing, would do no more than preserve it in this condition. It awaits the dawn of its being.

Ogotemmêli did not explain why this celestial germ could not develop in accordance with its essence. If asked, he would no doubt have answered that the "why" in the destinies of the universe was no part of his philosophy and that, if women brought perfect and celestial geniuses into the world, those destinies would not be what they are.

The germ must therefore be given a fresh start. It must also be given another substance, for its celestial nature was not fitted for life on earth. It is at this point that the man intervenes.

But it seems that this intervention, though necessary, bears the mark of certain primordial events. The amorous struggle of the human couple, in which the woman resists while her partner plays the aggressive part, reproduces the primal struggle between the jackal, God's eldest son, and his mother the earth. The male of today is the jackal digging into the anthill in search of the ant, an avatar of the earth. The woman is the incestuous mother, who finally confesses herself overcome by her son's superior strength, and mates with him.

The mating of the human couple in the darkness of the inner room with its four posts is consummated on the earth-platform, placed so that the man faces west, lying on his right side, while the woman faces east. The bed, symbolizing the primal field with the seeds in it ready for germination, is full of expectant life.

At the moment of union the Nummo guides the male seed, which encircles the womb with a spiral motion, as the Word did. This seed, coming as it does from an organ made of earth, is itself a symbol of the earth. It is also earth, because it comes from the man's joints, which were indicated in the original tomb by the covenant-stones cast up there.

"The stones," said the old man, "were put at the points where the joints lie, because the joints are the chief thing in the body of a man."

"The Nummo moulded this earth with the water of the germ, which is itself the produce of the words taught by Heaven."

"The water of the woman," said Ogotemmêli, "which the Nummo formed in his own image, is mingled by him with the seed of the man, who is earth."

As usual he went on to enlarge on a difficult point by retouching his first statement.

"Just as God shaped man out of earth and water, so the Nummo shapes the seed of the man with the water of the woman."

"The Nummo," he added finally, "with the words and the woman's seed forms a being of water after his own image. The man's seed enters into this germ as a man."

He meant that the human nature in its totality, "as a man," entered the being of celestial essence that was awaiting life in the womb.

The man's seed, originating in the joints, transmitted them, providing the being, whose limbs were supple like those of the Nummo, with a man's elbows and knees. Thus the male seed, extracted from the eight joints, directs itself within the embryo to places corresponding to those it occupies in the limbs of the man, in this way giving the first indication of the human frame.

It is also, by its earthly quality, both reminder and evidence of the debt which each of us owes to the earth, because it was of earth that the first pair were made; and this debt has to be paid by the shedding of blood, in circumcision and excision and in menstruation.

But Ogotemmêli postponed discussion of this debt till later and reverted to the effects of the Word in generation.

"Words spoken by day enter the bodies of women. Any man speaking to any woman is assisting procreation. By speaking to a woman one fertilizes her, or at least by introducing into her a celestial germ, one makes it possible for her to be impregnated in the normal way."

He compared a pregnant woman to an ear of millet beginning to swell within its leafy spiral. Such an ear is said to have "found its voice," perhaps by analogy with a fertilized woman, who also has found a voice, that is, the voice of a man.

But he insisted that the word, if it was to be good, must be spoken in the daytime. "Words of the day are the only good words; a word spoken by night is ill-omened." And that was why it was forbidden to talk loudly or shout or whistle in the villages by night.

"Words fly away," he said. 'No-one knows where they go; they are lost and that means a loss of force, for all the women are asleep at night; no ear, no sexual part will catch them."

Where could they vanish away, these words without echo and with no one to hear them? Was it right to utter, over enclosing walls, in the cracks of doors, in empty streets, words addressed to nobody?

But there was something even worse than lack of hearers. In fact in any village there are always some women who are not asleep. Words spoken by night may enter their ears. They say: "Who was that?" They never know. What is said at night is the word of an unknown speaker, falling into their wombs at random. If any women were impregnated in this way, the embryo would be the fruit of chance, like that of promiscuous and irregular unions.

But words spoken by night do not fertilize women, and just as blows on the ground at night undo the work done by the smith on his anvil by day, so the word of the night, entering a woman's ear and passing through her throat and liver, coils itself round the womb in an inauspicious way, unwinding the efficacious spirals formed by the word of the day.

Bad words therefore make women temporarily unfit for procreation by destroying, or rather disturbing, the "germ of water" which is waiting to receive the contribution of the male.

But its effects were more far-reaching. Ogotemmêli had already said that the bad word did not merely occupy the womb; it passed out thence in emanations, which also played a decisive part in the act of procreation.

"Bad words smell," he said. "They affect a man's potency. They pass from the nose to the throat and liver, and from the liver to the sexual organ."

They caused a man to feel aversion. Ogotemmêli then turned to the question of feminine hygiene, which could (he said) to a considerable extent, combat the effects of bad words. He referred to the celestial granary, in the middle of which was a round jar, symbolizing the womb and the sun, which contained the covenant-stones intended to mark the joints in which the human seed originated.

On this round jar was a smaller pot serving as a lid, full of *Lannea acida* oil intended for toilet purposes and symbolizing the foetus. This vessel had on top of it an even smaller pot containing sweet-scented roots.

Starting from these objects, Ogotemmêli developed rules of hygiene, which included details of the various measures taken by woman in order to attract men. Scent (he said) acted like a good word in combating the bad smell resulting from a bad word. From this theme he reverted to the uses of dress and ornaments, which he had already discussed at length.

In conclusion he dwelt on the continuous part played by words in the pitfalls and struggles associated with procreation. The same word which predisposed the womb for mating, also exerted an attraction for men in the folds of the loin-cloth, the warp and woof of which enclosed in their threads the words of the eight ancestors.

W. E. H. STANNER
The Dreaming

"Existence is elsewhere," wrote André Breton and pointed to the reintroduction of dream into everyday life, toward "the future resolution of these two states, dream and reality, which are seemingly so contradictory, into a kind of absolute reality, a surreality" (The First Surrealist Manifesto, 1924). A projection of Surrealist yearning, the idea of a process, an "act of dreaming" by which "the mind makes contact with whatever mystery it is that connects the Dreaming [the Eternal Dream Time] and the Here and Now," is fundamental to mythic thought throughout the world and is at its most developed in the traditions surrounding what the native Australians call by names like alcheringa. *In spite of some quibbles with Stanner's terminology, the following essay remains the clearest presentation of the Aborigine "Dreaming": a concept of the coexistence of multiple times and realities, and of a "dream-work"—in Freud's phrase—that works through language and imagination to show the repercussions of what it means to be living, genuinely and significantly, in a state-of-myth.*

Further reference to the Dreaming turns up, via Géza Róheim, in Robert Duncan's "Rites of Participation" (see below, p. 332). The reader may also want to reference it to Jungian notions of synchronicity (see above, p. 147) and to Senghor's presentation of the surreal image in traditional African poetics (see above, p. 119).

I

The blackfellow's outlook on the universe and man is shaped by a remarkable conception, which Spencer and Gillen immortalized as "the dream time" or *alcheringa* of the Arunta or Aranda tribe. Some anthropologists have called it "The Eternal Dream Time." I prefer to call it what the blacks call it in English—"The Dreaming," or just "Dreaming."

A central meaning of The Dreaming *is* that of a sacred, heroic time long long ago when man and nature came to be as they are; but neither "time" nor "history" as we understand them is involved in this meaning. I have never been able to discover any aboriginal word for *time* as an abstract concept. And the sense of "history" is wholly alien here. We shall not understand The Dreaming fully except as a complex of meanings. A blackfellow may call his totem, or the place from which his spirit came, his Dreaming. He may also explain the existence of a custom, or a law of life, as causally due to The Dreaming.

A concept so impalpable and subtle naturally suffers badly by translation into our dry and abstract language. The blacks sense this difficulty. I can recall one intelligent old

SOURCE: *William A. Lessa and Evon C. Vogt (eds.), Reader in Comparative Religion, pages 159–162. (Originally published in T. A. G. Hungerford, Australian Signpost, 1956.)*

man who said to me, with a cadence almost as though he had been speaking verse:

> White man got no dreaming,
> Him go 'nother way.
> White man, him go different,
> Him got road belong himself.

In their own dialects, they use terms like *alcheringa, mipuramibirina, boaradja*—often almost untranslatable, or meaning literally something like "men of old." It is as difficult to be sure of the objective effects of the idea on their lives as of its subjective implications for them.

Although, as I have said, The Dreaming conjures up the notion of a sacred, heroic time of the indefinitely remote past, such a time is also, in a sense, still part of the present. One cannot "fix" The Dreaming *in* time: it was, and is, everywhen. We should be very wrong to try to read into it the idea of a Golden Age, or a Garden of Eden, though it was an Age of Heroes, when the ancestors did marvelous things that men can no longer do. The blacks are not at all insensitive to Mary Webb's "wistfulness that is the past," but they do not, in aversion from present or future, look back on it with yearning and nostalgia. Yet it has for them an unchallengeably sacred authority.

Clearly, The Dreaming is many things in one. Among them, a kind of narrative of things that once happened; a kind of charter of things that still happen; and a kind of *logos* or principle of order transcending everything significant for aboriginal man. If I am correct in saying so, it is much more complex philosophically than we have so far realized. I greatly hope that artists and men of letters who (it seems increasingly) find inspiration in aboriginal Australia will use all their gifts of empathy, but avoid banal projection and subjectivism, if they seek to borrow the notion.

Why the blackfellow thinks of "dreaming" as the nearest equivalent in English is a puzzle. It may be because it is by *the act* of dreaming, as reality and symbol, that the aboriginal mind makes contact—thinks it makes contact—with whatever mystery it is that connects The Dreaming and the Here-and-Now.

II

How shall one deal with so subtle a conception? One has two options: educe its subjective logic and rationale from the "elements" which the blackfellow stumblingly offers in trying to give an explanation; or relate, as best one may, to things familiar in our own intellectual history, the objective figure it traces on their social life. There are dangers in both courses.

The first is a matter, so to speak, of learning to "think black," not imposing Western categories of understanding, but seeking to conceive of things as the black-fellow himself does.

In our modern understanding, we tend to see "mind" and "body," "body" and "spirit," "spirit" and "personality," "personality" and "name" as in some sense separate, even opposed, entities though we manage to connect them up in some fashion into the unity or oneness of "person" or "individual." The blackfellow does not seem to think this way. The distinctiveness we give to "mind," "spirit," and "body," and our contrast of "body" versus "spirit" are not there, and the whole notion of "the person" is enlarged. To a blackfellow, a man's name, spirit, and shadow are "him" in a sense which to us may seem passing strange. One should not ask a blackfellow: "What is your name?" To do so embarrasses and shames him. The name is like an intimate part of the body, with which another person does not take liberties. The blacks do not mind talking about a dead person in an oblique way but, for a long time, they are extremely reluctant even to breathe his name. In the same way, to threaten a man's shadow is to threaten him. Nor may one treat lightly the physical place from which his spirit came. By extension, his totem, which is also associated with that place, and with his spirit, should not be lightly treated.

In such a context one has not succeeded in "thinking black" until one's mind can, without intellectual struggle, enfold into some kind of oneness the notions of body, spirit, ghost, shadow, name, spirit-site, and totem. To say so may seem a contradiction, or suggest a paradox, for the blackfellow can and does, on some occasions, conceptually isolate the "elements" of the "unity" most distinctly. But his abstractions do not put him at war with himself. The separable elements I have mentioned are all present in the metaphysical heart of the idea of "person," but the overruling mood is one of belief, not of inquiry or dissent. So long as the belief in The Dreaming lasts, there can be no "momentary flash of Athenian questioning" to grow into a great movement of skeptical unbelief which destroys the given unities.

There are many other such "onenesses" which I believe I could substantiate. A blackfellow may "see" as "a unity" two persons, such as two siblings or a grandparent and grandchild; or a living man and something inanimate, as when he tells you that, say, the woolly-butt tree, his totem, is his wife's brother. (This is not quite as strange as it may seem. Even modern psychologists tend to include part of "environment" in a "definition" of "person" or "personality.") There is also some kind of unity between waking-life and dream-life: the means by which, in aboriginal understanding, a man fathers a child, is not by sexual intercourse, but by the act of dreaming about a spirit-child. His own spirit, during a dream, "finds" a child and directs it to his wife, who then conceives. Physical congress between a man and a woman is contingent, not a necessary prerequisite. Through the medium of dream-contact with a spirit an artist is inspired to produce a new song. It is by dreaming that a man divines the intention of someone to kill him by sorcery, or of relatives to visit him. And, as I have suggested, it is by the act of dreaming, in some way difficult for a European to grasp because of the force of our analytic abstractions, that a blackfellow conceives himself to make touch with whatever it is that is continuous between The Dreaming and the Here-and-Now.

The truth of it seems to be that man, society, and nature and past, present, and future are at one together within a unitary system of such a kind that its ontology cannot illumine minds too much under the influence of humanism, rationalism, and science. One cannot easily, in the mobility of modern life and thought, grasp the vast intuitions of stability and permanence, and of life and man, at the heart of aboriginal ontology.

It is fatally easy for Europeans, encountering such things for the first time, to go on to suppose that "mysticism" of this kind rules *all* aboriginal thought. It is not so. "Logical" thought and "rational" conduct are about as widely present in aboriginal life as they are on the simpler levels of European life. Once one understands three things—

the primary intuitions which the blackfellow has formed about the nature of the universe and man, those things in both which he thinks interesting and significant, and the conceptual system from within which he reasons about them—then the suppositions about prelogicality, illogicality, and nonrationality can be seen to be merely absurd. And if one wishes to see a really brilliant demonstration of deductive thought, one has only to see a blackfellow tracking a wounded kangaroo, and persuade him to say why he interprets given signs in a certain way.

The second means of dealing with the notion of The Dreaming is, as I said, to try to relate it to things familiar in our own intellectual history. From this viewpoint, it is a cosmogony, an account of the begetting of the universe, a story about creation. It is also a cosmology, an account or theory of how what was created became an orderly system. To be more precise, how the universe became a moral system.

If one analyzes the hundreds of tales about The Dreaming, one can see within them three elements. The first concerns the great *marvels*—how all the fire and water in the world were stolen and recaptured; how men made a mistake over sorcery and now have to die from it; how the hills, rivers, and water holes were made; how the sun, moon, and stars were set upon their courses; and many other dramas of this kind. The second element tells how certain things were *instituted* for the first time—how animals and men diverged from a joint stock that was neither one nor the other; how the black-nosed kangaroo got his black nose and the porcupine his quills; how such social divisions as tribes, clans, and language groups were set up; how spirit-children were first placed in the water holes, the winds, and the leaves of trees. A third element, if I am not mistaken, allows one to suppose that many of the main institutions of present-day life were *already ruling* in The Dreaming, e.g., marriage, exogamy, sister-exchange, and initiation, as well as many of the well-known breaches of custom. The men of The Dreaming committed adultery, betrayed and killed each other, were greedy, stole, and committed the very wrongs committed by those now alive.

Now, if one disregards the imagery in which the verbal literature of The Dreaming is cast, one may perhaps come to three conclusions.

The tales are a kind of commentary, or statement, on what is thought to be permanent and ordained at the very basis of the world and life. They are a way of stating the principle which animates things. I would call them a poetic key to Reality. The aborigine does not ask himself the philosophical types of questions: What is "real"? How many "kinds" of "reality" are there? What are the "properties" of "reality"? How are the properties "interconnected"? This is the idiom of Western intellectual discourse and the fruit of a certain social history. His tales are, however, a kind of answer to such questions so far as they have been asked at all. They may not be a "definition," but they are a "key" to reality, a key to the singleness and the plurality of things set up once-for-all when, in The Dreaming, the universe became man's universe. The active philosophy of aboriginal life transforms this "key," which is expressed in the idiom of poetry, drama, and symbolism, into a principle that The Dreaming determines not only what life *is* but also *what it can be*. Life, so to speak, is a one-possibility thing, and what this is, is the "meaning" of The Dreaming.

The tales are also a collation of *what is validly known* about such ordained permanencies. The blacks cite The Dreaming as a charter of absolute validity in answer to all questions of *why* and *how*. In this sense, the tales can be regarded as being, perhaps not a definition, but a "key" of Truth.

They also state, by their constant recitation of what was done rightly and wrongly in The Dreaming, the ways in which good men should, and bad men will, act now. In this sense, they are a "key" or guide to the norms of conduct, and a prediction of how men will err.

One may thus say that, after a fashion—a cryptic, symbolic, and poetic fashion— the tales are "a philosophy" in the garb of a verbal literature. The European has a philosophic literature which expresses a largely deductive understanding of reality, truth, goodness, and beauty. The blackfellow has a mythology, a ritual, and an art which express an intuitive, visionary, and poetic understanding of the same ultimates. In following out The Dreaming, the blackfellow "lives" this philosophy. It is an implicit philosophy, but nevertheless a real one. Whereas we hold (and may live) a philosophy of abstract propositions, attained by someone standing professionally outside "Life" and treating it as an object of contemplation and inquiry. The blackfellow holds his philosophy in mythology, attained as the social product of an indefinitely ancient past, and proceeds to live it out "in" life, in part through a ritual and an expressive art, and in part through nonsacred social customs.

European minds are made uneasy by the fact that the stories are, quite plainly, preposterous; are often a mass of internal contradictions; are encrusted by superstitious fancies about magic, sorcery, hobgoblins, and superhuman heroes; and lack the kind of theme and structure—in other words, the "story" element—for which we look. Many of us cannot help feeling that such things can only be the products of absurdly ignorant credulity and a lower order of mentality. This is to fall victim to a facile fallacy. Our own intellectual history is not an absolute standard by which to judge others. The worst imperialisms are those of preconception.

Custom is the reality, beliefs but the shadows which custom makes on the wall. Since the tales, in any case, are not really "explanatory" in purpose or function, they naturally lack logic, system, and completeness. It is simply pointless to look for such things within them. But we are not entitled to suppose that, because the tales are fantastical, the social life producing them is itself fantastical. The shape of reality is always distorted in the shadows it throws. One finds much logic, system, and rationality in the blacks' actual scheme of life.

These tales are neither simply illustrative nor simply explanatory; they are fanciful and poetic in content because they are based on visionary and intuitive insights into mysteries; and, if we are ever to understand them, we must always take them in their complex context. If, then, they make more sense to the poet, the artist, and the philosopher than to the clinicians of human life, let us reflect on the withering effect on sensibility of our pervasive rationalism, rather than depreciate the gifts which produced the aboriginal imaginings. And in no case should we expect the tales, *prima facie*, to be even interesting if studied out of context. Aboriginal mythology is quite unlike the Scandinavian, Indian, or Polynesian mythologies. . . .

CARL G. JUNG
On the Psychology
of the Trickster Figure

*A near-universal figure, Trickster appears both as human and animal—Raven,
Coyote, Rabbit, Jaguar, Spider, Fox, and so on: as the creator of the world and the
source of its confusion. In his prefatory note to his gathering and translation of the
Winnebago "trickster cycle," for which Jung's essay serves as commentary, Radin
writes:*

> Few myths have so wide a distribution as the one known by the name of *The
> Trickster*. . . . Among the North American Indians, Trickster is at one and the same time
> creator and destroyer, giver and negator, he who dupes the others and who is always
> duped himself. He wills nothing consciously. At all times he is constrained to behave as
> he does from impulses over which he has no control. He knows neither good nor evil
> yet he is responsible for both. He possesses no values, moral or social, is at the mercy of
> his passions and appetites, yet through his actions all values come into being. . . . As he
> is represented in the [Winnebago] version of the Trickster myth . . . he is primarily an
> inchoate being of undetermined proportions, a figure foreshadowing the type of man.
> In this version he possesses intestines wrapped around his body, and an equally long
> penis, likewise wrapped around his body with his scrotum on top of it.

The survival of Trickster in various forms and of his, or even her, *revival in our own
time, is a poetic event of major importance (see below, pp. 425 and 434). The
connection to Jung's own "archetypes" and to contemporary explorations of what
the neo-Jungian, James Hillman, presents to us as an "imaginal"—but vitally
"real"—underworld, may also be noted. Writes Hillman: "The persons of the
imagination are real" (1975: 17).*

It is no light task for me to write about the figure of the trickster in American-Indian
mythology within the confined space of a commentary. When I first came across Adolf
Bandelier's classic on this subject, *The Delight Makers* (1890), many years ago, I was
struck by the European analogy of the carnival in the mediaeval Church, with its reversal
of the hierarchic order, which is still continued in the carnivals held by student societies
today. Something of this contradictoriness also inheres in the mediaeval description of
the devil as "simia dei" (the ape of God), and in his characterization in folklore as the
"simpleton" who is "fooled" or "cheated." A curious combination of typical trickster
motifs can be found in the alchemical figure of Mercurius; for instance, his fondness for
sly jokes and malicious pranks, his powers as a shape-shifter, his dual nature, half
animal, half divine, his exposure to all kinds of tortures, and—last but not least—his
approximation to the figure of a saviour. These qualities make Mercurius seem like a
daemonic being resurrected from primitive times, older even than the Greek Hermes.

SOURCE: Paul Radin, The Trickster, *pp. 195−211.*

His rogueries relate him in some measure to various figures met with in folklore and universally known in fairy tales: Tom Thumb, Stupid Hans, or the buffoon-like Hanswurst, who is an altogether negative hero and yet manages to achieve through his stupidity what others fail to accomplish with their best efforts. In Grimm's fairy tale the "Spirit Mercurius" lets himself be outwitted by a peasant lad, and then has to buy his freedom with the precious gift of healing.

Since all mythical figures correspond to inner psychic experiences and originally sprang from them, it is not surprising to find certain phenomena in the field of parapsychology which remind us of the trickster. These are the phenomena connected with poltergeists, and they occur at all times and places in the ambience of pre-adolescent children. The malicious tricks played by the poltergeist are as well known as the low level of his intelligence and the fatuity of his "communications." Ability to change his shape seems also to be one of his characteristics, as there are not a few reports of his appearance in animal form. Since he has on occasion described himself as a soul in hell, the motif of subjective suffering would seem not to be lacking either. His universality is co-extensive, so to speak, with that of shamanism, to which, as we know, the whole phenomenology of spiritualism belongs. There is something of the trickster in the character of the shaman and medicine-man, for he, too, often plays malicious jokes on people, only to fall victim in his turn to the vengeance of those whom he has injured. For this reason his profession sometimes puts him in peril of his life. Besides that, the shamanastic techniques in themselves often cause the medicine-man a good deal of discomfort, if not actual pain. At all events the "making of a medicine-man" involves, in many parts of the world, so much agony of body and soul that permanent psychic injuries may result. His "approximation to the saviour" is an obvious consequence of this, in confirmation of the mythological truth that the wounded wounder is the agent of healing, and that the sufferer takes away suffering.

These mythological features extend even to the highest regions of man's spiritual development. If we consider, for example, the daemonic features exhibited by Yahweh in the Old Testament, we shall find in them not a few reminders of the unpredictable behaviour of the trickster, of his pointless orgies of destruction and his self-appointed sufferings, together with the same gradual development into a saviour and his simultaneous humanization. It is just this transformation of the meaningless into the meaningful that reveals the trickster's compensatory relation to the "saint," which in the early Middle Ages led to some strange ecclesiastical customs based on memories of the ancient saturnalia. Mostly they were celebrated on the days immediately following the birth of Christ—that is, in the New Year—with singing and dancing. The dances were the originally harmless *tripudia* of the priests, the lower clergy, children, and subdeacons, and they took place in the church. An *episcopus puerorum* (children's bishop) was elected and dressed in pontifical robes. Amid uproarious rejoicings he paid an official visit to the palace of the archbishop and distributed the episcopal blessing from one of the windows. The same thing happened at the *tripudium hypodiaconorum*, and at the dances for other priestly grades. By the end of the twelfth century the subdeacons' dance had already degenerated into a *festum stultorum* (fools' feast). A report from the year 1198 says that at the Feast of Circumcision in Notre-Dame, Paris, "so many abominations and shameful deeds" were committed that the holy place was desecrated "not only by smutty jokes, but even by the shedding of blood." In vain did Pope

Innocent III inveigh against the "jests and madness that make the clergy a mockery," and the "shameless frenzy of their playacting." Nearly three hundred years later (12th March, 1444) a letter from the Theological Faculty of Paris to all the French bishops was still fulminating against these festivals, at which "even the priests and clerics elected an archbishop or a bishop or pope, and named him the Fools' Pope" (*fatuorum papam*). "In the very midst of divine service masqueraders with grotesque faces, disguised as women, lions and mummers, performed their dances, sang indecent songs in the choir, ate their greasy food from a corner of the altar near the priest celebrating mass, got out their games of dice, burned a stinking incense made of old shoe leather, and ran and hopped about all over the church."[1]

It is not surprising that this veritable witches' sabbath was uncommonly popular, and that it required considerable time and effort to free the Church from this pagan heritage.[2]

In certain localities even the priests seem to have adhered to the "libertas decembrica," as the Fools' Holiday was called, in spite (or perhaps because?) of the fact that the older level of consciousness could let itself rip on this happy occasion with all the wildness, wantonness, and irresponsibility of paganism.[3] These ceremonies, which still reveal the spirit of the trickster in his original form, seem to have died out by the beginning of the sixteenth century. At any rate, the various conciliar decrees issued from 1581 to 1585 forbade only the *festum puerorum* and the election of an *episcopus puerorum*.

Finally, we must also mention in this connection the *festum asinarium*, which, so far as I know, was celebrated mainly in France. Although considered a harmless festival in memory of Mary's flight into Egypt, it was celebrated in a somewhat curious manner which might easily have given rise to misunderstandings. In Beauvais the ass procession went right into the church. At the conclusion of each part (Introitus, Kyrie, Gloria, etc.) of the high mass that followed, the whole congregation *brayed*, that is, they all went "Y-a" like a donkey ("hac modulatione hinham concludebantur"). A codex dating apparently from the eleventh century says: "At the end of the mass, instead of the words 'Ite missa est,' the priest shall bray three times (*ter hinhamabit*), and instead of the words 'Deo gratias,' the congregation shall answer 'Y-a' (*hinham*) three times."

Du Cange cites a hymn from this festival:

> Orientis partibus
> Adventavit Asinus
> Pulcher et fortissimus
> Sarcinis aptissimus.

[1]Du Cange, *Gloss. Med. et Inf. Lat.*, 1733, s.v. Kalendae, p. 1666. Here there is a note to the effect that the French title "sou-diacres" means literally "saturi diaconi" or "diacres saouls" (drunken deacons).

[2]These customs seem to be directly modeled on the pagan feast known as "Cervula" or "Cervulus." It took place in the kalends of January and was a kind of New Year's festival, at which people exchanged "strenae" (étrennes, gifts), dressed up as animals or old women, and danced through the streets singing, to the applause of the populace. According to Du Cange (ibid, s.v. cervulus), sacrilegious songs were sung. This happened even in the immediate vicinity of St. Peter's in Rome.

[3]Part of the *festum fatuorum* in many places was the still unexplained ball game played by the priests and captained by the bishop or archbishop, "ut etiam sese ad lusum pilae demittent" (that they also may indulge in the game of pelota). *Pila* or *pelota* is the ball which the players throw to one another. See Du Cange, ibid., s.v. Kalendae et pelota.

Each verse was followed by the French refrain:

> Hez, Sire Asnes, car chantez
> Belle bouche rechignez
> Vous aurez due foin assez
> et de l'avoine à plantez.

The hymn had nine verses, the last of which was:

> Amen, dicas, Asine (*hic genuflectebatur*)
> Jam satur de gramine
> Amem, amen, itera
> Aspernare vetera.

Du Cange says that the more ridiculous this rite seemed, the greater the enthusiasm with which it was celebrated. In other places the ass was decked with a golden canopy whose corners were held "by distinguished canons"; the others present had to "don suitably festive garments, as at Christmas." Since there were certain tendencies to bring the ass into symbolic relationship with Christ, and since, from ancient times, the god of the Jews was vulgarly conceived to be an ass—a prejudice which extended to Christ himself, as is shown by the mock crucifixion scribbled on the wall of the Imperial Cadet School on the Palatine—the danger of theriomorphism lay uncomfortably close. Even the bishops could do nothing to stamp out this custom, until finally it had to be suppressed by the "auctoritas supremi Senatus." The suspicion of blasphemy becomes quite open in Nietzsche's "Ass Festival," which is a deliberately blasphemous parody of the mass. (*Thus Spake Zarathustra*, Part IV, ch. LXXVIII.)

These mediaeval customs demonstrate the role of the trickster to perfection, and, when they vanished from the precincts of the church, they appeared again on the profane level of Italian theatricals, as those comic types who, often adorned with enormous ithyphallic emblems, entertained the far from prudish public with ribaldries in true Rabelaisian style. Callot's engravings preserved these classical figures for posterity— the Pulcinellas, Cucorognas, Chico Sgarras, and the like.[4]

In picaresque tales, in carnivals and revels, in sacred and magical rites, in man's religious fears and exaltations, this phantom of the trickster haunts the mythology of all ages, sometimes in quite unmistakable form, sometimes in strangely modulated guise.[5] He is obviously a "psychologem," an archetypal psychic structure of extreme antiquity. In his clearest manifestations he is a faithful copy of an absolutely undifferentiated human consciousness, corresponding to a psyche that has hardly left the animal level. That this is how the trickster figure originated can hardly be contested if we look at it from the causal and historical angle. In psychology as in biology we cannot afford to overlook or underestimate this question of origins, although the answer usually tells us

[4]I am thinking here of the series called "Balli di Sfessania." The name is probably a reference to the Etrurian town of Fescennia, which was famous for its lewd songs. Hence "Fescennina licentia" in Horace, Fescinninus being the equivalent of φαλλικός [phallikos].

[5]Cf. the article "Daily Paper Pantheon" by A. McGlashen in *The Lancet*, 1953, p. 238, pointing out that the figures in comic strips have remarkable archetypal analogies.

nothing about the functional meaning. For this reason biology should never forget the question of purpose, for only by answering that can we get at the meaning of a phenomenon. Even in pathology, where we are concerned with lesions which have no meaning in themselves, the exclusively causal approach proves to be inadequate, since there are a number of pathological phenomena which only give up their meaning when we inquire into their purpose. And where we are concerned with the normal phenomena of life, this question of purpose takes undisputed precedence.

When, therefore, a primitive or barbarous consciousness forms a picture of itself on a much earlier level of development and continues to do so for hundreds or even thousands of years, undeterred by the contamination of its archaic qualities with differentiated, highly developed mental products, then the causal explanation is that the older the archaic qualities are, the more conservative and pertinacious is their behaviour. One simply cannot shake off the memory image of things as they were, and drags it along like a senseless appendage.

This explanation, which is facile enough to satisfy the rationalistic requirements of our age, would certainly not meet with the approval of the Winnebagos, the nearest possessors of the trickster cycle. For them the myth is not in any sense a remnant—it is far too amusing for that, and an object of undivided enjoyment. For them it still "functions," provided that they have not been spoiled by civilization. For them there is no earthly reason to theorize about the meaning and purpose of myths, just as the Christmas tree seems no problem at all to the naïve European. For the thoughtful observer, however, both trickster and Christmas tree afford reason enough for reflection. Naturally it depends very much on the mentality of the observer what he thinks about these things. Considering the crude primitivity of the trickster cycle, it would not be surprising if one saw in this myth simply the reflection of an earlier, rudimentary stage of consciousness, which is what the trickster obviously seems to be.[6]

The only question that would need answering is whether such personified reflections exist at all in empirical psychology. As a matter of fact they do, and these experiences of split or double personality actually form the core of the earliest psychopathological investigations. The peculiar thing about these dissociations is that the split-off personality is not just a random one, but stands in a complementary or compensatory relationship to the ego personality. It is a personification of traits of character which are sometimes worse and sometimes better than those the ego personality possesses. A collective personification like the trickster is the product of a totality of individuals and is welcomed by the individual as something known to him, which would not be the case if it were just an individual outgrowth.

Now if the myth were nothing but an historical remnant one would have to ask why it has not long since vanished into the great rubbish heap of the past, and why it continues to make its influence felt on the highest level of civilization, even where, on account of his stupidity and grotesque scurrility, the trickster no longer plays the role of a "delight-maker." In many cultures his figure seems like an old river-bed in which the water still flows. One can see this best of all from the fact that the trickster motif does not crop up

---

[6]Earlier stages of consciousness seem to leave perceptible traces behind them. For instance, the chakras of the Tantric system correspond by and large to the regions where consciousness was earlier localized, *anahata* corresponding to the breast region, *manipura* to the abdominal region, *svadhistana* to the bladder region, and *visuddha* to the larynx and the speech consciousness of modern man. Cf. Arthur Avalon, *The Serpent Power*.

only in its original form but appears just as naïvely and authentically in the unsuspecting modern man—whenever, in fact, he feels himself at the mercy of annoying "accidents" which thwart his will and his actions with apparently malicious intent. He then speaks of "hoodoos" and "jinxes" or of the "mischieviousness of the object." Here the trickster is represented by countertendencies in the unconscious, and in certain cases by a sort of second personality, of a puerile and inferior character, not unlike the personalities who announce themselves at spiritualistic séances and cause all those ineffably childish phenomena so typical of poltergeists. I have, I think, found a suitable designation for this character component when I called it the *shadow*.[7] On the civilized level it is treated as a personal "gaffe," "slip," "faux pas," etc., which are then chalked up as defects of the conscious personality. We are no longer aware that in carnival customs and the like there are remnants of a collective shadow figure which prove that the personal shadow is in part descended from a numinous collective figure. This collective figure gradually breaks up under the impact of civilization, leaving traces in folklore which are difficult to recognize. But the main part of him gets personalized and is made an object of personal responsibility.

Radin's trickster cycle (Radin 1956) preserves the shadow in its pristine mytholog-ical form, and thus points back to a very much earlier stage of consciousness which existed before the birth of the myth, when the Indian was still groping about in a similar mental darkness. Only when his consciousness reached a higher level could he detach the earlier state from himself and objectify it, that is, say anything about it. So long as his consciousness was itself tricksterlike, such a confrontation could obviously not take place. It was possible only when the attainment of a newer and higher level of conscious-ness enabled him to look back on a lower and inferior state. It was only to be expected that a good deal of mockery and contempt should mingle with this retrospect, thus casting an even thicker pall over man's memories of the past, which were pretty unedifying anyway. This phenomenon must have repeated itself innumerable times in the history of his mental development. The sovereign contempt with which our modern age looks back on the taste and intelligence of earlier centuries is a classic example of this, and there is an unmistakable allusion to the same phenomenon in the New Testament, where we are told in Acts 17:30 that God looked down from above (ὑπεριδών, despiciens) on the χρόνοι τῆς ἀγνοίας, the times of ignorance (or unconsciousness).

This attitude contrasts strangely with the still commoner and more striking ideali-zation of the past, which is praised not merely as the "good old days" but as the Golden Age—and not just by uneducated and superstitious people, but by all those millions of theosophical enthusiasts who resolutely believe in the former existence and lofty civili-zation of Atlantis.

Anyone who belongs to a sphere of culture that seeks the perfect state somewhere in the past must feel very queerly indeed when confronted by the figure of the trickster. He is a forerunner of the saviour, and, like him, God, man, and animal at once. He is both subhuman and superhuman, a bestial and divine being, whose chief and most alarming characteristic is his unconsciousness. Because of it he is deserted by his (evidently human) companions, which seems to indicate that he has fallen below their

---

[7]The same idea can be found in the Church Father Irenaeus, who calls it the "umbra." *Advers. Haer.* I, ii, 1.

level of consciousness. He is so unconscious of himself that his body is not a unity, and his two hands fight each other. He takes his anus off and entrusts it with a special task. Even his sex is optional despite its phallic qualities: he can turn himself into a woman and bear children. From his penis he makes all kinds of useful plants. This is a reference to his original nature as a Creator, for the world is made from the body of a god.

On the other hand he is in many respects stupider than the animals, and gets into one ridiculous scrape after another. Although he is not really evil he does the most atrocious things from sheer unconsciousness and unrelatedness. His imprisonment in animal unconsciousness is suggested by the episode where he gets his head caught inside the skull of an elk, and the next episode shows how he overcomes this condition by imprisoning the head of a hawk inside his own rectum. True, he sinks back into the former condition immediately afterwards, by falling under the ice, and is outwitted time after time by the animals, but in the end he succeeds in tricking the cunning coyote, and this brings back to him his saviour nature. The trickster is a primitive "cosmic" being of *divine-animal* nature, on the one hand superior to man because of his superhuman qualities, and on the other hand inferior to him because of his unreason and unconsciousness. He is no match for the animals either, because of his extraordinary clumsiness and lack of instinct. These defects are the marks of his *human* nature, which is not so well adapted to the environment as the animal's but, instead, has prospects of a much higher development of consciousness based on a considerable eagerness to learn, as is duly emphasized in the myth.

What the repeated telling of the myth signifies is the therapeutic anamnesis of contents which, for reasons still to be discussed, should never be forgotten for long. If they were nothing but the remains of an inferior state it would be understandable if man turned his attention away from them, feeling that their reappearance was a nuisance. This is evidently by no means the case, since the trickster has been a source of amusement right down to civilized times, where he can still be recognized in the carnival figures of Pulcinella and the clown. Here we have an important reason for his still continuing to function. But it is not the only one, and certainly not the reason why this reflection of an extremely primitive state of consciousness solidified into a mythological personage. Mere vestiges of an early state that is dying out usually lose their energy at an increasing rate, otherwise they would never disappear. The last thing we would expect is that they would have the strength to solidify into a mythological figure with its own cycle of legends—unless, of course, they received energy from outside, in this case from a higher level of consciousness or from resources in the unconscious which are not yet exhausted. To take a legitimate parallel from the psychology of the individual, namely the appearance of an impressive shadow figure antagonistically confronting a personal consciousness: this figure does not appear merely because it still exists in the individual, but because it rests on a dynamism whose existence can only be explained in terms of his actual situation, for instance because the shadow is so disagreeable to his ego consciousness that it has to be repressed into the unconscious. This explanation does not quite meet the case here, because the trickster obviously represents a vanishing level of consciousness which increasingly lacks the power to take shape and assert itself. Furthermore, repression would prevent it from vanishing, because repressed contents are the very ones that have the best chance of survival, as we know from experience that nothing is corrected in the unconscious. Lastly, the story of the trickster is not in the least disagreeable to the Winnebago consciousness or incompatible with it, but, on the contrary, pleasurable and therefore not conducive to repression. It looks, therefore, as if the myth were actively sustained and fostered by consciousness. This may well be so, since that is the best and most successful method of keeping the shadow figure conscious and subjecting it to conscious criticism. Although this criticism has at first more the character of a positive evaluation, we may expect that with the progressive development of consciousness the cruder aspects of the myth will gradually fall away, even if the danger of its rapid disappearance under the stress of white civilization did not exist. We have often seen how certain customs, originally cruel or obscene, became mere vestiges in the course of time.[8]

This process of neutralization, as the history of the trickster motif shows, lasts a very long time, so that one can still find traces of it even at a high level of civilization. Its longevity could also be explained by the strength and vitality of the state of consciousness described in the myth, and by the secret attraction and fascination this has for the conscious mind. Although purely causal hypotheses in the biological sphere are not as a rule very satisfactory, due weight must nevertheless be given to the fact that in the case of the trickster a higher level of consciousness has covered up a lower one, and that the latter was already in retreat. His recollection, however, is mainly due to the interest which the conscious mind brings to bear on him, the inevitable concomitant being, as we have seen, the gradual civilizing, i.e., assimilation, of a primitive daemonic figure who was originally autonomous and even capable of causing possession.

To supplement the causal approach by a final one therefore enables us to arrive at more meaningful interpretations not only in medical psychology, where we are concerned with individual fantasies originating in the unconscious, but also in the case of collective fantasies, that is myths and fairy tales.

As Radin points out, the civilizing process begins within the framework of the trickster cycle itself, and this is a clear indication that the original state has been overcome. At any rate the marks of deepest unconsciousness fall away from him; instead of acting in a brutal, savage, stupid and senseless fashion the trickster's behaviour towards the end of the cycle becomes quite useful and sensible. The devaluation of his earlier unconsciousness is apparent even in the myth, and one wonders what has happened to his evil qualities. The naïve reader may imagine that when the dark aspects disappear they are no longer there in reality. But that is not the case at all, as experience shows. What actually happens is that the conscious mind is then able to free itself from the fascination of evil and is no longer obliged to live it compulsively. The darkness and the evil have not gone up in smoke, they have merely withdrawn into the unconscious owing to loss of energy, where they remain unconscious so long as all is well with the conscious. But if the conscious should find itself in a critical or doubtful situation, then it soon becomes apparent that the shadow has not dissolved into nothing but is only waiting for a favourable opportunity to reappear as a projection upon one's neighbour. If this trick is successful, then immediately there is created between them that world of primordial darkness where everything that is characteristic of the trickster can happen—

[8]For instance, the ducking of the ''Ueli'' (from Udalricus = Ulrich, yokel, oaf, fool) in Basel during the second half of January was, if I remember correctly, forbidden by the police in the 1860's, after one of the victims died of pneumonia.

even on the highest plane of civilization. The best examples of these "monkey tricks," as popular speech aptly and truthfully sums up this state of affairs in which everything goes wrong and nothing intelligent happens except by mistake at the last moment, are naturally to be found in politics.

The so-called civilized man has forgotten the trickster. He remembers him only figuratively and metaphorically, when, irritated by his own ineptitude, he speaks of fate playing tricks on him or of things being bewitched. He never suspects that his own hidden and apparently harmless shadow has qualities whose dangerousness exceeds his wildest dreams. As soon as people get together in masses and submerge the individual, the shadow is mobilized, and, as history shows, may even be personified and incarnated.

The disastrous idea that everything comes to the human soul from outside and that it is born a tabula rasa is responsible for the erroneous belief that under normal circumstances the individual is in perfect order. He then looks to the State for salvation, and makes society pay for his inefficiency. He thinks the meaning of existence would be discovered if food and clothing were delivered to him gratis on his own doorstep, or if everybody possessed an automobile. Such are the puerilities that rise up in place of an unconscious shadow and keep it unconscious. As a result of these prejudices the individual feels totally dependent on his environment and loses all capacity for introspection. In this way his code of ethics is replaced by a knowledge of what is permitted or forbidden or ordered. How, under these circumstances, can one expect a soldier to subject an order received from a superior to ethical scrutiny? It still hasn't occurred to him that he might be capable of spontaneous ethical impulses, and of performing them—even when no one is looking!

From this point of view we can see why the myth of the trickster was preserved and developed: like many other myths, it was supposed to have a therapeutic effect. It holds the earlier low intellectual and moral level before the eyes of the more highly developed individual, so that he shall not forget how things looked yesterday. We like to imagine that something which we do not understand does not help us in any way. But that is not always so. Seldom does a man understand with his head alone, least of all when he is a primitive. Because of its numinosity the myth has a direct effect on the unconscious, no matter whether it is understood or not. The fact that its repeated telling has not long since become obsolete can, I believe, be explained by its usefulness. The explanation is rather difficult because two contrary tendencies are at work: the desire on the one hand to get out of the earlier condition and on the other hand not to forget it.[9] Apparently Radin has also felt this difficulty, for he says: "Viewed psychologically, it might be contended that the history of civilization is largely the account of the attempts of man to forget his transformation from an animal into a human being" (Radin 1953: 3). A few pages further on he says (with reference to the Golden Age): "So stubborn a refusal to forget is not an accident" (ibid.: 5). And it is also no accident that we are forced to contradict ourselves as soon as we try to formulate man's paradoxical attitude to myth. Even the most enlightened of us will set up a Christmas tree for his children without having the least idea what this custom means, and is invariably disposed to nip any attempt at interpretation in the bud. It is really astonishing to see how many so-called superstitions

[9]Not to forget something means keeping it in consciousness. If the enemy disappears from my field of vision, then he may possibly be behind me—and even more dangerous.

are rampant nowadays in town and country alike, but if one took hold of the individual and asked him, loudly and clearly, "Do you believe in ghosts? in witches? in spells and magic?" he would deny it indignantly. It is a hundred to one he has never heard of these things and thinks it all rubbish. But in secret he is all for it, just like a jungle dweller. The public knows very little of these things anyway, and is convinced that superstition has long been stamped out in our enlightened society and that it is part of our general education to pretend never to have heard of such things: it is just "not done" to believe in them.

But nothing is ever lost, not even the blood pact with the devil. Outwardly it is forgotten, but inwardly not at all. We act like the natives on the southern slopes of Mt. Elgon, one of whom accompanied me part of the way into the bush. At a fork in the path we came upon a brand new "ghost trap," beautifully got up like a little hut, near the cave where he lived with his family. I asked him if he had made it. He denied it with all the signs of extreme agitation, and told us that only children would make such a "joujou." Whereupon he gave the hut a kick and the whole thing fell to pieces.

This is exactly the reaction we can observe today in Europe. Outwardly people are more or less civilized but inwardly they are still primitives. Something in man is profoundly disinclined to give up his beginnings, and something else believes it has long since got beyond all that. This contradiction was once brought home to me in the most drastic manner when watching a "Strudel" (a sort of local witch doctor) taking the spell off a stable. The stable was situated immediately beside the Gotthard line, and several international expresses sped past during the ceremony. Their occupants would hardly have suspected that a primitive ritual was being performed a few yards away.

The conflict between the two dimensions of consciousness is simply an expression of the polaristic structure of the psyche, which like any other energic system is dependent on the tension of opposites. That is also why there are no general psychological propositions which could not just as well be reversed; indeed, their reversibility proves their validity. We should never forget that in any psychological discussion we are not saying anything *about* the psyche, but that the psyche is always speaking about *itself*. It is no use thinking we can ever get beyond the psyche by means of the "mind," even though the mind asserts that it is not dependent on the psyche. How could it prove that? We can say, if we like, that one statement comes from the psyche, is psychic and nothing but psychic, and that another comes from the mind, is "spiritual" and therefore superior to the psychic one. Both are mere assertions based on the postulates of belief.

The fact is, that this old trichotomous hierarchy of psychic contents (hylic, psychic, and pneumatic) represents the polaristic structure of the psyche, which is the only immediate object of experience. The unity of the psyche's nature lies in the middle, just as the living unity of the waterfall appears in the dynamic connection of above and below. So, too, the living effect of the myth is experienced when a higher consciousness, rejoicing in its freedom and independence, is confronted by the autonomy of a mythological figure and yet cannot flee from its fascination, but must pay tribute to the overwhelming impression. The figure works, because secretly it participates in the observer's psyche and appears as its reflection, though it is not recognized as such. It is split off from his consciousness and consequently behaves like an autonomous personality. The trickster is a collective shadow figure, an epitome of all the inferior traits of character in individuals. And since the individual shadow is never absent as a component of personality, the collective figure can construct itself out of it continually. Not always, of course, as a mythological figure, but, in consequence of the increasing repression and neglect of the original mythologems, as a corresponding projection on other social groups and nations.

If we take the trickster as a parallel of the individual shadow, then the question arises whether that trend towards meaning, which we saw in the trickster myth, can also be observed in the subjective and personal shadow. Since this shadow frequently appears in the phenomenology of dreams as a well-defined figure, we can answer this question positively: the shadow, although by definition a negative figure, sometimes has certain clearly discernible traits and associations which point to a quite different background. It is as though he were hiding meaningful contents under an unprepossessing exterior. Experience confirms this; and what is more important, the things that are hidden usually consist of increasingly numinous figures. The first thing we find standing behind the shadow is the anima,[10] who is endowed with considerable powers of fascination and possession. She often appears in rather too youthful form, and hides in her turn the powerful archetype of the wise old man (sage, magician, king, etc.). The series could be extended, but it would be pointless to do so, as psychologically one only understands what one has experienced oneself. The concepts of complex psychology are, in essence, not intellectual formulations but names for certain regions of experience, and though they can be described they remain dead and irrepresentable to anyone who has not experienced them. Thus, I have noticed that people usually have not much difficulty in picturing to themselves what is meant by the shadow, even if they would have preferred instead a bit of Latin or Greek jargon that sounds more "scientific." But it costs them enormous difficulties to understand what the anima is. They accept her easily enough when she appears in novels or as a film star, but she is not understood at all when it comes to seeing the role she plays in their own lives, because she sums up everything that a man can never get the better of and never finishes coping with. Therefore it remains in a state of perpetual emotion which ought not to be touched. The degree of unconsciousness one meets with in this connection is, to put it mildly, astounding. Hence it is practically impossible to get a man who is afraid of his own femininity to understand what is meant by the anima.

Actually, it is not surprising that this should be so, since even the most rudimentary insight into the shadow sometimes causes the greatest difficulties for the modern European. But since the shadow is the figure nearest his consciousness and the least explosive one, it is also the first component of personality to come up in an analysis of the unconscious. A minatory and ridiculous figure, he stands at the very beginning of the way of individuation, posing the deceptively easy riddle of the Sphinx or grimly demanding answer to a "quaestio crocodilina."[11]

---

[10]By the metaphor "standing behind the shadow" I want to give a concrete illustration of the fact that in proportion as the shadow is recognized and integrated, the problem of the anima, i.e., of relationship, is constellated. It is understandable that the encounter with the shadow should have an enduring effect on the relations of the ego to the inside and outside world, since the integration of the shadow brings about an alteration of personality. Cf. Jung, *Aion*, 1951, pp. 22ff.

[11]A crocodile stole a child from its mother. On being asked to give it back to her, the crocodile replied that he would grant her wish if she could give a true answer to his question: "Shall I give the child back?" If she answers "Yes," it is not true, and she won't get the child back. If she answers "No," it is again not true, so in either case the mother loses the child.

If, at the end of the trickster myth, the saviour is hinted at, this comforting premonition or hope means that some calamity or other has happened and been consciously understood. Only out of disaster can the longing for the saviour arise—in other words, the recognition and unavoidable integration of the shadow create such a harrowing situation that nobody but a saviour can undo the tangled web of fate. In the case of the individual, the problem constellated by the shadow is answered on the plane of the anima, that is, through relatedness. In the history of the collective as in the history of the individual, everything depends on the development of consciousness. This gradually brings liberation from imprisonment in ἀγνοία, unconsciousness (Neumann 1954: passim), and is therefore a bringer of light as well as of healing.

As in its collective, mythological form, so also the individual shadow contains within it the seed of an enantiodromia, of a conversion into its opposite.

[Tr. R. F. C. Hull]

ELAINE PAGELS
God the Father/God the Mother

In an important synthesizing essay, "Passage to More than India," the poet Gary Snyder wrote:

> My own opinion is that we are now experiencing a surfacing (in a specifically "American" incarnation) of the Great Subculture which goes back as far perhaps as the late Paleolithic. This subculture of illuminati has been a powerful undercurrent in all higher civilizations. In China it manifested as Taoism . . . and the Zen Buddhists up till early Sung. Within Islam the Sufis; in India the various threads converged to produce Tantrism. In the West it has been represented largely by a string of heresies starting with the Gnostics, and on the folk level by "witchcraft." [1969: 104–105]

The aforementioned Gnostics—contemporary with and often a part of early Christianity—were a mix of Euro-Mediterranean religions, centered on the pursuit of gnosis (= "knowing") in the sense of "enlightenment" or "illumination." But what's of most interest for the present gathering is the projection—in writings such as those from Nag Hammadi in Egypt—of myth as process and conflict: a virtual "clash of symbols" (P. Ricoeur), in contrast to the fixed imagery and single vision of orthodox thought, whether religious or scientific. Of the Gnostics' poesis as ongoing creativity, Pagels writes:

> Like circles of artists today, gnostics considered original creative invention to be the mark of anyone who becomes spiritually alive. Each one, like students of a painter or

SOURCE: Elaine Pagels, The Gnostic Gospels, pages 48–57.

writer, expected to express his own perceptions by revising and transforming what he
was taught. . . . Like artists, they express their own insight—their own *gnosis*—by
creating new myths, poems, rituals, "dialogues" with Christ, revelations, and accounts
of their visions. [1979: 19−20]

*In this sense, too, the Gnostics may be seen—at least at their most heated—as
carrying forward the open field of earlier speculative poetry and religion. The
question, then, of a "female aspect of God" is only one example of the "ancient
[poetic] liberty" (Milton) that would be violently assaulted by the triumphant
Christian orthodoxy.*

*Pagels's ample discussion of the events behind the gnostic-orthodox disputes
follows the excerpt presented here (1979: 57−69). (For more on the suppression
and survival of the "goddess," etc., see above, p. 56, and below, pp. 303 and 441.)*

Unlike many of his contemporaries among the deities of the ancient Near East, the God
of Israel shared his power with no female divinity, nor was he the divine Husband or
Lover of any.[1] He can scarcely be characterized in any but masculine epithets: king,
lord, master, judge, and father.[2] Indeed, the absence of feminine symbolism for God
marks Judaism, Christianity, and Islam in striking contrast to the world's other religious
traditions, whether in Egypt, Babylonia, Greece, and Rome, or in Africa, India, and
North America, which abound in feminine symbolism. Jewish, Christian, and Islamic
theologians today are quick to point out that God is not to be considered in sexual terms at
all.[3] Yet the actual language they use daily in worship and prayer conveys a different
message: who, growing up with Jewish or Christian tradition, has escaped the distinct
impression that God is *masculine*? And while Catholics revere Mary as the mother of
Jesus, they never identify her as divine in her own right: if she is "mother of God," she is
not "God the Mother" on an equal footing with God the Father!

Christianity, of course, added the trinitarian terms to the Jewish description of
God. Yet of the three divine "Persons," two—the Father and the Son—are described in
masculine terms, and the third—the Spirit—suggests the sexlessness of the Greek neuter
term for spirit, *pneuma*. Whoever investigates the early history of Christianity (the field
called "patristics"—that is, study of "the fathers of the church") will be prepared for
the passage that concludes the *Gospel of Thomas*:

---

[1]Where the God of Israel is characterized as husband and lover in the Old Testament, his spouse is described as
the community of Israel (e.g., Isaiah 50:1, 54:1−8; Jeremiah 2:2−3, 20−25, 3:1−20; Hosea 1−4, 14) or as
the land of Israel (Isaiah 62:1−5).

[2]One may note several exceptions to this rule: Deuteronomy 32:11; Hosea 11:1; Isaiah 66:12 ff.; Numbers
11:12.

[3]Formerly, as Professor Morton Smith reminds me, theologians often used the masculinity of God to justify, by
analogy, the roles of men as rulers of their societies and households (he cites, for example, Milton's *Paradise
Lost*, IV.296 ff., 635 ff.).

Simon Peter said to them [the disciples]: "Let Mary leave us, for women are not worthy of Life." Jesus said, "I myself shall lead her, in order to make her male, so that she too may become a living spirit, resembling you males. For every woman who will make herself male will enter the Kingdom of Heaven." [NHL 130][4]

Strange as it sounds, this simply states what religious rhetoric assumes: that the men form the legitimate body of the community, while women are allowed to participate only when they assimilate themselves to men. Other texts discovered at Nag Hammadi demonstrate one striking difference between these "heretical" sources and orthodox ones: gnostic sources continually use sexual symbolism to describe God. One might expect that these texts would show the influence of archaic pagan traditions of the Mother Goddess, but for the most part, their language is specifically Christian, unmistakably related to a Jewish heritage. Yet instead of describing a monistic and masculine God, many of these texts speak of God as a dyad who embraces both masculine and feminine elements.

One group of gnostic sources claims to have received a secret tradition from Jesus through James and through Mary Magdalene. Members of this group prayed to both the divine Father and Mother: "From Thee, Father, and through Thee, Mother, the two immortal names, Parents of the divine being, and thou, dweller in heaven, humanity, of the mighty name . . . " (REF 5.6). Other texts indicate that their authors had wondered to whom a single, masculine God proposed, "Let us make man [*adam*] in our image, after our likeness" (Genesis 1:26). Since the Genesis account goes on to say that humanity was created "male and female" (1:27), some concluded that the God in whose image we are made must also be both masculine and feminine—both Father and Mother.

How do these texts characterize the divine Mother? I find no simple answer, since the texts themselves are extremely diverse. Yet we may sketch out three primary characterizations. In the first place, several gnostic groups describe the divine Mother as part of an original couple. Valentinus, the teacher and poet, begins with the premise that God is essentially indescribable. But he suggests that the divine can be imagined as a dyad; consisting, in one part, of the Ineffable, the Depth, the Primal Father; and, in the other, of Grace, Silence, the Womb and "Mother of the All" (AH 1.11.1). Valentinus reasons that Silence is the appropriate complement of the Father, designating the former as feminine and the latter as masculine because of the grammatical gender of the Greek words. He goes on to describe how Silence receives, as in a womb, the seed of the Ineffable Source; from this she brings forth all the emanations of divine being, ranged in harmonious pairs of masculine and feminine energies.

Followers of Valentinus prayed to her for protection as the Mother, and as "the mystical, eternal Silence" (AH 1.13.6). For example, Marcus the magician invokes her as Grace (in Greek, the feminine term *charis*): "May She who is before all things, the incomprehensible and indescribable Grace, fill you within, and increase in you her own knowledge" (AH 1.13.2). In his secret celebration of the mass, Marcus teaches that the wine symbolizes her blood. As the cup of wine is offered, he prays that "Grace may

---

[4]The gnostic texts cited in this piece are published in *The Nag Hammadi Library*, edited by James M. Robinson, referred to hereafter as NHL. Other sources used extensively are the third century *Refutation of All Heresies* (REF) and Irenaeus's second-century work, *Against Heresies* (AH).

flow'' (AH 1.13.2) into all who drink of it. A prophet and visionary, Marcus calls himself the *"womb* and *recipient* of Silence'' (AH 1.14.1) as she is of the Father. The visions he received of the divine being appeared, he reports, in female form.

Another gnostic writing, called the *Great Announcement*, quoted by Hippolytus in his *Refutation of All Heresies*, explains the origin of the universe as follows: From the power of Silence appeared ''a great power, the Mind of the Universe, which manages all things, and is a male . . . the other . . . a great Intelligence . . . is a female which produces all things'' (REF 6.18). Following the gender of the Greek words for ''mind'' (*nous*—masculine) and ''intelligence'' (*epinoia*—feminine), this author explains that these powers, joined in union, ''are discovered to be duality . . . This is Mind in Intelligence, and these are separable from one another, and yet are one, found in a state of duality.'' This means, the gnostic teacher explains, that

> there is in everyone [divine power] existing in a latent condition. . . . This is one power divided above and below; generating itself, making itself grow, seeking itself, finding itself, being mother of itself, father of itself, sister of itself, spouse of itself, daughter of itself, son of itself—mother, father, unity, being a source of the entire circle of existence. [REF 6.17]

How did these gnostics intend their meaning to be understood? Different teachers disagreed. Some insisted that the divine is to be considered masculo-feminine—the ''great male-female power.'' Others claimed that the terms were meant only as metaphors, since, in reality, the divine is neither male nor female (AH 1.11.5; REF 6.29). A third group suggested that one can describe the primal Source in either masculine or feminine terms, depending on which aspect one intends to stress. Proponents of these diverse views agreed that the divine is to be understood in terms of a harmonious, dynamic relationship of opposites—a concept that may be akin to the Eastern view of *yin* and *yang*, but remains alien to orthodox Judaism and Christianity.

A second characterization of the divine Mother describes her as Holy Spirit. The *Apocryphon [Secret Book] of John* relates how John went out after the crucifixion with ''great grief'' and had a mystical vision of the Trinity. As John was grieving, he says that

> the [heavens were opened and the whole] creation [which is] under heaven shone and [the world] trembled. [And I was afraid, and I] saw in the light . . . a likeness with multiple forms . . . and the likeness had three forms. [NHL 99]

To John's question the vision answers: ''He said to me, 'John, Jo[h]n, why do you doubt, and why are you afraid? . . . I am the one who [is with you] always. I [am the Father]; I am the Mother; I am the Son'' (NHL 99). This gnostic description of God—as Father, Mother and Son—may startle us at first, but on reflection, we can recognize it as another version of the Trinity. The Greek terminology for the Trinity, which includes the neuter term for spirit (*pneuma*) virtually requires that the third ''Person'' of the Trinity be asexual. But the author of the *Secret Book* has in mind the Hebrew term for spirit, *ruah*, a feminine word; and so concludes that the feminine ''Person'' conjoined with the

Father and Son must be the Mother. The *Secret Book* goes on to describe the divine Mother:

> [She is] . . . the image of the invisible, virginal, perfect spirit . . . She became the Mother of everything, for she existed before them all, the mother-father [*matropater*]. . . . [NHL 101]

The *Gospel to the Hebrews* likewise has Jesus speak of "my Mother, the Spirit." In the *Gospel of Thomas*, Jesus contrasts his earthly parents, Mary and Joseph, with his divine Father—the Father of Truth—and his divine Mother, the Holy Spirit. The author interprets a puzzling saying of Jesus' from the New Testament ("Whoever does not hate his father and his mother cannot be my disciple") by adding that "my (earthly) mother [gave me death], but [my] true [Mother] gave me life" (NHL 128–129). So, according to the *Gospel of Philip*, whoever becomes a Christian gains "both father and mother" (NHL 132) for the Spirit (*ruah*) is "Mother of many" (NHL 136).

A work attributed to the gnostic teacher Simon Magus suggests a mystical meaning for Paradise, the place where human life began:

> Grant Paradise to be the womb; for Scripture teaches us that this is a true assumption when it says, "I am He that formed thee in thy mother's womb" (Isaiah 44:2). . . . Moses . . . using allegory had declared Paradise to be the womb . . . and Eden, the placenta. . . . [REF 6.14]

The river that flows forth from Eden symbolizes the navel, which nourishes the fetus. Simon claims that the Exodus, consequently, signifies the passage out of the womb, and that "the crossing of the Red Sea refers to the blood." Sethian gnostics explain that

> heaven and earth have a shape similar to the womb . . . and if . . . anyone wants to investigate this, let him carefully examine the pregnant womb of any living creature, and he will discover an image of the heavens and the earth. [REF 5.19]

Evidence for such views, declares Marcus, comes directly from "the cry of the newborn," a spontaneous cry of praise for "the glory of the primal being, in which the powers above are in harmonious embrace" (AH 1.14.7–8).

If some gnostic sources suggest that the Spirit constitutes the maternal element of the Trinity, the *Gospel of Philip* makes an equally radical suggestion about the doctrine that later developed as the virgin birth. Here again, the Spirit is both Mother and Virgin, the counterpart—and consort—of the Heavenly Father: "Is it permitted to utter a mystery? The Father of everything united with the virgin who came down" (NHL 143)—that is, with the Holy Spirit descending into the world. But because this process is to be understood symbolically, not literally, the Spirit remains a virgin. The author goes on to explain that as "Adam came into being from two virgins, from the Spirit and from the virgin earth" so "Christ, therefore, was born from a virgin" (NHL 143)—that is, from the Spirit. But the author ridicules those literal-minded

Christians who mistakenly refer the virgin birth to Mary, Jesus' mother, as though she conceived apart from Joseph: "They do not know what they are saying. When did a woman ever conceive by a woman?" (NHL 134). Instead, he argues, virgin birth refers to that mysterious union of the two divine powers, the Father of All and the Holy Spirit.

In addition to the eternal, mystical Silence and the Holy Spirit, certain gnostics suggest a third characterization of the divine Mother: as Wisdom. Here the Greek feminine term for "wisdom," *sophia*, translates a Hebrew feminine term, *hokhmah*. Early interpreters had pondered the meaning of certain Biblical passages—for example, the saying in Proverbs that "God made the world in Wisdom." Could Wisdom be the feminine power in which God's creation was "conceived?" According to one teacher, the double meaning of the term conception—physical and intellectual—suggests this possibility: "The image of thought [*ennoia*] is feminine, since . . . [it] is a power of conception" (REF 6.38). The *Apocalypse of Adam*, discovered at Nag Hammadi, tells of a feminine power who wanted to conceive by herself:

> . . . from the nine Muses, one separated away. She came to a high mountain and spent time seated there, so that she desired herself alone in order to become androgynous. She fulfilled her desire, and became pregnant from her desire. . . .
> [NHL 262]

The poet Valentinus uses this theme to tell a famous myth about Wisdom: Desiring to conceive by herself, apart from her masculine counterpart, she succeeded, and became the "great creative power from whom all things originate," often called Eve, "Mother of all living." But since her desire violated the harmonious union of opposites intrinsic in the nature of created being, what she produced was aborted and defective (AH 1.2.2−3); from this, says Valentinus, originated the terror and grief that mar human existence (AH 1.4.1−1.5.4). To shape and manage her creation, Wisdom brought forth the demiurge, the creator-God of Israel, as her agent (AH 1.5.1−3).

Wisdom, then, bears several connotations in gnostic sources. Besides being the "first universal creator" (Clemens Alexandrinus, *Excerpta* 47.1), who brings forth all creatures, she also enlightens human beings and makes them wise. Followers of Valentinus and Marcus therefore prayed to the Mother as the "mystical, eternal Silence" and to "Grace, She who is before all things," and as "incorruptible Wisdom" (AH 1.13.1−6) for insight (*gnosis*). Other gnostics attributed to her the benefits that Adam and Eve received in Paradise. First, she taught them self-awareness; second, she guided them to find food; third, she assisted in the conception of their third and fourth children, who were, according to this account, their third son, Seth, and their first daughter, Norea (AH 1.30.9). Even more: when the creator became angry with the human race

> because they did not worship or honor him as Father and God, he sent forth a flood upon them, that he might destroy them all. But Wisdom opposed him . . . and Noah and his family were saved in the ark by means of the sprinkling of the light that proceeded from her, and through it the world was again filled with humankind.
> [AH 1.30.10]

Another newly discovered text from Nag Hammadi, *Trimorphic Protennoia* (literally, the "Triple-formed Primal Thought"), celebrates the feminine powers of Thought, Intelligence, and Foresight. The text opens as a divine figure speaks:

> [I] am [Protennoia the] Thought that [dwells] in [the Light]. . . . [she who exists] before the All . . . I move in every creature. . . . I am the Invisible One within the All. [NHL 461−462]

She continues: "I am perception and knowledge, uttering a Voice by means of Thought. [I] am the real Voice. I cry out in everyone, and they know that a seed dwells within" (NHL 462). The second section, spoken by a second divine figure, opens with the words

> I am the Voice . . . [It is] I [who] speak within every creature . . . Now I have come a second time in the likeness of a female, and have spoken with them. . . . I have revealed myself in the Thought of the likeness of my masculinity. [NHL 465−466]

Later the voice explains:

> I am androgynous. [I am both Mother and] Father, since [I copulate] with myself . . . [and with those who love] me . . . I am the Womb [that gives shape] to the All . . . I am Me[iroth]ea, the glory of the Mother. [NHL 467]

Even more remarkable is the gnostic poem called the *Thunder, Perfect Mind*. This text contains a revelation spoken by a feminine power:

> I am the first and the last. I am the honored one and the scorned one. I am the whore, and the holy one. I am the wife and the virgin. I am (the mother) and the daughter. . . . I am she whose wedding is great, and I have not taken a husband. . . . I am knowledge, and ignorance. . . . I am shameless; I am ashamed. I am strength, and I am fear. . . . I am foolish, and I am wise. . . . I am godless, and I am one whose God is great. [NHL 271−274]

What does the use of such symbolism imply for the understanding of human nature? One text, having previously described the divine Source as a "bisexual Power," goes on to say that "what came into being from that Power—that is, humanity, being one—is discovered to be two: a male-female being that bears the female within it" (REF 6.18). This refers to the story of Eve's "birth" out of Adam's side (so that Adam, being one, is "discovered to be two," an androgyne who "bears the female within him"). Yet this reference to the creation story of Genesis 2 (an account which inverts the biological birth process, and so attributes to the male the creative function of the female) is unusual in gnostic sources. More often, gnostic writers refer to the first creation account in Genesis 1:26−27 ("Then God said, Let us make man [*adam*] in our image, after our likeness . . . in the image of God he created him; male and female he created them''). Rabbis in Talmudic times knew a Greek version of the passage that suggested to Rabbi Samuel bar Nachman, influenced by Plato's myth of androgyny, that

> when the Holy one . . . first created mankind, he created him with two faces, two sets of genitals, four arms and legs, back to back. Then he split Adam in two, and made two backs, one on each side. [*Genesis Rabba* 8:1]

Some gnostics adopted this idea, teaching that Genesis 1:26—27 narrates an androgynous creation. Marcus (whose prayer to the Mother is given above) not only concludes from this account that God is dyadic (''Let *us* make humanity'') but also that ''humanity, which was formed according to the image and likeness of God (Father and Mother) was masculo-feminine'' (AH 1.18.2). His contemporary, the gnostic Theodotus (c. 160), explains that the saying ''according to the image of God he made them, male and female he made them,'' means that ''the male and female elements together constitute the finest production of the Mother, Wisdom'' (Clemens Alexandrinus, *Excerpta* 21.1). Gnostic sources which describe God as a dyad whose nature includes both masculine and feminine elements often give a similar description of human nature.

Yet all the sources cited so far—secret gospels, revelations, mystical teachings—are among those not included in the select list that constitutes the New Testament collection. Every one of the secret texts which gnostic groups revered was omitted from the canonical collection and branded as heretical by those who called themselves orthodox Christians. By the time the process of sorting the various writings ended—probably as late as the year 200—virtually all the feminine imagery for God had disappeared from orthodox Christian tradition. . . .

BARBARA G. MYERHOFF

Return to Wirikuta: Ritual Reversal and Symbolic Continuity in the Huichol Peyote Hunt

The following piece explores and illuminates ways in which this kind of traditional poetry and ritual has been able to "sustain contradictions" (S. Diamond) and to participate thereby in aspects of reality not recoverable by ordinary means. A Huichol summary, by Ramón Medina Silva, of the accompanying language of reversals, appears above on pages 116 to 118.

God is day and night, winter summer, war peace, satiety hunger—all opposites, this is the meaning.

—Heraclitus

THE PEYOTE HUNT OF THE HUICHOL INDIANS

Rituals of opposition and reversal constitute a critical part of a lengthy religious ceremony, the peyote hunt, practiced by the Huichol Indians of north-central Mexico.[1] In order to understand the function of these rituals it is necessary to adumbrate the major features and purposes of the peyote hunt. Annually, small groups of Huichols, led by a shaman-priest or *mara'akáme*, return to Wirikuta to hunt the peyote. Wirikuta is a high desert several hundred miles from the Huichols' present abode in the Sierra Madre Occidental. Mythically and in all likelihood historically, it is their original homeland, the place once inhabited by the First People, the quasi-deified ancestors. But Wirikuta is much more than a geographical location; it is *illud tempus*, the paradisical condition that existed before the creation of the world and mankind, and the condition that will prevail at the end of time. In Wirikuta, as in the paradise envisioned in many creation myths, all is unity, a cosmic totality without barriers of any kind, without the differentiations that characterize the mundane mortal world. In Wirikuta, separations are obliterated—between sexes, between leader and led, young and old, animals and man, plants and animals, and man and the deities. The social order and the natural and supernatural realms are rejoined into their original state of seamless continuity. Wirikuta is the center of the four directions where, as the Huichol describe it, "All is unity, all is one, all is ourselves."

[1] The Huichol Indians are a quasi-tribe of about 10,000 living in dispersed communities in north-central Mexico. They are among the least acculturated Mexican Indians and in part their resistence to outside influence is attributable to the complex and extraordinarily rich ritual and symbolic life they lead. A detailed presentation of the peyote hunt is presented in Myerhoff 1974. The fieldwork on which the present [essay is] based took place in 1965 and 1966.

SOURCE: Barbara A. Babcock (ed.), The Reversible World: Symbolic Inversion in Art and Society, pages 225–235.

In Wirikuta, the three major symbols of Huichol world view are likewise fused. These are the Deer, representing the Huichols' past life as nomadic hunters; the Maize, representing their present life as sedentary agriculturalists; and peyote, signifying the private, spiritual vision of each individual. To reenter Wirikuta, the peyote pilgrims must be transformed into the First People. They assume the identity of particular deities and literally hunt the peyote which grows in Wirikuta, tracking and following it in the form of deer footprints, stalking and shooting it with bow and arrow, consuming it in a climactic ceremony of total communion. Once the peyote has been hunted, consumed, and sufficient supplies have been gathered for use in the ceremonies of the coming year, the pilgrims hastily leave and return to their homes and to their mortal condition. The entire peyote hunt is very complex, consisting of many rituals and symbols; here I will only concentrate on one set of rituals, those which concern reversal and opposition, and the part they play in enabling the pilgrims to experience the sense of totality and cosmic unity that is their overarching religious goal.

MYTHOLOGICAL AND RITUAL ASPECTS OF REVERSALS

''In Wirikuta, we change the names of everything . . . everything is backwards.'' Ramón Medina Silva, the officiating mara'akáme, who led the Peyote Hunt of 1966 in which I participated, thus explained the reversals that obtain during the pilgrimage. ''The mara'akáme tells [the pilgrims], 'Now we will change everything, all the meanings, because that is the way it must be with the *hikuritámete* [peyote pilgrims]. As it was in Ancient Times, so that all can be united.' '' [See above, p. 117.]

The reversals to which he refers occur on four distinct levels: naming, interpersonal behavior, ritual behavior, and emotional states. The reversals in naming are very specific. Ideally, everything is its opposite and everything is newly named each year. But in fact, for many things there are often no clear opposites, and substitutions are made, chosen for reasons that are not always clear. Frequently the substitutions seem dictated by simple visual association—thus the head is a pot, the nose a penis, hair is cactus fiber. A great many of these substitutions recur each year and are standardized. Nevertheless, they are defined as opposites in this context and are treated as if they were spontaneous rather than patterned.

On the interpersonal-behavioral level, direct oppositions are more straightforward. One says yes when he or she means no. A person proffers a foot instead of a hand. Conversations are conducted with conversants standing back to back, and so forth. Behavior is also altered to correspond with the ritual identity of the participant. Thus the oldest man, transformed into a *nunutsi* or little child for the journey, is not permitted to gather firewood because ''this work is too heavy and strenuous for one so young.''

The deities are portrayed as the opposite of mortals in that the former have no physiological needs. Thus the pilgrims, as the First People, disguise, minimize, and forego their human physiological activities as much as possible. Sexual abstinence is practiced. Washing is forsworn. Eating, sleeping, and drinking are kept to an absolute minimum. Defecation and urination are said not to occur and are practiced covertly. All forms of social distinction and organization are minimized, and even the mara'akáme's leadership and direction are extremely oblique. The ordinary division of labor is suspended and altered in various ways. All forms of discord are strictly forbidden, and disruptive emotions such as jealousy and deceit, usually tolerated as part of the human condition, are completely proscribed for the pilgrims. No special treatment is afforded to children; no behavioral distinctions between the sexes are allowed. Even the separateness of the mara'akáme from his group is minimized, and his assistant immediately performs for him all rituals that the mara'akáme has just performed for the rest of the party.

In terms of ritual actions, reversals are quite clear. The cardinal directions, and up and down, are switched in behaviors which involve offering sacred water and food to the four corners and the center of the world. The fire is circled in a counterclockwise direction instead of clockwise as on normal ceremonial occasions. In Wirikuta, the mara'akáme's assistant sits to the latter's left instead of to his right.

Emotions as well as behaviors are altered on the basis of the pilgrims' transformation into deities. Since mortals would be jubilant, presumably, on returning to their pre-creation, mythical homeland, and grief-stricken on departing from it, the pilgrims weep as they reenter Wirikuta and are exultant on departing. This reflects the fact that they are deities leaving paradise, not mortals returning from it.

I should note also some of the attitudes and values toward the reversals that I observed. For example, there seems to be an aesthetic dimension since they regard some reversals as more satisfying than others. Humorous and ironic changes are a source of much laughter and delight. Thus the name of the wife of the mara'akáme was changed to "ugly *gringa*." The mara'akáme himself was the pope. The anthropologists' camper was a burro that drank much tequila. They also delight in compounding the reversals: "Ah what a pity that we caught no peyote. Here we sit, sad, surrounded by baskets of flowers under a cold sun." Thus said one pilgrim after a successful day of gathering baskets full of peyote, while standing in the moonlight. Mistakes and humorous improvisations are also the source of new reversals. When in a careless moment Los Angeles was referred to as "home," everyone was very pleased and amused; from then on home was Los Angeles and even in sacred chants and prayers this reversal was maintained. Accidental reversals such as this are just as obligatory as the conventional ones and the new ones "dreamed" by the mara'akáme. Mistakes are corrected with good will but firmly, and everyone shares in the responsibility for keeping track of the changes, reminding each other repeatedly of the changes that have been instituted. The more changes the better, and each day, as more are established, more attention by all is required to keep things straight. Normal conversation and behavior become more difficult with each new day's accumulation of changes. Sunsets are ugly. No one is tired. Peyote is sweet. The pilgrimage is a failure. There is too much food to eat, and so forth.

The reversals were not instituted or removed by any formal rituals, although it is said that there are such. It became apparent that the reversals were in effect at the periphery of Wirikuta when someone sneezed. This was received by uproarious laughter, for, the nose had become a penis and a sneeze, accordingly, was an off-color joke. After the peyote hunt, the reversals were set aside gradually as the group moved away from Wirikuta. On returning home, the pilgrims regaled those who had remained behind with descriptions of the reversals and the confusions they had engendered.

THE FUNCTIONS AND SYMBOLISM OF THE
REVERSALS

How should these ideas and actions concerning reversal and opposition be understood? In the Huichol context, they achieve several purposes simultaneously. Perhaps most familiar and straightforward is their function in transforming the mundane into the sacred by disguising the everyday features of environment, society, and behavior, and in the Durkheimian sense "setting it apart." As Ramón Medina Silva explained, "One changes everything . . . when [we] cross over there to the Peyote Country . . . because it is a very sacred thing, it is the most sacred. It is our life, as one says. That is why nowadays one gives things other names. One changes everything. Only when they return home, then they call everything again what it is." Here the totality and scope of the reversals are important—actions, names, ritual, and everyday behaviors are altered so that participants are conscious at all times of the extraordinary nature of their undertaking. Nothing is natural, habitual, or taken for granted. The boundaries between the ordinary and the sacred are sharply defined and attention to this extraordinary state of affairs cannot lag when one has to be perpetually self-conscious and vigilant against lapses. Reversals promote the essential attitude of the sacred, the *mysterium tremendum et fascinans*.

The transformation of mortals into deities is related to this purpose. Again and again in theological, mythological, and ethnographic literature one encounters the impossibility of mortals entering a supernatural realm in their normal condition. The shaman transforms himself into a spirit in order to perform his duties as soul guide or psychopomp. This is the essence of the Symplegades motif in shamanism—the passage into the other world through the crashing gates, as Eliade (1964) points out. The "paradoxical passage" to the supernatural domain is open only to those who have been transformed from their human state into pure spirit. An apotheosis is required of those who would "cross over" and achieve the "breakthrough in planes." The peyote hunt opens Wirikuta to all proper pilgrims, but they, like the shaman, cannot enter in mortal form. To enter Wirikuta, the Huichol peyote-seekers do not merely impersonate the deities by assuming their names and garb. Ritually and symbolically, they *become* supernatural, disguising the mortal coil, abrogating human functions and forms.

This "backwardness" operates on two levels: as the deities, they are the obverse of mortals; as deities, they are going back, going backwards, and signifying this by doing everything backwards. Backwardness is found frequently in connection with supernatural states, and with the denial of humanity. Lugbara witches are inverted beings who walk on their heads (Middleton 1960). And in Genesis we find that "the inhabitants of paradise stand on their heads and walk on their hands; as do all the dead" (Graves and Patai 1966:73, citing Gen. 24:65). The examples could be expanded indefinitely. Eliade suggests this widespread association of backwardness and the supernatural when he comments, "Consequently to do away with this state of [humanity] even if only provisionally, is equivalent to reestablishing the primordial condition of man, in other words, to banish time, to go backwards, to recover the 'paradisial' *illud tempus*" (1960: 72).

A third function of these reversals is their provision of mnemonic, or aid to the imagination and memory, for conception and action. For a time the peyote pilgrims in the Huichol religion live in the supernatural. They go beyond invoking and discussing it, for Wirikuta exists in ritual as well as mythical terms. Ritual, unlike myth, requires action. Ritual is a dramatization. Pilgrims must not only imagine the unimaginable, they must behave within it. It is through its action dimension that ritual makes religious values "really real," and fuses the "lived-in" and the "dreamed-of order," as Geertz puts it. Full staging is necessary. The unfathomable—*illud tempus*, the primordial state before time—is the setting. Props, costumes, etiquette, vocabulary, emotions—all must be conceived and specified. The theme of opposition provides the details that are needed to make the drama credible and convincing; the metaphor of backwardness makes for a concretization and amplification of the ineffable. Again Eliade's writings offer an insight along these lines. He points out that the theme of *coincidentia oppositorum* is an "eschatological symbol par excellence, which denotes that Time and History have come to an end—in the lion lying down with the lamb" (1962: 121). It is in the Garden of Eden that "opposites lie down together," it is there that conflicts and divisions are ultimately abolished and man's original innocence and wholeness are regained.

Separation, transformation, and concretization then are three purposes achieved by the reversals in Wirikuta. There is a fourth, perhaps the most important and common function of rituals of this nature. That is the capacity of reversals to invoke continuity through emphasis on opposition. How this operates in the Huichol case was explained in very precise terms by Ramón Medina Silva in a text he dictated about the 1966 peyote hunt five years later. He was elaborating on the beauties of Wirikuta and for the first time indicated that it was the state that would prevail at the end of time as well as that which characterized the beginning. When the world ends, the First People would return. "All will be in unity, all will be one, all will be as you have seen it there, in Wirikuta." The present world, it became clear, was but a shallow and misleading interlude, a transient period characterized by difference and separations, bracketed by an enduring condition of totality and continuity.

> When the world ends it will be like when the names of things are changed during the Peyote Hunt. All will be different, the opposite of what it is now. Now there are two eyes in the heavens, the Sun and the Moon. Then, the Moon will open his eye and become brighter. The Sun will become dimmer. There will be no more difference between them. Then, no more men and no more women. No more child and no more adult. All will change places. Even the mara'akáme will no longer be separate. That is why there must always be a *nunutsi* when we go to Wirikuta. Because the old man and the tiny baby, they are the same.

> [Personal communication, Los Angeles, 1971]

Polarity reaffirms continuity. The baby and the adult ultimately are joined, ends of a single continuum. Watts states it as follows: "What exactly is polarity? It is something much more than simple duality or opposition. For to say that opposites are polar is to say much more than that they are joined . . . , that they are the terms, ends, or extremities of a single whole. Polar opposites are therefore inseparable opposites, like the poles of the earth or of a magnet, or the ends of a stick or the faces of a coin" (1970: 45).

Surely the vision of an original condition of unity, before the world and mankind began, is one of the most common themes in religions of every nature and place. Again to draw on Eliade, ''Among the 'primitive' peoples, just as among the Saints and the Christian theologians, mystic ecstasy is a return to Paradise, expressed by the over-coming of Time and History . . . , and [represents] a recovery of the primordial state of Man'' (1960: 72).

The theme of nostalgia for lost paradise recurs so often as to be counted by some as panhuman. Theories attribute this yearning to various causes: a lingering memory of the undifferentiated state in the womb, the unfilled wish for a happy childhood, a fantasy of premortal blessedness and purity, a form of what the Jungians call uroboric incest, a fatal desire for nonbeing, and so forth (see Neumann 1954). Many theologians have viewed this vision of cosmic oneness as the essence of the mystical experience and of religious ecstasy. The particulars vary from one religion to the next but the ingredients are stable: paradise is that which existed before the beginning of time, before life and death, before light and darkness. Here animals and man lived in a state of easy companionship, speaking the same language, untroubled by thirst, hunger, pain, weariness, loneliness, struggle, or appetite. Humans knew neither discord nor distinction among themselves— they were sexless, without self-awareness, and indeed undifferentiated from the very gods. Then an irreversible and cataclysmic sundering took place and instead of whole-ness there was separation, the separation that was Creation. Henceforth, the human organism was no longer indistinguishable from the cosmos. The primordial splitting left mankind as we know it now, forever haunted by remembrance of and attraction for an original condition of wholeness.

The reversals, then, express the most lamentable features of the human condition by emphasizing the loss of the paradisical state of oneness. Humans are fragmented, incomplete, and isolated from the deities; they are vulnerable and literally mortal, which is to say helpless before the ravages of pain, time, and death. At the same time, the reversals remind mankind of the primordial wholeness that will again prevail when paradise is regained. Here is the theme expressed in a cultural form familiar to most of us, the Gospel according to Thomas:

> They said to Him: Shall we then, being children
> enter the Kingdom? Jesus said to them:
> When you make the two one, and
> when you make the inner as the outer
> and the outer as the inner and the above
> as the below, and when
> you make the male and the female into a single one,
> so that the male will not be male and
> the female [not] be female, when you make
> eyes in the place of an eye, a hand
> in the place of a hand, and a foot in the place
> of a foot, an image in the place of an image,
> then shall you enter [the Kingdom].
>
> [Logia 23—35, cited in Guillaumont et al. 1959: 17—19]

CONCLUSIONS

The theme of reversal, in all its permutations and combinations—opposition (complementary and binary), inversion, and dualism—has always been of great interest to anthropologists, mythographers, theologians, psychologists, linguists, and artists. The subject seems inexhaustible. In anthropology alone, we continue to unravel additional layers of meaning, to discover more and more functions fulfilled by reversals in various contexts. Recent studies especially have shown how reversals can be used to make statements about the social order—to affirm it, attack it, suspend it, redefine it, oppose it, buttress it, emphasize one part of it at the cost of another, and so forth. We see a magnificently fruitful image put to diverse purposes, capable of an overwhelming range of expression. Obviously there is no question of looking for the true or correct meaning in the use of reversals. We are dealing with a symbolic referent that has new meanings in every new context and within a single context embraces multiple and contradictory meanings simultaneously. In Wirikuta, the reversals accomplish many purposes and contain a major paradox. They emphasize the difference between Wirikuta and the mundane life, and the differentiated nature of the human condition. Also they stress the nondifferentiated nature of Wirikuta. The reversals thus portray differentiation and continuity at the same time. Both are true, separation and oneness, though this is contradictory and paradoxical. But this should come as no surprise, for paradox is the very quick of ritual. In ritual, as in the Garden, opposites are made to lie down together.

MIRCEA ELIADE
The Return of the Symbol

The headnote on the place and work of Mircea Eliade appears on page 59, above.

The surprising popularity of psychoanalysis has made the fortunes of certain key-words: image, symbol and symbolism have now become current coin. At the same time, systematic research devoted to the mechanisms of "primitive mentality" has revealed the importance of symbolism in archaic thinking and also the fundamental part it plays in the life of any and every primitive society. The obsolescence of "scientism" in philosophy, the revival of interest in religion since the first world war, many poetic

SOURCE: Mircea Eliade, Images and Symbols, *pages 9–11.*

developments and, above all, the researches of surrealism (with the rediscovery of occultism, of the "black" literature, of "the absurd," etc.) have, on various levels and with unequal effects, drawn the attention of the public in general to the symbol, regarded as an autonomous mode of cognition. The development in question is a part of the reaction against the nineteenth century's rationalism, positivism and scientism which became such a marked characteristic of the second quarter of the twentieth. But this conversion to the various symbolisms is not really a "discovery" to be credited to the modern world: in restoring the symbol to its status as an instrument of knowledge, our world is only returning to a point of view that was general in Europe until the eighteenth century and is, moreover, connatural to the other, non-European cultures, whether "historic" (like those of Asia or Central America for instance) or archaic and "primitive." . . .

A fortunate conjunction in time . . . has enabled Western Europe to rediscover the cognitive value of the symbol at the moment when Europeans are no longer the only peoples to "make history," and when European culture, unless it shuts itself off into a sterilizing provincialism, will be obliged to reckon with other ways and other scales of values than its own. In this respect, all the discoveries and successive fashions concerned with the irrational, with the unconscious, with symbolisms, poetic experience, exotic and non-representational art, etc., have been, indirectly, of service to the West as preparations for a more living and therefore a deeper understanding of non-European values, and in particular for a dialogue with the non-European peoples. One has only to reflect upon the attitude that nineteenth-century ethnography took up towards its subject, and above all to consider the results of its researches, to measure the progress made by ethnography during the last thirty years. The ethnologist of today has not only grasped the importance of symbolism in archaic thinking but has seen its intrinsic coherence, its validity, its speculative audacity, its "nobility."

Better still: today we are well on the way to an understanding of one thing of which the nineteenth century had not even a presentiment—that the symbol, the myth and the image are of the very substance of the spiritual life, that they may become disguised, mutilated or degraded, but are never extirpated. It would be well worth while to study the survival of the great myths throughout the nineteenth century: one would then see how they were humbled, minimized, condemned to incessant change of form, and yet survived that hibernation, thanks chiefly to literature. . . .

FOUR
Doings

ANTONIN ARTAUD
From "On the Balinese Theater"

Artaud's efforts "to break through language in order to touch life" placed him, finally, among the truly radical poets of the twentieth century and among those who pioneered a necessary ethnopoetics toward such ends. An actor by profession, he pursued a new overview of art and life, first as the director of the Paris-based Bureau of Surrealist Research and, after his break with the Surrealists, through his thwarted experiments with theater and film, his writings such as The Theater and Its Double (from which the present excerpt), and his collapse into a personal agony he could yet project through language. "All of which," writes Susan Sontag, "amounts to a broken, self-mutilated corpus, a vast collection of fragments . . . not achieved works of art"—she says—"but a singular presence, a poetics, an aesthetics of thought, a theology of culture, and a phenomenology of suffering" (Artaud 1976: xx).

As approximate models for his own work ("models and mysteries," writes Sontag), Artaud called on numerous traditional sources—non-Western and Western, "primitive" and "subterranean"—toward a reordering of the priorities of art and life, body and mind. His experiences with Asian theater were minimal—a Cambodian performance in Marseilles, a Balinese troupe in Paris—but in what the Thais, for example, distinguish as a poetics of the sounding of the text (rather than a poetics of the text) he found a proven instance of that more-than-verbal "poetry of space" and of the body—the true bases of what he called "the theater of cruelty" and played out—dying—through the instrument of his own voice and physical and mental being. (See also Lansing's essay on Balinese aesthetics, below, p. 241.)

The first performance of the Balinese Theater, which draws mainly on dancing, singing, pantomime, and music—and very little on psychological theater as we understand it here in Europe—restores the theater to its level of pure and autonomous creation, under the sign of hallucination and of fear.

It is quite remarkable that the first of the short plays that make up the program, which presents the admonishments of a father to a daughter who is rebelling against tradition, begins with an entrance of ghosts. The male and female characters who are going to serve the development of a dramatic but familiar subject appear to us first as personages in their spectral state, in that hallucinatory guise which is the attribute of every theatrical character, even before the situations in this sort of symbolic sketch are allowed to develop. And indeed, the situations in this play are merely a pretext. The drama does not develop as a conflict of feelings but of states of mind, which are themselves ossified and reduced to gestures—to structures. In short, the Balinese are carrying out with the utmost rigor the idea of pure theater, in which everything, conception and realization alike, has value or existence only in terms of its degree of objectification *on the stage*. They demonstrate triumphantly the absolute preponderance

SOURCE: Antonin Artaud, Selected Writings, pages 215–223.

of the director, whose creative power *eliminates words*. The situations are vague, abstract, extremely general. What brings them to life is the complex profusion of all the artifices of the stage, which impose on our minds, as it were, the idea of a metaphysics derived from a new utilization of gesture and voice.

What is really curious about all these gestures, these angular and abruptly broken attitudes, these syncopated modulations formed at the back of the throat, these musical phrases that break off short, these flappings of insect wings, these rustlings of branches, these sounds of hollow drums, these creaking of robots, these dances of animated puppets, is this: that out of their labyrinth of gestures, attitudes, and sudden cries, out of gyrations and turns that leave no portion of the space on the stage unused, there emerges the sense of a new physical language based on signs rather than words. These actors with their geometric robes seem like animated hieroglyphs. And it is not merely the shape of their robes which, shifting the axis of the human figure, creates next to the clothing of these warriors in a state of trance and of perpetual war a kind of symbolic or second clothing, which inspires an intellectual idea and which is related by all the intersecting lines to all the intersections of the spatial perspective. No, these spiritual signs have a precise meaning which impresses us only intuitively, but with enough violence to render useless any translation into logical or discursive language. And for lovers of realism at any price, who would tire of these perpetual allusions to secret and unusual attitudes of the mind, there is still the eminently realistic performance of the double who is terrified by these apparitions from the beyond. These tremblings, this childish yelping, this heel that strikes the ground rhythmically in time to the mechanism of the liberated unconscious, this double who at a certain point hides behind its own reality, offers us a portrayal of fear which is valid in every latitude and which shows us that in the human as well as the superhuman the Orientals have something to teach us in matters of reality.

The Balinese, who have a repertoire of gestures and mimetic devices for every circumstance of life, restore the superiority of theatrical convention; they demonstrate the power and the supremely effective force of a certain number of conventions that are well learned and above all masterfully executed. One reason for the pleasure we take in this flawless performance lies in the use these actors make of a precise number of unfailing gestures, tested bits of mimicry occurring on schedule, but above all in the spiritual ambiance, in the profound and subtle study that has governed the elaboration of these dramatic expressions, these powerful signs which give the impression that after many ages their power has not been exhausted. These mechanically rolling eyes, these pouts, these recurrent muscular contractions, whose studiously calculated effects rule out any recourse to spontaneous improvisation, these horizontally moving heads which seem to slide from one shoulder to the other as if on rollers—all this, which corresponds to immediate psychological necessities, also corresponds to a kind of spiritual architecture made up not only of gestures and sign language but also of the evocative power of a rhythm, the musical quality of a physical movement, the parallel and admirably fused harmony of a tone. All this may shock our European sense of theatrical freedom and spontaneous inspiration, but let no one say that this mathematics makes for sterility or monotony. The amazing thing is that a sense of richness, fantasy, and lavish abundance is created by this performance, which is governed by an attention to detail and a conscious control that are overwhelming. And the most compelling correspondences are constantly fusing sight with sound, intellect with sensibility, the gesture of a character with the evocation of the movements of a plant, across the scream of an instrument. The sighing of a wind instrument prolongs the vibrations of vocal chords with such a sense of identity that one cannot tell whether it is the voice itself that is being sustained or the senses that have absorbed the voice from the beginning. A frolicking of joints, the musical angle which the arm makes with the forearm, a foot that falls, a knee that bends, fingers that seem to fly off the hand—all this is like a perpetual play of mirrors in which the parts of the human body seem to send each other echoes, musical phrases, in which the notes of the orchestra, the whispers of the wind instruments evoke the idea of a violent aviary where the actors themselves provide the beating wings. Our theater, which has never conceived of this metaphysics of gesture, or known how to use music for such immediate and concrete dramatic purposes, our purely verbal theater which is ignorant of everything that constitutes theater, that is, everything that exists in the air of the stage, everything that is measured and surrounded by air, everything that has density in space—movements, forms, colors, vibrations, attitudes, cries—our theater would do well, in regard to what cannot be measured and what depends on the mind's power of suggestion, to ask the Balinese Theater for a lesson in spirituality. This purely popular and non-sacred theater gives us an extraordinary idea of the intellectual level of a culture that bases its civic festivals on the struggles of a soul in the grips of the specters and phantoms of the beyond. For it is a purely internal conflict that is going on in the last part of the spectacle. And, in passing, one may remark the degree of theatrical sumptuousness which the Balinese have been able to give it. Their sense of the plastic necessities of the stage is equaled only by their understanding of physical fear and of the means of releasing it. And there is in the truly terrifying appearance of their devil (probably of Tibetan origin) a striking similarity to a certain puppet within our memory, with swollen hands of white gelatin and nails of green foliage, which was the finest ornament of one of the first plays performed by the Alfred Jarry Theater.

We cannot approach this spectacle head on; it assails us with a superabundance of impressions, each richer than the last, but in a language to which it seems that we no longer possess the key. And this kind of irritation created by the impossibility of finding the thread, tracking down the beast, putting one's ear to the instrument in order to hear better, is only one more of its charms. And by language I do not mean the idiom that cannot be grasped on first hearing, but a kind of theatrical language which is external to all *spoken language* and which seems to contain a vast experience of the stage, an experience in comparison with which our productions, based exclusively on dialogue, seem like mere stammerings.

What is most impressive about this spectacle—so calculated to upset our Western conceptions of the theater that many people will deny that it has any theatrical quality at all, whereas it is the finest example of pure theater that we have been privileged to see—what is impressive and disconcerting for us Europeans is the admirable intellectuality that one feels sparkling throughout, in the dense and subtle fabric of the gestures, in the infinitely varied modulations of the voice, in that downpour of sound, as of a vast forest dripping and coming to life, and in the equally sonorous interlocking of the movements. From a gesture to a cry or a sound there is no transition: everything corresponds, as if through mysterious passageways etched right into the brain!

There is here a whole collection of ritual gestures to which we do not have the key and which seem to obey extremely precise musical indications, with something more which does not usually belong to music and which seems designed to surround thought, to pursue it, and to lead it into an inextricable and certain web. Indeed, everything about this theater is calculated in exquisite and mathematical detail. Nothing is left to chance or to personal initiative. It is a kind of superior dance in which the dancers are, above all, actors.

Time and again you see them perform a kind of recovery with measured steps. Just as you think they are lost in an inextricable maze of measures, just as you feel them about to fall into confusion, they have a characteristic way of recovering their balance, a special way of propping up the body, the twisted legs, that gives the impression of a wet rag being wrung out in time—and in three final steps, which always lead inexorably toward the middle of the stage, the suspended rhythm is over and the beat is resolved.

Everything about these dancers is just as disciplined and impersonal; there is not a movement of a muscle, not a rolling of an eye that does not seem to belong to a kind of studied mathematics which governs everything and through which everything happens. And the strange thing is that in this systematic depersonalization, in these purely muscular facial movements that are superimposed on the features like masks, everything works, everything has the maximum effect.

A kind of terror grips us as we contemplate these mechanized beings, whose joys and sorrows do not really seem to belong to them but rather to obey established rites that were dictated by higher intelligences. In the last analysis, it is certainly this impression of a Life that is higher and prescribed that impresses us most in this spectacle, which is like some rite that one might profane. And it has the solemnity of a sacred rite—the hieratic quality of the costumes gives each actor something like a double body, a double set of limbs—and the actor stiffly encased in his costume seems only the effigy of himself. There is also the broad, pounding rhythm of the music—an extremely insistent, droning, and fragile music, in which the most precious metals seem to be ground, in which springs of water seem to gush up as if in their natural state, and armies of insects march through vegetation, in which one seems to hear captured the very sound of light, in which the sound of deep solitudes seems to be reduced to flights of crystals, etc., etc.

Furthermore, all these sounds are connected to movements, as if they were the natural fulfillment of gestures that have the same quality they have; and this is done with such a sense of musical analogy that ultimately the mind is forced to confuse the two elements and to attribute to the articulated gestures of the performers the sonorities of the orchestra—and the reverse.

An impression of inhumanity, of divinity, of miraculous revelation is also created by the exquisite beauty of the women's headdresses: that series of luminous circles piled one on the other, composed of combinations of multicolored feathers or pearls so rich and beautiful that the total effect has a quality of *revelation*, whose crests sway rhythmically, responding *consciously*, it seems, to the slightest movements of their bodies.—There are also those other headdresses with a sacerdotal look, shaped like tiaras crowned with tufts of stiff flowers in oddly contrasting pairs of colors.

This dazzling blend of explosions, escapes, passages, and detours in all the directions of external and internal perception constitutes a supreme idea of theater, one which seems to have been preserved down through the ages in order to teach us what the theater should never have ceased to be. And this impression is reinforced by the fact that this spectacle—which is apparently popular and secular in its own country—is, as it were, the daily bread of the artistic feelings of these people.

Aside from the prodigious mathematics of the spectacle, what to me seems calculated to surprise and to astonish us most is this *revelatory aspect of matter*, which seems suddenly to scatter into signs in order to teach us the metaphysical identity of the concrete and the abstract, and to teach it to us *in gestures designed to last*. For the realistic aspect of matter is known in Western theater, but here it is carried to the nth power and definitively stylized.

In this theater all creation arises from the stage and finds its expression and even its origins in a secret psychic impulse which is Speech anterior to words.

It is a theater which eliminates the playwright in favor of what we in our Western theatrical jargon would call the director; but the director becomes a kind of magical conductor, a master of sacred ceremonies. And the raw material with which he works, the themes he brings to quivering life are not of himself but of the gods. They seem to come from the primitive connections of Nature which a double Spirit has favored.

What he sets in motion is the MANIFESTED.

It is a kind of primary Physics from which the Spirit has never been separated.

In a spectacle like that of the Balinese Theater there is something that eliminates entertainment, that quality of a pointless artificial game, an evening's diversion, which is the distinguishing characteristic of our theater. Its productions are carved directly from matter, from life, from reality. They possess some of the ceremonial quality of a religious rite, in that they extirpate from the mind of the spectator any idea of pretense, of the grotesque imitation of reality. This intricate gesticulation which we watch has a purpose, an immediate purpose toward which it moves by powerful means, means whose effectiveness we are in a position to experience directly. The ideas to which it aspires, the states of mind it seeks to create, the mystical solutions it offers are awakened, heightened, and attained without delay or equivocation. All this seems to be an exorcism to make our demons FLOW.

There is in this theater a low humming of the things of instinct, but brought to a point of transparency, intelligence, and malleability where they seem to offer us in physical form some of the most secret perceptions of the mind.

The situations presented may be said to have originated on stage. They have reached such a point of objective materialization that one cannot possibly imagine them outside of this dense perspective, this closed and limited sphere of the stage.

This spectacle gives us a marvelous complex of pure theatrical images for the comprehension of which a whole new language seems to have been invented: the actors with their costumes form true hieroglyphs that live and move around. And these three-dimensional hieroglyphs are in turn embellished with a certain number of ges- tures—mysterious signs which correspond to some fabulous and obscure reality that we Westerners have definitively repressed.

There is something that partakes of the spirit of a magical trick in this intense liberation of signs that are at first held back and then suddenly thrown into the air.

A chaotic turbulence, full of familiar landmarks, and at times strangely well organized, seethes in this effervescence of painted rhythms in which the single tone of the background is sustained throughout and comes through like a well-planned silence.

This idea of pure theater, which in the West is purely theoretical and which no one has ever tried to invest with the slightest reality, is realized in the Balinese Theater in a way that is astonishing, because it eliminates all possibility of resorting to words to elucidate the most abstract subjects; and because it has invented a language of gestures which are designed to move in space and which can have no meaning outside of it.

The space of the stage is utilized in all its dimensions and one might say on all possible levels. For in addition to a keen sense of plastic beauty these gestures always have as their ultimate purpose the elucidation of a mental state or a mental conflict.

At least this is the way they appear to us.

No point of space and at the same time no possible suggestion is lost. And there is an almost philosophical sense of the power that nature possesses of suddenly hurling everything into chaos.

One senses in the Balinese Theater a pre-verbal state, a state which can choose its own language: music, gestures, movements, words.

There is no doubt that this quality of pure theater, this physics of the absolute gesture which is itself idea and which forces the conceptions of the mind to pass, in order to be perceived, through the fibrous mazes and networks of matter—all this gives us a new idea of what properly belongs to the realm of forms and of manifested matter. These people who manage to give a mystical meaning to the mere shape of a robe and who, not content to place beside man his Double, attribute to each clothed man his double of clothing, who pierce these illusory or secondary garments with a sword that makes them resemble huge butterflies impaled on air, these people possess to a much greater degree than we the innate sense of the absolute and magical symbolism of nature, and offer us a lesson which it is only too sure that our theatrical technicians will be powerless to take advantage of.

This intellectual space, this psychic interplay, this silence ridden with thoughts which exists between the elements of a written sentence, is here traced in the space of the stage, between the parts of the body, the air, and the perspectives of a certain number of cries, colors, and movements.

In the productions of the Balinese Theater the mind has the feeling that the conception first collided with the gestures, that it first took root amid a whole fermentation of visual or auditory images, conceived as if in their pure state. In other words, something rather similar to the conditions for composing music must have existed for this *mise en scène* in which everything that is a conception of the mind is merely a pretext, a potentiality whose double has produced this intense poetry of the stage, this language of space and color. . . .

[Tr. M. C. Richards]

J. STEPHEN LANSING
The Aesthetics of the Sounding of the Text

What's "missing" from Artaud's spontaneous take on Balinese theater (see above, p. 235) is the awareness of a self-conscious body of discourse, an indigenous and fully formulated Balinese poetics, behind the work observed. This poetics— following from what J. Stephen Lansing, on a Southeast Asian model, calls "the aesthetics of the 'sounding of the text' "—illuminates not only Balinese performance per se but the nature of performance art in general. Such an "illumination in general" is, of course, what we've always posited for forms of Western discourse—the assumption, for example, that Aristotle's equally localized, Athenian Poetics is the basis, as in fact it may be, for a discourse on performance everywhere. Thus the Balinese poetics of performance, while working in and around an actual system of poesis, not only intensifies the flash of insight in Artaud's observations of theatrical and poetic alternatives in action but also has much to say about such matters as the overall nature of reflexivity, history, translation, poetry, and the interplay of audience and actors. And this in turn may be immediately relevant to a contemporary thought and praxis that has been shifting from the idea of a fixed text to that of a work emerging—newly, fully—in the process of performance.

For an example of the use of other-than-Western and Western performance models, see Schechner's "From Ritual to Theatre and Back," below, page 311.

"The word moves a bit of air and this the next until it reaches the ear of one who hears it and is therein awakened."

—Nachman of Bratzlav

"Homage to the god . . . who is the essence of written letters . . . concealed in the dust of the poet's pencil."

—The Sumanasantaka

The oppositions between language and culture, speech and writing, langue and parole, are the foundations of modern semiotics, the fruits of what Foucault has described as the "discovery of language" in the last two centuries in the West. They define the parameters of our discourse on language, a discourse based on our developing cultural awareness of language as more than a colorless medium of expression. Thus, for example, Paul Ricoeur investigates the nature of language by asking, "What is a text?"—a question which leads him to the oppositions between speaking and writing, and language and the world. For Ricoeur, the defining quality of a written text is precisely that it exists outside the world: "A text is somehow 'in the air,' outside of the world or without a

SOURCE: J. Stephen Lansing, "The Sounding of the Text" (previously unpublished).

world; by means of this obliteration of all relation to the world, every text is free to enter in relation with all the other texts which come to take the place of the circumstantial reality shown by living speech'' (D. Rasmussen 1971: 138). Speech, in other words, is physically present in the world—it occurs as an event in space and time—while texts hang in an unworldly suspension, awaiting a reader who may draw them into relationship with one another through the act of reading. Texts are in this sense timeless and detached from the world. Edward Said criticizes this view but regards it nonetheless as pervading, indeed defining our modern approach to texts. In a recent interview, Said wonders that ''our interpretive worldly-wisdom has been applied, in a sense, to everything except ourselves; we are brilliant at deconstructing the mystifications of a text, at elucidating the blindness of a critical method, but we have seemed unable to apply these techniques to the very life of the texts in the world . . .'' (1976: 41).[1] The subject of this essay is the ''life of texts in the world,'' a topic that, as Said observes, appears only on the distant horizons of the Western critical traditions, but is central for the literate cultures of Southeast Asia. The purpose of this essay, however, is not merely to show that others contrive to see the operations of speech and writing differently from us but that we aspire, after all, to a general theory of semiotics, a theory rich enough to accommodate the complex and interpenetrating relationships between language and culture. But our studies so far have been restricted to a very narrow range: the role of texts in Western cultures in the recent past. Texts are not always novels or advertisements; there is more to Language than French and English—ours, in short, is not necessarily a privileged position. Therefore, the distinctions between speech and writing, and language and the world, which seem to us to be a starting-point for analysis, are not necessarily obligatory.

The concept of the ''sounding of the text'' is drawn from the aesthetic vocabulary of several Southeast Asian cultures—in particular, the Balinese, whose libraries house texts in five languages, several of which are also commonly used in speech. This linguistic complexity, coupled with the brilliant theatrical traditions of the Balinese, makes Bali a particularly interesting case for studying the relationship of language to culture. But my purpose in this essay is not so much to explore the meaning of language in different cultures, but rather to attempt to introduce the notion of the sounding of the text as a semiotic principle.

I. THE POWER OF THE SOUNDED WORD

In the Thai language, the word for text is *bot*. To interpret a text in a reading or performance is to *ti bot*: to ''strike'' the text, in the same sense that one ''strikes'' a musical gong to emit a note. Mattani Rutnin writes of Thai dancers interpreting a bot: ''Those who can interpret the bot successfully, i.e. in terms of aesthetics, drama and emotion, are said to *ti bot taek* (literally, smash the text to pieces—interpret the text with utmost refinement and depth)'' (1980). Thai aesthetics is therefore divisible into two branches:

---

[1]For Said's critique of Ricoeur, see Edward Said, ''The Text, the World, the Critic,'' in *Harari* (1979), pp. 164–166.

1. the aesthetics of the text/instrument,
2. the aesthetics of the sounding of the text.

The first is analogous to modern Western aesthetics in that it involves a kind of iconographic analysis, concerned with questions of form, style, and composition. But the aesthetics of the *sounding* of the text is directed to the question of the ways a text becomes manifest in a reading or performance. In the Thai view, these are quite different, if complementary branches of aesthetics. We might summarize the differences thus: one set of questions is raised if we talk about a sonnet in terms of its intrinsic qualities, as though existing perpetually in some timeless Platonic realm of art. But very different questions suggest themselves if we consider the sonnet as it is performed, as an event occurring within a culture. There is a pervasive tradition in Southeast Asia which insists that the sounding of words or music has intrinsic power. This power is beautifully evoked in Shelly Errington's analysis of the role of prose stories (*hikayat*) in Malay culture:

> Hikayat were written, but they were written to be read aloud in a public place. As such, they are better considered notes for a performance than texts to be read in quiet solitude. People listened to, rather than read, hikayat. They were attracted into its realm through the voice of the narrator, which carried (membawa) and brought into being the hikayat.
>
> Not uncommonly, the reading of the hikayat is one of the events related in hikayat. Sejarah Melayu, for instance, tells of a hikayat being read when the Portuguese attacked Malaka. One particularly sinister passage in *Hikayat Hang Tuah* tells that Hang Jebat is asked by the raja to recite hikayat. His sweet, clear, melodious voice melts the hearts of listeners and renders them inexpressibly tender; the raja falls asleep on Hang Jebat's lap; and the palace women are inspired by lust and throw him betel nuts and perfume from behind the screen. The scene—or should we call it sound?—marks the beginning of Hang Jebat's treason. We hear of the power of words not only when hikayat are read. Words flow from Hang Tuah's mouth sweet as honey when he visits distant lands, and those around him feel love. The almost palpable physical imagery of the words flowing from his mouth points to their active presence in the world: they do not stand apart from the world, explaining it or representing it. They are a presence, having their effect in the world. Throughout the hikayat, the imagery of sounds and silence is pervasive. To *berdiam* is both to remain silent and do nothing. Of someone who is helpless the hikayat says, *tidak kata-kata lagi* ("he spoke no more"). Hang Tuah himself is wounded by the Portuguese near the end of the hikayat and falls overboard, to be retrieved quickly by his compatriots. The hikayat does not describe his wounds or the blood. Its significance falls upon us, rather, as we hear that for three days and three nights he cannot speak.

[1979: 237]

The concept of the sounding of the text is based upon belief in the power of what Errington calls "formed sounds, whether of words in spells, or the reading of the sacred texts, or of gamelan music, or of the combination of music, voices and sounds in *wayang* (shadow play)." This belief in the power of "formed sounds" is widespread among Southeast Asian peoples and appears to be very ancient. Certainly it has an archaic flavor, suggesting a rather naive or even "primitive" belief in word-magic.

But the impression of naiveté is shattered as soon as we confront even the earliest written texts. Consider, for example, the literature now known as "Old Javanese," which came into being in the Hindu/Buddhist courts of Java beginning around the ninth century A.D. The first texts were poems, written in the tradition of Sanskrit literature, in a language which drew upon both Sanskrit and Javanese styles and vocabularies. Each poem begins with a *manggala*: an invocation, which sets forth the poet's understanding of the relationship between himself, his text, and the world. The manggala begins by invoking one of many gods and goddesses, but

> it is not so much the identity of the god invoked as the manner of the invocation and the aspect in which the deity is viewed that matters. And these appear to be the same despite the variety of names. The god concerned is always the god who is present in everything that can be described as *langö*, the god of beauty in its widest sense. He is found in the beauty of the mountains and sea, in the pleasure-garden with its charms of trees and flowers and in the month when they are in full bloom, in feminine grace and charm. It goes without saying that he resides in the lover's complaint and in the description of nature, in the feeling that beauty arouses in the heart of the lover and of the poet. He resides in everything used for giving expression to that feeling, whether it is the spoken or written word, and therefore also in sounds and letters and even in the instruments of writing. He is the god of the board that is written on and the pencil that is written with, and of the dust that is sent whirling about, finally to settle, by sharpening the latter.

> [Zoetmulder 1974: 175]

The Sumanasantaka, for example, begins by invoking the god of "beauty" (langö), who is concealed in the dust of the pencil sharpened by the poet, and is asked to descend into the letters of the poem as if they were his temple. This god is considered to be both immanent and transcendent; immaterial (*niskala*); of a finer and subtler nature than the world, which is an object of the senses (*suksma*). It is through the apprehension of this "god" that one can pierce the veil of illusion (*maya*) to discover the nature of reality. This "god," then, is both the ultimate foundation of all that exists, and also its real essence—imperceptible because it is of a finer texture than the perceptible world, but nonetheless pervading everything "from the coarse to the fine" (*aganal alit*).

Obviously, the English words "god" and "beauty" are imperfect translations for the concept of such a being, or essence, or experience. After a brave attempt at translation, Zoetmulder (the foremost student of Old Javanese) throws up his hands with the remark that translators "must resign themselves to the fact that Old Javanese is exceptionally rich in this area of description, and has developed a variety of means of expressing (aesthetic emotion) which other languages simply do not possess." But Zoetmulder's remarks on the word *alangö* (which I have been rendering in the form "langö" as both "beauty" and "aesthetic experience") are helpful:

Alangö means both "enraptured" and "enrapturing." It can be said of a beautiful view as well as of the person affected by its beauty. It has what we might call a "subjective" and an "objective" aspect, for there is a common element—the Indians would say: a common *rasa*—in both subject and object, which makes them connatural and fit to become one. Objectively langö is the quality by which an object appeals to the aesthetic sense.

[Ibid.: 173]

Thus in one passage of the Sumanasantaka, the waves of the sea are described as "a flight of crystal stairs down which the poet descends when, in old age, he ends his life by plunging into langö." The same theme, of the way langö knits the essence of man and nature together, harmonizing the "Small" and "Great Worlds" (micro/macrocosm), is expressed in these lines from the poem quoted earlier, the Sumanasantaka:

When a woman wishes to die, she asks the gods to return her beauty to the month of Kartika, the loveliness of her hair to the rain-bearing clouds, the suppleness of her arms to the *welas-arep* creeper, her tears to the dew-drops suspended from the tip of a blade of grass.

[Ibid.: 209–210]

II. FROM LETTERS TO SOUNDS

The concept of langö defines an aesthetics, and with it an attitude toward language. Langö can be pursued in two directions: inward, through the letters of the poem, into the deep interior of the poet's soul; or outward, into the world, through the sounding of the text. In the second instance, aesthetic questions focus on congruence between the text (its overt meaning), the sounding of the text (the ways in which it becomes manifest), and its effects on the inner and outer worlds. Old Javanese poems were composed according to distinct metrical patterns, of which over two hundred are known to exist. It is clear that they were intended to be read aloud, and indeed such readings continue today among the "reading clubs" (*sekehe bebasan*) of Bali. These are actually performances in which the most careful attention is paid to both the sounds of the words and their meanings. A reader intones a line from the text, which may have to be repeated if he strays from the correct metrical pattern. Next, another reader proposes a spontaneous translation into modern colloquial Balinese. Once the "meaning" has been tacitly agreed on by all those present, the first reader chants the next line. The Balinese words for these "readings" (*mengidung, mekekawin*, etc.) are, I think, best rendered into English as "sounding" the text, in both the sense of turning its letters into sounds and that of searching for its meanings. From this "reading" or "sounding" it is but a short step to performance, where all the devices of music, language, and the theater are employed to carry the meaning, the langö into the world. Such performances are powerful—not because of word-magic, but because the more beautiful (alangö) a performance, the more attractive it will be. Sounding the texts dispels the illusions of ordinary consciousness and brings to light the underlying structures that bind man and nature, past and present, inner and outer. The events of everyday life are divested of their apparent uniqueness, and people become aware of themselves as acting in accordance with age-old scripts.

The sounding of the texts brings written order into the world, displaying the logos that lies beyond the illusions of mundane existence. Obviously, for this to be effective, the stories told must bear an important resemblance to events in the lives of the hearers or audience. Consequently, it is one of the distinguishing characteristics of serious Balinese drama, shadow-theater or other soundings of the text that the performers must not decide on the story to be told until they have assessed the needs of the audience. Here is Wija, a Balinese shadow-puppeteer, in an interview with an American storyteller, Diane Wolkstein (1979: 27):

> *Wolkstein:* "How do you choose which story you will tell?"
>
> *Wija:* "It is always different. Before performance begins we are served coffee and tea by the community or the people who have asked for the wayang. I talk with the people. Very often those who have sponsored the wayang will ask for certain things to be stressed."
>
> *Question:* "If you go to a village where there are troubles, do you try to solve them?"
>
> *Wija:* "Of course! That is my job! The wayang reflects our life. . . . Just as the Pandawas are always being tempted by the Kauravas, their enemies; we, too, are always being tempted by evil. By taking the shadows of the wayang into ourselves, we are strengthened by the struggle, and the victory of the Pandawas. The clashing of the swords and the heaving of the divine weapons is only the outer image of the internal battle."

In essence, a wayang performance is analogous to that of a reading club—a "sounding of the text." Line by line, an ancient text is sounded, and then an attempt is made at translation and interpretation. In a reading club, this is done orally, while in a wayang performance, music, puppets, and the theatrical skills of the puppeteer are used to enhance the interpretation. The whole performance is structured in such a way as to pose questions about the relationship of the text to those who see and hear it performed. The puppeteer is seated behind a cloth screen, which is illuminated by the flickering light of an oil lamp. Several hundred puppets are employed, representing the gods and heroes of Balinese mythology, inhabitants of the worlds that are ordinarily hidden from human sight by the veil of maya (illusion). The puppets are richly painted, but appear on the audience's side of the screen only as dark shadows, suggesting that the reality of the gods is so brillant as to be beyond human sight or imagination. The wayang screen is in one sense a window in maya, which allows us to peer into the dazzling world of the gods (for whom *we* are monochromatic shadows). In special wayang performances held for the entertainment of the gods, without a human audience, the screen is not used. The stories must be evoked by puppets speaking accurate Old Javanese; the sounds of their voices, enhanced by music from the wayang orchestra, are intrinsically powerful. Thus, on the Mountain of Poets in East Java, a wayang performance goes on continuously, day and night, sometimes with an audience but often not. The performance itself creates an order in the world, as in the story of the rampaging giant who was finally quieted by the sight of a wayang, which drew him in and made him cease his random destruction.

Before beginning a performance, a puppeteer ritually cleanses himself with holy water, holds the Tree of Life puppet to his forehead, closes his eyes and calls the gods to their places. The puppeteer Wija explains:

> There can be no world without direction. The gods have names and places in the compass. By calling their names, they go to their places—their homes. The last is the east which is the place of birth—the beginning. At this moment, too, the orchestra is playing the sunrise melody. In the wayang the puppeteer is god, and he is asking to be located in his proper place—his center—so that the creation can begin.
>
> [Wolkstein 1979: 27]

The gods whom he "calls to their places" have their homes equally at the ends of the world and within the self, according to Balinese belief. They are the gods of both the macrocosm and microcosm (in Balinese, "Great Realm"—*Buana Agung*; and "Small Realm"—*Buana Alit*). The structure of a wayang performance creates a rich and complex metaphor of inner and outer realities. The puppeteer constructs a world of pure illusion, which is paradoxically also the "real" world. Each audience—the gods and the human spectators—appears as a mere shadow to the other. The puppeteer animates the gods who in another sense animate him: gods who rule the "Great Realm" yet are found within himself. These paradoxes of illusion and reality are fully exploited in the wayang, and lead us deeper into the nature of the power Balinese attribute to sounding the text.

Within the context of Western notions of the "life of texts in the world," it is easy to see that wayang might possess what we might call an "illuminative" function. A well-told tale in a wayang might "instruct" the Balinese audience in essentially the same way that a biblical parable expounded in a church service is meant to edify a Christian congregation. But wayang performed without an audience, like endless performance on Poetry Mountain, is more mysterious. The Balinese explanation for such performances is that wayang can *create* order, in both the inner and outer worlds. To create order in the world is the privilege of gods, but the gods themselves are animated shadows in the wayang, whom the puppeteer calls to their places as he assumes the power of creation. It is significant that the effectiveness of wayang does not depend on the audience "really" believing that the puppeteer (or his puppets) are divine. In fact, quite the reverse is true. One of the most popular texts for wayang is the tenth-century poem *Arjuna Wijaya*. In this passage the god Indra, disguised as an elderly human, instructs the hero Arjuna:

> Blinded by the passions and the world of the senses, one fails to acquire knowledge of oneself. For it is as with the spectators of a puppet-performance: they are carried away, cry and are sad (because of what befalls their beloved hero or heroine), in the ignorance of their understanding. And this even though they know that it is merely carved leather that moves and speaks. That is the image of one whose desires are bound to the objects of the senses and who refuses to understand that all appearances are only an illusion and a display of sorcery without any reality.
>
> [Zoetmulder 1974: 209]

Yet despite this emphatic disavowal of "magical" powers in the puppets, puppeteers are regarded by the Balinese as a kind of priest. But they are priests whose aim is not to mystify with illusion but to clarify the role of illusion in our perception of reality. As Wija explained, "Wayang means shadow—reflection. Wayang is used to reflect the gods to the people and the people to themselves." Wayang reveals the power of language and the imagination to go beyond "illumination," to construct an order in the world which exists both in the mind and, potentially, in the outer world as well. The performance itself poses questions, in the minds of the audience, about the relations between imaginary worlds, perceptual worlds, and "real" worlds. In contemplating a wayang, one sees that the boundaries between inner and outer realities—imagined worlds, the world before our eyes, and the worlds of the past and present which we take to be "real"—are forever shifting and in flux.

III. LANGUAGE AND PERFORMANCE

It is characteristic of the sounding of the text in Balinese performances that several different languages are used. Usually they are juxtaposed—different characters speak in different languages—in order to exploit different properties of language. Balinese libraries house texts in Sanskrit, Old Javanese, Middle Javanese, Balinese, and Indonesian. The first three are ancient languages, now spoken only in performances, where they conjure up the worlds of the gods and the splendid kingdoms of the dim past. In Alton Becker's useful phrase, they are languages used for "speaking the past." To "speak the present," one uses Balinese or Indonesian. But spoken Balinese itself is divided into registers that carry distinct connotations of place: High Balinese is courtly language; Middle Balinese is formal speech between equals; Low Balinese, the vernacular of the villages. In the same way, the use of modern Indonesian invokes a modern urban context. All of these languages and registers may be employed in a theatrical performance, allowing a single actor to step adroitly from one historical/linguistic context to another:

REALM	LANGUAGE OR REGISTER
Modern World	Indonesian
Traditional Villages	Low Balinese
Recent Balinese Courts	High Balinese
Medieval Javanese Kingdoms	Middle Javanese
Legendary Past of "Indian" Epics—Heroic Age	Old Javanese
Timeless Realms of the Gods	Sanskrit

In the following excerpt from the first few minutes of a "mask theater" (*topeng*) performance, a single dancer shifts from language to language (and realm to realm) as he tells the story of the invasion of an East Javanese kingdom by a fifteenth-century Balinese king, Jelantik (Emigh 1979: 38–39).

Excerpt from "Jelantik Goes to Blambangan"

Pensar Kelihan, a clown/servant/storyteller, wearing a purple half-mask with round, bulging eyes emerges from behind a curtain and begins to dance, to the accompaniment of *gamelan* music.

LANGUAGE	SPEECH
Middle Javanese (excerpt from poem "Kidung Tantri")	A story is told of the King of Patali, rich, proud, and full of dignity. (Dances proudly.) Truly magnificent! Proceeding now! AAaat! Ah! Ha, ha, ha! Arah! Hi, hi, hi!
Old Javanese (excerpt from the Old Javanese version of the Mahabharata—tenth century)	At dawn, the red sun rises. The rustling of leaves on the mountainside joins the sounds of the frogs large and small.
Middle Balinese	I'm so happy! So happy! I never get bored, telling you about my happiness! Like today! Why don't I get bored, talking about my happiness? Ayah! Hi, hi, hi! Heh! Why am I so happy? Because I just now became a bachelor again! Hi, hi, hi!
High Balinese	Oh my lord and king, I try to follow you loyally. I beseech you, lay not your curse upon me, for I am going to tell your story now. Singeh! Singeh! Please! Please! I pay homage to the ancestors, to those who are already holy. And to the divine trinity, the Holy Lords Wisnu, Brahma, and Iswara. And I pay homage as well to all those who would make the country-side peaceful and prosperous here in ancient Bali. I ask for your blessings. I beseech you not to lay your curses upon me.
Middle Balinese	And why? Why do I offer up these prayers? Because, I am about to tell you of my Lord, the great King here in Gelgel, Klungkung, the great Dalem Waturrenggong.
Old Javanese (excerpt from the Old Javanese Ramayana)	Spinning round on his tail, the son of Subali rises higher and higher.
Low Balinese (the local dialect of Klungkung, where the performance is being held)	Aduh! What a chase those noblemen in the orchestra gave me! (He refers to the orchestra for this performance.) Now I'm worn out! Already too tired to give you a show! Mind you, I don't mean to criticize. Not just yet! It's my first time here. My first time dancing with these musicians. Their first time playing with me. And I'm very old-fashioned. Just like an old dog. There's not much fur left on my hide and what there is of it is very short. Huh! Moving on!

LANGUAGE	SPEECH
High Balinese	My Lord and Master, Dalem Waturrenggong, is the ruler of this kingdom. His mind is troubled now, filled with thoughts of His Royal Highness, His Majesty, the King of Blambangan.
Middle Balinese	What could have broken up their old friendship?

In the space of a few minutes, the actor has invoked four languages, of which most of his audience will understand only two or three. He has quoted from both of the great Hindu epics, the Ramayana and the Mahabharata, along with the Middle Javanese court poem, Kidung Tantri. He steps "out of character" for an instant to make fun of himself as a "mangy old dog of a performer," then instantly returns to his role of servant in a sixteenth-century Balinese court. In a manner unknown to Western theater, he weaves the story into the world of the audience and creates connections among the many worlds conjured up by the languages and poetry he uses.

Ancestral visitation is ancient in Indonesian cultures and continues to play a part in many Balinese theatrical performances in the phenomenon called "trance." The spirit of a performer can be "inhabited" by the spirit of the one he portrays. In this sort of drama, the performer always enters from behind a drawn curtain, after first shaking the curtain in such a way as to suggest some Power taking possession of it. There is thus a certain ambiguity about the dramatic figures who emerge from behind the curtain: are they actors, or visiting spirits? John Emigh comments on the entrance of the evil king, in a later episode of the performance quoted above:

> As the King of Blambangan shakes the curtain, thereby cueing a frenzied rush of percussive sound, he cries out in Old Javanese, "Behold, here I come, the King of Blambangan," and warns the audience that preparation is necessary to witness his powerful countenance. The curtain is yanked open and the King thrusts his animalistic hands forward, looking through the opened curtain into the performance oval, demanding to know whom it is he is facing. Is he talking to the warriors from Gelgel who have invaded his territory? Or is he speaking to the audience he sees revealed to him in a language which is no longer theirs? The ambiguity is deliberate. By shifting back and forth between the modes of illusion and visitation, the performer can playfully toy with the vantage point of the audience.

[Ibid.: 27]

The ability of different languages to evoke different "realms" is part of the reason why so many languages are employed in the theater. But from a Balinese perspective, differences between languages go deeper than their association with a particular time and place. Different languages are regarded as having different properties and hence different constraints on their use. Sanskrit and Old Javanese, the languages used to "speak the past," are intrinsically powerful and may not be lightly used. The nature of this power has been investigated by several scholars, beginning with C. C. Berg, who drew attention to passages in Old Javanese texts such as the *Hariwangsa*, which state the author's desire to promote, by the words of the text, "the invincibility of the king and the prosperity of the world." Following Berg, Zoetmulder observed that certain languages may create such effects because "there is a kind of identity between the word and what it stands for. But the degree of its effectiveness is dependent on various factors. It is high if the words are taken from a text or are borrowed from a language that is considered sacred (1974: 167).

In modern semiology this would be described as an iconic view of language. Michel Foucault has ascribed a similar view of language to sixteenth-century Europe:

> In its original form, when it was given to men by God himself, language was an absolutely certain and transparent sign for things, because it resembled them. The names of things were lodged in the things they designated, just as strength is written in the body of the lion, regality in the eye of the eagle, just as the influence of the planets is marked upon the brows of men: by form of similitude. This transparency was destroyed at Babel as a punishment for men. Languages became separated and incompatible with one another only insofar as they had previously lost this original resemblance to things that had been the prime reason for the existence of language.
>
> [1970: 36]

Thus, according to Foucault, in the "classical" sixteenth-century view, language lost its direct iconic nature at the Tower of Babel. For this reason, the oldest language (Hebrew), while no longer directly connected with the things it names, still contains, "as if in the form of fragments, the marks of that original name-giving." This seems very close to the Balinese view that Sanskrit is close to being a "perfect" language, in the sense that the connection between the word and what it signifies is not seen as arbitrary but intrinsic. Compare Foucault's example of this iconic view of language with Zoetmulder's:

> Foucault: "Paracelsus asks, 'Tell me, then, why snakes in Helvetia, Algoria, Swedland understand the Greek words Osy, Osya, Osy. . . . In what academies did they learn them, so that scarcely have they heard the word than they immediately turn tail in order not to hear it again? Scarcely do they hear the word, when, notwithstanding their nature and their spirit, they remain immobile and poison no one.' " [1970: 33]
>
> Zoetmulder (quoting Old Javanese texts): " 'Whosoever listens devotedly (*tuhagana*) to the story of Astika and the serpent-sacrifice has no need to fear serpents.' " [1974: 166]

For the Balinese, certain Sanskrit slokas possess this iconicity and are therefore "magical." Sanskrit is also supposed to be the oldest language. More recent languages—Old Javanese, Middle Javanese, Balinese, Indonesian—are less and less iconic, but the power of Old and Middle Javanese poetry resides in no small part in its iconicity, and for this reason, the manner of its "sounding" is critical for its efficacy.

Iconicity is dramatically portrayed as a possibility in texts such as the Old Javanese Ramayana, in which powerful words spoken by a character with sufficient *sakti* (power) *must* happen. It is not only the language in which the words are spoken but the circumstance of their utterance that makes the words come true. Sanskrit is the most iconic—the meaning of a mantra cannot be realized if it is not sounded correctly and in the proper circumstances. Words spoken in Indonesian or modern Balinese cannot be iconic under any circumstances. Thus, it is only in the total context of a performance that the issue of the relationship of a symbol to its referent can be settled. For an articulate Balinese, language can seemingly take on any resonance, from a sound that echoes music and is the true name of a thing, to words rich with archaic associations and social connotations, to mere weightless, arbitrary signs.

This suggests an important difference between the Western and Balinese attitudes toward the relationship of a particular language to the world. Foucault poses this question in an interesting way in the concept of the *episteme*: the principles of linguistic order, or classification, which establish preconditions for systems of knowledge. For Foucault there is no order,

> no similitude and no distinction, even for the wholly untrained perception, that is not the result of a precise operation and of the application of a preliminary criterion. A "system of elements"—a definition of the segments by which those segments can be affected, and lastly, the threshold above which there is a difference and below which there is a similitude—is indispensible for the establishment of even the simplest form of order.
>
> [1970: xx]

In *The Order of Things*, Foucault examines for postmedieval European culture "what modalities of order have been recognized, posited, linked with space and time, in order to create the positive basis of knowledge as we find it employed in grammar and philology, in natural history and biology, in the study of wealth and political economy."

Foucault traces the succession of epistemes as a linear process, in which one episteme succeeds another. Thus, in his view, "classical" thought crumbled at the end of the eighteenth century when language ceased to be iconic, and "words wandered off on their own." Foucault shares with Derrida a perception that the "modernity" of our thought is based on our discovery of language—our sense of language as the "empty play of signifiers." Foucault's perception of a linear succession of epistemes in Western culture, each ultimately grounded in a different linguistic order, provides a clear contrast to the relationship of language to culture in Bali. Here languages and textual traditions do not succeed one another; rather, they coexist and interact with one another. In the space of a few minutes, as we saw in the excerpt from "Jelantik Goes to Blambangan," a Balinese actor can employ the different properties of several languages to construct, in the minds of the audience, several distinct "realms" or realities. It is precisely the juxtaposition of different realms—or in Foucault's terminology, epistemes—that creates the drama. The plot of a "story" is secondary, almost unimportant; theatrical tension is created by the interaction of the "imaginary" realms with the present situation of the audience. Because stories must not be chosen beforehand, the challenge for performers is to bring the different textual traditions of the past to bear on the novelties of the present, molding them into continuing patterns of order.

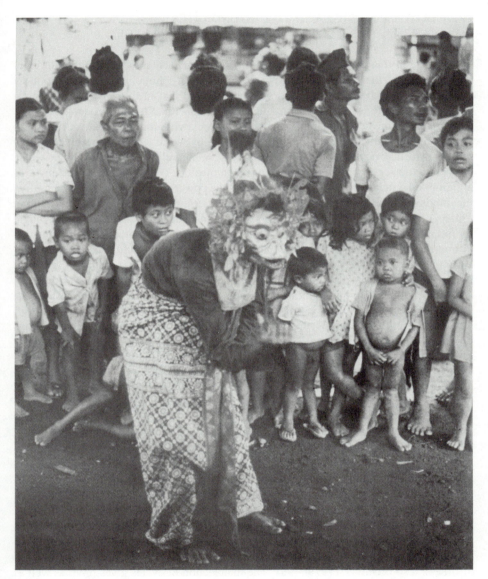

FIGURE 4. The Master Clown (*Parekan*) Twalen in a village temple performance. Photo by J. Stephen Lansing.

IV. CLOWNS, MUSIC, AND THE BOUNDARIES
OF TIME

We have seen that the different languages of Bali are each associated with a different realm, and that these realms are arranged in a sort of chronological order, from the ancient times to the present. It has also been hinted that in the context of dramatic performances different languages are often associated with different musical styles. This association of music with language may seem somewhat foreign to us, but from the standpoint of Balinese aesthetics, the sounding of words and music are intimately related. Music is never merely ornamental; it is an integral part of the process by which the boundaries between the worlds are made permeable. The sounds of powerful words are mingled with the flow of music, which has the power to shape and bend time itself in the minds of the hearers. The flow of sounds creates a tempo, a perceived rhythm of time. Thus, as the texts are sounded, performers and even members of the audience are caught up in the flow, experiencing sounds to which they fit their movements, their thoughts, ultimately perhaps their whole perception. Obviously this is not only a Balinese phenomenon but also the common human experience of music. But Balinese aesthetics emphasizes the power of music to shape people's perceptions, particularly of time and temporal rhythms. For the Balinese, absorption in the flow of sounds can finally be total, leading to the state of "trance" in which one is "in" the music-time or music-world. This is not simply a passive state of musical rapture, the absorption in the sounds alone that comes with listening attentively to a good performer. It is, or rather is described by the Balinese as being, an active experience of being *in* the music-world, the other-world. This is possible because the sounds of the music and the text are iconic for each other, and both point to a particular imaginary world. The music-world *is* the place spoken of in the text and portrayed by the dancers or puppets. Watching a performance on an admittedly rather bare and tatty stage or wayang screen, one is nonetheless carried along by the flow of sounds to lose oneself amid the images of the myths.

As Judith Becker has recently shown, the flow of music is the basic metaphor in Balinese thought for the flow of time. The Balinese conceptualize time not in terms of a linear flow, but rather as many repeating cycles, which reflect the rhythms of growth of the natural world. Calendars depict the intersections of different cycles or weeks. In a Balinese gamelan orchestra, each musician plays a cyclical, repetitive piece, and the fabric of the melody is created by the interlocking of the various cycles. Becker explains: "The fundamental governing principle in gamelan music is the cyclic recurrence of a melodic/temporal unit, which is a musical manifestation of the way in which the passage of time is also ordered" (1979: 198). The intersection of cycles gives time, as well as music, a kind of texture. Each day has a meaning, a quality, according to where it falls in the intersection of several cycles. This concept is essentially foreign to Western calendars, although we do have a single example: Friday the Thirteenth, a special kind of day, with a quality inherent in its position at the juncture of two cycles. By showing the qualities of different intersecting cycles, Balinese calendars tell, as Clifford Geertz put it, "not what time it is, but what *kind* of time it is." These cycles are not arbitrary units, but are regarded as expressing the true rhythms of time. According to Balinese cosmology, every living being is on its own temporal or developmental cycle, a process of growth followed by decay. Events occur as cycles touch, when beings interact with one another in the ''Middle World.'' In this way, past and present, man and nature are not separated, but woven together: ''The forest feels dejected in the month of Asadha, because its chill makes poets shiver and even sick from cold.''

But in the theater, there are special characters who alone are immune to the cycles of time—characters who move across the boundaries of time, music, and language. These characters are of special interest because they are not mentioned in any of the ancient texts, but play an important part nonetheless in the telling of most stories. They are called *parekan*, a word usually translated into English as ''clowns'' or ''fools,'' and they are indeed bumbling, odd-shaped, buffoonish creatures who play the role of servants to the gods and heroes of the stories. Their chief function appears to be one of translation: when it seems likely that members of the audience do not understand part of the story (probably because they do not understand the language being used, for few Balinese are fluent in all the languages of the theater), the clowns step in, translating and interpreting, making jokes, and rendering everything into Low Balinese.

The function of these clowns poses an interesting problem regarding the relationship of the text to the audience. In one sense they bring the drama to the audience as helpful translators. But their function as translators could easily be obviated by translating the text itself, as we perform Aeschylus in modern English. The structural effect of retaining the clowns is really the reverse: to create a space between the world of the audience and the text as it is invoked on-stage. The clowns create a liminal space for themselves, and they play with the structures that create the boundaries of the performance: music, language, and dramatic style. Mediating between performers and audience, they speak to themselves, to the audience, and to the mythical characters who speak the words of the ancient texts. Like all clowns, they have no social position and are therefore free to comment on the social dramas they observe. We might think of them as cousins to Shakespeare's fools—except that in Shakespeare, the clowns never speak directly to the audience, though they are forever trying to instill a reflexive awareness in their lords and masters, as the Fool does for Lear.

But what distinguishes Balinese clowns from those of the European tradition is their power of translation—the power to control the sounding of the text. Dancing back and forth between performers and audience, translating and enhancing some words while allowing others to pass into the void, they create the channels for the sounding of the text. In this sense, they are the masters of poesis—the use of words to create poetic worlds that are more true, more real than the everyday waking world of the audience.

That the Balinese recognize this power as supreme is shown in the worst-kept secret of the Balinese theater, the identity of the greatest of clowns, Twalen. Twalen is the prince of fools, a fat Falstaffian buffoon who usually plays the servant of the godlike Pandavas. But in reality, as everyone knows, Twalen is the elder brother of Siva, greatest of the gods, and is thus older and more powerful than all the gods.

CONCLUSION

One of the major trends in poststructuralist semiotics has been a progressive distancing of the author, and the reader, from the text. In part this derives from an early emphasis, in structural linguistics, on viewing languages as systems of signs, autonomous in the sense that they may be understood without reference to the minds of speaker or hearer, writer or reader. More recently, this view of language has been challenged. Chomsky's argument that language must be understood in relation to mind helped to inaugurate a poststructuralist phase in linguistics. Few linguists now see language from a strictly Saussurean perspective, as an "autonomous" system of signs.

Separation of language and mind has also been strongly challenged from an evolutionary, biological perspective. Increasingly studies of the role of language in the brain suggest that language and thought are inextricably linked and that the origin of human (as distinct from animal) language does not lie in social communication. For that purpose, according to most researchers, a much simpler language consisting of a few hundred signs would be ample. Harry J. Jerison provides a persuasive summary of research on the evolution of symbolic language in the human line:

> If there were selection pressures toward the development of language specifically for communication, we would expect the evolutionary response to be the development of "prewired" language systems with conventional sounds and symbols. These are the typical approaches to communication in other vertebrates, and they are accomplished (as in birds) with little or no learning and with relatively small neural systems. The very flexibility and plasticity of the language systems of the human brain argue for their evolution as having been analogous to that of other sensory integrative systems, which are now known to be unusually plastic, or modifiable by early experience. (Benjamin Lee Whorf and Edward Sapir pointed this out many years ago as one of the maladaptive features of this flexibility of the language system, which enables different societies to develop different languages and hence different realities, often with catastrophic effects on the interactions of human communities.)
>
> I am proposing here that the role of language in communication first evolved as a side effect of its basic role in the perception of reality. The fact that communication is so central to our present view of language does not affect the argument. It is, in fact, theoretically elegant to explain the evolution of an important novel adaptation in a species by relating it to the conversion of earlier patterns of adaptation. We can think of language as being merely an expression of another neural contribution to the construction of mental imagery, analogous to the contributions of the encephalized sensory systems and their association systems. *We need language more to tell stories than to direct action.*[2] In the telling we create mental images in our listeners that might normally be produced only by the memory of events as recorded and integrated by the sensory and perceptual systems of the brain. . . . In hearing or reading another's words we literally share another's consciousness, and it is that familiar use of language that is unique to man. [1976]

Language, then, is far more than a colorless medium of communication, more even than a system of signs—for it plays a continuous active role in the processes of imagining and interpreting the world. It is from this perspective on language that we can

---

[2]Emphasis mine.—J. S. L.

appreciate the richness of the Southeast Asian concept of "sounding the text." It is in the mind that the flow of sounds—music and language—can join with visual images, even shadows, in the process Rothenberg has called "world-making and self-making." The power to control the sounding of the text, as Twalen shows us, is the power to create the world.

ERNEST THEODORE KIRBY
From "Shamanistic Theater: Origins and Evolution"

The relation of shamans and their works to art, dance, music, poetry, performance—and, above all, to vision and healing—traces back to the Dancing Sorcerers of Europe's paleolithic caves. "Rain kings, magic protectors, chiefs, artisans and ambassadors," the shamans, now rediscovered, have become the prototypical "culture heroes . . . of all the European arts" (La Barre 1970: 422). Weston La Barre stresses the shaman's "secret magic, music," through "the harp-singing shaman Apollo . . . leader of the muses," but the shaman has also emerged as a kind of protopoet—"very much," writes Peter Furst, "Radin's own PRIMITIVE MAN AS PHILOSOPHER." (See above, pp. 31, 59.) Masters-of-language, "[these] shamans of the non-literate and pre-industrial world not only have accurate command over a body of oral literature that, if transcribed, could fill (indeed has filled) not hundreds but thousands of manuscript pages, but typically are masters of poetic vocabularies that far exceed those of their fellow tribesmen, and that equal, or exceed, those of the average educated individual in literate societies" (Furst 1977: 25−26).

If this image of the shamans is somehow equivalent to the shamans' own vision of a mythic First Shaman as their prototype, it isn't only a matter of a distant past from which we're totally cut off but a matter of works and acts common to all human cultures which the shamans first invented and developed. In what follows, we've selected from Kirby's almost definitive article those aspects of shamanistic performance most directly tied to the interests of this gathering, but his treatment of "the shamanistic origins of popular entertainments" is also and decidedly worth the reader's attention (for which see Kirby 1974 and/or Schechner 1976: 139−149).

The shaman is a "master of spirits" who performs in trance, primarily for the purpose of curing the sick by ritualistic means. Hunting magic, vegetation magic, conveying souls

SOURCE: *Ernest Theodore Kirby, Ur-Drama: The Origins of Theater, pages 1−31.*

to the realm of the dead, divination, and the giving of oracles are among the specialized functions that the shaman assumes. The distribution of shamanism among primitive peoples is virtually worldwide, and it has continued to exist side by side with developed religion or as a function of it. Despite Mircea Eliade's suggestion that we are not to think of shamanism as "primordial," there are several reasons to consider it so. The apparent diffusion of shamanist practices from Central Asia and Siberia through the Americas to the very extremity of the southern continent would attest to the great age of the phenomenon. Siberian-American shamanism represents the metaphysical practices of hunting peoples, strongly suggesting that the "mastery of animal spirits" was practiced by the nomadic hunting cultures that preceded cultivation. Andreas Lommel has traced prehistoric shamanism from the Early Magdalenian (13000−6000 B.C.) by means of the art and artifacts of the early hunters. Weston La Barre and others have made similar identifications in regard to mankind's earliest art. It also seems probable that shamanism occurs at times through parallel development rather than diffusion, because of the great and similar need and the similar structure of the psyche.

Shamanism seems to stand in a particular relationship to spirit mediumship. Eliade defines shamanism as a technique of ecstasy characterized by trance flight to spirit worlds and by a mastery over fire in rituals (Eliade 1964: 4 ff.). In this state the shaman does not become the instrument of the spirits but maintains control over them. Spirit mediumship, dominant in Africa, is possession in trance by a spirit who speaks from within the medium and determines his actions, essentially an "inhabitation" or "incarnation" of the spirit. I. M. Lewis, however, has questioned the distinction, feeling that Eliade was "seeking to drive a wedge between spirit possession and shamanism" (Lewis 1971: 50), and Rahmann has hesitated in regard to its applicability. The two modes of practice can exist in the same culture, as they do in China, and Jan de Groot reproduces an historical Chinese document which appears to discuss a cultural transition from trance flight to spirit mediumship (de Groot 1964: 1191). Definition can include the two modes: "The term 'shaman,' borrowed from the ethnography of Siberia, means a magician, healer and spirit medium combined, a person who is able to put himself into trance states in which he is thought to travel in heaven or in the underworld or to be possessed by spirits from these places" (Zerries 1968: 311). For our purposes, shamanism and spirit mediumship are identical, for they result in similar performances, affect audiences in the same way, and produce similar theatrical elaborations. On the other hand, it is shamanism as it is most rigorously defined, which has almost invariably been the antecedent of established theatre forms. It is on this basis then that we may speak of the shamanistic origins of theatre.

That shamanic performance may be considered the ur-theatre or prototheatre implies a very important distinction. Shamanistic ritual is unlike rites-of-passage or other forms of what may be called ceremonial ritual in that it depends upon the immediate and direct manifestation to the audience of supernatural presence, rather than its symbolization. All ritual and ceremony can be theatrical, but the theatricality of shamanistic ritual is related to its function in a particular way. In order to effect a cure of the patient, belief in what is happening must be held, reinforced, and intensified, not only in the patient, but in the audience as well, for their experience contributes directly to the effect. The audience actively reinforces the experience of the patient, and its own belief in a particular world view or cosmology is in turn reinforced by direct experience of it. Shamanistic theatre, founded upon manifestation of supernatural presence, develops from a small curing seance, which in effect needs only patient and shaman as participants, but actually depends upon an audience. This leads to more elaborate curing ceremonies and to rituals and trance dances for curing, exorcism, and other purposes. This complex develops finally into performances which are purely theatre, spectacles from which the functional element has disappeared. We may first trace a number of the significant aspects of performance and reconstruct general evolutionary sequences in this development, beginning with the basic element, the curing seance.

Lucile Hoerr Charles's study of 1953, "Drama in Shaman Exorcism," drew attention to the theatrical aspects of the shamanistic seance. Examples in her cross-cultural survey were drawn from Asia, Africa, North America, South America, and Oceania, and the summary of her findings reads as follows:

> Professional cure by a shaman who is the central actor usually involves careful preparations, full publicity, and an eager audience; impressive setting and lighting, costume and makeup, theatrical properties and sound effects. Actual performance includes dramatic invocation of evil or benevolent spirits, or both, for diagnosis and advice as to treatment; possession of or battle with the shaman by the spirits through ecstasy or frenzy which may be considered a supreme example of dramatic impersonation, often with elaborate use of voice, dialogue, and body pantomime; concretizing the disease demons, and driving them away, often with sucking out, sleight of hand, and display of disease objects; and luring home of the sick person's soul. The performance may require the help of stage assistants, and active participation by the patient and the audience. . . . The audience experiences entertainment, enlightenment, comforting, and renewed faith; and, occasionally, reactions of skepticism. The shaman afterwards may be exhausted, and collapse is common. Theatrical measures and paraphernalia throughout heighten the emotional quality of the seance and powerfully assist the shaman's psychotherapeutic function.
>
> [Charles 1953: 96]

The shamanic performance can occur indoors or out, in various types of setting or staging, during the night or during the day, but a rather small, darkened room, dimly illuminated, seems to be characteristic of the prototypical seance. The walls that contain the seance have the spirit world behind them; it can howl about outside, rap upon them, cause them to shake, and penetrate into the darkened, enclosed space. Close proximity to others gives the audience some reassurance. Close proximity to the shaman who will manifest the supernatural brings a degree of terror. The Evenk seance is typical of Siberian shamanism:

> At this moment, the song ceased and the sounds of the drum were gradually muffled, becoming a soft roll. The listeners with bated breath awaited the appearance of the spirit. The ensuing silence was broken by a sharp blow on the drum, changing into a short roll. In the silence following this, the voices of the spirits could be clearly heard: the snorting of beasts, bird-calls, the whirring of wings, or

others, according to the spirit appearing before the shaman at the moment. . . .
The journey of the *khargi* [an animal spirit helper] to the other world is described in
the shaman's songs in such fantastic form, so deftly accompanied by motions,
imitations of spirit-voices, comic and dramatic dialogues, wild screams, snorts,
noises, and the like, that it startled and amazed even this far-from-superstitious
onlooker. The tempo of the song became faster and faster, the shaman's voice
more and more excited, the drum sounded ever more thunderously. The moment
came when the song reached its highest intensity and feeling of anxiety. The drum
moaned, dying out in peals and rolls in the swift, nervous hands of the shaman.
One or two deafening beats were heard and the shaman leaped from his place.
Swaying from side to side, bending in a half-circle to the ground and smoothly
straightening up again, the shaman let loose such a torrent of sounds that it seemed
everything hummed, beginning with the poles of the tent, and ending with the
buttons on the clothing. Screaming the last parting words to the spirits, the shaman
went further and further into a state of ecstasy, and finally, throwing the drum into
the hands of his assistant, seized with his hands the thong connected to the tent pole
and began the shamanistic dance—a pantomime illustrating how the *khargi*,
accompanied by the group of spirits, rushed on his dangerous journey fulfilling
the shaman's commands. . . . Under the hypnotic influence of the shamanistic
ecstasy, those present often fell into a state of mystical hallucination, feeling
themselves active participants in the shaman's performance.

[Anisimov 1963: 101−102]

Dialogue, enactments, ventriloquism, incantations, music, dance, and song create
a swirling stream of images drawn from a number of performance modes. The effect is
literally hypnotic and hallucinatory, as we see also from Shirokogoroff's account of a
Siberian Tungus seance:

The rhythmic music and singing, and later the dancing of the shaman, gradually
involve every participant more and more in a collective action. When the audience
begins to repeat the refrains together with the assistants, only those who are
defective fail to join the chorus. The tempo of the action increases, the shaman
with a spirit is no more an ordinary man or relative, but is a "placing" (i.e.,
incarnation) of the spirit; the spirit acts together with the audience, and this is felt
by everyone. The state of many participants is now near to that of the shaman
himself, and only a strong belief that when the shaman is there the spirit may only
enter him, restrains the participants from being possessed in mass by the spirit.
This is a very important condition of shamanizing that does not however reduce
mass susceptibility to the suggestion, hallucinations, and unconscious acts produced in a state of mass ecstasy. When the shaman feels that the audience is with
him and follows him he becomes still more active and this effect is transmitted to
his audience. After shamanizing, the audience recollects various moments of the
performance, their great psychophysiological emotion and the hallucinations of
sight and hearing that they have experienced. They then have a deep satisfaction—
much greater than that from emotions produced by theatrical and musical per-

formances, literature and general artistic phenomena of the European complex, because in shamanizing, the audience at the same time acts and participates.

[Lewis 1971: 53]

Seances in other geographic areas can differ considerably from those of Siberia, often being less overtly spellbinding, but they develop the situation and the narrative of the cure in relation to the spirits and have definite aesthetic and theatrical qualities. John Beattie and John Middleton comment in regard to the spirit mediumship of Africa on "the degree to which spirit mediumship is, or may be, no more—and no less—than a kind of drama, differing perhaps in the degree of involvement (or dissociation) of the actors, but essentially a theatrical performance" (Beattie and Middleton 1969: xxviii). Dialogue, the hallmark of our drama, occurs in the seance as the shaman converses with his spirits or recounts the adventures of his trance journey to the spirit worlds. It also takes place in the form of interaction between the spirits and the participants in the ritual. This dialogue can be achieved by the ventriloquism of the shaman, as among the Tanala of Madagascar, described by R. Linton:

The people begin clapping and singing softly. After a time a knocking is heard on the walls, or voices are heard repeating: "We have come. We have come." There are sometimes as many as ten or twelve spirits, distinguishable by their different voices. The voices are nasal and seem to come from the east or west . . . sometimes high, sometimes low. . . . The head of the family, or the sick person, then tells the spirits why they have been called. After this the ombiasy [shaman] explains the situation fully and the spirits tell the cause of the illness and the medicine to be given. . . . After answering the questions, the spirits drink the rum, dance and sing . . . accompanied by rhythmic rappings on the floor and walls, but always near the ombiasy. . . . Finally they say they are tired and must go, and troop off noisily. The spirits are the souls of ancestors, but no individuals can be identified.

[Charles 1953: 109]

Dialogue also occurs when a spirit possesses or inhabits a shaman, as among the Yakuts, where the shaman in this example converses in trance with the master of the house in which the seance is being held. The spirit comes seeking a gift as propitiation.

The shaman rapidly approaches the entrance, beats the drum three times and repeats "Ba-ba-ba-ba," shaking his head.

"My one-sided Keeleeni, my one-eyed lame one, come quickly."

He goes to the audience, holding the drum behind his back and begins to speak in the name of his control, the spirit Keeleeni, stuttering:

Shaman (spirit): For what need have you caused me to be called.

Master of the House: I was not able to withstand the morning frost and evening dew.

Shaman (spirit): How will it be if you give me a present. If you will give me

something I will have yours who ran away and will bring back yours, who went
away!

Master of the House: Next time when you come!

Shaman (spirit): Is it because of that (I) am scampering away with nothing, eh?

The shaman goes to the left, mutters something (lets the spirit out of him) and
speaks, without stuttering, in his own name.

[Popov 1933: 266]

A series of spirits then inhabit the shaman in turn, each carrying on a dialogue with
the master of the house and seeking a gift as propitiation for leaving the patient. This
pattern of dialogue, in form and content, is remarkably similar to that found in the
Ceylonese *sanniyakuma* demon play, an exorcism which leads directly to drama, as we
shall see. It would also appear that conversation with the spirit developed into the
shamanic functions of giving oracles as prognostication, divination, or advice. There is
a transcript of an interesting dialogue between two trance mediums in Bali which served
to provide oracular advice to the community (Belo 1970: 119). Dialogue must be
considered a vital and active aspect of shamanist dramatic performance.

Another primary factor in the aesthetics of these performances is a magical
illusionism capable of inducing not only belief in the supernatural, in the virtually
impossible, but of contributing to a state of mind which further augments the actual
spectacle with hallucinatory perceptions, as in Siberia. The shamanistic seance is aptly
named. It is very like the seance of a medium in present Western culture, with its
levitation of tables, strange rappings, spectral apparitions, and voices from the dead.
Eliade notes how in a Chukchee shaman's seance ''suddenly the voices of the 'spirits'
are heard from every direction; they seem to rise out of the ground or to come from very
far away. . . . During this time, in the darkness of the tent, all sorts of strange phenomena occur: levitation of objects, the tent shaking, rain of stones and bits of wood, and so
on'' (Eliade 1964: 255). In an Evenk seance in Siberia ''wild screams, the snorting of
beasts, bird voices rushed about the tent with the shaman'' (Anisimov 1963: 104).
Shamans of the Algonquins used ventriloquism to represent rushing wind and the voices
of spirits underground and in the air (Hoffman 1896: 138−139). Hallowell describes the
characteristics of an Ojibwa seance as follows:

When a conjurer undertakes to divine, a small structure is built and, upon entering
it, he summons his spiritual helpers. They manifest themselves vocally, the voices
issuing from the conjuring lodge being distinguishable from the voice of the
conjurer who kneels within. Each *pawagan* [spirit] upon entering the tent usually
sings a song and sometimes he names himself. . . . Another manifestation of their
presence is the movement of the lodge itself. From the time the conjuror enters it is
seldom still. It oscillates and sways from side to side, behaving in a most animate
fashion.

[Hallowell 1942: 10]

South American shamans of the Mundurucú carry on similar dialogues with the
animal ''mothers'' while alone in a hut (Zerries 1968: 265). In South Africa, ventrilo-

quism is associated with a pseudo-shamanism, itinerant performances developed from
the functional rituals (Gelfand 1959: 106). It seems likely that shamanism represents the
actual, as well as the metaphorical or archetypal, origin of ventriloquism as a form of
modern Western popular entertainment. The same is true of the various forms of "magic
act," the visual illusionism which accompanies this auditory illusionism. . . .

[Discussions follow of what Kirby elsewhere calls "the shamanistic origins of
popular entertainments": e.g., sleight-of-hand, illusionism, sword-swallowing, escape
artistry, rope tricks, hypnosis, fire-walking, fire-handling, fire-eating, juggling, acro-
batics, puppetry, etc. (Eds.)]

*   *   *

The fundamental relationship of shamanism to the performing arts of a primitive
culture is most often established by its relationship to the dream and to the dreamlike
psychotic episode which there lie at the source of creativity. Contact with ghosts or
spirits who "give" new masks, songs, or dances when they are encountered in the bush
or forest is the source of creativity in New Guinea as in North America. Fugue states
accompanied by hallucination are often recorded in terms of the origin myths for
performances or masks. Such supernatural occurrences were the basis for the "vision
quest" prevalent throughout North America, in which the seeker was given magic songs
and ritual which, in effect, defined him for his lifetime. Particularly strong experiences
of this type characterize shamanic initiation, establishing a preeminence in regard to the
spirit-given creativity, so that often only the experiences of the shaman in trance or
dreams are considered strong enough to provide the mask images or rhythms for the
tribal performances. The winter ceremonies of the Iroquois center upon the shamanistic
False Face Society and are characterized by performances in which the participants act
out the particularly strong dreams they have had.

*   *   *

The basic concept of the mask seems to be associated with the use of body paint or
elaborated costume which transforms the wearer into an animated sculptural figure. . . .
Such figures are essentially abstract. One function of this abstraction is to create a
disjunction with ordinary visual reality, a disjunction which is similar to that presented
by the trance state itself. Like the spirit possession of puppets, the trance relationship to
actual statues suggests the relationship of trance to performance by "animated sculptural
figures." In China, the statue of the deity that possesses the medium is carried behind
him in processions, seated in a sedan chair like a person. In Tibet, a huge figure of the
goddess Lhamo on a massive structure is carried by men its spirit possesses.

The chief actors on such occasions are the "sorcerers," who wear no masks
themselves, but have the same type of hat and costume, bedecked with symbols, as
is worn by the image of the deity. These "sorcerers" are basically the same as
shamans; they not only represent the god and identify themselves with him, but are
possessed by him and are the medium through which he speaks.

[Lommel 1970: 97]

The masked "sculptural figure" is directly identified with what is undoubtedly the most instrumental phase in the evolution of shamanistic theatre. The costumed personi- fication of spirits, particularly of demons, is associated both with shamanistic ritual and with the dramas that then develop from these rituals. As a generalized category, such rituals and performances may be termed "demon plays." The Kwakiutl winter cere- mony is essentially one long demon play. In Asia, we may observe ritual exorcisms which appear archetypal of the demon play's development into drama. One important kind is represented by the *cham*, characteristic of the Mongolian-Tibetan area, where Buddhist Lamaism is pervaded by the practices of an antecedent Bon shamanism. Waddell's account of the *cham* in Tibet draws heavily upon E. F. Knight's description of 1893 and presents a vivid picture of this exorcistic spectacle:

> At a signal from the cymbals the large trumpets (eight or ten feet long) and the other instruments, pipes and drums, etc., and shrill whistling (with fingers in the mouth), produce a deafening din to summon the noxious demons and the enemies. "The music became fast and furious, and troop after troop of different masks rushed on, some beating wooden tambourines, others swelling the din with rattles and bells. All of these masks were horrible, and the malice of infernal beings was well expressed on some of them. As they danced to the wild music with strange steps and gesticulations, they howled in savage chorus. . . . The variously masked figures of Spirits of Evil flocked in, troop after troop—oxen-headed and serpent-headed devils; three-eyed monsters with projecting fangs, their heads crowned with tiaras of human skulls; Lāmas painted and masked to represent skeletons; dragon-faced fiends, naked save for tiger-skins about their loins, and many others . . . but no sooner did these [priests] exorcise one hideous band than other crowds came shrieking on. It was a hopeless conflict.

> [Waddell 1972: 524−525]

The impression is of a continuous flow of action, but the *cham* is actually a "compartmentalized" sequence of scenes and does not enact an overall dramatic or symbolized narrative. In the Mongolian *cham*, for example, the action seems somewhat more formalized, and this compartmentalization is clearly apparent. There the per- formers use a single passageway out of which the different groups are summoned in turn by the weird and cacophonous music of an orchestra of cymbals, horns, and flutes made of human thigh bones.

> Out of the gateway for the maskers, a pair of Gugor demons came into the arena. One of them wore a white mask with an angry expression and the other wore a plain white mask. They were accompanied by two skeletons, an old man with eight masked boys, two musicians playing the maskers' entrance music, two monks carrying censers, and one monk who showed the maskers the way.
> The two Gugor dancers, who personified the Guardians of Knowledge, chanted mystical incantations (the Kalarupa). Through the patterns of their dance

they called upon the fiends and spirits to spare their land from destruction. Concluding their dance, the Gugor left the arena.

[Forman and Rintschen n.d.: 111−112]

* * *

Ceylon provides a fourth area, with Bali, Tibet, and China and Japan, in which we may observe the development of a demon play. The Ceylonese *sanniyakuma*, a ritual curing ceremony, begins in the evening and lasts until the next morning. Much of the action is comprised of "devil dancing," the spectacular acrobatic trance-dancing with lighted torches. The main event, which occurs about midnight, is called the *pelapaliya*, "the series of spectacles of the eighteen [demons]." The appearance of each masked demon is preceded by a song recounting his life and death and is announced by a crescendo of drumming. Each demon participates in a particular ritual, such as the spectacle of the shawls, the spectacle of the torches, the spectacle of the sticks, and so on. The demon or *yakka* converses with the head drummer or with one of the other drummers, often in lengthy dialogues. As in the Siberian seance, the demons ask presents as the price for halting their affliction of the patient.

Yakka: What is going on here? What does this noise mean, gurunānsē?

Drummer: Somebody has fallen ill.

Yakka: What are you going to do about it?

Drummer: We will give him a medicine.

Yakka: That will not be of any use! There is no point in it! Give me twelve presents and I will cure him. But I must have my reward.

[Wirz 1954: 53]

The shamanistic priests also carry on dialogues with the patient while he is in a state of spirit possession. If this does not happen spontaneously, an arrow is placed on the patient's head, apparently as a kind of lightning rod or conductor for the descent of the demonic spirit, and trance is induced by incantations chanted over him. The patient, his voice altered, then speaks with the voice of the demon, and the exorcist bargains with it, threatens, and tries other means to get it to leave the patient.

Priest: Tell me, what demon has possessed you?

Demon: Maha Sohonā has possessed me. I am Maha Sohonā.

Priest: Why do you cause harm to this human being?

Demon: He ate a certain kind of food without giving me my share of it.

Priest: We are prepared to give you an offering if you will leave the patient.

Demon: I want a human victim. . . .

[Sarathchandra 1953: 32]

Shock effect is often used in the attempt to cure the patient. His view of the ceremony is blocked out by white cloth curtains hung before him.

> A demon wearing a black jacket, black "coat" and "trousers," black hat, his face and arms all coated with soot, enters the arena hooting and shrieking. He dances for a while and suddenly without warning throws apart the white curtain (*kada-turāva*) that had separated the patient from the preceding events and jumps at the patient as if to devour him. The patient gets a sudden shock; sometimes he shouts in alarm and always a startled reaction takes place. Even the audience is startled and there is a brief spell of silence. *Aturu Yaka* departs as suddenly as he arrived.

> [Obeyesekere 1969: 188]

The plot of the *sanniyakuma*, elaborated in terms of dialogue, centers upon the attempts to get the demons to leave the patient. This must be considered an active, continuous process, like that of narrative dramatic form. Yet the *sanniyakuma* essentially remains another example of the compartmentalized, serial-scene structure characteristic of the demon play. However, it provides important clues which aid in the reconstruction of the development from the demon play of various folk plays in this area and thus of the probable origins of Sanskrit drama itself. But the *sanniyakuma* is in part already comedy. Let us first observe the evolution of the demon play into comic spectacles and consider its relationship to the origins of comic performance.

Clowning, as such, arises from a differentiation of the shaman's function as well as from representation of an antagonistic reality based on portrayal of spirits or demons of disease. One of the Zuñi clown societies, the Ne'wekwe, was a curing society, exercising the basic functions of the shaman (Parsons and Beals 1934: 494). Another, the Koshare, specialized in shamanistic fertility magic. It is thought that "curing was almost certainly a primary function" of clowns among the Yaqui and Mayo (ibid.: 506). Among the Plains Indians, the "contrary" was often both clown and shaman. Ojibwa contraries masqueraded in grotesque costumes and practiced exorcism as a cure of sickness, particularly that caused by spirit possession, and the Canadian Dakota "consider the clown to be the most powerful of shamans" (V. Ray 1945: 84−86).

Primordial clowning is everywhere associated with the irrational and with the demonic. The shamanistic clown societies of the Southwest are sacred because they are associated with the antiworld, an anarchy identified with death which is opposed to the order established and maintained in ceremonies by the benevolent masked gods. One of the clowns' primary ceremonial functions is to parody the dances of these masked gods while they are in progress. The grotesque costumes of clowns manifest this identification with the demonic.

> The typical Koshare costume is that of the cadaverous-looking creature who represents death or the spirits of those dead: ancestors whom Indians call the Ancients. The effect is achieved by smearing bodies, faces, even hair with white clay, and painting the body with black stripes to suggest a skeleton. The head-dress

of dried cornhusks and the rabbit skins around the neck symbolize death, and sprigs of evergreen tied to the arms mean recurrent life.

[Fergusson 1933: 657]

These costumes are symbolic, rather than being intended for comic effect. Most often, they are awe-inspiring or frightening, rather than ludicrous. The Koshare clowns have been referred to as "these seeming monstrosities, frightful in their ugliness" (Bandelier 1954: 134).

Among the Pomo and Patwin the clown was primarily an antinatural being, a ghost, and the grotesque dress, strange behavior and contrary nature were as much an attempt actually to represent such a being as to produce a ludicrous impression. Moreover, within these tribes an atmosphere of sacred unnaturalness, even in regard to the buffoonery of the clowns, is attested by the fact that the audience was prohibited from laughing.

[Steward 1931: 199–200]

In the differentiation of shamanizing in the Kwakiutl winter festival, the Fool Dancers' trance possession tends toward the comic, and they often attack others, as clowns can do elsewhere. "This possession causes excitability, madness, unnatural behavior, and it is provoked by the members of the opposing moiety" (Steward 1931: 200). The Fool Dancers are represented with enormous noses, the striking of which drives them mad. They "personate fools and are characterized by their devotion to filth and disorder."

They do not dance, but go about shouting *wi . . . , wi . . . , wi . . .* ! They are armed with clubs and stones, which they use upon anything that arouses their repugnance for beauty and order. Excreta are sometimes deposited in the houses, and the "fools" fling nasal mucus on one another.

[Curtis 1915: 215–216]

One great paradox of clowning, which essentially manifests the anarchic, insane, and demonic, is represented by the fact that the Kwakiutl fools, like the clowns of the Southwest, are charged with keeping order, watching over the behavior of others during the ceremonies. This relates to the critical function of the comic exercised as a social corrective. If the function of the comic is therapeutic, as well-known theories hold, we perceive one basic reason for the identification of clowning with the shaman, the society's doctor. The evolution of function is from treatment of physical ills caused by disease spirits, to the treatment of psychological ills caused by spirits, to a broader social application in terms of the comic-demonic.

It is this evolution which characterizes the development of the demon play into comic performance. The Ceylonese *sanniyakuma* was undoubtedly once an awesome spectacle, but the behavior and dialogue of the demons is now essentially comic. Obeyesekere has shown in detail how the demons were originally representations of physical illness but then came to portray the psychological meanings of symptoms and of psychosomatic and psychological illness in particular. One reason for this development would certainly be the realization, in the course of time and with the development of physical medicine, that shamanistic rituals achieve a higher percentage of cures with psychological illness than they do with physical illness. But essential, perhaps determining, characteristics of comedy seem also to have played a primary role in this transformation. The Ceylonese demon-clowns "express bizarre, psychotic thinking and sense confusion" because these are characteristics of the maladies they are treating (Obeyesekere 1969: 202). A sense of strength and superiority is created in the patient and audience by demons who mock the sacred but are patently fools. The context, of course, is the actualized mysticism of the "devil dancing," and the element of fear plays an important part, as when the demon pounces suddenly upon the patient. The awesome, violent, and horrible aspects of the demon are first emphasized, but when he appears his behavior, except for his dancing, is comic. Obeyesekere observes that "these *inversions* not only ease the interaction situation, but prevent the attitudes one has towards demons in ordinary life from being generalized to the ritual situation" (ibid.: 205). The comedy is functional, having some therapeutic effect, by making the symptoms laughable in terms of bizarre and psychotic behavior, and it also functions against psychological repression in general by acting out vulgarities that are not represented in sanctioned behavior.

The relationship to shamanism and to the demon play is illustrated by a primal phase of clowning in which the comic is identified with the representation of the diseased and deformed. Aztec comedies portrayed stupidity, drunkenness, madness, and deafness, and "farces about syphilis, colds, coughs, and eye complaints were presented in the temple of Quetzalcoatl, who was believed to cause and cure these afflictions" (Mace 1971: 160). The six masked figures associated with the origins of the Yoruba Egungun masquerade are a hunchback, an albino, a leper, an individual with protruding teeth, a dwarf, and a cripple (Adedeji 1970: 81). In southern Nigeria, scrotal elephantiasis is considered a magical penalty inflicted on adulterers, and thus is an object of laughter. The masks of the *ekon* masquerades of the Nigerian Ibibio concentrate upon such physical deformities related to ghosts.

Traits condemned as ugly in songs sung at Ikot Ebak were the same (with the exception of protruding buttocks) as those carved and painted in *ekpo* masks to portray evil ghosts: swollen cheeks, bulging eyes, large ears, flat noses, sores of yaws and leprosy, swellings of elephantiasis, and black skin (members of *ekpo* when donning "ghost masks" blacken their bodies with yam charcoal to make them more ugly). Malformed genitals also figured in *ekon* satire.

[Messenger 1971: 221]

Physical deformity, a source of the comic, is thus an aspect of spirit possession. The origin of disease and other illness is ascribed by Iroquois mythology to the hunchbacked god Big Hump and his followers the "false faces," "gangling creatures with large heads and distorted features" who "are represented by the masked men who drive sickness from the village every spring and autumn" (Müller 1968: 192). Plains Indian contraries are identified with grotesque mythological beings with anatomical distortions such as large, flapping ears or enormous mouths (V. Ray 1945: 103). Cherokee clowns called Boogers wear grotesque masks, indulge in obscenity, and "distort their figures by stuffing abdomen, buttocks, or shins." The humpback was a source of the comic in Aztec performances, and it was characteristic of ancient Greek and Roman mimes, as it was of the Turkish Karagoz, of Pulcinella, Punch, and other Western comic types.

The physically grotesque distortion related to demonic representation of disease and abnormality then becomes transposed into caricature of social types and actions. In Malawi, undesirable character traits, such as drunkenness or senility, are considered diseases caused by immoral behavior and are represented in the twisted features of the masks (Blackmun 1972: 36). The face painting in Chinese drama shows it to be derived from the demon-play exorcism, and the social types who are represented with painted faces in the developed drama all have something in their character that is deserving of criticism; that is, they are to some degree still demons. Strangers, either from neighboring tribes or as satirical caricatures of the white man, are subjects of comic representations in African masquerades as by the clowns of the American Indian. Foreigners manifest the quality of "otherness" associated with the demonic world, and that which is feared or hated on a social level is made comic. The personifications of social satire replace the demons in demon plays.

* * *

ADDENDUM

[At the conclusion of his related article, "The Shamanistic Origins of Popular Entertainments" (1974), Kirby writes:] At their origin, popular entertainments are associated with trance and derive from the practices of trance, not of childhood play or imitation. They do not seek to imitate, reproduce, or record the forms of existent social reality. Rather, the performing arts that develop from shamanist trance may be characterized as the manifestation, or conjuring, of an immediately present reality of a different order, kind, or quality from that of reality itself. Shamanist illusionism, with its ventriloquism and escape acts, seeks to break the surface of reality, as it were, to cause the appearance of a super-reality that is "more real" than the ordinary. The illusionism is directly associated with delusionary experience, which is inherently surreal and more intense, more "real" than ordinary experience. The principle of the "more real" as the virtual ground of reality links spectacular and fraudulent trickery with demonstrations of the body's "supernatural" physical abilities in the trance state. Acts in which real danger is either present or the product of illusion show themselves to be present before an audience as virtual reality, "more real" than imitation. It is for this reason that Zuñi clowns will kill and dismember a dog or drink urine in the course of their activities. Such actions and the grotesque physical deformities of clowns relate them directly to the freaks of nature also exhibited at carnivals and in circus sideshows. Once a form of the "sacred," they represent a challenge to reality by the surreal as virtuality. Like fragments of the archaic, shamanist ur-drama, these various acts remain, each in its own form, elements of the "marvelous," of the surreal, that has been perpetuated in popular entertainments.

ALFONSO ORTIZ

The Sacred Clown

"[Among] the oldest pure performers in the history of settled human life," notes Alfonso Ortiz (1977 MS: 4−5), the sacred clowns in their Pueblo form "were around at least by the end of the 1st millennium, A.D., because petroglyphs and other representations of them are traceable to that period." As E. T. Kirby indicates (above, p. 266), the clown's "sacredness," like the shaman's, hooks into an extraordinary initiatory/visionary experience and rebirth. Ortiz terms this rebirth "a new, omnipotent mode of existence" (1977 MS: 22)—what Mircea Eliade speaks of as the "divine election," and Black Elk, with specific reference to the Sioux heyoka clown:

> Only those who have had visions of the thunder beings of the west can act as heyokas. They have sacred power and they share some of this with all the people, but they do it through funny actions. When a vision comes from the thunder beings of the west, it comes with terror like a thunder storm; but when the storm of vision has passed, the world is greener and happier; for wherever the truth of vision comes upon the world, it is like a rain.

> [Black Elk/Neihardt 1932, 1959: 192]

The clown's performance—where fully played out—was, again like the shaman's, an instance of life lived at its limits: "eating or drinking filth; drenching or being drenched with urine or water; simulating lust, fear or anger; playing games together with the lookers-on; begging from house to house; . . . burlesquing ceremonial; . . . acting or speaking by opposites" (Parsons 1939: 130). As sanctioned parodist of

SOURCE: Alfonso Ortiz (ed.), New Perspectives on the Pueblos, *pages 158−161.*

the sacred and of its language—"entertaining but also dangerous" (Parsons)—the clown is the embodiment of his culture's ability to sustain ambivalence and contradiction. He is therefore, in Ortiz's words, "an anti-ritualist presiding over an anti-rite"—attaining a position in performance and ritual to which our own poets and performance artists have only recently, sporadically, been moving.

[On] June 22 and 23 [1968] or about the time of the summer solstice, I had the good fortune to hear of a public ritual which was taking place on the 23rd in Hotavilla, the most conservative Hopi village, so I made plans to attend. The next day I climbed to a rooftop which commanded a good view of the proceedings and perched myself alongside some Hopis. The Hopis said we were witnessing a Navajo dance because, alongside the masked and somber Hopi kachinas, or ancestral raingod impersonators, were four other Hopi males dressed as Navajo women and doing a rather gross caricature of Navajo customs and behavior. The two parallel sets of dancers provided a striking contrast: the Hopi kachinas were dancing in perfect and restrained harmony in a straight line, while the Navajo "kachinas" were shuffling about, often out of step, and turning around frequently with awkward jerky motions.

Halfway through the afternoon the dancers went outside the village to rest and eat, and about a dozen sacred clowns trooped into the dance area, representing two different groups with marked differences in dress. One group, the Mudheads, were painted brown with a fine sandy mud and each had the familiar knob-eared cloth mask over his head. The second—in this case smaller—group were painted in broad, horizontal black and white stripes, each wearing a little leather skull cap culminating at the top in two cornhusk "horns." Pueblo clowns are much more than clowns; that is why I like to refer to them by the seemingly contradictory phrase "sacred clowns." For purposes of the present discussion, let me just point out that Pueblo clowns entertain the audiences in these mass public rituals while the kachinas are away. They do this by burlesquing missionaries, traders, government officials, members of neighboring tribes, anthropologists, and other people who touch on their lives; the clowns always pick on individuals, agencies and institutions which give them proper theatrical fodder for making some moral-ethical point about themselves. These alien personages may be annoying, funny, or both. They also burlesque the most sacrosanct of Hopi beliefs as on this occasion.

After doing a rather grotesque caricature of Hopi kachina behavior by hopping around and uttering loud grunts, they proceeded to mark out a race track on the dance area. After both groups agreed upon the boundaries, the Mudheads left, returning a short time later with large stems of the walking stick or cholla cactus suspended at the ends of strings made of yucca fibers. Because they were more numerous, pairs of the Mudheads proceeded to wrestle the others to the ground, tie the cactus "pendants" to their G-strings just beneath their penises, and then make them stand up. The reader can imagine how painful it was for everytime the clowns attempted to take a step, the cacti would swing from side to side between their legs.

Next, amidst much howling and yelping, the clowns with the cacti were lined up at one end of the racetrack and paired with Mudheads. The remaining Mudheads, also without cacti, armed themselves with brooms and other stout sticks and proceeded to make the others race down the makeshift track, two by two. It was a rout of course; the unencumbered Mudheads won hands down every time. In the meantime, those with sticks who were not racing added insult to injury by prodding the howling clowns with the cacti; each time one faltered or fell down, he would get the stick shoved at him in the region of his anus. So it went until the kachinas returned. The audience enjoyed the performance enormously, of course.

Now what was going on here? Let me say first that no one who witnesses Pueblo dramas like this for any length of time can fail to be just a bit entranced by them for they reveal a great deal about what the people regard as important or ludicrous about themselves, their world, and about others who impinge on it. Here are a people who can truly stand apart from themselves periodically, take an objective look, and laugh. Such indeed is the embarrassment of symbolic riches we have here that I can touch on only a few of the general themes directly relevant to the discussion. First, we have the role of the sacred clowns, a role which takes form under the impact of the solemn kachina performance itself, but which, in many respects, stands in direct contrast to the purpose of the dance. The dance serves to reaffirm the basic tenets of the Hopi world view and fuses it with the Hopi ethos while the clowns remind the audience-participants that this, after all, is only life that we are living, and that like life everywhere it is fraught with all sorts of paradoxes, uncertainties, and outright contradictions. Between the kachinas and the clowns, we obtain a well-balanced portrayal of what the Hopi know about living; the kachinas remind men that if they but join their hearts periodically in these rites of mass supplication to the ancestral deities, life will continue as before in abundance and harmony; the clowns, by injecting a bit of the mundane and the commonplace, the ludicrous and the whimsical, into these most solemn of occasions, remind the people that this other side of life, too, is their own and that it must not be forgotten in the commitment to an exacting calendar of religious observances. Perhaps one cannot go so far as to claim that the sacred clowns fuse the sacred and profane dimensions of existence, but they do at least serve to make the sacred relevant to the everyday.

The reader will also recall that this was the summer solstice, a time which all Pueblo Indians mark with a religious observance of some kind. This is a sacred time, a time between seasons, when the old rules are suspended briefly and new rules for conduct are brought into play. Quite often also, the Pueblo Indians pause during periods like this to redefine and reaffirm clearly who they are by showing through some symbolic act how unfortunate everyone else is. A typical pattern, as in our example, is to do a gross caricature or burlesque of some neighboring tribe. The Hopis, who are completely surrounded by more than 100,000 Navajo, almost always pick on them; thus the exaggerated dance movements of the Hopi men dressed as Navajo women performing right alongside the correct and proper Hopi kachinas.

Returning briefly to the clowns, the appearance of both groups can be explained by the suspension of rules on this occasion, by the fact that during this brief period ''when the sun stands still in the middle of the sky,'' man can enter into a period of pure sacra, when time past and time future are fused with time present. There is no winter nor summer, cold nor heat, so both groups of clowns may perform. On other occasions, only one group of clowns perform during ritual intermissions.

The solar symbolism of the solstice period gives rise to still another fundamental postulate of the Hopi world view reflected in this particular performance. The Hopi, as all Pueblo Indians, believe that after the summer solstice period the sun begins to travel to his winter home to the south, because the days proceed to grow shorter. So they not only dance during this period, but, to give the sun strength for its journey (and, perhaps, to slow it down a bit), they run relay races at dawn over a track running east to west like the sun. Like the dance, the relay races are carried out with high seriousness and with appropriate ritual precautions. As I learned later, the Hopi youths of the village did indeed have a relay race at dawn that morning.

But, as we have seen, the relay race conducted by the clowns differed in at least two important respects from the ritual one: the track ran from north to south rather than from east to west and one set of contestants was deliberately handicapped so that the races could not be conducted with any degree of fairness or seriousness. In brief, the clowns made shambles of both the dance and the races. By doing everything in a manner opposite that of ''normal'' they stood the normal social order absolutely on its head. Both sacred time and sacred space are here profaned.

EDWARD L. SCHIEFFELIN
From *The Sorrow of the Lonely and the Burning of the Dancers*

The interaction between performer and spectator has been an issue of performance theory—Western and other—from Aristotle's catharsis to contemporary experiments with participatory theater, etc. (see below, p. 311). In the Papua New Guinea instance following, the projection and expulsion, here of grief and anger, works through a language-centered, basically social and nonmystical exploitation of human feelings—a cathartic geography, a primal poetry of name and place. "Moving and violent," in Schieffelin's words, the Gisaro Ceremony is itself part of a larger series of ceremonial events involving ritual exchanges between kinsmen who are living at some distance from each other: "a drama of opposition initiated by the dancers but played out by everyone" (1976: 197). But the hosts as audience don't just grieve, nor are their counteractions limited to a responsive "burning of the dancers." Before the ceremony and through its early stages, some among the host

SOURCE: Edward L. Schieffelin, The Sorrow of the Lonely and the Burning of the Dancers, pages 21–25, 178–189.

group provoke the visitors in turn by clowning—as if to break the others' concentration and defuse their words and acts:

> Youths seated on the partition to the women's section stick their rear ends over the visiting women seated below and make loud, raucous, grunting noises as if about to defecate on their heads. At one performance, a man appeared with a huge penis carved from a banana stem hanging over his pubic covering. He waddled among the visitors, sticking it over the women's shoulders and rubbing it against the mouths of the chorus. It required considerable effort on the part of the performers not to laugh at this and destroy the elaborately maintained mood.
>
> [Schieffelin 1976: 173–174]

Once the clowning has ended, the "tension rapidly rises," and the nightlong performance continues, "serious and grim," until the crack of dawn.

THE GISARO CEREMONY

The most elaborate and characteristic [of Kaluli ceremonial dances] is called Gisaro. Like all Kaluli ceremonies, Gisaro takes place at night in the longhouse. It is performed by the guests at a formal social occasion for the benefit of their hosts and lasts until dawn. The first Gisaro I saw was held to celebrate the gathering of pigs for a forthcoming pork distribution. Preparations at the host longhouse at Wasu took two days. The Wasu people cooked large quantities of pandanus, a tropical fruit, and painted and decked themselves in their shell and feather ornaments.

The guests had been preparing for the ceremony for more than two weeks. They arrived at midday on the appointed day in a dramatic procession out of the forest accompanied by drums. They were entertained for the afternoon in the yard outside the longhouse. In the evening, the hosts went inside to wait for the performance to begin.

The dark interior of the longhouse was packed with spectators sitting on the sleeping platforms behind the row of houseposts that lined each side of the central hall. Light was provided by five or six resin-burning torches held by young men at the sidelines. Everyone was turned expectantly toward the front doorway for the dancers and chorus to enter.

A group of about twenty-five men came in, their faces downcast. They moved in a body quietly up the hall to the middle of the house. There they drew apart to reveal the resplendent figures of the four Gisaro dancers in their midst. After a moment, all whispered "shhhh" and sat down, leaving one dancer standing alone.

His body was painted in red ocher with black markings, his head crowned with feathery black cassowary plumes tipped with white cockatoo feathers. His chest was hung with shell necklaces; his wrists, arms, and legs decorated with bracelets and bands. His whole figure was outlined against waving streamers of stripped yellow palm leaf, which shot up to shoulder height from behind his belt and fell away to his feet: "break like a waterfall," as the Kaluli say. The dancer was slowly bouncing up and down in place, his eyes downcast, his manner withdrawn. A rattle suspended from his hand was clashing softly on the floor in time with his motion. As the house became quieter, his voice became audible, singing softly in a minor key.

The ceremony had a simple form. Throughout the night, one by one the four dancers took turns dancing in place or moving up and down the small space in the middle of the hall, singing songs in company with the choruses seated at each end. The songs concerned familiar places in the surrounding countryside known to most of those who were present. As dancer followed dancer, the songs began to refer to specific places on the host's clan lands and recalled to the listeners former houses and gardens and close relatives, now dead, who lived there.

One dancer sang a song that alluded to the dead son of a senior man of the host clan. The youth had died at a small house near a creek called Abo, and his soul was believed to have gone to the treetops in the form of a bird. The dancer sang:

> There is a *kalo* bird calling by the Abo waterfall, juu-juu-juu.
> Do I hear my son's voice near the Abo spring?
> Perched, singing in a *dona* tree, is that bird my son?

The senior man, who was sitting with the crowd at the sidelines, brooding and withdrawn, suddenly became overcome with grief and burst into loud wails of anguish. Enraged, he jumped up, grabbed a torch from a bystander and jammed the burning end forcefully into the dancer's bare shoulder. With a tremendous noise, all the youths and young men of the host community jumped into the dancing space, stamping and yelling and brandishing axes. The dancer was momentarily lost in a frightening pandemonium of shadowy figures, torches, and showers of sparks. Showing no sign of pain, he moved slowly across the dancing space; the chorus burst into song. The senior man broke away from the crowd and ran out the back door of the house to wail on the veranda. This scene was repeated over and over from dancer to dancer during the course of the night.

Finally, at dawn, when the first birds began to sing, the dancers, the chorus, and the rest of the visitors suddenly rose to their feet with a shout, "*Buuwɔɔɔ!*" breaking the spell of their performance and bringing it abruptly to an end. The dancers, whose shoulders were quite badly burned, then paid compensation to those they had made weep, and all the visitors trooped out of the house to go home. Since many people wept, the ceremony was felt to have been a good one. Some of the visitors left wailing out of sympathy with their grief-stricken relatives among the hosts. The rest were exhilarated, and hosts and visitors shouted to each other that they would surely live long.

For several days afterward, the performance loomed large as a topic of conversation. Men remarked on how well so-and-so had danced, how much they themselves had cried, and what they had received in compensation (or complained that they had not received enough). Young people and children sang the songs and played at dancing in off moments, while others responded with mock crying and mimed the plunging of the torch.

The Kaluli regard Gisaro with enthusiasm and affection. They find it exciting, beautiful, and deeply moving. The dancer in full regalia is a figure of splendor and pathos. This is not because of the ordeal of burning he must face; rather, it is the very beauty and sadness that he projects that causes people to burn him. From the Kaluli point of view, the main object of Gisaro is not the burning of the dancers. On the contrary, the point is for the dancers to make the hosts burst into tears. The hosts then burn the dancers in angry revenge for the suffering they have been made to feel. To the dancer and the chorus, this reflects rather well on their songs. Moreover, a well-decorated and graceful dancer may project such magnificence as to cause a girl among the hosts to lose her heart and elope by following him home after the performance—a significant social coup for the visitors.

The dancers are always volunteers. When it is decided to perform Gisaro, several men immediately step forward. For ceremonies involving less severe ordeal, I have seen boys of ten or twelve proudly and excitedly announce that they were going to participate.

Gisaro is the most widely known ceremony among the people of the plateau and seems to be historically the oldest. The Kaluli and their neighbors also perform five other kinds of ceremonies, which differ in the number of dancers, the nature of the songs, the appearance of the regalia. However, most of them have the same basic themes: they are staged in the communal house at night; the dancers are elaborately costumed; the songs concern people's lands and evoke grief, crying, and burning from the hosts for which the dancers offer compensation. They seem to be alternative ways of expressing the same things.

Kaluli ceremonies are not connected with any particular season or time of year, so long as there is sufficient food available to feed the guests. Any ceremony may be performed in connection with any important occasion that people wish to mark. The one exception is that ceremonies are not held at funerals, for Kaluli feel it is improper to jiggle a dead person with dancing. Besides, after a death people are grief-stricken, somber, and angry and are more in the mood for murder than for ceremonial dances. Which ceremonies will be performed depends largely on practical considerations, such as how elaborate the occasion is going to be, how long a time there is to prepare for it, and what people wish to do.

Ceremonies such as Gisaro are striking to an outsider at first because of their dramatic qualities; but, more important, one perceives that the people are deeply moved, in their grief and violence, and for that moment one glimpses something fundamentally important about their lives. Gisaro fascinated me while I was in Bosavi because I felt that, if I could grasp what it was about, it would provide a way to understand the people who performed it.

* * *

Of all the elements that contribute to an effective Gisaro, Kaluli emphasize the songs. It is the songs, they say, that move a person to tears. A Gisaro ceremony contains twenty-four to twenty-eight songs. Each is sung four times by a dancer and makes up one of his turns dancing before the torches (about fifteen to twenty minutes). Every song is composed of two parts, one called the trunk (*mɔ*) and the other the branches (*dun*), which he sings with the chorus. They are separated by lines (*talum*) that the dancer sings as he is about to progress from one end of the dancing space to the other (*sagulu*). The songs are long, containing between twenty-five and thirty-five lines, each of which is repeated twice in the singing (see fig. 5). The songs are not sung in Kaluli but in another related language said to be that of the Sonia people west of the Bosavis, the direction from which Gisaro is supposed to have originated. Whether or not this is so, everybody understands

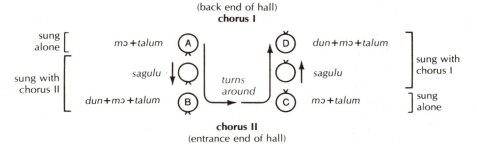

FIGURE 5. The Progression of the Dancer.
The turn begins as the previous dancer finishes his song and sits down. The dancer, who has been seated facing the chorus at his end, rises (*dasitaki*), takes a step backward, and turns around to face across the dancing space toward the opposite chorus. He sings the *mɔ* and *talum* by himself, bouncing in place. At the *sagulu*, he leans forward and starts his progression across the dancing space. The opposite chorus now answers him in the mode of overlapping call and response. When he arrives at the opposite end of the dancing space, the dancer sings the *dun* of his song, and then the *mɔ* again with the chorus, facing it. At the *talum*, he turns around, facing back toward the original end of the dancing space, and repeats the *mɔ* and *talum*—this time alone. At the *sagulu*, he moves back across the dancing space and sings the *dun*, followed by *mɔ*, *talum*, and *dun* again with the chorus. Then he sits down (*asitaki*). If the song was a particularly good or moving one, the aa *bišɔ* may request the dancer to sing it over again, and he does a repeat performance without sitting down.

the songs, and their peculiar language gives them a certain exoticism that adds to their appeal.

The songs refer to places and landmarks in various surrounding localities familiar to the listeners in a poignant, nostalgic way:

Mɔ	A *kalo* bird at Dubia Ridge is calling juu . . . juu.
	The *kalo* calling there is calling you.
	Go see the Walægomono pool,
	Go see the fruited *gala* sago.
	A *kalo* bird at Dubia Ridge is calling juu . . . juu.
	The *kalo* calling there is calling you.
	Go to the mouth of the Alim stream.
	Look at the fruited *safu* sago there.
	A *kalo* bird at Dubia Ridge is calling juu . . . juu.
	The *kalo* calling there is calling you.
Talum	Go look at the Masemonodugu pool,
	See the *bobolɔk* tree there.
Sagulu	Oooo-eeee.
Dun	Do you see? Do you see the Galinti pool?
	Do you see the crocodile?
	The *uf* tree up there at Wasisawel, will it break?
	Will the *uf* tree break?

Do you see the Galinti pool?
Do you see the crocodile?
The *mɔl* sago at Wasidugu, will it break?
Will the *mɔl* sago break?

Do you see the Galinti pool?
Do you see the crocodile?
The *beulin* tree up on top there at Gunisawel, will it break?

Do you see the Galinti pool?
Do you see the crocodile?
The base of the stone at Waimɔk, will it pull out?
Will the stone pull out?

Alas, the hill that is up there.
Alas, Balesawel that is up there.
The water pool,
The Gigidin water pool.

Oooo-eeee.

[Composed and danced by Hawe of Bonɔ at Wabisi Gisaro, April 17, 1968. In the original every line is repeated twice.]

All of the places mentioned—Dubia, Wasidugu, Balesawel, with their various trees, streams, and ridges—are real localities on the territory of the Sululib longhouse along the Isawa River.

The mood of the song is nostalgic. The voice of the *kalo* is a familiar, lonely sound of the forest and evokes such things as lost children. Fruited sago (which is no longer fit to eat) evokes the ruin and waste of food. The familiar *uf* and *beulin* trees on Dubia Ridge are seen as racked back and forth in the violent winds of a storm; the rock at Waimɔk is ready to uproot. The entire beloved landscape seems about to be destroyed. The image of desolation is completed with the reference to Balesawel, an abandoned house site on the opposite ridge. The composer told me he had made up the song one day on the way to his breadfruit garden by incorporating the names of various places he passed into song lines as he went along. Naturally the sago he sang about had not fruited, nor were trees cracking in the wind; he heard no *kalo* call, nor saw a crocodile. (A crocodile in a pool is another possible spirit image.) He had sung it as he did for effect. His metaphors of solitude, waste, and destruction are in fact entirely conventional metaphors and images and are aimed at awakening a sense of the passing of familiar things.

The sound of a woman beating sago at an isolated camp in the forest is a familiar sign of human presence and domestic activity. It carries some distance through the trees to the ears of passers-by. People often pause on the trail to wonder who it might be. In Gisaro this is transformed into an image of hunger and loneliness.

Mother, beat my sago
At the Gisæ mouth, beat *kalɔk*.
The Feleyowe hill hears it, the hill hears it.

> At Amalagalodo beat, beat the sago there.
> Iwalo hill hears it, the *bæ* tree hears it.

[Part of a song composed by Jubi of clan Bonɔ at Sululib.]

"A woman must work sago for her child," the composer explained, "but at the mouth of the Gisæ stream there is no sago or anything else to eat. She beats *kalɔk* [an inedible cane][1] in her sago trough. The sound of her working carries through the forest, but no one is there. Only the hill hears it." Next she works at Amalagalodo, where sago is abundant, but there is still no human presence. The passage clearly has a special poignancy for people whose personal affection is expressed in hospitality and gifts of food.

Framed in sentiments of loneliness or abandonment, the mention of particular trees, hills, and other details of the locality evoke for the listeners particular times and circumstances. The dancer continues:

> He has gone from the spring of the Waido stream,
> He has gone from his house by the Waido.
> I will sleep under the *dona* trees.
>
> Has he gone to the Hɔnsilen stream?
> Has he gone beneath the sago there? . . .

"A man [played by the dancer] has gone to visit his relative," my informant told me, "only to discover that he is not home and the house is closed up." He realizes he has no place to stay and must sleep the night in the forest by himself. He wonders where his relative may be. Perhaps he is at another stream, working at the sago he owns there. The house and places named in the song, and the people alluded to, were all familiar to the audience, and those who heard the song knew where and who they were. The people who owned the house felt sorry for their relative and wept for their abandoned house.

Each person knows the streams and landmarks of his longhouse territory, and these recall the people he worked and shared with there. This growth of young trees, that patch of weeds with a burned housepost, the huge *ilaha* tree that dominates the crest of a ridge reflect the contexts and personalities of his life. Here is an old garden planted by one's mother before she died; there is the site of a former *aa* where they killed many pigs. A stream recalls the fishing dam built there with one's affines some time ago. A swampy place littered with rotting sago trunks and broken-down processing troughs evokes a forgotten scene of domesticity.

Kaluli can discuss quite explicitly who or what they mourn for in regard to any particular place named in a song, though these persons and events are not obvious from the composition itself. When these names of particular places are projected in images of melancholy, hunger, and forsakenness, they evoke unbearable sorrow and nostalgia. One man wept at the song about the *kalo*, although it didn't concern his lands, because

---

[1]This is a poetic image. In reality no one would do this.

his brothers-in-law had invited him to pick pandanus from their garden at the Alim stream when he had none himself. The garden was now exhausted and left to weeds, but he wept because, I was told, "He used to go there, but doesn't anymore."

The deepest and most violent sorrow evoked by Gisaro songs is that evoked over death. About two months after Beli had lost his wife, Dasemi, at the small longhouse at Mundameyo, a Gisaro dancer rose and sang:

> [At] Mundameyo [one has] disappeared.
> A little *okari* tree disappeared.
>
> I have no brother. Where shall I go?
> A *jubɔlɔ* [bird] calls [from a leafless *malaf* tree]
> Come see the mouth of the Bibu stream.
> Come see the *okari* there.
>
> I have no brother. Where shall I go?
> I have no cross-cousin. Where shall I go?
> A *kalo* bird calls [in] a leafless *haido* tree.
> Come see the Sæluwæ stream.
> Come see the sago there.
>
> I have no brother. I'm hungry.
> A *muni* bird calls from a leafless *obora* tree. . . .

[Composed by Gaso and sung at Muluma Gisaro, February 1967. All lines are repeated twice in the original.]

The pathos of these lines needs little elaboration: Who is to work the sago at the Sæluwæ? Who is to share it? Beli and others drove torches into the dancer's shoulder. These things are unbearable because they are a poetic formulation of something that is real. Sometimes a composer knows an area well and makes up his songs with a particular person in mind, as above, but it is also common to find that several different men have each contributed a few locality names when no single one of them knows the area well enough to compose a song alone. They may have no idea who is associated with those localities, but if there are people from these places present at the ceremony, the song will ferret them out and cause them to weep. It is as though the place names (when appropriately framed in the melancholy images of the songs) are effective by themselves. The references to localities are anonymous, like the figures of the dancers, and the people in the audience see different things in them, each his own particular memories and sorrows (or those of dear friends). For a given song, some in the audience pay little attention, and others listen raptly. To an observer, it seems as if each listener thinks the dancer sings only to him. Sitting half-hidden in the shadows at the sidelines of the dancing space, each one seems to turn inward, lost in his own mood and thoughts.

As it refers first to one place and then to another, a Gisaro song represents a progression across some area of land. That is, the song traces an actual path, as if one were to travel that way across the ground. It is possible with any song to construct a map of the region concerned, including hills, streams, gardens, sago stands, and other resources, and from the allusions and associations of the sites trace a history of the area going back ten or fifteen years.

Kaluli develop the intensity of the ceremony and work the mood of the audience to the appropriate pitch by managing the order of the songs. Those sung early in the evening, as the dancers are newly arrived in the longhouse, do not usually concern the lands of the hosts but rather the guests' and dancers' home territories. The isolated bursts of wailing that occur at these times come mostly from women who married into the hosts' longhouse from the longhouse(s) of the guests or from in-laws of the guests who are familiar with these places through visiting. As the evening progresses, the songs gradually concern localities closer and closer to those belonging to the hosts, until finally (after five or six songs) they cross over into the hosts' lands themselves, and the weeping and violence begin in earnest. From this point on, the songs move back and forth across the hosts' lands, evoking enormous anguish in the audience until the morning comes and the ceremony ends.

The degree of subtlety and complexity in the interweaving of geography and personal allusion in some of the songs may be illustrated by a song composed by Seli of clan Bonɔ at Sululib. Seli intended his song for a Wabisi woman named Iše, whom he knew well. Iše was the widow of his mother's brother, Deina, who had died about four years previously. The "track" of the song leads from Deina's old garden house on Bonɔ ground to the place on Wabisi land where he died. It represents an imaginary journey such as Iše might take in returning with her children from Bonɔ to Wabisi after she had been widowed.

Mɔ	*Kalo* bird at the Alim waterfall; juu, father, juu.
	Do you hear father calling from the bank behind the Afo spring?
	Perched singing in a *dona* tree, do I hear my father?
	Kalo bird at the Alim waterfall; juu, father, juu.
	Do you hear father calling from the bank behind the Išen spring?
	Perched singing in the *ilaha* tree, do I hear my father?
	Kalo bird at the Alim waterfall; juu, father, juu.
	Do you hear father calling from the bank of the Bɔlu?
	Perched singing in the *ilaha* tree, do I hear my father?
	Kalo bird at the Alim waterfall; juu, father, juu.
	Do you hear father calling from the Bišan stream?
	Perched singing in the *til* tree, do I hear my father?
Talum	Eeeeee-oooooo.
Sagulu	I cross, I alone cross, I cross at the mouth of the Bišan stream.
Dun	At the Dædæ stream the trees stand out against the sunset.
	Ti sago at the Dædæ stream, the *ti* sago at the Dædæ stream has fruited; will a *howen* bird eat it?

At the Dædæ stream the trees stand out against the sunset.
Ti sago at the Anu spring, the *ti* sago at the Anu spring has
fruited; will a *bolo* bird eat it?

At the Dædæ stream the trees stand out against the sunset.
The *wayo* palm at the Bala spring is all dried out; will an
olɔn bird eat it?

(*Fɔs*)   A waterfall roars, the Dulu waterfall roars.
Gather at a high place! Gather at Baladagom hill.

[Composed by Seli and sung by Jubi at Wabisi longhouse, April 1967. Each line is
repeated twice in the original.]

The track followed by this song does not follow an existing trail (though in some
songs it does), but is rather a logical progression from landmark to landmark along the
ground. The relevant area (from a map drawn by the composer) is given in Map 1.

The first part of the song (the *mɔ*) refers to a place on the Alim stream where two
small waters run together as they go over a waterfall and down into a gorge. Between
them, above the waterfall, Deina and Seli had built a small house and planted a pandanus
garden together.[2] The call of the *kalo*, Seli told me, evoked the image of a child who is
hungry and calling for his father, and made people think of Deina's small son Kogowe,
who now doesn't have a father. At the same time, he said, it could be taken as the spirit of
Deina himself singing in the trees near where he used to live. Both images would be
poignant to Iše (Kogowe's mother, Deina's widow), who had shared the house at the
Alim. The image is repeated three times, each for a different stream and tree, moving
from place to place along the ground. At the *talum* and *sagulu*, the reference is to a place
on the Gamo River, which forms the border of Bonɔ and Wabisi land. The image evoked
is of Iše crossing the Gamo alone, returning home to her relatives now that her husband is
dead. The transition thus works on several levels: moving from the first part (*mɔ*) to the
second part (*dun*) of the song, from Bonɔ to Wabisi ground, and marking the movement
of the dancer across the dancing space.

The first lines of the *dun* complete the image. Iše arrives on her own clan lands in
the gathering dusk, through dark trees standing out against a red and yellow sky (Seli's
description). Here the song reference becomes more complex. The area referred to near
the Dædæ belongs to people of Bonɔ (through a complicated history of gift and
inheritance) but is on "Wabisi ground" (that is, the Wabisi side of the river) and the sago
palms mentioned belong to a prominent Wabisi man, Yayabo. Thus the verses are, for
the first time, aimed at someone besides Iše at Wabisi, namely, Yayabo.

The song continues with mention of sago and *wayo* palms at two other places
deeper in Wabisi land. (Seli knew where they were, but not who owned them.) The *wayo*
palm is near a place where the Bala stream runs into the Dulu, isolating a toe of the ridge.
A person standing there can hear the waterfall nearby. It was at this spot that Iše's brother
Kiliyæ had built a small *aa* (now burned down) and it was there that Deina had died. The
image is that of people being called together to build a house.

---

[2]Deina was a member of a lineage of clan Wɔsisɔ living with Seli's clan (Bonɔ) in the same longhouse (at
Sululib).

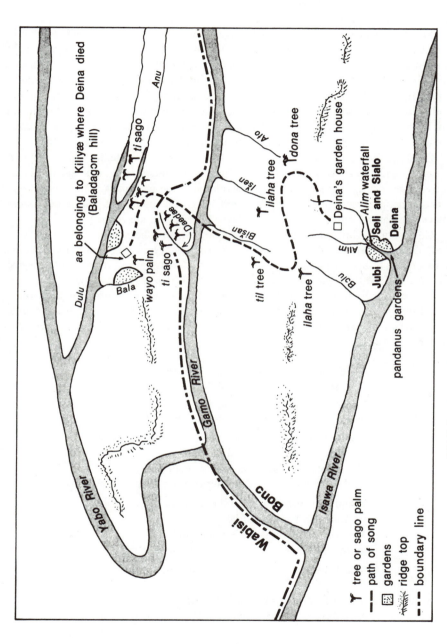

MAP 1. Sketch Map of the Area of Seli's Song for Iše.

Iše was not the only person to weep at this song. Suaga, Seli's sister, who was married to Kiliyæ, also grieved, though the song was not aimed at her. She wept for her former husband Dægili (also of Wabisi), who had died shortly after Deina and was associated by coincidence with some of the same lands in the song.

Seli commented that the song track went along a "marriage road" between Bonɔ and Wabisi. The song ended at the site of a house owned by Kiliyæ and other prominent Wabisi men so as to open the way for subsequent songs to be aimed at them. The various levels of allusion in the song; the self-conscious structural analogies between the land, the transitions in the ceremony, and the "marriage road"; and the transitional ending intended to open the way for new songs aimed at other people is unusual for the general run of Gisaro songs and reflects the gifted character of the composer. (Seli was a man of fast-rising prominence in the Bonɔ community at Sululib.)

Gisaro songs rarely attain this level of deliberate complexity. Less inspired composers, and those who do not know their hosts' lands well, manage nearly as effectively by fitting place names into conventional poetic images. The persons and events that people weep for are then organized, not by the intent of the composer, but in terms of the natural conformation of the land described in the song.

Conventional images (the call of the *kalo*, trees in the sunset, and so on) and appeals ("Sister, I am hungry, what shall I do?") indicate *types* of situations that become specific only in terms of a particular named location. Repetition and variation of the same poetic line diffuse the concrete place and event back into an abstract *type*.

The *kalo* calls from first one spring and then another, each time singing from a different tree. The song plays repeatedly on the image of a woman crossing a stream at sunset near ruined sago palms. The point is particularly clear in the following lines (also composed by Seli):

> I will beat fish poison in the Ɔidɔmin River pool.
> A *wagi* fish has turned belly up,
> Oh, father, won't you look at your child?
> Is the Auladugu cliff hanging in front of your eyes?
>
> I will beat fish poison in the Ɔidɔmin River pool.
> A *mobalo* fish has turned belly up,
> Oh, brother, won't you look at your child?
> Is the Isikaluɔ Ridge in front of your eyes?
>
> I will beat fish poison in the Ɔidɔmin River pool.
> A *halo* fish has turned belly up,
> Oh, cousin, won't you look at your child?
> Is the Olo swamp in front of your eyes?
>
> [Each line sung twice in the original.]

The song was aimed at a man whose son had died some time before and was believed to have gone to live in a river in the form of a *wagi* fish. It refers specifically to a time during a fishing trip when someone had caught a *wagi* and the boy's grief-stricken father had been unable to look at it.

Here the same allusion is repeated over and over, each time describing a different fish (all of which can be souls of the dead), appealing to a different kinsman, and naming a different place of "hiding the eyes." The lines are not addressed specifically to the father, for whom the song was composed, nor do they seem necessarily to concern only the one boy whose soul became a *wagi* fish. The lines use the actual incident as a basis on which to construct a number of poetic variations, changing the type of fish and the kind of kin feelings involved by the appeal to different relatives. Variations on the known incident open out a tragic type of Kaluli situation. Repetition brings abstractness to the event, rendering the particular people involved indistinct, and poetically elevates the incident from a concrete occurrence to a form. In this way, events referred to in Gisaro songs become embodiments of a general human condition.

ROBERT FARRIS THOMPSON
Nsibidi/Action Writing

Writing of African performance art, Robert Farris Thompson suggests that performance puts objects and words in motion toward a highly unified, even total art "in which one medium is never absolutely emphasized over others" (1974: xii). (Compare this with contemporary ideas of "intermedia," etc.) And again:

> Icon defines itself in act south of the Sahara. Things done, sculpture and dress, combine with things happening, music and dance. A fundamental principle is made manifest: action is a superior mode of thought. Movement serves long-term knowledge with sensuous uprush and spontaneity, answering to the imperatives of life. There is no turning back. The artist transcends particularity to illustrate, with authority, vital grace. [1974: 117]

The present piece about the Ejagham (Ekoi) of southeastern Nigeria and western Cameroon, takes not only dance but visual objects and language as "art in motion"—but equally, it would seem, as forms of writing in and on space: "an incomparable art [that] communicates a calligraphic sense of line, sensuous and superb" (1974: 173).

NSIBIDI: THE ANCIENT SCRIPT OF THE EJAGHAM

The traditional writing system of the Ejagham, at least as old as the basalt monoliths of the Nnam and neighboring Ejagham groups—*i.e.*, predating Western penetration of the

SOURCE: *Robert Farris Thompson, African Art in Motion, pages 177–182.*

area by several centuries—essentially functioned on two communicative levels, sacred and profane. The latter focussed on love and reconciliation, leading to birth and rebirth. Sacred signs were documents of death and initiation, matters of most important transition. Much of the former and a little of the latter can be rapidly illustrated by a sampling of recurrent motifs, which once were chalked on walls, embroidered or appliqued on cloth, painted and resist-dyed on cloth (fig. 6), incised on calabashes, hammered (at Duke Town) on brass containers, cut in divinatory leaves, painted on toy swords, and tattooed on human skin.

The forms today are fugitive, such as fading tattoos on the faces of elderly Ejagham and other Cross River peoples. The more recondite symbols survive within the Ngbe lodge, seen only by highly-initiated members at the moment of their swearing-in and at the death of their most important members. A sampling (fig. 7) of the signs includes: (1) the sign of love, a pair of interlaced curves; (2) the sign of hatred or discord, opposed curves, a line drawn between them; (3) the curved line of falsehood over the straight line of truth; (4) the crossed lines of speech, meaning a Ngbe command has stopped or blocked an action; (5) the intersection of equal lines within a circle, a sign of important discussion within an assembly hall; (6) the checkerboard, representing, in stylized form, the multiplication of the spots of the leopard's pelt; (7) the same motif rendered as a field of shaded or solid diamonds; (8) the Janus, a quartered circle, with one small circle within each quadrant, suggesting the meeting of the earth with the sky, or female with male, as in Janus-helmets; the four small circles standing for the four eyes of clairvoyance.

THE NGBE SOCIETY AND "ACTION WRITING"

The Ejagham Ngbe Society (*Ngbe* means leopard) is an all-male brotherhood devoted to the making and keeping of law, the maintaining of village peace, the hearing of disputes, and, above all, the pleasurable dancing in public of secret signs of magic prowess.

This secret idiom, called *egbe*, is a gesture language referring, in the main, to symbols and ideas which bind men together and lend them strength or inspiration for the hearing and resolution of discordant social situations. The positive character of nsibidi, their ability to notate fundamentals of social viability, love, trust, truth, and political efficacy, is given parallel substance by this tradition. The nsibidi mime is performed by two members in prolonged intellectual and artistic combat. Mime and calligraphic sign correspond. This can be demonstrated by the following gestures. For instance, the sign of love is rendered by hooking both forefingers together. The sign of hatred is conveyed by opposing the backs of the hand, thumbs down, "showing one's back to the husband." The sign of speech emerges in the crossing of two staffs. The presence of the leopard is variously expressed, either by crawling, or trembling, "when the leopard moves through the underbrush, he is shaking, shaking, moving the underbrush before him, stalking his prey, confounding everything before him." The elders of Ngbe mime transformation into leopards by other means, gently "pawing" invisible earth before their bodies, with a graceful gesture of the arms. These latter signs relate to checkered pattern ("leopard cloth") worn by messengers of the society, suggesting in the strong vibration of primary

FIGURE 6.   Cameroon, Bamun, textile, 11′6″.

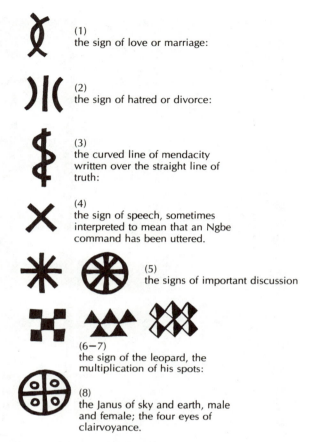

(1)
the sign of love or marriage:

(2)
the sign of hatred or divorce:

(3)
the curved line of mendacity
written over the straight line of
truth:

(4)
the sign of speech, sometimes
interpreted to mean that an Ngbe
command has been uttered.

(5)
the signs of important discussion

(6–7)
the sign of the leopard, the
multiplication of his spots:

(8)
the Janus of sky and earth, male
and female; the four eyes of
clairvoyance.

FIGURE 7. Nsibidi signs.

colors, one against the other, the quivering quality of the beast.

The sign of the Janus, fusing heaven and earth, is communicated by touching the region of the eye and pointing to the sky, the other person answering by indicating earth, pointing down. I have seen a single performer combine both gestures, answered by another who similarly brought the two together. Banyang gloss this sign: "God is in heaven, Ngbe on the earth" (*Mandem achi efe ne, Nyankpe achi ameke*).

The use of the signs is grammatical. They appear in sequence and they are almost always used *responsorially*, in the manner of call-and-response. Thus a Calabar informant: "before you make signs, you draw the attention of the person; you call him." The challenger calls the person by pointing, vigorously, with the right forefinger at his head. This has the force of "you!" and then the caller continues by passing his right forefinger over the eyes, meaning, "have you seen Ngbe?"—*i.e.*, "are you a member?" The person nods, if he is. Then an intellectual inquisition may begin. Each tests the other's knowledge and depth of initiation until one or the other receives a challenge for which he does not know the answer. The challenger may tap his right shoulder with his left hand ("what have you worn?"); the respondent activates both shoulders, alternately ("I have worn the Ngbe costume"). An elder, seated, may accost a young visitor with the following sign—he mimes washing, with his right hand, his left elbow, then his right elbow with his left hand, saying, cryptically, "before you eat with elders your hands must be clean and pure." This means: "we don't know you, explain yourself."

The member especially learns the form and meaning of masked figures who manifest the spirit of departed leopard-chiefs, and the "leopard voice," the most jealously guarded secret of the society. Every lodge includes at least two masked messengers, *ebongo*, who dance "very cool" and who are garbed in soft material. Abakpa Ejagham say ebongo represents the mother of the leopard spirit, hence the relative gentleness of the image. The corresponding image is "hard," the male spirit, *emanyankpe*.

Emanyankpe is a more elaborate mask, associated with fierceness and terror. It dances by itself. Non-members scatter when he appears: "this one will beat widows." He has the right to strike any woman who treated her husband with disrespect while he lived.

Emanyankpe combines a variety of nsibidi. Each unit of the costume is a symbol in itself, not a mere segment of a descriptive whole. The dancer becomes a document.

The conical headdress (*esi*), not unlike the conical head of the ancient basalt monuments, is an extraordinary abstraction. The mouth is not rendered: "because the leopard spirit does not speak; the moment it speaks it becomes a man." At the back of the head of the dancer, appears another head (*isun*), in the form of a disk. This disk, made of cloth over a circular cane frame, recenters us within the notion of Janus. The disk grants the spirit-dancer extra eyes, sometimes boldly rendered as appliqued mirrors. The mirrors guard his back, imparting magic vision. About the neck is wrapped a magnificent coil of raffia (*nki*) which, according to informants, adds, to the power of the leopard, the power of the lion. This ornamental coil is carefully trimmed and shaped, sometimes brilliantly colored with alternating bands of orange, black, and natural raffia.

The dancer is clothed in a tight skin-fitting knitted costume which covers his body entirely, from the conical hood to the ankles and wrists, leaving the feet and hands exposed. An opening in the region of the chest, through which the dancer enters the costume, is concealed by the raffia ruff. The costume is often checkered in brilliant gold, black, and red patterns, in allusion to the vitality and pelt of the leopard. A simpler costume from the village of Akriba, in upper Banyang, purchased at Calabar in 1963, is striped brown, orange, and white (fig. 8). The brown of this costume stands for "terror," the orange for "people dancing," and the white for "purity and peace." Terror, pleasure, and purity are commingled as flickering absolutes, within the striped pattern. Finally, like illuminating circles of forest ferocity, raffia fringing decorates the points of flexibility: ankles, wrists, and shoulders. The meaning of the raffia is: "when you meet raffia over a path, in the forest, you know it means a dangerous thing." A heavy bell is attached to the waist by two sashes, one red, the other white. The sashes are said to refer to mourning bands and to allude to the fact that the spirit has come from the dead. . . .

FIGURE 8.   Nigeria, Ejagham, Ngbe costume, 5'8".

EDWARD S. KLIMA and URSULA BELLUGI
Poetry without Sound

Even in its early, tentative stages, the signing poetry emerging as an aspect of the "culture of the deaf" challenges some of our cherished preconceptions about poetry and its relation to human speech. Ameslan (American Sign Language) represents, literally, a poetry without sound and, for its practitioners, a poetry without access to that experience of sound as voice that we've so often taken as the bedrock of all poetics and all language. In the real world of the deaf, then, language exists as a kind of writing in space and as a primary form of communication without reference to any more primary form of language for its validation. It is in this sense a realization of the ideogrammatic vision of a Fenollosa—"a splendid flash of concrete poetry" (see above, p. 24—but an ideogrammatic language truly in motion and, like oral poetry, truly inseparable from its realization in performance. (Ethnopoetic analogues—for those who would care to check them out—include Hindu and Tantric mudras, Plains Indian and Australian Aborigine sign languages, and Ejagham "action writing" [see above, p. 286]: a history of human gesture languages that would enrich our sense of poetry and language, should we set our minds to it.)

The reader may also want to relate this piece to recent discourse about "written-oral dichotomies" etc. (see above, p. 139); but the revelation of Ameslan, in that sense, isn't a denial of the powers of oral poetry but the creation of its possible and equally impermanent companion in performance.

The Greek poet Simonides once called poetry "painting with the gift of speech." We have discovered a different kind of poetry, one that lacks the gift of speech but possesses in its place the gift of gesture. For some years we have been studying the structure of American Sign Language (ASL or Ameslan), a manual-visual language used by most of the deaf people in this country to communicate with one another. Among those who have aided us in our research have been members of the National Theater of the Deaf, a remarkably talented group of actors who are either deaf or the hearing offspring of deaf parents. These creative artists are developing before our very eyes a poetic tradition unlike any other—a tradition based on the very special characteristics of "signing."

In order to appreciate the uniqueness of signed poetry, one must know something about the language in which it is composed. Hearing people, who have only limited contact with the deaf, sometimes confuse sign language with finger spelling, which is not a distinct language at all. Finger spelling is a derivative system based on written English, which, in turn, is a derivative system based on spoken English. One simply uses the fingers to form, in the air, symbols that represent the letters of the alphabet. Fluent ASL signers use finger spelling primarily for names and for borrowing English words. Some sign systems are also connected with spoken language. For example, Signing Essential

SOURCE: J. Rothenberg (ed.), New Wilderness Letter 9, pages 48–57.

English uses signs to match English word order in a virtual sign-for-word translation of English, down to the last, if, and, and but, including sign markers invented to match English affixes. Such English-based systems are often used in educational settings.

American Sign Language, on the other hand, is passed on from deaf parents to deaf children, and is a language in its own right, a full-fledged linguistic system. ASL signs are not based on English words, and a sign may or may not have an exact single-word English equivalent, just as a word in Russian or German may or may not have an exact English equivalent. Furthermore, ASL has its own methods for modifying the meanings of signs—for changing a sign from a verb to a noun, for indicating plural or temporal aspects, for extending the meaning of a sign from the purely literal to the metaphorical, for coining new terms, and so forth. Just as in a spoken language, ASL signs are not situation bound; signers can refer to other times, other places. And, as with spoken languages, individual signs may be combined into an unlimited number of statements. The syntax of ASL, the rules that determine what is and is not grammatical, is not based on any spoken language, but makes full use of mechanisms available to a visual-gestural language, including the elaborate use of spatial constructs.

The radical differences between signs and words are apparent from the way they are organized. A spoken word consists of a sequence of contrasting acoustical segments called phonemes, arranged sequentially. For instance, the word "feeling" breaks down into the phonemes f, i, l, ɪ, and ŋ. A sign, on the other hand, is essentially the *simultaneous* occurrence of particular values of a limited set of formational parameters. Every sign is composed of a hand configuration (or sometimes two, if both hands are used), a relationship between the two hands, a particular orientation of the hands, a place of articulation with respect to the rest of the body, and movements of the hands. To make the sign that translates as "feeling" in English [fig. 9], a signer uses one hand with the palm facing the body (orientation). The hand is flat and spread, with the middle finger bent in (configuration). It contacts the middle of the chest (place of articulation), making repeated upward strokes (movement).

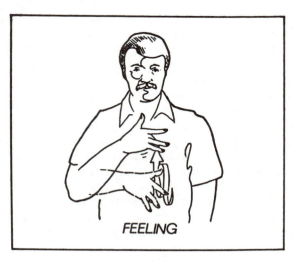

FIGURE 9.

Contrary to common belief, signs in American Sign Language are not merely pantomimic gestures. Just as the particular sounds of a word have no logical connection to its meaning, the way a sign is formed in ASL does not necessarily have anything to do with the meaning of that sign. It is true that many signs originate in pantomime, and certainly the mimetic aspects of the language are still very much alive. However, as a new sign comes into widespread use, it tends to lose some iconic aspects and become stylized and conventionalized. Usually a nonsigner will not be able to guess the meaning of a sign simply from the way it is made—and neither, for that matter, will a deaf person who knows only British Sign Language or Chinese Sign Language, which are quite different from ASL.

We became interested in the study of signed poetry not only for its own sake but also because we felt that by analyzing the heightened uses of ASL—poetry, wit, plays on signs—we could learn quite a bit about the linguistic features of the language. In a poem, linguistic features are more than just fleeting vehicles for the expression of meaning. A person who wishes either to write poetry or to appreciate it must be sensitive to the form of the language as well as to meaning: to grammatical categories as grammatical categories, and, in spoken poems, to sound as sound. Thus, as far as meaning is concerned, it matters little that ''June,'' ''moon,'' ''croon,'' and ''swoon'' have the same vowel and final consonant sounds—that they rhyme. But when the words are embedded in sentences patterned in a certain way, the sentences become verse, even though they may express inanities and the result is doggerel. We suspected that in signed poetry, too, we would find the manipulation of language for language's sake—the essence of the poetic function.

In spoken poetry, one finds various types of internal poetic structure, by which we mean structure that is formed by elements internal to the linguistic system proper: words, sounds, and so forth. At one level, there is a ''conventional'' structure determined by cultural tradition. In the English literary tradition, conventional structures make use of various metrical schemes, such as iambic pentameter, as well as end-rhyme schemes that dictate the recurrence of sounds in a predictable pattern. The Elizabethan sonnet is a conventional structure, as is the haiku form, borrowed from the Japanese poetic tradition. In structurally complex poetry, the conventional structure is overlaid by and interwoven with more innovative ''individual'' structures that involve the subtle patterning of sounds, words, grammatical forms, and meanings unique to the particular poem.

We have found that in signed poetry, the patterning of a poem is by and large individual rather than conventional. There is not yet anything analogous to the rigid, invariant structure of the Elizabethan sonnet. We have also learned that there are at least two types of structure that are special to signed poetry and that greatly enhance its poetic effect. We call one of these the ''external poetic structure''; it is produced by creating a balance between the two hands, or maintaining a flow of movement between signs. The other is a unique external structure that we call ''imposed superstructure'': a design in space, or a rhythmic and temporal pattern that is superimposed on the signs, just as in a song we may have melodic structure superimposed on the words.

In order to get at the distinctions between everyday signing and poetic signing, we asked Bernard Bragg, who is deaf and a master signer of the National Theater of the Deaf, to translate a poem by e. e. cummings, ''since feeling is first,'' into everyday sign and then into poetic form. The poem seemed peculiarly appropriate for linguists and artists to work on together:

> since feeling is first
> who pays any attention
> to the syntax of things
> will never wholly kiss you; . . .

We will discuss here only the first line. [Figure 10] shows the signs that Bragg used to represent this line in conventional signing. In this version, each sign is a literal translation of the corresponding English word.

Note that in the sign *since*, both hands are active, and they operate symmetrically. *Feeling* and *true* are one-handed signs. In *first*, one active hand operates on the other as a base. Since Bragg is right-handed, he makes the one-handed signs with his right hand and leaves his left hand lax, by his side. As Bragg shifts from one sign to another, there are several changes in hand shape. The right hand starts with an "index" hand, changes to a "mid-finger" hand, and then changes back again to an index hand for the last two signs. The left hand starts with an index hand, drops down toward the side of the body, and returns with a "fist" hand. There are various hand movements in the signs, and, although the illustration does not show them, there are also movements back and forth and up and down during transitions between signs. For example, at the end of *since*, the left hand relaxes and drops to the side, and the right hand moves down to the initial position of *feeling*.

Now consider the transformation of the poem into signed poetry, or "art-sign," in Bragg's capable hands [fig. 11]. First of all, Bragg replaces all of the signs except *feeling*. The first sign of the original version, *since*, is a literal translation of the English word, but it is not really semantically appropriate since in ASL it would ordinarily convey only the temporal sense of the word. The form of the new sign, *because*, is very different from that of *since*. Its final hand configuration is a fist with the thumb extended, and it moves from contact with the forehead to a final position off to the side of the head. The choice of *because* is related to the other choices in the line, because the other new signs share the same hand shape. Instead of *true*, Bragg uses *itself*, and instead of *first*, he creates a sign using a one-handed rendition of *most* (which is normally a two-handed

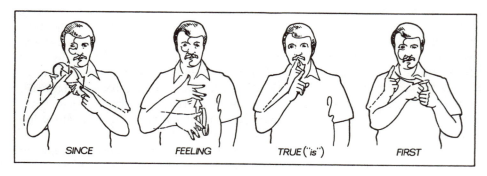

FIGURE 10.   Straight ASL.

BECAUSE — —/FEELING — ITSELF/— — FOREMOST/—

FIGURE 11. ART-SIGN. A dash and a slash before or after the name of a sign indicates that one hand from the preceding sign maintains the position and/or hand shape of that sign.

sign), combined with a marker for the superlative, *-est*. Bragg translated the new sign as "mostest" and we have called it "foremost." A deaf viewer would have no trouble interpreting it. The resulting line of poetry, then, has four signs made with one hand active, and the three made with the right hand share the same hand shape. We feel that this feature of hand shape similarity is probably analogous to the alliterative repetition of vowels or consonants in spoken poetry.

The choice of signs in a poem is part of its internal poetic structure. Bragg's translation also reveals an external poetic structure defined not by the choice of signs but by the pattern of their presentation. One aspect of this structure is balance. In ordinary conversation, a signer usually uses his or her dominant hand to make one-handed signs and as the active hand in signs requiring one hand to act on another. Since only about a third of all ASL signs involve the use of two active hands, most of the time there is an imbalance in the use of the hands. In the poetry being created by the National Theater of the Deaf, however, the signer may maintain balance by imposing a pattern of hand alternation that keeps both hands more equally in use. One method is to change hands with consecutive signs. Note that after signing *because* with his right hand, Bragg does not sign *feeling* with his right hand, as he ordinarily would, but with his left. He leaves *because* hanging in the air, as it were.

Another way to achieve balance is to overlap two distinct signs. After making the first sign, Bragg uses both hands at all times. While he signs *feeling*, he holds the sign *because* in its final position. Then he holds *feeling* (made with the left hand), and, in a way that would never occur in colloquial signing, he directs toward it the one-handed sign *itself* (made with the right hand). This emphasizes the fact that *itself* refers to *feeling*. Then Bragg continues to hold the hand configuration and final position of *feeling*, still with the left hand, while he makes *foremost* with his right hand.

Besides achieving a balance between the hands, Bragg also creates a continuous flow of movement of signs, another aspect of external poetic structure. We have found that to create this sort of continuity a poet may distort the form of the signs themselves, going beyond the grammatical code of the language, and may also manipulate the transitions between signs, as if to avoid any wasted movement.

[Figure 12] shows the signs *since* and *feeling* in ordinary signing. The center drawing shows the transition between the signs. Notice that after *since* Bragg drops his left hand to his side, because it is not used in the sign that follows. During the transition, he moves his right hand from the final location of *since* to the initial location of *feeling*, at the same time changing hand shapes. In the poetic version of the line, however, Bragg manipulates the form of the signs so that effectively there is no transition: the final position of the hand after making each sign is precisely the starting position of the next. The final position of *because*, which as we noted before is held during the signing of *feeling*, becomes the starting position of *itself*, and the final position of *itself* becomes the starting position of *foremost*. This continuity of movement would not exist in conversational signing of the same sequence of signs.

Finally, Bragg creates an imposed (kinetic) superstructure; it results partly from some of the distortions we have discussed, but is a separate level of structure. In this case a pattern of movement is superimposed on the signs of the line much as a melody is superimposed on the words of a song. We made flow charts of Bragg's hand movements in the non-poetic and poetic versions of the cummings line. From these [fig. 13] it

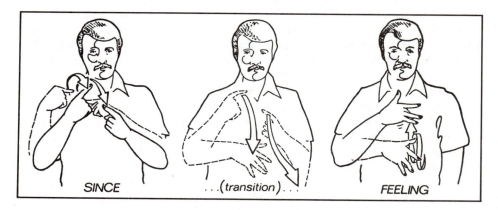

FIGURE 12.

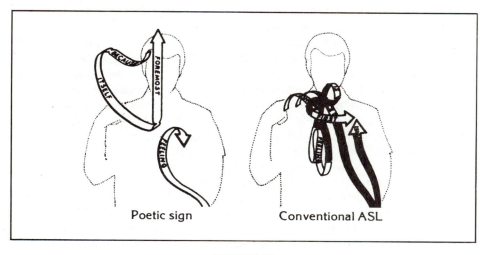

FIGURE 13.

becomes clear that in the poetic (art-sign) version there has been a further distortion of the signs, which creates an enlarged pattern of movement. This is enhanced by other types of distortions (such as those eliminating ''wasted'' movement in transitions), but this further, grosser distortion clearly seems an aim in its own right as well. Bragg has superimposed a special *design in space* on the signs chosen for his ASL rendition of the poem: a design in space characterized by large, open, nonintersecting movement as is shown in the flow chart of his ASL art-sign version of the line.

There are many problems in translating a poem from one language to another, and Bragg's task was even more challenging, since he was translating from one mode, the auditory, to another, the visual. In our laboratory we have also had the opportunity to study some original signed poetry. One of the poems we have analyzed, ''The Seasons,'' by Dorothy Miles, is special in that the poet composed it simultaneously in American Sign Language and in English. (Miles, who has been profoundly deaf since the age of eight, has a brilliant command of both languages.) ''The Seasons'' consists of four verses; in the English version each verse is in the standard haiku form: three lines, with five syllables in the first and last lines and seven in the middle line. The compression and rich imagery of poems in the haiku style seem especially suited to sign language.

Here is the English text of the verse entitled ''Summer'':

> Green depths, green heights, clouds
> And quiet hours, slow, hot,
> Heavy on the hands.

In addition to the conventional haiku structure, there is an individual structure that involves, among other things, repeated patterns of similar sounds. Here, though, we are more interested in the signed version. Miles's rendition suggests division into three ''lines'' as shown in [figure 14] (which we made by tracing images on a video tape of Miles performing her poem).

One of the most striking things about this verse is that it uses only a few of the possible hand configurations in ASL, variously estimated at between 19 and 40. Of the 16 signs in the verse, 13 use a ''five-finger'' hand in their citation form, either as the active hand or as a base, and sometimes both. The fingers may be bent and spread, straight and spread, or straight and compact, but in all 13 signs the five fingers are extended. Furthermore, through a distortion that is part of the external poetic structure, the five-finger hand becomes part of every sign in the verse after the first *green*. *High* and *green* are normally one-handed signs that do not use this hand shape, but Miles keeps the left hand in five-finger position as a kind of reference base or surface indicator throughout the signing of *deep below, green high above*. This modification provides a consistency to the forms of the signs in the first line.

In poetry, patterning is more important than mere frequency, and so we need to look at the patterning of hand shapes. The first line of the verse consists of two parallel halves, each beginning with an index hand (the first and second appearance of *green*). Each half ends with an active five-finger hand operating below or above a base five-finger hand (the signs *below* and *above*), in similar arcs. The second sign of the first half, *deep*, uses an index hand as the active hand; the second sign of the second half, *high*, uses what we call an index + mid hand shape, which is only slightly different from the index hand. The first line is semantically patterned as well. The first signs of each half are the same

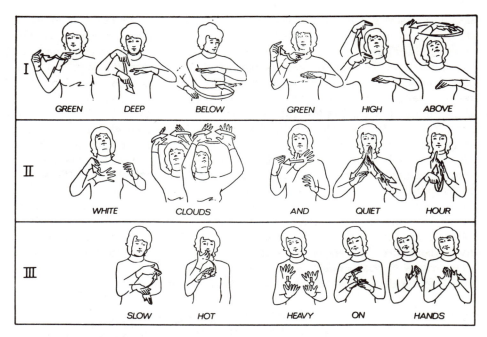

FIGURE 14. "SUMMER" by Dorothy Miles (Miles Rendition).

(*green* and *green*). The second signs in each half are opposites (*deep* and *high*), and so are the third signs in each half (*below* and *above*).

The second line, *white clouds and quiet hour*, also reveals internal poetic structure. Notice that *white* and *and* are each one-handed signs with a five-finger hand closing to a tapered *O*. Both *white* and *and* are followed by a two-handed, five-finger sign (*clouds* and *quiet*, respectively). It is clear that the pattern forms an intentional individual structure, especially since the sign *white*, the first sign in the pattern, is not represented by a word in the English version of the poem. Finally, the last sign in the line, *hour*, echoes in its active right hand the index-hand motif of the first line, and combines it with the five-finger motif that dominates the second line and, in fact, the entire verse.

The third and final line of the stanza, *slow, hot, heavy on hands*, consists exclusively of five-finger hands in signs made in front of the chest with the hands touching or close together. There is variation in movement, orientation, and intensity of the signs.

So far we have been discussing only the internal poetic structure of the poem. The patterns of external poetic structure that we found in Bernard Bragg's translation of "since feeling is first" are for the most part absent in Miles's rendition of "Summer." When we talked to Miles about her poem, we learned that she intended to keep the signs as close to their normal form as possible. In this rendition, she does not alternate hands in order to create a sense of balance; she uses her right hand in all one-handed signs and as the active hand in signs where one hand acts on another, just as she would in conversation. Nor does she make a special effort to overlap signs. During one-handed signs she leaves her left hand either by her side, as in *hot*, or off to the side and without a specific shape, as in *white* and *and*. She does make some minor variations in the forms of signs in order to produce certain effects, but she clearly does not make the major distortions necessary to create a design in space. Where Bragg displaced signs spatially to produce a kinetic superstructure, Miles makes all her signs within the normal signing space, not only in this verse but in her other ones as well.

However, a careful examination of "Summer" reveals a type of imposed superstructure that we did not find in the cummings poem. It is not spatial, but temporal and rhythmic. Each of the three lines in the verse takes about 7.5 seconds to perform, although the individual signs vary in length. The first and second halves of the first line and the second half of the last line have a similar rhythm, with four accents. The other three half-lines of the verse have fewer accents. We can represent this rhythmic-temporal superstructure in musical notation, and we are tempted to compare its effect with that of an operatic recitative, in which there is something of a cross between speaking and singing.

Different signers may favor different styles of signed poetry. Therefore we asked Lou Fant, who like Miles has been with the National Theatre of the Deaf, to perform his own rendition of "Summer," working from the English text alone. First of all, Fant [fig. 15] made the title a part of the first line of the poem. His other sign choices were not radically different from those of Miles, but neither were they identical. For example, he expresses the word "depths" from the English version not by a separate sign but by extending the sign *green* in a wide sweep of the arm, which gives the impression of *green* moving into the distance away from him. His rendition differs from Miles's in the

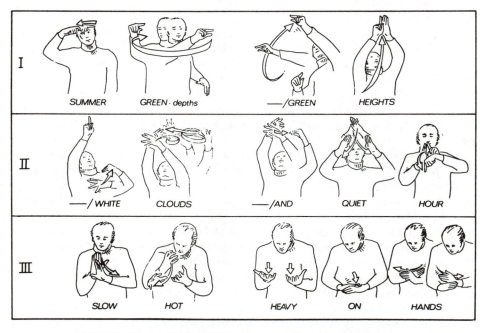

FIGURE 15. "SUMMER" by Dorothy Miles (Fant Rendition).

direction of more structural regularity. All four signs in the first line use an index hand as active, as this motif has an echo in the last sign of the second line, *hour*.

But the most significant distinction between Fant's version and Miles's is in external poetic structure. Fant, like Bragg, modifies the form of the signs or aspects of their presentation to create an external structure. If you examine the accompanying pictures, you will see that he uses patterned alternation of the hands throughout the poem: *green-depths* is with the right hand, the second *green* with the left; *heights* with the right hand, *white* with the left, and so on. He also uses the technique of overlapping signs. By alternating the hands he can overlap even one-handed signs that occur in sequence: he holds the form of a just-executed sign with one hand, while he makes the next sign with the other. For example, the final position and shape of the right hand for *heights* remain through the signing of *white* with the left hand. In this way Fant can present two signs simultaneously to the eye of the viewer.

When Bragg translated the cummings poem, he controlled the flow of movement for poetic effect. Fant does the same in "Summer." Signs do not begin and end in the same positions as in ordinary signing. Fant also manipulates the transitions so that the final position of one sign becomes the starting position of the next. This eliminates superfluous movement, and one sign simply flows into another. There is also an obvious design in space that is consistent with the theme of the verse: heaviness. Fant makes the signs of the first two lines much higher than they would otherwise be. Beginning with the second line, the signs slowly descend from far above the signer's head—a location not used in everyday signing—to below the waist. At the end of the verse, the body is bent over, the shoulders are hunched, and the hands are low in the signing space.

This rendition of "Summer" exhibits one other feature that is quite prominent in signed poetry: in some of the signs, Fant exaggerates the representational or pantomimic aspects. Consider the title sign, *summer*, which Fant incorporates into the body of the poem. The usual form of this sign involves a bent index finger that brushes across the central part of the forehead. When we asked Shanny Mow, a deaf signer, to review our video tapes of the poem, he noticed that Fant elaborates *summer* by "increasing its length . . . thus producing a more pantomime-like action." He uses an outstretched index finger that gradually bends to form the conventional hand shape, and he "wipes" the entire length of his forehead—as if to wipe away the sweat caused by the summer's heat.

Mow also pointed out that in signing *clouds*, the hands rotate slowly across the space overhead, to portray the drifting of the clouds. The sign *heavy*, Mow observed, "certainly looks heavy, so heavy that the bottom drops. . . . One begins to feel the oppressive claustrophobic heat and time standing still as the long summer drags on." The sign *slow*, in Miles's rendition as well as in Fant's, is longer than usual in terms of both time and space. Ordinarily the fingertips of the active, flat, five-finger hand brush once over the back of the base hand from the fingertips to the wrist. In Miles's version, the active hand, as it brushes over the base hand, continues well up toward the shoulder.

Poetry in sign language is still actively evolving and new poetic forms continually emerge. Joe Castronovo and Ella Lentz, two deaf signers who have worked with us, experimented with the signed equivalent of a duet [fig. 16]. They were inspired by a well-known children's game called Double Personality. One person stands with his arms at rest and allows them to be replaced by the arms of a second person standing behind him. The effect is reminiscent of the many-armed Hindu god, Shiva. In the culture of the deaf, the game often involves signing. Castronovo and Lentz noticed that when both

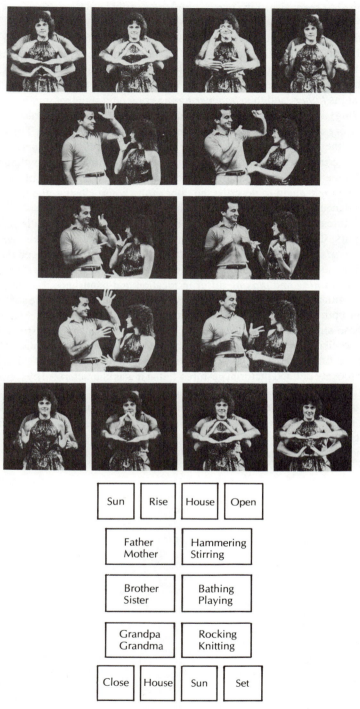

FIGURE 16. This poem for four hands has great symmetry, even though—except for the opening and closing lines—the actors are portraying different words.

people signed, it seemed as if the person in front was talking to himself and was answered by his "other voice." They decided to compose a poem for four hands.

At the beginning of the poem, a male stands behind a female, and both sign. The resulting blend describes the sun rising on the horizon, where there is a house. As we approach the house, the door opens. At this point the two signers split apart, the male going to the right and the female to the left. Now each begins to sign a separate message. The male signs *father*, and then *hammering* (a very iconic sign that mimics the motions of hammering). At the same time the female signs *mother* and *stirring* (also iconic). The male signs *big* and *brother* while the female signs *little* and *sister*. The male signs *bathing* and the female signs *playing*. The male signs *grandpa* and *rocking* while the female signs *grandma* and *knitting*. The signs are made with strong, rhythmic beats, in clusters of three beats at the end of each line. Then, in the final section of the poem, the signers blend once again to describe the door of the house closing, the house receding into the distance, and the sun setting on the horizon.

An interesting feature of this poem is that the signs in the middle section form minimal pairs. The signs *father, brother*, and *grandpa* are exactly like their matched pairs *mother, sister*, and *grandma*, except that the male signs are made on the forehead while the female signs are made near the lower cheek. *Big* and *little* are identical except for location. *Bathing* and *playing* differ in location and handshape, but they are made here with similar up and down movements. *Rocking* and *knitting* have different hand shapes, but both are made with the same strikingly similar to-and-fro rhythmic movements. These similarities give the poem a very symmetrical internal structure.

Studies like these have taught us much about this soundless language. Many years ago, when we first began to study ASL, we read that sign language was "a collection of vague and loosely defined pictorial gestures"; that it was characterized by "grammatical disorder, illogical systems, and linguistic confusion"; that it was "a pidgin form of English on the hands with no structure of its own." Although these views have been dispelled, most people are not aware of the poetic tradition developing in the language. This tradition shows how human beings, deprived of spoken language, devise ways to express the poetic imagination.

GERSHOM SCHOLEM
Kabbalistic Ritual
and the Bride of God

The "great subculture" (see above, p. 217) emerges as well in kabbalah: the last of
the Jewish oral traditions, connected at its source to what Scholem speaks of
elsewhere as "Jewish gnosticism." A catchall term "for the esoteric teachings of
Judaism and Jewish mysticism, especially the forms which it assumed in the Middle
Ages from the 12th century onward" (Scholem 1974: 3), kabbalah was often
carried on by mystics who were themselves extraordinary poets—Abraham
Abulafia, Isaac Luria, Moses de Leon (author of "The Zohar"), and others—"verbal
alchemists," in Rimbaud's phrase. This virtual poetics made an approach to reality
through forms of language—both voiced and written—not unrelated to contemporary language happenings: mystical exegesis, letter and number manipulation, magical and celestial alphabets, name-magic including chanted meditations
on the secret names of God, associative and metaphorical languages, and an
ongoing and persistently inventive mythopoeia. Such works, as Scholem shows in
the present piece, weren't without their performative and voiced side, even in a
culture thought to be so much devoted to the primacy of text. And along with the
voice and language happenings, there was a survival, equally surprising, of the
image of the Goddess—in Jewish mysticism, "the bride of God" or God's own
female aspect (Shekinah, or shekhina = God's exiled presence in this world), also
called "the daughter of the voice." Writes Raphael Patai in his book, The Hebrew
Goddess: "She is thus, if not by character, then by function and position, a direct
heir to such ancient Hebrew goddesses of Canaanite origin as Asherah and Anath"
(1967: 137).

A fuller exploration of kabbalistic poetics will be found in the present co-
editor's A Big Jewish Book (1978). For more on the survival of the Goddess, see
above, pages 56 and 217, and below, page 441.

Many of the Kabbalistic rites, needless to say, were strictly esoteric in character and
could only be performed by groups of initiates. Some of these were very old, going back
to the mystics who were the precursors of the thirteenth-century Kabbalists. In the oldest
literature we find descriptions of rites bearing the character of special initiations. Largely
theurgic in nature, they were not, like the Kabbalistic rites we shall discuss below,
accompanied by display that would also be understood by, and appeal to, the unlearned
public.

A rite of initiation in the strictest sense is that concerned with the transmission of
the name of God from master to pupil. Evidently a much older oral tradition concerning

SOURCE: Gershom Scholem, On the Kabbalah and Its Symbolism (tr. Ralph Manheim), pages
135–146.

the utterance of such names was still alive in Germany and France in the twelfth century. Eleazar of Worms (c. 1200) describes this initiation as follows:

> The name is transmitted only to the reserved—this word can also be translated as "the initiate"—who are not prone to anger, who are humble and God-fearing, and carry out the commandments of their Creator. And it is transmitted only over water. Before the master teaches it to his pupil, they must both immerse themselves and bathe in forty measures of flowing water, then put on white garments and fast on the day of instruction. Then both must stand up to their ankles in the water, and the master must say a prayer ending with the words: "The voice of God is over the waters! Praised be Thou, O Lord, who revealest Thy secret to those who fear Thee, He who knoweth the mysteries." Then both must turn their eyes toward the water and recite verses from the Psalms, praising God over the waters.

At this time the master evidently transmits the one among the secret names of God that the adept is permitted to hear, whereupon they return together to the synagogue or schoolhouse, where they recite a prayer of thanksgiving over a vessel full of water.

A theurgic ritual that has come down to us from the same school gives instructions for "putting on the Name"—a purely magical procedure. We possess numerous manuscripts of a "Book of the Putting on and Fashioning of the Mantle of Righteousness," in which the ancient Jewish conception that names can be "put on" is taken very concretely.[1] A piece of pure deerskin parchment is selected. From it are cut a sleeveless garment, modeled after the high priest's ephod, covering shoulders and chest down to the navel and falling along the sides to the loins, and a hat connected with the garment. On this magic garment the secret names of God are inscribed. Then the adept must fast for seven days, touch nothing unclean, eat nothing of animal origin, neither eggs nor fish, but only peas, beans and the like. At the end of seven days he must go at night to the water and call out the Name—evidently the name written on the garment—over the water. If he perceives a green form in the air above the water, it is a sign that there is still something unclean in the adept and that the same preparations must be repeated for another seven days, accompanied by alms and acts of charity. "And pray to your Creator that you will not be shamed once again. And if you see the form in bright red over the water, know that you are inwardly clean and fit to put on the Name. Then go into the water up to your loins and put on the venerable and terrible Name in the water." This ritual is thought to give the adept irresistible strength. He is advised, while "putting on the Name," to invoke the angels associated with it. They appear before him, but all he sees is a moving wisp of smoke. This magic significance of water as the only appropriate medium for such initiation—a conception widespread among non-Jews, e.g., baptism—does not occur in Talmudic literature or in any other Jewish traditions. I doubt whether this initiation in water was practiced after the fourteenth century.

It seems to me that the oldest instructions for making a golem must be regarded as a theurgic ritual, in which the adept becomes aware of wielding a certain creative power. These instructions are contained in the writings of the same Kabbalist to whom we owe

---

[1] A parallel to the baptismal ritual of certain Gnostic sects, in which the baptizee "puts on" the mystical name of Jesus; cf. Quispel in *Eranos-Jahrbuch*, XXI (1952), p. 126.

the preservation of the above-mentioned rites. The problem of the golem is exceedingly complicated. In the present context I should merely like to point out that these specifications for the making of a golem are not so much an element of legend as a description of a precise ritual, calculated to induce a very definite *vision*, namely a vision of the creative animation of the golem. It was from this rite as described in authentic sources that the popular mind developed a legend.

Let us now turn to those Kabbalistic rites developed on the basis of older conceptions, which were observed for centuries by large sections of the Jewish people and in some cases are still practiced today. Perhaps it will be best to begin with a few rites based on the sacred marriage, an idea that plays a central role in the *Zohar* and among all subsequent Kabbalists. What took place in this *hieros gamos* (*zivvuga kadisha*, as the *Zohar* calls it) was primarily the union of the two *sefiroth, tif'ereth* and *malkhuth*,[2] the male and female aspects of God, the king and his consort, who is nothing other than the *Shekhinah* and the mystical Ecclesia of Israel. The wide range of meaning contained in the symbol of the *Shekhinah* thus enabled the masses of the people to identify this sacred marriage with the marriage between God and Israel, which for the Kabbalists was merely the outward aspect of a process that takes place within the secret inwardness of God himself.

No holiday could more appropriately be interpreted as a sacred marriage feast in this sense than the Feast of Weeks on the fiftieth day after Passover. This festival, commemorating the Revelation on Mount Sinai, which according to the Torah took place fifty days after the exodus from Egypt, is the festival of the covenant between God and Israel. From covenant to marriage was only a short step for the Kabbalists. The *Zohar* relates that Simeon ben Yohai and his associates attached a special mystical significance to the night preceding this festival. For in this night the bride makes ready for marriage with the bridegroom, and it was thought fitting that all those ''belonging to the palace of the bride'' (i.e., the mystics and students of the Torah) should keep her company and partake, through a festive ritual, in the preparations for her marriage. It is the mystics who clothe the *Shekhinah* in the proper ornaments, with which on the following morning she will take her place beneath the bridal canopy. The complete bridal ornament, as the Talmudists had inferred from Isaiah 3, consisted of twenty-four items. But according to the *Zohar*, these twenty-four items are the twenty-four books of the Bible. Consequently, anyone who in this night recites selections from all twenty-four books and adds mystical interpretations of their secrets adorns the bride in the right way and rejoices with her all through the night. In this night the adept becomes the ''best man of the *Shekhinah*,'' and when next morning the bridegroom asks after those who have so splendidly adorned the bride, she points him out and calls him to her presence.

From the beginning of the sixteenth century a set ritual took form on the basis of this passage in the *Zohar*. The whole night before the mystical marriage was spent in vigil, songs were sung, and a specific selection from all the books of the Bible, from all the treatises of the Mishnah, and from the parts of the *Zohar* dealing with the festival, was recited. This rite became exceedingly popular and is widely practiced to this day.

[2]The *sefiroth*, in Jewish mysticism, are the ten emanations or stages by which God enters the world. For a description of the *Shekhinah* (identified with the emanation *malkhuth*), see editors' introduction to this piece. (Eds.)

Indeed, the conception of a marriage was carried so far that on the following morning, at the lifting up of the Torah in the synagogue and before the reading of the Ten Commandments, certain Kabbalists were in the habit of reading a formal contract, stating the terms of marriage between "Bridegroom God" and the "Virgin Israel."[3] Israel Najara, the [sixteenth century] poet of the Safed circle, wrote a poetic marriage contract, probably the first of its kind—a lyrical, mystical paraphrase of the marriage document prescribed by Jewish law. This and similar "documents," announcing consummation of the sacred marriage, achieved wide popularity. Here we have a mixture of allegory and the purest symbolism; for whereas the story of the marriage of Israel with God on the day of the Revelation is after all only an allegory, though a profoundly meaningful one, the conception of the *Shekhinah's* marriage with her Lord is a mystical symbol expressing something that transcends all images.

But it is the ritual of the Sabbath, and especially of the eve of the Sabbath, that underwent the most noteworthy transformation in connection with this idea of the sacred marriage. It would be no exaggeration to call the Sabbath *the* day of the Kabbalah. On the Sabbath the light of the upper world bursts into the profane world in which man lives during the six days of the week. The light of the Sabbath endures into the ensuing week, growing gradually dimmer, to be relieved in the middle of the week by the rising light of the next Sabbath. It is the day on which a special pneuma, the "Sabbath soul," enters into the believer, enabling him to participate in the right way in this day which shares more than any other day in the secrets of the pneumatic world. Consequently it was also regarded as a day specially consecrated to the study of the Kabbalah.

The Kabbalists cited three separate passages in the Talmud, which were brought together and presented in a new light by this conception of the Sabbath as a sacred marriage. The first tells us that on the eve of the Sabbath certain rabbis used to wrap themselves in their cloaks and cry out: Come let us go to meet Queen Sabbath. Others cried: Come, O Bride, come, O Bride. The second passage relates that on Friday evening Simeon ben Yohai and his son saw an old man hurrying through the dusk with two bundles of myrtle. They asked him, what are you doing with those bundles? He replied: I will honor the Sabbath with them. The third passage tells us that Torah scholars used to perform marital intercourse precisely on Friday night. These disparate reports are interpreted in the Kabbalistic books of ritual as indications that the Sabbath is indeed a marriage festival. The earthly union between man and woman, referred to in the third passage, was taken as a symbolic reference to the heavenly marriage.[4] These themes were combined with the mystical symbolism identifying Bride, Sabbath, and *Shekhinah*. Still another mystical notion that played a part in the Kabbalistic Sabbath ritual, was the "field of holy apple trees,"[5] as the *Shekhinah* is frequently called in the *Zohar*. In this metaphor the "field" is the feminine principle of the cosmos, while the apple trees define the *Shekhinah* as the expression of all the other *sefiroth* or holy orchards, which flow into her and exert their influence through her. During the night before the Sabbath the King is

[3]I have heard such reading in recent years in Sefardic synagogues in Jerusalem.

[4]This symbolism contradicts the thought of Simeon ben Yohai in the early Midrash, who termed the Sabbath and the community of Israel bride and groom and interpreted the sanctification of the Sabbath in the Ten Commandments as a marriage concluded through the "hallowing" of the Bride-Sabbath.

[5]On the strength of a Talmudic phrase (Ta'anith 29a)—"like an apple orchard"—which in the Talmud however merely characterizes a particularly pleasant odor.

joined with the Sabbath-Bride; the holy field is fertilized, and from their sacred union the souls of the righteous are produced.

On the basis of these conceptions, which are set forth at length in the *Zohar*, the Safed Kabbalists, beginning in the middle of the sixteenth century, developed a solemn and highly impressive ritual which is not mentioned in earlier sources. Its dominant theme is the mystical marriage. A strange twilight atmosphere made possible an almost complete identification of the *Shekhinah*, not only with the Queen of the Sabbath, but also with every Jewish housewife who celebrates the Sabbath. This is what gave this ritual its enormous popularity. To this day the Sabbath ritual is pervaded by memories of the old Kabbalistic rite, and certain of its features have been preserved intact.

I shall try to describe this ritual in its original and meaningful form. On Friday afternoon, some time before the onset of the Sabbath, the Kabbalists of Safed and Jerusalem, usually clad in white—in any case neither in black nor red, which would have evoked the powers of stern judgment and limitation—went out of the city into an open field, which the advent of the *Shekhinah* transformed into the "holy apple orchard." They "went to meet the Bride." In the course of the procession the people sang special hymns to the Bride and psalms of joyful anticipation (such as Psalm 29 or Psalms 95−99). The most famous of these hymns was composed by Solomon Alkabez, a member of Moses Cordovero's group in Safed. It begins:

> Go, my beloved, to meet the Bride,
> Let us receive the face of the Sabbath . . .

In this hymn, which is still sung in the synagogue, mystical symbolism is explicitly combined with Messianic hopes for the redemption of the *Shekhinah* from exile. When the actual procession into the fields was dropped, the congregation "met the Bride" in the court of the synagogue, and when this observance in turn fell into disuse, it became customary, as it is to this day, to turn westward at the last verse of the hymn and bow to the approaching Bride. It is recorded that Luria, standing on a hill near Safed, beheld in a vision the throngs of Sabbath-souls coming with the Sabbath-Bride. A number of our sources tell us that the Sabbath Psalms were sung with closed eyes, for as the Kabbalists explained, the *Shekhinah* is designated in the *Zohar* as "the beautiful virgin who has no eyes," that is to say, who has lost her eyes from weeping in exile.[6] On Friday afternoon the Song of Songs, traditionally identified with the indissoluble bond between "the Holy One, blessed be He, and the Ecclesia of Israel," but here taken also as an epithalamion for the *Shekhinah*, was also intoned. Only after the meeting-of-the-Bride were the traditional Sabbath prayers spoken.

After the prayer the mystical ritual was resumed at home. According to Isaac Luria, it was highly commendable and "rich in mystical significance" to kiss one's mother's hands on entering the house. Then the family marched solemnly around the table, from which they took in silence the two bundles of myrtle for the Bride and Bridegroom, and sang a greeting to the angels of the Sabbath, that is, the two angels who according to the Talmud accompany each man to his home at the onset of the Sabbath.

---

[6]In *Zohar*, II, 95a, this virgin is the Torah . . . and the literal meaning of the metaphor applied to a virgin "upon whom no eyes are directed" (whom no one sees).

The four stanzas of the hymn to the angels, "Peace be with you, you angels of peace," are followed by recitation of the thirty-first chapter of Proverbs, which seems to sing the praises of the noble housewife and her activities, but which the Kabbalists interpreted line by line as a hymn to the *Shekhinah*. Strange to say, it was through the mystical reinterpretation of the Kabbalists that this praise of the Jewish housewife found its way into the Sabbath ritual. This "hymn to the matron" is to be sung in a melodious voice by the seated company. Then, before the meal, as the *Zohar* prescribes, the master of the house "explicitly utters the mystery of the meal," that is, he introduces the sacred action in words which describe its secret meaning and at the same time conjure the *Shekhinah* to partake of the meal with her Bridegroom ("Small-faced," or better "Impatient") and the "Holy Old One." This solemn Aramaic invocation runs:

> Prepare the meal of perfect faith
> To rejoice the heart of the holy King,
> Prepare the meal of the King.
> This is the meal of the field of holy apples,
> And the Impatient and the Holy Old One—
> Behold, they come to partake of the meal with her.

What happens in this sacred action is described in Isaac Luria's great hymn, one of the few authentic works that have come down to us from the hand of this greatest of the Safed Kabbalists. Luria wrote hymns of this kind for each of the Sabbath meals. In the solemn drapery of their Zoharic Aramaic, they suggest the grandiloquent gesture of a magician, conjuring up a marvellous pageant for all to see. They read like the hymns of a mystery religion. Here I should like to quote the hymn for the Friday evening meal.[7]

I have sung
an old measure

would open
gates to

her field of apples
(each one a power)

set a new table
to feed her

& beautifully
candelabrum

drops its
light on us

Between right & left
the Bride

draws near in
holy jewels

clothes of the sabbath
whose lover

embraces her
down to foundation[8]

gives pleasure
squeezes his strength out

in surcease of
sorrow

& makes new faces
be hers

& new souls
new breath

---

[7]We have substituted Jerome Rothenberg's translation of Luria's "hymn to the Shekinah" (*Shekhinah*) from *A Big Jewish Book* (1978). (Eds.)

[8]The ninth *sefirah, yesod*, "the foundation," is correlated with the male and female sex organs.

gives her joy
double measure

of lights & of
streams for her blessing

o Friends of the Bride
go forth

all's sealed
within her

shines out from
Ancient of Days

Toward the south
I placed

candelabrum
(o mystical)

room in
the north

for table
for bread

for pitchers of wine
for sweet myrtle

gives power to
lovers

new potencies
garlands

give her many
sweet foods to taste

many kinds of
fish[9]

for fertility
birth

of new souls
new spirits

will follow the 32 paths
& 3 branches

the bride with
70 crowns[10]

with her King who
hovers above her

crown above crown in
Holy of Holies

this lady all worlds are
formed in

of words for her
70 crowns

50 gates
the Shekinah

ringed by
6 loaves

of the sabbath
& bound

all sides to
Heavenly Refuge

the hostile
powers

have left us
demons you feared

sleep in chains

In the eyes of the Kabbalists, this hymn was in a class apart. Unlike other table songs for the eve of the Sabbath, which could be sung or not, as one pleased, it was an indispensable part of the ritual. In Luria's hymn new meaning was not injected into an old prayer by means of mystical exegesis or *kavvanah*; rather, an esoteric conception creates its own liturgical language and form. The culmination of the hymn, the chaining

[9]The fish is a symbol of fertility. The widespread custom of eating fish on Friday is connected with the custom of consummating marriages on Friday night.

[10]Souls issue from "Wisdom" by 32 paths. The [three] branches are grace, judgment, and appeasing love, the three "pillars" of the world of the *sefiroth*, from which come the souls. The seventy crowns of the bride in the following line are mentioned in *Zohar*, II, 205a.

of the demons on the Sabbath, when they must flee "into the maw of the great abyss," recurs in Luria's hymns for the other two meals. The last song, sung at the dusk that ends the Sabbath day, strongly emphasizes this exorcism of the "insolent dogs," the powers of the other side—it is not a mere description of an exorcism, it *is* an exorcism:[11]

sons of his palace	those dogs
were shy	wild with *chutzpah*
who witness rays from	keep out
the small face	may not enter
these to be here	but send for
at this table	Ancient of Days
the king cuts	exchanging
grooves from his ring in	the jewel in his forehead
be pleased with	his peace
this meeting	as he sees it
this center of powers	releases the light from
all wingd	the shells
to bring joy to it	& will flow with it
now	into each orifice
is his hour of peace	these will conceal
without anger	under domes
draw near me	will be here
thou see my companions	in praise of the evening
be night without	a poem for
judgment	the small face[12]

I shall not go into all the other Sabbath rites of the Kabbalists. But there is still one point I should like to bring up in this connection. Just as the "reception of the Bride" marks a beginning of the holy day even before the onset of the actual Sabbath, so some Kabbalists attached great importance to a fourth Sabbath meal (mentioned very briefly in the Talmud as the custom of a single individual) which takes place after the *havdalah*, the prayer of division between Sabbath and weekday, and extends far into the night. This meal (at which among some of the Kabbalists nothing was eaten) escorts the Bride out of our domain, just as the ritual described above led her into it. Some Kabbalists attached the utmost importance to this mythical meal to "accompany the Queen." Whereas the three official Sabbath meals were associated with the patriarchs, Abraham, Isaac, and Jacob, this one was identified with David, the Lord's anointed, the Messiah. But according to the *Zohar*, these forefathers are the "feet of the divine throne," or *merkabah*. Small wonder that Nathan of Gaza, the prophet and spokesman of the Kabbalistic messiah, Sabbatai Zevi, prolonged this fourth meal until midnight. "He used to say: This is the meal of the King Messiah, and made a great principle of it."

[11]We have substituted Jerome Rothenberg's complete translation of the hymn from *A Big Jewish Book* (1978). (Eds.)

[12]*Ze'ir anpin* means in the *Zohar* the "Impatient One" in contrast to the "Patient One" as an aspect of God. In Luria it is taken literally as "he with the little face." He is the Godhead in its endless development and growth, as Lord of the *Shekhinah*.

RICHARD SCHECHNER

From Ritual to Theatre and Back: The Structure/Process of the Efficacy-Entertainment Dyad

In the late 1960s Richard Schechner, as director of the New York-based Performance Group and a leading shaper of contemporary "performance theory," pioneered a so-called "environmental theater" that could draw on all elements in and around the performance space, including the actor-audience nexus and that between both and "the larger environments outside the theatre." Schechner's deliberate use of models to "stimulate [the environmentalists'] creativity" turned from familiar Western sources to "American Indian, Oceanic, African, Siberian, or Eskimo societies," or back in history "to Altamira and the other caves, and then forward to Egypt, the Near and Middle East, Asia, and medieval Europe"—all "towards a poetics of performance" (Benamou and Rothenberg 1976: 42) that would return theater to the kind of "efficacy" he describes in the present essay. The search for a new poetics—at once a link between a future communalism, for which contemporary theater may be a model, and traditional, if distant, forms of participatory (communal) theater on which the contemporary theater may model itself—has engaged him as well with practitioners in the behavioral sciences (ethology, physical anthropology, ethnology, sociology, psychology, and so on). It has also led him to personal investigations in India and New Guinea ("the experiential background to this piece")—as in Herodotus's sense of history, often cited by Charles Olson, "to find out for oneself." In his exemplary mix of theory and performance, Schechner serves as a natural bridge to the contemporary discourse in Part 5.

The *kaiko* celebration of the Tsembaga of Highlands New Guinea is a year-long festival culminating in the *konj kaiko*—pig *kaiko*. *Kaiko* means dancing, and the chief entertainments of the celebrations are dances. During 1962 the Tsembaga entertained thirteen other local groups on fifteen occasions.[1] To make sure that the *kaiko* was successful young Tsembaga men were sent to neighboring areas to announce the shows—and to send back messages of delay should a visiting group be late: in that case the entertainments were postponed. The day of dancing begins with the dancers—all men—bathing and adorning themselves. Putting on costumes takes hours. It is an exacting, precise and delicate process. When dressed the dancers assemble on the flattened, stamped-down grounds where they dance both for their own pleasure and as rehearsal in advance of the arrival of their guests. The visitors announce their arrival by singing—they can be heard before they are seen. By this time many spectators have gathered, including both men and women from neighboring villages. These spectators come to watch, and to trade goods. Finally,

[1]In describing the *kaiko* I followed the account in Rappaport (1968). His study is a paradigm of how to examine ritual performances within an ecological context.

SOURCE: *Richard Schechner*, Essays on Performance Theory, *pages 63–78.*

the local dancers retire to a vantage point just above the dance ground, where their view of the visitors is unimpeded and where they continue singing. The visitors approach the gate silently, led by men carrying fight packages, swinging their axes as they run back and forth in front of their procession in the peculiar crouched fighting prance. Just before they reach the gate they are met by one or two of those locals who have invited them and who now escort them over the gate. Visiting women and children follow behind the dancers and join the other spectators on the sidelines. There is much embracing as the local women and children greet visiting kinfolk. The dancing procession charges to the center of the dance ground shouting the long, low battle cry and stamping their feet, magically treated before their arrival . . . to enable them to dance strongly. After they charge back and forth across the dance ground several times, repeating the stamping in several locations while the crowd cheers in admiration of their numbers, their style and the richness of their finery, they begin to sing.

[Rappaport 1968: 187]

The performance is a transformation of combat techniques into entertainment. All the basic moves and sounds—even the charge into the central space—are adaptations and direct lifts from battle. But the Tsembaga dance is a dance, and clearly so to everyone present at it. The dancing is not an isolated phenomenon—as theatre-going in America still is usually—but a behavior nested in supportive actions. The entry described takes place late in the afternoon, and just before dusk the dancing stops and the food which has been piled in the center of the dancing ground is distributed and eaten. It might be said, literally, that the dancing is *about the food*, for the whole *kaiko* cycle is about acquiring enough pigs-for-meat to afford the festival.

The visitors are asked to stop dancing and gather around while a presentation speech is made by one of the men responsible for the invitation. As he slowly walks around and around the food that has been laid out in a number of piles, the speechmaker recounts the relations of the two groups: their mutual assistance in fighting, their exchange of women and wealth, their hospitality to each other in times of defeat. . . . When the speech of presentation is finished they gather their portions and distribute them to those men who came to help them dance, and to their women.

[Rappaport 1968: 188]

After supper the dancing resumes and goes on all night. By dawn almost everyone has danced with everyone else: and this communality is a sign of a strong alliance.

With dawn the dancing ground is converted into a market place. Ornaments, pigs, furs, axes, knives, shells, pigments, tobacco are all traded or sold (money has come into the Tsembaga's economy).

The transactions that take place on the dance ground are completed on the spot; a man both gives and receives at the same time. . . . At the men's houses, however, a different kind of exchange takes place. Here men from other places give to their kinsmen or trading partners in the local group valuables for which they do not receive immediate return.

[Rappaport 1968: 189]

This orchestrated indebtedness is at the heart of the *kaiko*. At the start of the celebration the hosts owe meat to the guests and the guests owe items of trade to the hosts. In the first part of the *kaiko* the hosts pay meat to the guests; in the second part of the *kaiko* the guests pay the hosts trade items. But neither payment ends in a balance. When the *kaiko* is over the guests owe the hosts meat, and the hosts owe the guests trade items. This symmetrical imbalance guarantees further *kaikos*—continued exchanges between groups. Often trade items are not given back directly, but traded back through third or fourth parties. After the public trading and the gift-giving, some dancing resumes which ends by midmorning. Then everyone goes home.

The *kaiko* entertainments are a ritual display, not simply a doing but a *showing of a doing*. Furthermore, this showing is both actual (= the trading and giving of goods resulting in a new imbalance) and symbolic (= the reaffirmation of alliances made concrete in the debtor-creditor relationship). The entertainment itself is a vehicle for debtors and creditors to exchange places; it is also the occasion for a market; and it is fun. The *kaiko* depends on the accumulation of pigs and goods, and on a willingness to dress up and dance; neither by itself is enough. The dancing is a performance—and appreciated as such, with the audience serving as frequently acerbic critics—but it's also a way of facilitating trade, finding mates, cementing military alliances and reaffirming tribal hierarchies.

The Tsembaga say that "those who come to our *kaiko* will also come to our fights." This native interpretation of *kaiko* attendance is also given expression by an invited group. Preparations for departure to a *kaiko* at another place include ritual performances similar to those that precede a fight. Fight packages are applied to the heads and hearts of the dancers and *gir* to their feet so that they will dance strongly, just as, during warfare, they are applied so that they will fight strongly. . . . Dancing is like fighting. The visitors' procession is led by men carrying fight packages, and their entrance upon the dance ground of their hosts is martial. To join a group in dancing is the symbolic expression of willingness to join them in fighting.

[Rappaport 1968: 195−196]

The *kaiko* dance display is a cultural version of territorial and status displays in animals; the rituals of the Tsembaga are ethological as well as sociological. They are also ecological: the *kaiko* is a means of organizing the Tsembaga's relationships to their neighbors, to their lands and goods, to their gardens and hunting ranges.

A *kaiko* culminates in the *konj kaiko*. The *kaiko* lasts a year, the *konj kaiko* a few days, usually two. Kaiko years are rare. During the fifty to sixty years ending in 1963 the Tsembaga staged four *kaikos*, with an average of twelve to fifteen years between festivals. The whole cycle is tied to the war/peace rhythm which, in turn, is tied to the fortunes of the pig population. After the *konj kaito*—whose major event is a mass slaughter of pigs and distribution of meat—a short peace is followed by war, which continues until another *kaiko* cycle begins. The cycle itself lasts for enough years to allow the raising of sufficient pigs to stage a *konj kaiko*. The *konj kaiko* of November 7 and 8, 1963, saw the slaughter of 96 pigs with a total live weight of 15,000 pounds, yielding around 7,500 pounds of meat; eventually about 3,000 people got shares of the kill. What starts in dancing ends in eating; or, to put it in artistic-religious terms, what starts as theatre ends as communion. Perhaps not since classical Athenian festivals and medieval pageants have we in the West used performances as the pivots in systems involving economic, social, political and religious transactions. With the re-advent of holism in contemporary society at least a discussion of such performances becomes practical. It is clear that the *kaiko* dances are not ornaments or pastimes or even "part of the means" of effecting the transactions among the Tsembaga. The dances both symbolize and participate in the process of exchange.

The dances are pivots in a system of transformations which change destructive behavior into constructive alliances. It is no accident that every move, chant and costume of the *kaiko* dances are adapted from combat: a new use is found for this behavior. Quite unconsciously a positive feedback begins: the more splendid the displays of dancing, the stronger the alliances; the stronger the alliances, the more splendid the dancing. Between *kaikos*—but only between them—war is waged; during the cycles there is peace. The exact transformation of combat behavior into performance is at the heart of the *kaiko*. This transformation is identical in structure to that at the heart of Greek theatre (and from the Greeks down throughout all of Western theatre history). Namely, characterization and the presentation of real or possible events—the story, plot or dramatic action worked out among human figures (whether they be called men or gods)—is a transformation of real behavior into symbolic behavior. In fact, transformation is the heart of theatre, and there appear to be only two fundamental kinds of theatrical transformation: (1) the displacement of anti-social, injurious, disruptive behavior by ritualized gesture and display, and (2) the invention of characters who act out fictional events or real events fictionalized by virtue of their being acted out (as in documentary theatre or Roman gladiatorial games). These two kinds of transformation occur together, but in the mix usually one is dominant. Western theatre emphasizes characterization and the enactment of fictions; Melanesian, African and Australian (aborigine) theatre emphasize the displacement of hostile behavior. Forms which balance the two tendencies—Nō, Kathakali, the Balinese Ketchak, medieval moralities, some contemporary avant-garde performances—offer, I think, the best models for the future of the theatre.

Much performing among communal peoples is, like the *kaiko*, part of the overall ecology of a society. The *Engwura* cycle of the Arunta of Australia, as described by Spencer and Gillen in the late 19th century, is an elegant example of how a complicated series of performances expressed and participated in a people's ecology. The fact that the *Engwura* is no longer performed—that the Arunta, culturally speaking, have been exterminated—indicates the incompatibility of wholeness as I am describing it and Western society as it is presently constituted. Insofar as performing groups adapt techniques from the *kaiko* or *Engwura* they are bound to remain outside the "mainstream." But the chief function of the avant-garde is to propose models for change: to remain "in advance." The *Engwura* was an initiation cycle that spanned several years;

the last phase consisted of performances staged sporadically over a three-to-four-month period. Each phase of the *Engwura* took place only when several conditions meshed: enough young men of a certain age gathered in one place to be initiated; enough older men willing to lead the ceremonies (particularly important in a non-literate culture); enough food to support celebration. Then the sacred implements and sacred grounds were prepared painstakingly and according to tradition. Finally, there had to be peace among neighboring tribes—but the announcement of a forthcoming *Engwura* was sometimes enough to guarantee a peace.

The daily rhythm recapitulated the monthly rhythm: performance spaces were cleared, implements repaired and laid out, body decorations applied, food cooked. Each performance day saw not one but several performances, with rest and preparations between each. Each performance lasted on an average ten minutes, and was characteristically a dance accompanied by drumming and chanting. Then the performers rested for about two hours; preparations for the next performance began, and these preparations took about two hours.[2] The whole cycle recapitulates the life cycle of the Arunta male; and during his life he could expect to play roles co-existent with his status in society: initiate, participant, leader or onlooker. Thus on each day performers enacted condensed and concentrated versions of their lives; and the three-to-four-month culminating series of performances also replicated the life cycle. The whole cycle was, in fact, an important—perhaps the most important—set of events in an Arunta life. Each phase of the cycle was a replication (either an extension or a concentration) of every other phase.

The subject matter of each brief dance-drama was life events of mythical Dreamtime beings who populated the world "in the beginning."[3] These mythic events were very important to the Arunta and constituted for them a history and, since each Dreamtime event was connected to specific places and landmarks, a geography. The rituals are a concrete symbolization and reenactment of Dreamtime events, and to this extent the *Engwura* is familiar to us: it is not unlike our own drama except that we accept the reactualization of past events only as a convention. The Arunta, like the orthodox Catholic taking the Eucharist, accepted the manifestation of Dreamtime events as actual (see fig. 17).

The overall structure of the *Engwura* is analogic, while its interior structure is dramatic. The two structures are integrated because the Arunta believed concretely in the Dreamtime and experienced their own lives as divided between "ordinary" and "superordinary" realities. They experienced an interaction between these realities, and *Engwura* performers were the navel, or link, or point-of-time-and-place where the two realities meshed.

I saw an ecological ritual similar to the *konj kaiko* (but much less inclusive than the *Engwura*) in March, 1972, at Kurumugl in the Eastern Highlands of New Guinea. Surrounding the performance of the *kaiko* is no special self-consciousness—that is, the ritual functions without the Tsembaga being explicitly aware of its functions; and aside

---

[2]This rhythm of relatively long preparations followed by a brief performance, with a series of performances given on a single day, is common in Australia. Although we accept this rhythm in dance and music, it has not yet found acceptance in theatre. Still dominated by Aristotelian injunctions we act as if a work has to be of a certain length to acquire seriousness.

[3]See above, p. 201. (Eds.)

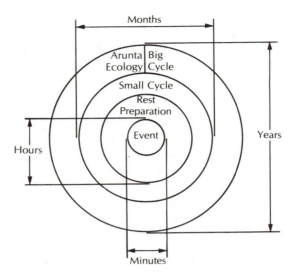

FIGURE 17. The *Engwura* of the Arunta.

from commendatory or critical comments on the dancing no aesthetic judgments are passed. In other words there are neither performance theorists nor critics among the Tsembaga. At Kurumugl the people know what the ritual does and why it was established—to inhibit warfare among feuding groups. The ritual at Kurumugl is already traveling along the continuum toward theatre in the modern sense. Knowing what the ritual does is a very important step in the development of theatre from ritual.

It's my purpose to outline a process through which theatre develops from ritual; and also to suggest that in some circumstances ritual develops from theatre. I think this process ought to be documented from contemporary or near-contemporary sources because so often the jump from ritual to theatre is assumed, or attributed to ancient events the evidence for which is suspect.

Unlike the *kaiko* dancing grounds, the "council grounds" (as they are called) at Kurumugl are near no regular village. The colonial Australian government set them up as a place where former enemies assemble to *sing-sing* (pidgin for drama-music-dance). The difference between the Tsembaga and the people at Kurumugl is that the *kaiko* brought together traditional allies while the Kurumugl *sing-sing* assembled traditional enemies. The performances at Kurumugl are always in danger of tipping over into actual combat, even though the performances are very much like those of the *konj kaiko*: dance movements adapted from combat, war chants, the arrival of a guest group at a dance ground piled high with freshly slaughtered, cooked pork. The celebration at Kurumugl that I saw took two days. The first consisted of arriving, setting up temporary house inside long rectanglar huts, digging cooking ovens. All the people gathered—about 350—were of one tribal group. They awaited the arrival of their guests, a group comparable in size, but recently their enemies. The second day began with the slaughter of about two hundred pigs. These are clubbed on the snouts and heads. As each owner kills his animal he recites—sings—a speech telling how difficult it was to raise the pig, who it is promised to, what a fine animal it is, etc. The *pro forma recitatives* are applauded with laughs and roars, as they often contain jokes and obscene invective. The orations are accompanied by the death squeals of the pigs. Then the animals are gutted, butchered and lowered in halves and quarters into earth ovens to cook. Their guts are hung in nets over the ovens and steamed. Their bladders are blown into balloons and given to the children. The sight and smell of so much meat and blood excites the people, including me. No special clothes are worn for the killing. The only ritual element I detected was the careful display of pig jawbones on a circular altar-like structure in the middle of the dance grounds. From each jaw flowers were hung.

As the cooking starts, the men retire to the huts to begin adorning themselves. From time to time a man emerges to try on a towering headdress of cassowary and peacock feathers. The women cook and tend to the children. After about four hours the meat, still nearly raw, is taken from the ovens and displayed in long rows. Each family lays out its own meat—the women doing most of the work—like so much money in the bank: pork is wealth in the Highlands. As more and more men finish dressing they emerge from the huts to show off and admire each other in a grudging way—the adorning is very competitive. Some women also adorned themselves, dressing much like the men. I couldn't determine if this was traditional or an innovation. A man invited Joan MacIntosh[4] and me into his hut to watch him put on his makeup. He set out a mirror and tins of pigment (bought from a Japanese trading store) and then applied blue, red and black to his torso, shoulders, arms and face. He painted half his nose red and the other half blue. I asked him what the patterns meant. He said he chose them because he liked the way they looked. The Australian aborigines, by contrast, adorn their bodies with patterns each detail of which is linked to ancestral beings, sexual magic or recent events. Aborigine body painting is map-making and myth-telling.

Our performer showed us his headdress of four-foot-long feathers, and stepped outside to try it on. As he emerged from the hut his casual air dropped and he literally thrust his chest forward, gave a long whooping call, put on his headdress and displayed himself. He was costumed for a social not a dramatic role—that is, not to present a fictional character whose life was separable from his own, but to show himself in a special way: to display his strength, his power, his wealth, his authority. It is not easy to distinguish between these kinds of roles, except that in drama the script is already fixed in its details, the precise gestures of the role are rehearsed for a particular occasion (and other occasions, other "productions," might eventuate in different gestures), while "in life" the script is "replaced by an ongoing process, this process is set in motion by the objective demands of the role, and the subjective motives and goals of the actor" [Burns 1972: 132]. An awareness that social and dramatic roles are indeed closely related to each other, and locating their points of convergence in the mise-en-scène rather than in the mind of the playwright, has been one of the major developments in contemporary theatre. This development has been helped by film and television—by film because it presents dramatic actions on location, as if in "real life," and by TV because all so-called news is staged. It is staged not only by the obvious editing of raw footage to suit TV format and the need to sell time (that is, to hold the viewer's attention), but also as it is actually made. Many guerrilla activities, terrorist raids, kidnappings, assassinations and street demonstrations are theatricalized events performed by groups of people in

[4]A leading member of the Performance Group. (Eds.)

order to catch the attention of larger masses of people by means of TV. This is the main way today in which powerless groups get a hearing. In response, the authorities stage their repressive raids, their assaults and their reprisals: to show the world how the insurgents will be dealt with, to display the power of authority and to terrorize the viewer. Thus an apparent two-person exchange between activist and authority is actually a three-person arrangement with the spectator supplying the vital link. Thus are we continually being educated to the histrionic structure of communication [Brustein 1974].

The seeds of this histrionic sense are at Kurumugl. As these people are "technified" (already they have planes before cars, TV before newspapers) they will leap not into the twentieth century but beyond, going directly from pre-industrial tribalism to automation-age tribalism. The big difference between the two is that pre-industrial tribalism scatters power among a large number of local leaders, there being no way for people to maintain themselves in large masses; automation-age tribalism is a way of controlling megalopolitic masses. I mean by tribalism the shaping of social roles not through individual choice but by collective formation; the substitution of histrionic-ritualized events for ordinary events; the sacralization or increasingly closely codified definition of all experience; and the disappearance of solitude and one-to-one intimacy as we have developed it since the Renaissance. Automation-age tribalism is medievalism under the auspices of technology. Such tribalism is good for the theatre—if by good one means that most social situations will be governed by conventional, external gestures loaded with metaphoric/symbolic significances. Anomie and identity crisis are eliminated and in their places are fixed roles and rites of passage transporting persons not only from one status to another but from one identity to another. These transportations are achieved by means of performances. I call these kinds of performances "transformances" because the performances are the means of transformation from one status, identity or situation to another.

When the performer at Kurumugl stepped outside his hut he joined a group of envious males whose costumes were, like his, peculiar amalgams of traditional and imported stuff: sunglasses and bones stuck through the septum; cigarette holders and homemade tobacco pipes; khaki shorts and grass skirts. But despite the breakdown in traditional costume an old pattern was being worked out. An ecological ritual where the pig meat was a "payback" (pidgin for fulfilling a ritual obligation) from the hosts to the guests. As among the Tsembaga every adult male at Kurumugl was in a debtor relationship to persons arriving in the afternoon of the second day. The nature of the payback is such that what is given back must exceed what is owed. (This is true even of war, where a perpetual imbalance in casualties must be maintained.) The payback ceremony involves an exchange of roles in which creditors become debtors and debtors become creditors. This insures that more ceremonies will follow when the new debtors accumulate enough pigs. Never is a balance struck, because a balance would threaten an end to the obligations, and this would lead to war. As long as the obligations are intact the social web transmits continuous waves of paybacks back and forth. The visitors approaching Kurumugl came not as friends but as invaders. The afternoon's performance was not a party but a ritual combat with the guests assaulting Kurumugl in a modified war dance, armed with fighting spears, and the campers at Kurumugl defending their ground and the immense pile of meat piled in the center of it. Instead of a secret raiding party there were dancers; instead of taking human victims, they took meat. And instead of doubt about the outcome everyone knew what was going to happen. Thus a ritualized social drama (as war in the Highlands often is) moves toward becoming an aesthetic drama in which a script of actions is adhered to—the script being known in advance and carefully prepared for.

Again, differences between social and aesthetic drama are not easy to specify. Social drama has more variables, the outcome is in doubt—it is more like a game or sporting context. Aesthetic drama is almost totally arranged in advance, and the participants can concentrate not on strategies of achieving their goals—at Kurumugl, to penetrate to where the meat was, or to defend the meat pile—but on displays; aesthetic drama is less instrumental and more ornamental than social drama. Also, it can use symbolic time and place, and so become entirely fictionalized.

Early in the afternoon of the second day I heard from outside the camp the chanting and shouting of the invaders. The people in camp returned these shouts so that an antiphonal chorus arose. Then the men in camp—and a contingent of about twenty women who were fully armed—rushed to the edges of Kurumugl and the ritual combat began. Both sides were armed with bows and arrows, spears, sticks and axes. They chanted in a rhythm common to the Highlands—a leader sings a phrase and is overlapped by the unison response of many followers. This call-and-response is in loud nasal tones, a progression of quarter and half notes. Such chants alternate with Ketchak-like staccato grunts-pants-shouts. From about one to five in the afternoon the two groups engaged in fierce ritual combat. Each cycle of singing and dancing climaxed when parties of warriors rushed forward from both sides, spears ready for throwing, and, at apparently the last second, did a rapid kick-from-the-knee step instead of throwing their weapons. The weapons became props in a performance of aggression displaced, if not into friendship, at least into a non-deadly confrontation.

The assaults of the invaders were repeated dozens of times; a lush and valuable peanut field was trampled to muck; each assault was met by determined counterattack. But foot by foot the invaders penetrated to the heart of the camp ground—to the pile of meat and the altar of jaw bones and flowers. All the meat previously laid out in rows was now piled three feet deep—a huge heap of legs, snouts, ribs and flanks all tangled together. Three live white goats were tethered to a pole at the edge of the meat pile. Once the invaders reached the meat they merged with their hosts in one large, whooping, chanting, dancing doughnut of warriors. Around and around the meat they danced, for nearly an hour. I was pinned up against a tree, between the armed dancers and the meat. Then, suddenly, the dancing stopped and orators plunged into the meat, pulling a leg, or a flank, or a side of ribs, and shouted-sung-declaimed things like:

> This pig I give you in payment for the pig you gave my father three years ago! Your pig was scrawny, no fat on it at all, but my pig is huge, with lots of fat, much good meat—much better than the one my father got! And my whole family, especially my brothers, will remember that we are giving you today better than what we got, so that you owe us, and will help us if we need you beside us in a fight!

Sometimes the speechifying rises to song; sometimes insults are hurled back and forth. The fun in the orating, and the joking, stands on a very serious foundation: the participants do not forget that not so long ago they were blood enemies. After more than an hour of orating, the meat is distributed. Sleds are made to carry it shoulder high and whole families, with much singing, leave with their share of meat.

The performance at Kurumugl consists of displaying the meat, ritual combat, the merging of the two groups into one, orating and carrying the meat away. Preparations for this performance are both immediate, the day before at the camp (and at the visitors' residence), and long-range: raising the pigs, acquiring costumes and ornaments. After the performance comes the cleanup, the travel home, the distribution of the meat, feasting and stories about the *sing-sing*. By means of the performance the basic relationship—one might say the fundamental relationship—between the invading and the host groups is inverted.

ACTUALITY 1	→	TRANSFORMANCE	→	ACTUALITY 2
Group A is debtor to Group B				Group B is debtor to Group A

As in all rites of passage something has happened during the performance; *the performance both symbolizes and actualizes the change in status*. The dancing at Kurumugl is the process by which change happens and it is the only process (other than war) recognized by all the parties assembled at Kurumugl. Giving and taking the meat not only symbolizes the changed relationship between Group A and B, it is the change itself. This convergence of symbolic and actual event is missing from aesthetic theatre. We have sought for it by trying to make the performer "responsible" or "visible" in and for his performance—either through psychodramatic techniques or other psychological means. This use of psychology is a reflection of our preoccupation with the individual. Where performances have been sociologically or politically motivated—such as happenings and guerrilla theatre—the authenticating techniques have included emphasis on the event in and for itself, the development of group consciousness and appeals to the public at large. But a fundamental contradiction undermines these efforts. At Kurumugl enough actual wealth and people could be assembled in one place so that what was done in the performance focused actual economic, political and social power. In our society only a charade of power is displayed at theatrical performances. When this is recognized, authenticating theatres preoccupy themselves with symbolic activities, feeling helpless in the face of the hollowness of the authenticating tasks they set up for themselves. So-called real events are revealed as metaphors. In a society as large and wealthy as ours only aesthetic theatre is possible. Or authenticating theatres must seek a basis other than economics; or fully ally themselves with established authority. None of these options is as easy as it sounds.

At Kurumugl the change between Group A and B is not simply the occasion for a celebratory performance (as a birthday party celebrates but does not effect a change in age). The performance effects what it celebrates. It opens up enough time in the right place for the exchange to be made: it is liminal: a fluid mid-point between two fixed structures. Only for a brief time do the two groups merge into one dancing circle; during this liminal time/place *communitas* is possible—that leveling of all differences in an ecstasy that so often characterizes performing. Then, and only then, the exchange takes place.

war parties	——————— transformed into ——————>	dancing groups
human victims	—————————————————————————————————>	pig meat
battle dress	—————————————————————————————————>	costumes
combat	—————————————————————————————————>	dancing
debtors	—————————————————————————————————>	creditors
creditors	—————————————————————————————————>	debtors
two groups	—————————————————————————————————>	one group

The transformations above the line convert actualities into aesthetic realities. Those below the line effect a change from one actuality into another. It is only because the transformations above the line happen that those below the line can take place in peace. All the transformations—aesthetic as well as actual—are temporary: the meat will be eaten, the costumes doffed, the dance ended; the single group will divide again according to known divisions; today's debtors will be next year's creditors, etc. The celebration at Kurumugl managed a complicated and potentially dangerous exchange with a minimum of danger and a maximum of pleasure. The mode of achieving "real results"— paying debts, incurring new obligations—was performing; the dancing does not celebrate achieving results, it does not precede or follow the exchange, it is the means of making the transformations; the performance is effective.

The Tsembaga, Arunta and Kurumugl performances are ecological rituals. Whatever enjoyment the participants take in the dancing, and however carefully they prepare themselves for dancing, the dances are danced to achieve results. In religious rituals results are achieved by appealing to a transcendent Other (who puts in an appearance either in person or by surrogate). In ecological rituals the other group, or the status to be achieved, or some other clearly human arrangement is the object of the performance. An ecological ritual with no results to show "below the line" would soon cease. The "above the line" transformations change aggressive actions into harmless and pleasure-giving performances (in the cases cited). One is struck by the analogy to certain biological adaptations among animals.

In the New Guinea Highlands, at first under the pressure of the colonial police, later under its own momentum, warfare is transformed into dancing. As above-the-line activities grow in importance, entertainment as such takes over from efficacy as the reason for the performance. It is not only that creditors and debtors need to exchange roles, but also that people want to show off; it is not only to get results that the dances are staged, but also because people like dancing for its own sake. Efficacy and entertainment are opposed to each other, but they form a binary system, a continuum.

EFFICACY <————————————————————> ENTERTAINMENT

EFFICACY	ENTERTAINMENT
(Ritual)	(Theatre)
results	fun
link to an absent Other	only for those here
abolishes time, symbolic time	emphasizes now
brings Other here	audience is the Other

EFFICACY ◄────────────────────► ENTERTAINMENT

performer possessed, in trance	performer knows what he's doing
audience participates	audience watches
audience believes	audience appreciates
criticism is forbidden	criticism is encouraged
collective creativity	individual creativity

The basic opposition is between efficacy and entertainment, not between ritual and theatre. Whether one calls a specific performance ritual or theatre depends on the degree to which the performance tends toward efficacy or entertainment. No performance is pure efficacy or pure entertainment. The matter is complicated because one can look at specific performances from several vantages; changing perspective changes classification. For example, a Broadway musical is entertainment if one concentrates on what happens onstage and in the house. But if the point of view expands—to include rehearsals, backstage life before, during and after the show, the function of the roles in the careers of each performer, the money invested by backers, the arrival of the audience, their social status, how they paid for their tickets (as individuals, expense accounts, theatre parties, etc.) and how this indicates the use they're making of the performance (as entertainment, to advance their careers, to support a charity, etc.)—then the Broadway musical is more than entertainment; it reveals many ritual elements.

Recently, more performances have been emphasizing the rehearsal and backstage procedures. At first this was as simple as showing the lighting instruments and using a half-curtain, as Brecht did. But within the last fifteen years the process of mounting the performance, the workshops that lead up to the performance, the means by which an audience is brought into the space and led from the space and many other previously automatic procedures, have become the subjects of theatrical manipulations. These procedures have to do with the theatre-in-itself and they are, as regards the theatre, efficacious: that is, these procedures are what makes a theatre into a theatre regardless of themes, plot or the usual "elements of drama." The attention paid to the procedures of making theatre are, I think, attempts at ritualizing performance, of finding in the theatre itself authenticating acts. In a period when authenticity is increasingly rare in public life the performer has been asked to surrender his traditional masks and be himself; or at least to show how the masks are put on and taken off. Instead of mirroring his times the performer is asked to remedy them. The professions taken as models for theatre are medicine and the church. No wonder shamanism is popular among theatre people: shamanism is that branch of doctoring that is religious, and that kind of religion that is full of ironies and tricks.

At present efficacy is ascending to a dominant position over entertainment. It is my belief that theatre history can be given an overall shape as a development along a core which is a *braided structure* constantly interrelating efficacy and entertainment. At each period in each culture one or the other is dominant—one is ascending while the other is descending. Naturally, these changes are part of changes in the overall social structure; yet performance is not a passive mirror of these social changes but a part of the complicated feedback process that brings about change. At all times a dialectical tension exists between efficacious and entertainment tendencies. For Western theatre, at least, I think it can be shown that when the braid is tight—that is, when efficacy and entertainment are both present in nearly equal degrees—theatre flourishes. During these brief historical moments the theatre answers needs that are both ritualistic and pleasure-giving. Fifth-century Athenian theatre, Elizabethan theatre, and possibly the theatre of the late 19th century and/or of our own times show the kind of convergence I'm talking about. When efficacy dominates, performances are universalistic, allegorical, ritualized, tied to a stable established order; this kind of theatre persists for a relatively long time. When entertainment dominates, performances are class-oriented, individualized, show business, constantly adjusted to suit the tastes of a fickle audience. The two most recent convergences—the rise of entertainment before the Elizabethan period and the rise of efficacy during the modern period—are necessarily opposites of each other. The model that I offer is of course a simplification. I present it as a help in conceptualizing my view of the progression of theatre history, which I think has its own logic and internal force. The late medieval period was dominated by efficacious performances: church services, court ceremonies, moralities, pageants. In the early Renaissance these began to decline and popular entertainments, always present, gained, finally becoming dominant in the form of the public theatres of the Elizabethan period. The private and court theatres developed alongside the public theatres. The private theatres were for the upper classes.

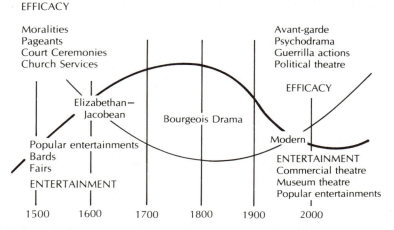

FIGURE 18.   Efficacy/Entertainment Braid: Fifteenth to Twenty-First Centuries in the English and American Theatres.

Although some professionals worked in both public and private theatres, and some spectators attended both, these entertainments were fundamentally opposed to each other. The conflicts between the public and private theatres never worked themselves out because all the theatres were closed in 1642. When theatres reopened at the Restoration the Elizabethan public theatre was gone and all the theatres resembled the private theatres and masques, the property of the upper classes. During the eighteenth and nineteenth centuries this aristocratic theatre developed into the bourgeois theatre, as that class rose to displace the aristocracy. The dominant efficacious mode of the medieval centuries went underground to re-emerge in the guise of social and political drama during the last third of the nineteenth century. This new naturalistic theatre opposed the commercialism and pomposity of the boulevards and allied itself to scientific theatrical styles and techniques. The avant-garde identified itself both with Bohemianism—the outcasts of bourgeois society—and science, the source of power. Avant-garde artists used terms like ''experimental'' and ''research'' to characterize their work, which took place in ''laboratories.'' Efficacy lies at the ideological heart of all aspects of this new theatre (see fig. 18).

In the twentieth century the entertainment theatre, threatened with extinction, broke into two parts: an increasingly outmoded commercial theatre typified by Broadway and a subsidized community museum typified by the regional theatres. The FACT [First American Congress of Theatre] meeting at Princeton [June 2—6, 1974] was an attempt by commercial interests to ally themselves with the regional theatres. Although such an alliance is inevitable, it's most likely that the regional theatres will absorb the commercial theatres. Whatever the outcome, the entertainment theatres remain fundamentally opposed by the avant-garde—which has itself, by mid-twentieth century, expanded to include direct political action, psychotherapy and other manifestly efficacious kinds of performances. It is my opinion that efficacious theatres are on the upswing and will dominate the theatrical world within the next twenty years. . . .

FIVE
Contemporary Moves

ROBERT DUNCAN
From "Rites of Participation"

"A multiphasic experience sought a multiphasic form," wrote Robert Duncan (D. Allen 1960: 435) toward a poetics, rich in influences and sources, that could set the work of an avant-garde alongside both the Western "mainstream" (Dante, Whitman, the Romantics) and those subterranean traditions (Kabbalah, Gnosticism, etc.) that had long been "neglected, even scorned" but "in which one begins to find the Gnosis of the modern world." Duncan is also, in both his poetry and poetics, a principal reinterpreter of myth as an ongoing human process, so crucial to him that he writes: "The meaning and intent of what it is to be a man and, among men, to be a poet, I owe to the workings of myth in my spirit, both the increment of associations gathered in my continuing study of mythological lore and my own apprehension of what my life is at work there" (1968: 7−8). Principal works: Opening of the Field, Bending the Bow, Roots and Branches, The Truth and Life of Myth.

The drama of our time is the coming of all men into one fate, "the dream of everyone, everywhere." The fate or dream is the fate of more than mankind. Our secret Adam is written now in the script of the primal cell. We have gone beyond the reality of the incomparable nation or race, the incomparable Jehovah in the shape of a man, the incomparable Book or Vision, the incomparable species, in which identity might hold & defend its boundaries against an alien territory. All things have come now into their comparisons. But these comparisons are the correspondences that haunted Paracelsus, who saw also that the key to man's nature was hidden in the larger nature.

In space this has meant the extension of our "where" into a world ecology. The O.E.D. gives 1873 as the earliest English use of the word in the translation of Haeckel's *History of Creation*—"*the great series of phenomena of comparative anatomy and ontogeny . . . oecology*." The very form of man has no longer the isolation of a superior paradigm but is involved in its morphology in the cooperative design of all living things, in the life of everything, everywhere. We go now to the once-called primitive—to the bush man, the child, or the ape—not to read what we were but what we are. In the psychoanalysis of the outcast and vagabond, the neurotic and psychotic, we slowly discover the hidden features of our own emotional and mental processes. We hunt for the key to language itself in the dance of the bees or in the chemical code of the chromosomes.

The inspiration of Marx bringing economies into comparison and imagining a world commune, of Darwin bringing species into comparison and imagining a world family of the living in evolution, of Frazer bringing magic, rituals and gods into comparison and imagining a world cult—the inspiration growing in the nineteenth century of imperialist expansions was towards a larger community of man. In time, this

SOURCE: Clayton Eshleman (ed.), A Caterpillar Anthology, pages 23−38.

has meant our "when" involves and is involved in an empire that extends into the past and future beyond times and eras, beyond the demarcations of history. Not only the boundaries of states or civilizations but also the boundaries of historical periods are inadequate to define the vital figure in which we are involved. *"For the intense yearning which each of them has towards the other,"* Diotima tells Socrates in Plato's Symposium, *"does not appear to be the desire of lover's intercourse, but of something else which the soul of either evidently desires and cannot tell, and of which she has only a dark and doubtful presentiment."*

The Symposium of Plato was restricted to a community of Athenians, gathered in the common creation of an *arete*, an aristocracy of spirit, inspired by the homoEros, taking its stand against lower or foreign orders, not only of men but of nature itself. The intense yearning, the desire for something else, of which we too have only a dark and doubtful presentiment, remains, but our *arete*, our ideal of vital being, rises not in our identification in a hierarchy of higher forms but in our identification with the universe. To compose such a symposium of the whole, such a totality, all the old excluded orders must be included. The female, the proletariat, the foreign; the animal and vegetative; the unconscious and the unknown; the criminal and failure—all that has been outcast and vagabond must return to be admitted in the creation of what we consider we are.

The dissolving of boundaries of time, as in H.D.'s *Palimpsest*, so that Egyptian or Hellenistic ways invade the contemporary scene—the reorganization of identity to extend the burden of consciousness—this change of mind has been at work in many fields. The thought of primitives, dreamers, children, or the mad—once excluded by the provincial claims of common sense from the domain of the meaningful or significant—has been reclaimed by the comparative psychologies of William James, Freud, Lévy-Bruhl, Piaget, by the comparative linguistics of Sapir or Whorf, brought into the community of a new epistemology.

"Past the danger point, past the point of any logic and of any meaning, and everything has meaning," H.D. writes in *Bid Me to Live: "Start superimposing, you get odd composites, nation on nation."* So, Malraux in his *Psychology of Art* hears *"a furtive colloquy in progress between the statuary of the Royal Portals of Chartres and the great fetishes"* beginning in museums of the mind where all the arts of man have been brought into the complex of a new idea of Art and Man in their being superimposed. *"Our art world is one,"* he writes in *The Metamorphosis of the Gods, "in which a Romanesque crucifix and an Egyptian statue of a dead man can both be living presences." "In our imaginary museum the great art of Europe is but one great art among others, just as the history of Europe has come to mean one history among others." "Each civilization had its 'high places',"* he concludes in the Introduction: *"All mankind is now discovering its own. And these are not (as the nineteenth century took for granted) regarded as successive landmarks of art's long pilgrimage through time. Just as Cézanne did not see Poussin as Tintoretto's successor, Chartres does not mark an 'advance' on Angkor, or Borobudur, or the Aztec temples, any more than its Kings are an 'advance' on the Kwannon at Nara, on the Plumed Serpents, or on Pheidias' Horsemen."*

If, as Pound began to see in *The Spirit of Romance*, *"All ages are contemporaneous,"* our time has always been, and the statement that the great drama of our time is the coming of all men into one fate is the statement of a crisis we may see as everpresent in

Man wherever and whenever a man has awakened to the desire for wholeness in being. *"The continuous present,"* Gertrude Stein called this sense of time and history, and she saw the great drama as man's engagement in a composition of the contemporary. Man is always in the process of this composition. *"The composition is the thing seen by every one living in the living they are doing,"* she writes in *Composition As Explanation: "they are the composing of the compositions that at the time they are living is the composition of the time in which they are living. It is that that makes living a thing they are doing."*

"Nothing changes from generation to generation," she writes later in her lecture *Portraits and Repetition, "except the composition in which we live and the composition in which we live makes the art which we see and hear." "Once started expressing this thing, expressing any thing there can be no repetition because the essence of that expression is insistence." "Each civilization insisted in its own way before it went away."* To enter into *"our time,"* she saw as *"a thing that is very troublesome,"* for life itself was a disturbance of all composition—*"a fear a doubt and a judgement and a conviction,"* troubling the waters toward some needed "quality of distribution and equilibration."

The first person plural—the "we," "our," "us"—is a communal consciousness in which the "I" has entered into the company of imagined like minds, a dramatic voice in which the readers and the man writing are gathered into one composition, in which we may find kindred thought and feeling, an insistence, in Plutarch or Dante, Plato or D. H. Lawrence, closer to our inner insistence than the thought and feeling of parents or neighbors. The discovery of self, time and world, is an entering into or tuning to possibilities of self, time and world, that are given.

"The single experience lodges in an individual consciousness and is, strictly speaking, incommunicable," Sapir writes in *Language: "To be communicated it needs to be referred to a class which is tacitly accepted by the community as an identity. Thus, the single impression which I have of a particular house must be identified with all my other impressions of it. Further, my generalized memory or my 'notion' of this house must be merged with the notions that all other individuals who have seen the house have formed of it. The particular experience that we started with has now been widened so as to embrace all possible impressions or images that sentient beings have formed or may form of the house in question. In other words, the speech element 'house' is the symbol, first and foremost, not of a single perception, nor even of the notion of a particular object but of a 'concept,' in other words, of a convenient capsule of thought that embraces thousands of distant experiences and that is ready to take in thousands more. If the single significant elements of speech are the symbols of concepts, the actual flow of speech may be interpreted as a record of the setting of these concepts into mutual relations."*

There is no isolate experience of anything then, for to come into "house" or "dog," "bread" or "wine," is to come into a company. Eros and Logos are inextricably mixed, daemons of an initiation in each of our lives into a new being. Every baby is surrounded by elders of a mystery. The first words, the "da-da" and "ma-ma," are keys given in a repeated ritual by parental priest and priestess to a locus for the child in his chaotic babbling, whereby from the oceanic and elemental psychic medium—warmth and cold, calm and storm, the moodiness previous to being—persons, Daddy and Mama, appear. But these very persons are not individual personalities but communal fictions of the family cultus, vicars of Father and Mother, as the Pope is a Vicar of Christ. The Child, the word "child," is himself such a persona, inaccessible to the personality of the individual, as the language of adult personal affairs is inaccessible to the child. To have a child is always a threat to the would-be autonomous personality, for the parent must take leave of himself in order to enter an other impersonation, evoking the powers of Fatherhood or Motherhood, so that the infant may be brought up from the dark of his individuality into a new light, into his Childhood. For the transition to be made at all, to come into the life of the spirit, in which this Kindergarten is a re-created stage set of the mythic Garden, means a poetry then, the making up of an imaginary realm in which the individual parents and infant participate in a community that exists in a time larger than any individual life-time, in a language. For "Father," "Mother," "Child," are living words, deriving their meaning from thousands of distinct experiences, and the actual flow of family life, like the actual flow of speech, "may be interpreted as the setting of these concepts into mutual relations." The toys of the nursery are not trivia but first given instruments of an extension in consciousness, our creative life. There is a travesty made of sacred objects when the building blocks that are also alphabet blocks, the animal and human dolls, the picture books, are rendered cute or babyish.

"*The maturity of man—*" Nietzsche writes in *Beyond Good and Evil:* "*that means, to have reacquired the seriousness that one had as a child at play.*" In *The Zohar* of Moses of Leon, God Himself appears as *Child-Creator-of-the-World:* "*When the Holy One, blessed be He, was about to make the world, all the letters of the Alphabet were still embryonic, and for two thousand years the Holy One, blessed be He, had contemplated them and toyed with them. When He came to create the world, all the letters presented themselves before Him in reversed order. The letter Tau advanced in front and pleaded: May it please Thee, O Lord of the world, to place me first in the creation of the world, seeing that I am the concluding letter of EMeTh (Truth) which is engraved upon Thy seal.*" One by one the letters present themselves. At the last, "*the Beth then entered and said: O Lord of the world, may it please Thee to put me first in the creation of the world, since I represent the benedictions (Berakhoth) offered to Thee on high and below. The Holy One, blessed be He, said to her: Assuredly, with thee I will create the world, and thou shalt form the beginning in the creation of the world. The letter Aleph remained in her place without presenting herself. Said the Holy One, blessed be His name: Aleph, Aleph, wherefore comest thou not before Me like the rest of the letters? She answered: Because I saw all the other letters leaving Thy presence without any success. What, then, could I achieve there? And further, since Thou hast already bestowed on the letter Beth this great gift, it is not meet for the Supreme King to take away the gift which He has made to His servant and give it to another. The Lord said to her: Aleph, Aleph, although I will begin the creation of the world with the Beth, thou wilt remain the first of letters. My unity shall not be expressed except through thee, on thee shall be based all calculations and operations of the world, and unity shall not be expressed save by the letter Aleph. Then the Holy One, blessed be His name, made higher-word letters of a large pattern and lower-word letters of a small pattern. It is therefore that we have here two words beginning with beth (Bereshith bara)* 'in-the-beginning He-created' *and then two words beginning with aleph (Elohim eth)* 'God the.' "

In this primal scene, before the beginning of the world that is also here before the beginning of a writing, the Self contemplates and toys in a rite of play until the letters present themselves and speak; as in another primal scene, in a drama or play of the family, the child contemplates and plays with the sounds of a language in order to enter a world in which Father and Mother present themselves and speak. So too in the fullness of the imagination, blocks and even made-up playmates present themselves. The teddy bear was once in the shaman world of the great northern forests Grandfather or Folk-Father. The figures we play with, the members of our play world, given as they are, like the Katchina dolls of the Zuñi child, are spirit figures. *"My unity shall not be expressed except through thee,"* the Child-Creator promises. It is the first promise of love. *"On thee shall be based all calculations and operations of the world."*

These powers, the ambience in which all things of our world speak to us and in which we in turn answer, the secret allegiances of the world of play, the psychic depth of time transformed into eternity in which the conceptual persons of Father and Mother, Child and Play-Thing, exist—these are pre-rational. Brother and Sister have such an existence in the unreal that, where actual brother and sister do not exist or are unwilling to play the part, imaginary brother and sister may appear.

For men who declare themselves partisans of the rational mind at war with all other possibilities of being, the pre-rational or the irrational appears as an enemy within. It was not only the Poet, but Mother and Father also, that Plato would exclude from his Republic. In the extreme of the rationalist presumption, the nursery is not the nursery of an eternal child but of a grown-up, a rational man. Common sense and good sense exist in an armed citadel surrounded by the threatening countryside of phantasy, childishness, madness, irrationality, irresponsibility—an exile and despised humanity. In that city where Reason has preserved itself by retreating from the totality of the self, infants must play not with the things of the imagination nor entertain the lies of the poets but play house, government, business, philosophy or war. Before the guardians of this state the voices and persons of the Child-Creator stand condemned as auditory and visual hallucinations, a dangerous non-sense.

In the world of the Zohar, dolls were not permitted. The Child plays with the letters of an alphabet and Logos is the creator of the world. Man is to take his reality from, to express his unity in, the letter. But this letter is, like the doll, alive to the mind. *Tau* presents herself and speaks, just as the bear in our nursery does. To the extent that once for us too alphabet blocks were animate, all future architectures and worlds are populated, and we are prepared to understand the world-experience of the Kabbalist.

In this world-experience rationality does not exist apart from the whole, but the understanding searches ever to picture the self in the ununderstandable. The human spirit draws its life from a tree larger and more various than knowing, and reason stands in need of a gift, *"the gift of the queen to them that wander with her in exile."*

There is a return in the imagination to the real, an ascent of the soul to its *"root,"* that Hayyim Vital describes in his life work, *The Tree of Life: "The imaginative faculty will turn a man's thought to imagine and picture as if it ascended in the higher worlds up to the roots of his soul . . . until the imagined image reaches its highest source and there the images of the supernal lights are imprinted on his mind as if he imagined and saw them in the same way in which his imaginative faculty normally pictures in his mind mental contents deriving from the world."* We seem to be in the description of the process of a poem, for here too the mind imagines, but then enters a real it had not imagined, where the image becomes informed, from above or below, and takes over as an entity in itself, a messenger from a higher real. In his ascent the mystic is irradiated by the light of the tree and in his descent the light finds a medium through which to flow back into the daily world: "*The thought of the prophet expands and rises from one level to another . . . until he arrives at the point where the root of his soul is. Next he concentrates on raising the light of the sefirah to* En Sof *and from there he draws the light down, from on high down to his rational soul and from there, by means of the imaginative faculty, down to his animal soul, and there all things are pictured either by the inner senses of the imaginative faculty or by the outer senses.*"

Returning from *En Sof*, the unknowable, unimaginable God, from beyond sense, the imaginer, no longer imagining but realizing, carries a light from station to station, sefiroth to sefiroth, irradiating the imagined with reality, transforming the sense of the divine—the articulated Tree of Life—the cosmos, the rational soul and the animal soul, in light of a source that is a numinous non-sense or beyond sense.

This Tree, too, we saw each year, for at the birthday of the Child-Christos, we were as children presented with a tree from which or under which gifts appeared— wishes made real. This Christmas tree came, we know, from the tree-cults of the German tribes, ancestral spirits—a burning tree. But it is also a tree of lights, and where, in the time of Jacob Boehme, in the early seventeenth century, the Jewish and the Germanic mystery ways are wedded in one, the Christmas tree may have also been the Divine Tree of the Zohar, lit with the lights of the sefirah.

In this ritual of the imagination of Hayyim Vital, there is not only the ascent by pretending, the "*as if*" of his text, the pretension then, but the mystic is pretender to a throne, a "*source*" or "*root*" in the Divine. In the descent a magic is worked and all the pretended way of the ascent is rendered "*greater than Reality.*" Not only the deep dream but the day dream enlightens or enlivens. "*Occasionally,*" Werblowsky relates from Vital, "*the imaginative faculty may even externalize or project the effects of this 'light' so that the experience becomes one of external sense impressions such as of the apparition of angelic messengers, the hearing of voices.*"

This Tree of Life is also the tree of generations, for its branches that are also roots are male and female, and the light or life is a mystery of the Shekinah, the ultimate Spirit-Mother of Israel as well as God's Glory. The root or seed is a quickening source in the immortal or eternal womb, wherein each man is immortal.

In his study of Australian tribal rites, the psychoanalyst Geza Roheim draws another configuration of source, dream, and transformation of reality, that may cast further light on our way towards a picture of what is involved in poetry when the images and personae of a dream greater than reality appear as active forces in the poet's world:

> Strehlow, who as a missionary living for decades among the Aranda was certainly an authority on their language, tells us that he cannot explain the meaning of the word *altjira*, but it seems that the natives connect to it the concept of something that has no beginning—*erina itja arbmanakala*, him none made. Spencer and Gillen, however, have given another interpretation of the word. In their glossary we find "*altjeringa:* name applied by the Arunta, Kaitish, and Unmatjera tribes to the far past or dream times in which their mythical ancestors lived. The word *altjeri* means dream." Strehlow denies this; he says the word for dream is *altjirerama*, and gives the following etymology: *altjira* (god) *rama* (to see).
> For one thing, it is clear that *altjira* means dream and not god or ancestor (as

Strehlow indicates) for I found that a folktale, a narrative with a happy end, is also called *altjira*.

It is evident that Strehlow, for his preoccupation with *Altjira* (God) of the Aranda Bible, managed to miss the real meanings of the word. *Altjira* = dream, altjireramaa = to dream; *altjirerinja* = dreaming. This is as near as I could get to Spencer and Gillen's *altjeringa*. Moses thought it must be a mistake for either *altirerindja* or *altjiranga*. There was no name for any mythical period. The time when the ancestors wandered on earth was called *altjiranga nakala*, i.e., "ancestor was," like *ljata nama*, i.e., "Now is." Other expressions were noted as equivalents of *altjiranga nakala*; these were *imanka nakala*, "long time ago was," or *kutata nakala*, "eternally was." This led us to the explanation and etymology of the word *altjiranga mitjina*. *Mitjina* is equivalent to *kutata*, "eternal"; *nga* is the ablative suffix *from*; therefore *altjiranga mitjina* = "the eternal ones from the dream" or "the eternal people who come in dreams." This is not my explanation, but that of the old men, Moses, Renana, and Jirramba. Another Aranda word for dream, ancestor, and story, is *tnankara*. It is not often used, and as far as I could see it means exactly the same as *altjira*.[1]

In story and tribal rite, the Australian native seeks to convert time and space into an expression of his unity, to create a language of acts and things, of devouring and being devoured, of giving birth and being born, in which man and the world about him come into one body. "*In an emu myth of the Aranda, Marakuja (Hands Bad), the old man emu, takes his bones out and transforms them into a cave . . . The kangaroo men take the mucus from their noses; it becomes a stone, still visible now. The rocks become black where they urinate.*" Here the *altjiranga mitjina*, the ones living in a dream of time more real than the mortality of the time past, invade the immediate scene. For the Australian as for Heraclitus, "*Immortal mortals, mortal immortals, their being dead is the other's life.*" The things lost in time return and are kept in the features of the place. "*Environment is regarded as if it were derived from human beings,*" Roheim observes.

In repeated acts—bleeding, pissing, casting mucus, spitting into the ground, or in turn, eating the totemic food and drinking the blood of the fathers—the boy is initiated into the real life of the tribe. "*An old man sits beside him and whispers into his ear the totemic name. The boy then calls out the esoteric name as he swallows the food. The emphasis on the place name in myth and ritual can only mean one thing, that* both myth and ritual are an attempt to cathect environment with libido . . . *The knowledge of the esoteric name 'aggregates' unites the boy to the place or to the animal species or to anything that was strange before.*"

The "beast, anus, semen, urine, leg, foot" in the Australian song, chant or enchantment, that is also hill, hole, sea, stream, tree or rock, where "*in the Toara ceremony the men dance around the ring shouting the names of male and female genital organs, shady trees, hills, and some of their totems of their tribe,*" are most familiar to the Freudian convert Roheim. He sees with a sympathy that rises from the analytic cult in which Freud has revived in our time a psychic universe in which dream has given a language where, by a "sexual obsession" (as Jung calls it), the body of man and the body of creation are united.

---

[1] See also above, page 201 and following. (Eds.)

The "blood" of the Aranda, the "libido" of the Freudian, may also be the "light" of our Kabbalist text. "En Sof," Gershom Scholem tells us in *Major Trends in Jewish Mysticism: "is not only the hidden Root of all Roots*

> it is also the sap of the tree; every branch representing an attribute, exists not by itself but by virtue of *En Sof*, the hidden God. And this tree of God is also, as it were, the skeleton of the universe; it grows throughout the whole of creation and spreads branches through all its ramifications. All mundane and created things exist only because something of the power of the Sefiroth lives and acts in them.
>
> The simile of man is as often used as that of the Tree. The Biblical word that man was created in the image of God means two things to the Kabbalist: first, that the power of the Sefiroth, the paradigm of divine life, exists and is active also in man. Secondly, that the world of the Sefiroth, that is to say the world of God the Creator, is capable of being visualized under the image of man the created. From this it follows that the limbs of the human body are nothing but images of a certain spiritual node of existence which manifests itself in the symbolic figure of *Adam Kadmon*, the primordial man. The Divine Being Himself cannot be expressed. All that can be expressed are His symbols. The relation between *En Sof* and its mystical qualities, the Sefiroth, is comparable to that between the soul and the body, but with the difference that the human body and soul differ in nature, one being material and the other spiritual, while in the organic whole of God all spheres are substantially the same.

"*The world of the Sefiroth[2] is the hidden world of language*," Scholem continues, "*the world of divine names.*" "*Totemic names*," Roheim calls the whispered passwords of the Australian rite. "*The creative names which God called into the world*," Scholem calls the Sefiroth, "*the names which He gave to Himself.*" It is the alphabet of letters revealed to the initiate as at once the alphabet of what he is and what the universe is and the alphabet of eternal persons.

As Scholem hints, "*the conception of the Sefiroth as parts or limbs of the mystical anthropos leads to an anatomical symbolism which does not shrink from the most extravagant conclusions.*" Man's "secret parts" are secret names or hidden keys to the whole figure of man, charged with magic in their being reserved. In the communal image, the human figure is male and female. Ass-hole, penis, cunt, navel, were not only taboo but sacred, words to be revealed in initiations of the soul to the divine body, as at Eleusis the cunt of a woman in the throes of birth was shown. In what we call carnal knowledge, in the sexual union of male and female nakedness, God and His creation, the visible and invisible, the above and the below are also united.

Ham, who sees the nakedness of his father, is the prototype of the Egyptian who in an alien or heretic religion knows the secrets of God. To steal a look, like the theft of fire, is a sin, for the individual seeks to know without entering the common language in which things must be seen and not seen.

"*At the initiation ceremony the point is to displace libido from the mother to the group of fathers*," Roheim writes. In the contemporaneity of our human experience with

---

[2]For more on the *Sefiroth*, and so forth, see above, page 305. (Eds.)

all it imagines, there may be not a displacement but an extension of libido: the revelation of the mother remains, the revelation of the male body is added. "*Some old men stand in the ring and catching hold of their genitals tell the boys to raise their eyes and take particular notice of those parts. The old men next elevate their arms above their heads and the boys are directed to look at their armpits. Their navels are exhibited in the same way. The men then put their fingers on each side of their mouths and draw their lips outward as wide as possible, lolling out their tongues and inviting the special attention of the novices. They next turn their backs and, stooping down, ask the novices to take particular notice of their posterior parts.*"

For Roheim, the images and magic of Australian story and rite are one with the images and magic of all dreams:

> After having withdrawn cathexis from environment, we fall asleep. But when the cathexis is concentrated in our own bodies we send it out again and form a new world, in our dreams. If we compare dream mechanisms with the narratives of dream-times we find an essential similarity between the two. The endless repetitions of rituals and wanderings and hunting are indeed very different from a dream; but when we probe deeper we find that they are overlaid by ceremony and perhaps also by history. The essential point in the narratives as in the ritual is that man makes the world—as he does in sleep.

> These natives do not wander because they like to . . . Man is naturally attached to the country where he was born because it, more than anything else, is a symbol of his mother. All natives will refer to their "place" as a "great place"; as they say "I was incarnated there" or "born there." Economic necessity, however, compels him time and again to leave his familiar haunts and go in search of food elsewhere. Against this compulsion to repeat *separation*, we have the fantasy embodied in myth and ritual in which he himself creates the world.

Where the nursing woman and the countryside itself are both "Mother," and where in turn the men of the tribe may initiate and reveal maleness as an other Mother, "Mother" means unity, what Gertrude Stein called the Composition. What we experience in dreaming is not a content of ourselves but the track of an inner composition of ourselves. We are in-formed by dreams, as in daily life we experience that which we are able to grasp as information. We see, hear, taste, smell, feel, what can be drawn into a formal relation; to sense at all involves attention and composition. "*It is very interesting that nothing inside in them, that is when you consider the very long history of how every one ever acted or has felt, it is very interesting that nothing inside in them in all of them makes it connectedly different,*" Stein writes in *Composition As Explanation*: "*The only thing that is different from one time to another is what is seen and what is seen depends upon how everybody is doing everything. This makes the thing we are looking at very different and this makes what those who describe it make of it, it makes a composition, it confuses, it shows, it is, it looks, it likes it as it is, and this makes what is seen as it is seen.*" The endless repetitions of rituals and wanderings and hunting as the pattern of life for the Australian is a living inside the Composition; and in their exhibiting the secrets of the male body to the boy, the men of the tribe are making a composition where what is seen depends upon how everybody is doing everything. In the ritual, song, parts of the body, parts of the landscape, man and nature, male and female, are united in a secret composite of magic names.

"*One of the main sources of male creative power*," Roheim tells us, "*is the incantation itself.*"

> When I asked old Wapiti and the other chiefs what makes the animals grow? the spirits? the ancestors? O, no, they said: *jelindja wara*, the words only. The form of the incantation is an endless, monotonous flow of words, and actually the men urinate very frequently while performing the ceremonies. This parallelism between the words and the fluid is brought out in a description by Lloyd Warner: "The blood runs slowly and the rhythm of the song is conducted with equal slowness. In a second or two the blood spurts and runs in a rapid stream. The beat of the song sung by the old men increases to follow the rhythm of the blood."

We may begin to see, given Stein's concept of insistence that informs composition, and then thinking of the pulse of the living egg-cell itself, that beat, rhythm, underlies every figure of our experience. Life itself is an endless, monotonous flow, wherever the individual cannot enter into it as revealed in dance and melody to give rhythmic pattern; the world about goes inert and dead. The power of the painter in landscape is his revelation of such movement and rhythm in seeing, information, in what otherwise would have been taken for granted.

Gertrude Stein, reflecting upon permanence and change in the artist's vision, sees that "*the only thing that is different from one time to another is what is seen and what is seen depends upon how everybody is doing everything.*" Close to the Cubist Movement in Paris, she had experienced how painting or writing in a new way had revealed coordinations of what was seen and heard towards an otherwise hidden unborn experience of the world, so that one saw and heard with a profound difference. "*A new cadence means a new idea,*" H.D. and Richard Aldington, writing in the Preface to the *Imagist Anthology* of 1916, declared. Here too, cadence is how it is done; to make clear the meaning of cadence they referred to the choral line of Greek poetry that was also the movement of the choral dance, strophe and antistrophe. So too, Roheim, initiate of Freudianism, as Stein was initiate of Cubism, or H.D. of Imagism, sees in the narratives of his Australian informants how "*in all of them environment is made out of man's activity,*" for he had himself experienced a conversion in which a new environment for man had been made out of analytic activity. The "*manmade world*" in which "*environment is regarded as if it were derived from human beings*" is the narrative itself; the unity of things in how the story is told. . . .

VICTOR TURNER
A Review of "Ethnopoetics"

Victor Turner has been a major and highly influential anthropologist since the late 1950s. His contributions to symbolic anthropology and to a unified theory of performance include concepts of liminality and communitas, social drama, reflexivity, and symbolic process, applicable to a wide range of human cultures but developed from particular situations such as that of the Ndembu of eastern Africa. In the present article, he reviews the proceedings of "the first international symposium on ethnopoetics" as gathered by Michel Benamou and Jerome Rothenberg in a special issue of Alcheringa *(Benamou 1976). Principal works:* The Forest of Symbols, The Ritual Process, *and* Dramas, Fields and Metaphors.

The first international symposium on ethnopoetics, held at the University of Wisconsin-Milwaukee on April 10–12, 1975, was obviously one of those transformative ingatherings which Richard Schechner discussed in his contribution. Poets, performers, and scholars of performative genres met, debated, performed, and came away with new ideas for distribution, much as Mexican pilgrims take consecrated zodiac bread from the sacred site home to their villages to share with their kith and kin. The participants were invited to define "ethnopoetics" and to present ethnopoetic performances, if reading, reciting, singing, acting and playing musical instruments were their métiers. Thought and act thus wrought upon one another to produce "something rich and strange" with which orthodox anthropology, to mention only one of the disciplines crucially involved, will have to reckon.

Anthropology itself is shifting from a stress on concepts such as structure, equilibrium, system, and regularity to process, indeterminacy, reflexivity, resilience (as I have tried to show in an article in the Summer 1977 volume of *Daedalus*, "Process, System, and Symbol: A New Anthropological Synthesis"). There is also a renewed interest in "performance," partly stemming from sociolinguists such as Dell Hymes, partly from modern folklorists (with Roger Abrahams, John Szwed, and Mihai Pop making important contributions), and partly from the fundamental work of Gregory Bateson and Erving Goffman. A recent focus on the dynamics of ritual (with contributions by Geertz, Leach, Douglas, Barth, Vogt, Barbara Myerhoff, Sally Falk Moore, Legesse, Ortiz, and Tambiah) partly accounts for this new "tuning in" to performative genres. Exciting new work on carnival, spectacle, sport, and theater is now in progress and should soon bear fruit in publications by a new generation of "processual" anthropologists (for example, Roberto Da Matta, John MacAloon, Bruce Kapferer). It is perhaps perfectly natural that an anthropology of performance should be moving to meet performers who are seeking some of their theoretical support from anthropology. With this renewed emphasis on society as a process punctuated by performances of various kinds, there has developed the view that such genres as ritual, ceremonial, carnival, festival, games, spectacles, and sports events may constitute, on various levels and in

SOURCE: *Boundary 2, volume six, number 2, Winter 1978, pages 583–590.*

various verbal and nonverbal codes, a set of metalanguages whereby a group or community not merely expresses itself but, more actively, tries to understand itself in order to change itself. In brief, such genres have a reflexive aspect, as well as providing an opportunity for participants to "flow" in unison even when the terms of interaction are agonistic. The dialectic between flow and reflexivity characterizes many performative genres: in fact, a successful performance of any may represent transcendence of the opposition between spontaneous and considered patterns of action.

This dialectic seems also to inform many of the reflections on ethnopoetics. For example, in his seminal "Pre-Face to a Symposium on Ethnopoetics," Jerome Rothenberg (who invented the term and the genre) sees *ethnos* as the *other* who is nevertheless *we*, or as Schechner puts it, the *not-not-me* beyond the *not-me*. For the Greeks the *ethnoi* were the barbarian nations, equivalent to "gentiles, *goyim*, pagan, heathen . . . people of the heath, the countryside, the wilderness, the unclaimed land, the ones in nature, natural, the lower foreign orders set apart from us, apart from cities, blocks to human progress, ancients, primitives, the fathers or mothers we must kill, the poets (Plato said) whom we must drive out of our cities, out of our bodies and minds in point of fact, those who scorn the new god, the abstraction, unity, the unconflicted single truth we worship" (p. 6). Rothenberg seeks to make ethnopoetics the major performative instrument of modern cultural reflexivity when he goes on to claim that poetry is "the very language of the *ethnoi*, in the equation Plato makes. As poets *we* are *them*." Reflexivity creatively democratizes: as we become on earth a single noosphere, the Platonic cleavage between an aristocracy of the spirit and the "lower or foreign orders" can no longer be maintained. To be reflexive is to be at once one's own subject and direct object. The poet subjectivizes the object, or, better, makes intersubjectivity the human mode. Cartesian dualism has insisted on distancing subject from object, us from them. It has made voyeurs of Western men, exaggerating sight by macro- and micro-instrumentation the better to learn the structures of the world "with an eye" to its exploitation. The deep bonds between body and mentality, unconscious and conscious thinking, species and self, have been treated without respect, as though they were irrelevant for analytical purposes. Ethnopoetics is a modality of the renewed recognizance of such ignored bonds. Historically, its resurgence comes at a time when knowledge is being increased of other cultures, other worldviews, other life styles, when Westerners, endeavoring to trap non-Western philosophies and poetries in the corrals of their own cognitive constructions, find that they have caught sublime monsters, eastern dragons, lords of fructile chaos, whose wisdom makes our knowledge look somehow shrunken and inadequate.

As Rothenberg admits, there is something romantic in this attempt to regain wholeness, hence identity, through seeking "a fundamental human nature"—particularly in the cultural productions of the *ethnoi*. And there is certainly the problem recently expressed by Harold Rosenberg in a review of "ethnic" art in *The New Yorker*: that of the necessary estrangement from his own society of every authentic artist, modern or tribal. As "exception" (in Kierkegaard's sense), the artist or poet among the Navajo or Zulu is in no better case than the novelist in Prague. Thus it is self-defeating for "ethnic" artists to present their collective achievement as at least as meritorious as that of the dominant group, for art is not measured by "General Forms," but, to cite Blake, each artwork has "definite and determinate Identity." Nevertheless, since all cultures have been produced by members of a single biological species, and since the core culture of each tradition (roughly its religion and art) represents a laminated sequence of insights into the human (species) condition regarded as worth preserving for their survival value in a given place under given historical circumstances, it is probable that any coherent perduring culture has a special gift to offer to mankind as a whole, a special aid.to panhuman reflexivity. Poets precisely because of their "otherness" in their home societies are attuned to otherness wherever it may be found. Hence they find an affinity, and to their own delight a *social* affinity, with the fruits of other cultures, particularly those of the "despised and rejected." The powerful of their own culture are blind to the wisdom in the traditions of those they like to consider "lesser breeds." But the poets see that wisdom and would make it over to the whole world, beginning with their own nation.

But ethnopoeticists, looking for information on ethnocultures, find that anthropologists in general have not too much to say on the performative genres and processes of traditional societies. They are mostly intent on economic processes, kinship systems, judicial processes, political action, or the analysis of texts of myths. The cognitive structures elicited by anthropologists are not usually presented as the outcomes of reflexive thought—often in crisis situations—but as sets of formal rules. They have been drained of the processual life, the volitions and emotions, the environmental pressures and changes, which challenged men and women to bring them into cultural existence. Some of the contributors to the special issue, however, notably Richard Schechner and Rothenberg (both of whom I recently had the pleasure of meeting at the Burg Wartenstein Symposium on "Cultural Frames and Reflections: Ritual, Drama and Spectacle," sponsored by the Wenner-Gren Foundation) have sought deliberately for anthropological analogues to their own "poetics of performance." Schechner, in fact, is now preparing a detailed study of the Ramlila cycle play of Ramnagar in India—a clear manifestation of his intent to make systematic controlled comparisons between the performative genres of several great cultural traditions. More than this, he has been developing a model, adumbrated in his article "Towards a Poetics of Performance," for relating "social drama," as I have defined the term, to "aesthetic drama" or "cultural performance" (to adopt Milton Singer's usage in *When a Great Tradition Modernizes*), showing how dramatic situations in political or domestic arenas borrow much of their rhetoric and style from stage drama and constitute their unmanifest dimension, while stage performances have for "subtext" the economic-political dynamical forms of their times and societies.

Here we have another mode of reflexivity. Performative genres have the function of letting a community's consciousness know periodically what its subconsciousness (preconscious awareness?) is up to. Certainly, many types of African ritual and divination have quite expressly this proclivity. In my book *Revelation and Divination in Ndembu Ritual*, I show how among the Ndembu of northwestern Zambia, the concept *kusolola*—"to make visible," "to produce to view"—underlies the entire class of rituals I call "rituals of affliction," performed to cure illness, remove bad luck, and, as their latent function, to redress conflicts. By public confession, by representing both negative and positive social forces by material symbols, and by naming the deceased relative believed to be responsible for the affliction—itself a reprimand to the living kin for failing to live well together in terms of the order bequeathed to them—things invisible are "revealed" and thus made available for public action, both symbolic and ritualized and nonsymbolic and rational. Ethnopoetics, as Rothenberg conceives it, has something of this ritual reflexivity about it; certainly his treatment of affinities between poet and shaman suggest this interpretation.

The mere fact that Westerners are now becoming aware of the potency of other traditions of thought and expressive culture is itself an act of "making visible" and at the same time an entering into reflexive relations with peoples, genders, classes, ethnicities, the sick, the marginal and the troubled, all of whom from beyond the pale or beneath our bureaucratic rationality insist that we are them. Their presence and their cultural product are "metacommentaries" on our own lifeways—in which we are becoming increasingly disappointed as their lack of grace or blessing becomes more obvious. Fredric Jameson puts the matter very well in his article "Collective Art in the Age of Cultural Imperialism": "It seems to me axiomatic that the use of other poetic forms—borrowed or reinvented from the chants, myths, lyrical fragments or epics, of other societies—is always an implied commentary on our own society" (p. 109).

Jameson is opposed to a view, advocated by the celebrated anthropologist Stanley Diamond (who spoke at the symposium), which opposes Western rationalism in binary fashion to primitive wisdom, Plato's totalitarian city to tribal *Gemeinschaft*. Jameson points out that there have been many forms of state centralization intervening between acephalous societies and modern capitalism. Collapsing them means to ignore the multiple, subtle cultural formations deposited in the noosphere by history, and to make renovation "a change not in the form of society but in the form of thinking" (p. 110). This is to ignore the whole genealogy of ameliorative forms of political action. And, indeed, the main problem of the symposium centers on this matter of the One and the Many. It is true, as Blake wrote, that "One Law for the Lion and the Ox is Oppression," and that this is "cultural imperialism." We do need not one but many "Prophets against Empire." But there are not a few *ethnoi*, both past and present, and not all of them are poets or prophets. There are many tribal Archie Bunkers, antiritualists, village atheists, and not a few philistines and despots. The value for reflexivity of the rediscovery of multiple differences within the historical existence of our species is not that of a single mirror which reverses or inverts. Rather we find ourselves in a hall of mirrors, or rather of magic mirrors, some of which enlarge, others diminish, some distort and some have X-ray properties; each mirror is a cultural field and each after its own fashion receives images from all the others and passes them on transmuted or transmogrified. Within each culture is its own hall of mirrors: the social division of labor, beginning with sex- and age-role oppositions, is charged with reflexivity, for although we are all members of one another, we are different members, both biologically and culturally. But this reflexive potential is actualized most patently in the performative genres, which often quite consciously hold their mirrors not up to nature but to the pre-existing system of mirrors which is humankind-in-culture. Culture is *re*mirrored by one of its own extensions—ritual or art. And this may even result in the *de*mirroring of the human incumbents of status-roles in the quotidian culture.

The more we are aware of the multiplicity of Others, the more we become aware of the multiple "selves" we contain, the social roles we have "internalized." Perhaps this awareness may help to free us from their domination over our deep Self, our principle of unity, that which Blake spoke of as Identity. The social selves may be demons, "their name is legion." But this is only in so far as they remain invisible. Once they are "made visible'' they are revealed as faintly comical figures, far removed from ''Man alive and Woman alive,'' to paraphrase D. H. Lawrence. It may be that the recognition of diversity in cultural voices has the therapeutic function of confronting us with the problem of the One and the Many—a new reflexivity in itself. Several authors in the symposium warn against the destruction that is going on of diversity on this planet. Gary Snyder writes, for example, in ''The Politics of Ethnopoetics'': ''What we are witnessing in the world today is an unparalleled waterfall of destruction of a diversity of human cultures; plant species; animal species; of the richness of the biosphere and the millions of years of organic evolution that have gone into it'' (p. 13).

''Monoculture'' is what Snyder fears. This is the very reverse of the One which lives in vital reciprocity with the Many, which, in a sense, *is* the Many. Monoculture is ''dedifferentiation,'' the erosion of outlines, the decomposition of complex cellular structures. Ethnopoetics may be said to provide one counterstroke to this by making visible and audible the multiple poetic and deeply human expressions of the *ethnoi*, by showing cultures as a complex flowering.

In my own technical vocabulary I would see ethnopoetics as a ''liminal'' phenomenon. By this I mean that it is in a ''threshold'' position, a betwixt-and-between state, like the seclusion phase in a tribal rite of passage in which the novices have been stripped of their antecedent status and have not yet acquired a new one and to which the categories and classifications of their previous sociocultural state have ceased to apply. Here, though, the ''limen'' is not determined by a cultural ''script'' or ''score,'' but is a historical moment to which old evaluative frames are ceasing to apply, fraught with perils and possibilities: dangers of nuclear extinction or slow starvation through overpopulation and environmental pollution; prospects of space travel and discovery of new power sources. It is an open limen, not a predetermined one. It is a characteristic of all liminal or ''liminoid'' processes or states that in them the factors of culture are ''deconstructed'' and often recombined in fantastic or improbable ways. For this reason, I call liminality culture's ''subjunctive mood,'' contrasting it with the ''indicative mood'' of everyday socioeconomic life. Customary *Gestälten* are ripped apart and their debris or ''elements'' are scrutinized and put together in accordance with principles of fantasy or aesthetics rather than law or ethics. Yet, as I have argued, a pool of variation is thus created, a set of utopian blueprints or models perhaps, if we are considering the political dimension, which, though presently functionless, may become functional under changed historical or environmental circumstances. It is in this sense that poets, liminoid ''makers,'' are the ''unacknowledged legislators of mankind.'' By ''liminoid'' I mean post-traditional, post-tribal modes of in-betweenness, characterized by optation rather than obligation, individual rather than collective authorship, and secular rather than sacred settings and goals. Thus ''the arts and all things common'' would be liminoid, as, indeed, would scientific research and hypothesis-forming. The liminoid is more flexible and multifarious than the liminal, which is bounded more firmly by ritual constraints: taboos and rubrics. It is a world of as if, may be, might have been, sometimes should be.

Ethnopoetics, then, is a liminoid genre in a (metaphorically) liminal phase of history—viewing the world as one vast initiatory seclusion camp. Ethnopoets are concerned with what I call *communitas*, with breaking down all social distinctions and status roles, political and other hierarchies, and segmentation into competing corporate groups. Thus they seek to make all people their "even-humans" (to adapt Julian of Norwich's phrase to the purpose of a final ecumenism) and to make new models from the outpoured cultures of all people—particularly formerly oppressed or colonized kinds of people. As Michel Benamou puts it in his "Postface: In Praise of Marginality": "Freely chosen marginality may be the necessary path if one wishes to meet half way the peoples whose marginality results from historical force" (p. 138).

To use Nathaniel Tarn's terms (from his fascinating paper "The Heraldic Vision: A Cognitive Model for Comparative Ethnopoetics") ethnopoeticists (poets?), and the convergent breed of anthropologists of liminality and reflexivity, seem now to aspire to the status of ritual specialists or "technicians of the sacred," in Rothenberg's phrase, in facilitating the last stages of a process which takes the form: *ecclesia* (primordial communitas) ——> *sparagmos* (equivalent to Lévi-Strauss's "detotalization," i.e., the rupture of tribal sociocultural bonds, the emergence of the competitive individual, a process also of movement from liminal to liminoid) ——> *ecclesia nova*. This could also be seen as a move from *membership* (in a sacred body) to *dismemberment* (in myriad secular bodies) to recovered *membership* (retotalization) in a "risen body" of human-kindness redeemed through "mutual forgiveness of each vice" (Blake), forgiveness made possible through radical, existential reflexivity.

The new technicians of the recovered "sacred," which is now aware of all that science can tell it, must recover also the magic of the word and break it out of its dull academic integument. George Quasha put this extraordinarily well ("The Age of the Open Secret: a writing piece on Ethnopoetics, the Other Tradition, and social transformation"):

> Countercultures, secret societies, academies—the tribes and the anti-tribes—collide, mix, change, and move towards an optimum membership of *one*. The secrets are out, Initiation becomes Self-initiation or the verb to "initiate" grows steadily intransitive. . . . As an interior sociology and archeology of the processual, [ethnopoetics] is also a tool for opening the secrets further, opening them into our lives. [p. 76]

The secrets—the knowledge and poetics of the *ethnoi*—are being made visible to and embodied in our modern retotalizing reflexivity; in the privileged liminal space-time of the new anthropology influenced by phenomenology and dialectics and given a new voice by ethnopoetics.

The sheer richness of ideas poured out in this counter-Platonic Symposium will take a while to assimilate. But if anthropologists take ethnopoetics seriously, it will mean that their discipline will have to cease being a cognitive game played in their heads. It will mean that they must take the performative modes seriously and become performers themselves. They must find ways of overcoming boundaries of structure by love and friendship even as they acquire deeper structural knowledge in reciprocity with the *ethnoi* and marginals in pursuit of common tasks.

DELL HYMES

Some North Pacific Coast Poems: A Problem in Anthropological Philology

As a major anthropological linguist, Hymes's early and ongoing contribution to an ethnopoetics has been a practical "structuralism" that attempts to examine and represent "ways in which narratives [or, as here, songs] are organizations of linguistic means"—a work he has pursued not by "leaping to universals" but by "the development of theories adequate and specific to each tradition." Beginning with the present essay—a criticism and virtual "deconstruction" of earlier translation work—Hymes later focused on the performative side of traditional oral poetry (i.e., on its "realization in performance") in ways akin to the proposals and practice of Dennis Tedlock (see below, p. 366) but with crucial divergences of his own. His work also influenced the discussions of "total translation" by Rothenberg and McAllester (see below, pp. 381, 393), particularly his foregrounding of the use of nonlexical vocables in tribal/oral song traditions and his encouragement of collaborative work by linguists and poets. All this he has seen as part of a larger project—the creation (as he describes it) of "a general poetics . . . a truly comparative, general literature, in which the verbal art of mankind as a whole has a place . . . expanding and deepening our understanding of what it can mean to be possessed of language" (1977: 455).

Hymes's work in this area has recently been brought together in In Vain I Tried To Tell You *(1981), a collection of his writings on Native American ethnopoetics. Principal works:* Language in Culture and Society, Reinventing Anthropology, *and* Foundations in Sociolinguistics.

INTRODUCTION

I wish to call attention to materials and problems that represent a neglected past, and, I believe, a neglected future, for American scholarship. The focus of the paper is upon texts from the Indian cultures of the North Pacific Coast, from a classic period of common cause among folklore, linguistics, and ethnology in the service of a general anthropology; but the problems are relevant to materials elsewhere.

On the American scene, the study of the structure of language is joining effectively again with the study of its use, after a period of relative separation. The full gamut of linguistic structures and their functions in social context is coming to be investigated in ways both structurally adequate and functionally interesting. As part of this, one more often finds an interest in linguistic method and an interest in the content of texts joined together—an interest both in texts as documentation for linguistics, and in linguistics as a source of insight into texts. Such joint interest takes various names and stems from

SOURCE: American Anthropologist, *volume 67, number 2, April 1965, pages 316–339.*

several sources, but for anthropology it is most noticeable in the structural study of myth
and in a surge of attention to stylistics and poetics. . . .

This changing climate is one of many changes now serving to bracket much of the
American scholarship from somewhat before until somewhat after the Second World
War, from perhaps about 1925 to 1950. To generalize oversimplifies unfairly, but, from
the standpoint of linguistics and the other disciplines that can constitute an anthropological philology, that period's dominant attitudes and interests and style of work no longer
seem unqualified advance, but in many respects the marks of a period now rapidly
becoming historical, some of whose steps were forward, some backward or to the side.
The period comes increasingly to seem an interregnum, regarding range, integration,
and depth.

The change of climate calls for reexamination of past contributions, so as to clarify
the base from which we advance. It has taken a French social anthropologist to dramatize
the value of our early resources of Amerindian prose narrative, particularly myth, by
relating them to our concern with structure, showing the possibility of novel insights and
structural relations.[1] Here I wish to deal with the largely neglected heritage of poetry, or,
more accurately, of the verbal component of song, and to show ways that it too may yield
new knowledge of structure. In particular, I wish to show that poems may have a
structural organization, and "nonsense" vocables,[2] or burdens, a structural function,
not hitherto perceived. (For novel structural organization, see especially "Comment" to
poems II−V. For the structural function of "nonsense" syllables, see "Comment" to
II−IV.)

My general thesis is twofold: our heritage of American Indian poetry must be
reanalyzed and revaluated, and from a linguistic basis, if its contribution to American
culture and to an anthropological science of culture is to be achieved with anything like
the validity expected of responsible disciplines. Such analysis and evaluation should
concern several intersecting activities, those of folklorists, anthropologists, linguists,
literary scholars, and poets, and each in turn has something to contribute. Hence the
analyses of six North Pacific Coast poems are preceded and followed by discussion
intended to relate them to the perspectives of the several activities just named. I begin
and end with emphasis upon the place of linguistics in an anthropological philology that
may serve the interests of all.

APPRECIATION (I): ANTHOLOGIES

In a presidential address to the American Folklore Society, MacEdward Leach (1963)
has called attention to the importance, to both scholarship and society, of concern with
the appreciation, as well as the collection and analysis, of folkloristic materials. He
stresses what should be the interdependence of appreciation and scholarship. Let me
consider appreciation of Amerindian poetry first in relation to the setting in which it is
most generally experienced by scholar and general public alike, that of the anthology.
The two major contemporary anthologies in English are Astrov (1946) and Day (1951).
The introductions to both are thoughtful, intelligent reflections of the situation of an
anthologist, and likewise a reader, in relation to the available materials.

Astrov (1946: 17) concludes her introduction with the observation: "In any case, in reading aboriginal prose and poetry, as it is compiled in this anthology, the reader is at the mercy of the translator, not only for bad but also for good.'' Elsewhere, however, she can only praise the translators whose results seem best, not indicating any basis for evaluating results other than by appreciation. In particular, independent recourse to the original texts is not mentioned. Astrov does state that the dual requirements, recreation of the spirit and linguistic fidelity to the letter, have been reconciled by Matthews, Cushing, Brinton, Densmore, Sapir, Spinden, Bunzel and Underhill, "to name only a few" (1946: 5). Yet it is doubtful if the letter of the originals was even available for consultation in some cases, not having been published with the translations in the sources upon which the anthology draws. It is doubtful if a knowledge of Navaho, Zuni, Nahuatl, Papago, Nootka, Keresan, Takelma, Tewa, etc., was drawn upon, for there were available no adequate grammars or dictionaries of several of these. Perhaps the word-for-word translations were compared with the poetic translations, a useful procedure, but even that could not have been available in every case. One cannot but suspect that the judgment of mutual recreation and fidelity is based solely on the reader's sense of the English and ethnological appropriateness of the translation, and respect for the linguistic ethnographer, each a redoubtable anthropological name.

Day (1951) goes further than Astrov to give Amerindian poetry its place as part of American literature.[3] He treats the Indian poetry both as something to be read as a part of American literature (1951: 26−27), and as something that can influence, if indirectly, the writing of it (1951: 33). Although he recognizes (1951: 18) that: "Judgment as to whether an English version is more or less faithful to the letter and spirit of the Indian original is properly a matter for an expert in linguistics," he must continue: "Since all the first-rate translators are specialists in the Indian dialects of the originals, they can presumably be criticized only by their peers in these studies."

In effect, Day, like Astrov, must fall back upon evaluating the translations by appreciation of their literary merit in English (1951: xi, 26−27), supported by the observation that the best translators from a literary point of view (he gives a somewhat different list: Boas, Brinton, Curtis, Densmore, Fletcher, Matthews, Russell, Spinden, Thalbitzer) were professional students of the Indian (and Eskimo). Although Day has recognized the possibility of an independent control of evaluation by recourse to the originals, he limits its status to that of one criterion among several, and one not primary; perforce, he seems to conclude, appreciation must rule alone. Nor is the possibility of other translations of the same poems, and of a living relation, through fresh translation and study of the originals, to modern poetry, envisaged. While noting the possibility of influence on modern poetry, as cited above, Day describes the influence only as coming through familiarity with translations.

Both anthologists think that something of the original stylistic features can be ascertained from the translations at hand. Astrov (1946: 11) states: "I have said that from translations one cannot perceive the particular style of a language. This statement, however, ought to be modified, since the ever-recurring patterns of stylistic expression may be recognized even from translations." Day (1951: 23) makes a similar, qualified statement: "Aside from repetition, stylistic devices such as contrast, monotony, variation, abbreviated expressions, poetic diction, parallelism, personification, apostrophe, euphony, and onomatopoeia are found which are used as they are used in European poetry. The best translations preserve a number of these effects, as may be seen in the selections in later chapters. Many patterns may be discovered in Indian poetry, even in translation.''

From the passages quoted, and the remainder of the discussions in the two books, a certain consensus of the situation seems to emerge. Much of it is not disputable. The part of concern here can be stated as a set of propositions: (a) the ethnologists who collected the material must be relied upon for the validity of the translations, and can be; (b) literary versions are to be preferred to literal ones; (c) the style, or structure, of the originals is accessible in significant part through the best translations.

I think it fair to say that these propositions would be widely assented to among those interested in Amerindian poetry (see discussion of attitude in the section after next). It may be unfair, but it is true, that the most preliminary linguistic study of original texts shows these propositions to be misleading enough to be effectively untrue, as will be shown in the two sections on ''Translation and Structure.'' Neither an understanding of the poetry in its own right, nor a use of it in the development of contemporary poetry, can accept these propositions without qualification. Remarkable works of imagination and beauty, to be sure, have been built with a base in similar sand (for its day, Longfellow's ''Song of Hiawatha'' is an apt case); but anthropologists cannot expect to deserve respect if scholarship is suspended within their own domain and appreciation alone left to judge. The more's the pity that it is so, because, I believe, the joining of scholarship to appreciation better serves the very ends of aesthetic reward and poetic knowledge that may counsel its suspension.

TRANSLATION AND STRUCTURE (I)

As a preliminary example, let me discuss a poem collected and translated by Henry School^raft, the pioneer ethnographer and afficionado of Amerindian verbal art, a man, indeed, moved to lifelong study of the Indian after experience of the verbal art of one group had awakened him to their humanity. The poem in question is cited by Day (1951: 27−28) in full, both for its role as a source of a portion of Longfellow's ''Song of Hiawatha'' and as source of a pattern of presentation still followed: text, literal translation, literary translation. (The example is also used by Greenway [1964], who makes some of the same points.)

Chant to the Fire-Fly

CHIPPEWA (OJIBWA) (Schoolcraft's orthography is preserved):

Wau wau tay see!	Wau wau tay see!
Wau wau tay see!	Wau wau tay see!
E mow e shin	Was so koon ain je gun.
Tahe bwau ne baun-e wee!	Was sa koon ain je gun.
Be eghaun—be eghaun—ewee!	Was sa koon ain je gun.

LITERAL TRANSLATION:

Flitting-white-fire insect! waving-white-fire bug! give me light before I go to bed!
give me light before I go to sleep. Come, little dancing white-fire-bug! Come, little
flitting white-fire-beast! Light me with your bright white-flame-instrument—your little
candle.

LITERARY TRANSLATION:

> Fire-fly, fire-fly! bright little thing,
> Light me to bed, and my song I will sing.
> Give me your light, as you fly o'er my head,
> That I may merrily go to my bed.
> Give me your light o'er the grass as you creep,
> That I may joyfully go to my sleep.
> Come, little fire-fly, come, little beast—
> Come! and I'll make you tomorrow a feast.
> Come, little candle that flies as I sing,
> Bright little fairy-bug—night's little king;
> Come, and I'll dance as you guide me along,
> Come, and I'll pay you, my bug, with a song.

Thanks to Schoolcraft's scholarship, we can appreciate in depth how bad his
translation is. Almost anyone sharing modern standards and taste, first of all, will prefer
the *literal* translation as more satisfactorily poetic, both in what it avoids and in what it
contains. Not only does the literal translation lack the supervening padding of the literary
translation (nine lines to the twelve of the literary version, the latter an expansion not to
express the original adequately, but to add a song, an overhead flight, a creep over grass,
a feast on the morrow, night's little king, a dance, a payment, and [intervening] merrily
and joyfully); but where both translations parallel the original in content, it is the literal
version that is the more concrete. Its specificity of image makes it the better version to an
audience familiar with the canons and accomplishments of Pound, Williams, and other
giants of twentieth-century American verse. (One may recall Sapir's likening of an
Algonquian verb to a tiny Imagist poem, and the interest of some Imagists in Amerindian
poetry.)

Second, neither translation conveys the structure of the original accurately. The
literal translation is far more faithful than the literary version in form, but it too
introduces, if not padding, elegant variation where there is none in the Chippewa text. In
the original, lines 1, 2, 6, 7 are constant; all are varied in the translation. Lines 8, 9 are
constant in the original, but not even parallel in the literal translation. In line 5 there is
internal repetition of which there is no indication in the literal translation. (For an
extreme example, changing an identity to contrast within a frame, see a song of the Hako
rite of the Pawnee cited by Day [1951: 25]. After an initial exclamation, the original
song consists of a line repeated six times, while the translation expands each line
differently.)

Third, as a consequence of the other two points, most of us, despite Schoolcraft's eminence as a pioneer ethnologist, would wish for a specialist in Algonquian languages, if not in Ojibwa (Chippewa) itself, to analyze the original text. Even better would be to have the text heard by an informant and redictated and retranscribed, a procedure that has been followed in the case of nineteenth-century Delaware (another Algonquian language) by [C. F.] Voegelin, for Kalapuya (a language of Oregon) by [Melville] Jacobs, and increasingly by contemporary specialists in such cases, where knowledge of the language, but not of certain valued texts, survives. By such a procedure, the defects of earlier materials in form can be remedied. By ascertaining the actual phonological, grammatical, and lexical structure of the texts, modern techniques bring out the full value of earlier enterprise in collection, something like the restoration of older paintings.

Merely on the basis of the information provided by Schoolcraft as to the form of the original text—its points of constancy and variation, repetition and contrast, and as to the literal content, one can do much better by way of an English expression for the Ojibwa song. Without consulting linguistic analysis and information (as I have deliberately restricted myself here), one cannot determine certain points, such as, principally, the content of the repetition and partial lack of repetition in lines 3−5. One can, however, suggest the following as a more adequate tribute to the original:

> Flitting insect of white fire!
> Flitting insect of white fire!
> Come, give me light before I sleep!
> Come, give me light before I sleep!
> Flitting insect of white fire!
> Flitting insect of white fire!
> Light me with your bright white instrument of flame.
> Light me with your bright white instrument of flame.

[As a contextual note could be added that "white-flame-instrument" is apparently a descriptive expression for "candle."]

One can perhaps smile and dismiss faults so patent to us in a predecessor of a century ago. Unfortunately, the same faults can occur in the translations from a half century ago on which we are accustomed to rely. The faults may be present in lesser degree, but are still the same in kind. When added to the sheer unavailability of the original texts in many cases, the potential presence of these faults means that the three propositions noted toward the end of the preceding section can not be relied upon by either the student or the appreciator of Indian poetry. Ethnologists *often* can be relied upon; literary versions *often* may be better than literal counterparts; structure may *often* be accessible in translation—but how is one to tell *when*? The only way to tell is by independent control of the results of translation, through access to the original texts, and, preferably, to the linguistic aids necessary for their analysis.

Some general implications of the latter point will be discussed in the concluding section "Appreciation II." I turn now to documentation of the statement that faults similar to those of Schoolcraft can be found in the more recent translations on which our anthologies, and, indeed, anthropologists, rely. The documentation also will show something of the gain in structural insight that fresh analysis can give.

TRANSLATION AND STRUCTURE (II): SOME NORTH PACIFIC COAST EXAMPLES

The term "structure" is used here because of my belief that the true structure of the original poem is essential to knowledge of it, both ethnological and aesthetic. By structure, I mean here particularly the form of repetition and variation, of constants and contrasts, in verbal organization. Such structure is manifest in linguistic form. It does not exhaust the structuring of poems, and in particular may not reveal other kinds of structural relations in their content (e.g., two Japanese haiku might be identical to all appearances in the respects in question, yet one have, and one lack, the "internal comparison," which partitions poems meeting the formal requirements into that which is "true" haiku and that which is not for some Japanese). But such structure is the matrix of the meaning and effect of the poem.

One of the particular results of the analyses is to indicate that in Kwakiutl something usually disregarded, the refrain or so-called "nonsense syllables," is in fact of fundamental importance. The refrain is both structural clue and microcosm.

Each poem is presented in the format of the preceding example: text, literal translation, literary translation (1), comment, literary translation (2).

The six poems presented (and their sources) are:[4]

I. *Cradle Song* (for boys) (Haida, Swanton [1912: 27]—not titled in the original text).

II. *Song of Chief's Daughter* (Kwakiutl, Boas [1921: 1314]).

III. *Workingman's Song of the Li: LəGi:d of the q'u:mky'ut'əs for his First-Born Son* (Kwakiutl, Boas [1921:1310]).

IV. *Love Song of the Dead, Heard on Shell Island* (Kwakiutl, Boas [1921: 1306−1307]).

V. *Song of Salmon* (Kwakiutl, Boas [1897: 474−475, 709]).

VI. *Cradle Song* (for boys) (Haida, Swanton [1912: 8]—not titled in the original text).

Poems I−IV are test cases, in that they have been reprinted in the major anthologies, so that the versions proposed here in the light of analysis can be used to judge the merit of the position I have taken, and the reassessment I propose, so far as the difference made to appreciation of Amerindian poetry is in question. As for the difference made to valid knowledge of the poetry, I think there can be little or no argument.

Poem V, not anthologized to my knowledge, may stand as a type of the additions to anthologizable, and publicly appreciated, material that structural analysis may provide, if, as seems likely, the song has not been reprinted because its presently published form does not reveal its structure and, hence, its effective power.

Poem VI, also not anthologized to my knowledge, may stand as a type of the additions that purely verbal restatement may provide. There are poems, of which this is one, whose published translations show no major departure from the structure of their original, but for which alternative translations suggest themselves. To offer fresh translations of such poems is to depend upon one's own verbal ability. The translation cannot claim to show significant new structure, but only to show new possibilities of verbal choice and rhythm. For the scholarly argument, such poems are not as significant, but for the possibility of a living relation between Amerindian poetry and new American poetry, such poems loom large. Only if it remains possible to accomplish something of value in new translation, even given accurate structure, can a permanently continuing relation thrive.

The absence of the musical portion of the songs may admittedly be a source of error. It is encouraging that the two recent structural analyses of the relations between text and music in North Pacific Coast songs (Yurok, Robins and McLeod 1956, 1957; Haida, Bursill-Hall 1964) have found precise parallelism at the level of the segmentation of musical and textual phrases, and their organization into the whole. Inspection of Tsimshian songs collected by Barbeau (1951) indicates that in some songs the patterning of the tune (often together with repetition of "nonsense syllables," sometimes with portions of text) is far more complex than the text as printed would indicate. The printed texts, however, seem intended as lexical abstracts, not as verse structures. As this article goes to press, I have not had the opportunity to hear tape recordings promised me of Kwakiutl song performance. The problem does not appear in the printed songs of Kwakiutl and Haida that I have examined (Boas 1896, 1897). In any case, the choice with the present texts is either to analyze them as texts or do nothing, since no music exists. I believe something useful is gained from their analysis as texts, despite the limitation of considering only part of actual performance.

I. Cradle Song (for boys)

dá:gua Gá:gwaiyá Gá:gwaiyá,
dá:gua Gá:gwaiyá Gá:gwaiyá.
dá:gua Gá:gwaiyá Gá:gwaiyá
sq'aos qa:s gü:sta gua
da gagwaiyá gagwaiyá
da gagwaiyá gagwaiyá.

You-? (whence)-have-been-falling, have-been-falling,
you-? (whence)-have-been-falling, have-been-falling.
you-? have-been-falling have-been-falling
Salmon-berry-bushes top-of from?
you have-been-falling have-been-falling
you have-been-falling have-been-falling.

"Whence have you fallen, have you fallen? Whence have you fallen, have you fallen?
"Did you fall, fall, fall, fall, from the top of the salmon-berry bushes?"

COMMENT:
The text and translations are printed as punctuated by Swanton, except that the hyphen is used uniformly to indicate English words translating a single Haida word. (Swanton published the literal translation in interlinear fashion under the Haida words.) Swanton did not distinguish all the lines in the original text, but ran together lines 1−2, and lines 4−5−6, capitalizing and placing at left margin only the first, third and fourth lines.

Day (1951: 57) prints the literary translation given above. But note that Swanton's literary translation (a) omits one of the three repetitions in the first half of the song; (b) translates essentially the same verbal phrase, when it recurs in the second half of the song, by a different repetition, differently placed. The structure of the original simply is not there. Especially since the poem in question is a cradle song, the exact structure of repetition and variation is significant both aesthetically and ethnographically. Swanton's second half, in literary translation, has a dynamic thrust in its repetition of four monosyllables hard on one another that is inappropriate and not authenticated.

LITERARY TRANSLATION (2):
The structure of the original poem can be carried over, as in the following version. In it, the variation as between the repeated phrases in the two stanzas reflects the change in accentuation and word order in Haida. (Note that Haida *gua* marks the interrogative.)

> ''From where have you been falling, been falling,
> From where have you been falling, been falling,
> From where have you been falling, been falling?
>
> The top of the salmonberry bushes, is it from there,
> You have been falling, have been falling,
> You have been falling, have been falling?''

(This version seems effective to my ear, but perhaps because it is associated with a tune I devised that gives its own rhythmic shape to the second stanza.)

II. Song of Chief's Daughter

1. *widzəl ya Gwa:LaLaLəq*
   dzu:dzaəyGəmi:ts dzi:dzəgyimi:ts yi:yqəyatsi:
   qaən tsa:'wənəmts'e:ts
   qadzən hi:'mi:dzən dza:dzəqi:Li:
   qaən dzi:dzəqi:yi:
   qən tsa:'wənəmtsa
   dzu:gwa ada:tsaxdzən
   wau:ts'a'atsi:ky
   ha ha aya,
   ha ha aya.

2. *wau:ts'a'atsəntsaxdzən dzaqi:ky*
   qats Gənəmu:ts
   dzu:dzaəyGami:ts dzi:dzəGəmi:ts yi:yqəyatsi:.
   ts'aqwadzən k'watsayi:tsu:kᵘ
   Gi:nəmdza ts'i:ts'əsu:
   dzu:gwa dzi:dzəGəmts
   qa yayu:tsdza ada:tsats
   yaqən tsa:'wənəmtsa,
   ha ha aya,
   ha ha aya.

3. *Qaxts ya'mi:ts GwaLdza*
   yipi:dzas a:da

qaən wətsi:dzanu:tsə
    qəntsu: La:yuqtsi:yax Li:lu:qəyi:Lalxdzi:tsa:sdza ada:tsa.
yaqən tsa:'wənəmtsa
    qu: wa:wadzətsi:s
Gi:nəmtsa hi:mau:matsu:q a:datsaq
    yaqən tsa:'wənəmtsa,
ha ha aya,
    ha ha aya.

1. Now-go-on be-ready / princes-of chiefs-of-the tribes / for-my future-husbands / for
   therefore-I ("I" is actually marked in qadzən) come that-I make-a-chief / my
   husband with-this my-father-who-I / his-master, / ha ha aya ha ha aya.
2. Master-I-shall come / to-be your-wife / princes-of-the chiefs-of-the tribes. / Coppers-
   my seat many privileges / and (cf. "with this" (#1)) names / for given-by my-father /
   to-my husband / ha ha aya ha ha aya.
3. For now-it-is finished / plated [sic]-by my-mother / for-my belt / when-I take-care-of
   the-future-house-dishes-of-my father / to-my future-husband / when-he-gives-in-
   the-marriage-feast many kinds-of-food my-father/ to-my future-husband / ha ha aya
   ha ha aya.

1. "Be ready, O chiefs' sons of the tribes! to be my husbands; for I come to make my
   husband a great chief through my father, for I am mistress, ha ha aya ha ha aya!"
2. "I, mistress, come to be your wife, O princes of the chiefs of the tribes! I am seated
   on coppers, and have many names and privileges that will be given by my father to
   my future husband, ha ha aya ha ha aya!"
3. "For my belt has been woven by my mother, which I use when I look after the dishes
   that will be given as a marriage present by my father to him who shall be my husband,
   when many kinds of food shall be given in the marriage-feast by my father to him who
   shall be my husband, ha ha aya ha ha aya!"

COMMENT:

The original text is not printed here as it was by Boas. Boas grouped the text of the
song into three block paragraphs (as numbered here), parallel to those of his translation.
The song, however, has a finer structure. The two-part repetition of the refrain suggests
an organization within the three blocks into paired lines. Further clues to such organization appear at clear junctures in content. Recurrences of forms occurring at such
junctures, and parallels and recurrences throughout the text, can be used as hints for
provisional segmentation.[5] On the hypothesis of short binary segments, paralleling the
organization of the refrain, it proves possible to organize the poem as a whole. Each
segmentation is justified in terms of parallelism within the poem, recurrence of initial
segments or types of segment being the chief key, save for one or two segments isolated
only by the segmentation and structure of the rest. The result is supported by the
consistency with which the whole can be so interpreted and by an analogous binary
structure (although different stanzaically) in another song (Boas 1921: 1293).

The refrain, as noted, has on the first level a binary structure in keeping with the
rest of the stanza. On a second level, the refrain, *ha ha aya*, consists of three elements,
grouped two against one (*ha ha: aya*). The number of elements parallels the number of

stanzas (three) and it is possible to find respects in which each possible pair of stanzas go together in contrast to a third.

1: 2, 3. The latter two stanzas end with "by my Father / to my husband-to-be," whereas stanza 1 ends "*with* my Father, / I am his master," pairing daughter and father, as against the father-in-law and son-in-law. Also, 2 and 3 both contain reference to "many" (a segment-initial element) and "to be gifts" (2, lines e−f, 3, line g, and 2g, 3d, f). Also, 2 and 3 alone contain mention of feminine roles (wife [2], mother [3], each in the second line); masculine roles are concentrated in 1 (6 occurrences [six out of eight lines], five types: sons of the chiefs, husband-to-be, chief, father, master), whereas 2 has four occurrences of four types (master, sons of the chiefs, father, husband-to-be) and 3 has four occurrences of but two types (father, husband-to-be). Each stanza does indicate five types of roles (counting the feminine types in 2 and 3), and the qualitative difference of the presence of feminine types versus their absence, supplemented by the relative concentration of masculine types, seems decisive.

2: 1, 3. The latter two stanzas show the "I" of the poem in an active role, although contrasting active dominance ("My making a chief") in 1 to active but subordinate tending ("when I care") in 3; stanza 2 shows the "I" of the poem in a passive or static role ("to *be* your wife," "sit on copper"). (This contrast is qualified by "As master I'll come" in 2, but its future reference lessens its active connotation from that of the "I come" in 1 preceding. There seems no future mark with "take care of" in 3.) Also, 1 and 3 each begin with a reference to a state of readiness ("now be ready," "now it is finished" [i.e., ready]) as opposed to the absence of such in 2.

3: 1, 2. The latter two stanzas agree in indicating sociopolitical roles and non-subsistence property, although contrasting the highest role, that of "chief," alone mentioned in 1, to mention as well of copper, privileges, and titles (generally shared by men of rank) in 2. In 3 the references are to domestic and more utilitarian or subsistence property, belt, house dishes, food. (Prestige, of course, accrued to the possession and giving of both kinds of property.) Also, 1 and 2 alone contain references to the coming of the "I" of the poem and to the "I" of the poem as "master." . . .

Grouping together the ways in which one stanza stands over against the other two, there is an implicit sequence characterizing the girl. In 1, she is identified with her father, not as concerned with gifts of wealth and privilege that link father-in-law and son-in-law, but as concerned or identified with power, as associated with the roles of chief, father, and master. In 2, she is passive, and, by possible implication of the contrast to 1, 3, not herself ready (note that "I come" has been modulated to "I shall come"). In 3, she is identified with domestic goods and activities; as not associated with mastery; and as stationary. From 1 to 3, masculine roles decline as feminine roles unfold.

There seems further symbolism, or structure, in the occurrence of *aya* as last element of the refrain. On the hypothesis (suggested first by poem IV) that the *ya* element of a refrain signals the "figure," against a ground represented by the *ha* elements, *ha ha aya* suggests a transition (*a*-) to a culminating -*ya*. Within each stanza, there is suggested an emphasis on the final statement, respectively, " . . . with my father, I am mistress (literally: master)," " . . . gifts by my father to my husband-to-be." " . . . many kinds of food (given by) my father to my husband-to-be." The succession of these final statements, and the succession of the three stanzas as wholes, in terms of their points of contrast analyzed above, go together to suggest a culmination in the third. The status and state as to change of identity, which become figure to ground in stanza 3 have, in the structure of both the poem and the refrain, the accent of finality.

It is not suggested that the refrain was consciously designed for the purpose, but rather that on an unconscious level, out of awareness, it reflects the structural principle of the whole, and by its position and concision, gives such structural principle expressively compelling statement.

It must be remembered that the song in question is not sung by the girl child, but sung for and to her by adults using a pronunciation ascribed to children. The values are those of adults, not ''out of,'' but ''put in'' the mouths of babes. (The phonic effect of the substitutions in pronunciation [Boas meticulously obtained and published the corresponding adult pronunciation] is one of much recurrence of substituted syllables with *dz*- plus varied vowels).

The prose translation given above from Boas is reprinted by Day (1951: 58). The discovered structure (and the translation below to which it gives rise) seem better suited to the context of a song associated with children than do the oratorical periods of the literary translation above. A verse translation following the structure discerned in the original text is as follows:

''Go now, be ready,

    Sons of the chiefs of the tribes,

My husbands-to-be,

    For I come for that,

My making a chief

    My husband-to-be,

And with my father,

    I am his master,

ha ha aya,

    ha ha aya.

As master I'll come,

    To be your wife,

Sons of the chiefs of the tribes.

    On copper I sit,

Many the privileges,

    And with titles,

To be gifts by my father

    To my husband-to-be,

ha ha aya,

    ha ha aya.

For now it is finished,

    Braided by my mother,

To be my belt,

    When I care for the dishes to be gifts by my father

To my husband-to-be,

    When in the wedding-feast he gives

Many kinds of food, my father,

    To my husband-to-be,

ha ha aya,

    ha ha aya.''

III. Workingman's Song of the Li:L Gi:d of the q'u:mky'uty s for his First-Born son

1. *hants'i:nuqwi' lakwi:ky la:qən gya:q'i:na'yi: bəgwa:nəmts'i:da dask'wɛ, ya ha ha ha.*
2. *a:li:winuqwi' lakwi:ky la:qən gya:q'i:na'yi: bəgwa:nəmts'i:da dask'wɛ, ya ha ha ha.*
3. *li:q'i:nuqwi' lakwi:ky la:qən gya:g'i:na'yi: bəgwa:nəmts'i:da dask'wɛ, ya ha ha ha.*
4. *lats'ai:nuqwi' lakwi:ky la:qən gyaq'i:na'yi: bəgwa:nəmts'i:da dask'wɛ, ya ha ha ha.*

5. *i:aqəlai:nuqwi'Ləky la:qən gya:q'i:na'yi: bəgwa:nəmts'i:da dask'wɛ, ya ha ha ha.*
6. *qats ky'iatsi:tsu:s tsa:yakwi:yatsu:s yaqi:s 'na:kwatsau:s agi:qs dəsu:tsu:s dask'wɛ*
   ya ha ha ha.

1. Born-to-be-a-hunter at-my becoming a-man, Father, *ya ha ha ha.*
2. Born-to-be-a-spearsman at-my becoming a-man, Father, *ya ha ha ha.*
3. Born-to-be-a-canoe-builder at-my becoming a-man, Father, *ya ha ha ha.*
4. Born-to-be-a-board-splitter at-my becoming a-man, Father, *ya ha ha ha.*
5. Will-be-a-worker at-my becoming a-man, Father, *ya ha ha ha.*
6. That-you you-will-nothing need of all you wanted-by-you, Father, *ya ha ha ha.*

1. "When I am a man, I shall be a hunter, O father! *ya ha ha ha!*"
2. "When I am a man, I shall be a harpooner, O father! *ya ha ha ha!*"
3. "When I am a man, I shall be a canoe-builder, O father! *ya ha ha ha!*"
4. "When I am a man, I shall be a board-maker, O father! *ya ha ha ha!*"
5. "When I am a man, I shall be a workman, O father! *ya ha ha ha!*"
6. "That there may be nothing of which you will be in want, O father! *ya ha ha ha!*"

(In Boas [1925], the second clause of each unit begins with "then (I shall) . . . ";
"carpenter" and "artisan" replace "board-maker" and "workman" in 4 and 5; and 6
becomes "That we may not be in want, O father! ya ha ha ha!")

COMMENT:
   The literal translation is more concrete and effective in some lexical respects:
"born to be" vs. "I shall be" especially; also, "board-splitter" vs. "carpenter," and
perhaps "spearsman" vs. "harpooneer." The choice of "artisan" in the literary
translation, as revised in 1925, avoids the culturally inappropriate associations of
"worker," but "craftsman," I think, may be better. The literary translation reverses the
order of the first two clauses, but the order in the literal translation and original text seems
more effective. Following the original order of the two clauses makes possible following
the variation in its content in 5, where "born" does not occur; Boas' choice of order and
words does not seem to permit recognizing the change. The reiteration of "you" in the
inflections of words in 6 seems purposive, and it would be desirable to reflect it in the
translation in some way.
   In terms of structure, each unit (1−6) would seem to be a stanza comprising four
segments, two invariable throughout ("Father, / *ya ha ha ha*"), one invariable through
the first five of the six stanzas ("when I become a man"), one variable within a constant
frame through the first five of the six stanzas ("[Born] to be a . . ."). The shift in the
sixth stanza from the regularities of the first two segments seems effective, enhancing by
direct address the recurring third segment, which, at the same time, together with the
fourth, reasserts and maintains the structure of the whole.
   This analysis of the structure is plausible in terms of the clear differences in content
of each of the four segments. The analysis is supported by consideration of the refrain, *ya
ha ha ha*. It comprises four elements, one different in part, three identical. In this it is a
direct image of the pattern established in the first five stanzas, in which the first element
varies as against the identical repetition of the remaining three (as between stanzas, of
course, not within). On the hypothesis that in refrains the *ya* element symbolizes the

"figure," the *ha* elements the "ground," the structure of stanzas 1—5 is confirmation, and the functional significance of line 1 of stanza 6 is highlighted.

Day (1951: 9) follows Boas in citing the poem (in its literary translation) as an example of rhythmic repetition with simple variation. Day uses the modified literary translation of Boas (1925: 494), which inserts "then" after the first comma in lines 1—5, changes "board-maker" to "carpenter," "workman" to "artisan," and the sixth line to "that we may not be in want. . . . "

In addition to the comments above, two more should be made. (1) Although the literal "spearsman" could only mean a user of the harpoon in the native context, "harpooneer" is perhaps better to convey the contrast of hunting at sea and at land that is involved. (2) "Boatwright" seems better in rhythm than "canoe-builder" and also in specific force. "Wright" seems to have the advantage of "builder" and the converse advantage of "canoe" may be offset if one knows that "boat" meant originally a hollowed tree trunk. "Canoewright" would combine the best of both, if not too saliently a neologism.

LITERARY TRANSLATION (2):

"Born to be a hunter,
    when I become a man,
        Father,
            Ya ha ha ha.
Born to be a harpooneer,
    when I become a man,
        Father,
            Ya ha ha ha.
Born to be a boatwright,
    when I become a man,
        Father,
            Ya ha ha ha.

Born to be a board-splitter,
    when I become a man,
        Father,
            Ya ha ha ha.
To be a craftsman,
    when I become a man,
        Father,
            Ya ha ha ha.
That you, you will need nothing,
    of all you want,
        Father,
            Ya ha ha ha."

IV. Love Song of the Dead, Heard on Shell Island

Lams wayadi:yahasgyas wayahadayəwahagyu:sahi: hai: gyiya'ya ha ha ye ya ha ha.
Lams aladiyahasgyas alahadayəwahagyu:sahi: hai: gyiya'ya ha ha ye ya ha ha.
Xgyin yayai:x' ali:si:ygyin nahənky'aGəmli:hisu:Lawa hai: gyiya'ya ha ha ye ya ha ha.
'ya u:gəxsali:hi:sLəhahən q'wats'i:ni:hi:la qahahas gyiya'ya ha ha ye ya ha ha.
'ya babanaxsali:hihi:sLahahən q'wats'i:ni:hi:La qahahas gyiya'ya ha ha ye ya ha ha.

You-are hard-hearted-against-me hard-hearted-against-me (the particle *hai:* is not rendered)
    my-dear *ha ha ye ya ha ha.*
You-are really-cruel-against-me really-cruel-against-me-my-dear *ha ha ye ya ha ha.*
For-I get-tired of-waiting-for-you-my-dear *ha ha ye ya ha ha.*
Oh differently-I-shall cry [sic] for-you my-dear *ha ha ye ya ha ha.*
Oh going-downward-I-shall shall-cry for-you my-dear *ha ha ye ya ha ha.*

"You are hard-hearted against me, you are hard-hearted against me, my dear, *ha ha ye*
    ya ha ha!

You are cruel against me, you are cruel against me, my dear, *ha ha ye ya ha ha!*
For I am tired of waiting for you to come here, my dear, *ha ha ye ya ha ha!*
Now I shall cry differently on your account, my dear, *ha ha ye ya ha ha!*
Ah, I shall go down to the lower world, there I shall cry for you, my dear, *ha ha ye ya ha ha!*"

COMMENT:

There are several points of difference between the three versions above. They become significant principally in the light of fresh possibilities of translation suggested by a hypothesis as to the structure. To indicate them: the identical repetition in the literary translation of lines (stanzas) 1 and 2 above is not identical in Kwakiutl, where "You are" occurs only initially. "Really" (*-gyas*) is omitted from the literary translation of 1 and 2 (and the literal translation of 1). "To come here" and "to the lower world" are not in the literal translations of 4 and 5, but seem added as explanation. The literal translation of the same form in 4 and 5 leaves its character uncertain, but the *-L* in the ending of *q'wats'i:ni:hi:La* is presumably a mark of the future in both occurrences. *'ya* is rendered "oh" in the literal translation, but neither as that, nor as the same thing, in its two occurrences initially in 4 and 5.

Despite the presentation of the five parts of the poem as each a single extended line (Boas 1921), each part can be considered a stanza. The justification is a hypothesis as to the structure of the poem, a structure mirrored on three levels, that of the poem, of the stanza, and of the refrain.

In terms of content and repetition, the *poem* is organized in three parts: A(1, 2), B(3), C(4, 5), of which the second, or B part, is the pivot. Stanzas 1 and 2, and 4 and 5, are alike in that there is repetition within each, between the initial portions, as against 3.

As the second literary translation below brings out, each *stanza* also is organized in three parts: A(lines 1, 2), B(line 3), C(line 4), of which the B part is again the pivot. Again, also, the A and C parts show repetition internally, as against B.

Finally, the *refrain* itself is organized in three parts: A (ha ha), B (ye ya), C (ha ha), of which the B part can be considered the pivot. The A and C parts show repetition (here, identity) as against B. If the repetition of initial consonant in B (ye ya) is compared to the nonidentical repetition on the stanza and whole poem levels, it remains the case that the *pattern* of (A, C): (B) is maintained in the refrain by the relative difference of identity: partial repetition. The intensification and compression of the structural pattern within the refrain into a single line and syllables may itself be a matter of functional significance for the poem as a whole.[6]

LITERARY TRANSLATION (2):

The first literary translation, given above before the Comment, is reprinted by both Day (1951: 54) and Astrov (1946: 280).

In the light of the above specific comments and structural analysis, the following translation may be more satisfactory both as a poem and as evidence of Kwakiutl poetics. (In point of fact, the translation was completed first, on the basis of hints from the specific details cited, and a desire to achieve something of an appropriate tone. Only sometime after the translation did the principle of examining the refrain for structural clues, added to recognition of the pivotal role of the middle stanza, bring the full hypothesis of structure to light.)

"You are hard-hearted against me,
    hard-hearted against me,
        my dear,
            ha ha ye ya ha ha.

You are really cruel against me,
    really cruel against me.
        my dear,
            ha ha ye ya ha ha.

For I get tired,
    waiting for you,
        my dear,
            ha ha ye ya ha ha.

O differently I'll
    cry for you, I shall,
        my dear,
            ha ha ye ya ha ha.

O going down I'll
    cry for you, I shall,
        my dear,
            ha ha ye ya ha ha.

V. Song of Salmon

1. *gyi:gyàxs' aisəla yu:xdenúguas mími:u:Xua:nakyasdi:.*
2. *hàlaqas gyágya:x' a:lagyilisi:ilu:L qáldu:yu:wi:'s lúwa. haiuXs' aisəlagyilitsəmXtəm núguas mími:u:Xua:nakyasdi:.*
3. *hàlaqais haixuanu:magyailuLai hi:iLgyu:tmi: is lúwa. LíLaxuya máya:Las aixyts' um-kyi:yaLi:Xdis mími:u:nakyasdi:.*

1. Many-are-coming-ashore they-with-me salmon-real-past.
2. For-they come-ashore-to-you post-in-middle-of heaven. Dancing-from-the-outside-to-the-shore-with me the-salmon-real-past.
3. For-they come-to-dance-to-you at-the-right-side-of-the-face of heaven. Overtowering surpassing outshining the-salmon-real-past.

1. "Many salmon are coming ashore with me."
2. "They are coming ashore to you, the post of our heaven."
3. "They are dancing from the salmon's country to the shore."
4. "I come to dance before you at the right-hand side of the world, overtowering, outshining, surpassing all; I, the salmon."

COMMENT:

Although the text is printed in three units, the formal translation in four, an inspection of the text shows that the recurrence of the final segments, "salmon-real-past" and "heaven (world)," organizes the poem into *five* units. In the original text the identification with the "ur-"salmon by the singer is subordinated to the coming and character of the salmon themselves; the "I come to dance" and "I the salmon" of the literary translation are not apparent in the text. Perhaps Boas supplied them because the song accompanies a dance in which the singer imitates the motion of jumping salmon (Boas [1897: 475] describes the context of the song). The order of the descriptive terms in line 5 is altered in the formal translation.

This song symbolizes in many ways the North Pacific Coast as a whole. Its culture, so remarkable and unrivalled among hunting-and-gathering peoples, depended for its richness on the sea, and especially the salmon; and with all its relative wealth and status-consciousness, the culture of the area retained its primitive sense of concreteness and of participant maintenance in relation to nature and gods. (The beliefs reflected in the song are perhaps also those reflected in a song in Chinook Jargon, told me by David French, which can be put in English as: "There is a land of light, / Far away, always light, / And from there the waters shine, / And from there the salmon come.")

LITERARY TRANSLATION (2):
Given the analysis of structure, it is possible to utilize the concrete imagery of the literal translation in a literary translation which is at once more faithful, and, I think, more effective. Indeed, the formal translation published by Boas in 1897 is not an attempt at a poem at all.

> "Many are coming ashore, they with me,
> > the true salmon that were.
> For they come ashore to you,
> > to the post at the center of the heavens;
> Dancing from the far side ashore with me,
> > the true salmon that were.
> For they come to dance to you,
> > at the right side of the face of the heavens;
> Overtowering, surpassing, outshining,
> > the true salmon that were."

VI. Cradle Song (for boys)

hao gí:na Gə+n dəng idjagá:djí:was é:dji.
hao gí:na Gə+n dəng i:djagá:djí:was é:dji.
NəngkílsLas agəng índaLxagá:Gəni
Skils naGá:ga ku:skíndias é:dji, wəstə Q'akúngwi Ga-iɬ gagáng dəngaɬ Ldju:dal.
Gwa-iskún xa:idəGaəi xənhao dəng ná:Ga ɬkiésiGei gut gut gunL'gəndias é:dji.
Hao gí:na Gə+n dəng i:djagá:djí:was é:dji.

(*ng* represents the back nasal of English "sing" except in the proper name *Q'akúngwi*)

"This thing for you sitting-as-a-boy are.
This thing for you sitting-as-a-boy are.
NəngkílsLas himself made-a-human-being.
Property in-the-house was, from-it Rose-Spit-towards (lit., "North-Point-towards"-D.H.) his-flood with tidal-wave-went.
North-Island (lit., "Island-point"-D.H.) people even your house towards-the-door are-as-
     many-as-when-waves-meet-each-other-and-are-packed-close-together.
This thing for you sitting-as-a-boy are."

"This is why you are a boy.
This is why you are a boy.
NəngkílsLas has become a human being.
From the property in his house a flood went out toward Rose Spit.

Even from North Island the people are crowded into your house, as when waves meet and are
packed together.
That is why you are a boy.''

COMMENT:

Lines 1, 2, 6 are identical in Haida, but the first word becomes "That" in line 6 in
the literary translation. The concreteness of the Haida lines (1, 2, 6) is not carried over,
but could be. The literary translation of line 3 conceals the sense of reincarnation of a
dead ancestor. (The name means literally, "One whose voice is obeyed," or, "the-
person-who-accomplished-things-by-his-words, that is, the Creator, Raven," according to Swanton's sketch of Haida grammar (1911: 242, 275).) The change in the literary
translation of "his flood" (line 4) to "a flood" loses some of the specificity of the
metaphor. The end of line 5 paraphrases and explains the Haida verb, for which there is
no easy English equivalent; the rhythm at least could be improved.

One point of structure does emerge. The recurrence of the sentence-final verb form
é:dji indicates a structure of seven lines, rather than the six of Swanton's version, for the
same verb form recurs within what Swanton treats as unit 4. Denoting lines ending in
é:dji with (a), and lines with other endings with (b), the structure of the poem is: a a b a b
a· a. The sixth line is considerably longer than the others, twice the average syllable
length, but shows no apparent internal segmentation, and syntactically parallels (with
expansion) line 4. The increasing length of line 5, then of line 6, can be interpreted as a
swelling of the pulse of the poem symbolic of the swelling of wealth being described, but
brought back within the structural frame by the final line, which repeats what has been
established by repetition at the beginning.

The song is part of a sequence, sung at potlatches. In effect, the child is said to be
born to give great potlatches, as if the great *NangkílsLas* were reborn. His property is like
the flood raised in the time of N., and people must crowd his house like waves. Both
images testify to his greatness, and, derivatively, to that of his kin.

LITERARY TRANSLATION (2):

"It is for this you sit a boy.
It is for this you sit a boy.
NangkílsLas himself is born again.
In the house was property,
From it, towards Rose Spit,
      his flood went a tidal wave.
From North Island even,
      people crowd your house to the door,
      as many converging, compacted waves.
It is for this you sit a boy.''

(An alternative rendering of line 3 of the original, but departing from the original
structure by requiring two lines, would translate the proper name, e.g., "One-whose-
voice-is-obeyed, himself, / Again is born a human being.'')

APPRECIATION (II): ATTITUDES AND PROSPECTS

In some quarters, appreciation of American Indian poetry has at present a strange, almost schizophrenic, quality. It insists on authenticity, but not on the original texts. It sees and values poetry as expression of Indian cultures, but in material that often is itself poor poetry or not poems at all.

There have been notable exceptions, but ethnologists and poets alike often share an attitude, such that a proper concern for objectivity and authenticity is improperly directed, displaced from the native poets and their native language texts onto the translations and the ethnologists. The qualities that American Indian poetry may have for us are frozen there. Why?

There are three reasons, I think, not all held by all, but mutually reinforcing within the society as a whole. First, the poems tend to be valued as outcroppings of a pristine primitivity, cherished just because responded to as something natural and untampered. The idea of conscious tampering is abhorred without much regard to what exactly it is proposed to tamper with. One wants to take the poems as found, like natural objects generally, as not having any part of us. Although there have been some serious studies, such are few. One mistrusts poets perhaps, as artificers, but is willing to take ethnologists as impersonal transmitters, or as personally assimilated to that which they transmit.

Second, as a consequence of the first, the poems tend not to be truly perceived as poems. What is asked of poems within our own poetry is not consciously asked of them (although it unconsciously may condition appreciation). It is almost enough that they be Indian, authentic, recognizably representative of Indian themes. Verbally, there is a minimum standard of presentableness to be met, to be sure, and verbal aptness, poetic effect, as judged by contemporary standards for contemporary poems, are valued. But they are not demanded. To be authentically Indian is to be given the benefit of the poetic doubt for the sake of other value ascribed to the text.

Third, and in some ways the necessary condition of the perpetuation of the whole, there is no continuing tradition of philology in most of the languages in which the poems exist. Appreciators, including anthologists, are willy-nilly forced to rely upon and rationalize the uncritical use of whatever English the ethnologists have provided. Even if they would, they cannot usually go behind the English to the original by means of adequate grammatical analyses and dictionaries. True, much can be done merely by scrutiny of literal translations and observation of patent repetitions in the structure of the original texts, as has been illustrated in the preceding section. To raise the question of alternatives to the printed translations, however, is to jeopardize the fabric of appreciation. In the absence of an adequate philology for the languages, nothing like the apprenticeship of translation known to so many poets is possible with the American Indian poetry. The poems being cut off, then, from a living place in contemporary poetry by lack of linguistics, the fabric of appreciation cannot raise linguistic questions. Without linguistics, as an active part of philology, the poems themselves disappear behind the veils of primitivity and preconception which we don to approach them. We approach, indeed, not the poems at all, but the ethnological translations. It is these our museum-like anthologies enshrine. There is little else, for now, they can do.

With regard to the first component of attitude above, we have seen that it is a mark of naïveté, not objectivity, to identify authenticity and pristineness with the ethnological translations. To say so is not to fault the ethnologists. In particular, the comments to the poems in the preceding section are not intended as criticism of Boas. Quite the contrary. It is with Boas' materials, and few others, that it is at present possible to work. His standards of careful checking of texts, of insistence upon collecting material in native text and of publishing it in full, and his ability and effectiveness in publishing linguistic descriptions as well, are at once the essential minimum without which nothing could now be done, and a minimum not many have achieved. In the period in which first Boas established and carried through his standards for philological work, and from which the materials here utilized stem, he had no peer in American anthropology, for the quality and responsibility of his work, save his students Sapir and Radin. He has had far too few peers since. Rather, it is that the present period can add one dimension to the tradition he exemplified. To the recording of texts as massive documentation, with lingustics as a means to the ends of ethnography and aesthetic appreciation, we can now add, materials being favorable, the influence of structural linguistics on our ability to perceive poetic structure.

What is objective, in short, is the native text itself, where this has been adequately recorded, a text perhaps subject to multiple interpretations in its own culture. The translation is an act of scholarship of a certain time, place, and person, variable in quality and character, as is all scholarship. As in all philology, new interpretations are possible, especially when new points of view and method emerge. There is no law that the first to examine a text exhausts it. Indeed, as can be argued in principle and supported from experience, a literary text is an open document, susceptible of different interpretation as the audience of interpreters differs, a document not necessarily exhausted by any one interpretation, but quite possibly enriched by many or all. Validity and interpretation have two aspects, the source and the receiver, and the exigencies of translation are such that any one translation is like a spotlight from one angle, highlighting some features, but shadowing others. A plurality of responsible translations can illumine more and in greater depth. All this, indeed, is obvious enough in respect to almost every literature and audience, save perhaps American Indian poetry among some anthropologists and poets.

With regard to the second component of attitude above, the consequence of special standards and of lack of a continuing relationship of translation is that the poems are fixed in the literary garb of the period in which the ethnologist worked, and of the ethnologist himself. In the case of Boas, it is the formal English of a native speaker of German trained in the third quarter of the nineteenth century. The reader who approaches the English versions without preconceived sympathy and suspension of verbal standards shares the lot of the student who is asked to believe, or act as if he believes, that certain Greeks wrote great dramatic poems, although what is before him in class is not a great dramatic poem, but English that he finds odd or distasteful or simply ineffective. The contemporary reader now has modern translations of Greek drama by Lattimore, Fitzgerald, Grene, Arrowsmith and others that are manifestly poems in a contemporary idiom; but for much Amerindian poetry, he has translations from two poetic generations ago, or more, many of which are not even by intention poems, but careful prose. Some of the early translations do still seem unimprovable, notably those by Washington Matthews of Navajo chants, having become classic in their own right. I hope to have shown, however, that such is not the case for all.

The third component in the attitude described is the crucial one. For the true values of the original structures and content of the poems to be realized, where now obscured, and for verbally effective translations to be newly made, the perspectives and tools of linguistics are indispensable.

One might think that the fact that aesthetically successful translations are recreations is in conflict with the linguistically motivated emphasis on structural analysis and verbal detail characteristic of the preceding section. There might seem conflict with an attitude such as the following:

> . . . the problem, in a sense, is not one of ''writing'' but one of ''visualizing.'' I have found this to be very true of Chinese poetry translation. I get the verbal meaning into mind as clear as I can, but then make an enormous effort of visualization, to ''see'' what the poem says, nonlinguistically, like a movie in my mind; and to feel it. If I can do this (and much of the time the poem eludes this effort) then I write the scene down in English. It is not a translation of the words, it is the same poem in a different language, allowing for the peculiar distortions of my own vision—but keeping it straight as possible. If I can do this to a poem the translation is uniformly successful, and is generally well received by scholars and critics. If I can't do this, I can still translate the words, and it may be well received, but it doesn't feel like it should.[7]

The question is in fact one, not of conflict, but of sequence and division of labor. As Snyder points out in the same communication, the recreation of a poem also requires, for knowledge of the verbal meaning of the text, the sort of materials that a linguistically-motivated approach puts in focus. In the present state of Amerindian texts, these materials have two necessary dimensions. Even minimal knowledge of verbal meaning requires the original texts in published form, interlinear translation, and some sort of usable grammar and dictionary, as check on interlinear translation and on alternative renderings. (Preferably, the text itself would be morphemically analyzed.) Given these materials, a talented and sympathetic translator can do much, and with most Amerindian poetry, the most one can expect in a living tradition of translation is philological recognition of the original, not bilingual control.[8] There is a second dimension as well, as the present paper has shown. For most Amerindian materials, an anthropological philology must provide analysis not only on the linguistic level, but on the level of metrics, or poetics, too. Formal structure of the sort set forth in the preceding section is as necessary as grammar and dictionary to the recognition of the verbal meaning of the original, for it is intrinsic to what in fact happens in the poem, to what there is to be felt in the verbal meaning. In its ritual-like function, a pattern of repetition is a pattern of insistence.[9]

For any body of Amerindian poetry, then, the two approaches to translation just sketched can be complementary, each contributing to the other. What may be lacking, unfortunately, is the contribution on which both must depend, that of anthropological philology. On this score, there has been considerable discontinuity more than cumulative progress since the classic period of Boas, Sapir, Radin, and others. As noted at the outset of this paper, their joint concern with texts and the best available linguistic method, as well as their unanimous insistence that anthropological study of other cultures meet the normal standard of scholarship, linguistic control, has lapsed in many quarters. On the one hand, some of those who concern themselves with the materials of verbal art assert or assume the irrelevance of linguistic control and analysis to their interpretive interest. Contrary to the experience and standards of scholarship in other fields, the style, content, structure, and functioning of texts seem to be declared ''translated'' (in the theological sense of the metaphor as well as the linguistic) bodily from their original verbal integument, and available for interpretation without it. Original texts are even declared in a scholarly review in the pages of the *American Anthropologist* to be of concern only to linguists—as if only linguists would mourn the loss of the original texts of Homer or the Bible! On the other hand, those who undertake linguistic description too often pursue it without effective concern for other students of the American Indian, or such fields as comparative poetics, to which American Indian studies should contribute.

The situation is absurd, and it is crippling. No scholarship ignorant of the linguistic foundations of its texts can survive the first breath of rigorous criticism. No American Indian descriptive linguistics which fails to make its material serviceable to general scholarship meets its responsibilities or fairly earns its support. Indeed, a descriptive account which erects *ad hoc* barriers to comprehension vitiates its author's own efforts, for no American Indian grammar today founds a general tradition, or contains such invaluable matter of general interest that a public, linguistic or other, will master all obstacles to gain access. It is not a seller's market, so far as American Indian linguistic accounts are concerned. The price of relevance and audience is clarity, and it is among other students of the American Indian, as much or more than among other linguists, that mutual audience and relevance are to be found.

We must hope that the renewed joining of interests described at the outset of this paper may integrate the study of American Indian languages and the values of American Indian texts more fully, proceeding on the conviction that the study of the languages is too important to be left solely to linguistics (in any narrow sense of the term), the texts too valuable to be interpreted by any who ignore linguistics. We must hope that the Alexandrianism of the one extreme and the shoddy foundations of the other both will be abandoned.

These are hard words, but better hard words within the disciplines concerned than to depend on an infinitely uncritical attitude to forestall criticism from others. In many branches of anthropology today there is an intensified concern with quality of workmanship, partly focused on the use of new tools. The tools of philology are in kind among the oldest the student of human culture knows, but so long as there are texts worth knowing they are indispensable.

NOTES

[Condensed from the Original]

¹To so single out Lévi-Strauss does not minimize the contributions of Paul Radin and Melville Jacobs, publishing and interpreting their own collections with an emphasis on interpretation couched in psychoanalytic

terms in part (for an evaluation of Jacobs's Clackamas Chinook work, see Hymes (1965)). Nor should it be overlooked that field work can still enlarge the resources with valuable result, as instanced by the Seneca work of Wallace Chafe and the Haida work of G. L. Bursill-Hall.

[2]I adopt *vocables* as a technical term from Powers (1960: 7, 1961: 41), and am indebted to W. C. Sturtevant for calling Powers's articles to my attention. I would rephrase Powers's definition, but the phenomena intended are the same.

[3]The place was recognized by Mark Van Doren (1928) in the American section of his *Anthology of World Poetry*, but has generally been neglected by anthologists of American poetry since. See, however, the appreciative essay, focused on the publications of the Bureau of American Ethnology, and particularly the work of Frances Densmore, by Kenneth Rexroth (1961); the interest of the poet and translator Jerome Rothenberg in his "From a Shaman's Notebook," including American Indian songs; and the weaving of North Pacific Coast material into the fabric of a set of original poems by Gary Snyder (1960).

[4]The orthographies of the originals have been partly retained, despite their supersession in current practice, and modified only where no unwarranted change of structure would result. Both retention and change have been governed by convenience of symbolization in a non-linguistic journal. To summarize main points: it is clear from Boas's own comments and later interpretation of his work that Kwakiutl has few phonemic vowels. It is assumed here that /i u a ə/ represent all phonemic distinctions (if not more). The colon /:/ symbolizes length. Long /i:/ and /u:/ have most often the qualities e: and o:, as is common on the North Pacific Coast. /ə/ takes various colorings according to phonetic environment and probably is often not distinctive but an incidental vocalic murmur. Among consonants, /L/ is retained for the lateral affricate; ł is its fricative counterpart. Palatalized consonants are marked by following /y/, e.g., /gy kg xy/. Palatal and velar consonants are indicated by /k/:/q/, /g/:/G/, /X/:/x/, with regard to voiceless stops, voiced stops, and voiceless fricatives, respectively (retaining for the last pair Boas's own usage). /'/ represents glottal stop, or glottalization. The original phonetic transcriptions are of course available in the sources.

[5]Such use of parallels and recurrences to delineate the poetic character of material hitherto handled as prose has a history reaching back at least into the eighteenth century, and linking contemporary anthropology with its antecedents in the Romantic movement. Perhaps the first anthropological exemplar is Herder, whose arrangement of Biblical passages as poetry in *Songs of Love* and *The Spirit of Hebrew Poetry* derives, through Michaelis, from Robert Lowth's *Sacra poesia Hebraorum* (1755). Lowth showed that passages of poetry were distinguishable from the rest of the Biblical text by "an accurate recurrence of clauses" (quoted in Emery Neff, *The Poetry of History* [New York: Columbia University Press, 1947], p. 60). The context of Herder's work is of course the first major movement toward an "emic" perspective in anthropology, associated with notions of the individual genius of each language and people, and hence of the form and content, respectively, of each national poetry.

[6]An analogous refrain pattern occurs in Songs 3 and 4, each a "Doctor Dance Song," in the excellent paper by R. H. Robins and Norman McLeod, "Five Yurok Songs: A Musical and Textual Analysis," Bulletin of the School for Oriental and African Studies 81(3); 592—609 (1956). A case can be made that the fourfold pattern of the closing refrain, *hahahaha*, does match the structure analyzed for song 3 (I have noted the details which support such an interpretation in a letter to Dr. Robins (25/IX/64); but no such case can be plausibly made for Song 4. Moreover, as Robins and McLeod point out, similar syllable groups occur in songs of the "Bird" series among the Yuman and Mohave. Yurok music falls within the area of the Yuman style as defined by Herzog. Robins and McLeod suggest that the refrain feature may have travelled independently of such, citing a Yurok formula from Kroeber (in which the formula occurs at the beginning, not end). The Yurok occurrence of such formulas, then, is limited to shamanistic contexts, possibly borrowed, lacking in internal structure of the sort found with Kwakiutl (with opposed elements in both h- and y-), and almost certainly not related to the internal structure of the song as a whole in one of the two known cases, only possibly so in the other. Having reviewed the evidence for the possibility, Dr. Robins does not think "that any connection can be established between the textual structure of Yurok songs and the sequence of 'nonsense' syllables that occur at the end of the doctor dance songs, of which type of song in Yurok they are characteristic." Calling attention to the use of such syllables at the beginning of a ritual formula, Dr. Robins writes: "This is, I think, the essence of these syllable sequences in Yurok, formulaic in nature, rather than linked in *internal* structure to the composition of the rest of the song" (personal communication, 2/X/64).

  In sum, the structural relationship between final refrain and the rest of a song, shown here for Kwakiutl is not general. Whether or not it is specific to Kwakiutl remains to be seen.

  Two Haida songs analyzed by Bursill-Hall (1964) on the model of the Yurok analyses of Robins and McLeod show diversity and complexity of patterning of vocables. In the first Haida song the vocables occur in somewhat modified forms of the same pattern at the beginning, middle, and end, not, as in the Kwakiutl songs here analyzed, at the end of each part. Bursill-Hall's concern is with the parallelism between text and music, but in personal communication he makes the important point that "the Haida themselves noted intuitively that it (the patterning of vocables) was to give the rhythm and *form* of the song.'' Bursill-Hall had himself suspected a structural role for the vocables from the music, and remarks that the slight but very important deviations from the pattern imply a formal principle at work. The exact pattern and structural role is not yet clear to either of us, but seem certain to differ from the Kwakiutl cases in some respects.

[7]A personal communication from Gary Snyder, whose translations of the Chinese Han Shan poems have been praised as superior to those of Waley and others. Snyder has himself an intimate knowledge of the North Pacific Coast oral literature, as evidenced in the poems cited in [note 3], and in his *Dimensions of a Myth* (Reed College dissertation, 1951), a study in multiple perspectives on a Haida myth. [Later published as *He Who Hunted Birds in His Father's Village* (Snyder 1979).]

[8]Cf. Hymes (1956: 601−602) (a sample translation to be included there was unfortunately omitted). Rexroth (1961: 19−40) is of interest for the view that philology is a necessary starting point in the study of a language and its literature, but something that must be left behind in most cases for successful translation, sympathy and talent being the requisites. Rexroth goes so far as to argue with examples that the best translations of Chinese poetry are almost wholly mutually exclusive with deep knowledge of Chinese. Cf. also the practice of Rothenberg (1962), whose versions of aboriginal poems are free workings from anthologized French texts and a literal English translation.

[9]With this sort of structure, and the structural significance discovered for refrains in mind, note Rexroth (1961: 57). Having stressed that the texts are mostly extremely simple and in their pure sensibility resemble classical Japanese poetry, Mallarmé, and certain other moderns, Rexroth continues: "It is possible, of course, to say that Miss Densmore greatly simplifies the poem by cutting out repetitions and nonsense vocables. But the Japanese poetry which we think of as so extremely compact on the printed page is similarly sung in extended fashion. Certainly the Indian singer does not feel that he is dulling the poignancy of the transcendental awareness of reality which he is communicating by musical elaboration, but rather the reverse. And, if the song is sung, or the record available, it is immediately apparent that this elaboration is insistence, not diffusion." Cf. also Lévi-Strauss (1955: 443; 1963: 229), "The function of repetition is to render the structure of the myth apparent." ("La répétition a une fonction propre, qui est de rendre manifeste la structure du mythe" [1958: 254].)

DENNIS TEDLOCK
"Tell It Like It's Right in Front of You"

Tedlock's breakthrough—for which his essay, "On the Translation of Style in Oral Narrative" (1971), was a first declaration—involves a recognition of the full dynamics of voice in oral narration, along with the development of new means of transcription and translation to bring it across on the page and in performance. To do this, he typically uses line and stanza breaks to note the natural pauses of all human speech, and he adapts such typographical devices as capital letters, reduced type-size, jagged lineation, and vowels followed by long dashes, to indicate such voice qualities as loudness, softness, (chanted) pitch variation and glissandi, and vowel elongation. His challenge to the old poetry-prose distinction and his introduction of spoken narrative into the poetic domain have influenced poets as well as those anthropologists and linguists who followed up on the experiments proposed by him. (See, for example, David Antin's attempt to base a poetics on "natural discourse genres"—below, p. 451.) With Jerome Rothenberg, Tedlock founded

SOURCE: *Michel Benamou and Jerome Rothenberg (eds.),* Ethnopoetics: A First International Symposium, *pages 120−132.*

Alcheringa: Ethnopoetics, *"a first magazine of the world's tribal poetries"* (1970–
1980). His translations of Zuni Indian narrative poetry (Finding the Center 1972)
show his translation method at its most developed, but he has also used it or a
simple variation thereof (as in the following) to chart his own voice in the act of
speaking and creating. *Principal works:* Finding the Center, Teachings from the
American Earth *(with Barbara Tedlock).*

---

*An intonational shift occurring without any pause is marked by a comma (,); a brief
pause occurring as a gap within an intonational period is marked by a raised point (·);
the end of an intonational period, marked by a lowering of the voice and a brief pause, is
marked with a period (.); a long pause, running from three to six seconds or more, is
marked with a double space.*

Speaker [walking up to Jerome Rothenberg, at the front of the room]: My father, my
   child · how have you been passing the days?
J. R. [to the speaker]: Happily, my father, my child.

   Now, for what reason have you entered upon our roads?
   You must have come because you have something to say · you would not come for no
reason.
   You must make this known to us · so that we may think about it as we pass the days.

Speaker [to J. R. and the audience]: Yes, in *truth* · my elders, my *children* · I have
   come because there is something to say.

   When I was eighteen months old · my parents moved west · and for some reason
they ended up · in New Mexico.
   And it was there · at eighteen months · that I met an Indian for the first time · in
Albuquerque in front of a tourist court.
   But the main way that I started off · on this · road · was through archaeology.
   Reading about the prehistoric past of New Mexico · visiting the ruins · going out
and copying rock drawings · those sorts of things.
   And · having no idea really · at that point at all · about how to deal with living
Indians · in high school · it just so happened · that · for one whole year · in my art
class · the instructor was Joe Herrera · from the Pueblo of Cochiti · near Santa Fe.
   He looked at my · drawings of the rock drawings and · very casually · told me
what they meant.
   The rock drawings that had been made at least five centuries ago.
   This man [feedback noise] · standing here · was telling me about them.
   The two things I remember most · were a spiral · just a spiral [draws a spiral] ·
and a set of concentric circles.
   The spiral · is the universe · and the concentric circles · are the earth.
   When I got to college I was still · focused on archaeology · spent every summer
on digs · sometimes as an unpaid laborer · this came to a climax · at a 15th century site

near Albuquerque called Pottery Mound · where there are kivas, underground ceremonial chambers covered with murals.

I was hired as a · draftsman and photographer · to make accurate copies of these murals.

One day · we were coming · back in · from the field · and there at the door to the anthropology department · was Ed Ladd · a · Zuni and so far as I know the only Zuni who has a · degree in anthropology · and Ed wanted to see the drawings.

One of the drawings · showed · an old lady sitting down on the ground · with a big black [cupping hands] round-bottomed pot in front of her over a fire · she was stirring it [hand as if grasping something] with a handful of something or other · he looked at it and said · *Oh · she's · parching corn, she's holding a bundle of willow sticks, parched corn has to be made · in a black round-bottomed pot or it'll stick, and you have to stir it all the time, you put sand in there too with it · you stir it around.*

Something like popcorn [as if holding a kernel at the fingertips] but it doesn't open up [opening the fingers] quite as far · you can do it with any kind of hard corn, not just · popcorn.

She's holding a bundle of · willow sticks, he saw the whole picture.

The picture he was looking at was five centuries old, or a copy rather of one five centuries old.

Later on · still talking about being at the University of New Mexico · one of my classmates there was Alfonso Ortiz · who's a Tewa · who's now a · Ph.D. in anthropology · he's now back at the University of New Mexico · we used to · get away from the campus by · driving about fifteen miles north of town · to a place on the Rio Grande where you're beyond all the light pollution from the city of Albuquerque · and where you can get right down through the alfalfa fields and right up to the edge of the river and the · bosques, the cottonwood groves · that grow up and down the · bottomlands.

We went there with several quarts of beer · it was a very · *clear* night · Alfonso looked up at the stars [looking up and pointing], he said, *You see that star there · that one that's steady and bright and right next to it there's one that's flickering constantly · there's a story about those stars*, and he told · what we would call an Orpheus story · about those two stars.

One of them following the other, the steady star following the flickering, the decaying star.

That's a · different kind of *literacy* than I had · been accustomed to.

To read everything that's around you.

In graduate school I was still doing archaeology [raps head with knuckles, audience laughs] · I got a job · for one of those summers as a dig foreman, I'd had so much archaeology experience by now I could tell · other people · where to [as if showing someone where to dig] · and reduce myself to a trowel and whisk broom, that's the way archaeology works as you rise [raising hand and arm] · up.

Lucky for me · the assignment was · to the Glen Canyon Project of the Museum of Northern Arizona · rescuing ruins that were going to be spoiled by · Glen Canyon Dam · what was lucky about it is that · it was in a very remote part of the Navajo Reservation.

Sixty miles of four-wheel drive.

From the nearest · pavement · and the · field hands were all Navajos.

And at every opportunity I went walking all over that country up there · and · met Navajos in the path · visited their gardens · stood with them while they herded sheep and so on and so forth · and it was at this time I first had to confront the business · of putting my tongue around an Indian *language*.

Never did learn much Navajo, but enough to · get around on those trails and to · talk to people.

If you're walking down a path · up in that country, and · you meet a gentleman coming in the opposite direction · you simply have to speak something of Navajo.

If only a few words, then the rest can be · gestures · whatever.

Whatever passes in that kind of a · that kind of a meeting.

Sometime during that summer, I don't know exactly when · I decided that there were other things in this world than to dig up *bones*.

Or at least, at least *literal* bones · and · announced that fall that I was not going to be an archaeologist.

And what happened gradually too is that I decided to · not only · try to be with *living* Indians · but to listen to what *they* had to say to *me*.

By the medium of · traditional stories especially.

Now · unfortunately for me · in a way · anthropology · prepares one rather elaborately for this field experience · a kind of preparation that I think is designed · with consummate skill to prevent one from learning anything whatsoever.

From · the people · one is supposed to be with.

Because they can tell you · exactly what to expect in advance, and *sure enough* [audience laughs] · if you · are really · completely back there, back there in your books and the classrooms instead of *here* [pointing to the spot he is standing on] · in the field · that's the way it'll turn out.

It's very tricky getting your *ears* opened up after, after being told · in elaborate detail exactly what you are going to expect.

In the case of the stories themselves · one is told that, *Well, there are several ways to look at stories* · and people tend to do just one of these, one of them is to · say, *Well, there must be some clues to* history *in here*.

We know that oral tradition is inaccurate history, but if we · *compared it with some other information and really looked at it really hard, we could figure out what was* real *history in there*.

And fill in · *the past in greater detail than we now know*.

Forget about the rest of the story · *let's see if we can* extract *the true history from it*.

It's, it's bad history, it's mistake history, this story · another way of going about it is · to focus in on the · *social* dimension of the story.

This story is some kind of an operating manual for this society, you tell yourself.

It's telling people exactly how they should do things, there's a certain amount of truth in that too of course.

Or, *This story is kind of like* their *constitution*.

Instead of a written one.

Then there's a · third way · this is the · psychological approach, used to be called Culture and Personality · now it's called Psychological Anthropology.

You decide here that · what you've really got here is like a · projective test for the whole society.

Or a collective *dream*.

This is very Freudian stuff, it's very *voyeuristic*.

Let's, let's see if we can see the bottom side of their lives · by spying on them by means of these stores.

These stories are going to · expose to us their dreams · and their private lives.

That's the psychological approach. *If* only *I could get* inside *there*.

And · people's guards are down when they're telling stories · it's a good, a good opportunity to go in there and · find out what a person's dreams are.

There are some other approaches too, I'm just giving you the · main sort of respectable ones.

A fourth one · a more recent one · called structuralism · is where · you discover that · the story is *really* an exercize in symbolic logic.

This is what they have instead of mathematics textbooks and logic textbooks.

Now if I had gone in there · really focused on the idea of · translating stories and making them *real* to other audiences · I could've been stopped right there · by · by getting confused · by the wonders of structuralism.

Claude Lévi-Strauss · says · in an article before I · ever went to the field that [reading] · *The mythical value of the myth remains preserved · even through the worst translation.*

And he goes on, this is a sort of paraphrase now, to say that · *it's not the music · it's not the · poetry · or anything like that, it's the* · story, he says · by which he means the structure · the logical exercise · That's *the essence of the thing · you can forget about the rest.*

In other words he's saying that · given that somebody had · already done the work of making a transcription of some sort · that *myths could just as well be studied by blind deaf-mutes who knew how to read braille.*

There was nothing at all in what I'd been taught that would have pointed me to · really thinking of · in terms of · the *art* of storytelling.

Itself.

Anthropologists always have some ulterior motive · they're doing *this* because it's going to mean something *else* to them.

It's going to, this is going to provide a clue *about something* else.

That's true of all those methods, all those four · methods · think about it in terms of my hand here [holds up the right hand showing four fingers] · there are four separate paths leading away from the story [traces a path along each of the four fingers] · and the story is down here [outlines the body of the hand].

So, off I went to Zuni [walks a few steps] · it took me a couple of months to · find [returns to the center] · to set things up with Andrew Peynetsa and Walter Sanchez · some other people too, but those were the main · two · gentlemen who told me most of · what I know · right away Andrew caught me up · with a remark [walks away again] that really didn't fit into the *program* of the field work, he said · [returns to the center] *You don't know the* time *when you're telling stories, it's not like working at a* desk.

You don't know the time *when you're telling stories* · then, things like this happen to you all the time · in the field if you're got your ears open.

One of the next things that happened is · I was laboriously working on a transcription and translation with Joseph Peynetsa, who helped me with those things · it's a very tedious process, sentence by sentence · tapes aren't good enough, you have to have somebody there to · to repeat the words to you, at least at first · so you both sit there listening to the tape · you write down the Zuni · then you work on · work out a translation of that and then you move on to the next line.

Joe had a · capacity · even with all that tediousness for · listening to the story and staying right with it, once in the middle of all this · laborious work · where I was madly scribbling down what he had just said · Joe said · *When I tell these stories* · *do you picture it?* · *or do you just write it down.*

At the moment he caught me he was · asking just the right question.

I was writing it down, that's all.

Writing it down to *read it later* [sniffs].

Some other kinds of things that happen · you're going by in a car, going by a mesa [faces west and gestures to the right] · with · pink and yellow stripes of sandstone and · about 300 feet up the side of it there's a cave up there.

You're going along with a Zuni and · the Zuni says · *That's the cave, you remember that story about the* · *Aatoshle ogress* · *that's the cave where she lived* · *when that little girl wandered into her cave to spend the night.*

Right there.

Or going by another mesa a little farther down the road on the left side [faces west and gestures to the left] · the one where the people went during the world flood, it's about · oh, five, 600 feet above the surrounding · countryside.

That's where the people went during the world flood · *those* stripes *on the side of the* mesa *are the* rings *the water* left *as it went* down.

Those two rocks in front of the mesa · *those are the two kids* · *the two little kids, the son and daughter of the priest, who were sacrificed to the flood to make it go down* · *they turned into* stone *as the water went* down.

Right there · *that's the place.*

And · sense of being *in place* · also · exists at the same moment the story is actually being *told*.

Even if you're telling it in Milwaukee · you've at least got · the directions.

And you always have to know before you can tell one of these stories · which way east is.

It's over there [gestures toward the east].

So that you can at least say · *He went over to the east, He went over to the south,* and so on.

And · set up the story right around there where you're standing.

So that begins to give you a sense of what *place* means · in stories · as you discover it · in the field · time works · very much the same way.

The narrator says · *It was a morning very much like this one*.

This one [indicates the spot where he is standing].

It was a night like this one, It was about this time of the winter, there was just a little bit of snow left on the ground.

Somebody came in the door [looks toward the door] · and so on.

Somebody came in the door [indicates the door] *and went up to the altar* [swinging around to indicate the stage behind him] · right there.

A good · storyteller can even make use of complete accident.

In the story of The Beginning in · Finding the Center · that *is* the story of The Beginning · there's a · passage in there · where most of the people have already emerged from the earth, they've gone some distance from the Place of Emergence · and they have · made a settlement · and they hear a sound like an earthquake.

Which means that somebody else has emerged from the earth after them · and they wonder about who it is · and it's going to turn out · that it's the emergence of the first witches, it's the entrance of evil into this world.

That's being announced by that earthquake · evil is sort of an afterthought of · of creation · it comes, it comes out *after*.

They send the twin war gods back there to investigate.

And the twin war gods being the first witch to them and they have to decide what to *do* about that.

Now · when Andrew was telling this story · on his farmstead about twenty miles from Zuni · it was late at night · in a very lonely · hamlet · the dogs are always outside · that's how you can always know whether something is going on outside or not · when dogs bark · it means that there's probably somebody or something out there · and sometimes they wonder whether it's a witch.

It's a · person out there · going around · late at night trying to do harm to someone perhaps · well, Andrew arrives at this point in the story · the noise of the earthquake · the · two Ahayuuta are going toward the Place of Emergence · and in the distance they · see somebody standing there · and at the moment · they come to that point of finding the first witch the dogs start barking outside · *this · house · here · now*.

The audience · freezes for a minute · everyone · looking · over toward the door [looks toward the door] · the narrator · sips this · perfect pause · to the full · and then proceeds with his story.

So that's how · you can even use · just incidental things that happened.

Even those can be · can be pulled into the story · if you're quick enough to do it.

They pull people into the story too · what the book doesn't show is that · I could tell one of those stories · and give the people in it · *names* of people in this audience.

I'd try to do it in a very appropriate way too, telling you that you're something like *that* person and [looking in a different direction] you're something like that *other* one.

Coming back to · everyday life outside · the event of the storytelling · itself ·

you even come to *this* kind of point · and this is where · you really begin to get the *message* of what stories are all about.

One summer, a time when people are not *allowed* to tell most of these stories · there are other things to do in the summer · snakes don't like stories, that's one reason you can't tell them in the · summer · or, in another way, I guess you might say they *do* like stories, it sends them right to you if they hear you doing it · but they bite you for it · but it's summer, we've got stories way at the back of our minds somewhere · one day instead of driving · to the farmstead from where I was staying · I decided to walk over the hill to it, it's about nine miles, and · I was going to see a lot of country by doing that that I was very curious about.

Make a direct on-the-ground connection between where I was and the farmstead in · Upper Nutria · or To'ya · and · I walked over the hill, I saw · all kinds of things on the way including several deer · and it turned out they were all · watching for me too, on the other side · and they spotted me · before I spotted them · I must have been an incredible speck when they started calling out to me.

When I got there · Andrew's eldest son was so taken with the whole crazy thing of walking over all that ground · that he said · *You're the Ahayuuta.*

The Ahayuuta is · there are two of them · they're the twin · sons of the Sun Father.

And they play a · big part in a lot of the stories · and they're spending all the time going over the ground just like that, step by step · just looking around and · seeing everything.

Only unlike myself, carrying · bows with quivers · on their backs.

Now it becomes · *you* · me · right here · now.
Ahayuuta.

The first way that remark struck my · Western mind · was that he'd almost been blasphemous · to use · the name of a god on *me.*

It was not intended as a · compliment either by the way, the Ahayuuta are rather · unreliable characters · who · among other things have nits in their hair [audience laughs].

Unreliable in the sense that you can't trust them to do exactly what you tell them to do.

They just *do* what they're doing.

So · I hope you begin to get the picture here that myth is coming to the surface all the time · whenever you happen to look for it.

They're looking for it all the time · it's a whole habit of life.

It's what · it means to be continuously and every day and in this moment always ·connected up with the whole past.

But I suppose · the best single awakening as to · the nature of storytelling itself came · really rather late · in my main stay out there · I finally got around to the business of saying, *Okay, what makes a good story, what is a story really all about, what do you think* about *that?*

One of Andrew's sons-in-law · said · *If you're really true to a story · you make it like it's right in front of you.*

Now if · Zunis were into making · statements that would fit into dialectical arguments · which they are definitely not · they might say · in reply to Lévi-Strauss, *The essential quality of myth · is that you be able to see it right in front of you* [moves hand up and down in front of himself].

Right in front of you.

The paradox is · that you're also forbidden to talk about anything modern in stories.

There are no cars in stories · horses sometimes sneak in · no sheep · except in a few cases · no machinery, no electricity · no Bureau of Indian Affairs · no taxes · it takes place · in something called the *inoote.*

Which I've translated, *long ago* · what I like about *long ago* is, that doesn't · *fix* it somewhere · gets a proper notion of a kind of · distance · and because that's true of stories that's why you have to keep the modern things out of them · the picture you have in front of you has to be true to some kind of vision of the long ago · at the same time you're seeing it right in front of you here and now.

It took me a long time to understand *this*, I understood it from such remarks as *these* · trying to explain inoote · Andrew said · *Well, you know, it's · back before 1800,* before *1700.*

What he means is · *it's before all those* numbers.

It's not datable.

In traditional Zuni culture you would never have a Bishop Usher · trying to figure out · that it was 4,000 and four B.C. on October the · whatever it was supposed to be, at · 9:00 A.M. Central Standard Time.

It's *before* all of that.

Or something other than · that kind of way of looking at the world.

There are other ways you can see this going on, that greeting that Jerry and I were doing · *My father, my child* · what does that mean, how can I call the same person both *my father* and *my child.*

What do I do · when I say that? [baby makes sounds in audience].

It's a timeless statement.

You could be · if we · remove this kind of time that's called *1700* and *1800* you could be my father · or my child.

It's an eternal statement.

Or you say more broadly, *My elders, Hom · aalhasshinaawe,* just means exactly that, the ones who are older than I.

Hom aalhasshinaawe · hom chawe, My children, the ones who are younger than I.

By which is meant · everybody, including everybody who ever *lived.*

There's no word for ancestor here, aalhasshinaawe, sometimes people think that means ancestor · there are no ancestors · in the sense that we know them, ancestor, that means the ones who are *dead*, right?

Aalhasshinaawe means everyone who is older than I am no matter how old they are · and no matter whether they're living or dead.

So, when I walk into a room and greet all of you, as *Hom aalhasshinaawe, hom chawe* · I am addressing all of · you who are either older or younger than I · and everybody else · in a way, who has ever lived.

Or who will.

They don't just wait around for stories to remind them of this kind of way of thinking · and it's not only when stories happen to occur to them as in those examples I gave · that they think in this way · that they look up and there's the cave that the Aatoshle lived *in* and so *on*.

One thing they do to keep them · constantly reminded of · this · is that every time they eat · they take a little bit of the meat, a little bit of the bread · they sacrifice it to the fire · they say · *Nanaakwe itonaawe* · which means, *Grandfatherly people, eat*, again meaning · all those who are old enough to be my grandfathers.

You might remember that line from a story [chuckles] · those people are all there, once you've done that, they're present at the meal.

You fed them, now you can sit down and eat yourself · and they're in a sense present there with you.

They use the fire in the fireplace in another way to remind them · if a fire makes a lot of noise in your fireplace, now remember this · I'm serious.

Remember this · when the fire makes a lot of noise in your fireplace, it means that you have forgotten to feed the ancestors.

Or rather, the elders · and you'd better take care of that · that's their voice, that loud noise that the fire makes sometimes.

So · in one way or another they manage to · live constantly · in the presence of the past.

We all do that, but they're aware of it · that they're doing that.

This doesn't mean · that in a traditional culture that lives always in the presence of the past · that you can't do anything new, it doesn't mean that you *can't*, absolutely *can't* have electricity · doesn't mean that you can't have a car · it just means that none of those things · had better make you forget · that you're also living with all of the past.

You are · responsible · for being · conscious · of the whole history of mankind · as often as you can · as you go about your daily life.

It's a responsibility.

It's a responsibility that · we trick ourselves out of · with history books, with archives · with museums · thinking we can file away the past · and appoint certain experts to worry about it.

Historians, anthropologists, archaeologists · but we haven't escaped it at all.

Just made it into an angry ghost.

So, we've got a mystery here · the story · has to be · connected up · with the past · and it has to be right here in front of us.

And it is precisely · the oral medium · which makes this possible.

An oral story is not an object [as if holding an object in the hand] · an object of art or any other kind of object · it is an action, it is something *I do*.

It's an action that's *now* · and that speaks · of ancient things.

If we get into · storing *that* in a *book* · we've begun · to forget.

We begin to attribute the past to that book which if we please we can put up on the shelf and forget.

A book that was published in 1789, that was published in 1801, that was published in 1902.

Those are like *tombstones*.

The story is what I'm telling · *now* · with my own breath.
With my own body.

Once you come to *that* realization · then you've got to figure out · if you want to · bring this experience back · from the field · if you're going to translate, if you're going to tell that story to other people who can't speak Zuni · you've got to figure out · how to turn that same trick · in English.

That means that · the work of translation isn't *done* when you've finished getting it all on the *page*.

It means you also have to figure out how · what's on that page · should be spoken · aloud by someone reading it.

The end point of the translation becomes not · *this* that I *hold* in my *hand* [as if holding a book] · but something that I might *say* sometime on a particular *occasion*.

This means · that · when you listen to those stories · figuring out how to translate them · how to tell them in English · you have to notice that · when a person *speaks* · as opposed to writing · he can [whispering] whisper or SHOUT · he can build up to a creSCENDO · he can insert a long · silence.

He can stretch out a word very lo——ng · he can go up like this, he can go · [continuously raising the voice] aaaaaaAAAH · when something in the story is going *up* · he can go [continuously lowering the voice] AAAaaaaaah · when somebody's going down a ladder in the story.

You can [muttering] mutter while you tell a story · and you can [speaking distinctly] speak very distinctly.

You can change your whole mode of delivery · you can make one of the characters speak a different dialect as the · Paiute do, and especially the peoples in the · Plateau.

You can give him a foreign accent · Coyote always speaks in another dialect or in a foreign accent or · sometimes · you make him, uh, have a speech defect of some sort.

Coyote, he might even have a harelip · [barely intelligible] and talk like this.

There are other ways of changing your whole mode of delivery.

[chanting] You may deliver a line like thiis · or else you may deliver a line that goes like this · you may even start singing · you may start to speak very · [uncertainly] weakly.

[hoarsely] You can speak hoarsely.

You can [low and gravelly] get low and gravelly.

You can speak [with strain] with pain, you can speak [expansively] with pleasure.

You can sigh · you can yawn · [smiling] smile · [scowling] scowl · suddenly look at someone [looking at someone] in the audience.

Say someone went *that* way [indicates east] · toward the east.

Show how big something is · *It was about that high* [indicates something about chest height].

You can rap [rapping three times] on the table.

You can blow cigarette smoke.

If you can take account of all those sorts of things in translation · working up a kind of performable script · you still haven't done your job, because now you've got to · tell *that* story · with your breath · you have to do it · more than once, too · to really begin, even begin to understand what it's all about · this is if you really finally want to understand what a story *is*.

[seriously] You have to tell it.

Put that another way, you must *be* · while you're telling it · everyone in that story, and you must be right there in the story.

If you're successful you make it like it's right in front of you, and if you're really successful · it's like it's right in front of the audience too.

Right in front of them.

And it's talking about ancient things.

Now we've begun to do our job.

Right there.

We've begun to do the the real job.

Now, whether they're expecting it or not, that story · will act upon the audience · in ways that they don't even suspect.

Might even make them just a tiny little bit · like a Zuni · in a way they didn't even suspect.

There are two ways of doing that, the other way is to eat Indian *food*.

There are two ways, eat the food · listen to the words.

Well · now · if we come right along until · just this past fall · I became aware for the first time · that this kind of stance · toward · the matter of storytelling · had a · kind of ready-made · philosophical argument.

To go with it · I feel all the surer · about adopting this particular · stance, if that's the word for it · because I arrived at it without · having it explained to me in the classroom.

The important things one learns are the things one *realizes*.

Not the things one takes on *faith*.

And that is hermeneutic phenomenology · which is quite a mouthful · all it really means · in the end · probably is learning to · tell the story, it means reducing your · distance · reducing the distance between you and that story · in the words of Paul Ricoeur · *living in the aura of the meaning* of the story · really opening up your ears to that text.

Not asking yourself all sorts of irrelevant · questions · that would attempt to pin that story down to a specific historical and cultural context.

Now what I haven't seen any of the phenomenologists · really explore is the fact that once you've *done* that · you can't really re-establish the distance · that you gave up for a moment.

If you've gone that far into · a story · you then have an obligation · to that story · if you like to think about it this way · it's now become a part of *your* past too · and the past of all the people that you've ever told it also · and like everything else about the past that's something we have to keep constantly · in mind · as the meaning is revealed to us constantly every day as we live.

I think · I can · sum up that point better though by using the words of · a Santo Domingo · named Larry Bird · who once · put it this way · [clearing throat] *When you grow up · you don't ask a lot of questions · you* listen.

You wait · and as you live your life · the answers to all the questions that you had will come to you · as you live.

Now · I'll · tell you one of those stories.

[opening a book] My apologies for · relying on the · script · this is the story of the Shumeekuli.

Shumeekuli · is something like a kachina, one of these · beings that wears a mask whenever you see him · when they're among themselves they don't wear masks, when they come to visit people they do.

Kachinas live over *there* [indicates west] · but the Shumeekuli live over here, to the east [indicates east].

It's a *flat* [hand as if pressing on a vertical surface] · kind of mask · they come in *six colors* · they come in · yellow [indicates north] · and in blue [indicates west] · and in red [south] · and in white [east] · and in multicolored [motions upward] and in black [motions downward].

And this is a story mostly about the Shumeekuli who · has to do with · the east · the white one.

I've chosen this particular story because · this is one that can be told at any time of year, it's getting a little late to tell stories, and they really shouldn't be told in the day like this either.

This is a story, though, that can be told at any time of day or night · and whether there are snakes around or not.

The thing about that · that's another · good point too · a book · you can take down off the shelf any time you please, 24 hours a day · twelve months a year.

Or any year.

In an oral culture · there are some kinds of words that you allow yourself to hear only maybe · at certain seasons.

Or at certain times of day · maybe even only once a year · and other things that you hear only every fourth year, and other things that you hear only · every · *eighth* year.

And that's part of the whole secret of making a story really *fit* · here · now · in *this place*.

It's got to fit the calendar, too.

Well then · there were villagers ar Hawikku · there were villagers at *Gypsum Place* · there were villagers at *Wind Place* · there were villagers · all around · and the priest · there at Gypsum Place · spoke of having a Yaaya, a Yaaya dance.

When the word went out, people from a——ll the villages started gathering.

The date had been set and · they lived on · for four nights · they practiced the Yaaya.

The Yaaya practice went on, and · they were gathering · for four nights they kept gathering · o——n it went, until · the day came · and the *Spiral Society* · went into session, and on the *eve* of the ceremony their *Shumeekuli* dancers came in.

The Shumeekuli came.

And · the next day · was to be the day · for dancing the Yaaya.

Then it was the morning of the dance.

On the morning of the dance · the villagers gathered · and then · they were going to · get up to dance.

O——n they went until at noon they stopped to eat, and when they had eaten they got up again · they got up in the afternoon · and when they had done about · two sets · there were four rings of dancers.

Then the *Spiral Society* brought in their · *Shumeekuli*.

And when these were brought in, the Horned Ones were also brought in.

They kept on dancing this way *until their* · White Shumeekuli came, he was brought in when · there were four rings of dancers · and a——ll the villagers had gathered · there was a *big crowd*, a big crowd and · the dance kept on · their White Shumeekuli · kept going around the tree, he danced around it, and for some reason · [softly] he went crazy.

The people *held on tight*, but somehow he broke through their rings and *ran away*.

He ran and ran · and they ran after him.

They ran after him, but · they couldn't catch him and still they kept after him shouting as they went · he was far ahead, the White Shumeekuli was fa——r ahead of them.

They kept on going until · they came near Shuminnkya.

Someone was herding out there.

He was herding, his sheep were spread out [sweeping gesture toward the east] when · they came along there shouting.

[chanting] *The——re goes our White Shu——meekuli running a—wa——y whoever is out there please help us* · CATCH HIM FOR US.

That's what they were shouting as they kept after him · [in a low voice] *Ah yes, there's a Yaaya dance today, something must've happened.*

That's what the herder was thinking about.

They were coming closer.

After a time their Shumeekuli · [looking westward] came into view.

He was still running.

The herder stood · under a tree [indicates an imaginary tree in front of him] · where he was going to pass [indicates a path from the west past the tree] and waited for him there [stands beside the tree facing west].

Then · going straight on · the Shumeekuli headed for the place [indicates the path again] · where the herder stood.

Sure enough, just as he · came up past the *tree* · the herder *caught* him [grabbing with both arms] for them.

[facing the audience again] There he caught him.

The White Shumeekuli · who had run away from the Yaaya dance.

The others came to get him · and took him back.

They brought him back, and when they · tried to unmask him · the mask · was stuck · to his face.

Some of his · flesh peeled off [pulls at his cheek].

He was changing over.

Then · the one who had come · as the White Shumeekuli · lived only four days · before he died.

They lived o——n until, at *Zuni* · when the Middle Place had become known · the date was again set for the Yaaya · and when the date had been set they gathered for four nights.

They gathered for practice, that is the way · they lived · and when the day of the Yaaya arrived · the villagers came together on the morning of the dance.

Again the *Yaaya* · dance began · and again the Shumeekuli dancers were brought in · they were brought in and they danced properly, but then there came one who costumed himself as the · [slowly] *White* Shumeekuli, and he went around · until it happened *again*.

He went crazy.

He struggled then, but · this time they held onto him.

It happens when · ever somebody impersonates that one · because of the *flesh* that got inside *that mask* in *former times* · when someone comes into the Yaaya dance as the White Shumeekuli · [with precision] something will inevitably happen to his mind.

This is what · happened and because this happened · the White Shumeekuli came to be feared.

That's all.

JEROME ROTHENBERG

Total Translation: An Experiment in the Presentation of American Indian Poetry

*Jerome Rothenberg has worked for two decades toward the enlargement of poetics by ethnopoetic and other means ("total translation," poetics of performance, etc.) involving a spectrum of assemblages and translations from multiple sources (see above, p. 99). The ethnopoetic aspects of the work are to be found in his own poetry (*Poland/1931, A Seneca Journal*), in anthologies such as the present one,* Technicians of the Sacred, Shaking the Pumpkin, America a Prophecy, *and* A Big Jewish Book, *and in magazines such as* Alcheringa *and* New Wilderness Letter.

At the time of this writing (1969), the other key works toward an approximately "total" translation were those of Dennis Tedlock, Dell Hymes, and David P. McAllester, each of whom is represented in the present volume.

It wasn't really a "problem," as these things are sometimes called, but to get closer to a way of poetry that had concerned me from years before, though until this project I'd only been able to approach it at a far remove. I'd been translating "tribal" poetry (the latest, still imperfect substitute I can find for "primitive," which continues to bother me) out of books; doing my versions from earlier translations into languages I could cope with, including English. Toward the end of my work on *Technicians* I met Stanley Diamond, who directed me to the Senecas in upstate New York, & David McAllester, ethnomusicologist at Wesleyan University, who showed me how a few songs worked in Navajo. With their help (& a nod from Dell Hymes as well) I later was able to get Wenner-Gren Foundation support to carry on a couple of experiments in the translation of American Indian poetry. I'm far enough into them by now to say a little about what I've been doing.

*   *   *

In the Summer of 1968 I began to work simultaneously with two sources of Indian poetry. Settling down a mile from the Cold Spring settlement of the Allegany (Seneca) Reservation at Steamburg, New York, I was near enough to friends who were traditional songmen to work with them on the translation of sacred & secular song-poems. At the same time David McAllester was sending me recordings, transcriptions, literal translations & his own freer reworkings of a series of seventeen "horse-songs" that had been the property of Frank Mitchell, a Navajo singer from Chinle, Arizona (born: 1881, died: 1967). Particularly with the Senecas (where I didn't know in the first instance what, if anything, I was going to get) my first concern was with the translation process itself. While I'll limit myself to that right now, I should at least say (things never seem to be clear unless you say them) that if I hadn't also come up with matter that I could "internalize," I would have foundered long before this.

The big question, which I was immediately aware of with both poetries, was if &

SOURCE: *Jerome Rothenberg, Pre-Faces, pages 76–92.*

how to handle those elements in the original works that weren't translatable literally. As with most Indian poetry, the voice carried many sounds that weren't, strictly speaking, "words." These tended to disappear or be attenuated in translation, as if they weren't really there. But they *were* there & were at least as important as the words themselves. In both Navajo & Seneca many songs consisted of nothing but those "meaningless" vocables (not free "scat" either but fixed sounds recurring from performance to performance). Most other songs had both meaningful & non-meaningful elements, & such songs (McAllester told me for the Navajo) were often spoken of, *qua* title, by their meaningless burdens. Similar meaningless sounds, Dell Hymes had pointed out for some Kwakiutl songs, might in fact be keys to the songs' structures: "something usually disregarded, the refrain or so-called 'nonsense syllables' . . . in fact of fundamental importance . . . both structural clue & microcosm." [See above, p. 349.]

So there were all these indications that the exploration of "pure sound" wasn't beside the point of those poetries but at or near their heart: all of this coincidental too with concern for the sound-poem among a number of modern poets. Accepting its meaning-fulness here, I more easily accepted it there. I also realized (with the Navajo especially) that there were more than simple refrains involved: that we, as translators & poets, had been taking a rich *oral* poetry & translating it to be read primarily for meaning, thus denuding it to say the least.

Here's an immediate example of what I mean. In the first of Frank Mitchell's seventeen horse-songs, the opening line comes out as follows in McAllester's transcription:

> dzo-wowode sileye shi, dza-na desileye shiyi,
> dzanadi sileye shiya'e

but the same segment given "as spoken" reads:

> dząądi silá shi dząądi silá shi dząądi silá shi

which translates as "over-here it-is-there·(&) mine" repeated three times. So does the line as sung if all you're accounting for is the meaning. In other words, translate only for meaning & you get the three-fold repetition of an unchanging single statement; but in the Navajo each time it's delivered there's a sharp departure from the spoken form: thus three distinct sound-events, not one-in-triplicate!

I know neither Navajo nor Seneca except for bits of information picked up from grammar books & such (also the usual social fall-out among the Senecas: "cat," "dog," "thank you," "you're welcome," numbers one to ten, "uncle," "father," & my Indian name). But even from this far away, I can (with a little help from my friends) be aware of my options as translator. Let me try, then, to respond to *all* the sounds I'm made aware of, to let that awareness touch off responses or events in the English. I don't want to set English words to Indian music, but to respond poem-for-poem in the attempt to work out a "total" translation—not only of the words but of all sounds connected with the poem, including finally the music itself.

*   *   *

Seneca & Navajo are very different worlds, & what's an exciting procedure for one

may be deadening or irrelevant for the other. The English translation should match the
character of the Indian original: take that as a goal & don't worry about how literal you're
otherwise being. Walter Lowenfels calls poetry ''the continuation of journalism by other
means,'' & maybe that holds too for translation-as-poem. I translate, then, as a way of
reporting what I've sensed or seen of an other's situation: true as far as possible to ''my''
image of the life & thought of the source.

Living with the Senecas helped in that sense. I don't know how much stress to put
on this, but I know that in so far as I developed a strategy for translation from Seneca, I
tried to keep to approaches I felt were consistent with their life-style. I can hardly speak
of the poetry without using words that would describe the people as well. Not that it's
easy to sum-up any people's poetry or its frame-of-mind, but since one is always doing it
in translation, I'll attempt it also by way of description.

Seneca poetry, when it uses words at all, works in sets of short songs, minimal
realizations colliding with each other in marvelous ways, a very light, very pointed
play-of-the-mind, nearly always just a step away from the comic (even as their masks
are), the words set out in clear relief against the ground of the (''meaningless'') refrain.
Clowns stomp & grunt through the longhouse, but in subtler ways too the encouragement
to ''play'' is always a presence. Said the leader of the longhouse religion at Allegany,
explaining why the seasonal ceremonies ended with a gambling game: the idea of a
religion was to reflect the *total* order of the universe while providing an outlet for *all*
human needs, the need for play not least among them. Although it pretty clearly doesn't
work out as well nowadays as that makes it sound—the orgiastic past & the ''doings''
(happenings) in which men were free to live-out their dreams dimming from generation
to generation—still the resonance, the ancestral permissiveness, keeps being felt in
many ways. Sacred occasions may be serious & necessary, but it doesn't take much for
the silence to be broken by laughter: thus, says Richard Johnny John, if you call for a
medicine ceremony of the mystic animals & it turns out that no one's sick & in need of
curing, the head-one tells the others: ''I leave it up to you folks & if you want to have a
good time, have a good time!'' He knows they will anyway.

I take all of that as cue: to let my moves be directed by a sense of the songs & of the
attitudes surrounding them. Another thing I try not to overlook is that the singers & I,
while separated in Seneca, are joined in English. That they have to translate for me is a
problem at first, but the problem suggests its own solution. Since they're bilingual,
sometimes beautifully so, why not work from that instead of trying to get around it?
Their English, fluent while identifiably Senecan, is as much a commentary on where they
are as mine is on where I am. Given the ''minimal'' nature of much of the poetry (one of
its *strongest* features, in fact) there's no need for a dense response in English. Instead I
can leave myself free to structure the final poem by using their English as a base: a
particular enough form of the language to itself be an extra means for the extension of
reportage through poetry & translation.

I end up collaborating & happy to do so, since translation (maybe poetry as well)
has always involved that kind of thing for me. The collaboration can take a number of
forms. At one extreme I have only to make it possible for the other man to take over: in
this case, to set up or simply to encourage a situation in which a man who's never thought
of himself as a ''poet'' can begin to structure his utterances with a care for phrasing &
spacing that drives them toward poetry. *Example*: Dick Johnny John & I had taped his
Seneca version of the thanking prayer that opens all longhouse gatherings & were

translating it phrase by phrase. He had decided to write it down himself, to give the translation to his sons, who from oldest to youngest were progressively losing the Seneca language. I could follow his script from where I sat, & the method of punctuation he was using seemed special to me, since in letters & such he punctuates more or less conventionally. Anyway, I got his punctuation down along with his wording, with which he was taking a lot of time both in response to my questions & from his desire ''to word it just the way it says there.'' In setting up the result, I let the periods in his prose version mark the ends of lines, made some vocabulary choices that we'd left hanging, & tried for the rest to keep clear of what was after all his poem. Later I titled it *Thank You: A Poem in 17 Parts*, & wrote a note on it for *El Corno Emplumado*, where it was printed in English & Spanish. This is the first of the seventeen sections:

> Now so many people that are in this place.
> In our meeting place.
> It starts when two people see each other.
> They greet each other.
> Now we greet each other.
> Now he thought.
> I will make the Earth where some people can walk around.
>
> I have created them, now this has happened.
> We are walking on it.
> Now this time of the day.
> We give thanks to the Earth.
> This is the way it should be in our minds.

> [*Note*. The set-up in English doesn't, as far as I can tell, reproduce the movement of the Seneca text. More interestingly it's itself a consideration of that movement: is in fact Johnny John's reflections upon the values, the relative strengths of elements in his text. The poet is to a great degree concerned with what-stands-out & where, & his phrasing reveals it, no less here than in any other poem.]

Even when being more active myself, I would often defer to others in the choice of words. Take, for example, a set of seven Woman's Dance songs with words, composed by Avery Jimerson & translated with help from his wife, Fidelia. Here the procedure was for Avery to record the song, for Fidelia to paraphrase it in English, then for the three of us to work out a transcription & word-by-word translation by a process of question & answer. Only afterwards would I actively come into it, to try to work out a poem in English with enough swing to it to return more or less to the area of song. *Example*. The paraphrase of the 6th Song reads:

> Very nice, nice, when our mothers do the
> ladies' dance. Graceful, nice, very nice, when our
> mothers do the ladies' dance . . .

while the word-by-word, including the ''meaningless'' refrain, reads:

> hey heya yo oh ho
> nice nice nice-it-is

> when-they-dance-the-ladies-dance
> our-mothers
> gahnoweyah heyah
> graceful it-is
> nice nice nice-it-is
> when-they-dance-the-ladies-dance
> our-mothers
> gahnoweyah heyah (& repeat).

In doing *these* songs, I decided in fact to translate for meaning, since the meaningless vocables used by Jimerson were only the standard markers that turn up in all the woman's songs: *hey heyah yo* to mark the opening, *gahnoweyah heyah* to mark the internal transitions. (In my translation, I sometimes use a simple "hey," "oh" or "yeah" as a rough equivalent, but let the movement of the English determine its position.) I also decided not to fit English words to Jimerson's melody, regarding that as a kind of oil-&-water treatment, but to suggest (as with most poetry) a music through the normally pitched speaking voice. For the rest I was following Fidelia Jimerson's lead:

> hey it's nice it's nice it's nice
> to see them yeah to see
> our mothers do the ladies' dances
> oh it's graceful & it's
> nice it's nice it's very nice
> to see them hey to see
> our mothers do the ladies' dances.

With other kinds of song-poems I would also, as often as not, stick close to the translation-as-given, departing from that to better get the point of the whole across in English, to normalize the word order where phrases in the literal translation appeared in their original Seneca sequence, or to get into the play-of-the-thing on my own. The most important group of songs I was working on was a sacred cycle called *Idos* (ee-dos) in Seneca—in English either *Shaking the Pumpkin* or, more ornately, *The Society of the Mystic Animals*. Like most Seneca songs *with* words (most Seneca songs are in fact *without* words), the typical pumpkin song contains a single statement, or a single statement alternating with a row of vocables, which is repeated anywhere from three to six or seven times. Some songs are nearly identical with some others (same melody & vocables, slight change in words) but aren't necessarily sung in sequence. In a major portion of the ceremony, in fact, a fixed order for the songs is completely abandoned, & each person present takes a turn at singing a ceremonial (medicine) song of his own choice. There's room here too for messing around.

Dick Johnny John was my collaborator on the Pumpkin songs, & the basic wording is therefore his. My intention was to account for all vocal sounds in the original but—as a more "interesting" way of handling the minimal structures & allowing a very clear, very pointed emergence of perceptions—to translate the poems onto the page, as with "concrete" or other types of minimal poetry. Where several songs showed a concurrence of structure, I allowed myself the option of treating them individually or combining them into one. I've deferred singing until some future occasion.

Take the opening songs of the ceremony. These are fixed pieces sung by the ceremonial leader (*hajaswas*) before he throws the meeting open to the individual singers. The melody & structure of the first nine are identical: very slow, a single line of words ending with a string of sounds, etc., the pattern identical until the last go-round, when the song ends with a grunting expulsion of breath into a weary "ugh" sound. I had to get all of that across: the bareness, the regularity, the deliberateness of the song, along with the basic meaning, repeated vocables, emphatic terminal sound, & (still following Johnny John's reminder to play around with it "if everything's alright") a little something of my own. The song whose repeated line is:

The animals are coming by *heh eh heh* (or *heh eh-eh-eh he*)

can then become:

<pre>
        T   H E H E H H E H
        h   H E H E H H E H
        e
The animals are coming by   H E H U H H E H
        n   H E H E H H E H
        i
        m   H E H E H H E H
        a
        l
        s
</pre>

& the next one:

<pre>
        T   H E H E H H E H
        h   H E H E H H E H
        e
The doings were beginning   H E H U H H E H
        o   H E H E H H E H
        i
        n   H E H E H H E H
        g
        s
</pre>

& so forth: each poem set, if possible, on its own page, as further analogue to the slowness, the deliberate pacing of the original.

The use of vertical titles is the only move I make without immediate reference to the Seneca version: the rest I'd feel to be programmed by elements in the original prominent enough for me to respond to in the movement from oral to paginal structure. Where the song comes without vocables, I don't supply them but concentrate on presentation of the words. Thus in the two groups of "crow songs," the first is a simple translation-for-meaning:

(1)

the crows came in

(2)

the crows sat down

while the other ("in the manner of Zukofsky") puns off the Seneca sound:

yehgagaweeyo (lit. that pretty crow) becomes "yond cawcrow's way-out"

&

hongyasswahyaenee (lit. that [pig]-meat's for me) becomes "Hog (yes!) swine you're mine"

—trying at the same time to let something of the meaning come through.

A motive behind the punning was, I suppose, the desire to bring across (i.e., "translate") the feeling of the Seneca word for crow (*gaga or kaga*), which is at the same time an imitation of the bird's voice. In another group—three songs about the owl—I pick up the vocables suggesting the animal's call & shape them into outline of a giant owl, within which frame the poems are printed. But that's only where the mimicry of the original is strong enough to trigger an equivalent move in translation; otherwise my inclination is to *present* analogues to the full range of vocal sound, etc., but not to *represent* the poem's subject as "mere picture."

The variety of possible moves is obviously related to the variety—semantic & aural—of the cycle itself.

[*Note*. Behind it all there's a hidden motive too: not simply to make clear the world of the original, but to do so at some remove from the song itself: to reflect the song without the "danger" of presenting any part of it (the melody, say) exactly as given: thus to have it while not having it, in deference to the sense of secrecy & localization that's so important to those for whom the songs are sacred & alive. So the changes resulting from translation are, in this instance, not only inevitable but desired, or, as another Seneca said to me: "We wouldn't want the songs to get so far away from us; no, the songs would be too lonely."]

*   *   *

My decision with the Navajo horse-songs was to work with the sound as sound: a reflection in itself of the difference between Navajo & Seneca song structure. For Navajo (as already indicated) is much fuller, much denser, twists words into new shapes or fills up the spaces between words by insertion of a wide range of "meaningless" vocables, making it misleading to translate primarily for meaning or, finally, to think of *total* translation in any terms but those of sound. Look, for example, at the number of free vocables in the following excerpt from McAllester's relatively literal translation of the 16th Horse-Song:

(nana na) Sun- (Yeye ye) Standing-within (neye ye) Boy

(Heye ye) truly his horses
('Eye ye) abalone horses
('Eye ye) made of sunrays
(Neye ye) their bridles

(Gowo wo) coming on my right side
(Jeye yeye) coming into my hand (yeye neyowo 'ei).

Now this, which even so doesn't show the additional word distortions that turn up in the singing, might be brought closer to English word order & translated for meaning alone as something like

Boy who stands inside the Sun
with your horses that are
abalone horses
bridles
made of sunrays
rising on my right side
coming to my hand
etc.

But what a difference from the fantastic way the sounds cut through the words & between them from the first line of the original on.

It was the possibility of working with all that sound, finding my own way into it in English, that attracted me now—that & a quality in Mitchell's voice I found irresistible. It was, I think, that the music was so clearly within range of the language: it was song & it was poetry, & it seemed possible at least that the song issued from the poetry, was an extension of it or rose inevitably from the juncture of words & other vocal sounds. So many of us had already become interested in this kind of thing as poets, that it seemed natural to me to be in a situation where the poetry would be leading me towards a (new) music *it* was generating.

I began with the 10th Horse-Song, which had been the first one Mitchell sang when McAllester was recording him. At that point I didn't know if I'd do much more than quote or allude to the vocables: possibly pull them or something like them into the English. I was *writing* at first, working on the words by sketching in phrases that seemed natural to my own sense of the language. In the 10th Song there's a division of speakers: the main voice is that of Enemy Slayer or Dawn Boy, who first brought horses to The People, but the chorus is sung by his father, the Sun, telling him to take spirit horses & other precious animals & goods to the house of his mother, Changing Woman. The literal translation of the refrain—*(to) the woman, my son*—seemed a step away from how we'd say it, though normal enough in Navajo. It was with the sense that, whatever distortions in sound the Navajo showed, the syntax was natural, that I changed McAllester's suggested reading to *go to her my son*, & his opening line:

Boy-brought-up-within-the-Dawn, it is I, I who am that one

(lit. *being that one*, with a suggestion of causation), to:

> Because I was the boy raised in the dawn.

At the same time I was, I thought, getting it down to more or less the economy of phrasing of the original.

I went through the first seven or eight lines like that but still hadn't gotten to the vocables. McAllester's more "factual" approach—reproducing the vocables exactly—seemed wrong to me on one major count. In the Navajo the vocables give a very clear sense of continuity from the verbal material; i.e., the vowels in particular show a rhyming or assonantal relationship between the "meaningless" & meaningful segments:

'Esdza shiye'	e hye-la	'esdza shiye'	e hye-la ŋaŋa yeye 'e
The woman, my son	*(voc.)*	*The woman, my son*	*(voc.)*

whereas the English words for this & many other situations in the poem are, by contrast to the Navajo, more rounded & further back in the mouth. Putting the English words ("son" here but "dawn," "home," "upon," "blown," etc. further on) against the Navajo vocables denies the musical coherence of the original & destroys the actual flow.

I decided to *translate* the vocables & from that point was already playing with the possibility of *translating* other elements in the songs not usually handled by translation. It also seemed important to get as far away as I could from *writing*. So I began to speak, then sing my own words over Mitchell's tape, replacing his vocables with sounds relevant to me, then putting my version on a fresh tape, having now to work it in its own terms. It wasn't an easy thing either for me to break the silence or go beyond the narrow pitch levels of my speaking voice, & I was still finding it more natural in that early version to replace the vocables with small English words (it's hard for a word-poet to lose words completely), hoping some of their semantic force would lessen with reiteration:

> Go to her my son & one & go to her my son & one & one & none & gone
> Go to her my son & one & go to her my son & one & one & none & gone
>
> Because I was the boy raised in the dawn & one & go to her my son & one & one & none & gone
> & leaving from the house the bluestone home & one & go to her my son & one & one & one & none & gone
> & leaving from the house the shining home & one & go to her my son & one & one & none & gone
> & from the swollen house my breath has blown & one & go to her my son & one & one & none & gone

& so on. In the transference too—likely enough because my ear is so damn slow—I found I was considerably altering Mitchell's melody; but really that was part of the translation process also: a change responsive to the translated sounds & words I was developing.

In singing the 10th Song I was able to bring the small words (vocable substitutions) even further into the area of pure vocal sound (the difference, if it's clear from the spelling, between *one, none & gone and wnn, nnnn & gahn*): soundings that would carry into the other songs at an even greater remove from the discarded meanings. [See fig. 19.] What I was doing in one sense was contributing & then obliterating my own level of meaning, while in another I was as much as recapitulating the history of the vocables themselves, at least according to one of the standard explanations that sees them as remnants of archaic words that have been emptied of meaning: a process I could still sense elsewhere in the Horse-Songs—for example, where the sound *howo* turns up as both a "meaningless" vocable & a distorted form of the word *hoghan* = house. But even if I was doing something like that in an accelerated way, that wasn't the real point of it for me. Rather what I was getting at was the establishment of a series of sounds that were assonant with the range of my own vocabulary in the translation, & to which I could refer whenever the Navajo sounds for which they were substitutes turned up in Mitchell's songs.

In spite of carryovers, these basic soundings were different for each song (more specifically, for each *pair* of songs), & I found, as I moved from one song to another, that I had to establish my sound equivalencies before going into the actual translation. For this I made use of the traditional way the Navajo songs begin: with a short string of vocables that will be picked up (in whole or in part) as the recurring burden of the song. I found I could set most of my basic vocables or vocable-substitutes into the opening, using it as a key to which I could refer when necessary to determine sound substitutions, not only for the vocables but for word distortions in the meaningful segments of the poems. There was a cumulative effect here too. The English vocabulary of the 10th Song—strong on back vowels, semivowels, glides & nasals—influenced the choice of vocables: the vocables influenced further vocabulary choices & vocables in the other songs. (*Note*. The vocabulary of many of the songs is very close to begin with, the most significant differences in "pairs" of songs coming from the alternation of blue & white color symbolism.) Finally, the choice of sounds influenced the style of my singing by setting up a great deal of resonance I found I could control to serve as a kind of drone behind my voice. In ways like this the translation was assuming a life of its own.

With the word distortions too, it seemed to me that the most I should do was *approximate* the degree of distortion in the original. McAllester had provided two Navajo texts—the words as sung & as they would be if spoken—& I aimed at roughly the amount of variation I could discern between the two. I further assumed that every perceivable change was significant, & there were indications in fact of a surprising degree of precision in Mitchell's delivery, where even what seemed to be false steps or accidents might really be gestures to intensify the special or sacred powers of the song at the points in question. Songs 10 & 11, for example, were structurally paired, & in both songs Mitchell seemed to be fumbling at the beginning of the 21st line after the opening choruses. Maybe it was accidental & maybe not, but I figured I might as well go wrong by overdoing the distortion, here & wherever else I had the choice.

So I followed where Mitchell led me, responding to all moves of his I was aware of & letting them program or initiate the moves I made in translation. All of this within

THE TENTH HORSE-SONG OF FRANK MITCHELL (BLUE)

Key: wnn Ngahn n NNN

Go to her my son N wnn & go to her my son N wnn N wnnn N nnnn
   N gahn
Go to her my son N wnn & go to her my son N wnn N wnnn N nnnn
   N gahn

Because I was thnboyngnng raised ing the dawn NwnnN go to
   her my son N wnn N wnn N nnnn N gahn
& leafing from thuhuhuh house the bluestone home N gahn N wnn
   N go to her my son N wnn N wnn N nnnn N gahn
& leafing from the (rurur) house the shining home NwnnnN go to
   her my son N wnn N wnn N nnnn N gahn
& leafing from thm(mm) (mm)swollen house my breath has blown
   NwnnN go to her my son N wnn N wnn N nnnn N gahn
& leafing from thnn house the holy home NwnnN go to her my son
   N wnnn N wnn ( ) nnnn N gahn
& from the house hfff precious cloth we walk upon N wnn N nnnn
   N go to her my son N wnn N wnn N nnnn N gahn
with (p)(p)rayersticks that are blue NwnnN go to her my son N
   wnn wnn N nnnn N gahn
with my feathers that're blue NwnnN go to her my son N wnn N
   wnn N nnnn N gahn
with my spirit horses that 're blue NwnnN go to her my son N
   wnn N wnn ( ) nnnn N gahn
with my spirit horses that 're blue & dawn & wnnN go to her
   my son N wnn N wnn N nnnn N gahn
with my spirit horses that rrr bluestone & Rwnn N wnn N go to
   her my son N wnn N wnn N nnnn N gahn
with my horses that hrrr bluestone & rrwnn N wnn N go to her
   my son N wnn N wnn N nnnn N gahn
with cloth of evree(ee)ee kind to draw (nn nn) them on & on N

FIGURE 19.   "The Tenth Horse-Song of Frank Mitchell" in a "total translation" by Jerome
Rothenberg (excerpt).

obvious limits: those imposed by the field of sound I was developing in English. . . .
Throughout the songs I've now been into, I've worked in pretty much that way: the
relative densities determined by the original, the final form by the necessities of the poem
as it took shape for me. Obviously too, there were larger patterns to keep in mind, when a
particular variation occurred in a series of positions, etc. To say any more about
that—though the approach changed in the later songs I worked on, towards a more
systematic handling—would be to put greater emphasis on method than any poem can
bear. More important for me was actually being in the stimulus & response situation,

certainly the most *physical* translation I've ever been involved in. I hope that that much comes through for anyone who hears these sung.

But there was still another step I had to take. While the tape I was working from was of Mitchell singing by himself, in actual performance he would be accompanied by all those present with him at the blessing. The typical Navajo performance pattern, as McAllester described it to me, calls for each person present to follow the singer to whatever degree he can. The result is highly individualized singing (only the ceremonial singer is likely to know all of it the right way) & leads to an actual indeterminacy of performance. Those who can't follow the words at all may make up their own vocal sounds—anything, in effect, for the sake of participation.

I saw the indeterminacy, etc., as key to the further extension of the poems into the area of total translation & total performance. (Instrumentation & ritual-events would be further "translation" possibilities, but the Horse-Songs are rare among Navajo poems in not including them.) To work out the extension for multiple voices, I again made use of the tape recorder, this time of a four-track system on which I laid down the following as typical of the possibilities on hand:

TRACK ONE. A clean recording of the lead voice.

TRACK TWO. A voice responsive to the first but showing less word distortion & occasional free departures from the text.

TRACK THREE. A voice limited to pure-sound improvisations on the meaningless elements in the text.

TRACK FOUR. A voice similar to that on the second track but distorted by means of a violin amplifier placed against the throat & set at "echo" or "tremolo." To be used only as a barely audible background filler for the others.

Once the four tracks were recorded (I've only done it so far for the 12th song)[1] I had them balanced & mixed onto a monaural tape. In that way I could present the poems as I'd conceived them & as poetry in fact had always existed for men like Mitchell—to be heard without reference to their incidental appearance on the page.

                                        *   *   *

Translation is carry-over. It is a means of delivery & of bringing to life. It begins with a forced change of language, but a change too that opens up the possibility of greater understanding. Everything in these song-poems is finally translatable: words, sounds, voice, melody, gesture, event, etc., in the reconstitution of a unity that would be shattered by approaching each element in isolation. A full & total experience begins it, which only a total translation can fully bring across.

---

[1]A final recorded version—composed along somewhat altered lines—appeared nearly ten years later as *6 Horse Songs for 4 Voices* (New Wilderness Audiographics, 1978). (Eds.)

By saying which, I'm not trying to coerce anyone (least of all myself) with the idea of a single relevant approach to translation. I'll continue, I believe, to translate in part or in any other way I feel moved to; nor would I deny the value of handling words or music or events as separate phenomena. It's possible too that a prose description of the song-poems, etc. might tell pretty much what was happening in & around them, but no amount of description can provide the *immediate* perception translation can. One way or other translation makes a poem in this place that's analogous in whole or in part to a poem in that place. The more the translator can perceive of the original—not only the language but, more basically perhaps, the living situation from which it comes &, very much so, the living voice of the singer—the more of it he should be able to deliver. In the same process he will be presenting something—i.e., making something present, or making something as a present—for his own time & place.

DAVID P. McALLESTER
The Tenth Horse Song of Frank Mitchell

Among the great American ethnomusicologists, David P. McAllester has had an eminent sense of the possibilities of an actual poetics emerging from the verbal materials with which he has dealt. His principal area of ethnographic concern has been Navajo, and he has worked with Navajo music and poetry (and their complex interworkings) for close to thirty-five years. The present essay was originally published alongside Jerome Rothenberg's experimental translations of the Navajo horse-songs (see above, pp. 381, 387), for which McAllester served as transmitter and adviser. Though their strategies for translation diverge significantly, McAllester's view, circa 1966, of the spirit of Navajo "ritual communication" is, in fact, a link still held between them:

> Given the emotional weight of mystery and danger, the structure of the poem itself intensifies the mood: much of the text is impenetrable because it is without overt meaning. . . . [The vocables] are specific to the song but at the same time they increase its mystery. . . . But . . . whether [the native listener] knows the story of Enemy Slayer or not, the poem has the double effect of reassuring him in the face of danger and of maintaining over him, as a participating member, the hold of the Navajo tradition. He knows that he is being identified with power and this provides protection in an immediate emergency . . . but the identification with the community is the deeper protection. (*Io* 3: 45–46)

SOURCE: Stony Brook, numbers 3–4, 1969, pages 306–311, 314–315.

Principal works: Enemy Way Music, Peyote Music, Readings in Ethnomusicology, Hogans *(in which he translates and arranges Navajo "house songs/house
poems" along the lines described here), and* Navajo Blessingway Singer *(his
editing, with Charlotte J. Frisbie, of the autobiography of the Navajo* hatali, *Frank
Mitchell).*

There are special responsibilities in writing down a work like this Horse Song for the first
time. The role of the collector is even more crucial than that of the translator. If the poem
has greatness it will undergo many translations, but they will all depend on the accuracy
and sensitivity with which the original text has been recorded. I will begin with some
observations about collecting and then go on to discuss some of my goals in the particular
kind of translation I attempted.

In recording poetic texts from the oral tradition some scholars have been tempted
to leave out repetitions and nonsense syllables on the grounds that they are repetitious
and nonsensical. Dell Hymes has shown how these features may be integral to the artistic
structure. He could have gone further and included the melody to which the poetry is
sung and the gestures, dance, and audience responses which are part of the total effect.
The ideal recording of a Navajo poetic event would be on sound film since an elaborate
ceremonial performance is usually involved, making use of sandpaintings, theater,
costumes, and large numbers of people. However, a complicating factor is that, in many
cases, the performers consider such a performance to be invalidated by the presence of
outsiders, especially obtrusive ones with notebooks, cameras and other equipment. In
the case of these Horse Songs, a private recording session was possible, as a second-best
alternative.

Making a film or tape is only the beginning of the recorder's task. Since poetic
texts are often in archaic or other unusual forms of the language, or distorted by
exigencies of meter or sung melody, very careful work in literal translation must be
carried out on the spot. Often the original performer is the only one who knows exact
shades of meaning, or even any meaning at all. Sensitive collaboration is required
between collector, interpreters and performer if there is to be any hope of accuracy. In
the case of the Horse Song, after the tape had been made I played it over and over while I
wrote out the Navajo text in the presence of the ceremonial practitioner. At the same time
I wrote out the text in its prosodic Navajo form as well, and made an interlinear
word-for-word literal translation.

This time of play-back and query and slow writing-out is an ideal opportunity for
finding out alternative versions, emotional responses to the poem, where the singer
learned it and why, and so on. All of this information is pure gold to the ethnographer and
it often has important implications for the translation. It should all be made available, in
voluminous notes, for the use of hoped-for generations of translators.

When it came to my own free translation, I tried to retain as much as possible of the
spirit of Navajo syntax. My hope was to present a Navajo poem in a form as close to the
original as English would allow.

The treatment of vocables was a half-way measure: the Navajo nonsense syllables

HORSE SONG NO. 10

Introduction: He neŋe yaŋa

Chorus: 'Esdza shiye' ehye-la,   'esdza shiye' ehye-la ŋaŋa yeye 'e,
        'Esdzáá shiye'   'esdzáá shiye'
        The Woman, my-son,   the Woman, my-son

        'Esdza shiye' ehye-la,   'esdza shiye' ehye-la 'aŋa yeye 'e,
        'Esdzáá shiye'   'esdzáá shiye'
        The Woman, my-son,   the Woman, my-son

1. Yikai hye' ne yane 'eshikiye shi nishliyigo 'ohye-la,
    Yikai yii'naayá   'eshkii   shi nishłįigo
    Dawn within-reared boy   I I-am-then

Burden: 'Esdza shiye' ehye-la,   'esdza shiye' ehye-la ŋaŋa yeye 'e,
        'Esdzáá shiye'   'esdzáá shiye'
        The Woman, my-son   the Woman, my-son,

2. Hogho hodotłiji hya'ałni-yido 'ohye-la, etc. (Burden)
    Hooghan hodootł' izhii ya''hałniidóó
    House place-turquoise within-from   The Woman, my-son

3. Hogho hodisǫs i hya'ałni-do 'ohye-la,   (Burden)
    Hooghan hodisǫs ya'hałniidóó
    House place-glitter within-from   The Woman, etc.

4. Hogho nohodzodi ya'ałni-do 'ohye-la,   (Burden)
    Hooghan nahatdzǫǫdi ya'ałniidóó
    House around-blown-in within-from

5. Hogho hodighin ni hya'ałni-do 'ohye-la,   (Burden)
    Hooghan hodighin ya'hałniidóó
    House place-holy within-from

6. Yodi be hostyeli tsi bakaŋado 'ohye-la,   (Burden)
    Yodi bee hastyeeli ts'ída bakạdóó,
    Fabrics spread-out truly its-top-from,
      with

FIGURE 20. Excerpt from David P. McAllester's transcription and literal translation of *Horse Song No. 10* of Frank Mitchell. Top lines: text as sung; center lines: as it would be in spoken Navajo; bottom lines: McAllester's literal translation.

do not fit with the English text, but by keeping them I was able to show the introductory function of the *He ŋeŋe yaŋa*, and how *'ohye-la*, or *'ehye-la* constitututed a semi-cadence at the end of the new material in each verse and the beginning of a full cadence at the end of each repetition of the burden.

The first meaningful phrase is simply, "The woman, my son." This is typical of the ambiguity and mystery of much of Navajo poetry in both ceremonial and popular songs. It is quite characteristic to begin with an obscure statement and then, bit by bit, reveal by the unfolding of more details what is meant. It is Navajo to "hold something back," to "not tell everything." In fact, the song never explains that the woman is the deity, Changing Woman, the mother of Enemy Slayer. This is one of the many things the outsider would have to learn by asking and should then record in his notes for the benefit of other outsiders. The singer explained, "The father (the Sun) is saying, 'Take these things to your mother's place.' " In my translation I conveyed something of who "the woman" is by capitalizing, but still left a degree of ambiguity.

In the first verse, Enemy Slayer reveals himself by one of his sacred names. Most Navajos would know that Enemy Slayer is speaking here; the phrase is such a familiar one in ceremonial poetry. By using parentheses I tried to separate this verse and the analogous declaration in the last verse, from the rest of the poem which is all spoken by the Sun.

Verses two to six begin the explanation of the idea of precious things being taken to "the Woman." The Sun reveals the source of the precious things to be a house of special beauty, but it is not until verse nineteen that he comes right out and says "my house."

Beginning with verse seven the precious things begin to be named. Here again, the meaning is hidden. Enemy Slayer did not take actual horses from the Sun's house. He did better than that, he took the prayer offerings and magical feathers containing spirit horses, from which all horses on earth would ultimately come forth. As the singer said, explaining the unusual word *nahadlǫ́ǫ́* (spirit horse, spirit animal):

> He is making the horses out of this (prayersticks and feathers) by stepping over them. Each time he steps over, a colt comes out; he does it four ways. On the East side a blue horse comes out, on the West side a White one, on the South an abalone horse and on the North a jet one.

Verses thirteen to eighteen concern lures or attractions to draw the spirit horses from the Sun's house in the sky to Changing Woman's home on earth. Verse nineteen refers to the transfer of good things from the Sun's house of precious fabrics to the most sacred place in Changing Woman's house, the back, or West corner. Verses twenty to twenty-three underscore the idea of plentiful things to be possessed during a long and happy life and this last idea enters into the new sacred name with which Enemy Slayer identifies himself.

Over the years I find myself getting closer to the original Navajo word order in my translations, even though it may sound forced in English. The Navajo sentence raps out the main idea and then, by qualifiers, begins to clarify what is intended about that idea. Thus verse fourteen, "Jewels, all kinds of them, now to her, leading them," might be given a more explicatory translation, spelling things out and in more conventional word order: "Now the spirit horses are drawn to Changing Woman by all kinds of jewels going to her from my house." It would be clearer, but the sinewy punch of the Navajo would be gone and a new main idea, not even mentioned explicitly in the original, would be introduced. . . .

THE TENTH HORSE SONG

(The Sun instructs Enemy Slayer to take spirit horses and all kinds of other precious things to Changing Woman's Home.)

Chorus: *He ŋeŋe yaŋa,*
       The Woman, my son, *'ehye-la,*
       The Woman, my son, *'ehye-la, ŋaŋa yeye, 'e,*

       The Woman, my son, *'ehye-la,*
       The Woman, my son, *'ehye-la, ŋaŋa yeye, 'e!*

1. (Dawn, Brought-up-within-it Boy
    I, I am that one, then, *'ohye-la!*)
    The Woman, my son, *'ehye-la, ŋaŋa yeye, 'e,*

2. The house, the place of turquoise,
    Within it, from there to her, *'ohye-la,*
    The Woman, my son, *'ehye-la, ŋaŋa yeye, 'e,*

3. The house, the place glittering,
    Within it, from there to her, *'ohye-la,*
    The Woman, my son, *'ehye-la, ŋaŋa yeye, 'e,*

4. The house, larger blown, in there,
    Within it, from there to her, *'ohye-la,*
    The Woman, my son, *'ehye-la, ŋaŋa yeye, 'e,*

5. The house, the place sacred,
    Within it, from there to her, *'ohye-la,*
    The Woman, my son, *'ehye-la, ŋaŋa yeye, 'e,*

6. Precious fabrics, with these spread out,
    Right on top of them, from there to her, *'ohye-la,*
    The Woman, my son. *'ehye-la, ŋaŋa yeye, 'e,*

7. Prayer offerings, blue, then, *'ohye-la,*
    The Woman, my son, *'ehye-la, ŋaŋa yeye, 'e,*

8. My feathers, blue, then, *'ohye-la,*
    The Woman, my son, *'ehye-la, ŋaŋa yeye, 'e,*

9. Spirit horses, blue, then, *'ohye-la,*
    The Woman, my son, *'ehye-la, ŋaŋa yeye, 'e,*

10. Dawn spirit horses, blue, then, *'ohye-la,*
    The Woman, my son, *'ehye-la, ŋaŋa yeye, 'e,*

11. Turquoise spirit horses, those ones, *'ehye-la,*
    The Woman, my son, *'ehye-la, ŋaŋa yeye, 'e,*

12. Turquoise horses, those ones, *'ehye-la,*
    The Woman, my son, *'ehye-la, ŋaŋa yeye, 'e,*

13. Precious fabrics, all kinds of them,
    Now to her, leading them, *'ohye-la,*
    The Woman, my son, *'ehye-la, ŋaŋa yeye,* *'e,*

14. Jewels, all kinds of them,
    Now to her, leading them, *'ohye-la,*
    The Woman, my son, *'ehye-la, ŋaŋa yeye,* *'e,*

15. Horses, all kinds of them,
    Now to her, leading them, *'ohye-la,*
    The Woman, my son, *'ehyè-la, ŋaŋa yeye,* *'e,*

16. Sheep, all kinds of them,
    Now to her, leading them, *'ohye-la,*
    The Woman, my son, *'ehye-la, ŋaŋa yeye,* *'e,*

17. Useful animals, all kinds of them,
    Now to her, leading them, *'ohye-la,*
    The Woman, my son, *'ehye-la, ŋaŋa yeye,* *'e,*

18. Servants, all kinds of them,
    Now to her, leading them, *'ohye-la,*
    The Woman, my son, *'ehye-la, ŋaŋa yeye,* *'e,*

19. Precious fabrics, of these my house,
    The very back corner, to that place, *'ihye-la,*
    The Woman, my son, *'ehye-la, ŋaŋa yeye,* *'e,*

20. Precious fabrics, with these spread out,
    Right on top of them, to that place, *'ihye-la,*
    The Woman, my son, *'ehye-la, ŋaŋa yeye,* *'e,*

21. Everything that was there before,
    Right on top of it all, to that place, *'ihye-la,*
    The Woman, my son, *'ehye-la, ŋaŋa yeye,* *'e,*

22. Increasing, then, not diminishing, *'ohi-la,*
    The Woman, my son, *'ehye-la, ŋaŋa yeye,* *'e,*

23. Now old age, lasting on,
    Now according to blessing, then, *'ohi-la,*
    The Woman, my son, *'ehye-la, ŋaŋa yeye,* *'e,*

24. (Now Old-age-lasting-on Boy,
    Now According-to-blessing Boy,
    I, I am that one, then, *'ohye-la!*)
    The Woman, my son, *'ehye-la, ŋaŋa yeye,* *'e,*

    The Woman, my son, *'ehye-la,*
    The Woman, my son, *'ehye-la, ŋaŋa yeye,* *'e,*

    The Woman, my son, *'ehye-la,*
    The Woman, my son, *'ehye-la, ŋaŋa yeye,* *'e!*

SIMON J. ORTIZ

Song/Poetry and Language— Expression and Perception

A poet of Acoma Pueblo (New Mexico), Ortiz's English writings have provided a significant continuity between old and new modes, with a strong sense of the possibilities and losses involved therein. To the questions, "Why do you write? Who do you write for?" he replies: "Because Indians always tell a story. The only way to continue is to tell a story and that's what Coyote says. The only way to continue is to tell a story and there is no other way. Your children will not survive unless you tell something about them—how they were born, how they came to this certain place, how they continued." And to the further question, "Who do you write for besides yourself?": "For my children, for my wife, for my mother and my father and my grandparents and then reverse order that way so that I may have a good journey on my way back home" (Ortiz 1977: 9). Principal works: Going for the Rain, A Good Journey, Howbah Indians, Fight Back.

My father is a small man, in fact almost tiny. I think it must be the way that the Pueblo people were built when they lived at Mesa Verde and Pueblo Bonito. That's a long time ago, around 800–1200 A.D. One thousand years ago—this man? He's very wiry, and his actions are wiry. Smooth, almost tight motions, but like currents in creek water or an oak branch in a mild mountain wind. His face is even formed like that. Rivulets from the sides of his forehead, squints of his eyes, down his angular face and under his jaw. He usually wears a dark blue wool cap. His hair is turning a bit gray, but it's still mostly black, the color of distant lava cliffs. He wears glasses sometimes if he's reading or looking closely at the grain swirls of wood he is working with.

My father carves, dancers usually. What he does is find the motion of Deer, Buffalo, Eagle dancing in the form and substance of wood. Cottonwood, pine, aspen, juniper which has the gentle strains of mild chartreuse in its central grains—and his sinewed hands touch the wood very surely and carefully, searching and knowing. He has been a welder for the ATSFRY railroad and is a good carpenter, and he sits down to work at a table which has an orderly clutter of carving tools, paints, an ashtray, transistor radio, and a couple of Reader's Digests.

His movements are very deliberate. He holds the Buffalo Dancer in the piece of cottonwood poised on the edge of his knee, and he traces—almost caresses—the motion of the Dancer's crook of the right elbow, the way it is held just below

SOURCE: Previously unpublished.

midchest, and flicks a cut with the razor-edged carving knife. And he does it again.
He knows exactly how it is at that point in a Buffalo Dance Song, the motion of
elbow, arm, body and mind.

He clears his throat a bit and he sings, and the song comes from that motion of his
carving, his sitting, the sinews in his hands and face and the song itself. His voice
is full-toned and wealthy, all the variety and nuance of motion in the sounds and
phrases of the words are active in it; there is just a bit of tremble from his thin chest.

I listen.

"Stah wah miayanih, Muukei-lra Shahyaika,
duuwahsteh duumahsthee Dyahnie guuhyouiseh mah-ah.
Wahyuuhuunah wahyuuhuu huu nai ah."

Recently, I was talking with a friend who is enrolled in a Navajo language course.
She is Navajo, but she does not know how to speak Navajo. That is the story at present
with quite a number of Indian young people who use English as the language with which
they express themselves. English is the main language in which they experience the
meaning and the uses of language.

She made a comment about not being able easily to learn Navajo as a course of
instruction. She said, "I can't seem to hear the parts of it," referring to inflections and
nuances of spoken sentences and words.

I referred to a remark I made sometime before. "The way that language is spoken
at home—Acu, the tribal people and community from whom I come—is with a sense of
completeness. That is, when a word is spoken, it is spoken as a complete word. There are
no separate parts or elements to it." And I meant that a word is not spoken in any
separate parts, that is, with reference to linguistic structure, technique of diction,
nuance of sound, tonal quality, inflection, etc. Words are spoken as complete words.

For example when my father has said a word—in speech or in a song—and I ask
him, "What does that word break down to? I mean, breaking it down to the syllables of
sound or phrases of sound, what do each of these parts mean?" And he has looked at me
with an exasperated—slightly pained—expression on his face, wondering what I mean.
And he tells me, "It doesn't break down into anything."

For him, the word does not break down into any of the separate elements that I
expect. The word he has said is complete.

The word is there, complete in its entity of meaning and usage. But I with my years
of formal American education and some linguistic training—having learned and experienced English as a language—having learned to recognize the parts of a sentence,
speech, the etymology of words, that words are separable into letters and sounds and
syllables of vowels and consonants—I have learned to be aware that a word does break
down into basic parts or elements. Like that Navajo friend who is taking the Navajo
language course, I have on occasion come to expect—even demand—that I hear and
perceive the *separated* elements of Indian spoken words.

But, as my father has said, a word does not break down into separate elements. A
word is complete.

In the same way, a song really does not break down into separate elements. In the minds and views of the people who are singing it at my home or in a Navajo religious ceremony, for whatever purpose that a song is meant and used—whether it be for prayer, a dancing event, or as part of a story—the song does not break down. It is part of the complete voice of a person.

Language, when it is regarded not only as expression but is realized as experience as well, works in and *is* of that manner. Language is perception of experience as well as expression.

Technically, language can be disassembled according to linguistic function that mainly deals with the expression part of it. You can derive—subsequently define—how a language is formed, how and for what purpose it is used, and its development in a context. But when the totality is considered—language as experience and expression—it doesn't break down so easily and conveniently. And there is no need to break it down and define its parts.

Language as expression and perception—that is at the core of what a song is. It relates to how my father teaches a song and how a poet teaches a poem.

There is a steel vise at one end of the table my father works at. He clamps a handlong piece of wood in it. This pine is the torso of an Eagle Dancer. The Dancer is slim and his chest is kind of concave. The eagle is about to fly aloft, and my father files a bit of the hard upper belly with a rasp. Later, he will paint the dancing Eagle Man who has emerged out of the wood.

My father built the small house in which we sit. The sandstone was brought from a simple quarry near Shuutuh Tsaigaiyamishrouh on the plateau uplift south of here towards Acu. This is his workshop. It has a couple of windows and a handmade door because he couldn't find the right size door at the lumberyard in Grants where he trades. The single room is very secure and warm when he has a fire built on cold days in the woodstove which is one of those that looks like a low-slung hog.

There are a couple of chairs on which we sit and the table with his work and a bed in a corner. There is a stack of shelves against the eastern wall. My mother stores her pottery there. The pottery is covered with some cloth that formerly was used to sack flour. I think there is a box of carpentry tools on the floor below the lowest shelf. Against another wall is a book case that doesn't hold books. Mainly there are pieces of wood that my father is carving—some he started and didn't feel right about or had broken and he has laid aside—and a couple of sheep vertebrae he said he is going to make into bolo ties but hasn't gotten around to yet. And a couple of small boxes, one of them a shoebox and the other a homemade one of thin plyboard in which are contained the items he uses for his duties as a cacique.

He is one of the elders of the Antelope people who are in charge of all of the spiritual practice and philosophy of our people, the Acumeh. He and his uncles are responsible that things continue in the manner that they have since time began for us, and in this sense he is indeed a 1,000-year-old man. In the box are the necessary items that go with prayer: the feathers, pollen, precious bits of stone and shell, cotton string, earth paints, cornmeal, tobacco, other things. The feathers of various birds are wrapped in several-years-ago newspaper to keep the feathers smoothed. It is his duty to ensure that the prayer songs of the many and various religious ceremonies survive and continue.

My father sings, and I listen.

Song at the very beginning was experience. There was no division between experience and expression. Even now, I don't think there is much of a division except arbitrary. Take a child, for example, when he makes a song at his play, especially when he is alone. In his song, he tells about the experience of the sensations he is feeling at the moment with his body and mind. And the song comes about as words and sounds— expression. But essentially, in those moments, that song that he is singing is what he is experiencing. The child's song is both perception of that experience and his expression of it.

The meaning that comes from the song as expression and perception comes out of and is what the song is.

> Stah wah maiyanih, Muukai-lra Shahyaika,
> duuwahsteh duumahsthee Dyahnie guuhyoutseh mah-ah.
> Wahyuuhuunah wahyuuhuu huu nai ah.

This is a hunting song which occurs to me because it is around deer hunting season. I look around the countryside here, the piñon and the mountains nearby, and feel that I might go hunting soon, in November. The meaning the song has for me is in the context of what I am thinking, of what I want and perhaps will do. The words are translatable into English and they are

> My helping guide, Mountain Lion Hunting Spirit Friend,
> in this direction, to this point bring the Deer to me.
> Wahyuuhuunah wahyuuhuu huu nai ah.

The latter part of the song is a chanted phrase that is included with all hunting songs. The meaning—the song for the hunt, asking for guidance and help—is conveyed in English as well. There is no problem in deciphering the original meaning, and I don't think there ever really is when a song is taken to be both expression and perception.

The meaning that it has for me is that I recognize myself as a person in an active relationship—the hunting act—with Mountain Lion, the spirit friend and guide, and Deer. It is a prayer. A prayer song. The meaning that it has, further, is that things will return unto me if I do things well in a manner that is possible, if I use myself and whatever power I have appropriately. The purpose of the song is first of all to do things well, the way that they're supposed to be done, part of it being the singing and performing of the song. And that I receive, again well and properly, the things that are meant to be returned unto me. I express myself as well as realize the experience.

There is also something in a song that is actually substantial. When you talk or sing with words that are just words—or seem to be mere words—you sometimes feel that they are too ethereal, even fleeting. But when you realize the significance of what something means to you, then they are very tangible. You value the meaning of the song for its motion in the dance and for the expression and perception it allows you. You realize its inherent quality by the feeling that a song gives you. You become aware of the quietness that comes upon you when you sing or hear a song of quiet quality. You not only feel it—you know. The substance is emotional, but beyond that, spiritual, and it's real and you are present in and part of it. The act of the song which you are experiencing is real, and the reality is its substance.

A song is made substantial by its context—that is its reality, both that which is there and what is brought about by the song. The context in which the song is sung or that a prayer song makes possible is what makes a song substantial, gives it that quality of realness. The emotional, cultural, spiritual context in which we thrive—in that, the song is meaningful. The context has to do not only with your being physically present but it has to do also with the context of the mind, how receptive it is, and that usually means familiarity with the culture in which the song is sung.

The context of a song can be anything, or can focus through a specific event or act, but it includes all things. This is very important to realize when you are trying to understand and learn more than just the words or the technical facility of words in a song or poem. That means that you have to recognize that language is more than just a group of words and more than just the technical relationship between sounds and words. Language is more than just a functional mechanism. It is a spiritual energy that is available to all. It includes all of us and is not exclusively in the power of human beings—we are part of that power as human beings.

Oftentimes, I think we become convinced of the efficiency of our use of language. We begin to regard language too casually, thereby taking it for granted, and we forget the sacredness of it. Losing this regard, we become quite careless with how we use and perceive with language. We forget that language beyond its mechanics is a spiritual force.

When you regard the sacred nature of language, then you realize that you are part of it and it is part of you, and you are not necessarily in control of it, and that if you do control some of it, it is not in your exclusive control. Upon this realization, I think there are all possibilities of expression and perception which become available.

This morning my father said to my mother and me, "On Saturday, I am going to go hunting. I am telling you now. I will begin to work on Tuesday for it." He means that he will begin preparations for it. He explained that my brother-in-law will come for him on Friday, and they are going to hunt in Arizona. This is part of it, I knew, the proper explanation of intention and purpose. I have heard him say that since I was a boy.

The preparations are always done with a sense of excitement and enjoyment. Stories are remembered.

Page was a good story teller. I don't know why he was called Page—I suppose there is a story behind his name but I don't know it. Page was getting older when this happened. He couldn't see very well anymore, but he was taken along with a group of other hunters. He said, "I was to be the kuusteenehrru." The camp cook sticks around the camp, sings songs and makes prayers for the men out hunting, and waits, and fixes the food. Page got tired of doing that. He said, "I decided that it wouldn't hurt if I just went out of camp a little ways. I was sort of getting tired of sticking around. And so I did; I wasn't that blind."

He walked a ways out of their camp, you know, looking around, searching the ground for tracks. And he found some, great big ones. He said, "It must be my good fortune that I am to get a big one. I guess I'm living right," and he reached into his cornfeed bag and got some meal and sprinkled it with some precious stones and beads and pollen into the big tracks. He said, "Thank you for leaving your tracks, and now I ask you to wait for me; I am right behind you." And putting his mind in order, he followed the tracks, looking up once in a while to see if the larger deer he could already see in his mind was up ahead.

"I was sure in a good mood," Page said, and he would smile real big. "Every once in a while I sprinkled cornfeed and precious things in the tracks. They were big," he said and he would hold out his large hand to show you how big, "and I would sing under my breath." He followed along, kind of slow you know because he was an old man and because of his eyes, until he came down this slope that wasn't too steep. There was an oak brush thicket at the bottom of it. He put his fingers upon the tracks, to let it know that he was right behind, and the tracks felt very warm.

He said, "Ah haiee, there you will be in the thicket. There is where we will meet," and he prayed one more time and concluded his song and set his mind right and checked to make sure his gun was ready—I don't know what kind of rifle he had but it was probably an old one too. And he made his way to the thicket very carefully, very quietly, slightly bent down to see under the branches of the oak. And then he heard it moving around in the thicket, and he said quietly, "Ah haiee, I can hear that you're a big one. Come to me now, it is time, and I think we are both ready," just to make sure that his spirit was exactly right. And he crouched down to look and there it was some yards into the thicket and he put his rifle to his shoulder and searched for a vital spot, and then it turned to him and it was a *pig*.

"Kohjeeno!" Page said, his breath exhaling. He lowered his rifle, cussed a bit, and then he raised his rifle and said, "Kohjeeno, I guess you'll have to be my Quuyaitih today," and shot the pig. He cut the pig's throat to let the blood, and then on the way back to camp he tried to find all the precious stones he had dropped in the tracks of the pig.

After that, until he went back North—passed away—his nephews and grandsons would say to him, "Uncle, tell us about the time the kohjeeno was your Quuyaitih." And Page would frown indignant a bit, and then he would smile and say, "Keehamaa dzee, we went hunting to Brushy Mountain. . . . "

The song is basic to all vocal expression. The song as expression is an opening from inside of yourself to outside and from outside of yourself to inside, but not in the sense that there are separate states of yourself. Instead, it is a joining and an opening together. Song is the experience of that opening, or road if you prefer, and there is no separation of parts, no division between that within you and that without you, as there is no division between expression and perception.

I think that is what has oftentimes happened with our use of English. We think of English as a very definitive language, useful in defining things—which means setting limits. But that's not supposed to be what language is. Language is not definition; language is all-expansive. We, thinking ourselves capable of the task, assign rules and roles to language unnecessarily. Therefore we limit our words, our language, and we limit our perception, our understanding, our knowledge.

Children don't limit their words until they learn how, until they're told that it's better if they use definitive words. This is what happens to most everyone in a formal educational situation. Education defines you. It makes you see with and within very definite limits. Unless you teach and learn language in such a way as to permit it to remain or for it to become all-expansive—and truly visionary—your expressiveness and perceptions will be limited and even divided.

My father teaches that the song is part of the way you're supposed to recognize everything, that the singing of it is a way of recognizing this all-inclusiveness because it is a way of expressing yourself and perceiving. It is basically a way to understand and appreciate your relationship to all things. The song as language is a way of touching. This is the way that my father attempts to teach a song, and I try to listen, feel, know, and learn that way.

When my father sings a song, he tries to instill a sense of awareness about us. Although he may remark upon the progressive steps in a song, he does not separate the steps or components of the song. The completeness of the song is the important thing, how a person comes to know and appreciate it, not to mark especially the separate parts of it but to know the whole experience of the song.

He may mention that a particular song was sung sometime before or had been made for a special occasion, but he remembers only in reference to the overall meaning and purpose. It may be an old, old song that he doesn't know the history of, or it may be one he has made himself. He makes me aware of these things because it is important, not only for the song itself but because it is coming from the core of who my father is, and he is talking about how it is for him in relationship with all things. I am especially aware of its part in our lives and that all these things are a part of that song's life. And when he sings the song, I am aware that it comes from not only his expression but from his perception as well.

I listen carefully, but I listen for more than just the sound, listen for more than just the words and phrases, for more than the various parts of the song. I try to perceive the context, meaning, purpose—all of these items not in their separate parts but as a whole—and I think it comes completely like that.

A song, a poem becomes real in that manner. You learn its completeness; you learn the various parts of it but not as separate parts. You learn a song in the way that you are supposed to learn a language, as expression and as experience.

I think it is possible to teach song and poetry in a classroom so that language is a real way of teaching and learning. The effort will have to be with conveying the importance and significance of not only the words and sounds but the realness of the song

in terms of oneself, context, the particular language used, community, the totality of
what is around. More complete expression and perception will be possible then.

Yesterday morning, my father went over to Diabuukaiyah to get oak limbs for the
Haadramahni—the Prayer Sticks. After he got back he said, ''The Haadramahni
for hunting are all of hardwoods, like the hahpaani.'' The oak grows up the
canyons which come out of the lava rock of Horace Mesa.

And at his worktable, he shows me. ''This is a Haitsee—a shield if you want to call
it that—and it is used as a guide.'' It is a thin, splitted strip of hahpaani made into a
circle which will fit into the palm of your hand. ''There is a star in the center—I
will make it out of string tied to the edges of the circle. This is a guide to find your
way, to know the directions by. It is round because the moon is round. It is the
night sky which is a circle all around in which the stars and moon sit. It's a circle,
that's why. This is part of it, to know the directions you are going, to know where
you are at.''

He shows me a stick about the thickness of his thumb. The stick is an oak limb split
in half, and he runs the edge of his thumbnail along the core of the wood, the dark
streak at the very center of the wood. The streak does not run completely straight,
but it flows very definitely from one end to the other. And my father says, ''This is
the Heeyahmani. This is to return you safely. This is so you will know the points on
your return back, the straight and safe way. So you will be definite and true on your
return. It is placed at the beginning point of your journey. This line here is that, a
true road.''

And then he explains, ''I haven't gotten this other stick formed yet, and it is of oak
also. It is pointed on both ends, and it is stout, strong.'' He holds up his right hand,
his fingers clutched around the stout oak limb. ''It's for strength and courage,
manliness. So that in any danger you will be able to overcome the danger. So that
you will have the stamina to endure hardship. It is to allow you to know and realize
yourself as a man. It is necessary to have also.''

He tells me these things, and I listen. He says, ''Later, we will sing some songs for
the hunt. There is a lot to it, not just a few. There are any numbers of prayer. There
are all these things you have to do in preparation before you begin to hunt, and they
are all meant to be done not only because they have been done in the past but
because they are the way that things, good things, will come about for you. That is
the way that you will truly prepare yourself, to be able to go out and find the deer,
so that the deer will find you. You do these things in the proper way so that you will
know the way things are, what's out there, what you must think in approaching
them, how you must respond—all these things. They are all part of it—you just
don't go and hunt. A person has to be aware of what is around him, and in this way,
the preparation, these things that I have here, you will know.''

My father tells me, ''This song is a hunting song; listen.'' He sings and I listen. He
may sing it again, and I hear it again. The feeling that I perceive is not only contained in

the words; there is something surrounding the song, and it includes us. It is the relationship that we share with each other and with everything else. And that's the feeling that makes the song real and meaningful and which makes his singing and my listening more than just a teaching and learning situation.

It is that experience—that perception of it—that I mention at the very beginning which makes it meaningful. You perceive by expressing yourself therefore. This is the way that my father teaches a song. And this is the way I try to learn a song. This is the way I try to teach poetry, and this is the way I try to have people learn from me.

One time my father was singing a song, and this is the instance in which this—perception by/and expression—became very apparent for me. He was singing this song, and I didn't catch the words offhand. I asked him, and he explained, "This song, I really like it for this old man." And he said, "This old man used to like to sing, and he danced like this," motioning like the old man's hands, arms, shoulders, and he repeated, "This song, I really like it for this old man."

That's what the song was about, I realized. It was both his explanation and the meaning of the song. It was about this old man who danced that way with whom my father had shared a good feeling. My father had liked the old man, who was probably a mentor of some sort, and in my father's mind, during the process of making the song and when he sang it subsequent times afterwards, he was reaffirming the affection he had for the old guy, the way "he danced like this."

My father was expressing to me the experience of that affection, the perceptions of the feelings he had. Indeed, the song was the road from outside of himself to inside— which is perception—and from inside of himself to outside—which is expression. That's the process and the product of the song, the experience and the vision that a song gives you.

The words, the language of my experience, come from how I understand, how I relate to the world around me, and how I know language as perception. That language allows me vision to see with and by which to know myself.

NATHANIEL TARN

Fragments from the Prayers Made on Behalf of Nathaniel Tarn by the Tzutujil-Maya Priest Nicolas Chiviliu Tacaxoy, Santiago Atitlan, Guatemala, 1953, 1959

Nathaniel Tarn's early work as an anthropologist (contemporary Mayan culture, popular Buddhism in Burma) informs the richness of reference in his later poetry (pre-Conquest and early post-Conquest themes in A Nowhere for Vallejo, Inuit [Eskimo] *observations in* Alashka, *etc.). He founded, in the 1960s, the Cape Goliard poetry series and the influential Cape Editions, a series of small books which forged significant links between poetics and contemporary social theory. Principal works:* Beautiful Contradictions, A Nowhere for Vallejo, Lyrics for the Bride of God, Alashka *(with Janet Rodney),* Rabinal Achi (Act IV). *Among recent writings on ethnopoetics is "The Heraldic Vision: Some Cognitive Models for Comparative Aesthetics" (Benamou 1976; see above, p. 342).*

---

in the name of the Creator God and Angel   O God   I meet you
prostrated   I meet you seated   may you be remembered God Creator of Day
and Light   Angel and Lord St. Simon   remembered before creation in the
fragrance of fruit your throne is adorned with   in your books   in your
accounts   before the world   before the Savior

Father God   elder among elders   in the fragrance of fruit
praised in a thousand prayers   son of the Incense and the Candle
because you existed through the centuries of existence that the World has
existed   because even below the clouds your hands and feet exist Lord
St. Simon   First Angel   you who are seated as one of the St. Simons of
Glory   remembered in your yellow cape   in your white cape   in your
yellow coat   in your white coat   in your yellow gaiters   in your white
gaiters   in your yellow overcoat   in your white overcoat   now I am
consulting you with the help of a bunch of wax candles   with the help of a bunch of
de-luxe candles   now I remind you of one of your sons   a descendant of yours O
God who has remembered your hands and your feet   O great Master and personage!

perhaps you are going about the World going up and down the Face of the
World using the crossroads who knows in the mission of your daily round like a

SOURCE: Nathaniel Tarn, Atitlan/Alashka, pages 99–104.

408

sentinel or a sergeant or a policeman and in your long march you take with you
two or three great thoughts and perhaps you meet with the sinners of the World
and the Face of the Earth   O Lord and Master we aren't spying we aren't
judging your acts do not drown us do not suffocate us it is not my thing that I
called your spirit that I called your sanctity it's the person here it's his thing
your son who comes to beg with wax and candlegrease with the savor of these
things that your son has brought here smoothly   and with the sound of violin
and guitar!

     perhaps you will have to go perhaps you will have to promenade through
the Holy Night the Holy Darkness   you great doctor and personage of the Holy
World and who will protect me then   O God   O World   who have
come crossing the World   from a far-off place   feels very poor in your hands
     poor and orphaned   to come to you Father-Mother   looking for your
hands   looking for your feet   looking for your lips that have been so highly
recommended to me   thanks to you Lord   I have a great desire to see you
and am very happy to talk to my Father today   I feel happy and am much
admired in the Face of the World because it is the Lord Angel who is leading me

O God   it is I who came as the custodian of the aroma and savor of the
God called Incense   the God called Candle   because Incense is the ancient
symbol of God you of the white eyebrows and hair   Lord of the World and the
Face of the Earth   ancient knower of things   remembered for your wisdom
in the aroma of *pataxte* and *cacao*   you Pedestal of the Sky   give your son
who has brought you so smoothly and so delicately and with such care these goods
before your table before your chair   Nathaniel Tarn his name   whose God
this is   whose Saint this is   give him all power!   I have come as his
helper   as his right-arm   as his foot before God and ask for life and health
on his behalf for that is what he wishes of this World and it is not because of
distance it is not because the leagues have been many he has covered to reach
you since he first heard of your name Don Pedro that he asks for your wisdom /
your fragrance / your books / your accounts / your secrets / your cape and coat /
your gaiters and scarves / your poncho and shawl   and so God don't depreciate
     don't discourage   he who looks for your sanctity   he who looks for
your hands and feet

     for he is not a liar he is not an evil-doer he is not a murderer before the
World for there exists a God whom he looks for and loves and we are looking for
the gallant Don Pedro   the Old God   to do him a ritual   so that we
don't forget his hands   his feet   his adornments   Don Pedro
     Don Pedro de Alvarado   Master and personality of the World and the Face
of the Earth who lives and rules among pines / firtrees / cypresses / flowers   he
who abandoned his father perhaps he who abandoned his mother he who came perhaps
from a hundred leagues' distance to arrive here before this Holy World to present himself
before the Holy Earth of Guatemala in the hands and before the table of Captain
Santiago Tzutujil and Martin-God!   O thanks to you Masters   I thank you

Lord   I thank you Lady   because I am looking for the son of the earth / the
son of cloud / the son of mist / the son of *pataxte* / the son of *cacao* / the son
of cypress / the son of palm / the son of *pacaya* / the son of stalk and the son of
flower!

        on Sunday your merits were remembered and your hands and feet before the
Holy World that he might not suffer fractures that he might not suffer harm in the
God Path   in the God called Footpath   before the spirit of the God called
Field   when he goes up   when he goes down among the fields   Lord
        perhaps out   perhaps down   but straight!   From San Juan I
        came to San Pedro   To Flores Peten   to Guatemala City   to
        Santo Tomas   to Visitacion   to Quezaltenango   to
        Huehuetenango   to Mazatenango   to Chicacao and San Antonio
        going through mountains   through valleys loving all the Gods   all
        the Angels who are on their hands   who are on their knees   before your
hands   before your feet!

        o that he might come here another time!   o Savior called World!   o
World of his day and his birth / of our Grandmothers and Mothers / of our Masters
and Great Gods and Angels of authorized speech and strong hands who lead the
World and the Face of the Earth   who bring the cloud and the mist / the
earthquake / the thunder and hail / who carry in their hands and palms the
Foundations of the Sky   o Lords and Masters of the World and the Face of the
Earth in this the navel of the World   Tziquinaha
. . . .

        I implore your hands your feet because you are our fathers our brothers of
great value our life and the health of our spirits O God this son of yours
Nathaniel Tarn his day Nathaniel Tarn's   he has remembered your hands he
has remembered your feet through the God called Incense through the God called
Candle the gum of the storax tree the gum of the frankincense here he is gathered
remembering in his own place his own essence so that I need remember only so
that I need ask only because you are the owners of *pataxte* and *cacao* / owners of
cloud and mist / gathered in the Sky and in Spain O Gods maintainers of the
Sun and Light before the essence of man and woman before the embrace and the
privacy of those two!

        your son does not ask for his voice for his speech he asks for his life for
his health he implores the Angels for the prayer of the holy table before our
Mothers before our Fathers chiefs of the World of mist and clouds / of rain and
lightning / and thunder

        our Father God in Glory our Father God in Sky made of twelve   Fathers
as well as Mothers   because they are found in each other's company   twelve
also are the Gods of Chiantla   who look after our sons   who look after our
offspring   who look after our shoots

Juan Martin / Diego Martin / King Martin / Pascual Martin / Parpeta
Martin / Nicolas Martin / Baltazar Martin / Chalela Martin / Staka Martin /
Palvera Martin / Balion Martin and St. John Martin of all the Martins
   Company of the Holy World   Masters of the wild animals in the forests

   and Maria Sabela / Maria Salina / Maria Madalena / Maria Losia / Maria
Candelaria / Maria Chiantla / Maria St. Annà / Maria Rosario / Maria
Concepcion / Maria Dolores / Maria Saragosta / Maria Niachotiya   Mothers of
the Holy World great procreators midwives experts in rocking
cradles and bundles and hammocks before the Face of the Earth and Maria
Yashper the tripes of woman

and Angel Semanera Pastor / Mayordomo / King Monarch / King Mateksun /
King Matektani / King Sakashol / Don Galisto / Francisco Sojuel / Juan Pablo
Baltazar Pablo / Jacobo Coo / Marcos Rujutch   Rainpriests of the Holy World
   with Anthony / John / Melchior / Baltazar / St. Philip of Galicia the oldest
of the Galicias and also Michael, Raphael and Gabriel and thousands of others
their houses in the hills their houses in the valleys their houses in the
clouds where they work and share out the plants and share out food and rain

   and St. Bernard the Sun who has maintained us in the World in tiled houses and in
houses of various materials who extends his flight across the World to see our past and to
see our future

   and you who suffered pain who suffered punishment from the moment the
World began from the moment the Face of the Earth began from the moment
your hands and feet existed Lord God Jesuschrist who walked in the God
called Cloud and in the God called Mist under the burning Sun who came bathed
in sweat remembering us when the Holy World was created you suffered pain
and punishment before the Cross of Passion with three hammers and a thousand
lashes they laid out your hands and your feet on the Cross of Passion and with
three nails held your divine body in place in order to pay for our sin for our
crime we are humankind we are sinners which is how man and woman
   youth and girl remained on this earth!

   and with San Pedro in the West / Atitlan-Toliman in the East /
Sambernawa in the North / Zunil in the South Volcanos of the Holy World

   and the various places of the Holy World

. . . .

   a yellow wine a white wine a yellow beer a white beer
   have come to your hands and to your feet Lord of white hair and white
eyebrows place him then under your power under your
miracle perhaps it is the Angel St. Michael who leads him to you because you are

our Father because you are our Mother because you are twelve you the Angels
        because you are the twelve chief Gods of the World   take him in your arms
then and embrace him World   which brings forth Justice   which brings forth
Sacrament   a thousand apologies   a thousand pardons   that the road
of your son might remain open   that he avoid harm to himself   that he avoid
fractures of the limbs to himself and   over the World come down perhaps Lord of
the white hair and eyebrows in the middle of the day in the middle of the hour to grant
permission to grant license to remain under your protection forever!

        I alone   I am people   I am people who live on a basis of food and
drink   I am not God   I am not Angel before the World and the Face of the
Earth   You Angels are of God because of your divinity   through being
Chiefs of the World and the Face of the Earth   perhaps you keep me here   in
the mountains in the valleys   perhaps you detain me in your hands in your feet
Lord St. Simon   perhaps you witness   perhaps you look down on me
        perhaps I have no destination in this World   but neither shall there be
anyone speaking before me or behind me God

        your son has remembered you Lord St. Simon because the God of the Day
looks after him   thanks then   to the World   to God-Father
        God-Son   God-Holy Ghost   Amenjesus

        thanks Jesuschrist   my Father   Ah God!   this will be my table
        this will be my book   now that I solicit pardon for our sins   for our
guilt before Lord St. Simon   when we go another time and come before Captain
Santiago when we come here another time before Captain St. James of Compostela
in this his town of Santiago which is also the House of Birds   Tziquinaha!

AUTHOR'S NOTE: The religion of the Highland Maya of Guatemala is syncretis-
tic: ancient Maya ideas and rites and icons underlie the surface Catholicism. Apart
from the Saints and Angels mentioned in these prayers, two major "pagan"
figures are referred to: St. Martin who masks an ancient Lord of the Wild Animals
(and whose female companion is Yashper, the First Mother) and St. Simon, alias
St. Michael Archangel, St. Peter Apostle, St. Andrew, Pedro de Alvarado Con-
quistador of Guatemala and Judas Iscariot, whose real identity is Mam (Mam-
shimon or Maximon) the Old-God of the Maya. Both the Martin and the Mam are
bundles rather than icons: but the Mam bundle contains the elements of a large
puppet which is taken out and dressed on certain ritual occasions. Mam is a great
walker, is bisexual and highly involved in love magic and witchcraft. Both Mam
and the Martin are looked after by special priests: among these, certain striking
figures are invoked in the prayers. These are dead priests who have become deities
and who are believed to return to earth—possibly as reincarnations—to help the
village in times of trouble. They are connected with the making of rain and the
bringing back of the good weather after the rainy season.
        These prayers were recited for me as part of an educational process which
involved the possibility of my becoming an apprentice of Nicolas Chiviliu

Tacaxoy. This priest's style was and is the finest I have heard and his systematization of belief the most impressive. One of his own idiosyncracies—although not unrelated to traditional calendrical lore—involved the listing of Powers by the dozen: twelve Martins, twelve Marias and so forth. This was also an aspect of a stylistic trick of the prayers: namely uttering one name and then repeating it as often as one can remember names to add to it. Some of these tricks became very well known to me after a while and I caught the habit of sensing which "slabs" of prayer Chiviliu would use at various times, when he would slow down and space out, when he would go fast to the limit of his breathing capacity and so forth.

I have taken liberties with the arrangement of these fragments and the presentation of data in them (though no information is deliberately perverted) not only as part of an experiment in attitudes towards translation and translators but also, in this case, because this is precisely what I would have done had I become an *ajkun* myself. The anthropologist I was knows where these "distortions" occur and readily forgives them. My teacher and friends would probably forgive them too if the case arose insofar as the religious status I was suspected of harboring would have allowed me the greatest possible latitude in creativity had I ever wished to avail myself of that power. And a last reason is that I do not have the Tzutujil texts with me: only an indifferent Spanish version and a certain pulsation in my ears.

Santa Fe, July 1970

Revered as a *nawal acha*, a living deity, before his passing, Chiviliu died full of years and earth-warming drink on April 21st, 1980. I had been fortunate to work with him one full year in his old age during 1979.

Santa Fe, August 1981

N. SCOTT MOMADAY
The Man Made of Words

Author of the Pulitzer Prize novel, House Made of Dawn, *N. Scott Momaday is the most prominent of the American Indian novelists and is a poet in the tradition of his teacher, Yvor Winters. His personal and familial works—drawing from his Kiowa Indian background and from the sense of a poetics offered in the present piece—include* The Way to Rainy Mountain *and* The Names.

When I was a child, my father told me the story of the arrowmaker; and he told it to me many times, for I fell in love with it. I have no memory that is older than that of hearing it. This is the way it goes:

> If an arrow is well made, it will have tooth marks upon it. That is how you know. The Kiowas made fine arrows and straightened them in their teeth. Then they drew them to the bow to see that they were straight. Once there was a man and his wife. They were alone at night in their tepee. By the light of a fire the man was making arrows. After a while he caught sight of something. There was a small opening in the tepee where two hides had been sewn together. Someone was there on the outside, looking in. The man went on with his work, but he said to his wife: "Someone is standing outside. Do not be afraid. Let us talk easily, as of ordinary things."
>
> He took up an arrow and straightened it in his teeth; then, as it was right for him to do, he drew it to the bow and took aim, first in this direction and then in that. And all the while he was talking, as if to his wife. But this is how he spoke: "I know that you are there on the outside, for I can feel your eyes upon me. If you are a Kiowa, you will understand what I am saying, and you will speak your name." But there was no answer, and the man went on in the same way, pointing the arrow all around. At last his aim fell upon the place where his enemy stood, and he let go of the string. The arrow went straight to the enemy's heart.

Heretofore the story of the arrowmaker has been the private possession of a very few, a tenuous link in that most ancient chain of language which we call the oral tradition; tenuous because the tradition itself is so; for, as many times as the story has been told, it was always but one generation removed from extinction. But it was held dear, too, on that same account. That is to say, it has been neither more nor less durable than the human voice, and neither more nor less concerned to express the meaning of the human condition. And this brings us to the heart of the matter at hand: the story of the arrowmaker is also a link between language and literature.

It is a remarkable act of the mind, a realization of words and the world that is altogether simple and direct, yet nonetheless rare and profound, and it illustrates more

SOURCE: *The New York Times Book Review, May 4, 1969, page 2.*

clearly than anything else in my own experience, at least, something of the essential character of the imagination—and in particular of that personification which in this instance emerges from it: the man made of words.

It is a fine story, whole, intricately beautiful, precisely realized. It is one of the Kiowa tales which I brought together in "The Way to Rainy Mountain." In a sense they are the milestones of an old migration in which the Kiowas journeyed from the Yellowstone to the Washita. They record a transformation of the tribal mind, as it encounters for the first time the landscape of the Great Plains; they evoke the sense of search and of discovery.

The story of the arrowmaker, especially, is worth thinking about, for it yields something of value; indeed, it is full of provocation, rich with suggestion and consequent meaning. There is often an inherent danger in the close examination of such a thing, a danger that we might impose too much of ourselves upon it. But this story, I believe, is exceptional in that respect. It is informed by an integrity that bears examination easily and well, and in the process it seems to appropriate our own reality and experience.

It is significant that the story of the arrowmaker returns in a special way upon itself. It is, after all, about language, and it is therefore part and parcel of its own subject; there is virtually no difference between the telling and that which is told. The point of the story lies not so much in what the arrowmaker does but in what he says—and indeed that he says it. The principal fact is that he speaks, and in so doing he places his very life in the balance. It is this aspect of the story which interests me most, for it is here that the language becomes most conscious of itself; we are close to the origin and object of literature, I believe; our sense of the verbal dimension is very keen, and we are aware of something in the nature of language that is at once perilous and compelling.

"If you are a Kiowa, you will understand what I am saying, and you will speak your name." Everything is ventured in this simple declaration, which is also a question and a plea. The conditional element with which it begins is remarkably tentative and pathetic; precisely at this moment is the arrowmaker realized completely, and his reality consists in language, and it is poor and precarious. All of this occurs to him as surely as it does to us. Implicit in that simple occurrence is all of his definition and his destiny, and all of ours. He ventures to speak because he must; language is the repository of his whole knowledge and experience, and it represents the only chance he has for survival.

Instinctively and with great care, he deals in the most honest and basic way with words. "Let us talk easily, as of ordinary things," he says. And of the ominous unknown he asked only the utterance of a name, only the most nominal sign that he is understood, that his words are returned to him on the sheer edge of meaning. But there is no answer, and the arrowmaker knows at once what he has not known before; that his enemy exists and that he has gained an advantage over him. This he knows certainly, and the certainty itself is his advantage; it is crucial, and he makes the most of it. The venture is complete and irrevocable, and it ends in success.

The story is meaningful. It is so primarily because it is composed of language and it is in the nature of language in turn that it proceeds to the formulation of meaning. Moreover the story of the arrowmaker, as opposed to other stories in general, centers upon this procession of words toward meaning. It seems in fact to turn upon the very idea that language involves the elements of risk and responsibility, and in this it seeks to confirm itself. In a word, everything is a risk. That may be true, and it may also be that the whole of literature rests upon that truth.

The arrowmaker is pre-eminently the man made of words. He has consummate being in language; it is the world of his origin and of his posterity, and there is no other. But it is a world of definite reality and of infinite possibility. I have come to believe that the arrowmaker has more nearly perfect being than other men have, and a more nearly perfect right to be. We can imagine him as he imagines himself, whole and vital, going on into the unknown darkness and beyond. This last aspect of his being is primordial and profound.

And yet the story has it that he is cautious and alone, and we are given to understand that his peril is great and immediate and that he confronts it in the only way he can. I have no doubt that this is true, and I believe that there are implications which point directly to the determination of our literary experience and which must not be lost upon us.

A final word, then, on an essential irony which marks this story and gives peculiar substance to the man made of words. The storyteller is nameless and unlettered. From one point of view we know very little about him, except that he is somehow translated for us into the person of the arrowmaker. But, from another point of view that is all we need to know. He tells us of his life in language, and of the awful risk involved. It must occur to us that he is one with the arrowmaker and that he has survived, by word of mouth, beyond other men. We said a moment ago that for the arrowmaker language represented the only chance of survival. It is worth considering that he survives in our own time and that he has survived over a period of untold generations.

ISHMAEL REED

Neo-HooDoo Manifesto/
The Neo-HooDoo Aesthetic

Ishmael Reed has long been a prolific and active poet and novelist, whose language and concerns reflect the particular and universal poles of a genuine ethnopoetics. As editor of the influential magazine, Y'Bird, and as a founder (with Bob Callahan, Frank Chin, Victor Hernandez Cruz, David Meltzer, and Simon Ortiz) of the San Francisco-based Before Columbus Foundation, he writes: "We welcome a time in history when 'American' is no longer interchangeable with rudeness, grossness and provincialism, but has begun to stand for a society where all of the cultures of the world may co-exist and in which cultural exchange is allowed to thrive." Principal works: Conjure, Chattanooga *(poetry);* Yellow Back Radio Broke-Down, Mumbo Jumbo *(novels).*

Neo-HooDoo is a "Lost American Church" updated. Neo-HooDoo is the music of James Brown without the lyrics and ads for Black Capitalism. Neo-HooDoo is the 8 basic dances of 19-century New Orleans' *Place Congo*—the Calinda the Bamboula the Chacta the Babouille the Conjaille the Juba the Congo and the VooDoo—modernized into the Philly Dog, the Hully Gully, the Funky Chicken, the Popcorn, the Boogaloo and the dance of great American choreographer Buddy Bradley.

Neo-HooDoos would rather "shake that thing" than be stiff and erect. (There were more people performing a Neo-HooDoo sacred dance, the Boogaloo, at Woodstock than chanting Hare Krishna . . . Hare Hare!) All so-called "Store Front Churches" and "Rock Festivals" receive their matrix in the HooDoo rites of Marie Laveau conducted at New Orleans' Lake Pontchartrain, and Bayou St. John in the 1880s. The power of HooDoo challenged the stability of civil authority in New Orleans and was driven underground where to this day it flourishes in the Black ghettos throughout the country. That's why in Ralph Ellison's modern novel *Invisible Man* New Orleans is described as "The Home of Mystery." "Everybody from New Orleans got that thing," Louis Armstrong said once.

HooDoo is the strange and beautiful "fits" the Black slave Tituba gave the children of Salem. (Notice the arm waving ecstatic females seemingly possessed at the "Pentecostal," "Baptist," and "Rock Festivals," [all fronts for Neo-HooDoo]). The reason that HooDoo isn't given the credit it deserves in influencing American Culture is because the students of that culture both "overground" and "underground" are uptight closet Jeho-vah revisionists. They would assert the American and East Indian and Chinese thing before they would the Black thing. Their spiritual leaders Ezra Pound and T. S. Eliot hated Africa and "Darkies." In Theodore Roszak's book *The Making of a*

SOURCE: *Ishmael Reed,* Conjure, *pages 20–26.*

Counter Culture—there is barely any mention of the Black influence on this culture even though its members dress like Blacks talk like Blacks walk like Blacks, gesture like Blacks wear Afros and indulge in Black music and dance (Neo-HooDoo).

Neo-HooDoo is sexual, sensual and digs the old "heathen" good good loving. An early American HooDoo song says:

Now lady I ain't no mill man
Just the mill man's son
But I can do your grinding
Till the mill man comes

Which doesnt mean that women are treated as "sexual toys" in Neo-HooDoo or as one slick Jeho-vah Revisionist recently said, "victims of a raging hormone imbalance." Neo-HooDoo claims many women philosophers and theoreticians which is more than ugh religions Christianity and its offspring Islam can claim. When our theoretician Zora Neale Hurston asked a *Mambo* (a female priestess in the Haitian VooDoo) a definition of VooDoo the Mambo lifted her skirts and exhibited her Erzulie Seal, her Isis Seal. Neo-HooDoo identifies with Julia Jackson who stripped HooDoo of its oppressive Catholic layer—Julia Jackson said when asked the origin of the amulets and talismans in her studio, "I make all my own stuff. It saves money and it's as good. People who has to buy their stuff ain't using their heads."

Neo-HooDoo is not a church for egotripping—it takes its "organization" from Haitian VooDoo of which Milo Rigaud wrote:

Unlike other established religions, there is no hierarchy of bishops, archbishops, cardinals, or a pope in VooDoo. Each oum'phor is a law unto itself, following the traditions of VooDoo but modifying and changing the ceremonies and rituals in various ways. [Secrets of VooDoo]

Neo-HooDoo believes that every man is an artist and every artist a priest. You can bring your own creative ideas to Neo-HooDoo. Charlie "Yardbird (Thoth)" Parker is an example of the Neo-HooDoo artist as an innovator and improvisor.

In Neo-HooDoo, Christ the landlord deity ("render unto Caesar") is on probation. This includes "The Black Christ" and "The Hippie Christ." Neo-HooDoo tells Christ to get lost. (Judas Iscariot holds an honorary degree from Neo-HooDoo.)

Whereas at the center of Christianity lies the graveyard the organ-drone and the cross, the center of Neo-HooDoo is the drum the anhk and the Dance. So Fine, Barefootin, Heard it Through The Grapevine, are all Neo-HooDoos.

Neo-HooDoo has "seen a lot of things in this old world."

Neo-HooDoo borrows from Ancient Egyptians (ritual accessories of Ancient Egypt are still sold in the House of Candles and Talismans on Stanton Street in New York, the Botanical Gardens in East Harlem, and Min and Mom on Haight Street in San Francisco, examples of underground centers found in ghettos throughout America).

Neo-HooDoo borrows from Haiti Africa and South America. Neo-HooDoo comes in all styles and moods.

Louis Jordon Nellie Lutcher John Lee Hooker Ma Rainey Dinah Washington the Temptations Ike and Tina Turner Aretha Franklin Muddy Waters Otis Redding Sly and the Family Stone B. B. King Junior Wells Bessie Smith Jelly Roll Morton Ray Charles Jimi Hendrix Buddy Miles the 5th Dimension the Chambers Brothers Etta James and acolytes Creedance Clearwater Revival the Flaming Embers Procol Harum are all Neo-HooDoos. Neo-HooDoo never turns down pork. In fact Neo-HooDoo is the Bar-B-Cue of Amerika. The Neo-HooDoo cuisine is Geechee Gree Gree Verta Mae's *Vibration Cooking*. (Ortiz Walton's Neo-HooDoo Jass Band performs at the Native Son Restaurant in Berkeley, California, Joe Overstreet's Neo-HooDoo exhibit will happen at the Berkeley Gallery Sept. 1, 1970 in Berkeley.)

Neo-HooDoo ain't Negritude. Neo-HooDoo never been to France. Neo-HooDoo is "your Mama" as Larry Neal said. Neo-HooDoos Little Richard and Chuck Berry nearly succeeded in converting the Beatles. When the Beatles said they were more popular than Christ they seemed astonished at the resulting outcry. This is because although they could feebly through amplification and technological sham 'mimic' (as if Little Richard and Chuck Berry were Loa [Spirits] practicing ventriloquism on their "Horses") the Beatles failed to realize that they were conjuring the music and ritual (although imitation) of a Forgotten Faith, a traditional enemy of Christianity which Christianity the Cop Religion has had to drive underground each time they meet. Neo-HooDoo now demands a rematch, the referees were bribed and the adversary had resin on his gloves.

The Vatican Forbids Jazz Masses in Italy
Rome, Aug. 6 (UPI)—The Vatican today barred jazz and popular music from masses in Italian churches and forbade young Roman Catholics to change prayers or readings used on Sundays and holy days.
    It said such changes in worship were "eccentric and arbitrary."
    A Vatican document distributed to all Italian bishops did not refer to similar experimental masses elsewhere in the world, although Pope Paul VI and other high-ranking churchmen are known to dislike the growing tendency to deviate from the accepted form of the mass.
    Some Italian churches have permitted jazz masses played by combos while youthful worshipers sang such songs as "We Shall Overcome."
    Church leaders two years ago rebuked priests who permitted such experiments.
[The New York Times, August 7, 1970.]

Africa is the home of the Loa (Spirits) of Neo-HooDoo although we are building our own American "pantheon." Thousands of "Spirits" (Ka) who would laugh at Jeho-vah's fury concerning "false idols" (translated everybody else's religion) or "fetishes."

Moses, Jeho-vah's messenger and zombie, swiped the secrets of VooDoo from old Jethro but nevertheless ended up with a curse. (Warning, many White "Black delineators" who practiced HooDoo VooDoo for gain and did not "feed" the Black Spirits of HooDoo ended up tragically.) Bix Beiderbecke and Irene Castle (who exploited Black Dance in the 1920s and relished in dressing up as a Nun) are examples of this tragic tendency.

Moses had a near heart attack when he saw his sons dancing nude before the Black Bull God Apis. They were dancing to a "heathen sound" that Moses had "heard before in Egypt" (probably a mixture of Sun Ra and Jimmy Reed played in the nightclub district of ancient Egypt's "The Domain of Osiris"—named after the god who enjoyed the fancy footwork of the pigmies).

The continuing war between Moses and his "Sons" was recently acted out in Chicago in the guise of an American "trial."

I have called Jeho-vah (most likely Set the Egyptian Sat-on [a pun on the fiend's penalty] Satan) somewhere "a partypooper and hater of dance." Neo-HooDoos are detectives of the metaphysical about to make a pinch. We have issued warrants for a god arrest. If Jeho-vah reveals his real name he will be released on his own recognizance de-horned and put out to pasture.

A dangerous paranoid pain-in-the-neck a CopGod from the git-go, Jeho-vah was the successful law and order candidate in the mythological relay of the 4th century A.D. Jeho-vah is the God of punishment. The H-Bomb is a typical Jeho-vah "miracle." Jeho-vah is why we are in Vietnam. He told Moses to go out and "subdue" the world.

There has never been in history another such culture as the Western civilization—a culture which has practiced the belief that the physical and social environment of man is subject to rational manipulation and that history is subject to the will and action of man; whereas central to the traditional cultures of the rivals of Western civilization, those of Africa and Asia, is a belief that it is environment that dominates man. [The Politics of Hysteria, *Edmund Stillman and William Pfaff.*]

"Political leaders" are merely altar boys from Jeho-vah. While the targets of some "revolutionaries" are laundramats and candy stores, Neo-HooDoo targets are TV the museums the symphony halls and churches art music and literature departments in Christianizing (education I think they call it!) universities which propogate the Art of Jeho-vah—much Byzantine Middle Ages Renaissance painting of Jeho-vah's "500 years of civilization" as Nixon put it are Jeho-vah propaganda. Many White revolutionaries can only get together with 3rd world people on the most mundane 'political' level because they are of Jeho-vah's party and don't know it. How much Black music do so-called revolutionary underground radio stations play. On the other hand how much Bach?

Neo-HooDoos are Black Red (Black Hawk an American Indian was an early philosopher of the HooDoo Church) and occasionally White (Madememoiselle Charlotte is a Haitian Loa [Spirit]).

Neo-HooDoo is a litany seeking its text
Neo-HooDoo is a Dance and Music closing in on its words
Neo-HooDoo is a Church finding its lyrics
Cecil Brown Al Young Calvin Hernton
David Henderson Steve Cannon Quincy Troupe
Ted Joans Victor Cruz N. H. Pritchard Ishmael Reed
Lennox Raphael Sarah Fabio Ron Welburn are Neo
HooDoo's "Manhattan Project" of writing . . .

A Neo-HooDoo celebration will involve the dance music
and poetry of Neo-HooDoo and whatever ideas the
participating artists might add. A Neo-HooDoo seal
is the Face of an Old American Train.
Neo-HooDoo signs are everywhere!
Neo-HooDoo is the Now Locomotive swinging
up the Tracks of the American Soul.

Almost 100 years ago HooDoo was forced to say
Goodbye to America. Now HooDoo is
back as Neo-HooDoo
You can't keep a good church down!

THE NEO-HOODOO AESTHETIC

Gombo Févi

A whole chicken—if chicken cannot be had, veal will serve instead; a little ham; crabs, or shrimps, or both, according to the taste of the consumer; okra according to the quantity of soup needed; onions, garlic, parsley red pepper, etc. Thicken with plenty of rice. (Don't forget to cut up the gombo or okra.)

Gombo Filé

Same as above except the okra is pulverised and oysters are used

Why do I call it "The Neo-HooDoo Aesthetic"?

The proportions of ingredients used depend upon the cook!

IMAMU AMIRI BARAKA (LeROI JONES)
Expressive Language

By the mid-1960s, Baraka had become one of the major figures (poetry, fiction, theater) of the "new American poetry." His contribution to an ethnopoetics was the articulation (both in theory and practice) of black cultural and linguistic values within a highly charged social/political context in which he participated notably from a home base in Newark, New Jersey. Changing over the years, his cultural writings are marked by early warnings of "cultural imperialism," etc. (see above, pp. 12, 340) and by a recent return to a universalism along Marxist-Leninist lines but drawing from the black instance still central to his poetry. Many of his principal works are included in the recently issued Selected Poetry and Selected Plays and Prose.

Speech is the effective form of a culture. Any shape or cluster of human history still apparent in the conscious and unconscious habit of groups of people is what I mean by culture. All culture is necessarily profound. The very fact of its longevity, of its being what it is, *culture*, the epic memory of practical tradition, means that it is profound. But the inherent profundity of culture does not necessarily mean that its *uses* (and they are as various as the human condition) will be profound. German culture is profound. Generically. Its uses, however, are specific, as are all uses . . . of ideas, inventions, products of nature. And specificity, as a right and passion of human life, breeds what it breeds as a result of its context.

Context, in this instance, is most dramatically social. And the social, though it must be rooted, as are all evidences of existence, in culture, depends for its impetus for the most part on a multiplicity of influences. Other cultures, for instance. Perhaps, and this is a common occurrence, the reaction or interreaction of one culture on another can produce a social context that will extend or influence any culture in many strange directions.

Social also means *economic*, as any reader of nineteenth-century European philosophy will understand. The economic is part of the social—and in our time much more so than what we have known as the spiritual or metaphysical, because the most valuable canons of power have either been reduced or traduced into stricter economic terms. That is, there has been a shift in the actual meaning of the world since Dante lived. As if Brooks Adams were right. Money does not mean the same thing to me it must mean to a rich man. I cannot, right now, think of one meaning to name. This is not so simple to understand. Even as a simple term of the English language, *money* does not possess the same meanings for the rich man as it does for me, a lower-middle-class American, albeit of laughably "aristocratic" pretensions. What possibly can "money" mean to a poor man? And I am not talking now about those courageous products of our permissive society who walk knowledgeably into "poverty" as they would into a public toilet. I mean, The Poor.

I look in my pocket; I have seventy cents. Possibly I can buy a beer. A quart of ale,

SOURCE: Amiri Baraka (LeRoi Jones), Home: Social Essays, *pages 373–377.*

specifically. Then I will have twenty cents with which to annoy and seduce my fingers when they wearily search for gainful employment. I have no idea at this moment what that seventy cents will mean to my neighbor around the corner, a poor Puerto Rican man I have seen hopefully watching my plastic garbage can. But I am certain it cannot mean the same thing. Say to David Rockefeller, "I have money," and he will think you mean something entirely different. That is, if you also dress the part. He would not for a moment think, "Seventy cents." But then neither would many New York painters.

Speech, the way one describes the natural proposition of being alive, is much more crucial than even most artists realize. Semantic philosophers are certainly correct in their emphasis on the final dictation of words over their users. But they often neglect to point out that, after all, it is the actual importance, *power*, of the words that remains so finally crucial. Words have users, but as well, users have words. And it is the users that establish the world's realities. Realities being those fantasies that control your immediate span of life. Usually they are not your own fantasies, *i.e.*, they belong to governments, traditions, etc., which, it must be clear by now, can make for conflict with the singular human life all ways. The fantasy of America might hurt you, but it is what should be meant when one talks of "reality." Not only the things you can touch or see, but the things that make such touching or seeing "normal." Then words, like their users, have a hegemony. Socially—which is final, right now. If you are some kind of artist, you naturally might think this is not so. There is the future. But *immortality* is a kind of drug, I think—one that leads to happiness at the thought of death. Myself, I would rather live forever . . . just to make sure.

The social hegemony, one's position in society, enforces more specifically one's terms (even the vulgar have "pull"). Even to the mode of speech. But also it makes these terms an available explanation of any social hierarchy, so that the words themselves become, even informally, laws. And of course they are usually very quickly stitched together to make formal statutes only fools or the faithfully intrepid would dare to question beyond immediate necessity.

The culture of the powerful is very infectious for the sophisticated, and strongly addictive. To be any kind of "success" one must be fluent in this culture. Know the words of the users, the semantic rituals of power. This is a way into wherever it is you are not now, but wish, very desperately, to get into.

Even speech then signals a fluency in this culture. A knowledge at least. "He's an educated man," is the barest acknowledgment of such fluency . . . in any time. "He's hip," my friends might say. They connote a similar entrance.

And it is certainly the meanings of words that are most important, even if they are no longer consciously acknowledged, but merely, by their use, trip a familiar lever of social accord. To recreate instantly the understood hierarchy of social, and by doing that, cultural, importance. And cultures are thought by most people in the world to do their business merely by being hierarchies. Certainly this is true in the West, in as simple a manifestation as Xenophobia, the naïve bridegroom of anti-human feeling, or in economic terms, Colonialism. For instance, when the first Africans were brought into the New World, it was thought that it was all right for them to be slaves because "they were heathens." It is a perfectly logical assumption.

And it follows, of course, that slavery would have been an even stranger phenomenon had the Africans spoken English when they first got here. It would have complicated things. Very soon after the first generations of Afro-Americans mastered this language, they invented white people called Abolitionists.

Words' meanings, but also the rhythm and syntax that frame and propel their concatenation, seek their culture as the final reference for what they are describing of the world. An A flat played twice on the same saxophone by two different men does not have to sound the same. If these men have different ideas of what they want this note to do, the note will not sound the same. Culture is the form, the overall structure of organized thought (as well as emotion and spiritual pretension). There are many cultures. Many ways of organizing thought, or having thought organized. That is, the form of thought's passage through the world will take on as many diverse shapes as there are diverse groups of travelers. Environment is one organizer of *groups*, at any level of its meaning. People who live in Newark, New Jersey, are organized, for whatever purpose, as Newarkers. It begins that simply. Another manifestation, at a slightly more complex level, can be the fact that blues singers from the Midwest sing through their noses. There is an explanation past the geographical, but that's the idea in tabloid. And singing through the nose does propose that the definition of singing be altered . . . even if ever so slightly. (At this point where someone's definitions must be changed, we are flitting around at the outskirts of the old city of Aesthetics. A solemn ghost town. Though some of the bones of reason can still be gathered there.)

But we still need definitions, even if there already are many. The dullest men are always satisfied that a dictionary lists everything in the world. They don't care that you may find out something *extra*, which one day might even be valuable to them. Of course, by that time it might even be in the dictionary, or at least they'd hope so, if you asked them directly.

But for every item in the world, there are a multiplicity of definitions that fit. And every word we use *could* mean something else. And at the same time. The culture fixes the use, and usage. And in "pluralistic" America, one should always listen very closely when he is being talked to. The speaker might mean something completely different from what we think we're hearing. "Where is your pot?"

I heard an old Negro street singer last week, Reverend Pearly Brown, singing, "God don't never change!" This is a precise thing he is singing. He does not mean "God does not ever change!" He means "God don't never change!" The difference, and I said it was crucial, is in the final human reference . . . the form of passage through the world. A man who is rich and famous who sings, "God don't never change," is confirming his hegemony and good fortune . . . or merely calling the bank. A blind hopeless black American is saying something very different. He is telling you about the extraordinary order of the world. But he is not telling you about his "fate." Fate is a luxury available only to those fortunate citizens with alternatives. The view from the top of the hill is not the same as that from the bottom of the hill. Nor are most viewers at either end of the hill, even certain that, in fact, there is any other place from which to look. Looking down usually eliminates the possibility of understanding what it must be like to look up. Or try to imagine yourself as not existing. It is difficult, but poets and politicians try every other day.

Being told to "speak proper," meaning that you become fluent with the jargon of power, is also a part of not "speaking proper." That is, the culture which desperately understands that it does not "speak proper," or is not fluent with the terms of social strength, also understands somewhere that its desire to gain such fluency is done at a terrifying risk. The bourgeois Negro accepts such risk as profit. But does *close-ter* (in the context of "jes a close-ter, walk wi-thee") mean the same thing as *closer*? Close-ter, in the term of its user is, believe me, exact. It means a quality of existence, of actual physical disposition perhaps . . . in its manifestation as a *tone* and *rhythm* by which people live, most often in response to common modes of thought best enforced by some factor of environmental emotion that is exact and specific. Even the picture it summons is different, and certainly the "Thee" that is used to connect the implied "Me" with, is different. The God of the damned cannot know the God of the damner, that is, cannot know he is God. As no Blues person can really believe emotionally in Pascal's God, or Wittgenstein's question, "Can the concept of God exist in a perfectly logical language?" Answer: "God don't never change."

Communication is only important because it is the broadest root of education. And all cultures communicate exactly what they have, a powerful motley of experience.

GARY SNYDER

From "The Incredible Survival of Coyote"

Gary Snyder's researches, which form a part of his own work, go back to the early 1950s and a thesis, He Who Hunted Birds in His Father's Village: The Dimensions of a Haida Myth, *only recently published as a book. A key contributor to the ethnopoetic discourse (see above, p. 90), his principal works include* Myths and Texts, Regarding Wave, *and* Turtle Island *(poetry);* Earth House Hold *and* The Old Ways *(essays); and* The Real Work *(talks and interviews).*

The Coyote figure discussed herein is, of course, only one instance of the widely diffused Trickster—for which, see above, page 206.

Of all the uses of native American lore in modern poetry, the presence of the Coyote figure, the continuing presence of Coyote, is the most striking. I could just as well say I am talking about the interaction between myth and place, sense of myth, sense of place, in our evolving modern poetry of the far West. Western American poets are looking back now at the history of the West, and how it is that they are using as much Native American

SOURCE: Gary Snyder, The Old Ways, *pages 67−85.*

lore as they are drawing on, say, the folklore of the cowboy or the mountain men. Why is this?

When the early mountain men, explorers, and then pioneers, cattle ranchers, moved into this Great Basin country a hundred and fifty years ago, they found, particularly on the west side of the Rockies, peoples, Shoshonean and others (Salishan peoples in the Montanas) that they regarded with some contempt, as compared say with the Indians of the plains, the Indians who put up a lot of fight and had a more elaborate material culture. The Shoshonean people of the Great Basin and the California Indians have received the least respect and have been accorded a position at the bottom of the scale in white regard for Indian cultures. The California Indians were called "diggers." The early literature is really contemptuous of these people. Ignorance of the California Indians is extraordinary. I find that very few people are aware of the fact that the population of native people in California was equal to native populations in all the rest of North America north of the Rio Grande, and the greatest density of North American Indian population north of Mexico was Napa County and Sonoma County California just north of San Francisco Bay. The image of California Indians as shiftless and as having no interesting material culture persists although they had elaborate dance, basketry, feather-working, ritual systems. That irony, then, is that these people who were the least regarded, have left modern poetry with a very powerful heritage—Coyote.

The coyote survives where the wolf is almost extinct throughout the West because, as I've been told, he took no poison bait. Strychnine-laced cow carcasses that ranchers put out for the wolf were what did the wolf in. The coyotes learned very early not to take poisoned bait, and they still flourish. In the same way, from the Rockies on westward, from Mexico and north well into Canada, in all of these cultures you find the trickster hero Coyote Man to be one of the most prominent elements.

Stories about Coyote, Coyote Man as he's sometimes called to distinguish him from coyote the animal, Coyote the myth figure, who lived in myth time, dream time, and lots of things happened then. Over on the other side of the Cascades, he switches names and becomes Raven. In the Great Lakes sometimes it's Hare, but out here it's Coyote Man. Now, is there anybody here who doesn't know what a Coyote tale is like? A Basin Coyote tale? In folklorist terms he's a trickster, and the stories of the far West are the most trickster-like of all. He's always traveling, he's really stupid, he's kind of bad, in fact he's really awful, he's outrageous. Now he's done some good things too, he got fire for people. The Mescaleros say he found where the fire was kept. It was kept by a bunch of flies in a circle, and he couldn't get into the circle, but he was able to stick his tail in there and get his tail burning, and then off he scampered and managed to start some forest fires with his tail, and that fire kept running around the world, and people are still picking it up here and there. So he's done some good things. He taught people up in the Columbia River how to catch salmon. He taught people which were the edible plants.

But most of the time he's just into mischief. Like, it's Coyote's fault that there's death in the world. This from California, Maidu. Earthmaker made the world so that people wouldn't get old, wouldn't die. He made a lake so that if people began to feel as if they were getting old, they'd go get in this lake and get young again, and he made it so that every morning when you wake up you reach outside your lodge and there's a cooked bowl, cooked mind you, of hot steaming acorn mush to eat. Didn't have to work for food in those days. Nobody died, and there was always plenty of food, you just reached outside the door every morning, and there's some nice hot acorn mush. But Coyote went around agitating the human beings saying "Now, you folks, don't you think this is kind of a dull life, there ought to be something happening here, maybe you ought to die." And they'd say "What's that, death?" And he'd say "Well, you know, if you die, then you really have to take life seriously, you have to think about things more." And he kept agitating this way, and Earthmaker heard him agitating this way, and Earthmaker shook his head and he said "Oh boy, things are going to go all wrong now." So Coyote kept agitating this death idea around, and pretty soon things started happening. They were having a foot race, and Coyote's son was running in the foot race. Coyote Man's son got out there, and by golly, he stepped on a rattlesnake and the rattlesnake bit him, and he fell over and lay on the ground, and everybody thought he was asleep for the longest time. Coyote kept shouting "Wake up, come on now, run." Finally Earthmaker looked at him and said "You know what happened? He's dead. You asked for it." And Coyote said "Well, I changed my mind, I don't want people to die after all, now let's have him come back to life." But Earthmaker said, "It's too late now, it's too late now."

There are plenty of stories about Coyote Man and his sheer foolishness. He's out walking along, and he watches these beautiful little gold colored Cottonwood leaves floating down to the ground, and they go this . . . this . . . this . . . this . . . this, this, this, this, and he just watches those for the longest time. Then he goes up and he asks those leaves "Now how do you do that? That's so pretty the way you come down." And they say "Well there's nothing to it, you just get up in a tree, and then you fall off." So he climbs up the Cottonwood tree and launches himself off, but he doesn't go all pretty like that, he just goes bonk and kills himself. But Coyote never dies, he gets killed plenty of times, but he always comes back to life again, and then he goes right on traveling.

When Coyote went to the world above this one, the only way to get back was to come down a spider web, and the spider told him, "Now, when you go down that spider web, don't look down, and don't look back, just keep your eyes closed until your feet hit the bottom, and then you'll be okay." So he's going down this spider web, and he's gettin' kind of restless, and he says "Well, now, I'm just sure I'm about to touch bottom now, any minute my foot's going to touch bottom, I'm going to open my eyes." And he opens his eyes, and naturally the spider web breaks, and he falls and kills himself. So he lies there, and the carrion beetles come and eat him, and some of his hair blows away and pretty soon his ribs are coming out. About six months go by and he really is looking messy, but he begins to wake up and opens one eye and the other, and he can't find the other eye, so he reaches out and sticks a pebble in his eye socket, and then a blue jay comes along and puts a little pine pitch on the pebble, and then he can see through that. And he sort of pulls himself back together and goes around and looks for a couple of his ribs that have kind of drifted down the hill, and pulls himself back together and says, "Well, now I'm going to keep on traveling."

He really gets into some awful mischief. There's a story we find all the way from the Okanogan country right down into the Apache country about how Coyote Man got interested in his oldest daughter. He just really wanted to have an affair with his oldest daughter, and he couldn't get over the idea so finally one day he told his family, "Well, I'm going to die now," or in some versions he says "I'm going on a long trip." So he just goes around the corner on the hill a ways, and he puts on a disguise. Oh, before he goes he tells them, "If a man comes along, some handsome man with a big satchel who has a couple of jack rabbits to offer you, now you be real nice to him, let him in, take good care of him.'' So then he goes off around the corner, puts on his disguise, picks up a couple of jack rabbits, and comes back, and the girls say to their mother, ''Why, sure enough, here's a man just like Daddy said we should be nice to.'' And so they take him into the house, and feed him and he sits in the corner and talks in kind of a muffled voice, and then he starts saying, ''That sure is a pretty oldest daughter you've got there, wouldn't you like to marry her to somebody?'' And he's almost going to get away with this, but then he asks them to go over his hair for lice or something like that, and so they're going over his hair for lice, and they find this wart on one cheek, and they say ''Why, it's just Daddy.'' Lots of stories like that.

How did this literature come down to modern American poetry? I was hitchhiking in 1951 from San Francisco to Indiana University where I was going to enter graduate school in anthropology. I got picked up by some Paiute men just outside of Reno in the evening. We drove all night to Elko. During that night it turned out they had a couple of cases of beer in the car, so we were doing that old far Western thing of driving and drinking a couple hundred miles, and they started telling Coyote tales. They had been working as steelworkers in Oakland, and they were heading back home somewhere near Elko, and they started telling Coyote tales. They started talking about Jesus, one said Jesus was a great gambler. He was perhaps the best gambler in the United States. And they told Coyote stories with obvious relish, as part of their own world, but also with that distance of having been urban, having worked on steelworking jobs, having been to BIA school. Still telling them. Another way we come on it is this. In my own poetry, back 20 years or so, the Coyote trickster theme began to crop up here and there. (I think I was one of the first to find something to use in that Coyote image, but I'm not the only one. There's been a magazine called *Coyote's Journal* that has had ten issues out now in the last seven years, edited by James Koller, who first lived in the state of Washington, then lived in the Bay Area and now lives in Maine, and the latest issue of *Coyote's Journal* was produced in Maine.)

Jaime de Angulo brought together a book that had originally started out as stories he told to his children, first published in the middle fifties as *Indian Tales*. [Jaime de Angulo was originally a Spanish M.D. who converted over to being an anthropologist and linguist first in the Southwest and then in California during the twenties and thirties, and then became a San Francisco and Big Sur post-World War II anarchist-bohemian culture hero. Now, he was one of the people who had direct contact with Coyote and other American Indian lore as a linguist and anthropologist. Jaime de Angulo was a friend of Robinson Jeffers, in fact I have heard it said that he was the only human being that Robinson Jeffers would let into his house any time of the day or night. He appears in some of Robinson Jeffers' poems as the Spanish cowboy, because at one time Jaime de Angulo was running a working ranch on Partington Ridge up above Big Sur.] So Jaime de Angulo's *Indian Tales*, which is full of California Indian Coyote lore, is filtered through Jaime's own peculiar way of seeing things and this became a direct influence on a lot of writers in the Bay Area. So there is a peculiar Western and particularly West Coast body of poetry which at one point or another refers to Coyote almost as though everybody knew what Coyote is all about already, and in some areas of the literary Western world Coyote is already taken for granted as a shorthand name for a particular figure which is out of the Native American Indian lore but also, in psychological terms, refers to something in ourselves which is creative, unpredictable, contradictory: trickster human nature.

I'd better step back and talk about the West again. I've noticed that all the experts here dodge off the question when anybody asks them "What is a Westerner, really, what is the West?" Nobody wants to say. So I'll offer my interpretation of that, hoping that I have proper credentials at least by being from an old Western family, who did what I would consider Western things, used Western speech, and had a certain kind of Western set of attitudes. A certain set, there are several sets. The usual literature of the West is concerned with the period of exploitation and expansion west of the tree line. This is what we mean when we talk about the "epic" or "heroic" period of the West. A period of rapid expansion, first-phase exploitation. It is not a literature of place. It's a history and a literature of feats of strength, and of human events; of specifically white, English-speaking-American human events. It's only about this place by accident. The place only comes into it as a matter of inhospitable and unfamiliar terrain; Anglos from temperate climates suddenly confronted with vast, treeless, arid spaces. Space and aridity; confronting that and living with it is a key theme in Western literature, but only incidentally. It could just as well be an Icelandic saga or a heroic epic of Indo-European people spreading with their cattle and wagons into any other unfamiliar and new territory as they did in 1500 B.C. when they moved down into the Ganges River Basin or into Greece. The West, then, presented us with an image of manliness, of vigor, of courage, of humor, of heroics which became a very strong part of our national self-image; perhaps the strongest part, the most pervasive, the one which has been most exported to the rest of the world. There are, of course, Southern images: the Daniel Boone image; there is the Yankee self-image and several others in American folk literature/folk lore history. But the Western image, which is a kind of amalgam of mountain man, cowboy, and rancher is one of the strongest self-images of America. The West ceases to be (whether it's geographically Western or not) when economy shifts from direct, rapid exploitation to a stabilized agricultural recycling base. Heroics go with first phase exploitation, hence fur trade, then cattle industry, then mining, then logging.

I grew up in an area where logging was going on. That's what made it the West, actually it was western Washington, which some people perhaps would exclude from the "Western literature" spheres since not arid & treeless, but it is within the West because it was within that sphere of direct exploitation which had the tall tales, the energy, the unpredictability, the mobility, and the uprootedness of that kind of work. The dairy farmers of the Willamette Valley of Oregon are not so much Westerners, they're New Englanders or they're Wisconsin People, they are in a different place. San Francisco was the jumping off point for the mines in Nevada—that's again the direct exploitation, the rapid growth. Which is why the oil fields are Western, they still have that rough and tumble angle to them, and why the North slope of Alaska is the West in the senses of which I'm talking. (And we can expect, or could have expected a few decades back that the oil fields of Alaska would produce some tall-tale-type lore of oil-men.)

Another aspect: men removed some distance from women. Leslie Fiedler has talked about this in a very interesting way: saying that one aspect of the heroic and epic West is that men have gotten away from home and away from women. You may all know the movie in which finally the Bible-totin' ladies come to town, and the men have to get all shiny and spruced up and there they are sitting in this little white New England style church singing hymns finally, and it's funny and it's also tragic, you know. The West is over when nice women come and start making you wash your hands before dinner. Something Fiedler didn't say is that it's also men removed from the father image. They're beyond the reach of the law, which is to say the Nation State patriarchal figure archetype. And so the West is in a sense psychologically occupied by boys without fathers and mothers, who are really free to get away with things for a while, and that's why there is so much humor in the lore of the West.

But something has happend, since World War II. I can see a little bit how it happened in myself. Our sense of the West is changing from a history of exploitation and westward expansion by white people, into a sense of place. Those old time Westerners did not know where they were. Except for the mountain men, who became almost Indians, they didn't really know the plants, they didn't really know animal behavior. The mountain men were the quickest and the first to learn that. The process of learning "where they were"—of becoming natives of the place—was underway. I know how my grandmother was able to pick wild plants in Kitsap County, Washington, how she was able to use things from the forest, making berry pies out of wild blackberries, she knew a few edible mushrooms. But my grandmother's generation was the last of it; the next generation grew up with supermarkets and canned food. The potentiality of a viable self-sufficient rural West evaporated after about one generation. What we have now in the West is really an urban population, small town and urban people who are all driving hundreds of miles, operating with fossil fuels, and getting their food from supermarkets (with a few outstanding exceptions). Comparisons can be made, of course, with people of the hills of the South, or of New England; who had a hundred and fifty to three hundred years of living in a self-sufficient rural manner, and who really did develop a much deeper knowledge and self-sufficiency related to the plants, animals, weather patterns, the lore of the place. There *is* a sense of place in the South and in New England, although it has eroded considerably. But the Far West didn't really quite get it. So that when some of my colleagues, poets, for example, talk about, "Let's make an anthology of Western Poetry" or "Who is a Western Poet? What is Western Poetry?" the first criterion should be sense of place, and how well that comes across. Poets who have lived in the West all their lives, teaching in universities, can speak only of the urban world, some of them, and they're not paisanos, you see, Paisanos in the sense of knowing a place. So there is a work to be done in the matter of knowing where we are, the old American quest, which I share with all of you, for an identity, a sense of place. To know the place well means, first and foremost, I think, to know plants, and it means developing a sensitivity, an openness, an awareness of all kinds of weather patterns and patterns in nature.

So, why do modern writers and some young people today, look to native American lore? Well, the first answer, there is something to be learned from the native American people about where we are. It can't be learned from anybody else. We have a Western white history of a hundred and fifty years; but the native American history (the datings are always being pushed back) was first ten thousand years, then it was sixteen thousand years, then people started talking about thirty-five thousand years, and now, the Santa Barbara skull, fifty thousand years. So, when we look at a little bit of American Indian folklore, myth, read a tale, we're catching just the tip of an iceberg of forty or fifty thousand years of human experience, on this continent, in this place. It takes a great effort of imagination to enter into that, to draw from it, but there is something powerfully there.

There is a remarkable body of Native American myth and lore which resides in our libraries in the form of the bulletins and reports of the Bureau of American Ethnology going back to the 1880's. Respectable, scrupulous, careful collections, for the most part unbowdlerized. (In the early days they took the more scatological sections and translated them into Latin, but then everybody knew Latin in those days so. . . . But in recent years they don't do that.) That is what I learned from, there is an irony in that too. I grew up knowing Indians and not too far from them, but the first way I got my hands on the material was going into the library. Franz Boas, Edward Sapir, John Swanton, Melville Jacobs, Thelma Jacobson, Alfred Lewis Kroeber and his students and disciplines, Harry Hoijer, M. E. Opler, almost all of them in one way or another disciples of Franz Boas, gave decades of their lives to the collection of texts in the original languages, and translations into English, of the lore of every cultural group that they could make contact with from British Columbia south. It is an extremely rich body of scholarship and some of us learned how to draw it into our own work, to enjoy it, first and foremost to enjoy it. The first thing that excited me about Coyote tales was the delightful, Dadaistic energy, leaping somehow into a modern frame of reference. The technical and scholarly collections of American Indian material have begun to creep into more popular availability and circulation. Jerome Rothenberg's book *Shaking the Pumpkin*, which is an anthology of American Indian poetry, is the best to be done so far, but I'm still dubious about what happens when modern white men start changing the old texts, making versions, editing, cleaning it up—not cleaning it up so much as just changing it around a little bit. There's nothing for me as useful as the direct transcription, as literally close as possible to the original text in whatever language it was, Kwakiutl or Apache. The true flavor seems to be there. (There is a perennial argument, do you get more out of something when somebody has made it more readable, more literary, taken the brackets and the parentheses out, and the dots and the ellipses and the footnotes, cleaned it up so you can read it? Is that better or is it better when you get down to the primary source and try to use that? Well, I'm all for the primary source in historical materials, whether American Indian or otherwise, because I would prefer to do the editing with my imagination rather than let somebody else's imagination do the work for me. At least, then, if there are errors in interpretation they're my own errors, and not somebody else's.) That's just a footnote on the side, and to point out that when these poets—such as Will Staple, Barry Gifford, Ed Dorn, Enrique Lamadrid, Margo St. James, James White, or James Koller—use Coyote material, usually some percentage of their inspiration started at the library. Peter Blue Cloud may be the only exception.

The other twenty percent is not to be overlooked, though. The other twenty percent comes from that direct experience of being in the space of the West. How does it feel to be out in the deserts of eastern Oregon, or eastern Washington? I spent a lot of time in eastern Oregon, and going into it. Sure, stories about the early stages and wagon trains going across eastern Oregon, tales of the early wheat ranchers, they're interesting, but they don't help with the place. To tune to the smell of it, and the feel of it I found that the sense of Coyote and some of the other materials that, say, Sapir collected, Wasco and Wishram texts, began to teach me something about the real flavor of the land, began to move me back just a trifle from historical time into myth time, into the eternal now of geological time for which our historical time, one hundred and fifty years, is an inconsequential ripple. Those flavors. . . . Looking forward, then, I can only speculate that (just to finish with comments on ideas of the West) future Western young people, whether in Utah, Idaho, Nevada, California, or whatever, are bound to become increasingly concerned with *place*. This will not be the same as regionalism. Regionalism, as it has existed in American literature in the past has been pretty much a human history; the story of particular human habits, and oddities and quirks, and ethnic diversities and whatever, that are established in a region. That's white human history, often very good literature, but "regional" has not been so specifically tuned to the spirit of place as I think it will in the future. That exploitative first phase economic and social behavior, although heroic and interesting, is not a viable long range model. Ecologists and economists are beginning to tell us now that harmony with the local place and a way of life that does not exhaust the resources and can be passed on to your children and grandchildren with no fear of depletion is the way we must learn to live. As people come to understand this, they will look back with few regrets, and say that the heroic period of the West was entertaining, but we're learning a lot from the Indians. And for the Indian peoples, Western history is not a glorious epic history with nice tall tales on the side, it's a history of humiliation, defeat and dispossession.

Now, then, what of the trickster, himself? Coyote, as I said, was interesting to me and some of my colleagues because he spoke to us of place, because he clearly belonged to the place and became almost like a guardian, a protector spirit. The other part of it has to come out of something inside of us. The fascination with the trickster. A world folk image of the trickster, suppressed or altered in some cultures; more clearly developed in others. For me I think the most interesting psychological thing about the trickster, and what drew me to it for my own personal reasons was that there wasn't a clear dualism of good and evil established there, that he clearly manifested benevolence, compassion, help, to human beings, sometimes, and had a certain dignity; and on other occasions he was the silliest utmost fool; the overriding picture is old Coyote Man, he's just always traveling along, doing the best he can. Growing up in the fifties in Portland, Oregon; going to Reed College, associated with still struggling ex-Communist Party professors, who had found the last haven, you know, somewhere to teach. Drawing on IWW lore, of my grandfather, native white grass-roots political radicalism of the Northwest. The trickster presents himself to us as an anti-hero. The West was heroics, but as you know, in the fifties and sixties we didn't feel like heroics, we felt more like anti-heroics, and the trickster is immediately an attractive figure for the same reasons that you find anti-heroics in the writings of post-World War II French and Italian or English writers. Artaud is a trickster, William Burroughs in his novels talks out of the side of his mouth with a kind of half Coyote, half Dashiell Hammett dry style. So the trickster image is basic; it has to do in part with that turning away from heroes. It's also interesting that there is a white American frontier language and story-telling which is often very much like Coyote lore—irresponsible, humorous, and unpredictable. Mike Fink stories and tall tales were being made up while these people were fighting with each other, the Indians telling their Coyote tales and the white men telling their tall tales, and they probably had very much the same sense of humor in some respects, but they weren't communicating across that gap. (I'm only reading Coyote as I can, namely twentieth century, West Coast white American. How the native American people themselves actually saw Coyote, actually used it, is another question which I may be able to touch on in a few minutes.)

So, when the Coyote figure comes into modern American poetry it is not just for a sense of place. It is also a play on the world-wide myth, tale, and motif storehouse. Poetry has always done this—drawing out, re-creating, subtly altering for each time and place the fundamental images. . . .

SIMON ORTIZ, PETER BLUE CLOUD, LEWIS MacADAMS
Coyote Poems

The emergence of Coyote as trickster-saint of the "new American poetry"—a primary event of ethnopoesis—is documented and discussed in the preceding piece by Gary Snyder. Three examples follow: from Acoma poet Simon Ortiz (see above, p. 399), who came at it from childhood, and from Mohawk poet Peter Blue Cloud and Texas-born poet Lewis MacAdams, who came at it in wanderings through the U.S.A. and through related adventures in poetry, etc. (But see also Diane di Prima's intuition of a female Loba (wolf) figure [below, p. 441], which is certainly related to the rest; or, at a still further remove, the English writings of Pierre Joris [born and raised in Luxembourg], who rediscovers ancient Trickster in the European Reynard = Fox Man.)

For classic examples of trickster-figures, see above, page 206, and Shaking the Pumpkin *(Rothenberg 1972: 102–116), among many other sources.*

TELLING ABOUT COYOTE (Simon Ortiz)

> Old Coyote . . .
> "If he hadn't looked back,
> everything would have been okay
> . . . . like he wasn't supposed to,
> but he did,
> and as soon as he did,
> he lost all his power, his strength."
> Never will learn will you.

SOURCE: Simon Ortiz, A Good Journey, *pages 235–237; Peter Blue Cloud (Aroniawenrate),* Back Then Tomorrow, *pages 71–74; Lewis MacAdams,* News from Niman Farm.

". . . . you know, Coyote
is in the origin and all the way
through. . . . he's the cause
of the trouble, the hard times
that things have. . . ."
"Yet, he came so close
to having it easy.

                                But he said,
"Things are too easy. . . ."
of course, he was mainly bragging,
shooting his mouth.
The existential Man,
a Dostoevsky Coyote.

"He was on his way to Zuni
to get married on that Saturday,
and on the way there,
he ran across a gambling party,
a number of other animals were there.

                                He sat in
for a while, you know, pretty sure,
you know like he is, he would win
something.

                                But he lost
everything. Everything.
and that included his skin, his fur,
which was the subject of envy
for all the other animals around.
Coyote had the prettiest,
the glossiest, the softest fur
that ever was. And he lost that.

                                So some mice,
finding him shivering in the cold
beside a rock, felt sorry for him.
'This poor thing, beloved,'
they said, and they got together
just some old scraps of fur
and glued them on Coyote with piñon pitch.
And he's had that motley fur ever since,
you know, the one that looks like
scraps of an old coat, that one."

Coyote, old man, wanderer,
where you going, man? Look up
and see the sun. Scorned,
an old raggy blanket at the back of the closet
nobody wants.

"At this conference of all the animals,
there was a bird with the purest
white feathers. The feathers were like,
ah . . . like the sun was shining on it
all the time, but you could look at it,
and you wouldn't be hurt by the glare;
it was easy to look at,
and he was Crow. He was sitting
at one side of the fire,
and the fire was being fed large pine logs,
and Crow was sitting downwind
from the fire, the wind was blowing that way

           . . . . and Coyote was there;
he was envious of Crow because
all the animals were saying, Wow,
look at that Crow, man, just look at him,
admiring him. Coyote began to scheme,
he kept on throwing logs into the fire,
and the wind kept blowing,
all night long . . .
    . . . . Let's see, the conference was about
deciding the seasons,
when they should take place,
and it took a long time to decide that. . . .
And when it was over, Crow was covered
entirely with soot, the blackest soot
from the pine logs,
and he's been like that since then."

"Oh yes, that was the conference
when Winter was decided
that it should take place
when Dog's hair got long.
                Dog said,
'I think Winter should take place
when my hair gets long.'
And it was agreed that it would. I guess
no one else offered a better reason."
            Who?
            Coyote?
O,
O yes, last time . . .
when was it,
I saw him somewhere
between Muskogee and Tulsa,

heading for Tulsy Town I guess,
just trucking along.
He was heading into some oakbrush thicket,
just over the hill was a creek.
Probably get to Tulsa in a couple days,
drink a little wine,
tease with the Pawnee babes,
sleep beside the Arkansas River,
listen to the river move,
. . . hope it don't rain,
hope the river don't rise.
He'll be back. Don't worry.
He'll be back.

BLACK COYOTE (Peter Blue Cloud [Aroniawenrate])

He was called Snowfox-running
of that large but scattered tribe
which hunted the frozen plains
and endless lakes of the far country,
born within the wail of a blizzard
his muzzle whiskered in frost
he whimpered an unknown hunger
his mother's milk could not quench.

He became a skilled hunter, and
even when very young often led
special hunting parties in the season
of the howling wind of hunger,
well respected by his people, he
had gained his hunting powers
by thinking hard and dreaming
himself to the places of food.

            It was a song brought to him
            on the wind of ice-breaking
            which gave him strange powers
            to see into the beyond;

            "I am given to sing it once,
            and then three times more,
            that I am to be a shadow
            cast upon unknown stone."

And his tribe and family wept
when he prepared to journey
for they thought he spoke of death

and would see them no more,
and he left a faint trail, soon
covered by snow, and was gone
crossing many plains and mountains
to the land of sage and sand.

He searched for and found the singular
circle of Coyote Old Man's sleep
and sat respectfully to await
the old man's own time,
and Coyote Old Man studied him
frowning at what was to be
having seen the whole process
in his lately dreaming sleep.

        "And so you are here and I
        am to ask what it is you seek
        and you will answer that you
        think you must become a shadow,

        and I must begin a ritual new
        to my mind's knowledge, and
        disagreeable to my thinking
        but I am Coyote, and will
                anyway.''

And Coyote Old Man built a fire
of sage and juniper in the sand
beneath the sky singing softly
feeding the fire slowly, slowly,
plucking out glowing coals
and blowing and talking to each
then setting them to rest on sand
to let them blacken and cool.

And all the while he ground the
charcoal, he spoke of and pointed
to moon shadows close and far
saying, "These you will become,
part of but separate, merging
like day into night, season
into season, back and
forth a running rhythm:

        now, as I rub you with charcoal
        now, as I rub-in shadow pigment
        now, I take away your voice
        now, I take away your body,
        you are a no one now,

you are a nothing, lost
like the memory of loneliness
the echo of a keening voice.

Now that you are nameless you
must follow me closely, making
every gesture I make and even
echoing my inner thoughts,
now when moon her fullness
lends us light, you are a motion
only, a shadow truly, moving
slowly across the cool night sand.

Nameless, you follow me and
become my footsteps, my
hind leg twitching in sleep, yes
you now enter my dreaming,
become as one with my ears
and nose, and soon you see
from my eyes and think
you think from my mind.

Yes, you are a shadow now
yes, as one with that which
is me we run barking,
                                    look
now I will give you a dance,
a moon dance, take it, it
is yours, and
                                    look
now I will give you a song
take that, too, and sing:

and watch me as you sing as I
tear you from me
                          see? Now you
I tear you from me laughing
yes, I am laughing now,
you are brother to me now
not blood of blood so much
as shadow of shadow, echo
of further echo, see?
You are a shadow cast in stone
and bigger in body than I
and your voice will also be
a more penetrating voice,

but your steps will not be seen
for even a solid shadow leaves
no trail, and you will travel
only at night, forever, at night.

       And you will turn the humans
       sleeping, with your voice, and
       they will worry in their dreams
       and wonder, and create a dance,

       and form a Coyote Clan of
       hunters and scouts, and all
       because they heard your voice
       and let it tell them what

they wished to think they heard.
And I will answer your keening
voice from the opposite hill
and though we never meet again,
we will sing together even until
the last human may perish
from having forgotten to dream
for the benefit of tomorrow.

And now I loose you wholly
and, see, now you have a shadow
of your own, to lead or follow
through the seasons' cycles,
and I name you
          Black Coyote,
dancer and singer of shadows,
disturber of human dreaming.
Go, the seasons await you!''

CALLIN COYOTE HOME (Lewis MacAdams)

Hey coyote. Welcome
back to the cartoon.

Thank you my fran. Excuse me boy,
you got a cigarette?

Here, have a camel.
Whaddya think's goin on?

All my frans are doing fine.

What do you think are the trends?
Do you think people are living a little more natural?

What do you mean natural?
Like when you're livin in a car
is that natural?

Right, but—

You must got to remember,
Illumination.
You got to give off some illumination
or the rest of us be thinkin
that the humans want it all for themselves.
And you pay for that in the long run, don't
you see.

I see.

Say. You know I don't have any money.

Oh. Well. I can go down to the liquor store
and cash a five. I have to go downtown anyway.

Heh-heh. No, that's alright man. Coyotes don't
use money. We usually naked. Don't have no pockets.

Coyote, are you a Buddhist?

I'm a *friend* of the Buddhist.

Coyote, what about marriage?

Boy, I'm afraid you're barking up the wrong tree.

It's just the same in your philosophy?

Boy, I don't have no philosophy.

Well how do you treat women?

I treat everybody good.
You have to,
if you're gonna live in a family,
which I'm hopin you're gonna do
because it's your ass if you *don't*.
Either way,
I'm gonna be a survivor.
If you know what I mean.

DIANE DI PRIMA
The Birth of Loba

The work of Diane di Prima—poetry, theater, autobiography—relates not only to European but to non-Western folklore and mythology: her anthology, Various Fables from Various Places; *her projected worldwide gathering on "the goddess"; her early staging of new ritual performances; and her long-running auto-mythological poem,* Loba, *to which the present lecture excerpt refers. The selection given here can be read in relation to the two preceding sections on Coyote, or to the Ainu version of the wolf goddess (see above, p. 156), or to the various discussions herein on the suppression and reemergence of the goddess figure (p. 36, 217, and 303). In the lecture itself, di Prima's description of Loba follows her self-identification with a gnostic/heretical visionary tradition brought into later poetry by such as Keats's "straining at particles of light in the midst of great darkness" or Pound's "In the gloom, the gold gathers the light against it." Principal works:* Loba, Selected Poems: 1956–1975, Dinners and Nightmares *(short stories),* Memoirs of a Beatnik.

There was a point at which I had been home for a number of years, and living as I thought I should live—zazen, macrobiotics, all that—and at one point I suddenly got a job teaching poetry in Wyoming to schoolchildren, and found that Wyoming, the parts that I was exposed to, was filled with so much pain, so much no-touching, so much no-loving, so much anger and these kids were in such a hungry place—all the usual boring stuff like teachers paddling people and all that, and Indian kids with almost no shoes having to run track in the snow, and nearly everyone always drunk or drinking—but there it was, there was so much for me to absorb, plus, also, I had lived on the kind of food I believed in, all those years, and I found myself thrown into a world where there was nothing to eat but steak and liquor. And you know, I came home from this experience, which was only a two-week experience, and I was sick for a month. I hurt all over my body. Everything hurt. I went to my homeopathic doctor, who was eighty-eight years old, and he said: "Toxins! Toxins in all the cells! A toxic condition of the system!" So, I went to bed and hurt a lot, and ate little homeopathic pills, and had a lot of dreams that were replays of various really heavy incidents: a girl at the reform school taking me on a tour of the building and showing me the solitary cells for thirteen to eighteen year olds, the face of a gay watercolorist who commits himself over and over to the state madhouse—trip after trip. I just had all these dreams, and slowly as I integrated this information, it got clear that there was nobody to blame. There was nobody in Wyoming that you could point to

SOURCE: Anne Waldmann and Marilyn Webb (eds.), Talking Poetics from Naropa Institute, *volume 1, pages 33–37.*

and say, "There's the villain, let's kill him!" and then it would all be OK. *There was no villain*. There was just a situation of people living in total pain. And as I began to absorb that information into my system, the dreams changed, they stopped being replays of classrooms and so on, and they got more and more symbolic. And finally, I had a very long dream one night. I won't go into all the parts of it, it had to do with having to find shelter somewhere, being in an outcast or vagabond situation with two of my children, and living in the cellar of this building in which some very rich people lived upstairs. They were getting ready to have one of their entertainments: they were going to watch through kind of skylight-things in the floor, while we were hunted down by a wolf. I found this out by going upstairs and spying on them, listening to the conversation. I decided I wasn't going to wait to be hunted. I picked up my baby, and had another kid following behind me, and I was with a friend whose baby was really noisy, and I was worried about the noise because I was afraid it was going to give us away, and we started to walk through this incredible stone labyrinth. As we were getting it together to go, down the ladder that I'd used to spy came two men with a wolf between them, trussed as if she had been killed in a hunt—you know, legs tied to a long piece of wood. When they got the wolf downstairs they untied it, and it's the wolf that's supposed to hunt us. We were already walking out. We weren't running—we were walking out. And this wolf digs that this is what's happening, and falls in behind us and starts walking with us. Keeping pace. And at some point, I turned around and looked this creature in the eye, and I recognized, in my dream, I recognized or remembered this huge white wolf, beautiful white head, recognized this as a goddess that I'd known in Europe a long long time ago. Never having read about any European wolf-goddesses, I just recognized this as deity. We stood and looked at each other for a long moment.

And then we emerged later—there's another part to the dream, which is interesting in terms of Wyoming. We emerged into the sunlight and all these rich folk were doing a dance in the rain, a circle dance with magical gestures. And the children without any question ran and joined the circle. I joined in, too, and then I began to wake up, and my head said—wait a minute, you can't join these folks, they're the bad guys. They're the bad guys and they're making all this pain and suffering, and you cannot dance this dance with them. And I was half awake and half asleep, and falling back asleep, and the voice of this friend of mine who'd been dead eight years at that point, said to me in his usual tone, annoyance and exasperation, Fred Herko said to me, "Di Prima, if you go on thinking like that, you're going to be sick for the rest of your life." And I woke up.

OK. I didn't start writing *Loba* then. The dream was a dream. I always write down my dreams. I wrote it down. A year later I was teaching in a classroom again, this time in Watsonville High School. There's barbed wire around the playing field, guards all over the place—an absolutely horrible situation full of the kids of the migrant farm workers. Out of the blue, I had to drop back and let the other poet continue the class alone, because there were some lines being spoken in my ear, and they had to be written down or they wouldn't go away. This happens to me sometimes. They turned out later to be the first lines of *Loba*, although at that point they didn't make any sense, I didn't know what they were about at all. "if he did not come apart in her hands, he fell / like flint on her ribs . . ." Who's writing that, I didn't know. The next day the process happened again, and when it happened a third time, those first three little sections, it began to zonk back in, not to that whole dream, but just to that vision of that wolf head, with the white ring

about it. And then, two years later, in Part Four of *Loba*, I finally got the dream down.
It's the first time I ever consciously turned a dream into a poem, although dreams turn
into poems all the time. Let me read that part to you. It's called

DREAM: THE LOBA REVEALS HERSELF.

she came
to hunt me down; carried down-ladder trussed
like game herself. And then set free
the hunted turning hunter. She came

thru stone labyrinths worn by her steps, came
to the awesome thunder & drum of her
Name, the LOBA MANTRA, echoing
thru the flat, flagstone walls
                    the footprints
                        footsteps of the Loba
                            the Loba
drumming. She came to hunt, but I did not
stay to be hunted. Instead
wd be gone again. silent
children in tow.

she came, she followed, she did not
pursue.
            But walked, patient behind me like some
big, rangy dog. She came to hunt, she strode
            over that worn stone floor
tailgating, only a step or two
                        behind me.
I turned to confront
        to face
                Her:
                            ring of fur, setting off
the purity of her head.
she-who-was-to-have-devoured me
stood, strong patient
                            recognizably
goddess.
            Protectress.
great mystic beast of European forest.
green warrior woman, towering.
                        kind watch dog I could
leave the children with.
            Mother & sister.
            Myself.

I have one little thought I want to throw in and then we can stop, and that's that we're all sitting or meditating or studying or whatevering in one form or another—this thing I was saying about the progression of European thought, the working out of a problem, whatever. Paganism, Gnosticism, alchemy and then what—where do we go. Way-seeking Mind, ''that which is creative must create itself.'' I want to say that the old religion and the old forms that we're all studying with such total devoutness—Eastern and Western—they have a lot of information and they have a lot of the means, but where we're all going they haven't mapped yet. We're mapping it now—or it's mapping us. If Buddha really had done it, we wouldn't be here.

CHARLES OLSON

The hinges of civilization to be put back on the door

Charles Olson was one of the major figures between Ezra Pound and the present in opening up American poetry to a range of ancient and contemporary/Western and non-Western cultures. (See above, p. 62.) His principal "ethnopoetic" works, as such, are The Mayan Letters, Causal Mythology, The Special View of History, *and the various lectures and writings assembled posthumously in* Muthologos—*but the same impulse is present throughout his cumulative masterwork,* The Maximus Poems.

Hinge #1	original 'town-man' put back to Aurignacian-Magdalenian, for evidence of a more primal & consequent art & life than the cultivation which followed (the Deglaciation & the Wet Period until 7000−5000 BC
Hinge #2	Indo-European, fr. the Bible or El Amarna Age: 1350 BC seen *prior* to itself, not forward of itself (such includes

| | texts | Hittite (& Sumerian behind it) Canaanite—as leading to the Old Testament, but showing |

SOURCE: *Charles Olson,* Additional Prose, *pages 25−26.*

earlier Cyprus & Cretan—
& Anatolian—conditions

invasion starts   *& roots:*   the linguistic values of Indo-
circa 2000 BC &   European languages, the
covers ¾s of   original minting of words
the millennium   & syntax
"Phoenician"
alphabet (Sinai)   [as in other hinges of the direct line, there
dates 1850 BC (?)   is an advantage to the leaping *outside* as
                       well as connecting *backward*: for example
                       American Indian languages offer useful
                       freshening of syntax to go alongside
                       Indo-European]

Hinge #3   to turn the 5th Century   Heraclitus
                       BC back toward the 6th   Buddha
                       & thus catch up Persian   Pythagoras
                       & Thracian & Milesian   Confucius
                                                  etc

                       forces not then lost   (Homer-Hesiod to
                                               be considered as
                                               Pisistratus of Athens
                                               made them texts
                                               etc; Miss Harrison
                                               clearest among
                                               moderns on Persian,
                                               & Cretan prepara-
                                               tions thus gained

Hinge #4   *the 2nd AD back to the 1st:*
                       an 'affective' time, the 2nd
                       —as well as brilliant
                       early secular: Maximus of Tyre
                                               Marinus of Tyre
                                               examples

                       but like the 17th later
                       costly in loss of some-
                       thing the 1st, as later the
                       15th & 16th still held, a
                       sense of the divine

                       (gain here is to get a load of Gnosticism,
                       & Hans Jonas particularly useful)

Hinge #5   the 50 years 1200−1250, to turn the corner
                       of what has been all we've known: Aquinas
                       Eckhart Bacon etc etc

Hinge #6   the 17th, seen as the brilliant secular it
                  was, without loss of the alchemy etc
                  it unseated

Hinge #7   the 20th, released fr
                  both the 18th—   inadequate ra-
                                           tionalizing after
                                           Locke & Descartes,
                                           & thus 'weakness'
                                           to increasing indus-
                                           trial revolution—

                  & 19th, the new progress of
                  Marxism

otherwise the present will lose what America is the inheritor of: a secularization which
not only loses nothing of the divine but by seeing process in reality redeems all idealism
fr theocracy or mobocracy, whether it is rational or superstitious, whether it is demo-
cratic or socialism.

CLAYTON ESHLEMAN
The Preface to *Hades in Manganese*

*From 1967–1973, Clayton Eshleman was the editor of Caterpillar, a seminal
magazine of the new poetry in which some of the early ethnopoetic discourse first
appeared. His own work draws from travels to Peru ("On Mule Back to Chavin")
and Japan (The House of Okomura, etc.)—an interplay in mind and at first hand
with those and other cultures—and from extensive translations of such poets as
Vallejo, Neruda, Artaud, and Césaire. The vision of the "paleolithic imagination"
and what he calls "the construction of the underworld" marks his distinctive
contribution to an expanded ethnopoetics—pursued over the last five years by
repeated trips to the great painted caves of France and Spain. Principal works:*
Indiana, Altars, Coils, The Gull Wall, What She Means, Hades in Manganese.

I first visited the paleolithic painted caves when I spent four months near Les Eyzies, in
the French Dordogne, in the spring/summer of 1974. I visited those caves that have been
fixed up for tourists a dozen or so times, along with making one trip to Lascaux, the most
famous cave in the area, which is officially closed.

SOURCE: Clayton Eshleman, Hades in Manganese, *pages 9–14.*

When I returned to Los Angeles, I became aware that nearly all of the material on paleolithic caves treated the art as reflective of daytime activities, i.e., success in the hunt or fertility magic. The only person who impressed me as having looked at the signs and animals as possessing a coherence relative to themselves (in contrast to one *reflective* of hunting and eating activity) was André Leroi-Gourhan.[1] Unfortunately, what he drew from his experience, while original, seemed to be inadequate and based on juggled and incomplete data. Leroi-Gourhan argued that the animal juxtapositions represented sexual pairing, and that there was a predictable distribution of sexual pairs, animal types, and signs at the entrances, and in the corridors and recesses of the caves that he had either visited or studied. Reading this, I was puzzled, as my experience in a cave like Les Combarelles, for example, led me to think that the corridors there had been visited and engraved over thousands of years and that there was no plan to it whatsoever.

In 1978 my wife and I returned to the Dordogne. When we revisited Les Combarelles, I took Leroi-Gourhan's map and compared it with that of the Abbé Henri Breuil's, in the possession of Claude Archambeau, the guide and caretaker at Les Combarelles. We found that Leroi-Gourhan had not indicated certain animals and signs that were on Breuil's earlier map, and that if all of Breuil's were added, along with at least two dozen engravings that Archambeau has discovered, Leroi-Gourhan's thesis made no sense. This has made me distrust his data for the other sixty-four caves mapped in his *Treasures of Prehistoric Art*. Beyond the empirical data itself, the thesis of sexual pairing is reductional and staticizes what in my experience is a tremendous sense of mobility and unpredictability in cave art.

Before returning to the Dordogne in 1978, I read an essay, later published as a book, by the archetypal psychologist James Hillman, called "The Dream and the Underworld." Hillman was not concerned with prehistory in this work, but what he had to say about dreams and the way we have used them, suggested a way for me to begin to think about cave art.

According to Hillman, modern man has interpreted his dreams and seen them as a reflection of daylight and daytime activity, thus denying them an autonomous realm, an archetypal place that corresponds with a distinct mythic geography—in short, an underworld that is not merely a reflection, i.e., a diminution, of an empirical sense world. I was astonished. This was exactly the same kind of interpretation that had been cast over the paleolithic painted caves! Like Plato's allegory of the cave, the caves themselves had, since the discovery of prehistory in the mid 19th century, been thought of as containing a blur of shadows in contrast to a "real" world blazing in at a distance from them.

It was not a matter of merely reversing such a verdict, but of acknowledging that the mysterious signs and animals which originated what might be called "the history of

---

[1]There are some minor but interesting exceptions to this statement. Georges Bataille's Skira monograph on Lascaux, which draws on his book, *Eroticism*, is provocative if terribly Catholic. Charles Olson's lectures on "The New Science Of Man," collected in *Olson #10*, are stimulating but, in contrast to his work on the Mayans, based entirely on the writing of others and hurriedly put together. Weston La Barre's chapter, "The Dancing Sorcerer," in his *The Ghost Dance*, while taking a traditional approach is thrilling to read. The Ucko/Rosenthal *Paleolithic Cave Art* is the best introduction to the subject from a critique-survey viewpoint. The drawings by Abbés Breuil and Glory, based on engravings, are worth more than anything written, as a meditation on this art.

image'' may very well represent the forging of the way to dream and image as such a way is conveyed to us today. In this way the signs and animals become a language upon which all subsequent mythology has been built, and the distinction between history and prehistory starts to look like the distinction between poetry and prose at the beginning of the 20th century.

I have been led to believe over the past few years of thinking about this, that it is not Dante's shoulders on which poets stand, but the shoulders of Neanderthal and Crô-Magnon men, women, and children, who made the nearly unimaginable breakthrough, over thousands of years, from no mental record to a mental record. Of course they were affected by all that was in and around them, and undoubtedly they brought their desire to live, i.e., to kill, eat and wear animal, into the depths of the caves. But the work on the cave walls has behind it a much more formidable crisis than depicting game.

When I crawled for four hours in Le Portel, or Les Trois Frères, glimpsing outlines of isolated animals (with only several exceptions no hunter/animal juxtapositions occur until *after* the upper Paleolithic period), wounded once to forty times—or crouched before massive "friezes" of hundreds of entangled animal outlines spanning thousands of years, often scratched on one great bison outline, as if the earth were seen as a ripe pelt of animals—and saw within this labyrinth little half-human animals beginning to appear, more often than not as mere dancing bits—I knew that "sympathetic magic" and "sexual pairing" interpretations only skimmed what had been recorded. I felt that I was witnessing the result of the crisis of paleolithic people separating the animal out of their thus-to-be human heads, and that what we call "the underworld" has, as its impulse, such a catastrophe behind it.

Which is to say that Eden, which most people regard as a primordial image, from the viewpoint of paleolithic art is the end of a truly primordial condition in which what is human and what is animal are bound together. It is possible to follow their separation as it is recorded in imagery. At around 15,000 B.C., a figure popularly referred to as the "dancing sorcerer" was engraved and painted in the "sanctuary" at Les Trois Frères. Wearing the antlers of a stag, an owl mask, wolf ears, bear paws and horsetail, a human appears to be dancing—or is he (he is male, with an animal-like penis) climbing a tree? Is he a shaman—or is he a Covering Shaman, the prototype not only for Shiva but also for the Covering Cherub? The armature of this figure is clearly human, yet his surface is stuccoed with a patchwork of animals. As we come forward in time, we can observe the animal anatomy falling away, until with the early Greeks most of the deities are sheerly human-looking, with animals as consorts—or in the case of some of the chtonian figures, such as the Medusa, bits of other kingdoms remain, like snakes for hair or tusks for teeth. It is possible in the case of the Medusa to imagine the snakes encircling her face as the winding corridors of a cave, and the tusks, in the center of her face, as the ghost of that dreadful encounter where in total blackness and at times more than a mile from the cave entrance a human met a 12-foot cave-bear.

By the end of the 18th century, in the "civilized" Western world, the "shaman" has lost even a consort relationship with the animal. In William Blake's "Glad Day," the shaman/poet displays himself naked and free of all animality, his left foot trodding on a worm while a bat-winged spirit, symbolizing evil, flies away.

*   *   *

The poems in *Hades In Manganese* were completed between January 1978 and April 1980, although I began work on the manuscript in 1974 when I first visited the Dordogne.

I was tempted to make two sections out of the book, one for poems dealing moreorless directly with paleolithic imagery and one for poems which do not. Then I realized that such a division would be against the way I try to write. I have no interest whatsoever in writing poems "about" the caves, or even doing poems that can be identified as "poems with the paleolithic as the subject." It is the present itself, with all its loop backs and deadend meanders, that is precious to establish. The meaning of paleolithic imagination that I spoke of before becomes a contour in my own poetic thinking precisely because we no longer live in Darwin's everglades. Species are becoming extinct and threatened while I write this. It is because the diverse fauna-flora fabric is really thinning out, that these first outlines—jabbings, gougings, tracings, retracings etc.—become especially dear, not as reflections, as I have argued, but as primal contours, shapes of first psyche, when Hades was a conjunction, say, of a bear paw buried in a hominid brain. . . .

By beginning to look at paleolithic cave art from the viewpoint of simultaneous psychic organization and disintegration, I hope to be extending our sense of "gods" and imaginative activity way beyond the Greeks, so that human roots may be seen as growing in a context that does not preclude the animal from a sense of the human. Up to this point, I have spoken of the crisis behind the making of what we call art as involved with the hominid separating the animal out of himself. To brood on this leads to several corollaries which do not necessarily follow. The size of the vast majority of paleolithic cave paintings, and the cramped circumstances in which they were executed, also suggests a drawing close of the animal depicted, as if the drawer were not only projecting an image but using the cave wall as a sort of microscope to work on and therefore examine the process of doing such work as well as considering what it came to.

The fact that many of these bisons, deer and horses, and occasionally human figures, are struck again and again with lines that look like arrows or lances (or possibly ferns—or fern/lances, ambivalent plunges/withdrawings, desires hooked on kill *and* live), suggests a testing of the drawn image, a wonder in attempting to make "it" go away—can I kill what I have made? Or, given the line/dot arena of an animal outline, can I gouge, in its rock interior, a deeper significance? Can I break through, given this ally, the substance in which I find myself hardening? Can I as bone/man make in rock a relief/island image of an earlier hominid branchiation? I set bone to rock in this question, as a kind of stone/flint fire friction, as if these engraved turns and twists were attempts to ignite a deep memory of Crô-Magnon's ape stem. There were no apes, of course, in the French and Spanish areas where the caves were marked and painted.

This writing . . . begins to envision the root ends of certain Humanistic divinities—such as Hermes, whose first appearance may be a meandering line looking for something to bind that, throughout the upper Paleolithic, is found in dots, dotted lines, solid abstract lines, and the more complex "closed" signs, traditionally referred to as claviforms and tectiforms. If Hermes is a god of boundaries, it may be possible to detect his archetypal activity in the earliest boundary signaling available to us today.

Recently, Gary Snyder wrote to me: "The '50s—'80s was the discovery of the depths of Far Eastern religious thought for Occidentals. The '90s should be the period of the beginning of the discovery of the actual shape of early Homo Sapiens consciousness: for both Occidental and Oriental seekers. A profound new step. Knowing more of the Paleolithic imagination is to know the 'Paleo Ecology' of our own minds. Planetwide human mental health in the twenty-first century may depend on arriving at these understandings. For it is in the deep mind that wilderness and the unconscious become one, and in some half-understood but very profound way, our relation to the outer ecologies seems conditioned by our inner ecologies. This is a metaphor, but it is also literal."

To which I would respond: the Hell in oneself, and its Hadic basin, must balance the poem as it capsizes or brims.

DAVID ANTIN
Talking to Discover

As an early participant in the ethnopoetic discussion, David Antin has explored a radically "new" source for poetry in speech and discourse. This has involved, as here, a tension with the idea of poetry's origins in song, and an intensification, touched on in the pieces that follow and elsewhere in this book, of the old dichotomy between the oral and the written. Antin's own poetry over the last decade has taken a form sometimes indistinguishable from "talking" per se, culminating in an ongoing series of written and elaborated poem-transcriptions. (See below, p. 469.) His principal works in this genre are Talking at the Boundaries *and* Tuning *(in preparation), and his earlier works include* Definitions for Mendy, Code of Flag Behavior, *and* Meditations.

"Talking to Discover" was originally spoken at the First International Symposium on Ethnopoetics (Center for Twentieth Century Studies, Milwaukee, April 1975). Other participants in the discussion were Nathaniel Tarn (see above, p. 408), Gary Snyder (see above, p. 90), Richard Schechner (see above, p. 311), and William Spanos, critic-editor of Boundary 2, *"an international journal of postmodern literature."*

I came to Milwaukee prepared to suggest that what is central to all language is discourse, and that there are, if you will permit the solecism, "natural discourse genres" that are

SOURCE: *Michel Benamou and Jerome Rothenberg (eds.),* Ethnopoetics: A First International Symposium, *pages 112—119.*

common to all cultures using language—and that are not only common but fundamental to the structure of language and to our humanness, our mental capacities and dispositions and the traffic problems of a semiotic. Genres, perhaps, of the sort Dell Hymes has called for an inventory and investigation of in his suggested ethnography of speaking. To paraphrase Hymes, all over the world in a great variety of languages people announce, greet, take leave, invoke, introduce, inquire, request, demand, command, coax, entreat, encourage, beg, answer, name, report, describe, narrate, interpret, analyze, instruct, advise, defer, refuse, apologize, reproach, joke, taunt, insult, praise, discuss, gossip. Among this grab-bag of human language activities are a number of more or less well-defined universal discourse genres, whose expectation structures are the source of all poetic activity. If there is any place that we should look for an ETHNOPOETICS it is here, among these universal genres, where all linguistic invention begins. For by an ETHNOPOETICS I mean Human Poetics. I suppose *ethnos* = people and therefore ETHNOPOETICS = People's Poetics or the poetics of natural language. So I think it is trivial for a structuralist like Todorov, for one example, to begin to look for the laws underlying narration in the socially dislocated literary tales of Boccaccio, though they should certainly be reflected there, when with Labov we can find them more completely articulated, with about equal elegance and greater clarity, in the street talk of the children of the black ghettoes of the United States, where story can be seen in the social and discourse context in which narrative normally occurs. I think it is also a mistake to begin an analysis of metaphor or the figures of rhetoric from Elizabethan or Roman examples, when there are virtually no known figures of speech, no idiosyncratic ways of talking that are not displayed more fully in some natural discourse setting, of which the literary examples are often merely atrophied specializations. For what I take the "poetics" part of ETHNOPOETICS to be is the structure of those linguistic acts of invention and discovery through which the mind explores the transformational power of language and discovers and invents the world and itself. What I was afraid of in the term ETHNO-POETICS was the historical legacy of the term *ethnos*, a kind of anthropological commitment to exoticism, to whatever is remote from us and somehow different—tribal if we are not tribal, religious if we are secular, dark if we are light, etc. Here *ethnos* = other, so not Human Poetics but the Poetics of the Other. Trying to avoid this I took a number of examples, fairly casually from several studies of black vernacular discourse in English, three of which I am including here. The first of these is reported by Claudia Mitchell-Kernan and involves an exchange between the author, a young black woman, and a young black man. The author was sitting on a park bench when the young man came up with a couple of friends and, finding her attractive, said approvingly

: Mama, you sho is fine!
She: That ain no way to talk to your mother.
(there is a laugh and his friends walk off while he sits down)
He: You married?
She: Uh huh.
He: Your husband married?
(they both laugh)

The second described by Thomas Kochman is also a dialogue, this time between a young black woman seated with her friends in a bar in which a black man happens to come out of the men's room with his pants still unzipped. This produces some laughter by the women, and the man, feeling somewhat put down and wanting to turn the tables says

> : Hey baby, did you see the big Cadillac with the full tires waiting to roll into action for you?
> She: No motherfuck, but I saw a little gray Volkswagon with two flat tires.

The third is a fight story told by a fifteen-year-old black kid and reported in a study by William Labov.

> An then three weeks ago I had a fight with this other dude outside. He got mad 'cause I wouldn't give him a cigarette. Ain't that a bitch? (Oh yeah?) Yeah, you know I was sitting on the corner and shit, smoking my cigarette, you know. I was high an shit. He walked over to me "Can I have a cigarette?" He was a little taller than me, but not that much. I said "I ain't got no more man" 'cause I ain gon give up my last cigarette unless I got some more. So I said "I don't have no more man." So he, you know, dug on the pack, 'cause the pack was in my pocket. So he said "Eh man, I can't get a cigarette, man? I mean, I mean we supposed to be brothers an shit." So I say "Yeah, well, you know man, all I got is one. You dig it? An I won't give up my las one to nobody." So, you know, the dude he looks at me an he . . . I don know . . . he just thought he gon rough that motherfucker up. He said "I can't get a cigarette." I said "That's what I said, my man," you know. So he said "What you supposed to be *bad* an shit?" So I said:
>
>> "Look here, my man,
>> I don't think I'm bad,
>> You understan
>> But I mean, you know,
>> If I had it you could git it
>> I like to see you with it,
>> you dig it?
>> But the sad part about it
>> You got to do without it
>> That's all, my man.
>
> So the dude, he on to pushin me, man. (Oh, he pushed you?) An why he do that? *Every time somebody fuck with me*, why they do it. I put that cigarette down, an boy, let me tell you, I beat the shit out that motherfucker. I tried to kill im—over one cigarette! I tried to kill im. Square business! After I got through stompin him in the face, man, you know all of a sudden I went crazy! I jus went crazy. An I jus wouldn't stop hittin the motherfucker. Dig it, I couldn't stop hittin im, man, till the teacher pulled me off o him. An guess what? After all that I gave the dude the cigarette, after all that. Ain't that a bitch? (How come you gave im a cigarette?) I don know. I jus gave it to him. An he smoked it too!

And I selected examples like these not because they were the best or because I thought that they were somehow "art" and therefore "poetry," but because they were convenient and vernacular, and exhibited all of the symmetrical and structural niceties conventionally associated with poetry, occurring here in rapid improvisational speech.

The first example is a pair of quibbles with precise parallels in Elizabethan drama, but here the quibbles have a quite clear social discourse function. A lone attractive woman is sitting on a bench and the young man is trying to make her acquaintance. He has to get past a social barrier that suggests it is perhaps not polite for a presumably "proper" young woman to strike up a flirting conversation with any passerby, and there is the danger, to his rep, that he might be rejected. So he begins with whimsical admiration placed firmly in Black Vernacular:

"Mama you sho is fine!"

She doesn't want to reject or offend him, but she parries his move by deliberately insisting on the supposedly literal meaning of "mama" as a kinship term instead of a term signifying "woman." She does this by shifting out of the vernacular to the more formal term "mother," but she keeps the whole transaction within the range of friendly rapping by keeping the rest of her return in the vernacular:

"That ain no way to talk to your mother!"

Which signifies that there is enough friendliness in her response for him to continue, and he does. He asks her a question that is an attempt to determine her reason for being (apparently) reluctant to engage:

"You married?"

It would constitute at least a formal excuse for unwillingness to play. Her answer seems minimal, but it constitutes a cautious acceptance of the line of reasoning he suggests:

"Uh huh."

He is asking "is it because you're married that you don't want to play" and she is responding to the effect that "you could say that." This sets up his decisive and comic counterargument.

"Your husband married?"

Which puts the question sharply and wittily of whether or not the term "married" is more than linguistically "symmetrical." Which is to say that it is a commonplace of the respectable culture to own this piece of linguistic and social knowledge: that if A is "married" to B, B is "married" to A. While his question suggests the socially verifiable argument: not necessarily. And perhaps: not usually, if B is male. Covertly it also proposes that what's sauce for the gander should also be sauce for the goose. Now this particular kind of linguistic compression and inventiveness has often been considered a distinguishing feature of poetry. And the second example is even stereotypical of traditional poetic analysis in that the entire exchange is based on the manipulation of a single extended metaphor, that serves as the basis of a sexual brag:

> . . . the big Cadillac with the full tires waiting to roll into action for you.

Here the woman accepts the automotive sexual metaphor as the basis for discourse and returns a point for point rejection of the car model, its value, size, color and condition, declaring it to be:

> . . . a little gray Volkswagon with two flat tires.

In which the word ''gray'' is an explicit answer to the unexpressed but probably well-understood (black) color of the Cadillac, which has considerably greater value— ''black'' is ''beautiful'' and the typical color of a limousine—than the drab or faded ''gray'' of the refutation. It is a devastating putdown within a well-defined verbal insult genre with literary equivalents in formal ''flytings'' and ''tenzone'' as well as African insult poetry. In fact, both ''brag'' and ''insult'' are well-defined genres in speech as well as in literary tradition. What is true of these genres is also true of narrative. The story I've quoted is an elaborate self-congratulating heroic tale, complete with a chivalric comic twist at the end:

> And guess what? After all that I gave the dude the cigarette, after all that . . . And he smoked it, too!

Which is the finishing touch in a representation of how just, how fierce, how noble the storyteller was, accomplished with a great array of details that never impede the forward course of the story. For all of the details are incorporated into the story's propulsive force. Larry is asked for a cigarette because he is smoking and the pack of cigarettes is visible in his shirt pocket. This allows the other boy to ask for one and expect to receive it, given the neighborhood code of manners. Larry's first answer is sufficient to himself, as a reason for not giving the cigarette—''I don't have no more, man.'' Which, if his story is to be believed, is honest but seems like a lie and a deliberate provocation. Since the pack is visible in his shirt pocket, while what Larry represents himself as meaning is that having one left leaves him not enough to share. But he is, in his depiction, too dignified, too cool to go into that much detail. The other boy ignores what he takes to be the lying response and looking at the pack, calls on the street code that requires sharing '' . . . I mean we supposed to be brothers, an shit.'' At this point Larry goes as far as his cool will allow toward explanation, the verbal response '' . . . you know man, all I got is one, dig it?'' Which at this point may no longer be convincing. Because if the first statement was a lie, this explanation is possibly also a lie. But it is as far as he can go without losing rep by say showing the nearly empty pack. Moreover, for these two kids the cigarette may only be a lightly-weighted issue, because they both have to be equally willing to enter a quarrel without too many reservations. So in the story both are represented as having a sense of their own rightness, with Larry being more in the right, and furthermore not the aggressor. At the end Larry gives him the cigarette, which is a gesture of magnanimity in the traditional sense of the term. For it shows how small a thing it is compared to his own dignity, which he has just so violently maintained. This is a didactic point of a truly heroic story—that the cause of a quarrel may be disproportionately small in comparison to the quarrel itself, as all material things are small to heroes in comparison with their own rep. Polonius's advice to Laertes is a good commentary on this system of values. Now throughout this skillful manipulation of the story, the teller never loses sight of the ostensible justification for telling the story:

> . . . He was a little taller than me . . .

For in discourse, stories, like all other elaborate genres that require extended speech by one of the partners, need either a stated or understood justification for the interruption of the normal "tit-for-tat" form of dialogue. And Larry never loses sight of the fact that this story was an answer to a question "Did you ever have a fight with a guy bigger than you?" and then "What happened?" Though in this case there is every reason to suppose that this justification, which is offered rather weakly (" . . . he was a little taller than me, but not that much"), serves more as pretext or a "formal justification" for telling the story, which Larry's listener will accept because of the inherent colorfulness of the narrative. But this "formal pressure" is felt by the teller sufficiently to make him suspend the narration long enough to offer his formal justification and receive silent permission to continue. For this "formal pressure" is really the social pressure of the discourse genre, that demands satisfaction of a socially-shared expectation: that when you are asked a question requiring some kind of explanation, that your explanation will be relevant to the question or at least contain a response to the unspoken but well-understood relevancy requirement. Many features that are requirements of extended speech genres in a real discourse context and that color the whole genre are often obscured in their literary equivalents, because literature has become, for many, its own justification and has pretty much lost its sense of address. And it may be difficult to remember now that even in a fully-literary novel like *Anna Karenina* the story is a powerful example that satisfies, though poorly, the relevancy requirements that would be imposed by a discourse about the value of certain types of family life, and that Tolstoy felt obligated to insert an explicit justification in the opening epigram: "All happy families are happy in the same way; all unhappy families are unhappy in different ways."

My attempt to discuss these and a number of other examples of vernacular genres drew me and a number of other discussants into frequently rather abstract analyses which led someone at the conference to challenge the "naturalness" of the discussion. And this in turn led to something of a discussion of the "naturalness" or "unnaturalness," or more precisely, the degree of self-consciousness of language acts, in which various special disciplines, among which linguistics and phenomenology, were invoked. It was this that formed the background for the following discussion.

(Participants include: Nathaniel Tarn, David Antin, Richard Schechner, William Spanos, and Gary Snyder.)

Tarn: There are two things, the monologue effect and the dialogue effect. Then there's the third thing of the monologue, telling a story dialogue. There's the true dialogue and there's the monologue about dialogue, and so on. Now if that's what you mean by phenomenology, that's O.K.

Antin: What you're talking about is the very considerable problem of the "naturalness" of describing something that presents itself in the course of events and is normally taken for granted and then one chooses to observe it. It's the observer problem. The question of whether an observer's understanding of something, formulated as a description, does not in fact change whatever is observed. Which summarizes in the aphorism that all observation is some kind of manipulation or transformation. But suppose it is. To begin with, there is a matter of degree in the deformation caused by any particular observation; and even if you can't easily determine that, the observation will be justified by the need for it and the usefulness of the description. The reason we're choosing to observe these speech acts here is that they have been very neglected and I want to restore the idea of the centrality of speech genres or discourse genres to any human poetics. I'm willing to put up with the fact that in order to talk about anything I can't deal with the taken-for-granted at the level that we take it for granted, because I've got to move something from here to there, from the periphery to center of attention, say. In doing this you can use different kinds of tools, but it's most convenient to use the tools that are ready to hand; like Lévi-Strauss' "handyman" you reach for the tools that are "handy." Now we might not have to mention Chomsky or William Labov or even grammatical analysis. But somehow we do have to be able to see the structure of the representation, that something like this narrative makes use of. What distinctions the storyteller makes, because he has to make them—to meet the intelligibility criteria of the genre. For the story to meet these requirements, given the nature of the events, the way they unfolded, and what Larry wants to communicate, you may have to observe with some precision the neat grammatical distinctions he makes in some parts of the story—like the aspects of the verb or something horribly technical like that and how the tense system and the aspect system are related in the story and how if we knew what was generally required by the genre we might find out how much he could screw around with requirements—the expectations set up by the system—and at what cost.

Schechner: Then what you're saying relates exactly to what was said earlier. It is that the dialectic between process and structure is probably biologically rooted. In other words, that evolution can only occur, in other words, structural changes can only occur as a process within a structural field but you can reverse it; structure can only occur within a processional field. And that's exactly what we're talking about, this balance between formalism and free play. That's also what happens in a lot of behavior both in animals and people as in rehearsal, we do a lot of rehearsing and animals do a lot of rehearsing. In other words, pre-playing and post-playing events and get a great deal of delight out of that.

Spanos: If we pay attention to the phenomenologists who have been referred to over and over again, I think one of the things that has to be brought into this whole discussion is the question of *origins*, especially since the stories that you repeated are formulaic, that is to say, they're teleological or logocentric. They're preconceived so that the process is more or less predictable. So when we equate this with orality, with the kind of oral expression we're talking about and have been talking about, a kind of oral expression which, in my understanding of it, is a second stage to a kind of orality that is even prior—ontologically prior—to that. In other words, the kind of thing that you were doing in speaking this more or less improvised and particular talk. If we're going to recover the oral impulse in poetry, and the new, the phenomenological way of looking at the lived world that this oral impulse implies, it seems to me that we have got to return to that kind of beginning. Not the beginning which is the logocentric beginning of an existential situation, the open beginning that is generating *this* talk, out of which emerges *my* response to *you* or your response to me. It seems to me that that's where real poetry has got to begin, and that's a poetry that is not teleological. It's a poetry which involves discovering or, as a Heideggerian phenomenologist would put it, a *dis*-covering. There's no discovery, no *periplus*, in those oral poems that Parry and Lord record in *The Singer of Tales* from the Yugoslavian *guslar* poets. Their subject matter is known from the end and their mode of telling is rigidly formulaic. It's a conservative logocentric poetry, a poetry of closed forms. There's room, of course, for explorative variation, but these stories are not being told, they're being re-cited, re-told. So I don't think we learn a hell of a lot about the origin of poetry in these poems. What we need, I think, is an orality of dis-closure.

Antin: I think probably there is something that you would call talking to discover and I think it exists in all societies, in all cultures, and I can't prove it. All I can say is that I think the invention of the self is an outcome of talking to discover, the outcome of a discourse genre. So is this discussion, we're doing it now, talking to discover. I think all cultures do it. But I would like to say that I think that what happens in some of the situations I was describing, where there were more or less ritualized settings, is that invention takes place in a different domain of the discourse. And although these inventions may be somewhat restricted and local, all invention is subject to some restriction. It seems to me for example that "soundings," these Black ritual insults, involve inventions within a particular arena in which it is conventionally insulting to be "thin" or "poor" or "small," and then there is a range of Pop culture products like Gainesburgers, Bosco, Apple Jack, or Cheerioats whose properties can be used to bring these insults home. So you get a game of invention with these counters and you get something like "Your mama's so skinny she can get in a Cheerioat and say 'Hula hoop! Hula, hoop!!' " or "Your mama so small she can play Chinese handball off the curb!" Which is pretty unexpected in its detail and virtuousity of selection.

Snyder: Right. Well, it seems to me that this whole discussion, David, as interesting as it is, only applies to poetry insofar as written rhetoric enters into poetics.

Antin: What do you mean by that, by "rhetoric" as opposed to what?

Snyder: All the other varieties of expression and concern that are involved in poetry.

Antin: But what are they? I mean, in what sense would you define this kid's narrative as "merely" rhetoric. Using the implied "merely" to characterize rhetoric as a pejorative term. To me the word "rhetoric" is not a pejorative term.

Snyder: Well, I don't mean it pejoratively. I mean it simply as the study of semi-formulaic ways of using language.

Antin: Well, I think the notion of discovery, the notion of invention, of combination and transformation that I was suggesting is central to poetry, though for me the notion of poetry is still open and I don't want to close it myself. I thought I was offering the notion that discourse, that talking that was transformative in a valuable way was central to poetry. Now I suppose there are other things that are also valuable.

Snyder: I object to the "central." Much of poetry has no meaning as discourse at all.

Antin: I don't know how you can say that. Though it depends on what you define as discourse, I suppose. And what you define as poetry.

Snyder: There's a useful definition of poetry as we all know, in the largest sense of it. Not definition, but the thing to remember about it is: that it's song.

Antin: I don't think so. Not only don't I think so, but I won't even argue the point. Personally, in poetry I have an intense dislike for song. Though I don't see why that should matter so much, because I don't think "taste" is all that important. And I suppose I could conceive of song as a type of discourse—the way I normally think of discourse. Because discourse is a very broad term for me. And it seems to me that if what we mean by song is the invention of song, improvisational song, like say Eskimo song . . .

Snyder: Well, it's curious to me that you said, yes, it may be possible that there is some self-discovering mode of discourse but we can't prove it when it seems to me that it is as obvious as the nose on my face that that's what poetry's been about for the last 50,000 years.

Antin: I point to the great corpus of poetry and most of that would deny that instantly. I mean most things that are called poetry certainly don't discover much at all, least of all self. And they're among the deadest artifacts in the world.

Schechner: I really would like you to explain more of what you said about song because that's a fundamental disagreement. It seems that discourse is a larger category that includes everything you think of as song and therefore what's the argument about?

Snyder: No, it doesn't include everything you think of as song. There are lots of songs which come as monologues, as chants, as ongoing self-contained chants, that unless your definition of discourse includes every possible variety of human behavior . . . Just take for example mantra chanting.

Antin: In a monologue, or what seems like a monologue, because the term is the result of a shallow linguistic analysis, you're conducting a discourse. But the discourse is not with another person. And it seems to me if there is not some auditor at some point in mantra chanting, you're not chanting mantra. I mean chanting is not an instantaneous act. It covers a perceivable duration. There is a before and after and during utterance, and you're listening, and you hear yourself either internally or externally, don't you, in mantra chanting? O.K. And if you hear yourself, during uttering and after, you're listening and uttering and remembering other uttering and uttering again maybe slightly differently, you are probably adjusting and tuning. So in some sense, through tuning, you're seeking some kind of agreement with some previous utterance, some image of previous utterance or some image of intended utterance, and to this degree you're making use of language-discourse habits and patterns. At least in the sense of seeking tuning, which requires seeking of agreement or concord and perceptions of failure of agreement (mistuning) and attempts at adjustment, which have a meaning for you. I don't want to make a big issue of this, because these utterances don't seem to have a specific meaning, but the form of meaning. Nevertheless such meaning as they have is language meaning. But you see, I don't tend to use meaning in such a restrictive way.

Snyder: They have no meaning in the sense of natural language.

Antin: Oh, well, I don't know about that. Even a cry is usually paralinguistic. That is, it functions, is uttered and understood, in a systematic way closely related to the rest of the language system. It seems to me that what is called song lies perhaps close to the intonation grammar of the language, and that if it doesn't, it's not anything at all except reflex. And it seems to me that it operates off a number of assumptions that come from particular forms of speaking and the discourse contexts within which they are appropriate, which these forms then evoke along with their contexts. Or at least they evoke the values associated with these contexts.

Schechner: Are you saying that all these things must be in terms . . . must be a dialogue, in other words there must be an other, assumed or actual, a Berkelian view . . .

Antin: I assume that in all language acts there is always an other, even when it is only the self alone, which takes at least two stances, before and after. I don't think there is any such thing as a true monologue. Somebody is always listening and somebody is always being talked to. Unless you yourself are deaf at some very profound level. For you to produce an utterance that you know is an utterance requires a dialogue, which is at least produced by you and addressed to yourself.

Schechner: Now let me ask you a Berkelian question. In your sleep you make a sound. The next morning somebody said, "Gee, that was a horrible sound. It scared me. What were you dreaming?" You say, I don't remember a thing, I don't even know I made a sound. Did you make the sound?

Antin: I'm perfectly willing to concede that there are discontinuous parts of the self. That I addressed myself at that time, in that sound or in that song, and I forgot. Besides, a sound is not a song. That is, a grunt may or may not be a part of a song, as it may or may not be a part of an utterance.

Schechner: You're saying the gregariousness of a species is fundamental, it's not divisible. And you're (Snyder) saying that it is not necessarily fundamental.

Snyder: I guess, in the midst of all this I would make a rough working distinction for purposes of discussion about poetry, between dialogues with oneself and dialogues with others.

In reading through this discussion I realize how tempted I was to respond to Gary's remark that "I wouldn't make such a distinction between discourse with others and discourse with oneself, or if I did, I wouldn't put a particularly high value on it." And as I thought this, I realized it would have corresponded more to the course of that conversation at the symposium than to what I believe. Because I do believe that there is a distinction between discourse conducted with the self and discourse conducted with others. That discourse conducted with the self is something of a special case and makes up only a small part of the great world of discourse, not because it's less or more valuable, but because it's more eccentric—a special case—like playing chess with yourself. But I also realize I went a long way in the discourse—as did almost everyone else—out of fellow feeling—in an attempt to come together. So much so, that perhaps we obscured our disagreements. For one, I don't think the notion of song is specially valuable in poetry, and I surely don't think it represents a self-discovering mode— certainly not what poets have commonly called song, which I think has very little in common with mantra chanting. About which I do not pretend to have any great fund of knowledge and in which I would like to say—if for no reason other than to clarify our disagreements—I am nearly totally uninterested. And I think I failed to answer Bill Spanos' pointed question about talking to discover, as I also failed in my own talking piece to avoid what some readers might consider exoticism. Since most of the examples I gave of discourse genres happened to be chosen from Black Vernacular English, and there are probably many people who regard this dialect and its speakers as exotic or specially colorful or gifted, which I do not. So I'd like to correct both of these faults by including a less-colorful story told by a fairly colorless man—a white Middle Western retired Post Office employee—a story that is nevertheless a clearer example of how a man can tell a story that he doesn't fully understand in advance, and can come to understand it as he talks, which is talking to discover.

DF: How did the work in the Post Office change over all those years?

PM: Huhh. We went . . . I went to the Post Office in thirty-six. And it was down on the corner of Main and Catherine—where it still is. And in 1950 they built the substation up on East University and they had that open for 10 years. Then they built the new Post Office out on West Stadium and we moved out there. And in about 1968 they moved a bunch of us right back down to the old Post

Office again. *So in 56 years, why, we made a full circle—from a dilapidated Post Office to a new Post Office to the original new Post Office and then back to the original old dump.* And that's all it is—an old dump down on Main and Catherine. And that was one reason—I could have worked a couple more years—but—I didn't want to work at that place a couple more years. It's nothing but—it was built for horse and buggy days and—it's unfit for present days. Docks are built for high trucks, not for the low trucks as they are now. And it was a pain in the neck to work there any more. So I just retired. I had a year. So to hell with it.

DF: Yeah.

PM: I made a full circle. From a dump to a new Post Office up there to a new Post Office out here and then back to the dump again. *That's the story of the Post Office.*

The samples of discourse quoted are from Thomas Kochman in *Afro-American Anthology*, eds. Whitten and Szwed; Claudia Mitchell-Kernan in *Readings in the Sociology of Language*, ed. Fishman; William Labov, *Language in the Inner City*; and William Labov and Joshua Wiletzky, "Narrative Analysis," in *Essays on the Verbal and Visual Arts*, ed. June Helm. The story of the retired Postman is from an unpublished doctoral dissertation at the University of California, San Diego, by Donald Forman, *Indirect Speech Acts, Speech Act Theory and Common Sense*.

GEORGE QUASHA

From "DiaLogos: Between the Written and the Oral in Contemporary Poetry"

George Quasha's wide-ranging magazine, Stony Brook, *provided a first forum, 1968–1969, to renew the discourse about ethnopoetics as such. (The term itself was first used here—by Jerome Rothenberg, who also acted as "ethnopoetics editor.") Quasha has also been co-editor of* America a Prophecy *(Quasha and Rothenberg 1973), editor of two anthologies of contemporary work,* Open Poetry *and* Active Anthology, *and author of the ongoing long poem,* Somapoetics. *His contribution to the issues of voicing/writing as mapped in this anthology has been to expand the idea of a poetics in a variety of ways (metapoetics, parapoetics, somapoetics, etc.) and to carry the methods of a redefined ethnopoetics into the center of contemporary poetry and its attendant discourse.*

SOURCE: New Literary History, *Volume VIII, number 3, 1976–1977, pages 485–506.*

I. FRAME

Buckminster Fuller formulating a law of modification: "Heisenberg said that observation alters the phenomenon observed. T. S. Eliot said that studying history alters history. Ezra Pound said that thinking in general alters what is thought about. Pound's formulation is the most general, and I think it's the earliest." Quoted by Hugh Kenner in *The Pound Era*, and extended: "To think of Pound in that way alters Pound." There is always discursive feedback because we communicate with the objects of our attention, and the quality of attention determines the quantity of communication. How conscious can we be of our contribution to world transformation? At last there is a species of anthropology that is processual and participatory; it has the candor to view its fieldwork as dialogue. The conversation between investigator and investigated is not a "means to an end" or a "necessary evil," but the Object itself in the process of projection. Such science grows accurate through self-study. It belongs to a larger and unnamed area of investigation, which *could* be called the History of Conscious Discourse or the Archaeology of Conversation. A participatory and processual poetics must be conscious of itself as dialogue—conscious, that is, of how the exchange between poetic discourse and the discourse about poetry is a process of mutual modification. The present writing-piece tries to break in on the conversation between the written and the oral in contemporary poetry.

II. OBJECT AT A DISTANCE

Oral vs. written—but that's too easy, that's the usual mistake, the simple opposition, rather than the dynamic of what Blake called "contraries," without which "there is no progression." If we restore to the "versus" its root meaning of "turning," we can make a new start: *the oral as contrary of the written*, speech turning with writing. The issue has probably always been there in our "history," or if we understand Heidegger aright, the possibility of choosing one over the other and so "getting stuck" with a literalist and one-direction option has marked our history from a very early axis of Western self-discrimination. *Logos*, he tells us in *What Is Called Thinking*, really meant "saying" and somehow went wrong at a crucial moment in the history of thought. But we are "back" now in the midst of that consideration; that is, we are again at the point where it is possible to know there is a choice. As I see it, we can do the same thing "we" did then, only turned the other way, or we can do something different, something truer to where we have come by way of a difficult history. And that would be to grasp the meaning of *middle*—the "between" zones (neither "active" nor "passive") signaled to us by the poet Blake and revived in our time by his rightful heirs, the poets. [Heidegger 1968: esp. 153 ff.] The issue, I gather from the evidence of a new or, rather, emergent language (we will variously see it as poetry, speech, talking, and discourse), is not the choice of oral or written modalities, but the problematic of *alignment* within language itself. And this problematic is rendered visible and audible in the event of poetic transformation in our time. I say "event" to stress the "coming out, happening" aspect of an emergent "other tradition."

It is tempting to begin with a history of the oral and the written as recurrent choices in poetic practice in the West, but as I turn the examples over in my mind, I realize that such choices have rarely if ever been made in the West, except very recently as aspects of complex strategies to "make it new," to use Pound's famous phrase. The supposed "evolution" from oral to written modalities does not in itself imply a choice in the sense which we might mean it now, or if it does, it may not be useful to speculate about it in a discussion of *present* options in poetry. Much has been written about oral poetry— Albert Lord's *The Singer of Tales* [see above, p. 158—Eds.] of course stands out as key text for many poets, and the notion of poetry as performance probably has a greater significance for contemporary poetry than at any time since Chaucer. But what *we* have to deal with is severalfold. There is the *presence of texts that raise the issue of the oral*—texts from the past and from the now enormous body of translated material from oral cultures. And there is the *presence of the oral modality as performance and as publicly generated "poem"*—contemporary "events" that are also in one sense or another texts. As difficult as these are to describe and discuss, there is the even more elusive phenomenon of *written poetry that is processual and "open" in its sensitivity to speech* (in Heidegger's meaning of Logos) and that figures crucially in the oral-written dynamic of the present. Added to these is the also large *"text" of discussion about the emergence of the oral*, statements by and dialogue with the poets who either do or do not identify with the oral. My approach here is to take the poets' discussion as primary to the event of what I will call *reoralization and further textualization* and to view it within the context of a renewed meaning for the *dialogical*.

In 1973 the poet Charles Stein and I initiated a long-range project which we called "dialogical criticism" or "DiaLogos," as an alternative both to conventional textual analysis—inappropriate for so much contemporary poetry, both oral and written—and to the interview structured by prepared questions. Our sense was then, and continues to be after some ten dialogical exercises,[1] that the useful "criticism" of new poetry often has occurred in the conversations of the poets who are making it and that something goes wrong in the commitment of even the best ideas to the written page in the form of critical articles. The energy not so much of the oral act as such but of *the immediate engagement with text* is easily dissipated or falsified in any attempt to structure it conceptually, too often leaving the impression that the poetic acts under discussion are somehow "about" the ideas they generate. The truer perspective seems to be that *text generates further text*, that is, any order of discourse makes more of itself. Furthermore, a "processual" and "open" poetry wants to be known processually and openly in a self-renewing language. If any abstraction remains in my mind after engaging the texts of the "new poetry," it's that the poetic is not a privileged and specialized use of language but *language itself in the act of being true to itself*. The "use" of the poetic is the activity it makes inevitable, *the further languaging in our discourse*.

That troublesome word *discourse* contains in its ambivalence almost the whole range of the oral-written conflict. Its dialectical history seems a consequence of the "contraction" (to use Owen Barfield's notion) [1957: esp. 72 ff., 116 ff., 122 ff.] of

---

[1]The dialogical exercises are focused conversations engaging the poet in exploring his own texts and/or working assumptions.

logos from "saying" into "logical reasoning," as Heidegger has described it. The Late
Latin *discursus* meant "conversation," a "running back and forth," rooted in the spoken
dynamic of human exchange, and not what it became as the lengthy argument of
reasonable men, language devoid of *listening to the other*. So that the poet Charles Olson
sometimes has used "discourse" to mean the very opposite of what he intends in the
poetic, what he calls the "projective" and "open verse": "discourse . . . has . . . so
worked its abstractions into our concept and use of language that language's other
function, speech, seems so in need of restoration that several of us got back to
hieroglyphs or to ideograms to right the balance. (The distinction here is between
language as the act of the instant and language as the act of thought about the instant.)"
[1967: 3–4] Olson is not arguing for speech over text but for a return to certain
immediate energies and *modalities of attention* that the history of discourse has diminished. He offers a strategy to "right the balance."

   This theme of "return" to primary *logos* is characteristic of the recent efforts at
restoring active language-consciousness, whether in Heidegger's or Barfield's medita-
tive etymologizing or in the reoralizing tendency of contemporary poetry. It is not
nostalgia, at least not in any simple sense, although there is often a mood of longing
(*Sehnsucht/Pothos*) in the more Romantic thinkers (Heidegger, Barfield) and poets
(Robert Duncan). The barely submerged longing is for the *primary*, the *direct*, that is
also locatable somewhere between Whitehead's "presentational immediacy" and
Olson's "one perception must immediately and directly lead to a further perception"
(credited to Edward Dahlberg). [1967: 52] The point is that, when Olson also says that
the poem must be the "issue of" the *time* of its composition, the poetic is now being
understood as *emergent language—language specifically energized by its processual
and eventual nature*, rather than by some set of qualities or formal conditions imposed
according to an aesthetic.

   We can no longer presume to get a handle on contemporary poetry by reference to
any one or even several traditions, although precedents may be found for even the most
radical innovations in poetic method. To observe, for instance, that Jackson Mac Low's
use of a performance modality that he calls "Simultaneities" (involving multiple readers
in realizing chance-generated texts) has a sort of precedent in Dada simultaneous
sound-poems, obscures as much as it clarifies. It does not help us to enter the necessary
relation to the text either as written or as performed, since it draws us away from a *radical
particularity*: the freedom of performer and audience to originate an unknown state of
attention or to enter an "anarchistic" social relationship through "authorless" language. Neither is it as useful as it may seem to notice the connection in general between
Mac Low's group performances and the ritual poetry of tribal/oral cultures, however
powerful the resemblance. And yet the advantage of such a connection is that it does not
posit a "tradition" in a linear or diachronic sense and that it opens a perspective on
altered states of language (as in "states of consciousness"). Jerome Rothenberg's
Ethnopoetic glossing of tribal poetries by reference to innovations in early and late
modern poetry both European and American (*Technicians of the Sacred*) *is* probably
more useful as a way into the former than the latter. And here too there is clearly a gain in
seeing both oral and literate in the same transcultural and synchronic context—as
synchronicity rather than literary history. The effort of the critical mind to get a handle on

processual/eventual poetries is itself belied by the nature of transformative poetics ("Metapoetics"),[2] which contrives by various strategies to *throw the reader/listener back on direct experience*—back to the root of composition itself, where the generalizing intelligence is shunned, altered, or supplanted.

We may ask what is the usefulness of speaking about these matters at all, although there is no necessity to ask the question so long as we are drawn to address the issues. The danger is that we come to believe that the issues have some ultimate meaning in themselves; they do not. They are only vectors in our continuous approach and perpetual indeterminate relation to the event of emerging language. In fact they are themselves crude poetic strategies to engage language in the midst of its process of self-alteration, or to bring ourselves more willingly to the place of that language. It is only necessary to urge a "willing suspension of disbelief" where there is a pervasive tendency toward belief. But the event of contemporary poetry—in the work of a Charles Olson or John Cage or Jackson Mac Low or Robert Kelly—is already functionally beyond the stage of belief in the issues it uses, uses, that is, to gain traction in eluding the grip of the intelligible. ("Our [society's] taboo is at root against unintelligible passions," writes Duncan.) [Allen 1960: 406] The threshold of the "postmodern" may well be this opening beyond belief (which Pound called a cramp of the mind in a certain position) and beyond the need to return text to intelligibility.[3] The most honest path for a "practical criticism" may be little more than an inventory of realized possibilities for emergent language, or criticism that is (in Robert Kelly's word) *deictic*—pointing out, showing, what now calls attention to itself.

And yet it will not help us much to advocate a field of easy agreement, however profound the perspectives, because agreement rigidifies quickly into consensus (and "without contraries there is no progression"). The traction of transformative poetics is largely polemical—or perhaps I should say, is still polemical—where the need to "destruct" lethargic, overconcretized, mechanized, or simply useless definitions (of one's own as well as of others) spurs the work to its further realization. Jerome Rothenberg is a rather good example of an "experimental" poet who has introduced useful theoretical perspectives that he has continually had to qualify in order to survive their consequences, and his definitional dance of veils illuminates the oral-written "debate" not only by what he says but by the mood of the saying. As the principal translator and anthologist of tribal/oral poetries, with a strong leaning toward modernist innovations, he has in the last several years developed a personal performance-orientation as what he calls a "stand-up" poet. For a recent issue of *Boundary 2* (Vol. III, No. 3, Spring 1975) on "The Oral Impulse in Contemporary American Poetry," he was asked by the editor, William V. Spanos, whether in the light of Heidegger's position on

[2]I now prefer "Parapoetics" to "Metapoetics," though there may be grounds for a distinction. My original definition is in "Metapoetry, or The Poetry of Changes," in *Open Poetry: Four Anthologies of Expanded Poems*, ed. R. Gross and G. Quasha (New York, 1973), pp. 3–8; also, "Metapoeia," in *America a Prophecy* (G. Quasha and J. Rothenberg 1973), p. 540. In an article to which this one is a sequel I defined Metapoetics as a "conscious transformation of discourse that yields 'discursive feedback' into the transformation of consciousness" ("The Age of the Open Secret: A Writing-piece on Ethnopoetics, the Other Tradition, and Social Transformation," in Benamou and Rothenberg 1976, pp. 65–77.)

[3]"Belief" here means *any* fixed perspective that leads to systematic judgment and that conditions language normatively and consensually.

Logos and Olson's on discourse he thinks "the effort to recover the oral impulse is a central and determining concern of contemporary American poets." Rothenberg's reply is long, but we can get the drift in a couple of paragraphs:

> Speaking for myself, then, I would like to desanctify & demystify the written word, because I think the danger of frozen thought, of authoritarian thought, has been closely tied in with it. I don't have any use for "the sacred" in that sense—for the idea of book or text as the authoritative, coercive version of some absolute truth, changeless because written down & visible. That isn't to say that our problems with what Blake called "single vision" begin with writing, or to push for a tactical illiteracy by way of solution. . . .
>
> But I've never thought of "oral" in this sense as my personal shibboleth, & I probably use it much less than you suppose. Because I happen to *write*—as do other "oral poets" you mention later—& I'm not going to undo that. I'm much more honest as a writer than as a speaker, although one going view of *the* oral seems to equate it with *the* truthful. (I'm writing this reply, for example, not speaking it, because I don't want my statements conditioned by our face-to-face interview or by my own awkwardness: a combination that doesn't do much for my love of the truth.) And in part—the simplest part—my attitude towards "oral" poetry has nothing to do with my criticism of literature & the written word, etc. It is only that I'm responding to a conventional & deeply entrenched view of poetry that excludes or minimizes the oral; & I'm saying that the domain of poetry includes both oral & written forms, that poetry goes back to a pre-literate situation and would survive a post-literate situation, that human speech is a near-endless source of poetic forms, that there has always been more oral than written poetry, & that we can no longer pretend to a knowledge of poetry if we deny its oral dimension. . . .
>
> The contrast isn't "oral & literate" (written) but "oral & literal," where by literal I mean what you, or Heidegger, present as a kind of closed *logos*, Final Cause, coercive propositional language, mastering the world rather than participating in it. Obviously the concern here isn't with a refinement of style, although as poets we have some difficulties in disengaging ourselves from an old-fashioned literary context. That context itself may be part of the trap of categorical thinking, & it's certainly under attack now from a number of different directions. So I can as easily expect to find allies among scientists & linguists & other generally turned-on people as among those specifically engaged in the business of literature. . . .
>
> The idea of the oral—of a source of forms renewed in each instance—remains germinal; so important in the end that some of us have come to see it as concurrent with, or prior to, that other ("visionary") business of the poem. And the way you've set it up in the question, it would now seem to cover whatever other anti-literal approaches—chance operations, say, or concrete poetry—develop the idea of each poem as a separate structural & cognitive instance. [Pp. 510–514]

It is difficult to know whether Rothenberg's interesting reply weighs more heavily toward "yes" or "no" to the editor's question about the centrality of "the oral impulse." Rothenberg takes the question very personally while also referring to a larger position on writing, literary conventions, innovative poetry, etc., and throughout it one senses a submerged polemic that never comes to full clarity because of the complexity of the issue and the paradoxical stand of the poet (a writer in favor of reoralization). He ends with a strong note on behalf of the oral as germinal by strategically including "anti-literal" approaches, which can only be considered oral if one wants them to be. Perhaps the most interesting maneuver—the shift from "oral/literate" to "oral/literal"—is finally the most problematic, for while it gains ground for the oral, it again ensnares the oral option in a binary opposition. This strategy, like the inclusion of antiliteral approaches, has the disadvantage of squaring off the sides too neatly, and it tends to obscure the relation of reoralization to textualization. The new textuality is as antiliteral as the new orality. Yet the position is also very attractive in that it allows the poet to find "allies" among scientists, linguists, and other nonliterary camps. The drift, however, is toward a kind of agreement that easily gets hazy around the edges, implying a consensus that may ultimately prove as troublesome as the "old-fashioned literary context" that Rothenberg wants to escape. The scientists and linguists may offer positions useful to an oral-modernist polemic, but their contribution to a living and emergent language is still an open question. The danger is that the partisans of reoralization may *win* their case a little too often, and then the poets among them will have to find a way to make the new consensus self-destruct.

I want to stress here the particular value of Rothenberg's presentation of the oral option and the further clarification of reoralization in his work. His oral performance of what he calls "total translation" from tribal/oral poetries—for instance, the chanted sound-poems from the Navajo called "Horse Songs"—has opened a genuine possibility for performance poetry [see above, page 391—Eds.]. The subdued polemic in his prose responses to questions about the oral impulse is partly defensive, intended to protect Rothenberg's vested interest in what might be called an "oral renaissance." Quite rightly, because, as he says in the same interview, "when I do a book like *Technicians [of the Sacred]* or *Shaking the Pumpkin*, it still seems to flush out those who can't see or hear beyond the written word on the printed page." Yet the extent to which his "total translations" and his own eminently performable work like *Poland/1931* (1970) and *Esther K. Comes to America* (1971) amount to a gain in poetics—a further textualiza-tion—is not clarified by his argument. In a recent dialogue on the oral, Robert Kelly refers to the "Horse Songs" as text—the self-conscious text that they, like any modernist appropriation, clearly are:

> I sense that the oralization of the poetic thing now—I mean oral as mimetic of a non-literary tribal context, as is often held up to us—is in fact speech reabsorbing itself, falling back into itself, the memory domain, and losing the opportunity of self-awareness, so its effect is always primary and dwindling, down to the navel, to its point of attachment to the primeval order of its being, and never is able to constellate a different order. Which I suppose is the particular value of the literary text, or the oral text reconsidered in the way Rothenberg would chant a "Horse Song," and if he pronounced a word in a different way and then if the next time the word occurs he is consciously repronouncing it, he is obviously reading from a written (however it may be "unwritten") text. Those things seem to me the most interesting parts of oral poetry: the thing that Rothenberg does with "Horse

Songs," that tells us what those Indians do as well, that continuously address themselves to a "same." And whenever we hear the word "same" in a meaningful way, a lexical way, we know we're talking about text [as opposed to a strictly oral context where a singer asked to repeat the "same" song comes out with something very different, but calls it the same]. And the other way we talk about all the time, the poetry is composed in a *mouth*; where else could it come from but what we are saying. [Unpublished DiaLogos with R. Kelly, C. Stein and G. Quasha, 15 December 1976]

The key phrase here is *opportunity for self-awareness* which Kelly sees as the special advantage of textualization—in this case of an oral/tribal song that, in performance, might well be regarded as a modernist experiment in *poésie phonétique*.

If Rothenberg's work can be seen as a new branch (via the tribal) of experimental European performance poetry, there are others such as David Antin who work without much connection with previous modernist experiments. While his earlier work—*Definitions* (1967), *Code of Flag Behavior* (1968), *Meditations* (1971)—grew out of collagist techniques and sometimes systematic procedures, he has since 1972 worked exclusively with a unique performance format that he calls, simply, "*Talking*," the title of his book of that year. He enters the "space" where a reading or lecture is to occur, and he talks. It isn't ordinary talk; it's a very intense and intricately woven talking, sometimes argumentative, sometimes narrative, often polemical, sharply amusing, annoying, etc. He is what Rothenberg calls a "stand-up poet" and something quite different. The anthropologist Stanley Diamond recently spoke of him as a *jongleur*. His talk-pieces are not adequately subsumed under the category of performance; they are public compositions, text-making in full view. Antin says they are "Improvised pieces that I have considered before doing, but which I have gone to a particular place to realize. I'm trying to reclaim for poetry a domain lying somewhere between the oral traditions of Homer and Socrates. . . . I want to get back to the intelligence inventing while talking-walking, while moving" (quoted by Hugh Kenner in "Antin, Cats, & c.," *Vort* 7 [1975]: 87). Antin's reoralizing intention is the clearest and most conscious among contemporary poets, and at the same time the poetic as category is only questionably applicable to his work—deliberately so. Trained as a linguist, Antin is interested in *language as such*. So indeed was Jack Spicer (though more conventionally in terms of linguistic theory), the first in what could become a subtradition of linguist-poets challenging (like Marcel Duchamp) the category of the art they practice. Thus Antin's infamous remark: "if robert lowell is a poet i don't want to be a poet   if robert frost was a poet i don't want to be a poet   if socrates was a poet i'll consider it" (*Boundary 2*, 1975: 575).

Socrates as poet calls up the dialogical model for poetic discourse, which isn't, however, what Antin has in mind. Not the least part of his strength is his uncommon ease in "thinking on his feet," peripatetic (appropriately he claims Aristotle's "poetics" as "talking lecture"), and he has always enjoyed argument in conversation, although his personal tendency is toward monologue. It would be a mistake, I think, to generalize about contemporary oral poetry on the basis of his talk-pieces, because they are very much *his* way of getting at the basic energy of the poetic. But the issues he raises have general significance:

I have this uncertain and emergent sense of what I regard as a poem. And there is something in the form of the question and the answer that's so clear cut in its demands, more clearly even than a conversation. And while I could imagine a conversation—some conversations—of being capable of moving into poems . . . I tend to think of a poem as having a certain . . . freedom . . . to move out into invention and discovery. To me shaping into a poem means steering it—the talk—into the open water—and not all kinds of talking—talking situations—have open water capabilities. There is a kind of demand you have to respond to, in this public situation, and I wanted it when I went out into these talking pieces, I wanted this sense of address, and the idea of writing struck me as lunatic, like trying to talk in a closet. And I was—am—glad to free myself from it, but there's also the claim of the domain into which you're beginning to be pointing your talking, after you've been talking for a while, and in some situations, the claims of the people you're addressing, talking toward, may begin to exert too much of a pull, violating the claims of the matter that you're moving toward. It's this pulse, this moving toward the matter, to break into the open, into the discovery and invention that gives the work its driving force. And without it, for me, the talking isn't a poem and it has no striking power. [*Vort* 7, 1975: 30]

The openness, the "emergent sense," before poetic process and the view of the poetic as "freedom to move out into invention and discovery" carry forward two pivotal developments in contemporary poetics, that of Olson's open verse/projective verse (shared by Duncan, the "opening of the field," and others) and that of Cage's systematic chance-operations (shared by Mac Low and others). Antin derives most from Cage's own talk-pieces (composed, however, before performance), such as the "Lecture on Nothing" (1949) and "Where Are We Going? What Are We Doing?" (1961). Along with Buckminster Fuller's tape-recorded (and much revised) oral discourse of "mental mouthfulls and ventilated prose," such as *No More Secondhand God* (1940/1963), these talk-pieces have contributed to a renewal of the didactic poem, the *poem as lecture*. (Antin's talk-poems arose out of his art lectures, in particular "The Metaphysics of Expectation: The Real Meaning of Genre," delivered at Cooper Union in 1972, which I happened to attend; it struck me then, as I told Antin at the time, that this was his most challenging "poetry.") Yet, however close Antin is to Cage (not least in the plain-talk and direct address), he does not use chance operations or systematic procedures in talking, and the actual generative process is probably closer to Olson, minus the latter's sense of musically measured verse. I mean that Antin's generative composition, the fluid process in which one perception immediately and directly leads to a further perception, constitutes a "stance toward reality," to use Olson's term, not wholly different from Olson's: "From the moment [the poet] ventures into FIELD COMPOSITION—puts himself in the open—he can go by no track other than the one the poem under hand declares, for itself." (1967: 52) Except that Antin's poem is no longer "under hand," but literally in the mouth.

I point to the closeness of Antin to Olson—and one could in *this* regard as easily say to Theodore Enslin or Robert Kelly—not to imply derivation or broad similarity but to suggest how much Antin's description of the poetic process (quoted above) stands for the larger development of "open," "processual," and "eventual" poetry. When we call Antin an Oral Poet, we are addressing the unusual radical of composition in which the poet exposes the process of making, but when we inquire of Antin's intentions in doing what he does, we enter the motive of processual work in the larger, and usually written, sense. The peculiar self-consciousness in which the poet notices (and often refers to) the thing he is doing as he does it—the opportunity for self-awareness mentioned by Kelly or the composer-poet Franz Kamin's "autoskreelik," "writing about something as you are writing about it"—manifests in Antin's talking about talking and links his particular language-consciousness to a lot of otherwise dissimilar contemporary work; I will have more to say on this later, as point of interface between oral and written composition.

Before I move to the question of the dialogical and certain aspects of performance-composition, I want to notice Antin's distinction between "modern" and "post-modern" as the latter's tendency away from the interruptive/collage and toward the fluid/processual—a useful if necessarily oversimple distinction:

> I . . . don't believe that "collage" is in conflict with "discourse" or even with "oral" impulses, at least not necessarily. The main feature of collage is not a spatial reference but disjunction, discontinuity, and, ordinarily, plurality of parts. To me this seems neither for or against "speech." Some terrific conversationalists are disjunctive, discontinuous and so on. At the moment I really don't think of my work in terms of collage organization. I think of my "talk pieces" as organized by my sense of "address." Talking toward some one, some others, talking discovery. So the idea of "collage" doesn't seem useful to me right now. I don't sense myself as putting things, pieces of things next to each other, not even successively. And so I see myself rather as "going on" however I have to "go on," which may be disjunctively—I might have to cross a river or street, scale a wall, maybe begin over again—sort of. I tend occasionally to arrive at a kind of narrative, sometimes, out of the process of going on. I don't object to it. It seems right now that what I'm doing is trying to find the sources of discourse in talking, and this situates what we used to consider the more conventional representational forms of narration and representation back in their emergent and more provisional domain, where they signify differently than in the fixed genres. This seems different. Everything here seems less disjunctive than fluid. And it seems true that many of the artists I would call postmodern—though they make no formal renunciation of collage or even of certain still valuable modernist strategies—seem tempted toward a more fluid, less disjunctive, (more natural?) way of proceeding. . . . [*Boundary* 2, 1975: 640–641]

I quote this at length to show a particularly impressive strategy toward giving poetic reoralization a historical function, that of initiating the postmodern. And I repeat here that Antin's statement is as applicable to written as to oral poetry (the example he gives is John Ashbery, a writing poet). But the strategy of preferring to think of the "sources of discourse" as literally *in* talking has this limitation: that it gives to the fluid tendency of postmodern discourse the rather limited *tonal* range of direct address. I point this out in order to protect us from simplistic preference for certain poetic events over others, which distorts the actual expansive energy of new discourse. (Note that Antin speaks personally above; the simplistic preference I guard against is a supposed consequence of his argument.)

In fact the reoralizing and fluidizing tendency in discourse often *appears* disjunctive in a collagist way where the fluid force is somehow concealed within the text—"projected," "energy transferred from where the poet got it (he will have some several causations), by way of the poem itself to, all the way over to, the reader" (Olson). The content may reach us through or in the midst of interruptions in linear thought and yet the movement within the text describe an inherently or "enstatically" unified field-energy. *Any* perception may lead immediately to *any other* perception without intervention of either a rational connective or a collagist gesture of cutting and pasting. And I cannot see it as anything more than a theoretical mystification to regard one method as more "natural" than another. If there is advantage in positing "nature," it cannot be in identifying its operations with any socially, linguistically, or otherwise consensually measurable manifestation, but only in seeing it as principle. Otherwise we lose both the opportunity for self-awareness of which Kelly speaks and the freedom to move out into invention and discovery of which Antin speaks.

The oral and written converse, and sometimes they do it by intensifying discourse polemically, by preferring one radical of composition over the other. But in poetry we are dealing with poetic mind in the process of knowing itself particularly, in the work of individuals seeking alignment with underlying principle. This is an abstraction which I offer to shift the present discussion onto a new footing. I had entitled this discussion "The Other Tradition: Between the Written and the Oral in Contemporary Poetry" in order to place myself in a tactical middle between preferences. I have briefly discussed two key poetic representations of reoralization, that of Rothenberg (performance of the written) and that of Antin (public, out-loud composition), both because of my deep admiration for these poets and because of the opportunity they provide me to get a hold on the issues. Rothenberg, Dennis Tedlock, and others engaged in the Ethnopoetic enterprise of mediating oral cultures are working to expand the Western poetic to include *other poetries* and, as Whorf did with Hopi, *other languages*. And I perceive David Antin, John Cage, Buckminster Fuller, and Franz Kamin—exemplars of a new lecture-poetry—as expanding the poetic to include an *extraordinary ordinary dimension of language*. It might be called the *undiscovered self of address, whether direct or indirect*, the social being that, as a by-product of our self-alienation, has fallen out of touch, lost its connection with *logos*—or as Olson quotes from Heraclitus, "We are estranged from that with which we are most familiar."

In both the Ethnopoetic and, to use my present favorite term, the Parapoetic, there is a dialogue with an *other*. The latter, the extraordinary ordinary, is only "other" in the sense of "alien" by reference to literary consensus and self-alienation, which for the postmodern have come to mean the same. The Parapoetic, including in its already enormous range not only lecture-poetry but performance-poetry (Mac Low et al.) and many varieties of further textualization (Kelly, Enslin, Blackburn, O'Hara, Ashbery, Lansing, Irby, Schwerner, Spicer, Eshleman, C. Stein, di Prima, Bialy, to sketch the beginning of a long list), *embodies a radical strategy to achieve realignment with a profounder or more essential intention to communicate*. It implies a critique of consensual language, and it offers its alternatives in the name of the New (good news, news that stays news, Novelty) towards the creation of an altered readership/auditorship. It insists on *new ways of reading and listening*, usually according to some notion of alignment within essential language or intentional sound-fields—Duncan's "resonance" and (after G. Stein) "equilibration," Cage's "unfocus," Mac Low's performance/listening instructions, Antin's "tuning," Kelly's "a poem is *ta'wil* [radical and processual exegesis] of its own first line," etc. *How we hear* these events is the root issue (pertaining to a new practical criticism); how we *use* them or relate to them consequentially is the further issue (pertaining to—what? A projective hermeneutics? A Parapoetics? A Dialogics? Let me dangle this parenthesis in a tactical openness. . . .

III. A FURTHER PART

This part of my work here is intended to practice a small degree of the "auto-skreelik" ("writing about writing about what you're writing about") in an effort to bring us closer to the almost indescribable interface between the oral and the written—to embody, in short, the opportunity for self-awareness which must have been an original motive for criticism.

John Cage's lecture-poems are self-conscious acts of language modeled both on musical structure (the method of his music applied to discourse) and on his own ordinary spoken language. Together these permitted him at once an extraordinary degree of certainty about the nature of poetry (viewed as musically structured language) and an unparalleled degree of openness ("random" choices), i.e., *un*certainty, in (rendering) the discourse. The best of two worlds: an almost eighteenth-century tidiness in the clarity of *ideas behind* the poetic act—a certainty that comes from the habit of writing—and a new sort of willingness to find advantage in not-knowing—an uncertainty that comes from the practice of listening to one's own speech as guide to the sayable. *This self-listening generates an "altered state" of discourse in that the saying does not follow expectation but gradual discovery along a constantly self-renewing route.* Writer-speaker shares with reader-listener a consciously dangerous delight: *the "self-manifestation" of speech-particles in uninterpreted relationship.* Whereas Western critical thought has typically found merit in interpretable verbal relationships, the new poetry seeks a strategic incursion into uninterpretable terrain—an enterprise shared even by so overinterpreted a poet as Wallace Stevens, who said that poetry must elude the intelligence almost successfully. (It may be that the "almost" has cost him nearly complete absorption into the securely intelligible world of the academic, which Gertrude Stein would say had rendered a work useless to its time. Yet Stevens's work is still readable in the light of contemporary poetry because its complexity allows one to disbelieve the critics; there is room for processual heresy.)

If reorealization in poetry has any "goal" at all, I think it is *to free the reader-listener from the anxiety of right interpretation.* Many who have studied literature in school know the narrowness of the space in which one is urged to let the spirit fly free, letting a butterfly loose in a jar. But it is hard to imagine how the academic mind can ever get a secure *enough* handle on a Cage or a Mac Low or an Olson, a Kelly, a Spicer. One cannot enter the work at all without a certain psychic adjustment into alignment, a "tuning" which, if it occurs in relation to a "faculty," is the oral-aural in action, whether or not its occurrence is out loud or in silence of the page.

The themes we are dealing with here are:

> self-awareness (auto-exegesis/*ta'wil*)
> uncertainty as practice (Negative Capability)
> altered states of discourse (Parapoetics)
> the difficulty of the text (uninterpretable complexity)
> processual and open alignment ("resonance"/"tuning")
> reoralization/further textualization (DiaLogos)

It would be possible to run down the consensual attitudes on each of these themes and then to locate their contraries in contemporary poetics, but that elenctic approach would hook us into the binary distinctions and polemical stances. Although a certain amount of this is unavoidable, *each "theme"* (from Greek, "thing placed" in discourse) *allows for development independently of counter-positions*. The purpose of my positing an *Other Tradition* is to suggest a notion of tradition (a "handing over") that is *fundamentally non- or anticonsensual*; that is, its strength does not come from a body of agreement, however small, however inchoate, but from an openness to transformation. This openness, however, is gradually encumbered by even the most flexible field of conceptual agreement—by anything that tells us we know what's there before it's there. The only thing I am aware of that sustains such a tradition, other than the poetic itself (in the transformative or "Parapoetic" sense), is the *dialogical*, the *process of discourse that remains between us without settling on a side, the "between-saying."* I do not understand the dialogical to mean only what occurs in the conversation format, anymore than I understand the oral as limited to the talk format. Rather, it implies an order of discourse in which the supposition of a one side or a right side is never made. Language at root implies the presence of the other, and in a sense *the poetic is language in dialogue with itself and with its otherness*, implying a certain consciousness on the part of the speaker/writer of the independent capabilities of his language. To invoke the dialogical is to emphasize the *directional*, in a sense other than teleological, and to notice that the speech-impulse is able to open out into unknown and perhaps unknowable territory. Uncertainty as practice.

The uttering of poetics is itself a central poetic activity in our time, and this tendency toward generative formulation may belong with the "conceptual" in art and the many moods of the theoretical in music. *Poetics is the point in discourse where all the arts commingle*—with each other and with other "disciplines" (philosophy, the sciences, etc.). Hence the lecture-poem (in Antin's case an oral presentation on art and an observation about linguistics join to open a path in poetry); hence the publication in recent years of almost every recorded lecture or conversation of a poet like Charles Olson; hence the reemergence of the dialogical not only in poetry (e.g., the popularity of interviews) but in phenomenological anthropology and in philosophy (Heidegger's "Conversation on a Country Path" or "A Dialogue on Language") where we first learn of it. What we are experiencing, then, is not only the reoralization of poetry but of poetics and of discourse in general, the bringing out, as it were, of the *logos* in the

-ologies. *And* their further textualization, because the principal way we know of these things is through texts. When the "talkers"—Antin or Fuller or Kamin, et al.—are going about their talking, it is clear that they are weaving text, that their experience as makers of texts fundamentally conditions the oral emergence. So that, again, it is not a matter of oral vs. written but of the way their continuous remarriage creates discourse and takes it beyond itself. . . .[4]

HENRY MUNN

Writing in the Imagination of an Oral Poet

The following essay by Henry Munn presents a necessary complication of the "orality" issue in ethnopoetics (see above, passim)—the location of a concept of "book" and "writing" at center of the genuine ethnopoetics of a major oral poet (see above, p. 187). The interested reader can relate it to the proposal of an archécriture (or primal writing)—the idea of writing itself as, in David Antin's term, a "natural genre" co-equal with speech, etc.—presented in the workings of such a contemporary philosopher as Jacques Derrida (see above, p. 139). Henry Munn is the author of an important introduction to Mazatec shamanism, "The Mushrooms of Language" (Harner 1973: 86–122) and is the translator-commentator of María Sabina: Her Life and Chants (Estrada 1981).

A brief excerpt from one of María Sabina's hours-long chants precedes Munn's essay.

I am the woman of the great expanse of the water
I am the woman of the expanse of the divine sea
the woman of the flowing water
a woman who examines and searches
a woman with hands and measure
a woman mistress of measure

SOURCE: New Wilderness Letter, *numbers 5–6, 1978, pages 6–10.*

[4]The final section of the essay, omitted here, presents actual conversations with contemporary poets, initiated by Quasha and offered as exhibits of the dialogical process. (Eds.)

* * *

I am a woman of letters, it says
I am a book woman, it says
nobody can close my book, it says
nobody can take my book away from me, it says
my book encountered beneath the water, it says
my book of prayers

* * *

I am a woman wise in words beneath the water, it says
I am a woman wise in words beneath the sea, it says

"You my Mother who are in the House of Heaven," sings María Sabina in 1956, "You my Father who are in the House of Heaven/ There do I go/ And there do I go arriving/ There do I go showing my book/ There do I go showing my tongue and my mouth/ There do I go signalling the tracks of the palms of my hands."

In this stanza she goes from the idea of writing, embodied in the book (a word she says in Spanish) to that of vocal speech to that of tracks. The image of footprints recurs throughout the shamanistic chants of the Mazatecs like an insistent reference in the course of the verbal flow of words to graphic marks. Frequently throughout the 1958 session she says: "The path of your hands, the path of your fists, the path of your feet." In other words: what one does, where one goes. "I am she who questions and sees," says the shamaness. "I am she who examines the tracks of the feet and of the hands."

Here we find the idea of reading in a more primordial sense than reading words. The hunter on the track of game is a reader of signs as is the shaman who interprets the symptoms of illness. The imprint of feet in the mud is the first writing of intentional existence. It is not by chance that the Minister of Houang-ti got the idea of writing from the tracks of birds in the sand. In the pre-Columbian codices footprints often appear, depicting the path of migration or used to mark intervals, as the tracks of moose and other animals appear in the petroglyphs of the North American Indians.

María Sabina is an oral poet; her society is one without writing, but curiously enough one of the principal themes of her chants is the book.[1] "I examine," she says in

[1]To R. Gordon Wasson belongs the credit for being the first person to discern the importance of this theme. Referring to the conjurations of the ancient Mexican sorcerers collected by Ruiz de Alarcón in the seventeenth century and recently retranslated and interpreted by López Austin, he writes: " 'The Book' is, I am sure, a permanent feature throughout much of Mesoamerican religious practice, and it goes back far into the past. . . . Ruiz de Alarcón quotes his Nahuatl informants as speaking of a Book, using the Nahuatl word, *amoxtli*. This word meant in pre-Conquest times the pictographic writings of the Nahuas and Mixtecs. . . . When Ruiz de Alarcón's informants spoke about the *amoxtli*, what did they mean? They would not have had access to the Codices, which were closely held by the powerful. Alfredo López Austin thinks this word was used by them metaphorically, by which I take it he means precisely what María Sabina means: the 'Book' in the Meso-american Indian mentality is a fount of mystical lore." (See Wasson, 1974. This book contains the text of the 1958 session I refer to, translated by the linguist George Cowan. The 1956 session, also recorded by Wasson, is on a Folkways record.)

1958, "because I have seen my clean book/ my ready book/ my clean pen/ my ready pen." And in 1970: "This is your book/ unique book/ book of the dew/ fresh book/ book of clarity/ I am a woman of the breeze."

She told Alvaro Estrada (1981) that once when she had eaten mushrooms to cure her sister she saw the following vision: "Some persons appeared who inspired me with respect. I knew they were the Principal Ones of whom my ancestors spoke. They were seated behind a table on which there were important papers. The Principal Ones were various, seven or eight. Some looked at me, others read the papers on the table, others seemed to be looking for something among the same papers. On the table of the Principal Ones, there appeared a book, an open book that went on growing until it was the size of a person. In its pages there were letters. It was a white book, so white it was resplendent. One of the Principal Ones spoke to me and said, This is the Book of Wisdom. It is the Book of Language. Everything written in it is for you. The Book is yours, take it so you can work."

The vision of these men sitting around a table moving papers like a group of lawyers or functionaries is worthy of Kafka. Here we see the influence of the modern state, which exists at the periphery of her indigenous world, with its offices and paperwork, on the imagination of a woman who can neither read nor write. For her, the heavenly lords are a kind of celestial bureaucracy, which corresponds with her concept of herself as a lawyer who goes up to heaven to argue the case of her patients with the powers that govern life. "I am a lawyer woman, a woman of transactions/ I go up to heaven/ there is my paper/ there is my book/ Before your gaze/ before your mouth/ even unto your glory." In 1956 she sings: "Paper/ Book of the Law/ Book of Government/ I know how to speak with the judge/ the judge knows me/ the government knows me/ the law knows me/ God knows me/ So it is in reality, I am a woman of justice/ A law woman."

The connection in her mind between writing and the law is founded in fact, for the law is primordially written and writing is in essence legislative. But even though her conception of the Principal Ones reflects the actual modern world of government with which she is familiar, it also has a precedent in the past: in the hierarchy of power of ancient Mexican society, the priests at the top of the pyramid were the ones who held the sacred books of oracle and wisdom. The wise men were described as those "loudly moving the leaves of the codices." The German scholar, Ernst Robert Curtius, in an essay (1956) about the metaphor of the book of nature in European literature, says that only in civilizations where writing was the prerogative of a religious ruling class does the image of the sacred book of wisdom appear. Such was the case, not only in Egypt and Mesopotamia, but in pre-Columbian Mexico as well.

They said of their wise men: "His is the ink red and black. His are the codices, the colored books of pictures. He himself is writing and wisdom." (Sahagún 1946) And María Sabina says: "It is your clean book/ It is your clean pen/ that I have Father/ Before your gaze, before your mouth, even unto your glory/ Look, I feel as if I were going up to heaven."

This woman of words, who is completely illiterate, is fascinated, haunted, obsessed by the idea of writing. "I am a woman of letters," she says. "I am a book woman."

The ancient Mexicans were the only Indians of all the Americas to invent a highly developed system of writing: a pictographic one. Theirs were the only Amerindian civilizations in which books played an important role. One of the reasons may be because they were a people who used psilocybin, a medicine for the mind given them by their earth with the unique power of activating the configurative activity of human signification. On the mushrooms, one sees walls covered with a fine tracery of lines projected before the eyes. It is as if the night were imprinted with signs like glyphs. In these conditions, if one takes up a brush, dips it into paint, and begins to draw, it is as if the hand were animated by an extraordinary ideoplastic ability.

Instead of saying that God speaks through the wise man, the ancient Mexicans said that life paints through him, in other words writes, since for them to write was to paint: the imagination in act constitutive of images. "In you he lives/ in you he is painting/ invents/ the Giver of Life/ Chichimeca Prince, Nezahualcoyotl."[2] Where we would expect them to refer to the voice, they say write. "On the mat of flowers/ you paint your song, your word/ Prince Nezahualcoyotl/ In painting is your heart/ with flowers of all colors/ you paint your song, your word/ Prince Nezahualcoyotl."

The psychedelics bring into play the same mechanisms that are at work in the production of dreams. One of the principal aspects of such awakenings are visions. Freud called dreams a hieroglyphic text. He said their language was closer to a pictographic form of writing than to verbal speech.

The metaphor of the book of life is as central to the mystical poetry of Nezahualcoyotl as it is to the thought of Plotinus, who said the art of the seer is "a reading of the written characters of Nature, which reveal its order and its law." "With flowers you write, Giver of Life," sings Nezahualcoyotl, "with songs you give color,/ with songs you shadow forth/ those who are to live in the earth/ Afterwards you will destroy eagles and tigers/ only in your book of paintings do we live/ here on the earth."

"The book," says Curtius, "received its supreme consecration from Christianity, religion of the sacred book. Christ is the only god whom antiquity represents with a volume in his hand." María Sabina stands at the convergence of the traditions of Mesoamerica and Christianity. When she sings in 1970, "I bring with me my sacred eagle/ Lord Saint John/ Father scribe in the House of Heaven," she refers to the statue of the patron of Huautla, the author of the Epistle according to Saint John, who stands in the Huautla church with a golden goblet of communion wine raised in one hand and a quill in the other, a lectern in the form of an eagle before him with a scroll over its shoulder on which is written in Latin: In the beginning was the Word.

In an interview with reporters from *L'Europeo* of Milan, she described in somewhat different terms the same capital, inaugural vision she later described to Estrada. She said that an elf appeared before her and asked her what she wanted to become. She replied that she would like to become a saint. "Then the spirit smiled and immediately he had in his hands something that was not there before, a big Book with many written pages. 'Here', he said, 'I am giving you this book so that you can work better and help the people who need help and know the secrets of the world where everything is known.'

---

[2]Nezahualcoyotl, the King of Tezcoco, was a mystic, architect, and poet. (See Miguel León-Portilla, *Trece Poetas del Mundo Azteca*, 1967.)

I thumbed through the leaves of the book many and many written pages, and alas I thought I did not know how to read. And suddenly I realized I was reading and understanding all that was written on the Book and it was as though I had become richer, wiser, and in a moment I learned millions of things'' (Wasson 1974).

The pages are covered with written characters. The designs one sees on the psychedelics, which many people have described as the motifs of oriental carpets, at least this once took the form of script in her imagination. She says the pages were covered with letters.

One can hardly imagine a more eloquent, poignant description of an oral poet's desire for the knowledge contained in books. She cannot read, but in her transcendental condition she can. The book is thus a perfect image of the divine wisdom which is beyond ordinary understanding but which the mushrooms enable one to comprehend.

One is reminded of the metaphor of the book of nature which occurs frequently in European literature, that ''universal and publick manuscript which lies expansed unto the eyes of all,'' as Sir Thomas Browne said, adding that its hieroglyphics were more familiar to heathens than to Christians. Paracelsus, ''doctor and alchemist, who established the role of chemistry in medicine,'' stated: ''It is from the light of nature that this illumination should come, so that the text of the books of nature may be comprehended and without this illumination, there would be no philosopher or naturalist.'' María Sabina is indeed enlightened with the light of nature and enabled thereby to read the text of nature which we know today is written in genetic script.

She told Estrada: ''The Principal Ones disappeared and left me alone in front of the immense book. I knew that it was the book of wisdom. The book was before me, I could see it but not touch it. I tried to caress it but my hands touched nothing. I limited myself to contemplating it and at that moment, I began to speak. Then I realized that I was reading the sacred book of Language.''

In the background as she sings, crickets chirp, near and far, throughout the mountain night. The chirps of crickets, say neurobiologists, are ''read-outs'' of impulse signals coded in the nucleic acid sequences of their genes. María Sabina, surprisingly enough, says that when she began to speak, she realized she was reading. One would think that for such an oral poet her inventions were wholly verbal, vocal ones, but for herself she is chanting what is written. She is reading at the same time as speaking as they must have done when they chanted their myths with the codices open before them like musicological scores. She is saying what she sees, which is, in a sense, to read. Where could such an idea come from, for her whose own language is an unwritten one, but from some sense of giving utterance to what has been coded in advance, what is inscribed in her brain, which is maybe what she means by saying that she has her knowledge from birth, that it is innate.

Of course it is not, but cultural in origin like the traditional form of her chant itself, yet the rhythms that vehicle her words are neurophysiological ones and her visions themselves are generated by the deep-lying mechanisms of the human cerebral cortex and nervous system.

''That is your book, my Father/ That is your clock,'' she sings. For her everything is written, predestined, foreordained. God has wound up the clock of existence and set it going, allotting to each his or her number of days. As Derrida has said, the metaphor of the book of the world is a theological one.[3] A universe in expansion, where events are the outcome of chance as much as necessity, can't be contained between the covers of a book; a reality which is not created once and for all but in course of realization is not written in advance but being written, it demands a text, an open-ended, unlimited play of signifiers in accord with the combinatory play of life itself.

It is as if, however, she goes back to the origins of writing. In her oral autobiography, she relates: "And as well I see that language falls, comes from up above, as if they were little luminous objects that fall from heaven. Language falls on the sacred table, falls on my body. So I catch word after word with my hands. That happens when I don't see the book." Words are invisible. If she sees them falling from heaven they must be changed into images, ideograms. Her words recall in a remarkable way the Chinese myth about the origin of writing recounted by Chang Yen-Yuan in the *Li Tai Ming Hua Chi*: "The K'uei star with pointed rays is the Lord of Literature on earth and as Tsang Chieh, who had four eyes, looked up (into heaven) he saw images dropping down (from the star) and these he combined with footprints of birds and tortoises."

EDMUND CARPENTER
The Death of Sedna

Edmund Carpenter's field studies and media experiments range from the Canadian Arctic and Siberia to Southeast Asia, Borneo, and New Guinea. His early collaboration with Marshall McLuhan gave the latter his principal link to areas of anthropological concern. A significant part of Carpenter's own work involves the impact of the new technology and its resultant monoculture on the world's surviving software cultures. Principal works: Eskimo Realities, They Became What They Beheld, Explorations in Communication *(ed., with Marhsall McLuhan), and* Oh, What a Blow that Phantom Gave Me!

SOURCE: *Edmund Carpenter,* Oh, What a Blow That Phantom Gave Me!, *pages 109–112.*

[3]Jacques Derrida, *De La Grammatologie* (Paris: Editions de Minuit, 1967). In connection with the image of the path as it occurs throughout the chants of the Mazatecs it is worth pondering his statement that "it would be necessary to mediate together . . . the history of writing and the history of the route." "It is difficult to imagine," he goes on, "that the access to the possibility of trails should not be at the same time access to writing" (p. 158).

In cigar stores, art galleries & museum shops across Canada, Eskimo stone art is available, popularly priced, popularly styled. Carvings of mermaids, those sexually frustrating figures from our own mythology, are especially popular. Here they are identified with the Eskimo goddess Sedna, though neither carvers nor buyers can be much concerned with accuracy, for these carvings always show a girl with two eyes, fingers & braided hair, whereas Sedna was one-eyed, fingerless & unkempt.

Of the myths that were once half-told, half-sung in the igloos, none was more important than that of Sedna. Every Eskimo knew it & had his own version, all equally true, for this myth was too complex for any single telling.

Sedna or Nuliajuk ("Young girl") rejected all suitors until a stranger induced her to elope with him. He was, in fact, a cruel dog disguised as a man, but she discovered this only after reaching her new home on a distant island.

Escape was impossible until one day when her family came to visit her. Her husband always refused to let her leave the tent, except to go to the toilet, and even then tied a long cord to her. But this time when she went outside and he called, asking why she delayed so long, she had the ball of cord reply that she would soon return.

In the meantime, she ran to the beach & joined her parents in their boat. But no sooner had they set out to sea, than her husband discovered the ruse and, transforming himself into a bird, swooped low over the fleeing family, turning the sea to storm, and threatening them with drowning. To save themselves, they cast Sedna overboard.

At first she clung to the gunwale. But her father cut off the first joints of her fingers; when she persisted, he cut off the second & third joints. They sank into the sea to become the seal, walrus & whale that the Eskimo hunt today.

In desperation, Sedna hooked her elbows over the side, but her father struck her with his paddle, gouging out an eye, and she sank into the sea, fingerless & one-eyed.

From the bottom of the sea, she ruled all creatures. Their floating bodies nearly filled her house. Periodically she sent animals forth to be taken by hunters, but only by hunters who showed respect for slain animals.

Other hunters returned empty-handed. That is, Sedna withheld life from them, for they could not survive without the food, clothing & fuel that came from her subjects.

She was the most feared of all spirits, the one who, more than any other, controlled the destinies of men.

In the various versions of this myth, Sedna was sometimes an unwanted daughter cast into the sea by her father, or a girl who has rejected all eligible men, or an orphan nobody wanted; in one version she was already a mother, abandoned by her own children. In each, she was someone the family abandoned for its own safety.

Abandonment of people was not purely mythical. The Eskimo did, in fact, abandon old people. Killing new-born girls was common. And the position of orphans was precarious: one's own family always took precedence. These were normal experiences in Eskimo life—cruel necessities forced on them by scarcity.

The Sedna myth represented this dilemma as the Eskimo saw it. They never asked that the universe be this way. But—*ayornamut* ("it cannot be otherwise")—they accepted life on its own terms.

They did more than accept: they took upon *themselves* the responsibility for the fact that life was the way it was. They gave Sedna the power of life & death over man.

Those who were forced to abandon her now placed themselves in her power, dependent upon her good will, her respect for life.

The hunter Aua, asked by the ethnologist Rasmussen to explain why life was as it was, took him outside and, pointing to hunters returning empty-handed after long hours on the ice, himself asked, "Why?" He then took him into a cold igloo where hungry children shivered and into another igloo where a woman, who had always worked hard and helped others, now lay miserably ill. Each time he asked, "Why?" but received no reply.

"You see," said Aua, "you are equally unable to give any reason when we ask why life is as it is. And so it must be. All our customs come from life and turn toward life; we explain nothing, we believe nothing, but in what I have just shown you lies our answer to all you ask."

The last part of the Sedna myth told of a maze to be entered & come out of alive, bringing the innocent to safety. In this maze there lived the dog whose name was Death. It fell to the *angakok*, or shaman, to find the door that opened the past, unravel the tangled traces of time, rescue the innocent & beware the dog. The occasion was a séance where the *angakok* sought to cure the sick & save the dying. If he failed & his patient died, its soul went beneath the sea to Sedna's home. The *angakok* followed, traveling on the sound of his drum. Sedna's husband, a snarling dog, guarded the entrance to her home, but the *angakok* paralyzed him with a chant & entered her strange house, confronting her directly. He tried to reason with her, arguing that she had taken a life without cause. But she ignored him. He begged for pity, but she laughed contemptuously. In anger, he twisted her arm & struck her with a walrus penis bone. But she was not afraid. Then he appealed to her vanity, combing out her tangled hair. But she was still unrelenting. Finally, ignoring her altogether, he stepped back and, with drum held high, sang of life.

Sedna was sometimes so touched by his song, so moved by his singing, she released the soul of the dead person, and the *angakok* returned with it to the land of the living.

In a life where neither reason nor strength prevailed, where cunning counted for little & pity least of all, the Eskimo sang of life, for only that availed, and even that, not always.

A people may be fairly judged by their uses of the past. The myth of the hero who goes to the land of the dead to unravel the threads of time & save the innocent has been shared by many people & woven into their most magical dreams. The ancient Greeks knew the hero as Orpheus. Literate man knew the goddess of the nether world as the Ice Queen in a Hans Christian Andersen fairy tale for children. Modern man knows the goddess as mermaid, debased into a paperweight.

BIBLIOGRAPHY

Bibliography

The listing below is by no means exhaustive and is intended to function primarily as a reference resource for works cited in the selections and in the editors' headnotes—at least insofar as data for the former are readily available. While we may think of all ethnography and poetry as ultimately related to the ethnopoetic, those works which bear principally on other than ethnopoetic concerns—for example, the individual books of poetry mentioned in the headnotes to Section Five—have generally not been referenced.

Abimbola, W. "The Odù of Ifá," *African Notes*, vol. 1. no. 3. Ibadan, 1964.

———. "Yoruba Oral Literature," *African Notes*, vol. 2, nos. 2, 3. Ibadan, 1965.

Abraham, Roy Clive. *Dictionary of Modern Yoruba*. London: University of London Press, 1958.

Abrahams, Roger D. "Concerning African Performance Patterns." *Neo-African Literature and Culture: Essays in Memory of Janheinz Jahn*. Ed. B. Heymann. Mainzer Afrika-Studien. Mainz, 1976.

Alcheringa. Ed. Jerome Rothenberg and Dennis Tedlock. 10 vols. New York and Boston, 1970–1980.

Allen, Donald. *The New American Poetry: 1945–1960*. New York: Grove Press, 1960.

Angulo, Jaime de. *Indian Tales*. New York: Hill and Wang, 1953.

Anisimov, A. F. "The Shaman's Tent of the Evenks and the Origin of the Shamanistic Rite." *Studies in Siberian Shamanism*. Ed. Henry N. Michael. Toronto: University of Toronto Press, 1963.

Antin, David. *Talking at the Boundaries*. New York: New Directions, 1976.

Archer, W. G. "Baiga Poetry," *Man in India*, Vol. XXIII, no. 1 (1943). Reprint. Amsterdam: Swets and Zeitlinger N.V., 1972.

———. *The Hill of Flutes: Life, Love, and Poetry in Tribal India*. Pittsburgh: University of Pittsburgh Press, 1974.

Armstrong, R. G. "Talking Drums in the Benue-Cross River Region of Nigeria," *Phylon* 15 (1954).

Artaud, Antonin. *Selected Writings*. Ed. and intro. Susan Sontag. New York: Farrar, Straus and Giroux, 1976.

Astrov, Margot. *The Winged Serpent*. New York: John Day, 1946. Reprinted as *American Indian Prose and Poetry*. New York: Capricorn, 1962.

Avalon, Arthur. *The Serpent Power*. Reprint of 7th edition. New York: Dover Books, 1974.

Awoonor, Kofi. *The Breast of the Earth: A Survey of the History, Culture and Literature of Africa South of the Sahara*. Garden City, N.Y.: Anchor Press, 1975.

Babcock, Barbara A., ed. *The Reversible World: Symbolic Inversion in Art and Society*. Ithaca, N.Y.: Cornell University Press, 1978.

Bandelier, Adolph. *The Delight Makers*. New York: Harcourt Brace Jovanovich, 1971.

Baraka, Amiri [LeRoi Jones]. *Home: Social Essays*. New York: Morrow, 1966.

Barbeau, Marius. "Tsimshian Songs." *The Tsimshian: Their Arts and Music*. Ed. Viola E. Garfield, Paul S. Wingert, and Marius Barbeau. New York: Publications of the American Ethnological Society 18, 1951.

Barea, Arturo. *Lorca: The Poet and His People*. New York: Grove Press, 1958.

Barfield, Owen. *Saving the Appearances: A Study in Idolatry*. New York, London: Faber and Faber, 1957.

Barthes, Roland. "The Written Face," *The Drama Review*, vol. 15, no. 3 (Spring 1971).

Bascom, W. R. "The Sanctions of Ifa Divination," *Journal of the Royal Anthropological Institute*, no. 71 (1941).

————. "The Relationship of Yoruba Folklore to Divining," *Journal of American Folklore*, no. 56 (1943).

————. "Folklore Research in Africa," *Journal of American Folklore*, no. 77 (1964).

————. "Folklore and Literature." *The African World: A Survey of Social Research*. Ed. R. A. Lystod. New York: Praeger Publishers, 1965a.

————. "The Forms of Folklore: Prose Narratives," *Journal of American Folklore*, no. 78 (1965b).

Bataille, Georges. *Lascaux or the Birth of Art*. New York: Skira Press, 1955.

————. *Eroticism*. London: John Calder, 1962.

Beattie, John, and John Middleton, eds. *Spirit Mediumship and Society in Africa*. New York: Africana Publishing Corp., 1969.

Becker, Alton L. "Notes on the Ramayana in Modern Java." Presented to the Association for Asian Studies panel on the Ramayana, Toronto, March 1973.

Becker, Judith. "Time and Tune in Java." *The Imagination of Reality: Essays in Southeast Asian Coherence Systems*. Ed. Alton L. Becker and Aram Yengoyan. Norwood, N.J.: Ablex, 1979.

Belo, Jane. *Traditional Balinese Culture*. New York: Columbia University Press, 1970.

Benamou, Michel, and Jerome Rothenberg, eds. "Ethnopoetics: A First International Symposium," *Alcheringa*, n. s., vol. 2, no. 2 (1976).

Benedict, Ruth. *Zuni Mythology*. Columbia University Contributions to Anthropology 21 (1935).

Bergin, Thomas Goddard, and Max Harold Fisch. *The New Science of Giambattista Vico*. Ithaca, N.Y.: Cornell University Press, 1948.

Berndt, R. M. *Kunapipi: A Study of an Australian Aboriginal Religious Cult*. New York: International Universities Press, 1951.

————. *Djanggawal: An Aboriginal Religious Cult of North-Eastern Arnhem Land*. New York: Philosophical Library, 1953.

Berry, Jack. *Spoken Art in West Africa*. London: School of Oriental and African Studies, University of London, 1961.

Black Elk. *The Sacred Pipe*. Ed. Joseph Epes Brown. New York: Penguin Books, 1971.

Black Elk, and John G. Neihardt. *Black Elk Speaks*. Lincoln: University of Nebraska Press, 1961, Bison Books, 1979.

Blackmun, Barbara, and Matthew Schoffeleers. "Masks of Malawi," *African Arts*, vol. 5, no. 4 (Summer 1972).

Blake, William. *The Poetry and Prose of William Blake*. Ed. David V. Erdman. Garden City, N.Y.: Doubleday, 1965.

Blue Cloud, Peter [Aroniawenrate]. *Back Then Tomorrow*. Brunswick, Me.: Blackberry Press, 1978.

Boas, Franz. "Songs of the Kwakiutl Indians," *Internationales Archiv für Ethnographie*, 9. Supplement. Leiden, 1896.

———. "The Social Organization and Secret Societies of the Kwakiutl Indians," *Report of the U.S. National Museum for 1895*. Washington, D.C.: Government Printing Office, 1897.

———. "Ethnology of the Kwakiutl," *Bureau of American Ethnology Annual Report* 35 (1913–1914). Washington, D.C.: Government Printing Office, 1921.

———. "Stylistic Aspects of Primitive Literature," *Journal of American Folklore* 38 (1925). Reprinted in *Race, Language, and Culture*. New York: Macmillan, 1940.

Boundary 2. Ed. William Spanos. Special issue: "The Oral Impulse in Contemporary American Poetry," Vol. III, no. 3 (Spring 1975).

Bowra, C. M. *Primitive Song*. Cleveland and New York: World, 1962.

Breton, André. "The First Surrealist Manifesto." *Manifeste du Surréalisme*. Paris: Editions du Sagittaire, 1924. English trans. in A. Breton, *Manifestos of Surrealism*. Ann Arbor: University of Michigan Press, 1969.

Brustein, Robert Sandford. "News Theatre," *New York Times Magazine*, 16 June 1974.

Bryant, Alfred T. *Olden Times in Zululand and Natal*. Capetown: C. S. Struik, 1929, 1965.

Bunzel, Ruth L. "Zuni Origin Myths," *Annual Report of the Bureau of American Ethnology* 47 (1932).

———. "Zuni Texts," *Publications of the American Ethnological Society* 15 (1933).

Burns, Elizabeth. *Theatricality*. New York: Harper and Row, 1972.

Bursill-Hall, G. L. "Linguistic Analysis of North American Indian Songs," *Canadian Linguistic Journal* 10 (1964).

Bury, J. B. *A History of Greece to the Death of Alexander the Great*. 3d ed. London: Macmillan, 1956.

Caillois, Roger, and Jean-Clarence Lambert, eds. *Trésor de la Poésie Universelle*. Paris: Gallimard, 1958.

Carpenter, Edmund. *They Became What They Beheld*. New York: Outerbridge and Dienstfrey, 1970 (distributed by E. P. Dutton).

———. "The Eskimo Artist." *Anthropology and Art: Readings in Cross-Cultural Aesthetics*. Ed. Charlotte M. Otten. Garden City, N.Y.: Natural History Press, 1971.

———. *Eskimo Realities*. New York: Holt, Rinehart and Winston, 1973.

———. *Oh, What a Blow That Phantom Gave Me*. New York: Bantam Books, 1974.

Carpenter, Edmund, and Marshall McLuhan, eds. *Explorations in Communication*. Boston: Beacon Press, 1960.

Carrington, J. F. "The Drum Language of the Lokele Tribe," *African Studies* 3 (1944).

———. *Talking Drums of Africa*. London: Carey Kingsgate Press, 1949a. Reprint. New York: Negro Universities Press, 1969.

———. "A Comparative Study of Some Central African Gong Languages," *Mémoires*, vol. 18, no. 3. Brussels: Institut Royal Colonial Belge, 1949b.

Castaneda, Carlos. *Tales of Power*. New York: Simon and Schuster, 1974.

Cendrars, Blaise, ed. *The African Saga: Anthologie Nègre*. Trans. Margery Bianco. New York: Payson and Clarke, 1927.

Césaire, Aimé. *Discourse on Colonialism*. Trans. Joan Pinkham. New York and London: Monthly Review Press, 1972.

———. "Notebook of a Return to the Native Land." Trans. Clayton Eshleman and Annette Smith. *Montemora* 6 (1980).

Chapman, Abraham. *Literature of the American Indians: Views and Interpretations.* New York: New American Library, 1975

Charles, Lucile H. "Drama in Shaman Exorcism," *Journal of American Folklore*, vol. 66, no. 260 (April–June 1953).

Childe, V. Gordon. *Man Makes Himself.* New York: New American Library, 1955.

Clarke, R. T. "The Drum Language of the Tumba People," *American Journal of Sociology* 40 (1934).

Cope, Trevor, ed. *Izibongo: Zulu Praise Poems.* London: Oxford University Press, 1968.

Corbin, Henry. *Avicenna and the Visionary Recital.* Trans. Willard Trask. New York: Pantheon, 1960.

Cornford, F. M. *The Unwritten Philosophy and Other Essays.* Cambridge: Cambridge University Press, 1950.

Curtis, Edward S. *The North American Indian.* 20 vols. New York, 1915. Reprint. New York: Johnson, 1970.

Curtis, Natalie, ed. and recorder. *The Indians' Book: Songs and Legends of the American Indians.* New York: Dover Books, 1968.

Curtius, Ernst Robert. *La Littérature Européene et le Moyen Age Latin.* Trans. Jean Bréjoux. Paris: Presses Universitaires de France, 1956.

Cushing, Frank Hamilton. *Zuni Folk Tales.* New York: Putnam, 1901, 1931. Reprint. New York: AMS Press, 1976.

Dauenhauer, Richard, and Fr. Julius Jetté. "Koyukon Riddle-Poems," *Alcheringa*, n. s., vol. 3, no. 1 (1977).

Day, A. Grove. *The Sky Clears: Poetry of the American Indian.* New York: Macmillan, 1951.

Demetracapoulou, D., and Cora DuBois. "A Study of Wintu Mythology," *Journal of American Folklore* 45 (1932).

Densmore, Frances. "Chippewa Music," *Bureau of American Ethnology Bulletin* 45, 53 (1910–1913).

———. "Teton Sioux Music," *Bureau of American Ethnology Bulletin* 61 (1918).

Derrida, Jacques. *Of Grammatology.* Baltimore: Johns Hopkins University Press, 1976.

Desoille, R. *Le Rêve Eveillé Dirigé en Psychothérapie.* Paris: Payot, 1973.

Diamond, Stanley. "Dahomey: A Proto-State in West Africa." Ph.D. dissertation, Columbia University, 1951. Ann Arbor: University of Michigan Microfilms.

———. "Kibbutz and Shtetl: The History of an Idea," *Social Problems* 5 (Fall 1957).

———. *In Search of the Primitive: A Critique of Civilization.* New Brunswick, N.J.: Transaction Books, 1974.

———. "Anaguta Cosmography," *Anthropological Linguistics*, vol. 2, no. 2 (1960), Bloomington: University of Indiana Press.

Di Prima, Diane. "Light/and Keats." *Talking Poetics from Naropa Institute.* Vol. I. Eds. Anne Waldman and Marilyn Webb. Boulder and London: Shambhala, 1978.

H. D. [Hilda Doolittle]. *Bid Me to Live.* New York: Grove Press, 1960.

Doria, Charles, and Harris Lenowitz. *Origins: Creation Texts from the Ancient Mediterranean.* Garden City, N.Y.: Anchor Books, 1976.

Duncan, Robert. *The Opening of the Field.* New York: Grove Press, 1960.

———. *Roots and Branches.* New York: Scribners, 1964.

————. *Bending the Bow*. New York: New Directions, 1968.

————. *The Truth and Life of Myth*. Fremont, Mich.: Sumac Press, 1968.

————. "Rites of Participation: Parts I and II." *A Caterpillar Anthology*. Ed. Clayton Eshleman. New York: Anchor Books, 1971.

Dundes, Alan. *The Study of Folklore*. Englewood Cliffs, N.J.: Prentice-Hall, 1965.

Durkheim, Emile. *The Elementary Forms of the Religious Life*. Trans. Joseph Ward Swain. New York: Collier Books, 1961.

Durkheim, Emile, and Marcel Mauss. *Primitive Classifications*. Trans. Rodney Needham. London: Cohen and West, 1963.

Eliade, Mircea. *Myths, Dreams and Mysteries*. U.K.: The Fontana Library, 1960.

————. "The Yearning for Paradise in Primitive Tradition." *Myth and Mythmaking*. Ed. H. A. Murray. New York: Braziller, 1960.

————. *Images and Symbols*. New York: Sheed and Ward, 1961.

————. *The Two and the One*. New York: Harper Torchbooks, 1962.

————. *Shamanism: Archaic Techniques of Ecstasy*. Bollingen Series, 76. New York: Pantheon, 1964.

————, ed. *From Primitives to Zen: A Thematic Sourcebook on the History of Religions*. New York and Evanston: Harper and Row, 1967.

Emigh, John. "Playing with the Past," *The Drama Review*, vol. 23, no. 2 (1979).

Errington, Shelly. "Some Comments on Style in the Meanings of the Past," *Journal of Asian Studies*, Vol. XXXVIII, no. 2 (1979).

Eshleman, Clayton, ed. *A Caterpillar Anthology*. New York: Anchor Books, 1971.

————. *Hades in Manganese*. Santa Barbara, Ca.: Black Sparrow Press, 1981.

Estrada, Alvaro. *María Sabina: Her Life and Chants*. Santa Barbara, Ca.: Ross-Erikson Publishers, 1981.

Feldman, Burton, and Robert D. Richardson, eds. *The Rise of Modern Mythology*. Bloomington: Indiana University Press, 1972.

Fenollosa, Ernest. *The Chinese Written Character as a Medium for Poetry*. Ed. Ezra Pound. San Francisco: City Lights Books, 1963.

Fergusson, Erna. "Laughing Priests," *Theatre Arts Monthly* (August 1933).

Fergusson, Francis. *The Idea of a Theater*. New York: Doubleday, 1949.

Field, Edward. *Eskimo Songs and Stories*. New York: Delacorte Press, 1973. (1st ed. Cambridge, Mass.: Education Development Center, Inc., 1967.)

Finnegan, Ruth. *Oral Literature in Africa*. London: Oxford University Press, 1970.

————. *Oral Poetry: Its Nature, Significance, and Social Context*. Cambridge: Cambridge University Press, 1977.

————, ed. *A World Treasury of Oral Poetry*. Bloomington: Indiana University Press, 1978.

Fischer, John L. "The Sociopsychological Analysis of Folktales," *Current Anthropology* 4 (1963).

Fishman, Joshua A., ed. *Readings in the Sociology of Language*. The Hague: Mouton, 1968.

Forman, Warner, and Bjamba Rintschen. *Lamaistische Tanzmasken: Der Erlik-Tsam in der Mongolei*. Leipzig, n.d.

Foucault, Michel. *The Order of Things*. New York: Pantheon, 1970.

Fox, Hugh, ed. *First Fire: Central and South American Indian Poetry*. Garden City, N.Y.: Doubleday-Anchor, 1978.

Freud, Sigmund. *On Creativity and the Unconscious*. New York: Harper and Brothers, 1958.

―――. *The Interpretation of Dreams*. New York: Avon Books, (1900), 1965.

Furst, Peter T. "To Find Our Life: Peyote among the Huichol Indians of Mexico." *Flesh of the Gods: The Ritual Use of Hallucinogens*. Ed. P. T. Furst. New York: Praeger, 1972.

―――. "The Roots and Continuities of Shamanism." *Stones, Bones and Skin: Ritual and Shamanic Art*. Ed. A. Brodzky. Toronto: Artscanada, 1977.

Furst, Peter T., and Barbara G. Myerhoff. "Myth as History: The Jimson Weed Cycle of the Huichols of Mexico," *Anthropologica* 17 (1966).

Gbadamosi, B., and Ulli Beier. *Yoruba Poetry*. Ibadan: Ministry of Education, Nigeria, 1959.

Geertz, Clifford. *The Interpretation of Cultures*. New York: Basic Books, 1973.

Geertz, Clifford, and Hildred Geertz. *Kinship in Bali*. Chicago: The University of Chicago Press, 1975.

Gelfand, Michael. *Shona Ritual: With Special Reference to the Chaminuka Cult*. Capetown: Juta, 1959.

Geronimo. *Geronimo: His Own Story*. Ed. S. M. Barett. New York: Ballantine Books, 1968.

Gleason, Judith. *A Recitation of Ifa, Oracle of the Yoruba*. New York: Grossman Publishers, 1973.

Goldman-Eisler, Frieda. "Discussion and Further Comments." *New Directions in the Study of Language*. Ed. Eric H. Lenneberg. Cambridge, Mass.: MIT Press, 1964.

Graves, Robert. *The White Goddess: A Historical Grammar of Poetic Myth*. New York: Vintage Books, 1958.

Graves, Robert, and Raphael Patai. *Hebrew Myths: The Book of Genesis*. New York: McGraw-Hill, 1966.

Greenway, John. *Literature Among the Primitives*. Hatboro, Pa.: Folklore Associates, 1964.

Griaule, Marcel. *Conversations with Ogotemmêli*. London: Oxford University Press, 1965.

Groot, J. J. M. de. *The Religious System of China*. 6 vols. Taipei: Ch'eng-nsu Publishing Company, 1964.

Guillaumont, A., et al. *The Gospel According to Thomas*. New York: Harper, 1959.

Haberland, Eike, ed. *Leo Frobenius 1873–1973: An Anthology*. Wiesbaden: Franz Steiner Verlag, 1973.

Hale, Kenneth. "Introduction to Walbiri Domains and Selection." Unpublished MS. N.d.

Hollowell, A. Irving. *The Role of Conjuring in Salteaux Society*. Philadelphia: Publications of the American Philosophical Society, 1942.

Harari, Josue. *Textual Strategies: Perspectives in Post-Structuralist Criticism*. Ithaca: Cornell University Press, 1979.

Harner, Michael. *Hallucinogens and Shamanism*. New York: Oxford University Press, 1973.

Heidegger, Martin. *What Is Called Thinking*. Trans. and intro. J. Glenn Gray. New York: Harper and Row, 1968.

———. *On the Way to Language*. Trans. Peter D. Hertz. New York: Harper and Row, 1971.

Helm, June, ed. *Essays on the Verbal and Visual Arts*. Proceedings of the 1966 Annual Meeting, American Ethnological Society. Seattle: University of Washington Press, 1967.

Hendricks, William O. "On the Notion 'Behind the Sentence,' " *Linguistics* 37 (1967).

Herskovits, M. J. "Negro Folklore." *Encyclopedia of Literature*. New York: 1946. Reprint. *Cultures and Societies of Africa*. Ed. S. and P. Ottenberg. New York: 1960.

Hillman, James. *Re-visioning Psychology*. New York: Harper and Row, 1975.

———. *The Dream and the Underworld*. New York: Harper and Row, 1979.

Hoffman, Walter James. "The Menomini Indians," *14th Annual Report of the Bureau of American Ethnology*. Washington, D.C.: 1896.

Holmer, Nils M., and Henry Wassén. *Mu-Igala or the Way of Muu: A Medicine Song from the Cunas of Panama*. Göteborg, Sweden, 1947.

Hungerford, T. A. G., ed. *Australian Signposts*. Melbourne: Longman Cheshire, 1956.

Hymes, Dell. "Review of Papers from the Symposium on American Indian Linguistics," *Language* 32 (1956).

———, ed. *Language in Culture and Society*. New York: Harper and Row, 1964.

———. "Some North Pacific Coast Poems: A Problem in Anthropological Philology," *American Anthropologist*, vol. 67, no. 2 (April 1965).

———, ed. *Reinventing Anthropology*. New York: Pantheon, 1972.

———, ed. *Foundations in Sociolinguistics: An Ethnographic Approach*. Philadelphia: University of Pennsylvania Press, 1974.

———. "Discovering Oral Performance and Measured Verse in American Indian Narrative." *New Literary History*, Vol. VIII, no. 3 (Spring 1977).

———. *In Vain I Tried To Tell You*. Philadelphia: University of Pennsylvania Press, 1981.

Jacobs, Melville. *Clackamas Chinook Texts*. Publications of the Indiana University Research Center in Anthropology, Folklore and Linguistics 8 (1958) and 11 (1959), Bloomington.

———. *The Content and Style of an Oral Literature*. Viking Fund Publications in Anthropology 26 (1959).

Jerison, Harry J. *Evolution of the Brain and Intelligence*. New York: Academic Press, 1973.

———. "Paleoneurology and the Evolution of Mind," *Scientific American*, vol. 234, no. 1 (January 1976).

Jetté, Fr. Julius. "Riddles of the Ten'a Indians," *Anthropus* 8 (1913).

Jowett, Benjamin, trans. *The Dialogues of Plato, Vol. II: The Republic*. New York: Bigelow, Brown, 1914.

Jung, Carl G. *Aion*. Zurich: Rascher, 1951.

———. "On the Psychology of the Trickster Figure." In Paul Radin. *The Trickster: A Study in American Indian Mythology*. New York: Schocken Books, 1972.

Kaplan, Bert. "Psychological Themes in Zuni Mythology and Zuni TAT's." *The Psychoanalytic Study of Society*. Ed. Warner Muensterberger and Sydney Axelrod. Vol. II. New York, 1962.

Kenner, Hugh. *The Pound Era*. Berkeley, Los Angeles, London: University of California Press, 1971.

Kirby, Ernest T. "The Shamanistic Origins of Popular Entertainments," *The Drama Review* 18 (March 1974).

―――. *Ur-Drama: The Origins of Theatre*. New York: New York University Press, 1975.

Klima, Edward S., and Ursula Bellugi. *The Signs of Language*. Cambridge: Harvard University Press, 1979.

―――. "Poetry Without Sound," *New Wilderness Letter* 8 (1980).

Kroeber, Alfred L. *Anthropology: Race, Language, Culture, Psychology, Prehistory*. Rev. ed. New York: Harcourt Brace Jovanovich, 1948.

―――. "A Mohave Historical Epic," *Anthropological Records*, University of California (1951).

Kroeber, Theodora. *The Inland Whale*. Berkeley and Los Angeles: University of California Press, 1963.

Kroeber, Theodora, and Robert F. Heizer. *Almost Ancestors: The First Californians*. Ed. F. David Hales. San Francisco: Sierra Club, 1968.

La Barre, Weston. *The Ghost Dance: Origins of Religion*. Garden City, N.Y.: Doubleday, 1970.

Labov, William. *Language in the Inner City: Studies in the Black English Vernacular*. Philadelphia: University of Pennsylvania Press, 1972.

Lame Deer [John Fire], and Richard Erdoes. *Lame Deer Seeker of Visions: The Life of a Sioux Medicine Man*. New York: Simon and Schuster, 1972.

Landes, Ruth. *Ojibwa Religion and the Midéwiwin*. Madison: University of Wisconsin Press, 1968.

Lansing, J. Stephen. "The Sounding of the Text." Unpublished MS. N.d.

Laoye I, Oba Adetoyese. "The Orikis of the Timis of Ede," Ede, 1965.

Leach, MacEdward. "What Shall We Do with 'Little Matty Groves?' " *Journal of American Folklore* 76 (1963).

Lenneberg, Eric H. *New Directions in the Study of Language*. Cambridge, Mass.: MIT Press, 1964.

Leon, Moses de. *The Zohar*, 5 vols. London: The Soncino Press, 1934, 1958, 1970.

León-Portilla, Miguel. *Trece Poetas del Mundo Azteca*. Mexico, D.F.: Universidad Autónoma de Mexico, 1967.

―――. *Pre-Columbian Literatures of Mexico*. Norman: University of Oklahoma Press, 1969.

Leroi-Gourhan, A. *Treasures of Prehistoric Art*. New York: H. N. Abrams, 1967.

Lessa, William A., and Evon C. Vogt, eds. *Reader in Comparative Religion*. Evanston, Ill.: Row Peterson, 1952, 1965.

Lévi-Strauss, Claude. "The Structural Study of Myth," *Journal of American Folklore* 78 (1955). Reprints. *Anthropologie Structurale*. Paris: Plon, 1958. *Structural Anthropology*. New York: Basic Books, 1963.

―――. *The Savage Mind*. Chicago: University of Chicago Press, 1966.

―――. *Structural Anthropology*. Garden City, N.Y.: Anchor Books, 1967.

―――. *Tristes Tropiques*. New York: Atheneum, 1967.

Lewis, I. M. *Ecstatic Religion: An Anthropological Study of Spirit Possession and*

Shamanism. Harmondsworth, England: Penguin Books, 1971.

Lindsay, A. D., trans. *The Republic of Plato*. New York: Dutton, 1940.

Lommel, Andreas. *Shamanism: The Beginnings of Art*. Trans. Michael Bullock. New York: McGraw-Hill, 1967.

————. *Masks: Their Meaning and Function*. New York: McGraw-Hill, 1972.

Lorca, Federico García. *Poet in New York*. Trans. Ben Belitt. New York: Grove Press, 1955.

Lord, Albert B. *The Singer of Tales*. New York: Atheneum, 1970.

Lowenstein, Tom. *Eskimo Poems from Canada and Greenland*. (From material originally collected by Knud Rasmussen.) London: Allison and Busby, 1973.

MacAdams, Lewis. *News from Niman Farm*. Bolinas, Ca.: Tombouctou Press, 1977.

McAllester, David P. *Peyote Music*. New York: Viking Fund Publications in Anthropology, 1949.

————. *Enemy Way Music: A Study of Social and Esthetic Values As Seen in Navajo Music*. Cambridge, Mass.: Papers of the Peabody Museum of Archaeology and Ethnology, Harvard University, vol. 41, no. 3 (1954).

————. "Ritual Communication." *Io*, ed. R. Grossinger, no. 3 (1966–67).

————. "The Tenth Horse Song of Frank Mitchell: Translation and Comments." *Stony Brook*, ed. G. Quasha, 1969.

————, ed. *Readings in Ethnomusicology*. New York and London: Johnson Reprint, 1971.

————. *Hogans: Navajo House and House Songs / House Poems from Navajo Ritual*. Middletown, Conn.: Wesleyan University Press, 1980.

McAllester, David P., and Charlotte J. Frisbie, eds. *Navajo Blessingway Singer: The Autobiography of Frank Mitchell 1881–1967*. Tucson: University of Arizona Press, 1978.

Mace, Carroll Edward. *Two Spanish–Quiche Dance Dramas of Rabinal*. New Orleans, 1971.

McGlashen, A. "Daily Paper Pantheon," *The Lancet* (1953).

Mac Low, Jackson. *The Pronouns: A Collection of Forty Dances for the Dancers*. Barrytown, N.Y.: Station Hill, 1979.

McNickle, D'Arcy. *Native American Tribalism: Indian Survivals and Renewals*. London: Oxford University Press, 1973.

Malinowski, Bronislaw. *Argonauts of the Western Pacific*. New York: Dutton, 1922.

————. *Sex and Repression in Savage Society*. New York: Harcourt Brace, 1927.

————. *Magic, Myth and Religion*. Garden City, N.Y.: Doubleday, 1954.

————. *Coral Gardens and Their Magic*. Bloomington: Indiana University Press, 1965.

Malraux, André. *Psychology of Art*. Trans. Stuart Gilbert. Bollingen Series, 24, 1949–1950. New York: Pantheon.

Marriott, Alice. *Kiowa Years: A Study in Culture Impact*. New York: Macmillan, 1968.

Marriott, Alice, and Carol K. Rachlin. *American Indian Mythology*. New York: Mentor Books, 1968.

Marx, Karl, and Friedrich Engels. *Basic Writings on Politics and Philosophy*. Ed. Lewis S. Feuer. Garden City, N.Y.: Anchor Books, 1959.

Matthews, Washington. "Songs of Sequence of the Navajos," *Journal of American Folklore*, Vol. VII, no. 26 (July–Sept. 1894).

————. *Night Chant: A Navajo Ceremony*. New York: The Knickerbocker Press, 1902. Also New York: Memoirs of the American Museum of Natural History, 1902.

Maupoil, B. "La géomancie à l'ancienne Côte des Esclaves," *Travaux et mémoires de l'Institut d'Ethnologie* 42 (1961).

Messenger, John C. "Ibibio Drama," *Africa*, vol. 41, no. 3 (1971).

Middleton, John. *Lugbara Religion: Ritual and Authority among an East African People*. London: Oxford University Press, 1960.

Momaday, N. Scott. *House Made of Dawn*. New York: Harper and Row, 1968.

————. *The Way to Rainy Mountain*. Albuquerque: University of New Mexico Press, 1969.

————. *The Names*. New York: Harper and Row, 1976.

————. "The Man Made of Words: The Story of the Arrowmaker," *New York Times Book Review*, 4 May 1969.

Mooney, James. *Ghost Dance Religion and the Sioux Outbreak of 1890*. Chicago: University of Chicago Press, 1965. Reprint of 14th Annual Report, Pt. 2, Bureau of American Ethnology, Washington, D.C., 1896.

Morton-Williams, P., W. Bascom, and E. M. McClelland. "Two Studies of Ifa Divination," *Africa* 36 (1966).

Müller, Werner. "North America." *Pre-Columbian American Religions*. Ed. Walter Krickeberg, Hermann Trimborn, Werner Müller, and Otto Zerries. New York, 1968.

Munn, Henry. "Writing in the Imagination of an Oral Poet," *New Wilderness Letter*, ed. J. Rothenberg, no. 5/6, 1978.

Munn, Nancy. "Totemic Designs and Group Continuity in Walbiri Cosmology." *Aborigines Now*. Ed. M. Reay. Sydney: Angus and Robertson, 1964.

————. *Walbiri Iconography: Graphic Representation and Cultural Symbolism in a Central Australian Society*. Ithaca: Cornell University Press, 1973.

Myerhoff, Barbara G. "The Deer-Maize Peyote Symbol Complex among the Huichol Indians," *Anthropological Quarterly* 43 (1970).

————. "The Revolution as a Trip: Symbol and Paradox." *The New Pilgrims*. Ed. P. G. Altback and R. S. Laufer. New York: McKay, 1972.

————. *Peyote Hunt: The Sacred Journey of the Huichol Indians*. Ithaca: Cornell University Press, 1974.

Neff, Emery. *The Poetry of History*. New York: Columbia University Press, 1947.

Neihardt, John G. *Black Elk Speaks: Being the Life Story of a Holy Man of the Oglala Sioux*. Lincoln: University of Nebraska Press, 1961; Bison Books, 1979.

Neumann, Erich. *The Origins and History of Consciousness*. Bollingen Series, 42. New York: Pantheon Books, 1954.

Newman, Stanley. "Vocabulary Levels: Zuni Sacred and Slang Usage," *Southwestern Journal of Anthropology* 11 (1955). Reprint. Hymes, 1964.

Nietzsche, Friedrich W. *Beyond Good and Evil: Prelude to a Philosophy of the Future*. Trans. Walter Kaufmann. New York: Vintage Books, 1966.

Nketia, J. H. K. *Drumming in Akan Communities of Ghana*. Legon: T. Nelson for University of Ghana, 1963.

Nordenskiöld, E. *An Historical and Ethnological Survey of the Cuna Indians*. Ed. Henry Wassén. *Comparative Ethnographical Studies*. Vol. X. Göteborg, Sweden: 1938.

Norman, Howard. *The Wishing Bone Cycle: Narrative Poems from the Swampy Cree*

Indians. New York: Stonehill Publications, 1976. Reprint. Santa Barbara, Ca.: Ross-Erikson, 1982.

Obeyesekere, Gonanath. "The Ritual Drama of the Sanni Demons: Collective Representations of Disease in Ceylon," *Comparative Studies in Society and History*, vol. 11, no. 2 (April 1969).

Olson, Charles. *The Mayan Letters*. London: Jonathan Cape, 1953, 1968.

———. *The Maximus Poems*. New York: Jargon/Corinth Books, 1960.

———. *Charles Olson Reading at Berkeley*. San Francisco: Coyote Press, 1966.

———. *Human Universe*. New York: Grove Press, 1967.

———. *Causal Mythology*. San Francisco: Four Seasons Foundation, 1969.

———. *The Special View of History*. Berkeley: Oyez, 1970.

———. *Additional Prose*. Bolinas, Ca.: Four Seasons Foundation, 1974.

———. "The Science of Mythology," *Olson: The Journal of the Charles Olson Archives* 10 (Fall 1978).

———. *Muthologos: The Collected Lectures and Interviews*. 2 vols. Bolinas, Ca.: Four Seasons Foundation, 1979.

Ortiz, Alfonso, ed. *New Perspectives on the Pueblos*. Albuquerque: University of New Mexico Press, 1972.

———. "On Becoming a Pueblo Sacred Clown." MS, 1977.

Ortiz, Simon J. *A Good Journey*. Berkeley: Turtle Island, 1977.

———. "Song/Poetry and Language: Expression and Perception." Unpublished MS. N.d.

Ortner, Sherry B. *Sherpas through Their Rituals*. Cambridge: Cambridge University Press, 1978.

Pagels, Elaine. *The Gnostic Gospels*. New York: Random House, 1979.

Parrinder, G. *West African Religion*. London: Epworth Press, 1961.

Parry, Milman. "The Homeric Language as the Language of Oral Poetry." *Harvard Studies in Classical Philology*, vol. 43 (1932).

Parry, Milman, and Albert Lord, eds. and trans. Vol. I. *Serbocroation Heroic Songs*. Cambridge: Harvard University Press, 1953.

Parsons, Elsie Clews. "Zuni Tales," *Journal of American Folklore* 43 (1930).

———. *Pueblo Indian Religion*. Chicago: University of Chicago Press, 1939.

Parsons, Elsie Clews, and Ralph L. Beals. "The Sacred Clowns of the Pueblo and Mayo-Yaqui Indians," *American Anthropologist*, vol. 36, no. 4 (October–December 1934).

Patai, Raphael. *The Hebrew Goddess*. New York: Ktav Publishing House, 1967.

Peterson, Elmer. *Tristan Tzara: Dada and Surrational Theorist*. New Brunswick, N.J.: Rutgers University Press, 1971.

Philippi, Donald L. *Songs of Gods, Songs of Humans: The Epic Tradition of the Ainu*. Princeton: Princeton University Press, 1979.

Popov, A. "Consecration Ritual for a Blacksmith Novice Among the Yakuts," *Journal of American Folklore* 46 (1933).

Pound, Ezra. *Guide to Kulchur*. New York: New Directions, 1970; 1st ed. 1918.

———. *The Spirit of Romance*. New York: New Directions, 1952.

Powers, William. "American Indian Music: An Introduction," *American Indian Hobbyist*, vol. 7, no. 1 (1961).

————. "American Indian Music, Part Two: The Language," *American Indian Hobbyist*, vol. 7, no. 2 (1961).

Prince, R. *Ifa*. Ibadan, 1964.

Quasha, George. "DiaLogos: Between the Written and the Oral in Contemporary Poetry," *New Literary History*, Vol. VIII, no. 3 (Spring 1977).

Quasha, George and Jerome Rothenberg, eds. *America a Prophecy: A New Reading of American Poetry from Pre-Columbian Times to the Present*. New York: Random House, 1973.

Radin, Paul. "The Culture of the Winnebago as Described by Themselves," *Memoirs of the International Journal of American Linguistics* 2 (1949).

————. *The World of Primitive Man*. New York: E. P. Dutton, 1953, 1971.

————. *Primitive Man as Philosopher*. New York: Dover Books, 1957.

————. *The Trickster: A Study in American Indian Mythology*. New York: Schocken Books, 1956, 1972.

Rappaport, Roy A. *Pigs for the Ancestors: Ritual in the Ecology of a New Guinea People*. New Haven: Yale University Press, 1968.

Rasmussen, David. *Mythic-Symbolic Language and Philosophical Anthropology*. The Hague: Nijhoff, 1971.

Rasmussen, Knud. *The Netsilik Eskimos: Social Life and Spiritual Culture*. Copenhagen: Gyldendalske Boghandel, Nordisk Forlag, 1931.

Rattray, R. S. "The Drum Language of West Africa," *Journal of African Society* 22 (1923). Reprint. *Ashanti*, Oxford, 1923.

Ray, Verne F. "The Contrary Behavior Pattern in American Indian Ceremonialism," *Southwestern Journal of Anthropology*, vol. 1, no. 1 (Spring 1945).

Redfield, Robert. *Tepoztlan—A Mexican Village: A Study of Folk Life*. Chicago: University of Chicago Press, 1930.

Reed, Ishmael. *Conjure: Selected Poems 1963—1970*. Amherst: University of Massachusetts Press, 1972.

Rexroth, Kenneth. *Assays*. New York: New Directions, 1961.

Rimbaud, Arthur. *A Season in Hell*. Trans. Louise Varèse. New York: New Directions, 1945.

Robins, R. H., and Norman McLeod. "Five Yurok Songs: A Musical and Textual Analysis," *Bulletin of the School for Oriental and African Studies*, vol. 18, no. 3 (1956).

————. "A Yurok Song Without Words," *Bulletin of the School for Oriental and African Studies* 20 (1957).

Robinson, James M., ed. *The Nag Hammadi Library*. New York: Harper and Row, 1977.

Róheim, Géza. *The Eternal Ones of the Dream: A Psychoanalytic Interpretaton of Australian Myth and Ritual*. New York: International University Press, 1945, 1969.

Rothenberg, Jerome. "From a Shaman's Notebook." *Poems from the Floating World* 4. New York: Hawk's Well Press, 1962.

————. "Total Translation: An Experiment in the Presentation of American Indian Poetry." *Stony Brook*. Ed. G. Quasha. 3—4 (1969).

————. *Poland/1931*. New York: New Directions, 1974.

————. *6 Horse Songs for 4 Voices*. New York: New Wilderness Audiographics, 1978.

————. *Pre-faces and Other Writings*. New York: New Directions, 1981.

————, ed. *Technicians of the Sacred: A Range of Poetries from Africa, America, Asia, and Oceania*. New York: Doubleday, 1968.

————, ed. *Shaking the Pumpkin: Traditional Poetry of the Indian North Americas*. New York: Doubleday, 1972.

————, ed. *New Wilderness Letter*. New York: New Wilderness Foundation, 1976–present.

————, ed. *A Big Jewish Book: Poems & Other Visions of the Jews from Tribal Times to the Present*. New York: Doubleday, 1978.

Russell, Frank. "The Pima Indians," *23rd Report of the Bureau of American Ethnology*. Washington, D.C.: 1908.

Rutnin, Mattani. "Transformations of Thai Concepts of Aesthetics." Paper presented to the Second S.S.R.C. Conference on Southeast Asian Aesthetics, Cornell University, August 24–26, 1980. MS.

Rycroft, D. K. "Melodic Features in Zulu Eulogistic Recitation," *African Language Studies* 1 (1960).

Sahagún, Fray Bernardino de. *Historia General de las Cosas de la Nueva España*. Mexico: Editorial Nueva España, 1946.

————. *Florentine Codex: General History of the Things of New Spain*. Trans. Charles E. Dibble and Arthur J. O. Anderson. Salt Lake City: University of Utah Press, n.d.

Said, Edward. "Interview with Edward Said," *Diacritics*, vol. 6, no. 3 (1976).

————. "The Text, the World, the Critic." *Textual Strategies: Perspectives in Post-Structuralist Criticism*. Ed. Josue Harari. Ithaca: Cornell University Press, 1979.

Sapir, Edward. *Language*. New York: Harcourt Brace, 1921.

Sarathchandra, C. R. *The Sinhalese Folk Play and Modern Stage*. Ceylon, 1953.

Schechner, Richard. *Essays on Performance Theory 1970–1976*. New York: Drama Book Specialists, 1977.

Schechner, Richard, and Mady Schuman, eds. *Ritual, Play, and Performance: Readings in the Social Sciences/Theatre*. New York: Seabury Press, 1976.

Schieffelin, Edward L. *The Sorrow of the Lonely and the Burning of the Dancers*. New York: St. Martin's Press, 1976.

Scholem, Gershom. *Major Trends in Jewish Mysticism*. New York: Schocken Books, 1954, 1961.

————. *On the Kabbalah and Its Symbolism*. New York: Schocken Books, 1965.

————. *Kabbalah*. New York: New York Times Book Company, 1974.

Sechebaye, M. A. "La Réalisation Symbolique." Supplement no. 12. *Revue Suisse de Psychologie et de Psychologie Appliquée*. Bern, 1947.

Senghor, Léopold Sédar. *Prose and Poetry*. Selected and trans. John Reed and Clive Wake. London: Oxford University Press, 1965.

Singer, Milton. *When a Great Tradition Modernizes: An Anthropological Approach to Indian Civilization*. London: Pall Mall Press, 1972.

Snyder, Gary. *Earth House Hold*. New York: New Directions, 1969.

————. *Myths and Texts*. New York: New Directions, 1978.

————. *The Old Ways*. San Francisco: City Lights Books, 1977.

———. *He Who Hunted Birds in His Father's Village: The Dimensions of a Haida Myth*. Bolinas, Ca.: Grey Fox Press, 1979.

———. *The Real Work: Interviews and Talks 1964 – 1975*. New York: New Directions, 1980.

Stein, Gertrude. *Composition as Explanation*. London: Hogarth Press, 1926. Reprint. *Selected Writings*. New York: Random House, 1946.

———. *Lectures in America*. New York: Random House, 1935. Reprint. Boston: Beacon Press, 1957.

———. "Portraits and Repetition." *Gertrude Stein, Writings and Lectures 1909 – 1945*. Middlesex, England: Penguin Books, 1967.

Stevenson, Matilda Coxe. "The Zuni Indians," *Annual Report of the Bureau of American Ethnology* 23 (1904).

Steward, Julian H. "The Ceremonial Buffoon of the American Indian." *Papers of the Michigan Academy of Science, Art and Letters*, vol. 14 (1931).

Storm, Hyemeyohsts. *Seven Arrows*. New York: Harper and Row, 1972.

Swanton, John R. "Haida." *Handbook of American Indian Languages*, Bureau of American Ethnology, bulletin 40, Part I. Ed. Franz Boas. Washington, D.C.: Government Printing Office, 1911.

———. "Haida Songs." *Publications of the American Ethnological Society* 3. Leiden, 1912.

Tarn, Nathaniel, and Janet Rodney. *Atitlan/Alashka*. Boulder: Brillig Works, 1979.

Tedlock, Dennis. *The Ethnography of Tale-Telling at Zuni*. Ann Arbor: University of Michigan Microfilms, 1968.

———. "On the Translation of Style in Oral Narrative," *Journal of American Folklore*, vol. 84, no. 331 (January–March 1971).

———. *Finding the Center: Narrative Poetry of the Zuni Indians*. New York: Dial Press, 1972.

Tedlock, Dennis, and Barbara Tedlock, eds. *Teachings from the American Earth*. New York: Liveright, 1975.

Thompson, Robert Farris. *African Arts in Motion*. Berkeley, Los Angeles, London: University of California Press, 1974.

Thompson, Stith. *Tales of the North American Indians*. Bloomington: Indiana University Press, 1929, 1966.

Thoreau, Henry David. *The Writings of Henry David Thoreau*. Riverside Edition, 1894.

Trask, Willard, ed. *The Unwritten Song: Poetry of the Primitive and Traditional Peoples of the World*. 2 vols. New York: Macmillan, 1967.

Turner, Victor. *The Forest of Symbols: Aspects of Ndembu Ritual*. Ithaca: Cornell University Press, 1967.

———. *The Ritual Process: Structure and Anti-Structure*. Ithaca: Cornell University Press, 1969.

———. *Dramas, Fields, and Metaphors: Symbolic Action in Human Society*. Ithaca: Cornell University Press, 1974.

————. *Revelation and Divination in Ndembu Ritual*. Ithaca: Cornell University Press, 1975.

————. "A Review of 'Ethnopoetics: A First International Symposium,' " *Boundary 2*, Vol. VI, no. 2 (Winter 1978).

Tylor, Edward B. *Researches Into the Early History of Mankind*. Chicago: University of Chicago Press, 1964.

Tzara, Tristan. *Oeuvres Complètes*. Vol. I, 1912–24; Vol. IV, 1947–1963. Paris: Flammarion, 1975.

Ucko, Peter J., and Andrée Rosenfeld. *Paleolithic Cave Art*. London: Weidenfeld and Nicolson, 1967.

Van Doren, Mark. *Anthology of World Poetry*. New York: Reynal and Hitchcock, 1928.

Vort 7. Ed. Barry Alpert. Antin/Rothenberg issue. Silver Springs, Md., 1975.

Waddell, L. Austine. *The Buddhism of Tibet or Lamaism*. Reprint. Cambridge: W. Heffner, 1972.

Waldmann, Anne, and Marilyn Webb, eds. *Talking Poetics from Naropa Institute*. Boulder and London: Shambhala, 1978.

Wallace, Anthony F. C. *The Death and Rebirth of the Seneca*. New York: Alfred A. Knopf, 1970.

Wasson, R. Gordon. *María Sabina and Her Mazatec Mushroom Velada*. New York: Harcourt Brace Jovanovitch, 1974.

Watts, Alan W. *The Two Hands of God: The Myths of Polarity*. New York: Collier, 1970.

Whitman, Walt. *The Poetry and Prose of Walt Whitman*. New York: Simon and Schuster, 1949.

Whitten, Norman E., and John F. Szwed, eds. *Afro-American Anthology*. New York: Free Press, 1970.

Whorf, Benjamin Lee. *Language, Thought and Reality*. Cambridge, Mass.: MIT Press, 1956.

Wilhelm, Richard, trans. *The I Ching or Book of Changes*. English trans. Cary F. Baynes. New York: Pantheon, 1950.

Wirz, Paul. *Exorcism and the Art of Healing in Ceylon*. Leiden: E. J. Brill, 1954.

Wittgenstein, Ludwig. *Preliminary Studies for the "Philosophical Investigations."* (Generally known as *The Blue and Brown Books*.) Oxford: Blackwell, 1969.

Wolkstein, Diane. "Master of the Shadow Play," *Parabola*, Vol. IV. no. 4 (1979).

Zerries, Otto. "Primitive South America and the West Indies." *Pre-Columbian American Religions*. Ed. Walter Krickeberg, Hermann Trimborn, Werner Müller, and Otto Zerries. New York: 1968.

Zoete, Beryl de, and Walter Spies. *Dance and Drama in Bali*. New York: Harpers, 1939.

Zoetmulder, P. J. *Kalangwan: A Survey of Old Javanese Literature*. The Hague: Nijhoff, 1974.

ACKNOWLEDGMENTS

The following publishers and individuals have kindly granted permission to include material in *Symposium of the Whole*: George Allen & Unwin for excerpt from *Elementary Forms of the Religious Life* by Emile Durkheim; Paula Gunn Allen for ''The Sacred Hoop: A Contemporary Indian Perspective on American Indian Literature''; American Anthropological Association and Dell Hymes for ''Some North Pacific Coast Poems: A Problem in Anthropological Philology'' by the author; Andrews and McNeel for excerpt from *Images & Symbols* by Mircea Eliade; David Antin for ''Talking to Discover'' by the author; Atheneum Publishers for excerpt from *Tristes Tropiques* by Claude Lévi-Strauss (copyright © 1973 by Jonathan Cape Ltd.; New York: Atheneum, 1973), and for excerpt from *The Singer of Tales* by Albert B. Lord (copyright © 1960 by the President and Fellows of Harvard College); Bantam Books, Inc. for excerpt from *Oh, What a Blow That Phantom Gave Me!* by Edmund Carpenter (copyright © 1972, 1973 by Edmund Carpenter, reprinted by permission of Bantam Books, Inc., all rights reserved); Ursula Bellugi and Edward S. Klima for ''Poetry without Sound'' by the authors (originally appeared in *Human Nature*, 1978, 1 (10), 74–83); Black Sparrow Press for ''Preface'' by Clayton Eshleman (copyright © 1981 by Clayton Eshleman and published in *Hades in Manganese* published by Black Sparrow Press); Peter Blue Cloud for ''Black Coyote'' by the author (from a book of coyote stories and poems entitled *Back Then Tomorrow*, Blackberry Press, Brunswick, Maine); *Boundary 2* and William V. Spanos for ''A Review of 'Ethnopoetics''' by Victor Turner; City Lights Books for excerpt from *The Old Ways* by Gary Snyder (copyright © 1977 by Gary Snyder, reprinted by permission of City Lights Books); Cornell University Press for excerpt from *The New Science of Giambattista Vico*, translated from the Third Edition by Thomas Goddard Bergin and Max Harold Fisch (copyright © 1948 by Cornell University and used by permission of the publisher, Cornell University Press), for excerpt from *Walbiri Iconography: Graphic Representation and Cultural Symbolism in a Central Australian Society* (copyright © 1973 by Cornell University and used by permission of the publisher, Cornell University Press), and for excerpt from *Peyote Hunt: The Sacred Journey of the Huichol Indians* by Barbara G. Myerhoff (copyright © 1974 by Cornell University and used by permission of the publisher, Cornell University Press); Richard Dauenhauer for ''Koyukon Riddle-Poems'' by the author; Stanley Diamond for ''Plato and the Definition of the Primitive'' by the author; Doubleday & Company, Inc. for excerpts and poems from *The Breast of the Earth* by Kofi Awoonor (copyright © 1975 by Kofi Awoonor and reprinted by permission of Doubleday & Company, Inc.); Dover Publications for excerpt from *Primitive Man as Philosopher* by Paul Radin; Robert Duncan for excerpt from ''Rites of Participation'' by the author; Farrar, Straus & Giroux, Inc. for excerpt from *The White Goddess* by Robert Graves; Librairie Ernest Flammarion and Pierre Joris for excerpt in the English language only from *Oeuvres complètes*, volumes I and IV, by Tristan Tzara; the Four Seasons Foundation and the Estate of Charles Olson for ''the hinges of civilization to be put back on the door'' by Charles Olson (copyright © 1974 by Charles Boer, literary executor of the Estate of Charles Olson, and reprinted by permission of the Four Seasons Foundation); Editions

Gallimard for translated excerpt from *Images et Symboles* by Mircea Eliade; Grove Press, Inc. for excerpt from "On Balinese Theater" by Antonin Artaud; Johns Hopkins University Press for excerpt from "DiaLogos: Between the Written and the Oral in Contemporary Poetry" by George Quasha, as it appeared in *New Literary History*, volume VIII, number 3 (1976−77); Indiana University Press for "From a Correspondence on Ossian," reprinted from *The Rise of Modern Mythology* by Feldman and Richardson; the International African Institute and Germaine Dieterlen for the excerpt from *Conversations with Ogotemmêli* by Marcel Griaule; J. Stephen Lansing for "The Sounding of the Text" by the author; Lewis MacAdams for "Callin Coyote Home" from *News from Niman Farm* by Lewis MacAdams; David P. McAllester for "The Tenth Horse Song of Frank Mitchell" by the author; Macmillan Publishing Co., Inc. for excerpt from *The Elementary Forms of Religious Life* by Emile Durkheim, trans. by Joseph Ward Swain (copyright © 1915, Allen & Unwin, Ltd., First Free Press Paperback Edition, 1964); The MIT Press for "An American Indian Model of the Universe" from *Language, Thought & Reality* by Benjamin Lee Whorf (reprinted by permission of The MIT Press, Cambridge, Massachusetts, copyright © 1956 by the Massachusetts Institute of Technology); Monthly Review Press for excerpt from *Discourse on Colonialism* by Aimé Césaire (copyright © 1972 by Monthly Review Press, reprinted by permission of Monthly Review Press); William Morrow & Company, Inc. for "Expressive Language" from *Home: Social Essays* (1966) by LeRoi Jones (Amiri Baraka), © 1963 by LeRoi Jones and reprinted by permission of William Morrow & Company; Henry Munn for "Writing in the Imagination of an Oral Poet" and the accompanying "Shaman Songs" by María Sabina; Barbara Myerhoff for "Return to Wirikuta: Ritual Reversal and Symbolic Continuity in the Huichol Peyote Hunt" by Barbara Myerhoff; New Directions Publishing Corp. for "The Duende" from *The Poet in New York* by Federico García Lorca (copyright 1940 by Francisco García Lorca, copyright © 1955 by Ben Belitt, reprinted by permission of New Directions), for excerpt from *Guide to Kulchur* by Ezra Pound (copyright © 1970 by Ezra Pound, all rights reserved, reprinted by permission of New Directions), for excerpts from *A Season in Hell* by Arthur Rimbaud, translated by Louise Varèse (copyright © 1946, 1957, by New Directions and reprinted by permission of New Directions), and "Poetry and the Primitive" from *Earth House Hold* by Gary Snyder (copyright © 1967 by Gary Snyder and reprinted by permission of New Directions); The University of New Mexico Press for excerpt from *New Perspectives on the Pueblos* by Alfonso Ortiz; The *New York Times* for "The Story of the Arrowmaker" by N. Scott Momaday (copyright © 1969 by The New York Times Company, reprinted by permission); Howard Norman for excerpt from *The Wishing Bone Cycle: Narrative Poems from the Swampy Cree Indians* by the author; New York University Press for excerpt from *Ur-Drama: The Origins of Theatre* by E. T. Kirby (copyright © 1975 by New York University and reprinted by permission of New York University Press); George Butterick and the Estate of Charles Olson for "Human Universe" (copyright © 1965 by Charles Olson); Simon J. Ortiz for "Song/Poetry and Language—Expression and Perception" and "Telling About Coyote" by the author; Peter Owen Ltd. for British Commonwealth rights to excerpt from *Guide to Kulchur* by Ezra Pound; Oxford University Press for excerpt from *Izibongo: Zulu Praise Poems* by Trevor Cope (copyright © 1968 by Oxford University Press), for excerpts from *Oral Literature in Africa* by Ruth Finnegan (copyright © 1970 by Oxford University Press), and for excerpt from *Prose and Poetry* by Léopold Sédar Senghor, selected and translated by John Reed and Clive Wake (copyright © 1965 by Oxford University Press); Princeton University Press for excerpt from *Shamanism: Archaic Techniques of Ecstasy* by Mircea Eliade, trans. Willard R. Trask (copyright © 1964 Princeton University Press), and for excerpt and "Song of the Wolf Goddess" from *Songs of Gods, Songs of Humans: The Epic Tradition of the Ainu* by Donald L. Philippi (copyright © 1979 by University of Tokyo Press, reprinted by permission of Princeton University Press); Random House, Inc. for excerpt from *The Gnostic Gospels* by Elaine Pagels; Ishmael Reed for "Neo-HooDoo Manifesto" by the author; Paul R. Reynolds, Inc. for excerpt from *Coral Gardens and Their Magic* by Bronislaw Malinowski; Ross-Erikson Publishers for excerpt from *María Sabina, Her Life and Chants* by Alvaro Estrada; Routledge & Kegan Paul Ltd. and Schocken Books Inc. for Carl Jung: "On the Psychology of the Trickster Figure" from *The Trickster* by Paul Radin; St. Martin's Press, Inc. for excerpt from *The Sorrow of the Lonely and the Burning of the Dancers* by Edward Schieffelin (copyright © 1976 by St. Martin's Press, Inc. and reprinted by permission of the publisher); Richard Schechner for excerpt from "From Ritual to Theatre and Back" by the author; Schocken Books, Inc. for excerpt from *On the Kabbalah and Its Symbolism* by Gershom Scholem (English translation by Ralph Manheim, copyright © 1965 by Schocken Books, Inc.); Shambhala Publications, Inc. for excerpt from "Light/and Keats" by Diane di Prima in *Talking Poetics from Naropa Institute* edited by Anne Waldman and Marilyn Webb (copyright © 1978 by Diane di Prima); Simon & Schuster for excerpt from *Lame Deer: Seeker of Visions* by John Fire/Lame Deer and Richard Erdoes (copyright © 1972 by John Fire/Lame Deer and Richard Erdoes); Mrs. W. E. H. Stanner for excerpt from "The Dreaming" by W. E. H. Stanner; Franz Steiner Verlag GMBH, Wiesbaden, Germany, for excerpts from *Leo Frobenius 1873–1973: An Anthology*, edited by Eike Haberland; Nathaniel Tarn for "Fragments from the Prayers Made on Behalf of Nathaniel Tarn by the Tzutujil-Maya Priest Nicolas Chiviliu Tacaxoy" with comments and emendations by Nathaniel Tarn; Dennis Tedlock and *Alcheringa: Ethnopoetics* for "Tell It Like It's Right in Front of You" by Dennis Tedlock, originally published under the title, "Toward a Restoration of the Word in the Modern World" (copyright © 1976 by the Editors and the Trustees of Boston University); the UCLA Art Council for excerpts from *African Art in Motion* by Robert Farris Thompson (copyright © 1974 by the UCLA Art Council).

An exhaustive effort has been made to locate all rights holders and to clear reprint permissions. This process has been complicated, and if any required acknowledgments have been omitted, or any rights overlooked, it is unintentional and forgiveness is requested.

Designer: Linda Robertson
Compositor: Trend-Western
Printer: Malloy Litho
Binder: Malloy Litho
Text: Times Roman
Display: Auriga